Inside
Microsoft Office
for Windows 95

Bruce Hallberg

Kathy Ivens

New Riders

New Riders Publishing, Indianapolis, Indiana

Inside Microsoft Office for Windows 95

By Bruce Hallberg, Kathy Ivens

Published by:
New Riders Publishing
201 West 103rd Street
Indianapolis, IN 46290 USA

Printed in the United States of America 1 2 3 4 5 6 7 8 9 0

```
***CIP data available upon request***
```

Warning and Disclaimer

This book is designed to provide information about the NetWare computer program. Every effort has been made to make this book as complete and as accurate as possible, but no warranty or fitness is implied.

The information is provided on an "as is" basis. The author and New Riders Publishing shall have neither liability nor responsibility to any person or entity with respect to any loss or damages arising from the information contained in this book or from the use of the disks or programs that may accompany it.

Publisher	*Don Fowley*
Associate Publisher	*Tim Huddleston*
Marketing Manager	*Ray Robinson*
Acquisitions Manager	*Jim LeValley*
Managing Editor	*Tad Ringo*

Product Development Specialist
Ray Robinson

Acquisitions Editor
Alan Harris

Software Specialist
Steve Weiss

Production Editor
Cliff Shubs

Technical Editor
Robert L. Bogue

Assistant Marketing Manager
Tamara Apple

Acquisitions Coordinator
Stacey Beheler

Publisher's Assistant
Karen Opal

Cover Designer
Karen Ruggles

Book Designer
Sandra Schroeder

Photographer
Larry Ladig

Manufacturing Coordinator
Paul Gilchrist

Production Manager
Kelly Dobbs

Production Team Supervisor
Laurie Casey

Graphics Image Specialists
Jason Hand
Laura Robbins
Craig Small
Todd Wente

Production Analysts
Angela D. Bannan
Bobbi Satterfield

Production Team
Angela Calvert
Kim Cofer
Kevin Foltz
David Garratt
Shawn MacDonald
Joe Millay
Erika Millen
Beth Rago
Gina Rexrode
Erich J. Richter
Christine Tyner

Indexer
Bront Davis

About the Author

Bruce Hallberg is the Director of Information Systems for Genelabs Technologies, Inc., a biotechnology company located in Redwood City, California. He has been heavily involed with PCs since 1980 and has specialized in accounting and business control systems for the past seven years. He has consulted with a large number of local and national companies in a variety of areas and has expertise in networking, programming, and system implementations. He works with a wide variety of PC computing platforms, including DOS, Windows, OS/2, Unix, and Macintosh.

Kathy Ivens has been a Computer Consultant/Management Consultant in private practice since 1984. Operating as Ivens Consulting, Inc., her company specializes in accounting applications for micro and mini computers; network design and installation; database design and development; word processing training and operating system training.

Trademark Acknowledgments

All terms mentioned in this book that are known to be trademarks or service marks have been appropriately capitalized. New Riders Publishing cannot attest to the accuracy of this information. Use of a term in this book should not be regarded as affecting the validity of any trademark or service mark. Office, Windows, Word for Windows, Access, Excel, and PowerPoint are all trademarks of the Microsoft Corporation.

Dedication

From Bruce Hallberg. For Becky.

From Kathy Ivens. To her three sets of youngens: Debbie & Allen, Beverly & Bill, and Judy & Mike.

Acknowledgments

There are a lot of wonderful, talented people at New Riders Publishing, and we owe thanks to everyone who worked on this book. We extend special kudos to Alan Harris, a warm, funny man who is a dream as an Acquisitions Editor; Cliff Shubs, who made the necessary changes when we did wrong, and did so with such humor and humanity that he had his way with us; Ray Robinson, who made sure this book would be literate and readable, not always an easy task when you're dealing with computer writers; and Stacey Beheler, who juggled brilliantly as she dealt with the millions of details involved with authors on opposite coasts, and all the editors and support personnel located between them.

Contents at a Glance

Part IV: Schedule+   635

Part V: Data Sharing and Integration   687

Table of Contents

Part II: Excel

13   Excel Data Management   443

16 PowerPoint Tools and Concepts 533

Part IV: Schedule+

Introduction

Welcome to *Inside Microsoft Office for Windows 95*! This book is designed specifically to meet the needs of users who have invested in the Microsoft Office suite of applications, including Microsoft Word for Windows, Microsoft Excel for Windows, Microsoft PowerPoint, and Microsoft Schedule+.

How *Inside Microsoft Office* Is Designed

Four of the six parts in this book are dedicated to the separate applications in the suite. The other parts show you how to get more out of your Office suite of products by using more advanced features such as integration and networking. This approach enables you to use Office as most users use it—as separate applications—as well as understanding how to use these applications in harmony.

Inside Microsoft Office is written for those users who might be comfortable or even expert with one or two of the Office suite applications, but who must or want to learn the other applications in the Office line. Many users find that they spend so much time in one application, such as Word, that when they have to use another application, such as PowerPoint, they really are not that comfortable with it.

How many times have you had to complete a presentation, but you didn't know how to use PowerPoint, so you just created it in Word? Or, perhaps, your boss wants that report with charts, graphs, and pretty pictures done in "FIVE MINUTES," or else. But when you get back to your workstation, you can't get that sales history out of Excel so that it imports into Word just right. Eventually, you get frustrated with this approach, so you close Excel in a huff and rekey the data into a Word table and hand in a report blander than ice cubes boiled in water. The information is there, but it is not as presentable as you would like.

What's Different about This Book

The power of a suite of programs like Microsoft Office is the integration, or as Microsoft labels it, *component reuse,* you get when all your major applications work together seamlessly. This integration enables you to create sparkling presentations, "smart" spreadsheets, highly automated word processing documents, and powerful databases.

What Is Integration?

Although Windows has made it easier to integrate your applications, not many users are comfortable designing elaborate OLE and DDE links to make their various applications work together. Office is designed around the theory that users want to use two or three applications at once without having to reengineer or reformat data once time has been spent creating it. Users don't want to create worksheets in Excel that are filled with thousands of numbers, only to have that data available only to Excel. Why not use that data in another applications, such as Word or PowerPoint? This is the magic of Microsoft Office, and *Inside Microsoft Office* shows you how to do this.

Integration enables you to create a Word document, such as a sales letter, using an Excel worksheet to plug in sales figures in the letter. Or, you might have an Excel database that keeps your inventory. For accounting purposes, you can have Excel send specific inventory data to Word to create a monthly report that you can turn in to your accountant or manager. Microsoft Office enables you to do all this and more.

Part I: Word for Windows

Part I is devoted to Microsoft Word for Windows. Many users devote most of their working time using a word processor for correspondence, business proposals, memos, or other reports. For these users, the word processor is the key application on their desktop, with all other applications supporting its documents.

Using Word for Windows to complete your work is easy. The goal of Part I is to introduce you to the basics of Word, including creating a document, changing text formats, and printing documents. Part I also gets you up and running on the more advanced uses and features of Word. You learn, for example, how to create tables and customize dictionaries, macros, and graphics.

Word is a powerhouse application and is simple enough that you can work with it as soon as it is installed. Word's more advanced features enable you to build complex documents such as an office newsletter. Whether you want to type a quick to-do list or create a one-page trifold brochure containing pictures and drop caps, you can do it in Word with equal ease. Word's advanced capabilities are as easy to use as its simple features.

Part II: Excel

The second part of *Inside Microsoft Office* is devoted to Microsoft Excel for Windows. Excel is one of the most popular spreadsheets available for Windows and is probably the second most popular application in the Office suite. With Excel, you can quickly and easily create powerful worksheets, colorful charts, and focused reports and presentations.

In Part II you are introduced to Excel's new features; how to create and format worksheets; and how to build charts from the data you have in your worksheets. In later chapters, more advanced features are covered to help you get the most out of your Office investment. If you are interested in setting up loan calculations, mortgage analysis, or other powerful spreadsheet applications, *Inside Microsoft Office* shows you how to use functions, macros, and Visual Basic for Applications to get what you want.

Part III: PowerPoint

When you need to put together a presentation replete with slides, handouts, and reports, use Microsoft PowerPoint. Part III gives you an introduction into this easy-to-use Office application. Although you might not do all of your work in PowerPoint, you might need to use it from time to time to put together that "perfect" presentation for the board of directors. For that reason, Part III shows you the best information and instructions to get the job done.

After you have put together your presentations on the computer, you can transfer them onto plain paper, color or black-and-white overheads, or 35mm slides, or you can show them on a video screen or computer monitor. To complete your presentation package, PowerPoint's printing options include formats ranging from audience handouts to speaker's notes.

Part III discusses using the PowerPoint AutoContent Wizard, entering presentation text in the outline, and viewing slides. You also learn ways to apply PowerPoint templates to a presentation, add to presentation shapes with text inside, and insert a new slide and clip art into a presentation.

What you will learn with PowerPoint and other Office applications is that many design and formatting tools are identical to those in Word and Excel. If you know how to use these applications, you already know how to use many functions in PowerPoint. This feature helps transfer your skill in one application to another, making the learning curve for that application much smaller.

Part IV: Schedule+

Everyone working in a typical business environment needs to manage their contacts, schedule, and tasks. In Part IV, you learn how to use Microsoft Schedule+ to help you manage, manipulate, and use all your productivity-based information. Do you have a stack of business cards you've received from business contacts, hairdressers, and friends sitting in your desk drawer with a rubber band around them? Would you like a better way to manage them? Do you manage a number of people, and need to keep track of who's working on what projects, and when they're due? Would you like a better way to coordinate your schedule with others in your company?

If you answer yes to these or any other questions that deal with productivity data, you should consider using Schedule+ to manage your information.

In Part IV, you learn how to add contacts, set appointments (both single and recurring), create projects and delegate tasks within the project, and print your data in easy-to-use formats for quick reference.

The nicest thing about Microsoft Schedule+ is that it has been designed for normal people like you. Part IV is designed to give you more than just a basic understanding of what you can do with Schedule+; it shows you how to manage your busy life with it.

Part V: Data Sharing and Integration

Have you ever created a Word document and decided to include a summary of data that you have stored in an Excel spreadsheet? Do you wish you could just place the data in there and not worry about updating that same data in the Word document every time you change or manipulate it in the Excel worksheet? With the integration features of Word and Excel (and the other Office applications), you can do just that. Link the data you want from Excel into the Word document using dynamic data exchange (DDE) and rest assured that your data will always be updated. No need to enter the same updates in two different documents.

DDE is an internal communications protocol Windows uses to enable one application to "talk to" or exchange data with another application. Normally used to transfer information between applications, DDE also can be used within an application. Part V shows you ways to create and use DDE links, use macros to control DDE, and share information between applications.

CD-ROM

The CD-ROM that accompanies this book contains the files that go with the exercises and examples. Because Windows 95 automatically plays discs that are placed in the CD-ROM drive, no installation instructions are needed; all you need to do is put the disc in the drive and follow the instructions.

Special Conventions and Sidebars

Inside Microsoft Office includes special conventions that help you follow along with various discussions and procedures. Most New Riders Publishing books use similar conventions to help you distinguish between various elements of the software, Windows, and sample data. This means that once you purchase one New Riders book, you will find it easier to use all the others.

Before you look ahead, you should spend a moment examining these conventions.

Typeface Conventions

When you see the following typeface, you know that the same information literally appears on-screen:

```
This appears on-screen
```

When you see this same typeface with bold lettering, you know that you are supposed to type the information, as in the following example:

```
Type this information.
```

Anytime you see a word, letter, or number highlighted with boldface, you know to type it in. You might, for example, be instructed to type **WIN** at the DOS prompt. When you see this, you should type WIN as instructed.

New terms, when defined, appear in *italic*. Sometimes italic is also used to provide *emphasis* in a sentence.

Key Combinations

Inside Microsoft Office uses a special convention to help you know which keys to press and in what order:

◆ Key1+Key2: When you see a plus sign (+) between key names, hold down the first key while pressing the second key. Then release both keys.

◆ Key1,Key2: When a comma (,) appears between key names, press and release the first key, then press and release the second key.

Hot Key Characters

The Microsoft Office applications adhere to Windows functionality and specifications, including menu placement, dialog box functionality, and command syntax. One of these specifications includes the use of hot key characters in menu names, commands, and dialog box items. *Hot keys* enable you to use Alt+hot key to activate that menu, command, or dialog box item. The hot key character for the File menu, for example, is F. To activate this menu, press Alt+F.

Inside Microsoft Office shows hot keys for these application elements by boldfacing and underscoring the hot key character. The hot key character for the File menu, for example, is shown as **F**ile.

Notes, Tips, Warnings, and Disk Elements

One way to fully understand and exploit the power of the Office applications is to find shortcuts, enhancements, tips, and other insider information. *Inside Microsoft Office* is packed with Notes and Tips to give you those shortcuts and enhancements just when you need them!

Another way to take advantage of the power of Office and to increase your efficiency with its applications is to know when you might get in trouble with a feature or procedure. *Inside Microsoft Office* provides warnings to help you get around these problem spots.

The following gives you more information about the special icons in this book:

Tip This icon marks a shortcut or neat idea that will help you get your work done faster.

Note A Note includes extra, useful information that complements the discussion at hand, instead of being a direct part of it. A Note, for example, might describe special situations that can arise when you use Word 7 under certain circumstances, and tells you what to do.

This icon flags documents, worksheets, or other resources that are found on the *Inside Microsoft Office* companion disk you can use to test the concepts you are learning.

On the CD

Stop This icon tells you when a procedure might be dangerous—that is, when you run the risk of losing data, locking your system, or damaging your software. These warnings generally tell you how to avoid such losses or describe the steps you can take to remedy them.

New Riders Publishing

The staff of New Riders Publishing is committed to bringing you the very best in computer reference material. Each New Riders book is the result of months of work by authors and staff, who research and refine the information contained within its covers.

As part of this commitment to you, New Riders invites your input. Please let us know if you enjoy this book, if you have trouble with the information or examples, or if you have a suggestion for the next edition.

Please note, though: New Riders staff cannot serve as a technical resource for Microsoft Office or for related questions about hardware- or software-related problems. Please refer to the documentation that accompanies Microsoft Office or to the applications' Help systems.

If you have a question or comment about any New Riders book, there are several ways to contact New Riders Publishing. We will respond to as many readers as we can.

Most effectively, you can use the registration card included in the back of this book. This will help us continue to bring you the best books possible. You can also write to us at the following address:

New Riders Publishing
Attn: Associate Publisher
201 W. 103rd Street
Indianapolis, IN 46290

If you prefer, you can fax us your letter or registration card at (317) 581-4670.

As well, you can leave a voice mail message to New Riders at (317) 581-3871.

You can send electronic mail to New Riders from a variety of sources. NRP maintains several mailboxes organized by topic area. Mail in these mailboxes will be forwarded to the staff member who is best able to address your concerns. Substitute the appropriate mailbox name from the list below when addressing your e-mail. The mailboxes are as follows:

ADMIN	Comments and complaints for NRP's Publisher
APPS	Word, Excel, WordPerfect, other office applications
ACQ	Book proposals inquiries by potential authors
CAD	AutoCAD, 3D Studio, AutoSketch, and CAD products
DATABASE	Access, dBASE, Paradox and other database products
GRAPHICS	CorelDRAW!, Photoshop, and other graphics products
INTERNET	Internet
NETWORK	NetWare, LANtastic, and other network-related topics
OS	MS-DOS, OS/2, all OS except Unix and Windows

UNIX	Unix
WINDOWS	Microsoft Windows (all versions)
OTHER	Anything that doesn't fit the above categories

To send NRP mail from CompuServe, use the following to address:

>INTERNET: *mailbox* @ NEWRIDERS.MCP.COM

To send mail from the Internet, use the following address format:

mailbox@newriders.mcp.com

If you would like to review our products online, please visit us at our Web site at http://www.mcp.com/newriders for our latest offerings and information.

NRP is an imprint of Macmillan Computer Publishing. To obtain a catalog or information, or to purchase any Macmillan Computer Publishing book, call (800) 428-5331.

Thank you for selecting *Inside Microsoft Office for Windows 95*!

Part I

Word for Windows

Word for Windows Quick Start

U sing Microsoft Word for Windows to accomplish your work is easy. The goal of this chapter is to introduce you to using Word rapidly and efficiently. You will be given a guided tour of getting started with Word, with an emphasis on showing you the following steps:

◆ Creating a document

◆ Changing the format of the text

◆ Changing the text

◆ Using some advanced formatting features

◆ Printing your document

By the time you have finished this chapter, you will have created, formatted, and printed your first Word document. You will have learned the features of Word that you use most often, and you will be ready to create and work on the documents that get your job done.

Word for Windows, the word processor in Microsoft Office, probably is the application you will use most as you work with Office. Word is a powerhouse application. It is simple enough that you can work with it as soon as it is installed, yet it contains all the features that you need to build complex documents such as an office newsletter. Whether you want to type a quick to-do list or create a one-page trifold brochure containing pictures and drop caps, you can do it in Word with equal ease. Word's advanced capabilities are as easy to use as its simple features.

Word also possesses the capability of teaching you how to use it as you work. The most obvious feature that helps you learn appears on the screen as soon as you start Word—the Tip of the Day (see fig. 1.1). Each time you start Word, this dialog box presents one new feature of the word processor that you might not be using effectively. Over time, these daily reminders add up to a stronger knowledge of the less frequently used features of your software than if you rely on recalling information from the manual.

Figure 1.1

Word's Tip of the Day bar, just above the ruler.

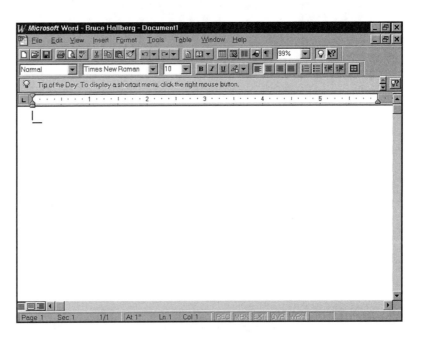

In addition to the Tip of the Day, Word for Windows contains *Wizards* and *Helpers*, special programs that step you through complex tasks. Even when you are working on a familiar task, a Wizard or Helper can be useful. These programs structure your thinking around making your decisions in the right order and with the correct options. For example, you never need to worry about whether you did everything you needed to do to set up a mail merge correctly. The Mail Merge Helper, shown in figure 1.2, makes sure that you did. You activate the Helper by selecting **M**ail Merge from the **T**ools menu.

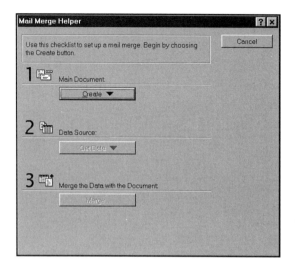

Figure 1.2

The Mail Merge Helper included in Word.

Tip Have you ever puzzled over what the picture on a toolbar button means? Word for Windows ends such puzzling. Place the mouse pointer over any toolbar button and wait. In about two seconds, a ToolTip window appears, giving the name of the command or feature represented by the button. Also, the status bar at the bottom of the screen shows an explanation of what the command or feature does.

Creating a Document

The first step in learning to accomplish a task with Word for Windows is learning how to create a new document or open an existing document. A *document* in Word is the data you type onto the screen and the file that contains the saved data. Word provides powerful document-management features that enable you to handle both these tasks.

Creating a New Document

Word enables you to create both simple and complex spaces into which you can type information. At the simple end of the scale, you can create a blank screen into which you can insert characters. At the complex end, you instantly can create an invoice form into which you can enter the sales information necessary to enable the purchasing party to complete payment. You create both simple and complex documents in just a few easy steps. In the examples included in this chapter, you create three different documents.

Using the Toolbar or Menu

The easiest way to create a new document is to use the Standard toolbar. Table 1.1 describes the buttons found on the Standard toolbar.

TABLE 1.1
Standard Toobar Buttons

Name	Description
New	Creates a new file based on the Normal template
Open	Displays the Open dialog box so that you can select an existing file to open
Save	Saves the current document
Print	Prints the current document
Print Preview	Activates Word's print preview features
Spelling	Initiates a spelling check
Cut	Cuts selected material to the Windows Clipboard
Copy	Copies selected material to the Clipboard
Paste	Pastes material from the Clipboard into your document
Format Painter	Copies the formatting of a selection to the text you specify
Undo	Undoes the commands you select from the list presented
Redo	Redoes the commands you select from the list presented
AutoFormat	Formats your document automatically
Insert Address	Inserts an Address
Insert Table	Inserts a table into your document
Insert Excel	Inserts an Excel worksheet into your document Worksheet
Columns	Formats your document using columns
Drawing	Opens the drawing application and enables you to draw a picture in your document
Show/Hide Paragraph	Shows or hides the paragraph, tab, and space symbols
Zoom Control	Scales your view of the document by the percentage you select
TipWizard	When it turns yellow, click it to get a tip about how to do whatever you just did more quickly
Help	Activates context-sensitive help

To create a new document by using the Standard toolbar, follow these steps:

1. Point with the mouse to the left button on the Standard toolbar, the one representing a page with the upper-left corner folded down (see fig. 1.3).

2. Click with the left mouse button.

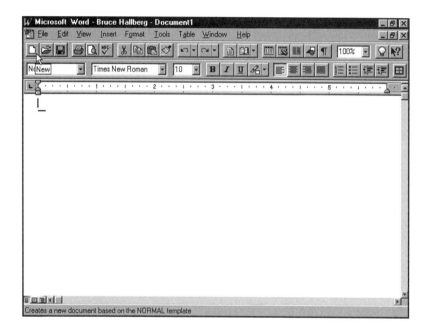

Figure 1.3

Using the New Document button on the Standard toolbar.

In response to your click on the New Document button, Word creates a new document and displays it in a *document window*, the workspace that displays the information you type. If you have a document on your screen already, the new document window appears in front of the existing document window. Both documents, however, are active in the word processor. The section "Navigating the Document" later in this chapter shows the way to move among and within your documents.

The New Document button creates the simplest kind of document Word for Windows uses, a blank workspace with a default font and margins into which you can insert text. Word uses a *document template*, a file that contains instructions for creating a document, to create this simple document. The name of the document template associated with this basic document is Normal, and it is stored in a file called NORMAL.DOT. NORMAL.DOT contains instructions about the margin width, the default font, the page size, and so on that define the appearance of a Normal document.

You also can create a document using Word's menu by performing the following procedure:

1. Open the **F**ile menu.

2. Select the **N**ew menu item (see fig. 1.4).

3. In the New dialog box, select the template on which the document should be based in the **T**emplate combination box. (Normal is selected by default for you, even though the scroll list starts at the top.)

4. Click on the OK button.

 Note You also will see items named Wizards in the **T**emplate combination box. Ignore them for now. The next section explains how to use them.

Figure 1.4

Using the File menu to create a new document.

If you used Word's default template selection, you just created a new document based on the Normal template, exactly as you did when you clicked on the New Document button. However, for purposes of illustration, use the menu procedure to open a new document based on the Invoice template (first select the Other Documents tab and then the Invoice document template; see figure 1.5 for the resulting document). The Invoice template illustrates how useful (and complex) document templates can be. The document you create using the Invoice template appears with all the standard text necessary for the invoice already on-screen. You need only to fill in the appropriate amounts and customer information and print the invoice.

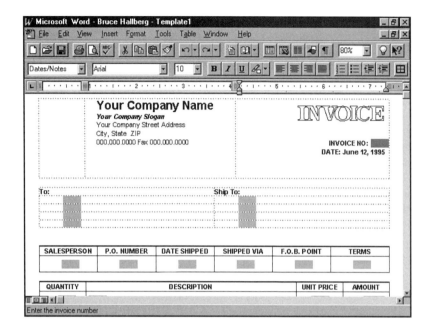

Figure 1.5

A document based on the Invoice template.

There are two reasons to use the File New dialog box instead of the Standard toolbar to create a new document. First, you can access the menu from the keyboard by pressing Alt and the underlined hot keys in the menu name and menu items. (For instance, Alt+F, N selects the **N**ew menu item on the **F**ile menu.) If you prefer to keep your hands on the keyboard instead of reaching for the mouse while you are working, the menu provides you with a more convenient option for creating a new document. Second, the menu gives you access to the New dialog box and its associated list of templates and Wizards. If you want to create a document based on an alternate template or a Wizard, the menu is your only choice.

Note It might not seem like it now, but soon you will come to know the hot keys. By knowing these hot keys, you will be able to dramatically improve your speed with Word.

Using a Wizard

Wizards are Microsoft's answer to the problem of improving the usability of software. Software manufacturers have known for some time that many features always lie just outside a user's knowledge of the program. In Word, for instance, there are many features that you might not use because you do not use them frequently enough to remember how to use them. Calendar-making is an example of such a feature for the average user of a word processor. Small offices might create calendars only a couple of times each year, often enough to want to use the feature but not often enough to remember how to use it. Wizards step you through such procedures, serving as your memory in such instances.

 Stop   Although Wizards are nice features, they do take up memory. When you try to run one, you might receive an out-of-memory error message if you have lots of documents or other applications open. Close unnecessary documents and applications to free memory if you receive such a message.

Microsoft provides 10 Wizards in Word for Windows 95 to help you create complex documents from document templates. Each Wizard is listed in table 1.2 with a brief explanation of what it helps you create.

TABLE 1.2
Word for Windows New Document Wizards

Wizard	Function
Agenda	Creates an agenda for a meeting in one of three styles
Award	Creates an award to honor an achievement in one of four styles
Calendar	Creates calendars
Fax	Creates forms for faxed documents in several styles
Letter	Creates a standard letter and enables you to select text from prewritten letters
Memo	Creates a standard memorandum
Newsletter	Creates a newsletter document in one of two styles
Pleading	Creates a standard pleading document for use by lawyers
Resumé	Creates a standard resumé in one of four types
Table	Creates tables of text in several different formats

To use a Wizard, follow this procedure:

1. Open the **F**ile menu.

2. Select the **N**ew menu item.

3. Using the appropriate tab, select the Wizard you want to use.

4. Click on the OK button.

5. Follow the directions provided by the Wizard dialog box and use the **N**ext and **B**ack buttons provided by the Wizard to move among the steps.

Each Wizard offers different choices specific to its tasks. To get a sense of how a Wizard works, start the Agenda Wizard. The initial screen for the Agenda Wizard appears, as shown in figure 1.6.

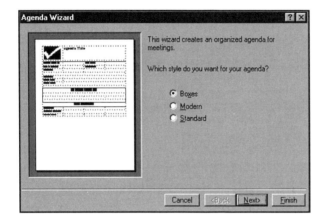

Figure 1.6

The first screen offered by the Agenda Wizard.

Next, perform the following procedure:

1. Select the Bo**x**es style for the agenda and click on the **N**ext button.

2. Enter the correct date and time and click on the **N**ext button.

3. Enter the title and location for the meeting, then click on the **N**ext button.

4. Select the headings you want to use on the agenda by clicking on the check boxes. Click on the **N**ext button to move to the next screen.

5. Select the names you want to use on the agenda by clicking on the check boxes. Click on the **N**ext button to move to the next screen.

6. Enter the topics of discussion, people responsible, and time allocated in the text boxes provided. Click on the **N**ext button when you are finished.

7. Arrange the topics by selecting one and clicking on the Move **U**p or Move **D**own button. Click on the **N**ext button when you are finished.

8. Indicate whether you want a form for recording minutes, using the option buttons provided. Click on **N**ext to move to the final screen.

9. You have reached the end of the information you need to provide to the Wizard. Indicate whether you want Help displayed as the Wizard creates the agenda using the option buttons provided. (Display Help if you want to learn the exact steps the Wizard follows in creating the agenda.) Then click on the **F**inish button. The Wizard next creates your agenda and displays it in a document window.

10. Fill in the agenda with the appropriate information and print the number of copies you need. A sample of such an agenda is shown in figure 1.7.

Figure 1.7

An agenda completed using the Agenda Wizard.

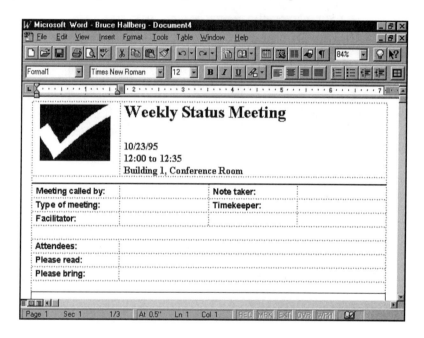

As you can see, you can use Wizards to create complex documents quickly and easily. Wizards save you time and energy, and they give your work a professional look. They let you use the advanced features of Word right from the start, even though you might not understand what all those features are when you use them. With the Wizards on your side, knowing how to use the basic **N**ew command on the **F**ile menu gives you an extraordinary amount of power over Word.

Entering Text

To enter text into a document, type at the keyboard. The text you type enters at the *insertion point,* the flashing vertical bar that appears in the document window. If you already have some text in your document—as you do if you created the agenda or the invoice—you can position your insertion point anywhere in the existing text by clicking at that point with the mouse.

Note The insertion point cursor is different from the mouse pointer. The mouse pointer takes on the appearance of an "I" shape and never flashes, while your insertion point is always flashing.

Closing a Document

If you have been working along with the examples, you have created three to five documents using Microsoft Word. You might find it useful at this point to know how to close a document. Word provides several methods.

The fastest method for closing a document is to press Ctrl+F4 while the document is active. If there are no changes to save, the document closes immediately. If there are changes to save, a Microsoft Word dialog box appears asking if you wish to save changes. Click on **Y**es to save, **N**o to close the document without saving changes, or Cancel to cancel the document closing operation. If you click on **Y**es and the document is not yet named, the Save As dialog box appears, which enables you to enter a name for the document (see fig. 1.8). Enter a name in the File **N**ame text box and click on OK to complete the document closing operation. Clicking on Cancel cancels the close operation entirely.

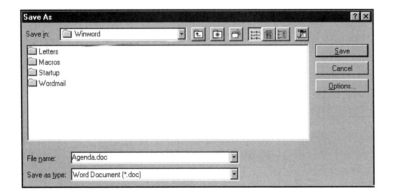

Figure 1.8

Word's Save As dialog box appears automatically when you exit a document that has unsaved changes.

You also can close a document from one of two menus. From the Word menu, open the **F**ile menu and select the **C**lose item (see fig. 1.9). Alternatively, from the document window's control menu, select the **C**lose command. Both these menu actions initiate the same sequence of dialog boxes and actions as pressing Ctrl+F4.

Tip A document window's control menu always appears in the upper left corner of the document window as the control menu box. The control menu box might be difficult for you to locate if the document window is maximized. Look to the immediate left

continues

of the **F**ile menu on Word's menu bar. The control menu box for a maximized window always appears in this position. Click on this box or press Alt+- (hyphen) to open the menu.

Figure 1.9

Using the Close command from Word's File menu.

To follow through with the exercises you have done so far, close your active documents and save at least one of them. The agenda is a good one to save because it is reused later in this chapter. In the next section you learn how to open a document that you have created, saved, and closed.

Opening an Existing Document

Word provides two methods for opening a document you have created, saved, and closed. To use the Standard toolbar, perform the following procedure:

1. Click on the Open Folder button (the second button from the left) to bring up the Open dialog box (see fig. 1.10).

2. In the Open dialog box, select the file you want to open from the window.

3. Click on OK.

At this point, Word opens the file and displays it in a document window.

Alternatively, you can open a file from Word's menu. Click on the **F**ile menu and select the **O**pen menu item. Word displays the Open dialog box; from here, the procedure is the same as using the Standard toolbar.

Look in Favorites   Add to Favorites
Up One Level   File and folder displays
File and folder window   Special commands

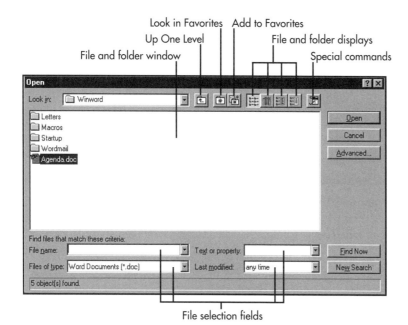

File selection fields

Figure 1.10

The Open dialog box is used to select a file to open.

The Open dialog box enables you to select any file from any directory or drive to be opened. To change the directory or drive whose contents are displayed in the window, access the drop-down menu labeled Look **in**. Click on a drive or open folder by double-clicking on it; this displays the contents of the window. To move up a level in the folder hierarchy, click on the Up One Level button (it appears as a button with a picture of a folder that has an up arrow and two dots).

The Open dialog box also controls which files are displayed in a directory. When it opens, it shows only Word documents that end in a DOC file extension, the default extension for Word documents. If you want to see files that end in other extensions, access the Files of **t**ype drop-down list to choose a different extension (or even All Files).

Navigating the Document

Word for Windows provides you with several methods for *navigating* within a document—that is, changing which portion of the document is displayed and where the insertion point is. There are many key assignments available in Word; table 1.3 lists the basic ones.

TABLE 1.3
Basic Key Assignments for Navigating a Document

Key	Action
Up arrow	Moves the insertion point up one line
Down arrow	Moves the insertion point down one line
Right arrow	Moves the insertion point right one character
Left arrow	Moves the insertion point left one character
Ctrl+up arrow	Moves the insertion point to the beginning of the previous paragraph
Ctrl+down arrow	Moves the insertion point to the beginning of the next paragraph
Ctrl+right arrow	Moves the insertion point right one word
Ctrl+left arrow	Moves the insertion point left one word
Home	Moves the insertion point to the beginning of the line
End	Moves the insertion point to the end of the line
PgUp	Moves the insertion point up one screen
PgDn	Moves the insertion point down one screen
Ctrl+PgUp	Moves the insertion point to the top left of the current screen (Word overrides Windows default action of scrolling the screen to the right)
Ctr+PgDn	Moves the insertion point to the bottom right of the current screen (Word overrides Windows default action of scrolling the screen to the left)
Alt+Ctrl+PgUp	Moves the insertion point to the beginning of the previous page
Alt+Ctrl+PgDn	Moves the insertion point to the beginning of the next page
Ctrl+Home	Moves the insertion point to the beginning of the document
Ctrl+End	Moves the insertion point to the end of the document
Tab	Moves the insertion point to the next cell in a table
Shift+Tab	Moves the insertion point to the previous cell in a table
Alt+Home	Moves the insertion point to the first cell in a row in a table
Alt+End	Moves the insertion point to the last cell in a row in a table
Alt+PgUp	Moves the insertion point to the first cell in a column in a table
Alt+PgDn	Moves the insertion point to the last cell in a column in a table

In addition to these key assignments, you can navigate by clicking the mouse where you want the insertion point to appear on your screen.

You also can use the scroll bars that border the right and bottom edges of a document window to navigate in a document. Clicking on the arrow at either end of a scroll bar moves you one line or one column in that direction. Clicking on the scroll bar itself to the right or left of (or above or below) the scroll box moves you one screen in the direction of the arrow at that end of the scroll bar. Dragging the scroll box moves you several screens at a time in the direction you drag.

Tip   When you drag the scroll box, Word displays the resulting page number next to the scroll box as you drag.

If you have multiple documents open, you also need to know how to move from one document window to another. When you open a document, its name is appended to the end of the **W**indow menu (see fig. 1.11). Opening the **W**indow menu and clicking on the name of the document you want to view moves its document window to the top of the stack.

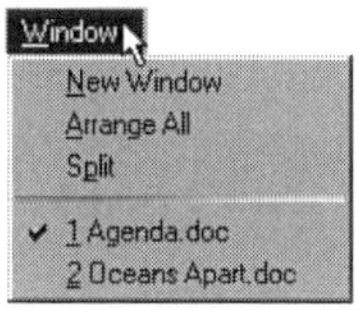

Figure 1.11

Using the Window menu to navigate among open document windows.

In addition to using the **W**indow menu, you can press Ctrl+F6 to move to the next document window and Ctrl+Shift+F6 to move to the previous document window.

Tip   Word for Windows provides many more keyboard shortcuts for navigating documents and windows. For the complete listing divided by category, select **S**earch for Help from the **H**elp menu and go to the topic "Shortcut Keys."

Note   Some people use the term "hot keys" when referring to what Microsoft calls "shortcut keys." The names are interchangeable.

Changing the Format of the Text

The second step in learning to accomplish a task with Word for Windows 95 is learning how to define the appearance of your document. Word provides you with several options for defining the basic look of your document. You can select different fonts, change the size of the text, select a style, and work with a variety of special features.

 Tip   Before you begin this section, open a document so that you can practice each procedure. A good choice would be your agenda. You can fill in some of the blanks and adjust its look to suit your needs.

Choosing a Font

The most noticeable element in the appearance of your document is the font you use to create it. A *font* in Word refers to the physical and artistic design of the letters as they appear on the page. In different fonts, the same character is designed in a different way. Table 1.4 shows the same words presented in several fonts.

TABLE 1.4
A Comparison of Fonts

Font Name	Sample
Zapf Chancery	*The lazy red dog jumped over the wall*
New Century Schoolbook	The lazy red dog jumped over the wall
Tekton	The lazy red dog jumped over the wall
PostCrypt	THE LAZY RED DOG JUMPED OVER THE WALL

A font in Word also refers to the particular collection of characters that can be displayed in a typeface. A particular font in Word may not have exactly the same characters in it as any other font you use in Word. A good example is the Wingdings font that ships with Windows. The example sentence in table 1.4 appears as follows when typed using the Zapf Dingbats font:

✳✳✳ ●❂❙❙ ❑✳✳ ✳❑✳ ✳◆○❑✳✳ ❑❖✳❑ ▼✳✳ ❱❂●●

Obviously, Zapf Dingbats does not contain the same collection of characters as any of the four fonts shown in table 1.4. In fact, it contains no alphabetic characters at all. Remember, when working with fonts, the concept really refers to two things: the

design of the characters and the selection of characters available. On occasion, as in choosing to use Wingdings or a special foreign language font, your choice will be based on the selection of characters the font makes available rather than the look of the characters.

 Note If you feel you need more fonts than you have, you can purchase several different font packs from both Microsoft and other vendors. Fonts are also available as downloadable shareware or freeware programs from sources such as the Desktop Publishing Forum on CompuServe. Some software vendors include fonts with their programs; CorelDRAW!, for instance, includes 750 fonts!

Word provides you with two methods for selecting a font for use in your document. First, there is a drop-down list box on the Formatting toolbar from which you can select the font for use. The Formatting toolbar displays three drop-down list boxes. The one that displays the current font is the middle one. To select a font, perform the following procedure:

1. Click on the arrow button to the right of the drop-down list box to open it (see fig. 1.12). (Pressing Ctrl+Shift+F activates the drop-down list box. After it is activated, pressing the down arrow opens the drop-down list.)

Figure 1.12

Opening the font drop-down list box in the Formatting toolbar.

2. Scroll through the list box by clicking on the scroll bar, and select a font by clicking on it. (You also can use the standard navigation keys to move up and down the list. Once the font you desire is highlighted, press Enter to select it.)

3. Begin typing. Your text will appear in the font you just selected.

 Tip If the Formatting toolbar is not visible, open the **V**iew menu and select the **T**oolbars item. In the Toolbars dialog box, check the box next to Formatting in the **T**oolbars list box. The Formatting toolbar then will appear on-screen. If it appears as a floating toolbox and you would rather it appear as a toolbar beneath the menu, double-click on it. Double-clicking switches any toolbar's appearance between toolbar and floating toolbox.

The second way to choose a font is to use the Font dialog box by performing the following steps:

1. Open the Format menu and select the **F**ont item.

2. If the Fonts tab is not on top, click on it.

3. Select the font you want by clicking on it in the **F**ont list box (see fig. 1.13).

4. Click on the OK button.

5. Begin typing. Your text appears in the font you selected.

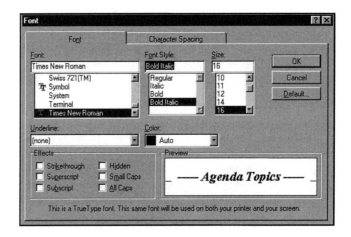

What happens when you select a new font depends on whether you have text selected. If you select text by dragging over it with the mouse and then select a font, the text in the selection changes to the font you selected. The font used for typing depends on which font is active for the area of the screen in which you type next.

If you have a document for which the Arial font is the active font, for example, but you want your section headings to appear in Monotype Corsiva, you can set the font for the headings only by using the following steps:

1. Select a heading by dragging over it with the mouse.

2. Select Monotype Corsiva as the font.

The selected heading changes to Monotype Corsiva. However, if you move your insertion point to the end of the document and start typing, your text appears in Arial. Changing the font for a selection affects the selection only, not the entire document.

If you have no selection active and choose a new font, the new font appears when you start typing—as long as you do not move the insertion point before you start typing. Moving the insertion point before typing causes the font selection to revert to the font active for that region in the document.

Tip

To change the font for an entire document, open the Edit menu and choose the Select **A**ll command. Then select a new font. The new font affects the entire selection. If the selection is large, you have to click on the selection before the new font displays on the screen.

Choosing a Size

You can adjust the size of the font displayed on your screen by using either the Formatting toolbar or the Font dialog box. On the Formatting toolbar, the font size is adjusted using the right drop-down list box. To use the Formatting toolbar, perform the following procedure:

1. Click on the arrow button to the right of the drop-down list box to open it (see fig. 1.14). (Pressing Ctrl+Shift+P activates the drop-down list box. After it is activated, pressing the down arrow opens the drop-down list.)

2. Scroll through the list box by clicking on the scroll bar, and select a size by clicking on it. (You also can use the standard navigation keys to move up and down the list. Once the size you desire is highlighted, press Enter to select it.)

3. Begin typing. Your text will appear in the font size you just selected.

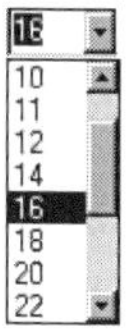

Figure 1.14

Opening the font size drop-down list box in the Formatting toolbar.

To adjust the size of a font using the Font dialog box, follow this procedure:

1. Open the Fo**r**mat menu and select the **F**ont item.

2. If the Fo**n**ts tab is not on top, click on it.

3. Select the size you want by clicking on it in the **S**ize list box (see fig. 1.15).

4. Click on the OK button.

5. Begin typing. Your text appears in the font size you selected.

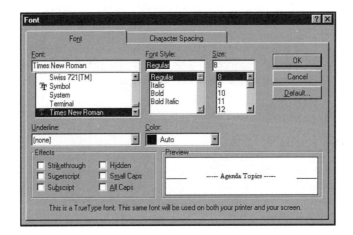

What happens when you select a font size depends on whether you have a selection active, just as when choosing a font. If a selection is active, the change in font size affects the selection only. If a selection is not active, the change in size affects the next character you type—as long as you do not move the insertion point first. If you move the insertion point before you begin typing, the font size reverts to the size already set for that region in your document.

Note   The font sizes available depend on the design of the font. Typically, for the TrueType fonts shipped with Windows, you can select from a range of sizes between 8 and 72 points. A *point* is a unit of measurement used by printers that is equal to $1/72$ of an inch. The size of a font refers to its height rather than its width. A common font size for composing letters is 10 or 12 points.

Choosing a Style

A font's *style* describes whether the font has any special attributes, such as bold, italic, or underline.

You adjust a font's style using either the Formatting toolbar or the Font dialog box. On the Formatting toolbar, you adjust style with the three buttons to the right of the Size drop-down list box labeled B, I, and U (see fig. 1.16).

Figure 1.16

Using the Formatting toolbar to set the font style.

Perform any of the following procedures to change a font's style:

◆ Click on the button labeled B to set the bold feature on. (You also can press Ctrl+B from the keyboard.)

◆ Click on the button labeled I to set the italic feature. (You also can press Ctrl+I at the keyboard.)

◆ Click on the button labeled U to set the underline feature. (You also can press Ctrl+U at the keyboard.)

◆ Click on any combination of buttons to set the appropriate mix of styles. (You also can press Ctrl+I followed by Ctrl+B at the keyboard, for example.)

◆ To clear any feature, click its button again (or press its keyboard shortcut again).

To use the Font dialog box to set the font style, perform the following procedure:

1. Open the For mat menu and select the Font item.

2. If the Fonts tab is not on top, click on it.

3. Select the style you want by clicking on it in the Font Style list box (see fig. 1.17).

4. Click on OK.

5. Begin typing. Your text appears in the font style you selected.

What happens when you select a font style depends on whether you have a selection active, just as when choosing a font or choosing a font size. If a selection is active, the change in font style affects the selection only. If a selection is not active, the change in style affects the next character you type—as long as you do not move the insertion point first. If you move the insertion point before you begin typing, the font style reverts to the style already set for that region in your document.

Tip   In Word for Windows 95, style is a word that can refer to two things: font style or document style. For an explanation of document styles, see the section "Understanding Styles" in Chapter 2, "Understanding Word for Windows Concepts."

Figure 1.17

*Selecting Bold in
the Font Style
list box.*

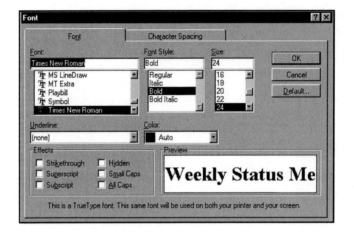

Selecting Special Features

You can set several special features that affect the appearance of your document.
Using the Font dialog box, you can set these features for your text:

◆ Underlining

◆ Color

◆ Special effects

Using the Paragraph dialog box, you can set the following features for your paragraphs:

◆ Indentation

◆ Spacing

◆ Alignment

◆ Pagination

◆ Other text-flow features

Some of these features can be set from the Formatting toolbar, but many of them
must be set using the dialog boxes.

Setting the Underline

You can set underlining for text from both the Formatting toolbar and the Font dialog box. To set underlining from the Formatting toolbar, use the following procedures (see fig. 1.18):

◆ Click on the button labeled U to set the underline feature on. (You also can press Ctrl+U from the keyboard.)

◆ To clear the underline feature, click on its button again (or press Ctrl+U again).

Figure 1.18

Setting the underline feature using the Formatting toolbar.

When you set underlining using the Formatting toolbar, the underline is a single, solid underline that appears under both words and spaces, as in the following example:

Here is an example of underlining from the Formatting toolbar.

To set underlining using the Font dialog box, use the following procedure:

1. Open the Format menu and select the Font item.

2. If the Fonts tab is not on top, click on it.

3. Select the type of underline you want by opening the Underline drop-down list box and selecting it from the list.

4. Click on OK.

5. Begin typing. Your text appears with the type of underline you selected.

The Font dialog box gives you much greater control over the type of underline you can use in your text than does the Underline button. The possible types are listed in table 1.5.

TABLE 1.5
Underlining Available in Word for Windows 95

Underline	Example
Single	Here is an example of single underlining.
Words Only	Here is an example of words only underlining.
Double	Here is an example of double underlining.
Dotted	Here is an example of dotted underlining.

What happens when you select a type of underlining depends on whether you have a selection active, just as when choosing a font or choosing a font style. If a selection is active, the change in underlining affects the selection only. If a selection is not active, the change in underlining affects the next character you type—as long as you do not move the insertion point first. If you move the insertion point before you begin typing, the type of underlining reverts to the type already set for that region in your document.

Setting the Color

Word for Windows 95 enables you to use up to 16 different colors for text. You can use colored text for display purposes only, or you can print colored text if you have a color printer. You can set the color of text by performing the following procedure:

1. Open the Format menu and select the Font item.

2. If the Fonts tab is not on top, click on it.

3. Select the color you want by opening the Color drop-down list box and selecting it from the list (see fig. 1.19).

4. Click on OK.

5. Begin typing. Your text appears in the color you selected.

One item in the list of colors is not a color: Auto. When you select this color, Word uses the text color set by the Color dialog box in Control Panel. This color is determined by the overall Windows color scheme or the custom color scheme that you use. Choosing one of the color names from the list overrides the default text color and causes text to appear in the color you have selected.

Tip   Colored text is useful for identifying section headers of different types in a long document. You might see this technique used in New Riders books. Section headings are often set in a different text color from the body text.

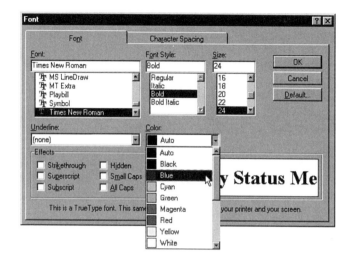

Figure 1.19

Selecting Blue in the Color drop-down list box.

What happens when you select a color depends on whether you have a selection active, just as when choosing a font or choosing a font style. If a selection is active, the change in color affects the selection only. If a selection is not active, the change in color affects the next character you type—as long as you do not move the insertion point first. If you move the insertion point before you begin typing, the color reverts to the type already set for that region in your document.

Setting Special Effects

In Word, you can use a variety of special text effects:

◆ Strikethrough

◆ Superscript

◆ Subscript

◆ Hidden

◆ Small caps

◆ All caps

To set any of these features, use the following procedure:

1. Open the Format menu and select the **F**ont item.

2. If the Fo**n**ts tab is not on top, click on it.

3. In the Effects group box, select the check box that represents the special effect you want to turn on.

4. Click on OK.

5. Begin typing. Your text appears with the special effects you selected.

You can combine up to four of the special effects if you want. The strikethrough and hidden features combine with either the small caps or all caps features and with either the superscript or subscript features. You can combine only four effects because superscript and subscript are mutually exclusive effects, as are small caps and all caps. Text cannot be both superscript and subscript, or small caps and all caps, at the same time.

Setting the Indentation

If you are used to a typewriter or to one of the early word processors, you probably are familiar with handling indentation with tabs. In Word for Windows 95, the word processor handles indentation for you. Using the Paragraph dialog box, you can tell Word how to set up paragraph indentation. Each paragraph you create then fits that template.

To set up paragraph indentation, use the following procedure:

1. Open the Format menu and select the Paragraph item.

2. If the Indents and Spacing tab is not on top, click on it (see fig. 1.20).

3. In the Indentation group box, use the Left and Right spin boxes to set the indentation from the left and right margins. Click on the arrow buttons until the measurement is correct, or select the text in the box by highlighting it with the mouse and then type the exact measurement you want.

4. To set first-line or hanging indentation, open the Special drop-down list box by clicking on its arrow, and select the appropriate item. Then use the By spin box to set the measurement for the first-line indentation or the hanging indentation.

5. Click on OK. Your current paragraph takes on the indentation you just set. Each subsequent paragraph you create takes on this pattern, unless you reset the indentation using the dialog box.

Typical indentation patterns are easy to apply. Typical paragraph settings include those shown in table 1.6.

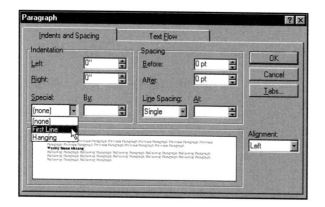

Figure 1.20

Setting indentation using the Indents and Spacing tab of the Paragraph dialog box.

TABLE 1.6
Indentation Settings for Common Paragraphs

Paragraph Type	Left	Right	Special	By
Standard	0	0	First line	.5
Blocked quote	.5	.5	(none)	blank
Hanging (bibliographic entry)	0	0	Hanging	.5

Because the Paragraph dialog box shows you an example of what the paragraph looks like in the Preview box, you easily can experiment with the indentation settings until you have the paragraph format that meets your needs.

 Tip

You can use two buttons on the Formatting toolbar to increase or decrease the left indentation setting by .5 inches (or the equivalent metric setting) with each click. These buttons are the second and third from the right on the toolbar.

When you change indentation settings, they affect your current paragraph and each subsequent paragraph you create. You do not have to select your current paragraph for the effect to take place. However, if you want to affect a group a paragraphs—putting them all into the same format—select them and then open the Paragraph dialog box. The changes then occur in all the selected paragraphs.

 Tip

You also can adjust indentation settings by dragging the pointers on the ruler. The right pointer adjusts the right margin. The left pointer has upper and lower halves. Drag the lower half to adjust the left margin. Drag the upper half to adjust the first line or hanging measurement. Drag the box at the bottom of the lower half to adjust both halves of the pointer at the same time.

Setting Line Spacing

You also can use the Paragraph dialog box to set the line spacing within each paragraph:

1. Open the Format menu and select the Paragraph item.

2. If the Indents and Spacing tab is not on top, click on it.

3. In the Spacing group box, use the Before and After spin boxes to set the distance in points from the previous paragraph and from the following paragraph. Click on the arrow buttons until the measurement is correct, or select the text in the box by highlighting it with the mouse and then type the exact measurement you want.

4. To set line spacing within the paragraph, open the Line Spacing drop-down list box by clicking on its arrow, and select the appropriate item. Then use the At spin box to set the measurement for number of lines or distance between lines, whichever is active.

5. Click on OK. Your current paragraph takes on the line spacing you just set. Each subsequent paragraph you create takes on this pattern, unless you reset the line spacing using the dialog box.

The Line Spacing drop-down list box offers the settings shown in table 1.7.

TABLE 1.7
Line Spacing Settings in the Paragraph Dialog Box

Setting	Explanation
Single	Single spacing, with the line set to a height just a bit greater than that of the font
1.5 Lines	One and one-half line spacing, with the height calculated as 1.5 times the height of a single-spaced line
Double	Double spacing, with the height of the line calculated as twice that of the single-spaced line
At Least	A minimal height for each line, in points, that Word can adjust to accommodate larger fonts or inserted objects
Exactly	A fixed height for each line, in points, that Word cannot change
Multiple	A line height, expressed as a multiple of the single-spaced line height, that you can adjust to any value you want (the default is three, triple-spaced, but you can enter any factor to serve as a multiplier—1.4, for example)

As with indentation, because the Paragraph dialog box shows you an example of what the paragraph spacing looks like in the Preview box, you can experiment with the spacing settings until you have the paragraph format that meets your needs.

When you change line spacing settings, they affect your current paragraph and each subsequent paragraph you create. You do not have to select your current paragraph for the effect to take place. However, if you want to affect a group of paragraphs—setting them all to the same line spacing—select them and then open the Paragraph dialog box. The changes then occur in all the selected paragraphs.

Setting Alignment on the Page

Word offers you two means of setting the alignment of paragraphs on the page. You have four choices for paragraph alignment:

- ◆ **Left justified.** A straight left margin and a ragged right margin.

- ◆ **Right justified.** A straight right margin and a ragged left margin.

- ◆ **Centered.** Each line centered and both right and left margins ragged.

- ◆ **Fully justified.** Straight right and left margins.

You can set the paragraph alignment using the four buttons on the Formatting toolbar to the right of the underline button (see fig. 1.21). Click on the button that represents the alignment you want. The pictures on the buttons graphically illustrate the type of alignment that the button provides. These buttons are mutually exclusive. Only one can be pressed at a time, and one must always be pressed.

You also can set paragraph alignment from the Paragraph dialog box by performing the following steps:

1. Open the F**o**rmat menu and select the **P**aragraph item.

2. If the **I**ndents and Spacing tab is not on top, click on it.

3. Open the Alignment drop-down list box by clicking on its arrow, and select the type of alignment you want from the list.

4. Click on OK. Your current paragraph takes on the alignment you just set. Each subsequent paragraph you create takes on this pattern unless you reset the alignment using the dialog box.

Note Many desktop publishers feel that a ragged right margin is easier to read than fully justified text. This is because the letters and words always have a consistent amount of space between them, whereas fully justified lines often have inconsistent letter—and word—spacing that makes them harder to read.

Figure 1.21

The paragraph alignment buttons on the formatting toolbar.

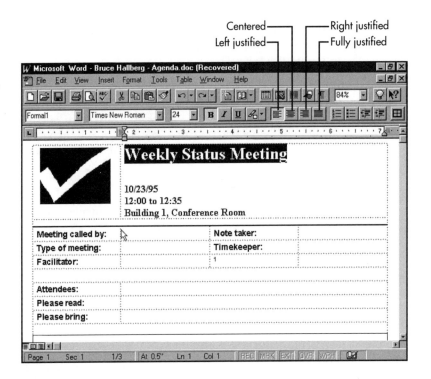

Changing the Text

The third step in learning to accomplish tasks with Word for Windows 95 is learning how to edit the text of your document. The feature that captivated most users of the original word processors was the capability to edit the text of a document. As word processors have developed, the editing features have become more flexible and useful.

Note   Open a document to practice with before you start reading these sections. Again, try working on the agenda. You can fill it out for your next meeting while you practice.

Inserting Text

By now you have discovered how to insert text. When you press text keys, characters are inserted at the insertion point, and the insertion point moves to the right of the last character inserted. You can move the insertion point with the navigation keys or

by clicking with the mouse. (See the section "Navigating the Document" earlier in this chapter.) Inserting text probably is the most intuitive action you take with Word.

Overtyping Text

There are times, however, when you want to type over existing text. To switch to this editing mode, press the Insert key. When you type, the characters you type replace any characters to the left of the insertion point. To turn off the overtype mode, press the Insert key again. Use this mode when you need to replace a section of text completely with one of about the same length. Using overtype saves you the time of removing the outdated text by some other means.

Tip You can switch the overtype mode on or off by double-clicking on the OVR box on the status bar at the bottom of the Word window. Note that you cannot activate overtype mode when revision marks are turned on.

Cutting and Pasting

As you work with your document, there are, of course, times when you want to delete a block of text or move a block of text. In Word, you perform these tasks with the cutting and pasting features.

Before you can cut and paste text, however, you first must select the block of text on which you want to take action. You select text using one of two methods:

◆ Drag the mouse pointer over the text to be selected.

◆ Hold down the Shift key and press any of the navigation keys. (Table 1.3 provides a list of the navigation keys.)

Selected text is highlighted in inverse screen colors, usually a black background with white text. (The actual colors depend on the color scheme you have selected using the Control Panel.)

Tip You can lock Word in the text selection mode by pressing F8 or double-clicking on the EXT box in the status bar at the bottom of the Word window. As long as EXT remains highlighted, you can extend your selection using any of the navigation keys or by dragging with the mouse. You will not stop extending your selection until you double-click again on the EXT box.

Once you select a block of text, you can perform on it the operations listed in table 1.8.

TABLE 1.8
Cutting and Pasting Operations in Word for Windows

Operation	Result
Cut	Removes text from your document and places it on the Clipboard
Copy	Copies the selected text to the Clipboard, but does not remove it from your document
Paste	Inserts text from the Clipboard, placing the text at the current insertion point (if you have a block of selected text active, it replaces the selected block with the text on the Clipboard)

Note   The Clipboard is an area of memory in which Windows stores material that is cut or copied.

These operations are the same as in any other Windows program that enables editing in this manner. Word provides a standard **E**dit menu with the usual Cu**t**, **C**opy, and **P**aste items for performing these operations. (Accelerator key combinations for these three menu items are Ctrl+X, Ctrl+C, and Ctrl+V, respectively.) However, the Standard toolbar provides buttons for these three common operations (see fig. 1.22).

Figure 1.22

The Cut, Copy, and Paste buttons on the Standard toolbar.

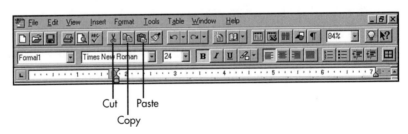

Cut   Paste
Copy

Tip   The Windows standard keys Ctrl+Ins, Shift+Ins, and Ctrl+Del also are available to Cut, Copy, and Paste.

Undoing and Redoing

When you are editing, you can, of course, make mistakes. Nothing is more disappointing than deleting an entire section of a document and then realizing it was the wrong section! Word for Windows 95 helps you recover from such mistakes by offering undo and redo features.

If you do make a mistake, you can undo it by selecting the **U**ndo option from the **E**dit menu. This procedure undoes the last change you made to the file. (The accelerator key combination for this undo operation is Ctrl+Z.) Word always will add the name of the operation you are about to undo as the second word of the **U**ndo menu item. If you cannot undo anything, this option changes to Can't Undo and is dimmed.

However, what if you have made lots of changes and discovered you made them in the wrong place? Word helps you compensate for such problems by offering the Undo button on the Standard toolbar. The Undo button is the one with an arrow curved to the left on it. Click on the arrow to the right of the button to display a list of the things you can undo (see fig. 1.23). Select the items on the list you want to undo by dragging with the mouse or extending the selection with the down-arrow key. Then release the mouse button (or press Enter if you are working from the keyboard). Word undoes the last set of actions you indicated. You must always undo actions in the sequence they were taken.

Figure 1.23

Using the Undo button on the Standard toolbar.

You also can redo actions. To redo a single action from the **E**dit menu, select the **R**epeat option from the **E**dit menu. Word always will add the name of the operation you are about to redo as the second word of the **R**epeat menu item.

You can redo multiple actions using the Redo button on the Standard toolbar. The Redo button is the one with the picture of an arrow curved to the right. It works the same way as the Undo button (see fig. 1.24). Click the arrow to the right of the button, select the sequential items you want to redo, and release the mouse button (or press Enter if you are working from the keyboard). Word redoes the set of actions you have indicated.

Figure 1.24

Using the Redo button on the Standard toolbar.

Using Advanced Formatting Features

The fourth step in learning to accomplish work with Word for Windows 95 is learning how to apply advanced formatting features. Word gives you almost all the capabilities associated with desktop publishing programs. Taking advantage of these advanced features enables you to give your documents a professional look.

 Tip   If you don't have a document open, it is a good idea to open one now so that you can practice with these advanced features. The Normal document you created earlier is a good choice. This document gives you a chance to experiment without spoiling the formatting of your agenda.

Adding a Border

In Word, you can add borders around paragraphs to create lines and boxes of different styles on the page. Such borders can be useful for highlighting information, dividing sections of documents, or giving some artistic flair to a document. You also can shade sections of a document using Word's bordering tools. These features enable you to underscore the relative emphasis each section of the document should have.

Word provides two methods for creating borders and shading sections of your document. The most accessible is the Borders toolbar, which you can show by clicking on the last button on the Formatting toolbar. (Clicking on this button again hides the Borders toolbar.) As shown in figure 1.25, the Borders toolbar provides seven buttons and two drop-down list boxes, which enable you to specify the nature of the border and the amount of shading for a block of text.

Figure 1.25

The Borders toolbar.

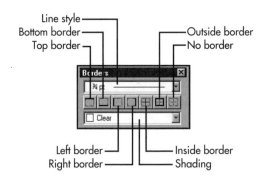

Tip An inside border is a border that appears between paragraphs in a multiparagraph section surrounded by a border or between the cells of a table.

To use the Borders toolbar, follow this procedure:

1. Place the insertion point inside the paragraph, or select the group of paragraphs you want to surround with a border.

2. Click on the button that provides the kind of border you want.

3. Open the upper drop-down list box and select the line style for the border.

4. Open the lower drop-down list box and select the shading for the bordered area. (Keep in mind that you can shade an area that does not have a border around it.)

The second method for creating borders and shading sections of text is by using the Borders and Shading dialog box. This dialog box, shown in figure 1.26, gives you more control over the nature of the borders and shading. You can set colors for each line or shading, for instance, which you cannot do from the Borders toolbar. You also can define shadow borders and set the distance of the border from the text.

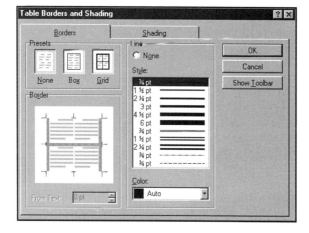

Figure 1.26

The Paragraph Borders and Shading dialog box showing the Borders tab.

To set a border using the dialog box, perform the following procedure:

1. Place the insertion point inside a paragraph or select the group of paragraphs you want to surround with a border.

2. Open the Format menu.

3. Select the **B**orders and Shading item.

4. Click on the **B**orders tab if it is not on top.

5. Use the Preset controls to select the type of border, or click on the junction point (defined by the angle markers) in the Border control to define where the border should be.

6. Use the **F**rom Text spin box to set the distance in points of the border line from the text.

7. Select the line style from the St**y**le list box.

8. Select the color from the **C**olor drop-down list box.

9. Click on OK to implement your border.

To set shading using the dialog box, perform the following procedure:

1. Place the insertion point inside a paragraph or select the group of paragraphs you want to surround with a border.

2. Open the Format menu.

3. Select the **B**orders and Shading item.

4. Click on the **S**hading tab if it is not on top (see fig. 1.27).

5. Select the type of shading from the Sha**d**ing list box.

6. Select the foreground color for the shaded area, using the **F**oreground drop-down list box.

7. Select the background color for the shaded area, using the B**a**ckground drop-down list box.

8. Click on OK to implement the shading you have designed.

Tip   You can set both borders and shading in one session with the Paragraph Borders and Shading dialog box.

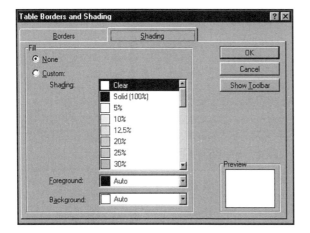

Figure 1.27

The Shading tab in the Borders and Shading dialog box.

Building Tables

Word for Windows includes an advanced table editor that enables you to create tables that include the following features:

- ◆ Split cells

- ◆ Formulas that define the contents of cells

- ◆ Complex formatting

- ◆ Predefined table formats

Word provides three methods for creating tables; the method you choose depends on how you want to use the table. If you need a quick table with just a few cells, or a table with lots of cells that are of equal sizes, use the Insert Table button on the Standard toolbar by performing the following steps:

1. Place the insertion point where you want the table to appear in your document.

2. Click on the button to open the grid.

3. Drag across the grid until the appropriate number of cells is highlighted (see fig. 1.28).

4. Release the mouse button to insert the table.

5. Insert your data into the table's cells.

Figure 1.28

Using the Insert Table button on the Standard toolbar to define the table's size.

 Tip   Table 1.3 explains how to use key combinations to navigate a table.

If you need to have more control over column widths or you want more control over the format of your table, use the Insert Table dialog box to create your table. To use this dialog box, perform the following steps:

1. Place the insertion point where you want the table to appear in your document.

2. Open the T**a**ble menu.

3. Select the **I**nsert Table item. This brings up the Insert Table dialog box (see fig. 1.29).

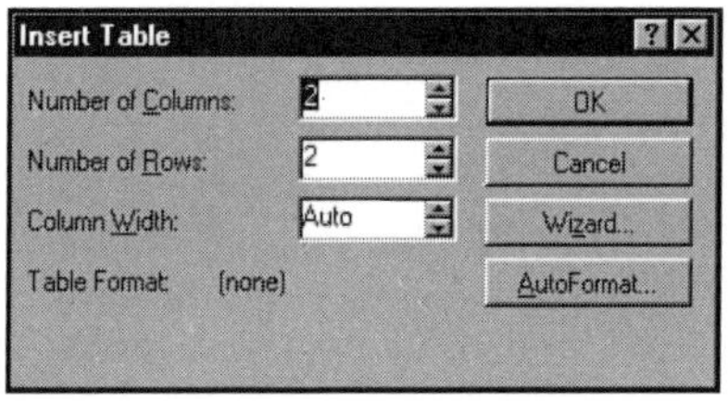

Figure 1.29

The Insert Table dialog box.

4. In the dialog box, use the three spin boxes to set the Number of **C**olumns, Number of **R**ows, and Column **W**idth.

5. To select a special format, click on the **A**utoFormat button to bring up the Table AutoFormat dialog box (see fig. 1.30).

6. In the Table AutoFormat dialog box, select one of the predefined formats in the Forma**t**s list box. (The Preview box shows you what each table format looks like.)

7. Use the check boxes in the Formats to Apply group to select whether to use **B**orders, **S**hading, **F**onts, **C**olors, Auto**F**it, or any combination of these features. (You can experiment with different combinations of these features and view the results in the Preview box.)

8. Use the check boxes in the Apply Special Formats To group to select whether the formats you chose in step 7 are applied to Heading **R**ows, First C**o**lumn, **L**ast Row, Last Col**u**mn, or any combination of these. (You can experiment with different combinations of these features and view the results in the Preview box.)

9. Click on OK to accept the AutoFormat you have chosen.

10. Click on OK in the Insert Table dialog box to insert your table.

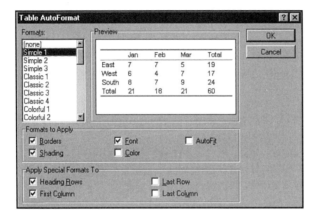

Figure 1.30

The Table AutoFormat dialog box.

Stop If you have an active selection in your document when you choose the **I**nsert Table item from the T**a**ble menu, Word converts the text in the selection to a table and does not display the Insert Table dialog box. If you did not intend such a conversion, use the Undo feature to remove the table and return your text to its former state.

The final method for inserting a table is to use the Table Wizard, shown in figure 1.31. Use this method when you want to build a complex table with row and column headings preinserted. The Table Wizard is best at building tables for storing time-oriented data, such as monthly reports.

To use the Table Wizard, follow these steps:

1. Place the insertion point where you want the table to appear in your document.

2. Open the T**a**ble menu.

3. Select the **I**nsert Table item.

4. Click on the Wi**z**ard button to bring up the initial Table Wizard screen.

5. Select the table format from the six presented, using the option buttons. Click on the **N**ext button to move to the next screen.

6. Use the drop-down list box to set the number of columns. Click on the **N**ext button to move to the next screen.

7. Use the option buttons to set the type of column headings you want. Click on the **N**ext button to move to the next screen.

8. Use the option buttons to set the type of row headings you want. Click on the **N**ext button to move to the next screen.

9. Use the option buttons to indicate the contents of the cells. Click on the **N**ext button to move to the next screen.

10. Use the option buttons to select the printing orientation for the table. Click on the **N**ext button to move to the next screen.

11. Use the option buttons to determine whether you want to see each step in the table's creation on your screen. Click on the **F**inish button.

12. When the Table AutoFormat dialog box appears (refer to figure 1.30), select one of the predefined formats in the Forma**t**s list box. (The Preview box shows you what each table format looks like.)

13. Use the check boxes in the Formats to Apply group to select whether to use **B**orders, **S**hading, **F**onts, **C**olors, AutoF**i**t, or any combination of these. (You can experiment with different combinations of these features and view the results in the Preview box.)

14. Use the check boxes in the Apply Special Formats To group to select whether the formats you chose in step 13 are applied to Heading **R**ows, First C**o**lumn, **L**ast Row, Last Col**u**mn, or any combination of these. (You can experiment with different combinations of these features and view the results in the Preview box.)

15. Click on OK to accept the AutoFormat you have chosen. The Wizard then inserts your table in the document.

Word's T**a**ble menu provides robust table editing features. If you create a simple table and decide later you want to apply AutoFormat to it, for instance, select the table and then select the Table Auto**F**ormat item from the T**a**ble menu. If you want to split a cell into two subcells, select the cell (or cells) and then choose S**p**lit Cells from the T**a**ble menu. You can split a table into two sections using the **S**plit Table menu option. You also can convert text to a table using the Con**v**ert Text to Table option, which divides the text into cells based on the appearance of a special character in the text. If you have a list in which the items are separated by commas, for instance, the chunks of text between the commas are inserted into separate cells.

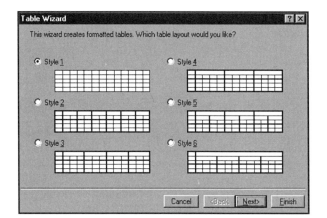

Figure 1.31

The initial screen of the Table Wizard.

Perhaps the most exciting table feature in Word for Windows 6.0, however, is the capability to assign formulas to cells in a table. The contents of the cell are the results of the calculation. You can, as a result, build miniature spreadsheets into your Word tables. If you are familiar with entering formulas into Microsoft Excel spreadsheet cells, you already know how to enter formulas into Word table cells. The process is very much the same.

To insert a formula in a cell, follow these steps:

1. Place the insertion point in the cell.

2. Open the Table menu.

3. Select the Formula option. The Formula dialog box appears, as shown in figure 1.32.

Figure 1.32

The Formula dialog box.

4. In the Formula dialog box, type the formula in the Formula text box after the equal sign. Use standard mathematical operators (+, -, *, /) and parentheses to build your formula.

5. If you want a number format associated with the cell, select one from the Number Format drop-down list box. The *number format* determines the way the

number is displayed in the cell, governing such things as number of decimal places and whether a dollar sign is present.

6. If you want to use one of Word's mathematical functions, select it from the Paste F**u**nction drop-down list box.

7. If you want to use a cross-reference to a bookmark, paste it in using the Paste **B**ookmark drop-down list box.

8. Click on OK. The result of your formula now appears as the cell's contents.

Tip   If you have a formula stored at a bookmark, you can reference it in the formula you are building by pasting in the bookmark name. You can create cross-references to formulas outside the table in this manner.

Inserting Pictures

In addition to providing robust table creation and editing, Word also makes it easy to insert pictures into your document. Word can import graphics in most graphics file formats. If your drawing program's file format is not supported directly, chances are that your drawing program can convert the graphic to one of Word's supported file formats.

To insert a picture into your Word document, perform the following steps:

1. Place the insertion point where you want the picture to go.

2. Open the **I**nsert menu.

3. Select the **P**icture menu item.

4. In the Insert Picture dialog box, select the graphics file from the File **N**ame list box. You can navigate to other drives and directories using the **D**irectories and Dri**v**es controls just as you can in the Open dialog box. You can limit the type of file displayed in the File **N**ame list box by selecting a new file type descriptor from the Files of **T**ype drop-down list box (see fig. 1.33).

5. If you want to preview the picture before inserting it, click the Preview button.

6. If you want to create a link to the graphics file, check the Lin**k** to File check box. (See Part V of this book, "Data Sharing and Integration," for more information about links. If you choose to link, you can uncheck the **S**ave Picture in Document check box if you want.)

7. Click on the OK button. Word then inserts the picture into your document.

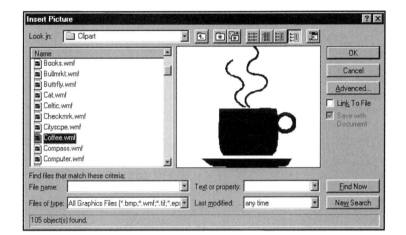

Figure 1.33

The Insert Picture dialog box showing a picture previewed.

Tip   If you cannot find the file you want, use the **F**ind File button in the Insert Picture dialog box to invoke Word's file finder. This feature searches your drive for files that match the specifications you provide.

If you want to edit the picture after you have inserted it, double-click on the picture. This action starts Microsoft Picture, which enables you to edit the picture while it is in place in your Word document. *See Chapter 4, "Sharing Data with Word," for more information about picture editing.*

Printing the Document

The fifth and final step in learning how to accomplish tasks with Word for Windows 95 is learning how to print your document. Word provides access to all its document formatting features from the printing menu commands. Although you can access these same features at any time as you work, you probably don't think much about them until you are ready to print. The remaining sections in this chapter explain how to get ready to print by saving and formatting your document, and finally how to print your document.

Tip   Be sure to have a document open so that you can practice with Word's printing features. Your agenda is a good choice. If you filled it out in the earlier exercises, you can print enough copies to distribute for your next meeting.

Saving Your Work

Although not required before printing, it is a good idea to save your work at this time. If your computer locks up because of a printer problem, your document is protected as a file on disk. Word offers several save options, the easiest of which is the Save button on the Standard toolbar. This button is third from the left and has a picture of a 3.5-inch floppy disk on it (see fig. 1.34).

Figure 1.34

The Save button on the Standard toolbar.

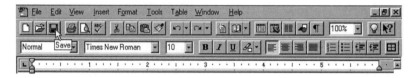

To save using this button, click on it with the mouse. The following actions take place:

◆ If the file already has a name, Word saves the file.

◆ If the file has not been named, Word displays the Save As dialog box, prompting you to name the file (refer to fig. 1.8). After you provide a name for the file and click on OK, Word saves the file.

◆ After Word starts to save the file, it might display a dialog box asking for information. If the file is not in Word format, for instance, the dialog box asks if you want to convert to Word format, save in the existing format, or cancel the save operation.

The Word **F**ile menu offers three save options (see fig. 1.35). The first, **S**ave, initiates the same actions as clicking on the Save button on the Standard toolbar. The second option, Save **A**s, brings up the Save As dialog box. Use this option when you wish to save a file under a new file name or in a new location. The third option, Save Al**l**, initiates the save action for all files that currently are open in Word.

Tip

The AutoSave option is a useful option to set. Click on the **O**ptions button in the Save As dialog box and check the Automatic **S**ave Every check box. Enter the number of minutes to wait between saves in the spin box just to the right of the check box. The default is 10 minutes, but if you work quickly you might want to reduce that setting to 3 minutes. Click on OK, and then cancel the Save As dialog box. Word now will save your document at the regular interval you specified.

The only disadvantage to this is that if you have AutoSave turned on and you are working on large files it might take Word a few seconds to respond to your command when it is saving—which can become a nuisance.

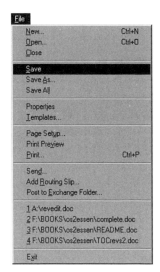

Figure 1.35

The three save options on Word's File menu.

Setting Up the Page

You always can print a document without checking the page setup, but when you do, you accept default values that might not be what you want for your document. By checking the page setup, you can make sure that all the settings for your document are correct. You get access to all the page features through one dialog box, so the process does not take much time.

Tip The one feature that Word does not let you check from the print dialog boxes is page numbering. Before you print, be sure you have the pages numbered if you so desire. To add page numbers, select Page Numbers from the Insert menu.

To check page setup, perform the following steps:

1. Open the File menu.

2. Select the Page Setup option.

3. Click on the Margins tab (see fig. 1.36).

4. Use the Top, Bottom, Left, and Right spin boxes to adjust the width of these margins.

5. Use the Header and Footer spin boxes to adjust the distance between the header and footer and the edge of the page.

Figure 1.36

*The Margins tab
in the Page Setup
dialog box.*

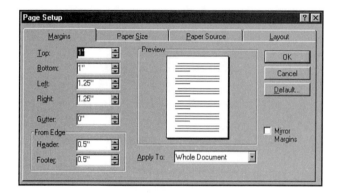

6. Use the G**u**tter spin box to create a gutter if you plan to bind the document. The
   gutter is an additional margin added to allow room for binding. An extra margin
   is added to the left side of odd-numbered pages and to the right side of even-
   numbered pages.

7. Check the M**i**rror Margins check box if your document needs to be printed with
   right and left pages. This can be used in a similar manner to the gutter.

8. Use the **A**pply To drop-down list box to determine if these settings apply to the
   whole document or to the document from the insertion point forward.

9. Click on the Paper **S**ize tab (see fig. 1.37).

Figure 1.37

*The Paper Size
tab in the Page
Setup dialog box.*

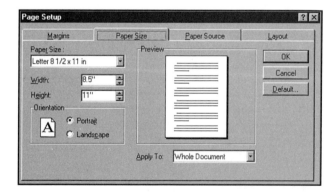

10. Use the Pape**r** Size drop-down list box to select predefined paper dimensions, or
    the **W**idth and H**e**ight spin boxes to set custom dimensions.

11. Use the option buttons in the Orientation group to set Portra**i**t or Lands**c**ape as
    the printing direction.

12. Use the **A**pply To drop-down list box to determine if these settings apply to the whole document, to the document from the insertion point forward, or to the current section of a multiple-section document.

13. Click on the **P**aper Source tab (see fig. 1.38).

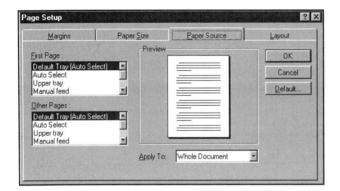

Figure 1.38

The Paper Source tab in the Page Setup dialog box.

14. Use the **F**irst Page and **O**ther Pages list boxes to determine from which tray the paper for those pages feeds.

Tip   Being able to set a different paper source for the first page can enable the first page to be printed on letterhead and the remaining pages to be printed on standard stock.

15. Use the **A**pply To drop-down list box to determine if these settings apply to the whole document, to the document from the insertion point forward, or to the current section of a multiple-section document.

16. Click on the **L**ayout tab (see fig. 1.39).

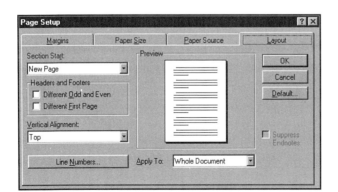

Figure 1.39

The Layout tab in the Page Setup dialog box.

17. Use the Section Sta<u>r</u>t drop-down list box to determine whether the document is one continuous section or new sections starting at New Columns, New Pages, Odd Pages, or Even Pages. *See Chapter 3, "Using Advanced Formatting Features," for an explanation of sections.*

18. Use the check boxes in the Headers and Footers group to set whether headers and footers will be different on odd and even pages and whether the first page will have a different header and footer than the rest.

19. Use the <u>V</u>ertical Alignment drop-down list box to set the alignment of text on the page relative to the top of the page, relative to the center of the page, or justified between the top and bottom edges of the page.

20. Check the <u>S</u>uppress Endnotes check box to prevent endnotes from printing.

21. Click on the Line <u>N</u>umbers button to open a dialog box with controls that enable you to add line numbers to your document.

22. Use the <u>A</u>pply To drop-down list box to determine if these settings apply to the whole document or to the document from the insertion point forward.

23. Click on OK to close the dialog box and make your settings effective.

After you are satisfied with the page settings, you should preview the document to make certain that it looks the way you want.

Previewing the Document

The print preview feature of Word for Windows 95 enables you to see the way your document will appear on the page before you print it. This option gives you a chance to verify that the formatting is correct and to make any final changes before the document goes to paper. In fact, you can edit your document in the print preview mode if you notice any details that need to be adjusted.

 Tip   You can work with your document in the page layout view mode at all times if you want, which is like being in the print preview mode except that the Print Preview toolbar is not available. Open the **V**iew menu and select the **P**age Layout menu option, or click on the center button to the left of the horizontal scroll bar at the bottom left edge of the document window.

To enter the print preview mode, open the **F**ile menu and select the Print Pre**v**iew option. (You can also click on the Print Preview button on the Standard toolbar; it's to the right of the Print button). Your screen adjusts to show a reduced picture of your documents page, and the Print Preview toolbar appears (see fig. 1.40). The percentage of reduction depends on your screen resolution.

Figure 1.40

The Print Preview toolbar.

While in the print preview mode, you can use the Print Preview toolbar to perform the following actions:

◆ You can print the document by clicking on the Print button.

◆ You can switch the magnifier on and off by clicking on the Magnifier button.

◆ You can switch to a one-page view by clicking on the One Page button.

◆ You can switch to view multiple pages by clicking on the Multiple Pages button and dragging across the grid that appears, releasing the mouse button when you have the multiple-page view you want to use.

◆ You can zoom in or out on your document by adjusting the zoom percentage in the Zoom Control drop-down list box.

◆ You can switch the view of the ruler on and off by clicking on the View Ruler button.

◆ You can squeeze a small amount of text on the final page into the other pages by clicking on the Shrink to Fit button.

◆ You can expand the preview screen to show only the page, the toolbar, and the status bar by clicking on the Full Screen button.

◆ You can get context-sensitive help by clicking on the Help button and then clicking on other buttons or screen elements.

◆ You can exit the preview mode by clicking on the **C**lose button.

When the magnifier is on, your mouse pointer becomes a magnifying glass. You can switch between a 100 percent view of a document page and the reduced view of a document page by clicking on that page. You have to shut off the magnifier, however, to do any editing while in the preview mode.

When you are satisfied with the document in the preview mode, the next step is to print the document.

Printing

Word provides three methods of initiating printing. You can click on the Print button on either the Standard toolbar or the Print Preview toolbar. When you do so, Word prints one copy of the document, using the settings in place at the time you clicked on the Print button.

For more control over the printing process, you can select the **P**rint option from the **F**ile menu. (The accelerator key combination for this menu action is Ctrl+P.) This action causes the Print dialog box to appear (see fig. 1.41).

Figure 1.41

The Print dialog box.

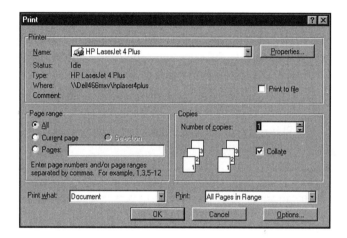

To exert maximal control over your print job, perform the following steps from the Print dialog box:

1. Select the object to be printed using the **P**rint What drop-down list box. Word enables you to print the document or several items ancillary to the document, such as Summary Info, Annotations, Style, AutoText Entries, and Key Assignments.

2. Use the **C**opies spin box to set the number of copies to print.

3. Use the option buttons in the Page range group to determine how much of the document to print. You can print **A**ll the document, the Curr**e**nt Page, or selected Pa**g**es. (If you select Pa**g**es, you must enter the page range to print in the text box. Separate discontinuous pages with commas, and express page ranges using a hyphen; for example: 2,4,6-8,12.) If a selection is currently active, you can opt to print the Selectio**n**.

4. Use the P**r**int drop-down list box to specify whether to print All Pages in Range, just the Odd Pages, or just the Even Pages.

5. Check the Collate check box to cause Word to finish printing the first copy before printing the second copy. Otherwise, Word prints all the copies of one page, then all the copies of the next, and so on.

Tip

By not selecting Collate Copies, some printers might print the document faster because Word will attempt to tell the printer to print copies of the page itself, using the printer's built-in memory to quickly duplicate each page. If the printer supports this it will reduce the size of the file being sent to the printer, and should improve printing time.

6. Check the Print to File check box to cause Word to print the document to a disk file. When you print to a file, you then can print the document on a computer that does not have Word installed with the operating system print command.

7. If the Printer line at the top of the dialog box does not list the printer you want, use the drop-down list box to choose a different available printer (see fig. 1.42). This enables you to choose from a list of available printers. If you need to adjust the setup of the printer, click on the **P**roperties button to open the dialog box provided by the printer driver that enables adjustment of printer settings.

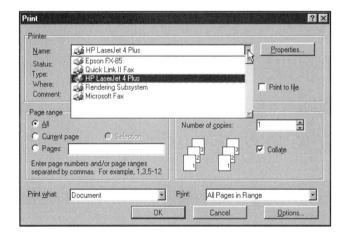

Figure 1.42

Choosing a different printer.

8. To adjust Word's printing options from the Print dialog box, click on the **O**ptions button. This action opens the Print tab in the Options dialog box, shown in figure 1.43. You can use the Include With Document check boxes to determine which of the ancillary materials to print along with the document. You can use the Printing Options check boxes to set output quality, the print order, whether fields and links are updated before printing, and whether printing can occur in the background. You can use the Default **T**ray drop-down list box to set the default paper tray for your printer. And you can set the Options for Current Document Only controls to set up settings that refer only to the current document.

Figure 1.43

*The Print tab in
the Options
dialog box.*

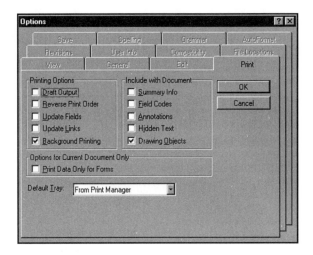

9. When all is set correctly, close all the dialog boxes you have opened from the Print dialog box, and click on the Print dialog box's OK button. Word then prints your document.

Understanding Word for Windows Concepts

Every piece of software has a set of concepts—a mindset—behind it. To exploit Word to your best advantage, you have to get used to a few metaphors and concepts that drive the design of the software. In this chapter, you will learn the following items:

- What a document is

- What a template is

- How styles work

- When to use document tools

- The way in which macros structure Word

This chapter also will acquaint you with toolbars, headers and footers, and multiple document handling. After you are familiar with all these concepts, your work with Word will become more intuitive.

Defining "Document"

Word uses the metaphor of a *document* to describe the data you can enter and maintain with the word processor. A Word document has a lot in common with the typical document you could produce with a typewriter; for instance, both types of documents consist of printed pages containing text. However, a Word document can be much more.

Word documents can exist in your computer's memory and can be stored on a disk. Word documents can be viewed on your computer's screen or can be printed on your printer. Because they are electronic in form, Word documents can be sent by electronic mail as well as postal mail. In addition, Word documents can contain several different kinds of data. They are not just text documents, as typewritten documents are.

The Document Window

Probably the best way to begin understanding how Word for Windows extends the document metaphor is to look at the way a document appears on the screen.

Each document appears in a *document window,* a child window that Word creates in its workspace when you create a document (see fig. 2.1). Essentially, a document window is an on-screen container for your document. This window not only controls the appearance of your document, but also provides you with means of interacting with your document.

A Word document window is like the standard document window that you see in any other Windows application. It has the familiar title bar, control menu box, minimize button, maximize button, and scroll bars. These items are standard for any document window. They enable you to view the contents of a document and to scroll that view.

Word adds two elements to this familiar scheme that give you much greater control over your document. At the top of the document underneath the title bar is a horizontal ruler. At the left edge of the horizontal scroll bar are three view buttons.

Using the Ruler

The ruler enables you to control the margins, the paragraph indentation, and the tab settings for your document. (Figure 2.2 shows the ruler and its parts in detail.) The margin settings are controlled by the upward facing pointers at the bottom edge of the ruler. Dragging these pointers adjusts the position of the right or left margin. When you drag these pointers, Word displays a vertical dashed line down your screen showing the position of the margin in the document. You can align margins easily in different portions of your document by matching this line to the position of the relevant characters on the screen.

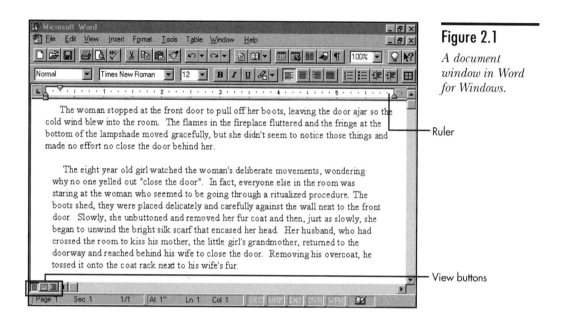

Figure 2.1

A document window in Word for Windows.

Ruler

View buttons

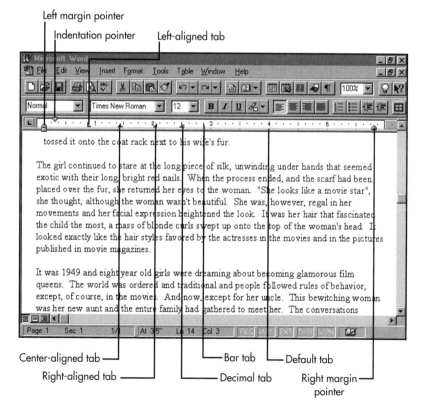

Left margin pointer

Indentation pointer   Left-aligned tab

Center-aligned tab

Right-aligned tab

Bar tab   Default tab

Decimal tab

Right margin pointer

Figure 2.2

The details of Word's horizontal ruler.

The paragraph indentation setting is controlled by the downward-facing pointer at the top edge of the ruler. Dragging this pointer adjusts the indentation of the first line of a paragraph. When you drag the pointer, Word displays a vertical dashed line down your screen so that you can see the exact position of the new indentation setting.

You can align indentations easily in different portions of your document by matching this line to the position of the relevant characters. You can use the ruler to create both hanging and standard indentations.

Tip You also can adjust the paragraph settings using the Paragraph dialog box as explained in Chapter 1, "Word for Windows Quick Start." To do this, select the **P**aragraph option from the F**o**rmat menu.

After setting the indentation for a paragraph, you will often want to move both the left margin setting and the indentation setting at one time. In this way, you preserve your indentation pattern while adjusting the margin. You can accomplish this type of adjustment by dragging the box under the left margin pointer.

As in the other margin and indentation adjustments, Word displays a vertical dashed line down your screen to indicate the position of the left margin. In this mode, Word does not display a line to indicate the position of the indentation pointer.

You can adjust tab settings by clicking or double-clicking on the ruler. Clicking on the box at the left edge of the ruler enables you to select which type of tab you will place on the ruler. Clicking on the box cycles you through the following four kinds of tab types:

◆ **Left-aligned.** Characters extend to the right of the tab as you type; indicated by an L-shaped angle in the box.

◆ **Center-aligned.** Characters are centered about the tab position; indicated by an angle with the vertical member centered over the base line.

◆ **Right-aligned.** Characters extend to the left of the tab as you type; indicated by a reverse L-shaped angle.

◆ **Decimal.** The decimal point aligns with the tab position; indicated by the symbol for a center-aligned tab with a decimal point to the right of the vertical member.

After you have selected the type of tab you want, follow these procedures to set the tabs:

◆ Click once on a marked position on the ruler to place a tab at that position.

◆ Double-click on the ruler to place a tab at an unmarked position.

As you are clicking or double-clicking to set a tab, Word displays a vertical dashed line down your screen to show you the position of the tab relative to the text on the screen.

The action of double-clicking not only places the tab but opens the Tabs dialog box, shown in figure 2.3. In this dialog box you can specify the exact position of the tab on the ruler as well as the tab's type and the positions of default tabs on the ruler.

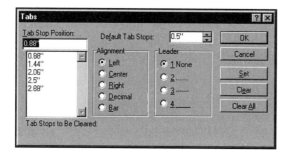

Figure 2.3

The Tabs dialog box.

 Tip   You also can access the Tabs dialog box by selecting the **T**abs option from the F**o**rmat menu.

The exact position of the tab you are setting appears in the **T**ab Stop Position combination box in the Tabs dialog box; the positions of other tabs you have set appear in the list box portion of the combination box. To adjust the position and character of the tab, perform the following steps:

1. To specify a more exact position for the tab, enter a number representing the exact position you want in the text box portion of the **T**ab Stop Position combination box.

2. Select the type of the tab using the option buttons in the Alignment group. You can select from the four options already discussed plus the **B**ar tab option. A *bar tab* places a vertical line through a paragraph at the tab position.

3. Use the option buttons in the Leader group to select characters that fill in the space between the last text on the line (or the margin, if there is no text) and the tab position.

4. Click on the **S**et button, then click on OK to complete the action of setting a tab at an unmarked position on the ruler.

Tip A tabs leader enables you to place all the periods, or leader dots, between a chapter title and a page number in a table of contents or similar document. You do not have to type all those periods by hand!

The Tabs dialog box also enables the three following actions:

◆ You can clear the tab indicated in the **T**ab Stop Position combination box by clicking on the Cl**e**ar button and then clicking on OK.

◆ You can clear all the tabs you have set by clicking on the Clear **A**ll button and then clicking on OK.

◆ You can adjust the width between the default tab stops using the De**f**ault Tab Stops spin box.

Note Default tabs are present in the document even when you have set no other tabs. They are indicated on the ruler by faint dots along the bottom edge.

As you can see, a Word document adds all the settings provided on the ruler to the design of a document. Embedded in each document is the equivalent of the tabulator bar and margin setting controls on a typewriter. Word merges these concepts related to document control into the concept of a Word for Windows document.

Changing the View

Word merges concepts of three different types of documents into its formula for the document. Writers often talk of outlines, drafts, and final copy. Word enables you to view any document in any of these three ways; you do not need to create separate documents for your outlines, drafts, and final copies. In Word for Windows, you shift among these points of view on a document by clicking on the view buttons at the left edge of a document's horizontal scroll bar (see fig. 2.4).

To see a document as an outline, click on the outline button. The Outlining toolbar appears, as shown in figure 2.5. Now when you type, each block of text is either a heading for the outline or body text. The single arrow buttons on the Outlining toolbar reformat a block of text as a heading. The left and right arrows also promote and demote headings to different levels within the outline's structure, whereas the up and down arrows move a heading up and down the list within its level in the outline.

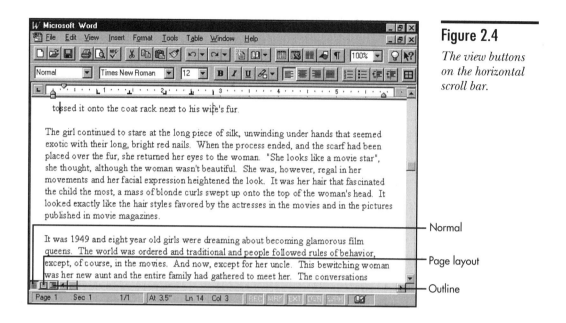

Figure 2.4

The view buttons on the horizontal scroll bar.

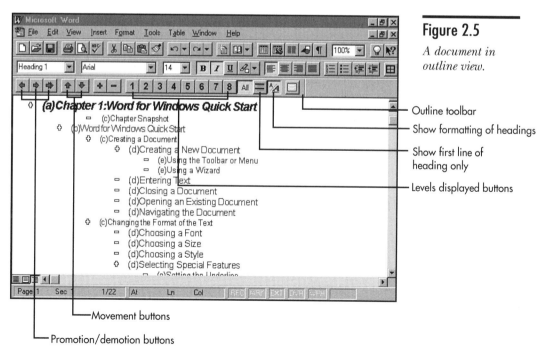

Figure 2.5

A document in outline view.

You do not have to display every level of the outline at once. The number buttons indicate how many levels are displayed. Headings that contain undisplayed, or collapsed, levels appear underlined. The plus and minus buttons expand and collapse the topic containing the insertion point. You also can limit the display to the first line of any heading with the Show First Line button.

You can switch between using special font and paragraph formats for each level of heading and not using these formats by using the Show Formatting button.

 Tip You also can adjust the view of your document by selecting the appropriate options from the **V**iew menu.

To see a document as a draft, click on the Normal button. You see a simplified version of your document, without special formatting applied, as shown in figure 2.6. In this view, you can enter text the fastest, scroll the fastest, and apply proofreading tools the fastest. It is the best view for rapidly developing your document.

Figure 2.6

A document in normal view.

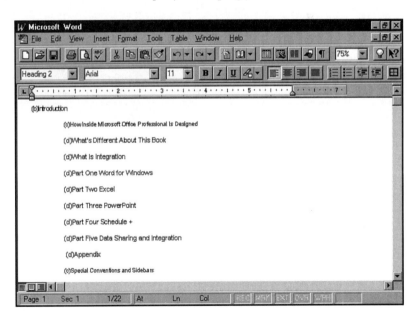

To see a document as final copy, click on the Page Layout button (see fig. 2.7). The view you have now shows you exactly how the document looks when printed. All formatting is applied and all the document's contents are shown in their correct position on the page. You can edit the document to adjust its final appearance in preparation for printing, and Word provides some additional tools to help you.

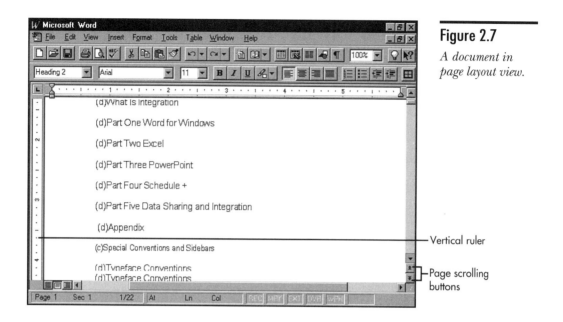

Figure 2.7

A document in page layout view.

Vertical ruler

Page scrolling buttons

Down the left side of the active page is a vertical ruler that displays the vertical margin settings. If you need to adjust these settings, double-click on the vertical ruler to display the **M**argins tab of the Page Setup dialog box. On the vertical scroll bar are two additional buttons displaying double arrows. These buttons advance you through the document, up or down, a page at a time.

Using Word's tools, you can rapidly shift among outline, draft, and final views of your document. A single document can represent what you ordinarily might see as three different documents.

Zooming and Splitting

Word adds the capability to view more and less of a document. You can zoom in or zoom out on portions of a document, exploding and reducing the size of your view, and you can split a document into two window panes so that you can see different portions of the document simultaneously.

To zoom in or out on your document, follow this procedure:

1. Open the Zoom drop-down list box on the Standard toolbar, the next-to-last control on the right (see fig. 2.8).

2. Select the reduction or enlargement factor you want to use.

Your document immediately shifts to that size on the screen.

Figure 2.8

*Using the Zoom
drop-down list
box on the
Standard toolbar.*

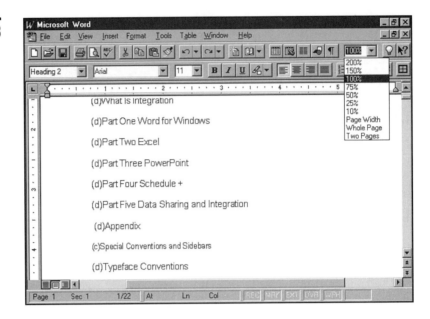

Note   Zooming out beyond 50 percent makes a document difficult to read and edit, but does give you a sense of its overall look and structure. Zooming above 100 percent can ease eyestrain and help you to examine details like fine print at the bottom of a contract. To gain the maximum amount of screen space for viewing your document, open the **V**iew menu and select the F**u**ll Screen option.

To split your document into two panes, double-click on the split bar, the black region at the top of the vertical scroll bar, as shown in figure 2.9. You can drag the split bar to adjust the relative dimensions of the two panes. Click on either pane to make it active for editing, just as you would on any other window. To return to a single-pane view of your document, double-click on the split bar again.

By merging the concepts of enlargement, reduction, and multiple views with its concept of the document, Word provides you with greater flexibility and control over your documents. Documents become objects that you manipulate electronically within your computer's memory the same way you might by spreading them out on a table and using a magnifying reader to study details. Documents provide you with all the tools you need to create and use them as a part of their functionality. You do not need lots of external tools to be able to use your documents.

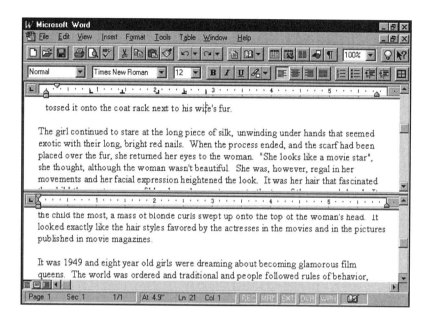

Figure 2.9

Using the split bar.

The Document's Contents

Another way to see how Word revises your concept of a document is to look at the contents of a document. Normally a document contains words and, at a higher end of publishing, pictures, graphs, and tables. In Word for Windows 95, documents can contain any type of data. You can create documents whose contents cannot be presented on paper.

To illustrate this concept, you need to examine only one of the applets that comes with Windows, the Sound Recorder. If you have a microphone attached to the sound system in your computer, try the following exercise:

1. Open any Word document.

2. Position the cursor to a location where you would like to add a voice annotation to the document.

3. Open the **I**nsert menu and select the **O**bject option.

4. If the **C**reate New tab is not on top, click on it.

5. In the **O**bject Type list box, select Sound, and then click on OK.

6. Click on the microphone button.

7. Record your message by speaking into the microphone.

8. Click on the Sound Recorder's stop button.

9. Open the Sound Recorder's **F**ile menu and choose **U**pdate. A sound icon appears in your Word document, as shown in figure 2.10.

10. Close the Sound Recorder by selecting E**x**it from the **F**ile menu.

11. To play back your voice annotation, double-click on the sound icon.

Figure 2.10

*A Word document
that contains a
voice annotation.*

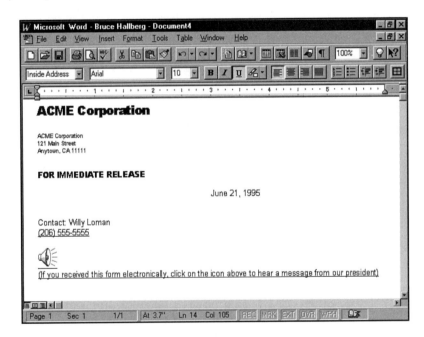

As you can imagine, you can add all sorts of nontext data into a Word for Windows document. If you own Video for Windows, you can embed full-motion video clips to illustrate your text. You can include sound files of all types to illustrate your points. Using the options in the **I**nsert menu, you can include data of any type prepared by any other application that can run under Windows.

Of course, you also can include pictures, tables, spreadsheets, and other typical illustrations that can be printed on paper. If you are using electronic mail to route documents for review and revision, you easily can include voice comments as well as written comments in the documents. If you are creating the text of a presentation slide show, you can embed the kind of data you need to make your points and present the slides electronically.

The application of Word's document metaphor radically redefines the nature of a document. Think of a Word document as a stack of paper with a home theater system hooked up to one of the futuristic interactive cable systems attached to it, along with an information service like CompuServe. These are the capabilities that Word can provide for you if your computer has the hardware to use them.

Master Documents

In Word for Windows, documents can serve to contain other documents. A document that serves this function is called a *master document*—a collection of separate documents, each contained in its own file, managed by another document file. As a result, the master document features of Word facilitate working with long documents like the text of a 1,000-page book. Scrolling from the beginning to the end of such a work would take forever.

Using the master document features, you can work with smaller chunks of the full document so that scrolling and spell-checking time no longer become horrendous problems. You also can work with the whole document.

Master documents are really special types of outlines. If you look back at figure 2.5, you will note that there is an extra button on the Outlining toolbar. It is the last one on the right—the Master Document button. When you click on that button you enter master document mode, in which you can convert an existing set of documents into a master document.

Note   You can view a master document in master document view, in which case you see the list of subdocuments. You also can view it in normal view, in which case you see the entire document as a single document. In normal view, sub-documents are indicated by section boundaries in the continuous text that you see. (Click on the Paragraph button on the Standard toolbar to make the section boundaries visible.)

To create a master document from scratch, follow these steps:

1. Click on the New button on the Standard toolbar to create a new file.

2. Open the **V**iew menu and select the **M**aster Document item.

The new document you created is now a master document. You can outline your overall document using Word's outlining features, and you can group headings on your outline and define them as subdocuments.

After writing your outline, perform the following procedure to create subdocuments:

1. Select the headings on the outline that should represent the subdocument.

2. Click on the Create Subdocument button on the Master Document toolbar (see fig. 2.11).

Figure 2.11

The Master Document toolbar, an extension to the Outlining toolbar.

Create subdocument

Remove subdocument

Insert subdocument

Merge subdocument

Split document

Lock document

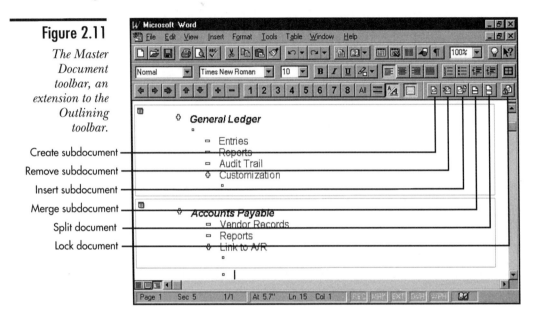

Word encloses each subdocument that you create on the outline in a box and identifies that the box's contents are a subdocument by displaying the subdocument icon in the upper left corner of the box.

To open a subdocument for editing, double-click on its subdocument icon. Word creates a new file, displays it in a document window, and displays the contents of the subdocument's segment of your outline for your additions and editing. To save the changes you have made to a subdocument, open the **F**ile menu and select the **S**ave option, and accept the file name that Word has assigned. Close a subdocument just as you would close any other document.

To save your work on the entire project, return to the master document and select one of the save options from the **F**ile menu. Word automatically provides file names for the subdocuments based on the first header in the outline for the subdocument. As long as you keep the file name Word assigns to a subdocument file, you can edit it either outside of the master document as a separate file or from within the master document.

Stop Never change the name of a subdocument file when you edit it outside the master document. Doing so destroys the link between the subdocument and the master document.

If you need to rename a subdocument, first open it from within the master document. You then can use the **F**ile, Save **A**s menu option to rename the file. After renaming the subdocument, you should save the master document as well so that the new file name is recorded as a part of the master document.

You can remove subdocuments just as easily as you can create them by following these steps:

1. In master document view, place the insertion point inside the subdocument you want to remove.

2. Click on the Remove Subdocument button.

When you remove a subdocument, you do not lose any of its contents. Word makes the contents of the subdocument into a new segment of the master document. Instead of appearing as a subdocument that you open from the master document, the information appears as a part of the master document. If you want to delete the information, you should delete it from the master document.

If you need to add information stored in a separate file as a part of a master document, perform the following steps:

1. Open the master document.

2. Click on the Insert Subdocument button to display the Insert Subdocument dialog box (see fig. 2.12).

3. Select the name of the file to insert in the File **N**ame list box.

4. Click on OK.

The file becomes a part of the master document, and its original file name is reserved.

Figure 2.12

*The Insert
Subdocument
dialog box.*

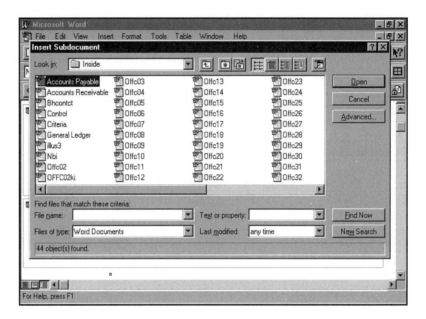

 Note   Master documents and subdocuments can be based on different templates. When you open subdocuments from the master document, however, Word applies the formatting used by the master document's template first and then picks up the nonconflicting features of the subdocument's template.

When you open the subdocument outside the master document, Word applies the formatting used by the subdocument's template. You should eliminate as many conflicts as possible between the master document's template and subdocument templates to avoid surprise changes in a document's format.

When managing a long project using a master document, you eventually will find the need to merge two subdocuments into a single subdocument. This situation might occur when you discover that two chunks of text covering the same issue in separate places need to be combined into one. To merge two subdocuments, you need to make sure they are next to each other in your master document's outline. If they are not, follow these steps:

1. Click on the subdocument icon for the subdocument you want to move up or down in the outline.

2. Drag the subdocument into its new position and drop it into place.

After the two subdocuments are next to each other, perform the following actions to merge them:

1. Select the subdocuments to merge. Holding the mouse button down but not pointing to the subdocument icon, drag the mouse over the text of the documents.

2. Click on the Merge Subdocument button.

Word merges the selected subdocuments into a single subdocument.

You might want to split a long subdocument into shorter ones to improve the speed of working with the text. To split a subdocument, open the master document and perform the following steps:

1. Select the text that should be in the first new subdocument.

2. Click on the Split Subdocument button.

3. Select the text that should be in the second new subdocument.

4. Click on the split subdocument button.

Word breaks the old single subdocument into the chunks you have defined.

 Tip   For information about printing master documents, see Chapter 5, "Understanding Printing and Printers."

When you are working as a part of a workgroup, you will want to lock subdocuments to prevent confusion about who is working on what section of the master document. Word keeps track of who created which subdocuments. When workgroup members open the master document, they have read-write editing privileges on the subdocuments they created, but those created by others are locked, providing only read-only access.

You can open a document created by another user to make changes, but you must first unlock it. After you are done, you should lock it again.

To unlock a document, follow these steps:

1. In master document view, place the insertion point in the subdocument to be unlocked.

2. Click on the Lock Document button.

To lock a document, follow the same procedure. The Lock Document button switches the state of the document lock. When a document is locked, Word displays a padlock icon underneath the subdocument icon.

Tip If you want to avoid making accidental changes to a subdocument, always lock your subdocuments. You can read and review them, but you will not be able to make changes unless you first unlock the document.

By bundling the document window, the ruler, the capability to split and zoom, and master documents into the concept of a document, Word for Windows extends the document metaphor considerably. Working with a Word document now can mean editing a graphic, changing the volume of a sound, or adjusting the playback characteristics of a movie. These extensions can make your Word document a multimedia experience without requiring you to be a multimedia expert.

Defining Template

Word uses a *template* to describe a set of directions for creating a document. Whenever Word creates a new document, it follows the directions stored in one of its templates. Templates all carry the file extension DOT. If you open a file with this extension, it looks just like an ordinary Word document—in fact, it is. When Word constructs a new document, it copies all the characteristics of the template to the new document. When you save the new document, you save it as a file with its own name.

The characteristics of the document template are not modified when you save the document based on the template unless you have taken an action that explicitly modifies the template, such as recording a macro or creating a new style.

Tip Chapter 3, "Using Advanced Formatting Features," explains styles, and Chapter 6, "Word's Word Basic Macros," explains how to record macros.

Templates in Word are files from which characteristics are inherited. As a result, to build a template, you simply create a Word document that has the characteristics you want, and save it as a template. When you create a new document based on the template, the new document inherits all the features you gave to the template. It appears on your screen with all those features in place, ready for you to make additions.

The best way to see how to create a template is to make and save one. Suppose that you want a memo format that clearly shows that a document is confidential. You

would like to have your company name and information on the document and a clear indication that the information in the document is to be treated with confidentiality. You could create a template for such documents by following these steps:

1. Open the **F**ile menu and select the **N**ew option.

2. In the New dialog box, select the T**e**mplate option button and click on OK.

3. Enter the information you want for your company into the workspace; figure 2.13 shows an example.

4. Place the insertion point where you would like a confidential label to appear.

5. Open the **I**nsert menu and choose the **P**icture option.

6. In the Insert Picture dialog box, select the file CONFIDEN.WMF in the File **N**ame list box and click on OK.

7. Place the insertion point where you would like to begin typing once the new confidential memo document is created.

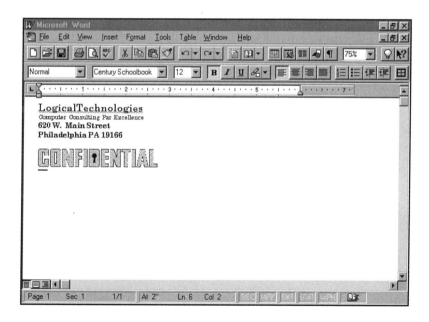

Figure 2.13

Creating a confidential memo template.

You now have created the image of the documents you want based on this template. To save the template, follow these steps:

1. Open the **F**ile menu and select the **S**ave option, or click on the Save button on the Standard toolbar.

2. Word selects a portion of the first line you entered and offers it as a name. You can accept the name, edit it, or enter a new name for the document template, then click on OK. Word has limited the Save As dialog box to saving a template because you already defined the file as a template.

Word automatically saves the template file to your template directory, where it is ready for use the next time you create a new document.

 Tip   You actually can save any file as a template. After you have entered a file name in the Save As dialog box, open the Save File as **T**ype drop-down list box and select Document Template, then click on OK.

Templates can contain anything a document can contain. They can be simple, like this confidential letterhead, or they can be complex. Imagine setting up a standard contract as a document template. All the text that never changes could become a part of the template. You could use bookmarks, a feature of Word explained later in this chapter, to indicate where you need to add the text related to each client who signs the contract. Writing a contract is then as simple as creating the document, moving to each bookmark, and entering the text necessary there.

You also can change a document's template if you find it necessary to do so. You might have formatted a document using the Normal template, and discovered afterward that the person sitting two desks over has created a template for just that kind of memo. To substitute the new template for the old one, you attach the new template to the document, following this procedure:

1. Select the **T**emplates option from the **F**ile menu to display the Templates and Add-ins dialog box (see fig. 2.14).

2. Click on the **A**ttach button to display the Attach Template dialog box. Select the template to attach from the File **N**ame list box.

3. Click on OK in the Attach Template dialog box and then click on OK in the Templates and Add-ins dialog box.

Templates also are the repository for things like styles and macros, both explained briefly later in this chapter and in more detail in Chapters 3 and 6. The template can contain toolbars, custom menus, and default settings for dialog boxes. Using templates, you can set up each type of document you work with so that your work is focused on exactly the options of Word necessary to the task at hand.

 Tip   If you want styles, toolbars, or other such items stored in a special template available to any document you open, load the template globally. Open the **F**ile menu, select the **T**emplates option, click on A**d**d, select the name of the template in the File **N**ame list box, and click on OK.

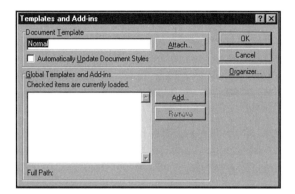

Figure 2.14

Using the Template and Add-ins dialog box to attach a template to a document.

Templates define a plan of action for creating a document. When you create the template, you decide how the document will be created and how you will interact with the document after it is created. As a result, you should plan templates with your work flow in mind. Let the template perform repetitive tasks for you so that you save time and focus on the items in the document that demand your attention.

Understanding Styles

Word for Windows uses style to mean a way of doing things with a format. Word extends this meaning into a concept that helps you accelerate much of the typical work you do in formatting a document.

A *style* is a collection of formats that you save as a unit. After you have saved this collection of formats, you can apply them to any block of text by placing the insertion point within the paragraph to be formatted and selecting the style from the Style drop-down list box on the Formatting toolbar (which is just above the Ruler). The Style drop-down list box is always the one farthest left on this toolbar. It contains the styles currently in use in the document.

Tip Word provides two kinds of styles: paragraph styles and character styles. Paragraph styles contain formatting information that applies to paragraphs, including font formats. Character styles contain formatting information that applies only to characters. Paragraph style names appear in bold characters, while character style names do not.

Word provides a number of built-in styles that you can use to format your own documents. The Style drop-down list box on the Formatting toolbar shows you only the styles currently in use. If you want to see all the styles available to you, perform the following steps:

1. Open the Format menu and select the **S**tyle option.

2. In the Style dialog box, use the **L**ist drop-down list box to select All Styles. The **S**tyles list box then displays all the styles available in the current template and in templates available globally (see fig. 2.15).

3. To apply any style built into Word, select its name in the **S**tyles list box and click on **A**pply. The paragraph containing the insertion point takes on the formats saved as that style.

Figure 2.15

Displaying available styles in the Style dialog box.

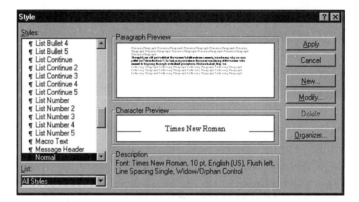

Note   To see how to create a style, turn to "Creating Custom Styles" in Chapter 3, "Using Advanced Formatting Features." To learn how to make a template available globally, see the preceding section.

Styles are saved as a part of a document or a document template. Because of this fact, document templates can serve as collections of styles that you can apply to format the document based on the template. If you are wondering whether Word includes a template with appropriate styles for the document you need to create, investigate the Style Gallery. Open the Format menu and select the Style **G**allery option. The Style Gallery dialog box appears, as shown in figure 2.16.

The **T**emplate list box displays the list of document templates in the \OFFICE95\TEMPLATE directory. By selecting a template from the list, the document shown in the **P**review of box takes on the style of that template.

By default, Word shows you a preview of the document you currently are working on. Unfortunately, the current document is probably the worst example of the template and its styles, because none of the contents of the template are added to the document and only the default paragraph text style is applied. As a result, you see very little of the automatic formatting available to you in the template. Better examples

are provided by the alternate option buttons in the Preview group. You can choose to see an example document or a list of the styles available in the template, with each item in the list formatted in the style it names.

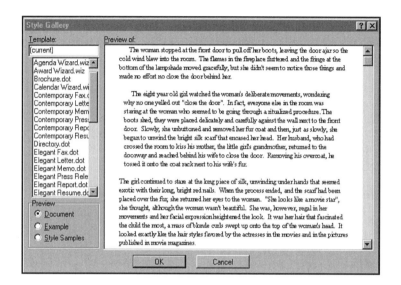

Figure 2.16

The Style Gallery dialog box.

If you find styles available in a template that you would like to use in your current document, you have four choices:

◆ Copy the styles from their home template into your current document. The styles are available in that document only, unless you copy them again to another document. To exercise this choice, click on OK in the Style Gallery dialog box.

Use this option if you are interested only in formatting your current document but not in creating similar documents on a regular basis.

◆ Attach the template to the document. Do this by canceling the Style Gallery dialog box and selecting the **T**emplates option from the **F**ile menu. Click on the **A**ttach button and select the template to attach from the File **N**ame list box in the Attach Template dialog box. Click on OK in the Attach Template dialog box and then click on OK in the Templates dialog box. Keep in mind that the template you attach replaces the template that previously was attached.

Use this option when you want to take advantage of other items that might also be stored in the template, such as macros and toolbars, and when you are certain that the template is not missing features you might need.

◆ Copy the styles into the NORMAL.DOT template. See Chapter 3, "Using Advanced Formatting Features," for more information about how to perform this operation.

Use this option when you expect to use the styles stored in the template in the documents you create by choosing <u>N</u>ew from the <u>F</u>ile menu. Keep in mind that the styles will not be available in templates from which you have deleted some of the items stored in NORMAL.DOT.

◆ Make the template available globally. In this case the styles in the template become available to every document in the Style dialog box. For the procedure, see the preceding section of this chapter.

Use this option when you want the styles to be available to every document.

 Tip   You can remove a character style from a selection by pressing Ctrl+spacebar.

Understanding Toolbars

Word provides toolbars to assist you with various editing tasks. Each toolbar consists of a bar-shaped window that appears beneath Word's menu and contains buttons and other controls that enable you to perform with a single mouse click tasks that otherwise might take several keystrokes or mouse clicks.

Toolbars display visual images that Word uses to represent to you how to perform these tasks. A toolbar therefore serves as a visual reminder of the nature and organization of the task represented by the toolbar. To facilitate your work, Word presents sixteen different toolbars, described in table 2.1.

TABLE 2.1
Word for Windows Toolbars

Toolbar	Function
Borders	Helps in placing borders around paragraphs and selecting shading
Database	Assists in inserting, building, and maintaining databases in Word documents
Drawing	Enables the drawing of pictures in Word documents
Equation Editor	Enables you to insert mathematical and scientific equations into a document

Toolbar	Function
Formatting	Helps you to format a document
Forms	Enables you to insert custom fields on templates so that you can create online forms
Header and Footer	Enables you to edit headers and footers for your documents
Macro	Assists in editing, testing, and debugging macros
Mail Merge	Helps in conducting a mail merge operation
Master Document	Enables you to manage a master document
Microsoft	Enables you to launch other Microsoft applications from within Word
Outlining	Helps you to create and manage outlines
Standard	Contains typical tools that you want to access frequently
TipWizard	Provides access to a generic "Tip of the Day" and tips about the current task, including a Show Me function
WordArt	Helps in constructing artful text
Word for Windows 2.0	Provides the Word for Windows 2.0 toolbar for those who need to use it

To use a toolbar, you manipulate the controls on the bar just as you would if they appeared in a dialog box. You can adjust your view of the toolbars in two ways. First, you can determine which of several toolbars are displayed. The easiest way to adjust which toolbars appear on your screen is to click on any toolbar with the right mouse button. A floating menu that gives you access to all toolbar functions appears, as shown in figure 2.17.

On the toolbar floating menu you can choose to have up to 7 of the 15 toolbars on-screen just by clicking on the menu item that bears the toolbar's name. A check appears next to the names of toolbars already showing on-screen. To hide a toolbar from this menu, click on its checked menu item, and the toolbar will disappear.

In addition to being able to control your view of toolbars, you can select the Toolbar and Customize dialog boxes from this menu. For more about customizing toolbars, see Chapter 7, "Customizing Word for Windows."

Also, you need to know how to float toolbars so that you can avoid limiting a document's workspace. The toolbars shown in figure 2.17 are *anchored;* that is, they are stationary and fixed underneath the Word menu. To make them *float* over your work as separate, movable, and sizable windows, double-click on the toolbar some-where outside the controls. The toolbar floats away from its anchored position and into the body of the document (see fig. 2.18).

Figure 2.17

The toolbar floating menu.

Figure 2.18

A floating toolbar.

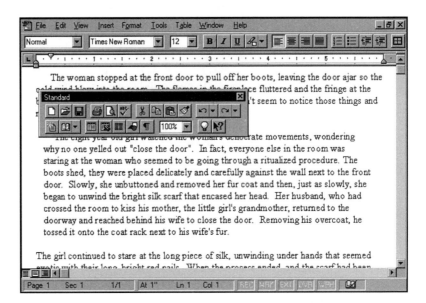

You can adjust the size of the toolbar just as you would any window. To anchor the toolbar again, double-click on it.

To manage toolbars effectively, you must know how to access the Toolbar dialog box from the View menu. If you have hidden all your toolbars, you have no other means of getting access to them again. To change your view of the toolbars, follow this procedure:

1. Open the **V**iew menu.

2. Select the **T**oolbars option.

3. Check the toolbars you want to appear in the **T**oolbars list box. Uncheck those you do not want to appear.

4. Click on OK.

Using the Toolbars dialog box, you can also create new toolbars, customize existing toolbars, and reset toolbars to default tools. For more information about these processes, see Chapter 7, "Customizing Word for Windows."

Defining Headers and Footers

Word enables you to place headers and footers in your documents. These are special regions of the page in which you can insert information you want repeated on each page. The header appears at the top of the page and the footer appears at the bottom. Common uses for these regions are displaying running titles, printing page numbers, and printing information about the document itself, such as file name, print date, last edit date, or version number. Headers and footers remind us of the process printers use to place running titles, tool lines, and other graphics on each page.

Tip The footer of a document is a good place to store any version tracking information you want to keep as you revise a collaborative document.

Word reserves space for a header and footer in each document. If you insert nothing into these regions, then your text takes them over. On the other hand, if you do insert information, the header or footer is displayed.

One of the most common uses for either the header or footer is to display page numbers. To add page numbers, perform the following procedure:

1. Open the **I**nsert menu and select the Page N**u**mbers option to display the Page Number dialog box (see fig. 2.19).

2. Open the **P**osition drop-down list box and select whether you want the page number in the header or the footer.

3. Open the **A**lignment drop-down list box and select whether you want right, left, center, inside, or outside alignment for the page number. Right, left, and center place the page number at the corresponding position within the header or footer. Inside and outside place the page number at the inside of the binding edge or the outside of the binding edge if you are using mirror margins. The Preview box displays the exact position you have selected.

4. Check the **S**how Number on First Page check box if you want to display a page number on the first page of your document.

5. Click on the **F**ormat button to open the Page Number Format dialog box, shown in figure 2.20.

Figure 2.19

*The Page
Numbers dialog
box.*

Figure 2.20

*The Page Number
Format dialog
box.*

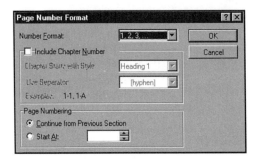

6. Use the Number **F**ormat drop-down list box to select the number format you want to use.

7. Use the option buttons in the Page Numbering group to determine whether the number sequence should **C**ontinue from Previous Section or Start **A**t a particular number. If you choose Start **A**t, enter the starting number in the spin box.

8. Check the Include Chapter **N**umber check box to include the chapter number as a part of the page number. If you select this option, you must select a style using the Cha**p**ter Starts with Style drop-down list box. This tells Word how to recognize chapter beginnings. You also must open the Use S**e**parator drop-down list box to indicate what character separates the chapter number from the page number in the page number string.

9. Click on OK in the Page Number Format dialog box and in the Page Number dialog box.

You also can directly edit the header and footer for each page. To prepare to do so, open the **V**iew menu and select the **H**eader and Footer option. Your screen will switch to page layout view and the Header and Footer toolbar appears, as seen in figure 2.21.

Tip   You can float the Header and Footer toolbar by double-clicking on it.

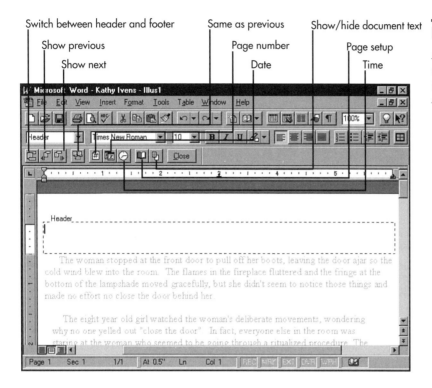

Switch between header and footer

Show previous

Show next

Same as previous

Page number

Date

Show/hide document text

Page setup

Time

Figure 2.21

Editing the header and footer using the Header and Footer toolbar.

While the Header and Footer toolbar is visible, you can take the following actions to define your headers and footers:

◆ You can enter and edit text in the header or footer section of the document. You can use any text, field, or control that you can use anywhere else in a Word document.

◆ You can switch between editing the header and footer by clicking on the Switch Between Header and Footer button.

◆ You can move between headers and footers for each section of your document by clicking on the Show Previous or Show Next buttons.

◆ If you want to continue a header or footer from the previous section of the document, click on the Same as Previous button. The button stays depressed to indicate that all sections have the same header and footer. If you want to use different headers and footers in a section, place the insertion button in that section and click on the Same as Previous button again. It pops up to indicate that each section has different headers and footers.

Note Word enables you to define sections in your document, each of which can have different formatting characteristics.

◆ You can insert page number, date, and time fields by clicking on the buttons with those names.

◆ You can hide the document text if it distracts you, or re-show it, by clicking on the Show/Hide Document Text button.

◆ You can access the Page Setup dialog box by clicking on the Page Setup button. See the section "Setting Up the Page" in Chapter 1 for more information about how to use the controls in this dialog box. The most important controls for headers and footers appear in the Headers and Footers group on the **L**ayout tab and the From Edge group on the **M**argins tab. These controls enable you to select Different **O**dd and Even and Different **F**irst Page for headers and footers, as well as to set the distance from the edge of the page to the header and footer.

◆ You can exit the header and footer editing mode by clicking on the Close button or by selecting the **H**eader and Footer option from the **V**iew menu.

Explaining Document Tools

Word uses the metaphor of a tool to represent an electronic automation of a proofing process that you ordinarily would perform by hand in preparing a document. Word provides you with several tools that help you improve your documents in one way or another. These tasks range from proofreading to maintaining lists of common phrases to automatically changing a date to match the current day. Using these tools simplifies and speeds up your work.

Spelling Checker

Probably the most familiar document tool is the *spelling checker,* which compares each word in your document to the correct spellings stored in its dictionary and asks you to verify the spelling of any words not in the dictionary. You can add words not in the standard dictionary to a custom dictionary, and you can maintain several custom dictionaries specific to specialized types of documents. The spelling checker, therefore, is a flexible tool that automates the process of proofreading for spelling errors.

Stop Spelling checkers are wonderful, but they do not eliminate typographical errors. In fact, they can serve to hide certain kinds of typos. After the spelling check is over, you can be certain that all the words in the document have correct spellings; however, you cannot be certain that you have used the correct form of the word in the right place. The spelling checker, for instance, will not point out that "to" should have been spelled "too" when you meant "also." Such incorrect forms can be difficult to find once they all are correctly spelled.

Word has two processes for checking the spelling of documents: automatic and manual.

The *automatic* spelling checker works in the background while you are creating or editing documents. When the automatic spelling checker encounters a word that might be spelled incorrectly, it places a wavy red line under the word. Your work on the document is not interrupted and you can choose whether or not you want to correct the word. If you do want to change the spelling, click the wavy red line with the right mouse button to display a list of suggested spelling corrections.

The *manual* spelling checker lets you stop your work on the document to launch Word's spelling check program. To access Word's spelling checker, perform the following steps:

1. Click on the Spelling button on the Standard toolbar, open the **T**ools menu and select the **S**pelling option, or press F7. The Spelling dialog box appears, as shown in figure 2.22.

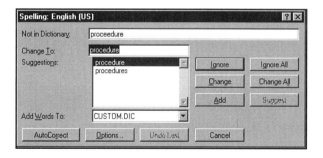

Figure 2.22

The Spelling dialog box.

2. Verify the spelling of the word in the Not in Dictionary text box. If it is correct, take one of the following steps:

   ◆ Click on the **I**gnore button.

   ◆ If you expect that the word will occur later in your document, click on the **I**gnore All button. Word then will ignore the word for all spelling checks during the current Word session.

◆ If you frequently use the word, select a dictionary in the Add **W**ords To drop-down list box and click on the **A**dd button. Word then will accept the word as being correctly spelled during all Word sessions.

3. If the word in the Not in Dictionary text box is incorrect, select one of the suggestions from the Suggestio**n**s list box so that the word in the Change **T**o text box is the word you want. Or type the correct word in the Change **T**o text box, then perform one of the following steps:

◆ Click on the **C**hange button to change to the correct form displayed in the Change **T**o text box.

◆ Click on the Change A**ll** button if you expect to encounter the same misspelling throughout the document. Word then will change all encountered forms of the word to the form you specified as correct.

Stop   Be careful when selecting the Change A**ll** button, especially if the incorrect form is close to the correct spelling of two different words. You might encounter the word all incorrectly spelled as al in a document containing the male first name Al. You could accidentally misspell Al's name throughout the document by clicking on the Change A**ll** button.

4. If you recognize the misspelling in the Not in Dictionary text box as a common typing error that you make, click on the AutoCo**r**rect button. Word adds this wrongly typed word and its correction to the AutoCorrect list, and will perform the correction on the fly as you type. (For more information about AutoCorrect, see the section "AutoCorrect" later in this chapter.)

5. If the Not in Dictionary box is empty, the **C**hange and Change A**ll** buttons take on the labels **D**elete and Delete A**ll**. Usually this change occurs when the spelling checker encounters a repeated word or some similar occurrence. Use **D**elete and Delete A**ll** just as you would **C**hange and Change A**ll** in dealing with these circumstances.

6. Click on the **U**ndo Last button to undo the last spelling correction. Using this button, you can reverse the course of the spelling checker through the file to correct any errors you might have made when clicking on buttons. **U**ndo Last remains active as long as you can back up to an earlier correction and undo the action.

7. Click on the **O**ptions button to set the options for the spelling checker. The Options dialog box appears with the Spelling tab active, as shown in figure 2.23.

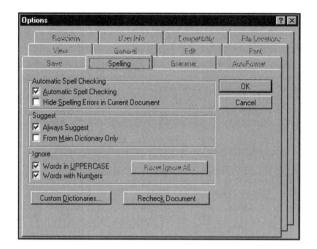

Figure 2.23

The Options dialog box with the Spelling tab active.

In the Options dialog box, perform the following steps:

◆ Use the check boxes in the Automatic Spell Checking section to turn automatic spell checking on and off. Click on the Hide **S**pelling Errors in Current Document box to hide the wavy red line that appears under words that could be spelled incorrectly.

◆ Use the option buttons in the Suggest group to control how the spelling checker suggests possible correct forms. Select A**l**ways Suggest if you want Word always to suggest alternate forms. (If you uncheck this box, you can always get suggestions by clicking on the **S**uggest button in the Spelling dialog box.) Check From **M**ain Dictionary Only if you want suggestions only from the main dictionary. Uncheck this box if you want suggestions from custom dictionaries as well.

Tip   The fewer suggestions the spelling checker has to make, the faster it runs.

◆ Use the controls in the Ignore group to control the way in which the spelling checker ignores certain words. Check the Words in **U**PPERCASE box to ignore words in all capitals. Check the Words with Num**b**ers box to ignore such words. Click on the Reset **I**gnore All button to clear the Ignore All list for the current session.

◆ Use the controls in the Custom Dictionaries group to set up and maintain your custom dictionaries. Use the Custom **D**ictionaries list box to select which dictionaries are active by checking or unchecking the box next to the dictionary's name. Use the La**n**guage drop-down list box to select the language formatting that applies to the dictionary. Use the **N**ew button to create a new custom dictionary. This button opens a dialog box that enables you to create a file in dictionary format. Use the **E**dit button to open a dictionary as a Word document so that you can add words to it. Use the **A**dd button to open a dialog box that permits you to add a third-party dictionary to the list of custom dictionaries. Use the **R**emove button to remove a custom dictionary from the list.

◆ Click on Rechec**k** Document to check the spelling of a document again after you have changed options or opened another dictionary.

Word's spelling checker enables you to define words that should not be included in the spelling check. The list of words to exclude from the spelling check is called the *exclude dictionary.* It must have the same name as the main dictionary it should work with, end in an EXC extension, and be stored along with its main dictionary in the \OFFICE95\WINWORD directory. For example, the American English dictionary shipped with Word is named MSWDS_EN.LEX. The corresponding exclude dictionary must be named MSWDS_EN.EXC.

This capability permits you to use variant spellings not accepted by the main dictionary. For example, if you prefer *judgement* to *judgment,* a commonly accepted spelling variant in American English, you should add *judgment* to the exclude dictionary. This action causes Word's spelling checker to question the spelling *judgment,* so that you can change it to your preferred spelling of *judgement.*

To create an exclude dictionary, perform the following procedure:

1. Create a new file by clicking the New button on the Standard toolbar or by opening the **F**ile menu and selecting the **N**ew option.

2. Type the list of words to exclude. Press Enter after each word.

3. Open the **F**ile menu and select the Save **A**s option.

4. Open the Save As File **T**ype drop-down list box and select Text Only.

5. Enter the appropriate name for the exclude dictionary in the File **N**ame text box.

6. Click on OK.

7. Start the spelling checker to complete the installation of the exclude dictionary.

Grammar Checker

Word for Windows provides a grammar checking tool that can help you catch common errors in writing. The grammar checker examines your document sentence by sentence, searching for patterns that might indicate errors. This tool also can suggest improvements to each sentence that it flags as containing a possible error. You can accept the suggested change, seek an explanation of the possible error, edit the sentence, or ignore the possible error.

 Stop   Although grammar checkers get better and better all the time, they do not catch all errors and they flag some sentences as containing errors that are in fact correctly formed. For example, Word's grammar checker responds to the sentence "This here be a boo boo" by suggesting only that you consider deleting the repeated word. You should proofread your document after checking the grammar to catch any errors the grammar checker missed.

To use the grammar checker, open the **T**ools menu and select the **G**rammar option to display the Grammar dialog box, as shown in figure 2.24.

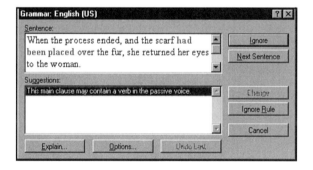

Figure 2.24

The Grammar dialog box.

In the Grammar dialog box, examine the sentence containing the possible problem in the **S**entence text box and read the suggested course of action in the Su**g**gestions text box. Then take one of the following courses of action:

◆ Click on the **I**gnore button to ignore the suggested change.

◆ Click on the **N**ext Sentence button to move to the next sentence without either correcting the error or ignoring the error. You can bypass an error this way so that you can return later with the grammar checker after considering how you want to express the sentence.

◆ Edit the sentence in the **S**entence text box, making the changes you desire.

◆ Click on the **C**hange button to make the suggested change or to substitute your edited version of the sentence for the original. Your edited version takes precedence over the suggested change.

◆ Click on the Ignore **R**ule button to prevent the grammar checker from applying the rule indicated during the remainder of the grammar check.

◆ Click on the **E**xplain button to open a dialog box, seen in figure 2.25, that offers a more detailed explanation of the possible problem.

Figure 2.25

Getting an explanation of a grammar checker rule.

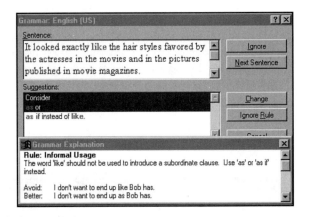

◆ Click on the Cancel or Close button to end the grammar checking session.

◆ Click on the Undo **L**ast button to reverse the last action you took with the grammar checker. You can repeat this undo action to move backwards through the actions you have taken with the grammar checker.

You can adjust which rules the grammar checker applies to your text by clicking on the **O**ptions button or opening the **T**ools menu and select the **O**ptions item. When the Options dialog box appears, click on the Grammar tab if it is not active (see fig. 2.26).

Now, perform the following steps:

1. Use the Check **S**pelling check box to control whether the grammar checker runs a spelling check on each sentence before checking its grammar. Turning off the spelling check speeds the grammar checker, but you need to perform a spelling check before you check your document's grammar.

2. Check or uncheck the Show **R**eadability Statistics check box to control whether the grammar checker shows readability statistics after the grammar check is completed.

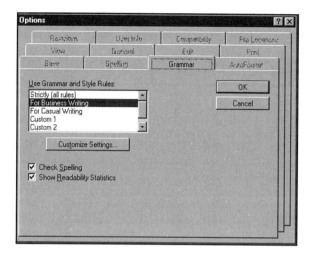

Figure 2.26

The Grammar tab in the Options dialog box.

3. Select the type of writing whose grammar you are checking in the **U**se Grammar and Style Rules list box.

4. If you want to create a custom set of grammar and style rules or to change the rules applied in a predefined type of writing, click on the Cus**t**omize Settings button and take one or more of the following actions:

   ◆ In the Customize Grammar Settings dialog box (see fig. 2.27), open the **U**se Grammar and Style Rules list box to select the type of writing for which you want to modify the rules applied.

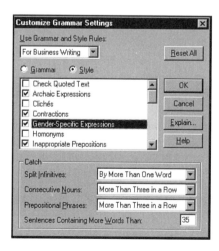

Figure 2.27

The Customize Grammar Settings dialog box.

◆ Use the **G**rammar and **S**tyle option buttons to select which set of rules to modify.

◆ Click on the sets of rules displayed in the list box to switch whether they will be used in the grammar check.

◆ Open the Split **I**nfinitives, Consecutive **N**ouns, and Prepositional **P**hrases drop-down list boxes to determine how the grammar checker handles these constructions.

◆ Enter a number in the Sentences Containing More **W**ords Than text box to determine the largest sentence (in number of words) that the grammar checker considers acceptable.

◆ Click on the **E**xplain button to open a dialog box that explains more about each rule set.

◆ Click on the **R**eset All button to change a rule group back to its default settings if you feel you have made an error in making changes.

◆ Click on OK to accept the changes you have made in the rule settings.

At the end of each grammar checking session, Word displays a set of readability statistics unless you have turned this feature off using the Grammar tab in the Options dialog box. These statistics can help you to determine whether you have matched your writing appropriately to your intended readers.

Each of the means of calculating readability applies a slightly different method of calculating reading ease. In general, the lower the value the easier the reading. You can use these statistics as guidelines for determining how well you meet the reading ability of your intended audience.

Note Under certain circumstances, you might want to have your document meet rigid reading ease guidelines, such as when preparing technical repair manuals for an aircraft maintenance crew. In this setting, the need to understand the steps to follow on first reading is mission critical, since errors in procedure can lead to airplane crashes. In other settings, however, you might not need to adhere tightly to such guidelines. Many of the classics often recommended to adolescents for enjoyment score well off the top of the Flesch and Flesch-Kincaid scales.

Thesaurus

Word for Windows includes a thesaurus to help you vary your vocabulary and find more useful words by association with the less useful word you might be able to think

of. To use the thesaurus, place the insertion point on the word you want to look up. Then, open the **T**ools menu and select the **T**hesaurus option, or press Shift+F7, to display the Thesaurus dialog box (see fig. 2.28).

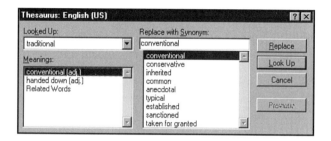

Figure 2.28

The Thesaurus dialog box.

In the Thesaurus dialog box, perform one of the following actions:

◆ Verify that the word you want to look up appears in the Loo**k**ed Up drop-down list box. (If the word was not found, Loo**k**ed Up becomes the **N**ot found drop-down list box.) If it does not, enter the word in the text box portion of the Replace with **S**ynonym combination box and click on the **L**ook Up button.

   If the insertion point is not on a word when you invoke the thesaurus, the dialog box will be empty and the Replace with **S**ynonym combination box will be labeled **I**nsert. Type the word to look up in the **I**nsert control and click on **L**ook Up.

◆ Select the meaning you want to work with in the **M**eanings list box. (If the word was not found, **M**eanings becomes the **A**lphabetical List list box.) You can select antonyms and related words if you want to explore opposites or related word families.

◆ Select a synonym you want to work with in the list box portion of the Replace with **S**ynonym combination box.

◆ Click on the **L**ook Up button to look up synonyms for the word that currently appears in the text box portion of the Replace with **S**ynonym combination box.

◆ Click on the **P**revious button or open the Loo**k**ed Up drop-down list box to select words previously looked up during the thesaurus session.

◆ Click on the **R**eplace button to replace the word containing the insertion point with the word that appears in the text box portion of the Replace with **S**ynonym combination box.

Hyphenation

Word provides a hyphenation facility that enables you to give your documents a professional look by reducing excessive raggedness along a margin or unusually long spaces between words in a fully justified document.

Word enables you to insert two types of hyphens into words. *Optional hyphens* break a word only when the word appears at the end of a line and using the hyphen would improve the appearance of the ragged margin. *Nonbreaking hyphens* always appear in the word but never break at the edge of a line. They are useful in compound words such as *Somerset-Upon-Thyme* or hyphenated personal names in which you do not wish parts of the compound to wrap around a line. To insert an optional hyphen, press Ctrl+- (hyphen). For a nonbreaking hyphen, press Ctrl+Shift+-.

 Tip   Word treats a hyphen typed using the hyphen key only as an ordinary punctuation mark.

You can read your text on-screen and guess where hyphens ought to appear if you want. Word, however, provides two alternative methods of inserting hyphens in a text: automatic and manual. Ordinarily, it is best to apply hyphenation toward the end of the writing process. Changes in the text alter the locations at which you need to apply hyphenation.

To apply hyphenation automatically, perform the following procedure:

1. Open the **T**ools menu and select the **H**yphenation option. The Hyphenation dialog box appears, as shown in figure 2.29.

Figure 2.29

The Hyphenation dialog box.

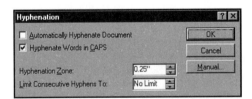

2. Check the **A**utomatically Hyphenate Document check box.

3. Check the Hyphenate Words in **C**APS check box if you want to hyphenate words in caps; otherwise, Word will not hyphenate these words.

4. Use the Hyphenation **Z**one spin box to adjust the width of the zone between the word and the margin where the hyphen break can occur. A wider zone produces a more ragged margin.

5. Use the **L**imit Consecutive Hyphens To spin box to set the maximum number of consecutive lines that can be hyphenated. (A text in which many consecutive lines are hyphenated can be difficult to read.)

6. Click on OK, and Word hyphenates the text.

To insert hyphens manually, follow this procedure:

1. Open the **T**ools menu and select the **H**yphenation option to display the Hyphenation dialog box (refer to figure 2.29).

2. Click on the **M**anual button to display the Manual Hyphenation dialog box (see fig. 2.30).

Figure 2.30

The Manual Hyphenation dialog box.

3. Word searches through your document, displaying each word to be hyphenated in the Hyphenate **A**t text box. For each word, perform one of the following actions:

◆ Click on the **Y**es button to accept the suggested hyphenation.

◆ If you disagree with the location of the suggested hyphen, click on the word in the Hyphenate **A**t text box to indicate where the hyphen should go.

◆ Click on the **N**o button to prevent Word from hyphenating the word shown.

Automatic hyphenation is faster and more convenient, but you should proof your document to make certain you agree with the hyphens inserted. Manual hyphenation is slower, but gives you control over the process at the screen. If hyphenation is the last step in producing your document, you can switch from manual hyphenation to print preview (see the section "Setting Up a Document" in Chapter 5) to verify the final look of the document. You then are ready for printing.

Tip   You can turn off hyphenation for individual paragraphs by opening the F**o**rmat menu, selecting the **P**aragraph option, selecting the Text **F**low tab, and checking the **D**on't Hyphenate check box.

AutoCorrect

AutoCorrect is a Wizard that runs in the background as you type, watching for preprogrammed patterns in the stream of characters that you type. When AutoCorrect encounters one of these patterns, it substitutes a corresponding preprogrammed pattern.

AutoCorrect can therefore watch for your most frequent typing errors of common words and automatically correct them for you. As a result, *teh* automatically becomes *the* as soon as you press the space bar after typing the word. You can extend this capability, however, to cover more than spelling errors. Common phrases can be AutoCorrect entries. You can set up the string *slogan* to expand into your company's slogan. You can set up quick key combinations that expand into frequently used addresses, chemical formulas, specialized vocabulary, and so on.

Stop   Keep in mind that AutoCorrect entries can take effect at unwanted times. If you store lots of specialized AutoCorrect entries, you will want their invoking strings to be unique and infrequently used words.

To build an AutoCorrect entry, perform the following steps:

1. Open the **T**ools menu and select the **A**utoCorrect option to display the AutoCorrect dialog box (see fig. 2.31).

Figure 2.31

The AutoCorrect dialog box.

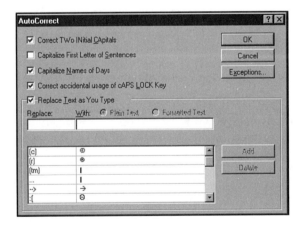

2. In the AutoCorrect dialog box, type the text to replace in the **R**eplace text box.

3. Type the text to substitute in the **W**ith text box.

4. Click on the **A**dd button.

5. Make sure the Replace **T**ext as You Type check box is checked; otherwise, AutoCorrect is turned off and will not substitute text as you type.

6. Click on OK.

You can also designate exceptions to the AutoCorrect function by selecting the **Ex**ceptions button. Enter any abbreviations or terms that must appear with mixed capitalization and, therefore, should not be changed by AutoCorrect.

The next time you type the sequence of characters you designated to be replaced, AutoCorrect substitutes the characters you typed in the **W**ith text box.

AutoCorrect also can substitute graphics and formatted text for a string of characters. Suppose you need your company logo and slogan to appear in the first heading for each section of your document. You have the logo and slogan already entered in your letterhead template. The logo has been scanned as a clip art graphic, and the slogan is a block of 14 point text sitting to its right. To make the logo and slogan an AutoCorrect entry, perform the following procedure:

1. Select the graphic and the text as a unit.

2. Open the **T**ools menu and select **A**utoCorrect.

3. Type a name for the entry in the **Re**place text box.

4. Select either the **P**lain Text or **F**ormatted Text option button. **F**ormatted Text preserves the formatting of the text and the graphic image. **P**lain Text converts both formatted text and graphics to characters in the system font. The **W**ith box previews your entry for you.

5. Click on the **A**dd button.

6. Make sure the Replace **T**ext as You Type check box is checked.

7. Click on OK.

The following check boxes in the AutoCorrect dialog box enable you to correct additional text problems:

◆ Replace **T**ext as You Type switches the AutoCorrect Wizard on and off.

◆ Change Straight Quotes to Smart **Q**uotes switches the substitution of curly quotation marks for straight quotation marks on and off.

◆ Correct TWo INitial **C**Apitals switches the correction of this common Shift key error on and off.

◆ Capitalize First Letter of <u>S</u>entences switches this self-explanatory correction feature on and off.

◆ Capitalize <u>N</u>ames of Days switches the capitalization of these names on and off.

 Tip If AutoCorrect corrects something you did not want corrected, just click on the Undo button on the Standard toolbar.

AutoCorrect enables you to change your entries any time you want by simply editing the <u>R</u>eplace or <u>W</u>ith text boxes. You can insert any entry into these boxes by clicking on it in the list box. (If your entry is formatted text or graphics, make the change in your document, select the changed material, and then open the AutoCorrect dialog box.) To complete the change, click on the <u>A</u>dd or <u>R</u>eplace button, whichever appears.

If you are editing the <u>R</u>eplace box, the <u>A</u>dd button appears. When you click on it, the entry you changed is not deleted in its original form. Instead, a new entry is added as a new <u>R</u>eplace segment paired with the same <u>W</u>ith segment. If you edit the <u>W</u>ith text box, the <u>R</u>eplace button appears, and the new entry is substituted for the old.

You will need on occasion to delete an AutoCorrect entry. To do so, select the entry in the list box and click on the <u>D</u>elete button.

Document Statistics

Often you need to make a document fit into guidelines of various lengths. Word has a document statistics facility that provides you with various length statistics. To use this facility, open the <u>T</u>ools menu and select the <u>W</u>ord Count option. The Word Count dialog box appears, as shown in figure 2.32, and Word updates the counts for you. If you wish to include footnotes and endnotes, check the Include <u>F</u>ootnotes and Endnotes check box.

The counts reported are based on the counting rules shown in table 2.2.

TABLE 2.2
Counting Rules for Document Statistics

Count	Rule
Word	Words in the document, exclusive of footnotes and endnotes unless the check box is checked, and exclusive of headers and footers
Pages	Number of pages as defined by page breaks in document and section breaks where relevant

Count	Rule
Characters	Alphabetic characters, numeric characters, and punctuation marks
Paragraphs	Number of paragraphs defined by paragraph marks
Lines	Number of lines, including blank lines following paragraphs even if they are defined by paragraph marks

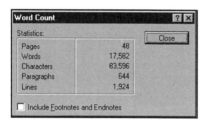

Figure 2.32

The Word Count dialog box.

Stop   Every time you use the word count feature, Word repaginates your document and counts the relevant items. In a long document, this can take quite some time. You might want to use this feature sparingly as a result.

Multiple Language Support

Word enables you to work in multiple languages, even within the same document. You will not even know that Word is changing from one language format to another as you are working. You need only to designate which sections of your text are written in which language, and Word handles the rest automatically.

If you have to work with people in Quebec with whom you must use French Canadian words, for instance, you can designate such words as French Canadian using the **L**anguage option on the **T**ools menu. When Word encounters such a word in a spelling check, for example, it automatically switches to the French Canadian dictionary to look up the words designated as French Canadian. If such a dictionary is not installed, Word switches to the nearest equivalent if possible—in this case, a French dictionary.

Tip   If you work with multiple languages frequently, make sure you have the appropriate dictionaries installed. If Word does not ship with the dictionary you need, you might be able to purchase one from a third party or find one available as shareware. You install such dictionaries as custom dictionaries. See the section "Spelling Checker" earlier in this chapter for the procedure.

To change the language support for a portion of your document, perform the following procedure:

1. Select the text to be treated as a different language.

2. Open the **T**ools menu and select the **L**anguage option to display the Language dialog box (see fig. 2.33).

Figure 2.33

The Language dialog box.

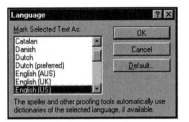

3. Select the language you want to use from the **M**ark Selected Text As list box.

4. If your text is primarily in a language other than the one you normally work with, you might want to set this language as the default language for Word. To do so, click on the **D**efault button, then click on the **Y**es button in the dialog box that appears.

5. Click on OK.

After you have adjusted the language format, use the proofing tools just as you normally would. Word will treat appropriately the blocks of text you marked as being in particular languages.

 Tip If you often work in multiple languages, consider creating a style for each language. Such styles can contain all the appropriate language formatting, and you can set them from the Formatting toolbar quite easily.

AutoText

Word provides the AutoText facility to enable you to create *boilerplate text,* common chunks of text that you use frequently. AutoText is the perfect place to store addresses, standard contract paragraphs, openings and closings for letters, distribution lists you use frequently, fax headers for clients, and other such items. Using AutoText, you can create boilerplate items, save them, and insert them into documents easily.

AutoText items are stored in a document template. Each item has a name that by default is the first few characters in the entry. You can, however, supply a name for each AutoText item when you create it. Because these items appear as entries in the AutoText dialog box, they frequently are called AutoText entries.

To create an AutoText entry, perform the following steps:

1. Enter the text, including graphics if you want, exactly as you want it to appear in any document.

2. Select the text (and graphics, if they are included). If you want the text to retain its formatting, be sure to select the paragraph mark as well. (Click on the Show/Hide Paragraph button on the Standard toolbar to reveal the paragraph mark, if necessary.)

3. Click on the Edit AutoText button on the Standard toolbar, or open the Edit menu and select the AutoTe**x**t option. This displays the AutoText dialog box, as shown in figure 2.34.

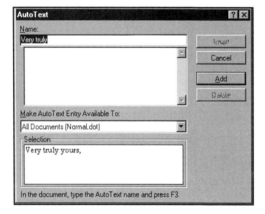

Figure 2.34

The AutoText dialog box.

4. In the AutoText dialog box, enter a name in the **N**ame text box if you do not like the default. Names can contain up to 32 characters, spaces included.

5. Open the **M**ake AutoText Entry Available To drop-down list box and select the document tcmplate in which you want the entry stored.

6. Click on the **A**dd button.

Tip Because AutoText entries are stored in document templates, you easily can customize templates with boilerplate text that meets typical goals for documents based on that template. A client letter template, for instance, might contain the addresses of your 10 most frequent clients, three typical opening paragraphs, three typical closing paragraphs, and frequently used enclosure and copy lists

To insert an AutoText entry, follow these steps:

1. Place the insertion point at the beginning of a line or in an area surrounded by spaces.

2. Open the **E**dit menu and select the AutoTe**x**t option. The AutoText dialog box presents the insert options, as shown in figure 2.35.

Figure 2.35

The AutoText dialog box showing insert options.

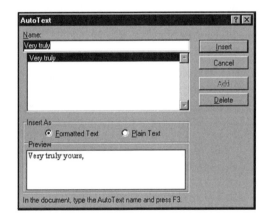

3. Select the name of the entry in the **N**ame combination box.

4. Select either the **F**ormatted Text or **P**lain Text option button in the Insert As group.

5. Click on the **I**nsert button.

Alternatively, you can type the name of the entry in your document and press F3 or Alt+Ctrl+V to invoke AutoText. AutoText inserts the entry you have named, or the closest match to the characters you have typed, at the insertion point.

You can also add an Insert AutoText button to the Standard toolbar and use it to invoke AutoText. *See Chapter 7, "Customizing Word for Windows," for information about adding buttons to toolbars.*

If you ever need to change the content of an AutoText entry, insert it into a document, make the changes you want, and then repeat the entry creation process described previously using the same name for the entry as it had before editing. To delete an AutoText entry, open the AutoText dialog box, highlight the name of the item to delete, and click on the **D**elete button.

The Spike

The Spike is a special AutoText entry that functions as a multiple cut and paste tool. (Microsoft uses the visual image of a desktop spindle holding several slips of paper to represent the Spike in the Word manual.) You can use the Spike to cut several items from a document and insert them elsewhere in the same document or in another document. When you insert the items, they are inserted in the order you cut them.

To cut multiple items using the Spike, follow these steps:

1. Select the text or graphics you want to cut from the document.

2. Press Ctrl+F3. Word cuts the selection and places it on the Spike.

3. Repeat steps 1 and 2 for each item you want to cut.

To paste items from the Spike, locate the insertion point at which the items should appear, but make certain that it is at the beginning of a line or surrounded by spaces. Then, perform one of the following steps:

◆ If you want to paste the material and clear the Spike, press Ctrl+Shift+F3.

◆ If you want to paste the material without clearing the Spike, type **spike** and click on the Insert AutoText button on the Standard toolbar. You can also open the **E**dit menu, select the AutoTe**x**t option, select the Spike in the **N**ame combination box, and click on the **I**nsert button.

Find and Replace

Word provides a powerful search and replace routine to help you locate information in your documents. Using this utility, you can locate just about anything and substitute something else for it if you want. To access the find utility, perform the following steps:

1. Open the **E**dit menu and select the **F**ind option, or press Ctrl+F, to display the Find dialog box (see fig. 2.36).

Figure 2.36

The Find dialog box.

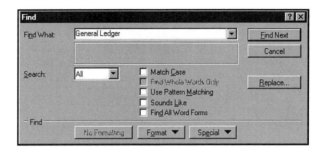

2. Enter the text to find in the Find What drop-down list box. The find strings from previous searches are stored in the list box portion of the control to facilitate repeated searches.

3. Select a search direction using the Search drop-down list box. The choices are Up, Down, and All.

Use the check boxes to set the following search specifications:

◆ Checking Match Case requires the matching item to be an exact upper- and lowercase match for the Find What string. *Intern* would not match *intern*, for example. Leaving the box unchecked allows a match with a string containing the same letters, but not necessarily the exact cases. *Intern* would match *intern*, *Intern*, and *INTERN*, for example.

◆ Checking the Find Whole Words Only box allows matches only with whole words. *Intern* would not match *internment*, for example. Leaving the box unchecked allows the Find What string to be matched with parts of words; therefore, *Intern* would match *internment*.

Stop Be careful of using Replace without checking Find Whole Words Only. You can replace the string in fragments of words, an action you probably do not intend.

◆ Checking the Use Pattern Matching check box enables the use of the advanced wild cards shown in table 2.3 in your Find What string.

TABLE 2.3
Advanced Search Wild Cards

Wild Card	Use	Example
?	Single character	w?t finds *wit* and *wet*
*	String of characters	w*t finds *wit, wet, wheat,* and so on

Wild Card	Use	Example
[]	One of the characters	w[ie]t finds *wit* and *wet*
[-]	Any character in range	[p-t]at finds *pat, rat, sat,* and *tat*
[!]	Any single character except these	p[!a]t finds *pit, pet, pot,* and *put,* but not *pat*
[!*m-n*]	Any single character except in this range	p[!a-e]t finds *pit, pot,* and *put,* but not *pat* and *pet*
{*n*}	*n* occurrences of the character or expression to the left	ble{2}d finds *bleed* but not *bled*
{*n,*}	*n* or more occurrences of the character or expression to the left	ble{1,}d finds *bleed* and *bled*
{*n,m*}	From *m* to *n* occurrences of the character or expression to the left	20{1,4} finds *20, 200, 2000,* and *20000*
@	One or more occurrences of the character or expression to the left	ble@d finds *bled* and *bleed*
<	Character or characters to the right at the beginning of a word	<(intern) finds *internment* and *internally*
>	Character or characters to the right at the end of a word	(intern)> finds *commintern*

◆ Checking the Sounds **L**ike check box enables Word to find words that sound like the one in your Fi**n**d What string, but are spelled differently. Common variants like *Katherine* and *Catherine* or *sum* and *some* can be found this way.

◆ Checking the Find All Wor**d** Forms box enables Word to find a variety of forms of a word. For example, if you search for *looking,* Word will also find *looked* and *looks.*

◆ Click on the F**o**rmat button to select **F**ont, **P**aragraph, **L**anguage, and **S**tyle formats to search for. The items that appear on this button's menu open the same dialog boxes that you can open from Word's F**o**rmat menu, in which you specify the format you want to look for. Using these options, you could look for italic text in paragraphs with hanging indents, for example. You do not need to enter text in the Fi**n**d What drop-down list box to search for a format—you can search for the format alone. Click on the No Forma**t**ting button to clear formatting information from a search.

◆ Click on the Sp**e**cial button to search for one of the special characters that Word uses, like paragraph characters or section breaks.

◆ Click on the **F**ind Next button to execute the search.

◆ Click on the **R**eplace button to switch to the Replace dialog box in the midst of a find operation

To replace text with some other text, perform the following steps:

1. Open the **E**dit menu and select the **R**eplace option, or press Ctrl+H. The Replace dialog box appears, as shown in figure 2.37.

Figure 2.37

*The Replace
dialog box.*

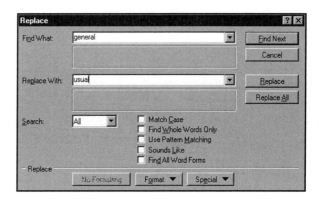

2. Set the controls in the dialog box exactly as you would for a find operation.

3. Enter the text or format to replace with in the Re**p**lace With drop-down list box. You can use the F**o**rmat and Sp**e**cial buttons to enter formats or special characters.

4. Perform one of the following actions:

◆ Click on the **F**ind Next button to find the next occurrence of the Find What string without replacing the currently found selection.

◆ Click on the **R**eplace button to replace the currently found selection and find the next selection.

◆ Click on the Replace **A**ll button to replace all matching strings without having to confirm each replacement.

Tip You can change the order of the words in the Fi**n**d What drop-down list box and insert them into the Re**p**lace With drop-down list box by entering the number of each word in the Re**p**lace With drop-down list box preceded by a backslash. If the Find What string is Darrow Clarence, you can enter \2\1 in the Re**p**lace With control to make the Replace With string Clarence Darrow.

Bookmarks

Word provides a bookmark facility so that you can easily find specific locations in a document. A *bookmark* is a named location in a document. It functions like a Post-it note inserted as a reminder tab in a book, except that each electronic reminder tab has its own name so that you can find it easily. After you have named a location in your document, however, you not only can move to that location quickly, but you also can insert information at that location.

To create a bookmark, perform the following steps:

1. Select the item you want to mark with a bookmark. This item can be text, graphics, or an insertion point location.

2. Open the **E**dit menu and select the **B**ookmark option, or press Ctrl+Shift+F5, to display the Bookmark dialog box (see fig. 2.38).

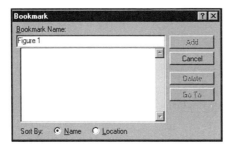

Figure 2.38

The Bookmark dialog box.

3. Enter a name for the bookmark in the text box portion of the **B**ookmark Name combination box. The name must begin with a letter and can contain only letters, numbers, and underscore characters. The name must be 40 or fewer characters in length.

4. Click on the **A**dd button.

Tip   You can choose to view or hide your bookmarks. You make this selection using the View tab in the Options dialog box. Open the **T**ools menu and select the **O**ptions item to gain access to these settings.

The most common use for a bookmark is to provide a speedy means of locating a particular spot in a document. To move to a location marked by a bookmark, follow these steps:

1. Open the **E**dit menu and select the **B**ookmark option, or press Ctrl+Shift+F5.

2. Select the name of the bookmark in the **B**ookmark Name combination box.

3. Click on the **G**o To button.

 Tip   You also can move to a bookmark using the Go To dialog box. Double-click on the Status Bar or open the **E**dit menu and select the **G**o To option. Select Bookmark in the Go To **W**hat list box and select the bookmark name using the **E**nter Bookmark Name drop-down list box. Then click on the Go **T**o button.

When you edit items marked with bookmarks, you can use the following procedures to get the corresponding actions:

◆ Copy a marked item, or part of it, to another place in the same document. The bookmark stays in place. It is not moved or copied. The copy is not marked by a bookmark.

◆ Cut a marked item and paste it somewhere else in the same document. The bookmark moves with the item cut and marks the item at its new location.

◆ Copy or cut a marked item and paste it to a location in another document. The bookmark both stays in place and moves to the other document. Both documents contain an identical bookmark. If the other document already has a bookmark of the same name, the bookmark does not move and the pasted text is not marked with a bookmark.

Bookmarks enable you to perform calculations on marked numbers. Suppose you mention three sales figures in a memo and want to add them to present a grand total at the end of the memo. If each figure is marked with the bookmarks figure1, figure2, and figure3, you can use this procedure to perform the calculation:

1. Open the **I**nsert menu and select the Fi**e**ld option.

2. In the Field dialog box, select = (Formula) in the Field **N**ames list box. It is the first item in the list when (All) is selected in the **C**ategories list.

3. Enter **= figure1+figure2+figure3** in the **F**ield Codes text box (see fig. 2.39).

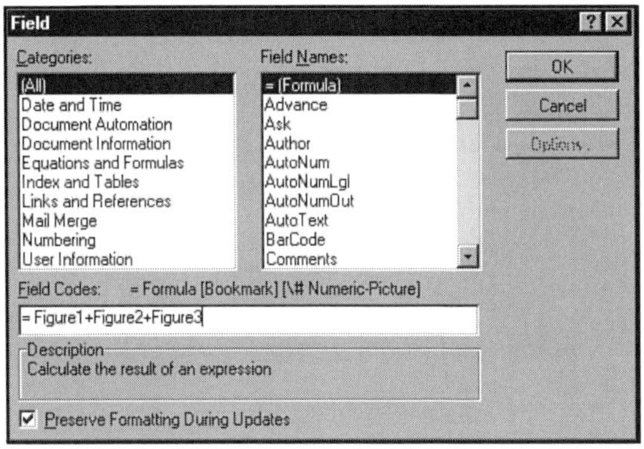

Figure 2.39

Entering a formula based on bookmarks in the Field dialog box.

4. Click on OK.

You will, of course, want to delete a bookmark occasionally. Word offers the following three methods for doing so:

◆ Open the **E**dit menu, select **B**ookmark, select the name of the bookmark in the dialog box, and click on the **D**elete button. The bookmark is deleted, and none of the text or other items marked are affected.

◆ Select the item marked by the bookmark, then press Del or Backspace. Both the item marked and the bookmark are deleted.

◆ Create a bookmark in a new location with the same name. The bookmark is moved to the new location, and the item previously marked is no longer marked by a bookmark. The item previously marked is not otherwise affected.

Highlighting

Word provides a new feature, highlighting, to let you mark parts of your document for special attention, similar to the way a highlighting marker is used on printed documents. You can use this feature to draw your own attention to a particular section of the document or to note places that need attention when you share the file with another Word user.

There are two ways to apply highlighting to text: selecting the text and then applying the highlight, or painting the highlight color directly over text.

To highlight selected text, click the Highlight icon on the Formatting tool bar. By default, the highlight color is yellow. If you want to change the color, press the arrow to the right of the Highlight icon and choose a color.

To maneuver through your document as if you were holding a highlighting marker, follow this procedure:

◆ Press the Highlight icon with no text selected. The icon appears to have been pressed into the Formatting toolbar and your pointer changes its shape to resemble a marker.

◆ Drag the marker across any text you want to highlight. Continue to lift and then drag the marker until you have applied a highlight to every part of the document you want to draw attention to.

◆ To stop highlighting text, click the Highlight icon.

If you change the color of the highlight as you work with the marker, the text you have already highlighted does not change its highlight color. The new color takes effect with the next text you highlight. As a result, you can highlight different types of items with different colors. The Highlight icon contains a color indicator showing the current highlight color.

Fields

Word uses fields to enable the entry and updating of information automatically. A *field* is a set of codes that instructs Word to perform an action of this sort. Although you can enter a field by hand, you have to know the appropriate codes for doing so. Word does not require you to learn these codes. The Field dialog box assists you in creating any type of field you want to use, and Word provides many types of fields to choose from.

As an example of how to use fields, consider how often you need to create a letter to a client, typing the date each time you do. You could place a date field in the template for the document that would automatically insert today's date when the document is created. To insert such a field, perform the following procedure:

1. Open the document template and place the insertion point where you want the date to go.

2. Open the **I**nsert menu and select the Fi**e**ld option to display the Field dialog box (refer to figure 2.39).

3. Select the category of field you want to insert from the **C**ategories list box. In this case, select Date and Time. Select the type of date and time field you want in the Field **N**ames list box—in this case, Date.

4. Click on the **O**ptions button to display the Field Options dialog box. Select the **G**eneral Switches tab and select the date format you want, as shown in figure 2.40.

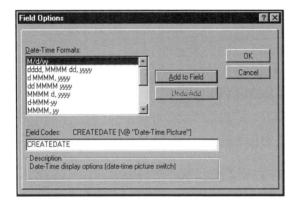

Figure 2.40

The Field Options dialog box, enabling the choice of date formats.

5. Click on the **A**dd to Field button and click on OK. Click on OK in the Field dialog box to insert the field.

6. Close and save the template.

Now each time you create a letter based on the template, the date is automatically inserted in the format you have chosen. When you reopen the document you have created, the date is not updated unless you specifically request it by selecting the field and pressing F9.

If you want to see the codes Word uses in a field, select the field and press Shift+F9; this keystroke switches the display of the actual codes. To switch all fields in this way at the same time, press Alt+F9. You can lock a field, preventing any updates, by pressing Ctrl+F11 or Ctrl+3. You can unlock the field by pressing Ctrl+Shift+F11 or Ctrl+4. If you need to *unlink* a field, that is, convert it to text that displays the last result of the field, select it and press Ctrl+Shift+F9.

If your service bureau uses a desktop publisher that does not recognize Word fields, you can unlink your fields to convert them to plain text that can be imported into the desktop publisher.

Symbols

Word has a special utility that enables you to insert symbols into a document from any font, as well as from a list of commonly used special symbols like em dashes and trademark symbols. Using this utility, you can give your documents a professional look without having to look up and remember all the special character codes that enable you to enter such symbols using the ASCII character set.

To insert a symbol, perform the following procedure:

1. Open the **I**nsert menu and select the **S**ymbol option to display the Symbol dialog box.

2. In the Symbol dialog box, select either the **S**ymbols or S**p**ecial Characters tab (see figs. 2.41 and 2.42), depending on whether you want to select the symbol from a font or from the list of special characters.

3. Using the **S**ymbols tab, shown in figure 2.41, perform one of the following actions:

Figure 2.41

The Symbol dialog box showing the Symbols tab.

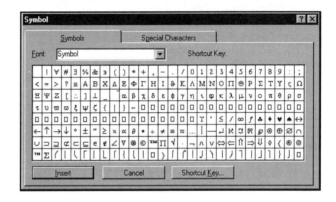

Figure 2.42

The Symbol dialog box showing the Special Characters tab.

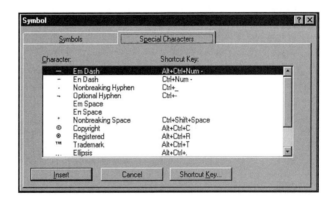

◆ Select a font using the **F**ont drop-down list box.

◆ Select a character from the grid displayed and click on the **I**nsert button. The character is inserted at the insertion point.

◆ Select a character from the grid displayed and click on the Shortcut **K**ey button. When the Customize dialog box appears, press the keystroke you want to use to insert the character in the future, click on the **A**ssign button, and click on the Close button. You can insert the character now using the keystroke you just assigned.

4. Using the S**p**ecial Characters tab, shown in figure 2.42, perform one of the following actions:

◆ Select a character from the list displayed and click on the **I**nsert button. The character is inserted at the insertion point.

◆ Select a character from the list displayed and click on the Shortcut **K**ey button. When the Customize dialog box appears, press the keystroke you want to use to insert the character in the future, click on the **A**ssign button, and click on the Close button. You can insert the character now using the keystroke you just assigned.

Defining Macros

You might think that macros are mysterious things that you will never use. *Macros,* after all, are user-created commands, and you must use some sort of programming language to create them. Word for Windows, however, has you using them all the time. Macros are a part of the document metaphor, so much so that you could not have a document without macros. Each Word command that you invoke from the menu is, in fact, a macro created by the Word programmers for your use.

To demonstrate this point, follow these directions:

1. Open the **T**ools menu and select the **M**acro option to display the Macro dialog box.

2. In the Macro dialog box, use the Macros **A**vailable In drop-down list box to select Word Commands (see fig. 2.43).

3. Scroll through the **M**acro Name combination box and select the InsertSymbol macro.

4. Click on the **R**un button.

The Symbol dialog box should now be on your screen, and you can work with it just as you can if you had invoked it from the menu. The macro and the menu command are equivalent. (The menu, however, makes the Symbol dialog box much easier to find and use.)

Figure 2.43

The Macro dialog box with Word Commands selected in the Macros Available In list box.

All the Word commands are stored in the document template NORMAL.DOT. Any macro is stored as a part of a document template. As a result, you can keep macros that relate to special document types in the templates for those documents. In this way, Word integrates commands and documents entirely. Commands are parts of documents.

You might wonder why Word is structured this way. Building a word processor as a set of macros that you run as you work on your document has the following advantages:

◆ You can choose to use any command in any way at any time, whether it is on the menu, attached to a button, hidden away, or dimmed on the menu. You always can get access to a command through the macro dialog box.

◆ You can decide which commands are attached to the menu and to the toolbars.

◆ You can build your own Word commands that perform custom functions by combining the already familiar commands you use from the menu. You can use your own commands or Word's commands interchangeably.

◆ User-created commands are composed of already existing, already tested Word commands.

◆ With this structure, most users never need to learn the command names in order to create new commands. They can use the macro facility to record the command sequences generated by using the menu and to play these back to Word at will.

In Word, macros are not mysterious—you use them all the time. They are the core of the word processor, a part of every document, and a key concept behind the software. Chapters 6 and 7 show the way to create your own Word macros and how to assign them to the menu or to toolbar buttons. For now, just be aware of how important these macros are to you.

Working with Multiple Documents

The reason that Word couples a document and a window together as a part of the document metaphor is that Word enables you to open multiple documents without having to open a separate copy of the word processor. Each open document runs in its own window and has all the capabilities associated with that window.

You can have open as many documents as can fit in the available computer memory. As a result, you need to know how to manage multiple documents.

Each document window has the familiar maximize and minimize buttons. When a document is maximized, it occupies the entire Word workspace. Its ruler tucks up under the toolbars, its maximize button appears at the right end of the menu bar, and its control menu button appears at the left end of the menu bar. These features define the default appearance of any new document you open when you start Word.

When a document is not maximized, its window has a title bar and looks like any other document window used by any other Windows program, with the addition of the ruler and the view buttons already noted earlier in this chapter. When a document is minimized, it appears as an icon at the bottom of Word's workspace.

You can manage multiple document windows using Word's **W**indow menu, shown in figure 2.44.

Figure 2.44

Word's Window menu.

The commands on the menu control the following actions:

◆ The **N**ew Window command opens a copy of the active document window. When you close the document, all copies of its window close as well.

◆ The **A**rrange All command arranges all the open document windows so that they are visible on-screen. If you have only a few documents open, their windows appear as horizontal bands in your workspace. If you have more windows open, Word automatically arranges them in a tiled fashion in the workspace. To change the active window, simply click on the window you want to be active.

◆ The S**p**lit command activates the split bar. Click in the active window where you want the split to occur.

◆ The list of document names enables you to switch to any document at any time. Simply select the name from the list. If your **M**ore Windows option is available, selecting it opens the Activate dialog box (see fig. 2.45), which gives you access to the list of windows by means of a list box. Scroll through the list, select the document you need, and click on OK.

Figure 2.45

The Activate dialog box.

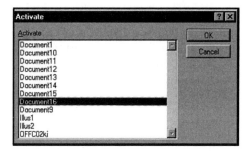

Through the facilities provided by the Window menu, you can keep track of all the documents on your screen. Word makes it easy to have multiple documents open and to avoid getting lost in the maze of multiple documents.

Using Advanced Formatting Features

Now that you know the basic concepts on which Word is built, it is time to teach Word how to support the way you work. In this chapter, you will learn the following advanced features and techniques for customizing Word:

- ◆ Creating a custom template

- ◆ Modifying and deleting styles

- ◆ Merging existing styles

- ◆ Changing case

- ◆ Using drop caps

- ◆ Creating document sections

- ◆ Using columns

- ◆ Using bullets and numbering

- ◆ Using numbered headings

- ◆ Using AutoFormat

Using these features, you can create professional-looking documents with a minimum of effort.

Having mastered the basics, you can apply your knowledge of Word to create sophisticated documents. Most users accommodate themselves to their software—that is, they learn how to perform tasks the way the software was designed to perform them. Word, however, accommodates itself to your working style. You don't need to build your documents a certain way because Word does it that way; you can teach Word to build documents your way.

You need only two tools to set up Word to work the way you do: document templates and styles. The templates you create provide your documents with the formatting you want, and the styles you create and store in your templates define how you work with your documents. This combination provides you with a tool that facilitates your work by automating it as much as possible.

To illustrate how to use templates and styles to teach Word the way you work, this chapter presents a scenario to help you imagine building your own solutions to working problems. This scenario involves a consulting firm, Write Solutions, Inc., that specializes in helping companies find ways to simplify and automate writing tasks by taking advantage of the features built into their word processing software. The firm has clients in the United States, the United Kingdom, Belgium, and France. Members of the firm have French language skills, and often both correspondence and contracts must contain some passages in French. Of course, Write Solutions practices what it preaches—all its documents are based on Word templates, including its letterhead.

As an employee of this firm, your job is to set up Word for Windows to handle the letters its representatives must write. You do not write in French, but you need to incorporate passages written in French by others in your correspondence. You also want to match your writing as closely as possible to the conventions used in the United Kingdom when you write to clients in that country.

Creating a Custom Template

The first step in setting up Word to meet your goals is to create a new document template. Follow these steps to perform this task:

1. Open the **F**ile menu and select the **N**ew option.

2. In the New dialog box, select the **T**emplate option button on the lower right (see fig 3.1).

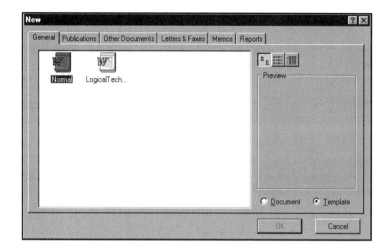

Figure 3.1

Creating the new template using the New dialog box.

3. If the General page is not displayed, click on the General tab.

4. Click the icon for the existing template—in this case the normal template—on which you want to base this new template.

5. Click on OK to create the file.

After you create the new template, click on the Save button in the standard toolbar to save it under its own name. When the Save As dialog box appears, give the template the name **WRITESOL** and click on SAVE. After you name and save the template, you can add to it the information you need each document to have whenever you create correspondence.

Because documents based on this template will bear the Write Solutions letterhead, you can use the document header to contain the letterhead information. Open the **V**iew menu and select the **H**eader and Footer option.

Note   The Write Solutions letterhead information is in the Arial font that ships with Windows. The upper line is in 14-point Arial, and the lower line is in 9-point Arial. The phone number is placed at the first default tab after the address text. The rule between the two lines of text is the upper border for the second paragraph of the letterhead information. To create the rule, place the insertion point on the second line, open the F**o**rmat menu, and select the **B**orders and Shading option. In the **B**orders tab of the Paragraph Borders and Shading dialog box, click on the upper border line in the Bo**r**der box and click on OK.

Follow these steps:

1. Click on the Page Setup button in the Header and Footer toolbar and select the **L**ayout tab in the Page Setup dialog box. In the Headers and Footers group, check the Different **F**irst Page check box to prevent the letterhead information from appearing on each page of a multipage letter. Then click on the OK button.

2. Enter the letterhead information. Click on the **C**lose button in the Header and Footer toolbar.

3. Enter a page break to create a second page. Open the **V**iew menu and select **H**eader and Footer again. Click on the Switch Between Header and Footer button on the Header and Footer toolbar to move to the footer for the second page.

4. Click on the Align Right button in the standard toolbar.

5. Click on the Page Number button in the Header and Footer toolbar. Press Enter.

6. Click on the Date button in the Header and Footer toolbar. Press Enter.

7. Type **Write Solutions**. Select the text you have just entered and use the Font drop-down list box in the formatting toolbar to set the font to Arial.

8. Click on the **C**lose button on the Header and Footer toolbar, and delete the page break that you entered into your template file. (You no longer need it there.)

Your completed header, as shown in figure 3.2, can now serve as your letterhead.

The people to whom you send correspondence now know the name of your firm from the letterhead you have created. They also can tell from the second and following pages which company the correspondence is from and on what date it was sent. This information helps if the pages of a long letter ever become separated. The final step in preparing this template is to add your name on the first line of the first page. Your clients can then tell who to contact in response to the correspondence.

After performing all these steps, save the template again to protect your work against loss. At this point, you are ready to consider what styles you might want to add to the document template you have just created.

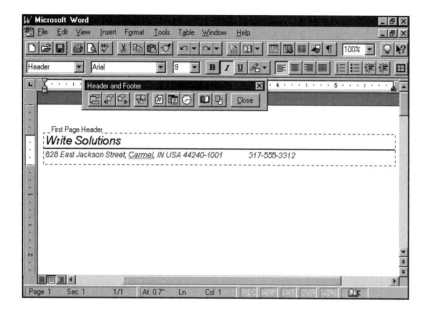

Figure 3.2

The letterhead information for Write Solutions entered on the template.

Creating Custom Styles

To simplify working with documents based on your new template, you can create a selection of styles that automate the formatting of the document. The easiest way to create a style is by example. Format a paragraph of text the way you want it, then perform the following steps:

1. Open the Style drop-down list box on the formatting toolbar.

2. Clear the current style name by pressing Del.

3. Type a new name for the style.

4. Press Enter.

You can perform those steps on the WRITESOL.DOT template as follows:

Format your name the way you would like it to appear beneath the letterhead on the document. To keep the font consistent, select your name and set the font to Arial using the Font drop-down list on the formatting toolbar. Set the size to 8 points using the Font Size drop-down list. Next, open the F**o**rmat menu and select the **P**aragraph option. In the Paragraph dialog box, select the **I**ndents and Spacing tab. Use the Aft**e**r spin box to set the space after your name to 12 points. Choose OK. Then open the Style drop-down list box, clear the current style, type **Name**, and press Enter. You've just created a style for the name block on your letter.

Press Enter and type a date. Select the date text and change the font size to 9 points. Name this style **Date**. You will use it to format the date block on all documents.

Next type a sample inside address and apply formats from the appropriate dialog boxes until it looks the way you want it to. For example, set the font to Arial and the size to 9 points. Set the space after the paragraph to 0 points. Name this style **Address**. You now have a style for the inside address of letters you might write.

 Tip   Figure 3.5 later in this section shows an example of each of these formats, if you need a visual target for creating these styles.

Create a similar style for the greeting. Set the space before the paragraph and after the paragraph to 12 points so that the greeting automatically spaces itself between the inside address and the body of the letter. Name this style **Greeting**.

Creating Language Styles

The body of your planned document places considerable demand on Word. You might be working with text in U.S. English, U.K. English, or French. As a result, you need to create three body paragraph styles, one for each language. In this way, you signal to Word's document tools to apply the appropriate language information as they operate on the document. As a result, during a spelling check the French dictionary applies to the French paragraphs, the U.K. English dictionary to the U.K. English paragraphs, and the U.S. English dictionary to the U.S. English paragraphs automatically. Word also automatically applies the appropriate exception dictionaries that you might have created.

To create styles for the body of your document, type some sample text. Keep the 9-point Arial font and set the paragraph spacing to 0 points before and 12 points after. Select the text, open the **Tools** menu, and select the **L**anguage option. Select English (US) from the **M**ark Selected Text As list box and click on the OK button. Then open the Style drop-down list box and create a style named **BodyUS**. Repeat the process of selecting the language, this time choosing English (UK). Create a style called **BodyUK**. Repeat the process one last time, selecting French and creating a style called **BodyFR**. You now can create paragraphs in all three languages, and Word will automatically handle them appropriately.

Create a style in U.S. English that has no lines before or after the paragraph. It should remain in the 9-point Arial font. Name this style **Close**. You will use it to format the closing of letters.

Creating Character Styles

The styles you have created so far are *paragraph styles,* so named because they involve paragraph formats. When you apply these styles to text, the paragraph containing the text is modified to fit the style. You also can create *character styles*—styles that apply only a font format to text. To create character styles, you must use the **S**tyle command on the **Fo**rmat menu.

Tip You also can create paragraph styles using the **S**tyle command. The process is the same as for creating character styles, except that you set Style **T**ype to Paragraph. The one advantage of creating paragraph styles in this way is that you can set the style of the text following the paragraph using the **S**tyle for Following Paragraph drop-down list box. The **Fo**rmat button in the New Style dialog box provides access to all the Format dialog boxes applicable to paragraphs.

To create a character style, perform the following steps:

1. Open the **Fo**rmat menu and select the **S**tyle option to bring up the Style dialog box (see fig. 3.3).

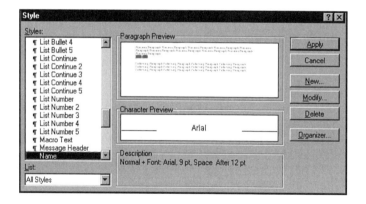

Figure 3.3

The Style dialog box.

2. In the Style dialog box, click on the **N**ew button to bring up the New Style dialog box (see fig. 3.4).

3. In the New Style dialog box, open the Style **T**ype drop-down list box and select Character.

4. Enter a name for the style in the **N**ame text box.

Figure 3.4

The New Style dialog box.

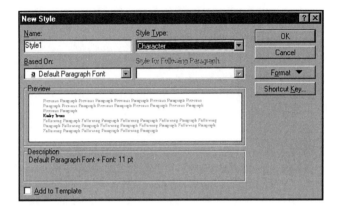

5. Select the style to base the new style on from the **B**ased On drop-down list box. Word must always use information about an existing style as the basis for creating the new one.

6. Click on the F**o**rmat button and select either **F**ont or **L**anguage from the list that appears. Use the Font and/or Language dialog boxes to set the characteristics for your style.

7. Check on the **A**dd to Template check box if you want to store the style to the current document template; otherwise, it is stored in the document only.

8. Click on OK. Word creates your new style.

9. Click on the Close button in the Style dialog box.

For the WRITESOL.DOT template, you might need a number of character styles: bold italics for foreign words and phrases embedded in your document, for example, and superscript and subscript styles for use in describing some elements of the programs your firm writes. Create these styles according to the procedure outlined. Name them **ForeignPhrase**, **Subscript**, and **Superscript**.

Tip   Style names can contain up to 253 characters, but cannot contain backslashes, braces, or semicolons.

Putting the Styles Together

To get a sense of the usefulness of your custom styles, create a brief document based on WRITESOL.DOT. Follow these steps:

1. Create a new document based on the WRITESOL template.

2. Press the End key to move to the end of the name block, press Enter, select the Date style, and type the date.

3. Press Enter, select the Address style, and type the address.

4. Press Enter, select the Greeting style, and type the greeting.

5. Press Enter, select the Body style appropriate to the country of your client, and type a body paragraph. Repeat this process until the body of the letter is complete.

6. Press Enter, select the Close style, and type the closing.

A portion of the completed letter is shown in figure 3.5 with the styles applied to each paragraph showing in the style area. As you can see, the appropriate formatting is automatically applied to each section of the letter. You do not need to make repeated adjustments using the menu to change the format for each section of the letter. Each section is also set up for the appropriate spelling check procedures.

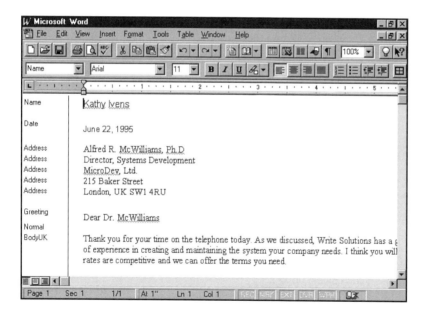

Figure 3.5

A sample letter based on WRITESOL.DOT, showing the use of custom styles.

Tip

You can open the style area on your screen by choosing **O**ptions from the **T**ools menu. Then use the Style Area Width spin box in the Window section to adjust the size.

Figure 3.6 shows the same letter in page layout view, showing the advantage of using the document template to contain the boilerplate text of the letterhead. Entering the text and the styles in the template once saves you a considerable amount of work as you create subsequent documents.

Figure 3.6

The sample letter based on WRITESOL.DOT in page layout view.

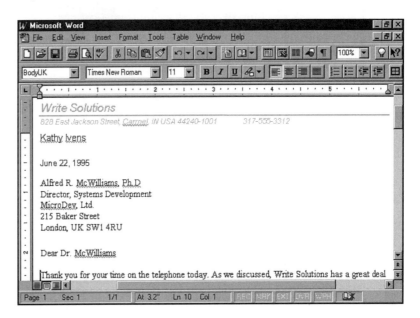

Modifying and Deleting Styles

Occasionally you might need to modify a style that you use for creating documents with the WRITESOL.DOT template. You might decide that because you write most of your documents in U.S. English, for example, you would like to limit your use of U.K. English and French to single paragraphs only. You might like to automatically reset the following paragraph to the U.S. English style. Making this change requires you to modify the style.

To modify a style, perform the following steps:

1. Open the **F**ormat menu and select the **S**tyle option to bring up the Style dialog box (refer to figure 3.3).

2. Open the **L**ist drop-down list box and select the view that causes the style you want to modify to appear in the **S**tyles list box.

3. Select the style in the **S**tyles list box and click on the **M**odify button. The Modify Style dialog box appears (see fig. 3.7).

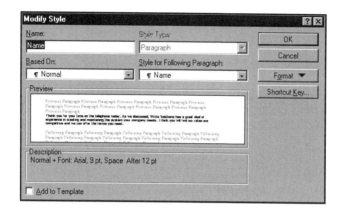

Figure 3.7

*The Modify Style
dialog box.*

4. To change the name, enter a new name in the **N**ame text box.

5. Open the **B**ased On and **S**tyle for Following Paragraph drop-down list boxes to change these aspects of the style. (If you are working on a character style, the **S**tyle for Following Paragraph control will not be active.)

6. Click on the F**o**rmat button and select the appropriate formatting dialog boxes. Make the changes you want to the style.

7. When you are finished, click on the OK button, then click on the Close button in the Style dialog box.

To change the BodyUK and BodyFR styles, select each in the Style dialog box, click on the **M**odify button, and set the **S**tyle for Following Paragraph for each to BodyUS. When you press Enter after you write a paragraph in either of these formats, the style for the new paragraph reverts to BodyUS.

Tip   When styles logically follow one another in a document, you might want to modify them so that each style selects the style for the next paragraph as the next style in the sequence. Address, for example, could format the next paragraph as Greeting. After you complete the inside address for the letter, press Enter to type the greeting using the appropriate style.

Occasionally you will need to delete a style from a document template. To delete a style, open the Style dialog box and select the style in the **S**tyles list box. If you can delete the style, the **D**elete button becomes active. Click on the **D**elete button to delete the style.

Merging Existing Styles

As noted in Chapter 2, "Understanding Word for Windows Concepts," Word provides a large number of built-in styles you can use in documents. You might want to use some of these styles in your own custom templates, or you might want to move some of your custom styles from a custom template into NORMAL.DOT to make them available globally. Word provides a facility for doing this type of copying and moving—the Organizer dialog box.

To access the Organizer dialog box, follow these steps:

1. Open the F**o**rmat menu and select the **S**tyle option.

2. In the Style dialog box, click on the **O**rganizer button to display the Organizer dialog box. Then select the **S**tyles tab (see fig. 3.8).

Figure 3.8

*The Organizer
dialog box
displaying the
Styles tab.*

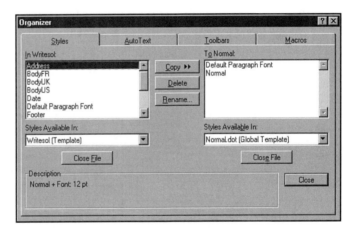

3. In the left half of the style organizer, set up one of the documents or templates that you want to work with. By default, Word places your current document in the left portion of the Organizer and NORMAL.DOT in the right portion. If this arrangement suits you, proceed to step 8. If not, follow steps 4–7.

4. Click on the Close **F**ile button on the left.

5. Click on the Open **F**ile button that replaces the Close **F**ile button.

6. In the Open dialog box that appears, select the file you want to work with and click on OK.

7. Repeat steps 4–6 with the Clos**e** File button under the list box and drop-down list box in the right portion of the style organizer.

8. Select a style in either list box, then choose from the following options

◆ Click on the **C**opy button to copy the style to the other document or template. (The arrow on the **C**opy button reverses direction depending on which list box contains the selected style.)

◆ Click on the **D**elete button to delete a style. Confirm the deletion by clicking on the **Y**es button in the confirmation dialog box. The list boxes in the style organizer allow multiple selections. You can select contiguous style names using Shift+left mouse button. You can select discontiguous style names using Ctrl+left mouse button.

◆ Click on the **R**ename button to rename a style. Type the new name in the Rename dialog box and click on the OK button.

9. When you have finished with the style organizer, click on the Close button.

Using the style organizer, you can copy styles among documents and templates, rename styles within documents and templates, and delete styles from documents and templates. After you have defined a set of styles, those styles need not stay isolated in your template or on your machine. You can easily make them available to colleagues, just as colleagues can share styles with you. You can mix and match styles to your advantage.

Changing Case

Word also provides the capability to alter the capitalization of your text on the fly. This capability goes beyond changing the case of selected letters from upper to lower. Word provides several options.

The easiest way to become familiar with Word's case-changing capabilities is to type a sentence, select it, and then press Shift+F3. When you first press this key combination, the sentence changes to all uppercase letters. On the next press, the sentence changes to all lowercase. On the third press, the sentence changes to normal sentence capitalization: an uppercase first letter for the first word and the remainder in lowercase. For any group of selected characters, press Shift+F3 repeatedly to cycle the text through these three options. Just press this key combination until you have the results you want.

 Tip Shift+F3 works on blocks of text longer than a single sentence. This key combination can be useful if you are not a skilled typist. Keep in mind, however, that Word will not preserve the capitalization of proper names in the sentences for which you adjust capitalization using this technique.

In addition to the Shift+F3 key combination, Word provides the Change Case command on the Format menu. This command offers you even more flexibility. When you choose this command, if no text is selected, Word automatically selects the nearest word for you. If text is selected, Word operates on the selection you have made.

When you select the Change Case menu option, the Change Case dialog box appears, as shown in figure 3.9. Choose from the following options:

◆ Select **S**entence case to place an initial capital letter on the selection and make the rest of the characters lowercase.

◆ Select **l**owercase to make the selection all lowercase characters.

◆ Select **U**PPERCASE to make the selection all uppercase characters.

◆ Select **T**itle Case to make the selection have initial uppercase characters on each word.

◆ Select tO**G**GLE cASE to reverse the capitalization of the characters in the selection.

After you have made your selection in the dialog box, click on OK. Word applies the formatting you have chosen to the selection on the screen.

Figure 3.9

The Change Case dialog box.

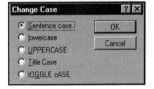

Using Drop Caps

Word also provides you with a simple way to create *drop caps,* large capital letters that mark the beginning of the first word in a section. Drop caps can make your documents visually exciting. They also serve a practical purpose—you can use them like bullets on a list. Drop caps help the person reading the document to find the relevant sections. While you might not use them in formatting a letter that you prepare using WRITESOL.DOT, you might use them in preparing a report using that template. Figure 3.10 shows an example of a drop cap in use in a report prepared with the Write Solutions template.

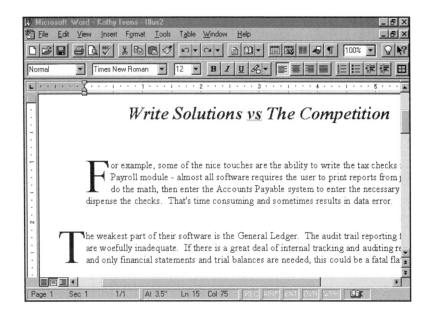

Figure 3.10

A drop cap in a report prepared with WRITESOL.DOT.

To create a drop cap, follow this procedure:

1. Place the insertion point in the paragraph that will receive the drop cap.

2. Open the F**o**rmat menu and select the **D**rop Cap option. The Drop Cap dialog box appears, as shown in figure 3.11.

3. In the Drop Cap dialog box, select the position of the drop cap, either **D**ropped or In **M**argin.

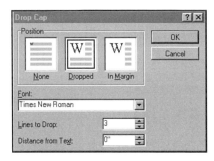

Figure 3.11

The Drop Cap dialog box.

4. Using the **F**ont drop-down list box, select the font for the drop cap. The default is the font of the text in the paragraph.

5. Using the **L**ines to Drop spin box, adjust the size of the drop cap in lines.

6. Using the Distance from Te**x**t spin box, adjust the distance of the drop cap letter from the rest of the text on the right.

7. Click on OK. If you are not in page layout view, Word will ask if you want to switch to that view before you insert the drop cap. You need to be in page layout view to adjust the position and size of the drop cap by dragging with the mouse.

Tip

You often will want to use a different font from the rest of your text for the drop cap. To create visual unity, however, it helps to use no more than two fonts. If you use Universal for titles and subheads and Palatino for body text, for example, use Universal for the drop cap at the head of a section to tie the elements together visually.

If, after creating your drop cap, you do not like it, you have the following options:

◆ Open the **E**dit menu and select **U**ndo Drop Cap. You can select this option from the Undo button on the standard toolbar if the option no longer shows on the menu.

◆ Select the drop cap and press Del. You will need to retype the character you deleted from your text.

◆ Select the drop cap, open the F**o**rmat menu, and select the **D**rop Cap option. You can adjust the controls in the Drop Cap dialog box to change the font, distance, and position of the drop cap until you are satisfied with it.

◆ Select the drop cap, select **D**rop Cap from the F**o**rmat menu, and then select None in the Position group.

Creating Document Sections

Word enables you to control the formatting you apply to any part of a document completely. In Word, a *section* is a part of a document that can be formatted separately from other sections. You define a section by inserting a section break into a document. Whatever comes before the section break can be formatted differently from whatever comes after the section break. You can create as many sections as you want in a document, and sections can be as short or long as you want them to be.

When you create a new Word document, it has a single section by default. To break a document into more than one section, you must perform the following steps:

1. Position the insertion point where you want to insert the section break.

2. Open the **I**nsert menu and select the **B**reak option.

3. In the Break dialog box, shown in figure 3.12, use the option buttons in the Section Breaks group to select one of the following kinds of section breaks:

   ◆ **N**ext Page: The new section begins on a new page.

   ◆ Con**t**inuous: The new section begins on the same page, unless the two sections have different settings for page size or page orientation, in which case the section starts on a new page.

   ◆ **E**ven Page: The new section begins on the next even-numbered page.

   ◆ **O**dd Page: The new section begins on the next odd-numbered page.

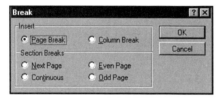

Figure 3.12

The Break dialog box.

Word inserts a visible break line labeled End of Section into your document, which you can see in Normal view. If you ever need to delete a section break, select it and press the Backspace or Del key. If you delete a section, the formatting of the section above the break in the document becomes the same as the following section.

Defining sections enables you to mix all sorts of formatting styles in the same document. Suppose you are creating a report on recent research and development efforts undertaken by Write Solutions. You want to have an abstract that occupies the full page width, the research report in two-column format, and the bibliography in full-page format. You can accomplish this formatting using sections.

To set this document up, enter the text, applying the styles you have created. To format this document, create a TitleWS style that formats a centered title, a HeadingWS style that formats a left-aligned bold title, and a BiblioWS style that formats each bibliography entry. After you format your text, break it into three sections so that you can separately format the column section.

To create the sections, position the insertion point at the title of the research report, open the **I**nsert menu, select the **B**reak command, select a Con**t**inuous section break, and click on OK. Repeat these steps with the insertion point at the title for the bibliography. Figure 3.13 shows this report with the section break inserted after the abstract.

Figure 3.13

A report for Write Solutions that uses sections.

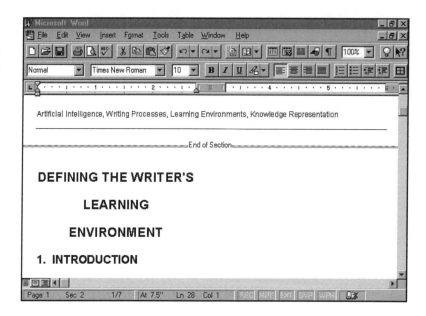

Tip To give each section a different header and footer, make sure that the Same As Previous button is not active on the Header and Footer toolbar. If the button is active, your new section has the same headers and footers as the previous section. To break this link, click on the button.

Using Columns

To create columns in a section of a document, you have two courses of action: you can use the Columns button on the standard toolbar, or you can use the Columns command on the Format menu. Each action achieves the same result. But as usual in Word, the menu command gives you more control over the column creation process.

To use the Columns button, place the insertion point in the section that is to have columns. Point to the Columns button, depress the left mouse button, and drag over the grid until the correct number of columns is highlighted (see fig. 3.14). Release the mouse button, and Word formats your section with the number of columns you indicated.

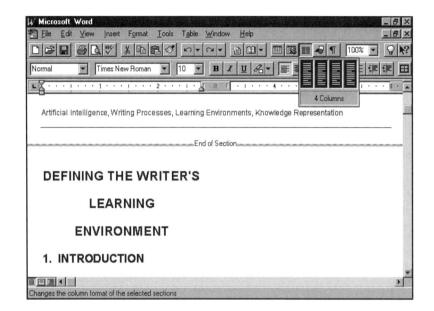

To use the menu command to create columns, perform the following steps:

1. Open the Format menu and select the **C**olumns command.

2. In the Columns dialog box, shown in figure 3.15, you can set the following options:

   ◆ To set up columns quickly in one of five preset formats, click on one of the controls in the Presets group to select **O**ne, T**w**o, **T**hree, **L**eft (two columns, the narrower on the left), or **R**ight (two columns, the narrower on the right).

   ◆ To set a custom number of columns, enter the number using the **N**umber of Columns spin box.

   ◆ To place a vertical line between the columns, check the Line **B**etween check box.

   ◆ To set up custom column widths and spaces between columns, use the W**i**dth and **S**pacing spin boxes in the Width and Spacing group. Select which column you are working on using the **C**ol. # control. To set equal column widths easily and quickly, check the **E**qual Column Width check box.

◆ To start a new column at the insertion point, check the Start New Column check box, located beneath the Preview box.

◆ Use the **A**pply To drop-down list box to control whether the column formatting applies to the entire document or simply from the insertion point forward. Word inserts a section break to protect the previous formatting if you elect to apply the column format from the insertion point forward.

3. When you have the column format set up properly, click on the OK button.

Figure 3.15

The Columns dialog box.

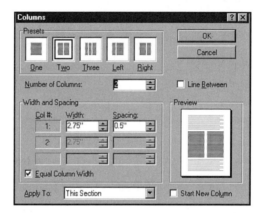

To create the columns in the second section of your Write Solutions report, place the insertion point in the second section. Use the Columns button on the standard toolbar to select two columns. Word adjusts the format of the section as shown in figure 3.16.

To fine-tune your columns, you need to master a few tricks:

◆ If you have unbalanced columns on the final page of your document, insert a continuous section break at the end of your document. Word automatically balances the columns for you when a continuous section break follows them.

◆ If a heading or text is orphaned at the bottom of a column, insert a column break ahead of the problem text to force it into the next column. Open the **I**nsert menu, select the **B**reak command, select **C**olumn Break in the dialog box, and click on the OK button.

◆ If you need two paragraphs or some text and a graphic to stay within the same column, select the items that need to stay together, open the F**o**rmat menu, select the **P**aragraph command, select the Text **F**low tab, check the Keep With Ne**x**t check box, and click on the OK button.

New Riders Publishing
INSIDE
SERIES

◆ If you have a document with a different header on the first page and you want to start your section on a new page, the first page header will appear on the first page of the new section. If you want to maintain the same header and footer for the remaining pages throughout your document, do not want the first page header to appear in the new section, and need the new section to start on a new page, insert a continuous section break followed by a page break.

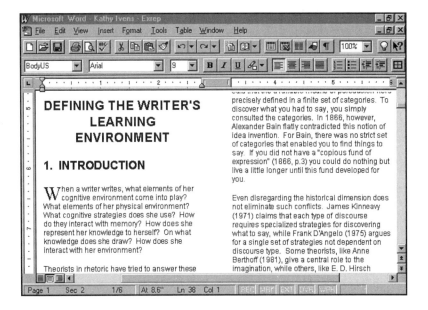

Figure 3.16

The Write Solutions report with two-column format in the second section.

Using Bullets and Numbering

Word automates the process of using bulleted and numbered lists for you. Word offers two buttons on the right side of the formatting toolbar: the Numbering and Bullets buttons. These buttons switch numbered and bulleted lists on and off. When you are numbering or bulleting, these buttons appear pressed. When you are not using these features, these buttons appear normally. Click on the button to turn this feature on and off.

To enter a bulleted or numbered list, follow these steps:

1. Set up the paragraph's left indent the way you want it to be. If you want your list indented further than the rest of your text, you need to set that up in advance.

2. Click on the Bullets or Numbering button. The first bullet or number will automatically appear.

3. Type the items in your list. Each time you press Enter, a new bullet or the next number appears. Figure 3.17 shows this process in action.

4. When you finish your list, click on the button to exit bullet or numbering mode.

Figure 3.17

Entering a numbered list.

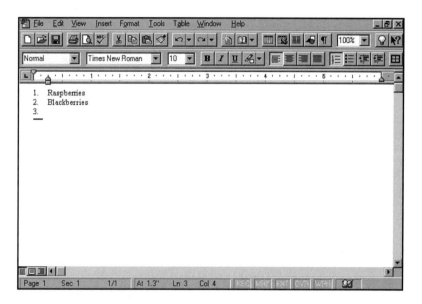

If you've already entered a list of items and decide later that it should be bulleted or numbered, select the list and click on the appropriate button. Word converts your list by adding the appropriate bulleting or numbering.

Tip Word supplies styles for formatting lists, bulleted lists, and numbered lists, which you can apply using the **S**tyle command on the F**o**rmat menu. There are five forms of each list style. Each form is increasingly indented. The number ending the style name indicates the level of indentation. List5, for instance, is the furthest indented of the standard list styles.

The buttons on the standard toolbar offer default bullets and numbering. Your list items are formatted with hanging indentation. The numbers are Arabic numbers followed by periods. The bullets are a standard round dot in a default size based on the font size associated with the paragraph marker.

If you want to modify these defaults or to use a different style of bullets and numbering, you need to apply the format using the Bullets and **N**umbering command from

the F**o**rmat menu. Using this command, you can create lists that are bulleted, numbered, or multilevel with the levels indicated by alternating numbers and bullets. To use this command, perform the following procedure:

1. Place the insertion point where you want to begin your list, or select the text that will be formatted as a list.

2. Open the F**o**rmat menu and select the Bullets and **N**umbering option. The Bullets and Numbering dialog box, shown in figure 3.18, appears.

3. The three tabs in the dialog box, **B**ulleted, **N**umbered, and M**u**ltilevel, offer different default styles. Select the style you want by clicking on its preview box; then click on the OK button.

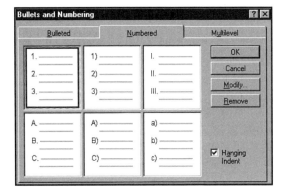

Figure 3.18

The Bullets and Numbering dialog box.

Word applies the bullet, numbering, or multilevel style that you select. If you apply the style to a selection, the list is formatted. If you enter the list after applying the style, Word applies the style as you type.

Tip   When you are working with a list, point the mouse to the list and click the right button. Word displays the shortcut menu for lists. You can use this menu to stop numbering, skip numbering an item, or access the Bullets and Numbering dialog box.

You can create custom bullet and numbering styles using the Bullets and Numbering dialog box. On any of the tabs, click on the **M**odify button. A Modify dialog box for the tab appears, offering controls that enable you to adjust the settings for the type of list you want to have. The Modify dialog box for the **B**ulleted tab is shown in figure 3.19.

Figure 3.19

*The Modify
Bulleted List
dialog box.*

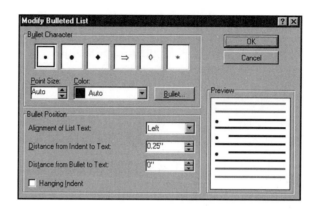

To modify the bulleted list options, you can choose from the following options:

◆ Select the bullet character from the B**u**llet Character control by clicking on the preview that suits your needs. If you want a different bullet character, click on the **B**ullet button and select one from the Symbol dialog box that appears. Click on OK after you make your selection.

◆ Set the point size and color of the bullet character using the **P**oint Size spin box and the **C**olor drop-down list box.

◆ Use the drop-down list box in the Bullet Position group to set the Ali**g**nment of List Text.

◆ Use the spin boxes in the Bullet Position group to set the **D**istance from Indent to Text and Dis**t**ance from Bullet to Text.

◆ Check the Hanging **I**ndent text box if you want your list to have hanging indents.

Click on the OK button to apply your custom format.

Stop   When you create a new style, you replace one of the existing styles displayed by the tab.

The remaining two Modify dialog boxes have basically identical controls in the Position group; however, they offer different controls in the top portion of the dialog box specific to the format being modified. The Modify Numbered List dialog box is shown in figure 3.20.

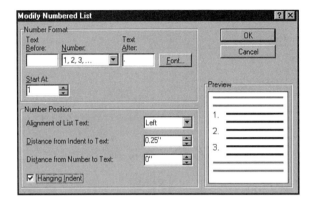

Figure 3.20

The Modify Numbered List dialog box.

To adjust the numbered list format, you can choose from the following options:

◆ Enter any text that should appear before the number in the Text **B**efore text box.

◆ Use the **N**umber drop-down list box to select a number format.

◆ Enter any text that should follow the number in the Text **A**fter text box.

◆ Click on the **F**ont button to select the font and character styles from the Fo**n**t tab in the Font dialog box. Click on OK after you have made your selection.

◆ Set the starting number in the **S**tart At spin box.

◆ Use the drop-down list box in the Number Position group to set the Ali**g**nment of List Text.

◆ Use the spin boxes in the Number Position group to set the **D**istance from Indent to Text and Dis**t**ance from Number to Text.

◆ Check the Hanging **I**ndent text box if you want your list to have hanging indents.

Click on the OK button to apply your custom format.

The Modify Multilevel List dialog box is very similar to the Modify Numbered List dialog box, except that it adds a control for specifying the level of the list you are modifying (see fig. 3.21).

Figure 3.21

*The Modify
Multilevel List
dialog box.*

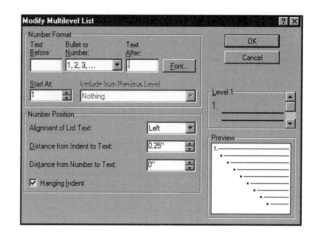

Choose from the following options to modify a multilevel list:

◆ Select the list level to modify using the **L**evel 1 list box. Your list can have up to nine levels.

◆ Enter any text that should appear before the number in the Text **B**efore text box.

◆ Use the Bullet or **N**umber drop-down list box to select a number format.

◆ Enter any text that should follow the number in the Text **A**fter text box.

◆ Click on the **F**ont button to select the font and character styles from the Fo**n**t tab in the Font dialog box. Click on OK after you have made your selection.

◆ Set the starting number in the **S**tart At spin box.

◆ Select what to include from the previous level using the Include from **P**revious Level drop-down list box. The Preview box shows the results of your selection.

◆ Use the drop-down list box in the Number Position group to set the Al**i**gnment of List Text.

◆ Use the spin boxes in the Number Position group to set the **D**istance from Indent to Text and Dis**t**ance from Number to Text.

◆ Check the Hanging **I**ndent text box if you want your list to have hanging indents.

Click on the OK button to apply your custom format.

Using Word, you can create lists of any type you want—bulleted, numbered, multi-level, or plain. You can convert list types easily. After you have formatted a list as one style, select it and open the Bullets and Numbering dialog box. The tab representing the format of the list is automatically selected, and the **R**emove button is active. To remove the list format, click on the **R**emove button. You then can apply a new list format (or not) as you like.

Tip   You can sort a list using Word. Select the list, open the **Ta**ble menu, and select the Sor**t** Text option. Word sorts numbered lists alphabetically and automatically renumbers numbered lists after sorting.

Bibliographies often appear in different formats for different audiences. Some publishers prefer the items numbered, for example, whereas some do not. Write Solutions is a company that has to work for both kinds of clients. Converting the bibliography from numbered to unnumbered format is a simple proposition once the basic list is typed into a document. Select the list, apply the appropriate list format, and the job is done. Figure 3.22 shows the converted bibliography in the Write Solutions report you have been preparing in this chapter.

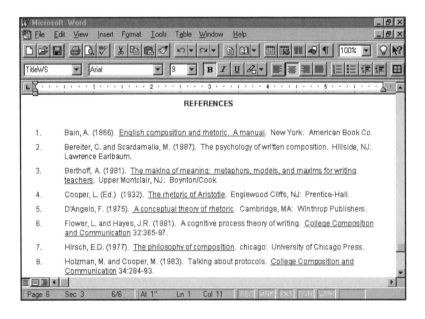

Figure 3.22

A portion of the finished bibliography for the Write Solutions report.

Using Numbered Headings

Word provides you the same flexibility with numbered headings as it does with numbered and bulleted lists. As long as you use the built-in heading styles, you can choose among several formats for these styles using the Heading Numbering dialog box. You apply the built-in heading formats using the **S**tyle command on the F**o**rmat menu, and you adjust the formatting of these styles using the **H**eading Numbering command on the F**o**rmat menu.

Tip   If you are creating a custom document template, you might want to copy the heading styles from NORMAL.DOT to your custom template using the style organizer. See the section "Merging Existing Styles" in this chapter for more information.

To adjust the formatting of heading styles, perform the following steps:

1. Open the F**o**rmat menu and select the **H**eading Numbering command to bring up the Heading Numbering dialog box (see fig. 3.23).

Figure 3.23

The Heading Numbering dialog box.

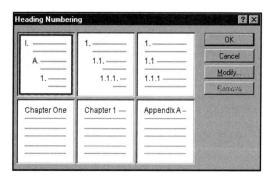

2. In the Heading Numbering dialog box, select the style you want by clicking on its preview box.

3. Click on OK to apply the format.

You could, for example, number the headings in your Write Solutions report by applying the built-in Heading 1 style to all headings except the elements of the learning environment. These should be formatted in Heading 2. Open the Heading Numbering dialog box and choose either the Roman or Arabic numbering style. Click on OK, and the headings are numbered.

Note   If you want, you can redefine the built-in styles to meet your needs. You probably want to copy them to your custom template beforehand to preserve the default formats in NORMAL.DOT. If NORMAL.DOT becomes hopelessly changed in unwanted ways from the default, you can always reinstall it.

If you outline your document before you apply heading numbering, Word automatically applies the default heading styles as you create the outline. You easily can apply heading numbers to documents created using this procedure. If you use numbered headings often, you might want to develop the habit of using Word's outline capabilities as you develop the structure of your document.

Using AutoFormat

Word can automatically format a document for you after you have typed it. Word applies the built-in styles associated with the template on which the document is based, according to rules Word contains that allow the analysis of a document's parts. Word can recognize titles, headings, lists, and so on. When it recognizes such a structure in your document, Word applies the appropriate style to it.

Word comes with several document templates that it can use with the AutoFormat feature, each representing different types of documents. To take advantage of these templates, you can either base your document on the template when you create it (see Chapter 1) or copy the styles associated with the template using the Style Gallery (see Chapter 2). To see a list of the document types available to you, open the F**o**rmat menu and select the Style **G**allery option. The Style Gallery dialog box offers previews of Word's companion document templates.

You can automatically format a document in two ways. To automatically format without reviewing Word's changes, click on the AutoFormat button on the standard toolbar (see fig. 3.24). Word formats the document and presents the finished version to you. If you do not like the changes, you can use the Undo feature to reverse them.

Figure 3.24

The AutoFormat button on the Standard toolbar.

You can use AutoFormat to review the changes Word makes, accepting some and rejecting others. Open the F**o**rmat menu and select the **A**utoFormat option. Word then displays the AutoFormat dialog box, as shown in figure 3.25. Use the controls in the AutoFormat dialog box to control the formatting process.

Figure 3.25

The AutoFormat dialog box.

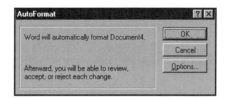

At this point, you can click on OK to proceed with the AutoFormat process or Cancel to cancel it, or you can choose **O**ptions to set options for the process. If you click on **O**ptions, Word displays the AutoFormat tab in the Options dialog box, shown in figure 3.26.

Figure 3.26

The AutoFormat tab in the Options dialog box.

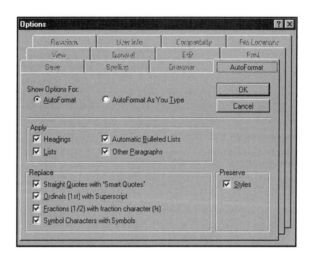

The AutoFormat tab controls what Word does as a part of the AutoFormat process. Word can perform the following types of actions:

◆ Word can preserve existing formats. Check the **S**tyles check box in the Preserve group to enable this.

◆ Word can apply styles to various document structures. Check any or all of the Hea**d**ings, **L**ists, Automatic **B**ulleted Lists, and Other **P**aragraphs check boxes in the Apply group to enable these actions.

◆ Word can replace certain characters with other characters. In the Replace group, check Straight **Q**uotes with 'Smart Quotes' to replace regular quotation marks with the curly kind; check **O**rdinals to replace 1st with 1st; check **F**ractions to change numbers separated by a slash to true fraction symbols such as $^{1}/_{2}$; check S**y**mbol Characters with Symbols to replace, for example, (C) with a true copyright symbol.

If you select the AutoFormat As You **T**ype radio button, you can see the formatting changes Word is making automatically as you enter text. You can adjust those AutoFormat changes to suit your own needs.

Tip If you work with a typist who formats text the way you would on a typewriter, AutoFormat can convert such formatting to standard Word styles.

If you click on OK in the AutoFormat dialog box, the AutoFormat dialog box changes to show different options (see fig. 3.27). Use the buttons in this dialog box to control which changes you accept for the document.

Figure 3.27

The AutoFormat dialog box after clicking on OK to start the AutoFormat process.

Review the new format Word has given the document. You can choose from among the following options:

◆ Click on the **A**ccept button to accept all changes. (You can always undo the changes using Word's Undo feature.)

◆ Click on the **R**eject All button to reject all changes.

◆ Click on the **S**tyle Gallery button to open the Style Gallery dialog box. Here you can review the types of document formats available by selecting each in the list box, preview them in the Preview box, and choose the one you like by clicking on OK after having selected it in the list box. Word then repeats the AutoFormat process.

◆ Click on the Review **C**hanges button to review each change, accepting or rejecting each change on an individual basis.

If you click on the Review **C**hanges button, the Review AutoFormat Changes dialog box appears (see fig. 3.28). Use the controls in this dialog box to determine which changes to accept and which to reject.

Figure 3.28

The Review AutoFormat Changes dialog box.

You can perform the following actions:

◆ Click on the F**i**nd button or the **F**ind button to scroll to the previous change or the next change, respectively.

◆ Click on the **R**eject button to reject a change.

◆ Click on the Hide **M**arks/Show **M**arks button to turn the display of paragraph marks off and on.

◆ Click on the **U**ndo Last button to undo previous actions. Each click undoes one action.

◆ Check Find **N**ext after Reject to automatically move to the next change after you click on the **R**eject button.

◆ Click on the Close or Cancel button (whichever appears) to accept all remaining changes.

 Tip   You can also scroll through your document using the scroll bars while reviewing AutoFormat changes.

While you are reviewing changes, Word represents its AutoFormat changes to you visually using the cues shown in table 3.1.

TABLE 3.1
Visual Cues to AutoFormat Changes

Cue	Change Made
Blue Paragraph Mark	New style applied to paragraph
Red Paragraph Mark	Deleted this existing paragraph mark

Cue	Change Made
Strikethrough Character Style	Deleted these characters or spaces
Underline Character Style	Added these characters
Bar in Left Margin	Changed the formatting of this text

AutoFormat thus helps you to identify its changes quickly and efficiently. You can easily recognize which parts or elements of the document have changed.

AutoFormat is a useful feature in Word for Windows. It enables you to type as you are comfortable typing and to convert what you do to a correctly formatted document using styles. It also enables the quick conversion of a document from one style to another. If AutoFormat makes a mistake, you can easily correct it. AutoFormat can be a very useful first step, if nothing else, in the final formatting of a complex document.

Sharing Data with Word

When you use a suite of applications, you find occasions to want to use the data stored by one application in the other suite applications. Word makes it easy for you to include data from other applications in documents, and to include documents in other applications. In this chapter, you will learn ways to perform the following tasks:

- ◆ Linking data to and from documents

- ◆ Embedding data in documents

- ◆ Embedding documents in other applications

- ◆ Using the applets that accompany Word to place drawings, graphs, and charts in documents

After you know how to share data, you easily will find opportunities to take advantage of your new skills in your work with Word.

Part of the power of Word for Windows is its capability to accept data from other applications as if the data had been generated by Word itself. A block of such data is called an object. Word can both contain and display objects without the other applications being installed on your machine.

Word can also maintain links to files created by other applications. A *link* is simply a channel of communication with a file of data. Using links, portions of the data in another application's file can be brought into a Word document as an object. These links can be *automatic,* so that every time the other application changes the data the changes are reflected in your Word document. They also can be *manual,* so that after data is brought in it is not updated unless you request the update. They also can be *locked,* so that no updates are possible unless the link is first unlocked.

Using objects and links, you can use Word documents to present pictures, sounds, spreadsheet data, presentation graphics, and other types of data. You can plan to display these documents on-screen, or you can plan to print the documents for display. Some types of data, such as sound, might be useful only in on-screen presentation, whereas others might make sense only in paper presentations. The capability for including objects in your documents removes the limits from your word processor. You now can create documents that include any kind of data that your Microsoft Office applications can create.

Understanding OLE and DDE

For our purposes, OLE is not something you shout at a bullfight and DDE is not a mistaken stutter. These are the technical specifications that enable Windows programs to accept data as objects and maintain links with other applications. DDE, or dynamic data exchange, is the earliest of these specifications. OLE, or object linking and embedding, is the later specification. Both OLE and DDE give applications names that indicate the application's role in the exchange of data. Sometimes you hear the names *client* and *server* applications. At other times you hear the name *container* and *source* applications.

At present, discussions of these two technical specifications confuse the two names, but they are really very easy to keep straight. Equivalent names begin with the same letter. *Client* applications are *container* applications; they receive the data from another application and hold it within their data file. *Server* applications are *source* applications; they possess data that they share with other applications. *Container* and *source* are the later, more explanatory, terms. As a result, they will be used in this chapter.

Applications can be container applications, source applications, or both. They can play each role at the same time in relationship to any of the applications running on your computer or your network. Sometimes understanding which application is playing which role can be confusing. To you it is mostly unimportant, except that you need to understand container and source applications well enough to manage a data exchange. Which is container and which is source is dependent on your point of view at the moment you initiate a data exchange. If your application is accepting data, it is the container. If it is providing data, it is the source.

It is easiest to understand these technologies if you look at the metaphors that drive them. The metaphor behind DDE is that of a conversation. Imagine that each application on your computer that supports DDE has a phone.

If a container application needs some data, it goes to its phone booth, checks the directory of which applications are available, and dials each one, asking if it can borrow a cup of data. Each source application can do one of two things in response to the phone call. It can answer the phone, or, it can ignore the ring because it is too busy to be bothered. In this case, the container and source never have a conversation.

If the source application answers the phone, the container asks if it can borrow the cup of data. If the source application does not have the data, it tells the client application that it has no data, and both applications hang up the phone.

If the source application has the data, it sends the data down the phone line. The container application receives the data and thanks the source application after the data has arrived. When the source application hears the thank you message, it sends an acknowledgment to the container application and both applications hang up the phone. However, if the link is an automatic link, the phone line stays open between the applications permanently, and the applications call each other back if the line is broken. If the link is locked, the container application has padlocked its phone booth, and you must unlock the phone to call the source application back.

OLE also depends on the conversation metaphor, only not as completely. In an OLE exchange, especially in Word, the container application calls the source application to ask if the source can share data with the container or custom design some data for the container. If the source is available, it answers the phone, but the conversation is very different. The source application does not send just the data down the phone line. Instead, it sends part of itself down the phone line to become a temporary part of the container application.

The source application sends either its menu or a toolbar to the container application. The container application displays the menu or toolbar along with any data that is sent. The user manipulates the data using the menu or toolbar. When the user is finished, the container accepts the data, removes the menu or toolbar from the screen, and hangs up the phone. If the container application ever needs the source application to manipulate the data again, the container calls the source and the conversation is repeated.

Under the earliest version of OLE, the container is the only application that possesses the data. Today, containers and sources can maintain DDE-style links with one another.

 Stop   You need to remember that not all application programs are DDE- or OLE-enabled. Some of them simply have no phone. In such cases, you cannot link to or embed from the application.

Linking to Data in Other Applications

Translating these example telephone conversation metaphors into your work with Word is straightforward. In the example of a link, you establish the link using the Windows Clipboard as your telephone booth. Both the container application and the source application use the Clipboard as a shared phone booth, and both applications place and answer calls using the **C**opy and **P**aste commands on the **E**dit menu.

This section shows you the way to create links between Word and other applications. The first example demonstrates using Word as a source application, and the second example shows using Word as a container application.

Creating Links with Word as the Source Application

To create a link between a Word document (as source) and another application (as container), perform the following procedure:

1. Save and name your Word document.

2. Select the material to be linked.

3. Place your call by opening Word's **E**dit menu and selecting the **C**opy option to place the selected material on the clipboard (see fig. 4.1).

Figure 4.1

Creating a link by copying material from a Word document to the clipboard.

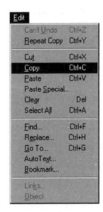

4. Switch to the intended container application—in this case Excel.

5. Receive the call by opening the **E**dit menu and selecting Paste **S**pecial.

6. In the Paste Special dialog box, examine the options available in the **A**s list box, shown in figure 4.2. The options in the **A**s list box describe the format the data can take in the container application. The Result box contains an explanation of the currently selected data format.

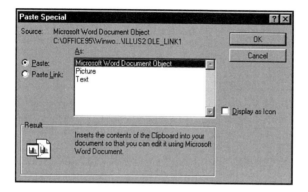

Figure 4.2

The Paste Special dialog box in the container application, Excel.

7. Select a data format in the **A**s list box and select the Paste **L**ink option button.

8. If you want the data to be hidden by an icon, check the **D**isplay as Icon check box. When the data are hidden by an icon, you must double-click on the icon to see the data. When you double-click, Word starts, if it is not already running, and displays the data.

Tip   Only some data formats can use all the options offered in the Paste Special dialog box. When you select a data format, the options it can use are active and the options it cannot use are not active. If you cannot link a certain data format, you might be able to paste it as an embedded object. The container application determines which data formats it can accept and whether it can link to the source application or only accept objects from the source application.

9. Click on the OK button to complete the conversation and create the link. Figure 4.3 shows two links from Word to Excel involving the same data. In the first case, the data is not hidden by an icon. In the second case, the data is hidden by an icon.

Links always are maintained by the container application. To see how Word maintains links, open Excel's **E**dit menu and select the Lin**k**s option. The Links dialog box, shown in figure 4.4, appears.

Figure 4.3

An Excel file showing two links.

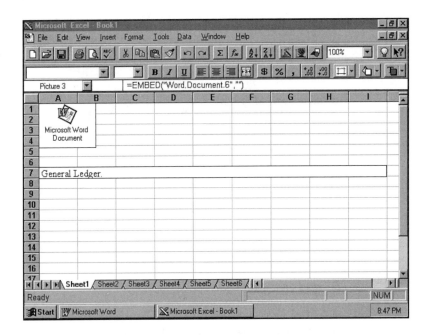

Figure 4.4

Excel's Links dialog box.

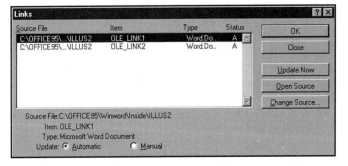

Link maintenance really involves only the following three actions:

◆ You can specify a link as automatic or manual by selecting the **A**utomatic or **M**anual option buttons. If you make a link manual, you can update it only by opening this dialog box, selecting the link in the **S**ource File list box, and clicking on the **U**pdate Now button.

◆ You can open the source application (if it is not running) and load the linked data file by clicking on the **O**pen Source button.

◆ You can change the name of the source file associated with the link if the file has been renamed. Click on the **C**hange Source button and edit the file name in the Change Links dialog box (see fig. 4.5). The file name appears between the vertical bar (I) and the double exclamation points (!!).

Figure 4.5

The Change Links dialog box in Excel.

Stop You should always name a file before creating links from it and you should never change the name of a file that has links. The file name is a critical part of the link. If a file name changes after a link is created, the container application can no longer find the source application data for the link and the link is broken. You must repair it by supplying the correct file name.

Creating Links with Word as the Container Application

To create a link between another application (as source) and Word (as container), reverse the process you used to link Word as source to another application and perform the following procedure:

1. Save and name your file in the other application—in this case, Excel.

2. Select the material to be linked.

3. Place your call by opening Excel's **E**dit menu and selecting the **C**opy option to place the selected material on the Clipboard (see fig. 4.6).

Figure 4.6

Initiating a link with Word from Excel.

4. Switch to the intended container application—in this case, Word.

5. Receive the call by opening the **E**dit menu and selecting Paste **S**pecial.

6. In the Paste Special dialog box, examine the options available in the **A**s list box, shown in figure 4.7. The options in the **A**s list box describe the format the data can take in the container application. The Result box contains an explanation of the currently selected data format.

Figure 4.7

Word's Paste Special dialog box.

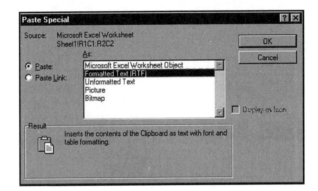

7. Select a data format in the **A**s list box and select the Paste **L**ink option button.

8. If you want the data to be hidden by an icon, check the Display as Icon check box. When the data are hidden by an icon, you must double-click on the icon to see the data. When you double-click, Excel starts, if it is not already running, and displays the data.

9. Click on OK to complete the conversation and create the link. Figure 4.8 shows two links from Excel to Word involving the same data. In the first case, the data is not hidden by an icon. In the second case, the data is hidden by an icon.

To see how Word maintains links, open Word's **E**dit menu and select the Lin**k**s option. The Links dialog box, shown in figure 4.9, appears.

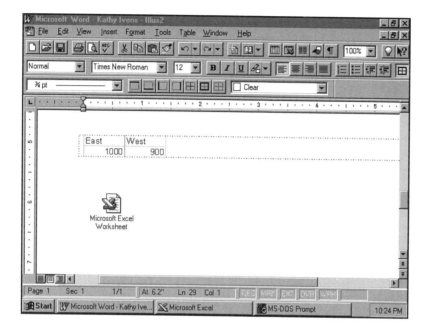

Figure 4.8

A Word document showing two links.

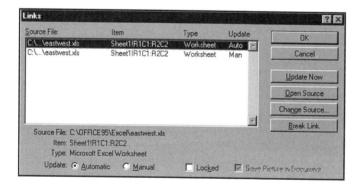

Figure 4.9

Word's Links dialog box.

Link maintenance in Word involves the following four actions after you have selected a link in the list box:

◆ You can specify a link as automatic (the default), manual, or locked by selecting the **A**utomatic, **M**anual, or Loc**k**ed option buttons. If you make a link manual, you can update it only by opening this dialog box, selecting the link in the **S**ource File list box, and clicking on the **U**pdate Now button.

Tip

If you are linking your Word document to several graphics files, you can choose where the actual graphic image is stored. If you do not mind having a large file size for your Word document, store the graphic in the document itself by checking the Save **P**icture in Document check box (the default). If you need to reduce the file size for the Word document, clear this check box so that Word saves only the link to the graphics file in the document.

◆ You can open the source application (if it is not running) and load the linked data file by clicking on the **O**pen Source button.

◆ You can change the name of the source file associated with the link if the file has been renamed. Click on the Cha**n**ge Source button and change the link information using the familiar controls in the Change Source dialog box (see fig. 4.10). This dialog box works in the same way as the Open dialog box, except it provides an **I**tem text box for editing the name of the data item involved in the link.

Figure 4.10

Word's Change Source dialog box.

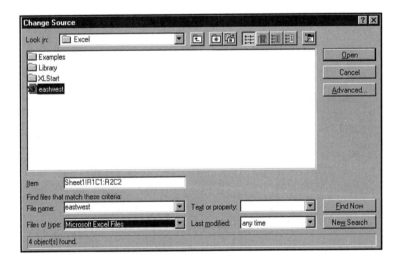

◆ You can break a link, leaving the data as it is intact in your document, by clicking on the **B**reak Link button.

Note

A link name consists of four items. The first is the source file name. The second is the link item, which specifies the location of the data. This might be a specification like a spreadsheet range and column, or it might simply be a name like DDE_LINK10. The third is the type of link; an indication of the nature of the data linked to. The

most common type is a document link. The final item is the update item, which indicates whether the link is automatic, manual, or locked. These items are concatenated for use by Windows using the vertical bar and exclamation point concatenators you saw in the Excel Change Links dialog box. In most cases, the only part of the link name that should concern you is the source file name.

You should use links to data objects whenever the data object meets the following criteria:

◆ The data is likely to change on a frequent basis.

◆ You plan to use copies of the data in several different documents or files.

◆ You want to have the latest copy of the data available in each place the data appears.

Links are especially useful, for example, for spreadsheet data that needs to appear as charts in documents that you have to produce on a weekly or monthly basis, such as sales summaries. They also are useful for database queries that you need to use in mailmerge documents, in which you know that the data is updated on a continuing basis and you want the latest addresses for your labels and form letters. Links like these, coupled with boilerplate text inserted from a template, can save you hours of time. When you open the document to create the report, standard text is inserted and the latest data appears. The data is updated automatically as long as you use automatic links. You need only do a quick edit of the document to make it say what it needs to say this time.

Inserting Objects from Other Applications

In the example of embedding an object, you embed the object using the Windows Clipboard as your telephone booth, just as you do with a link. As with links, both the container application and the source application use the Clipboard as a shared phone booth. Both applications place and answer calls using the **C**opy and **P**aste commands on the **E**dit menu, just as with links.

This section shows you the ways to embed objects in Word documents and Word objects in other applications. The first example demonstrates the use of Word as a container application. The second example shows the use of Word as a source application.

Embedding with Word as the Container

To embed an object in a Word document (as container) and another application (as source), perform the following procedure:

1. Select the material to be embedded in the source application—Excel in this example.

2. Place your call by opening Excel's **E**dit menu and selecting the **C**opy option to place the selected material on the Clipboard (refer to figure 4.6).

3. Switch to Word and position the insertion point where you want the object to appear.

4. Receive the call by opening the **E**dit menu and selecting Paste **S**pecial.

5. In the Paste Special dialog box, examine the options available in the **A**s list box, shown in figure 4.11. The options in the **A**s list box describe the format the data can take in the container application. The Result box contains an explanation of the currently selected data format.

Figure 4.11

The Paste Special dialog box in the container application Word.

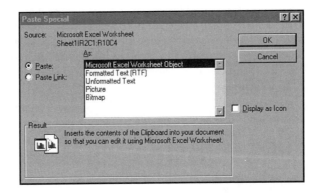

6. Select a data format in the **A**s list box and select the **P**aste option button.

7. If you want the data to be hidden by an icon, check the **D**isplay as Icon check box. When the data are hidden by an icon, you must double-click on the icon to see the data. When you double-click, Excel starts, if it is not already running, and displays the data.

8. Click on OK to complete the conversation and embed the object. Figure 4.12 shows an object embedded in a Word document. When you want to edit the data in the object, you must double-click on the object. Excel starts, if it was not already running, and enables the capability of editing the object.

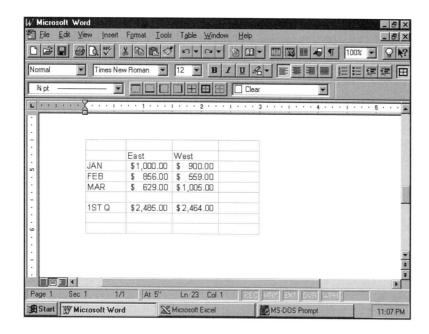

Figure 4.12

An Excel object embedded in a Word document.

The difference between a link and an object is that objects are always contained in the container application and not in a file maintained by the source application. While you can have several copies of the same object in several different documents, they are independent of one another. They can be changed at different times independently of one another. The changes are made in one copy of the object and are not reflected in other copies of the object.

 Tip   If you want changes in one copy to be reflected in all copies of the object, link them.

Maintenance for embedded objects is different from maintenance for links. If you need to change an object, simply double-click on it to open its source application and make the changes. In most cases, when you double-click, the source application replaces Word's menu with its own and provides a toolbar for your use. (This is the case with Excel.)

You also can access an object for maintenance from the **E**dit menu. As figure 4.13 shows, the last item on this menu is the object option. It changes name according to the type of object selected. This option opens a cascading menu that offers different options depending on the type of object.

Figure 4.13

Word's Edit Object option.

In the case of an Excel worksheet object, you have the following options:

◆ **E**dit causes Excel's menu toolbar to replace Word's so that you can edit the worksheet object while it is in place in the document. This form of editing is called *in-place editing.*

◆ **O**pen causes the Excel window to open and load the object. This is the form of object editing that you might be used to from version 2.0 of Word for Windows. When you close the Excel window, the worksheet object is updated in the Word document.

◆ Con**v**ert opens the Convert dialog box, shown in figure 4.14, which enables you to convert the object from one form to another or to make active the object for editing in one of its possible forms. Select the form of the object you prefer in the list box, select the conversion or activation action that you want, and click on OK to carry out the action.

Figure 4.14

Word's object conversion dialog box.

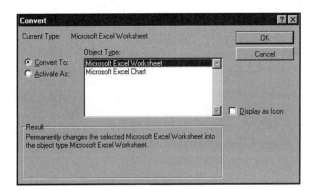

Tip

Embedded objects can take several possible forms, as determined by the source application. Just because you embedded the object in one form does not mean that it must remain embedded in that form. The object conversion option enables you to change the form of the object. Be aware, however, that some non-Microsoft applications might include one-way conversions as an option.

Embedding Data Using Word as the Source

To embed Word data (using Word as the source) in another application (as the container), reverse the process for embedding an object in Word and perform the following procedure:

1. Select the material to be embedded from your Word document.

2. Place your call by opening Word's **E**dit menu and selecting the **C**opy option to place the selected material on the Clipboard (see figure 4.15).

Figure 4.15

Preparing to embed Word data in another application using the Copy option.

3. Switch to the intended container application—in this case Excel.

4. Receive the call by opening Excel's **E**dit menu and selecting Paste **S**pecial.

5. In the Paste Special dialog box, examine the options available in the **A**s list box, shown in figure 4.16. The options in the **A**s list box describe the format the data can take in the container application. The Result box contains an explanation of the currently selected data format.

Figure 4.16

Excel's Paste Special dialog box.

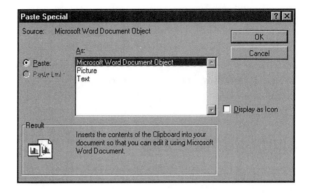

Figure 4.16

Excel's Paste Special dialog box.

6. Select a data format in the **A**s list box and select the **P**aste option button.

7. If you want the data to be hidden by an icon, check the **D**isplay as Icon check box. When the data are hidden by an icon, you must double-click on the icon to see the data. When you double-click, Word starts, if it is not already running, and displays the data.

8. Click on OK to complete the conversation and create the link. Figure 4.17 shows a Word object embedded in an Excel worksheet.

Figure 4.17

Word text embedded in an Excel worksheet.

Objects in Excel are maintained in exactly the same way as they are in Word. Double-click on the object to edit it in place, or use the **O**bject option on the **E**dit menu to **E**dit, **O**pen, or Con**v**ert the object.

In general, you should embed data objects whenever they meet the following criteria:

◆ The data are not likely to change on a frequent basis.

◆ You do not plan to use copies of the data in several different documents or files.

◆ You are not concerned whether this copy of the data remains the latest copy of the data.

Embedded objects are useful any time that data from external applications needs to appear in a document. You might need to include a spreadsheet table, for example, in a Word document. Rather than build the spreadsheet in Excel and have to maintain the file with Excel, you can keep the spreadsheet in the document that uses it. As a result, the spreadsheet is never divorced from the document. You can never accidentally delete the file from your Excel directory and need to re-create the worksheet from the data in your Word document. Embedded objects keep related data in the same container, making your work with that data much more efficient. Very often, Word documents make the best containers for your data.

Using Word's Drawing Capabilities

A good example of the usefulness of embedded objects in Word documents is the insertion of pictures that you can create using Word's Drawing application. You can access this application by clicking on the Drawing button on the Standard toolbar. When you click on this button, the button stays depressed and Word displays the Drawing toolbar (see fig. 4.18). You then can use the tools on the Drawing toolbar to embed graphics in your Word document. Clicking on the Drawing button again removes the toolbar and returns you to editing your document.

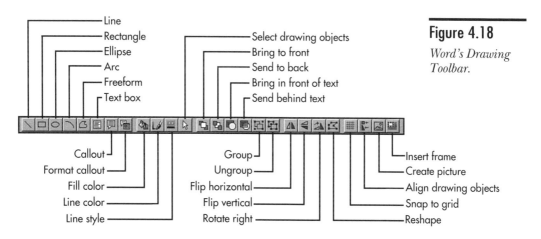

Figure 4.18

Word's Drawing Toolbar.

Drawing in Word

To draw in your Word document, you must be in page layout view. When you click on the drawing button, you enter page layout view. You can switch to any view you want while working on your drawing, but use of any of the drawing tools on the toolbar will return you to page layout view.

You can draw in one of two ways in your document. First, you can use any drawing tool to draw directly on your document. You can create the line shown in figure 4.19, for instance, by selecting the Line button and dragging in your document. In this way, you can add graphics to emphasize text, draw arrows that demonstrate the relationship between text elements, or add callouts to tables to make special points. No matter which way you choose to draw, the graphics are embedded as objects in your Word document.

Figure 4.19

A line drawn directly in a Word document.

President

Vice President

You also can create a picture by clicking on the Create Picture button. When you click on the button, the draw picture screen appears, as does the Picture toolbar (see fig. 4.20).

Figure 4.20

Word displaying the draw picture screen and toolbar.

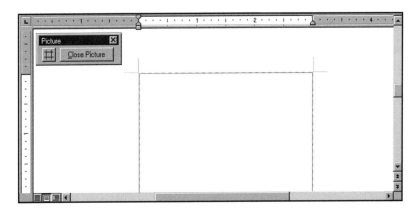

The drawing screen shows you the current picture boundary. You can draw on this screen using the drawing tools. After selecting a drawing tool, drag to draw the shape you have selected. Adjust its dimensions using the sizing handles that are visible when you select the shape by clicking on it. You are not limited to the picture boundary shown on the screen—you can draw beyond it.

When you are finished with your drawing, click on the Reset Picture Boundary button on the Picture toolbar. Word then makes the picture boundary fit what you have drawn. To exit the drawing screen and see the picture in place in the document, click on the **C**lose Picture button. Word inserts the picture at the current location of the insertion point.

Tip   You can remove the Picture toolbar from the screen before you have closed your picture by clicking on its control menu box. Without the toolbar on the screen, however, you cannot close the picture. To get the toolbar back, open the **V**iew menu and select the **T**oolbars option. In the Toolbars dialog box, check the box next to the Picture item in the list box and click on the OK button.

Fine-Tuning Your Word Drawing

After you have inserted a picture, it appears wherever the insertion point was when you clicked on the Create Picture button. Text does not flow around it, and it might create large white spaces in your document that you do not want.

To control the way the picture fits into your document more effectively, you should place it in a frame. To do so, select the picture and click on the Insert Frame button. Word places a frame around your picture. Text will now flow around your drawing, you can place your drawing more effectively by dragging it on the screen, and you can resize your drawing by selecting the frame and dragging the sizing handles.

Word's drawing application provides you with additional drawing tools that you might need. You can select the fill color by clicking on the Fill Color button and selecting a color from the palette that appears (see fig. 4.21). You can select the line color in similar fashion using the Line Color button. The Line Style button enables you to select the type of line you want to draw from a palette as well.

Figure 4.21

The fill color palette.

You can insert text boxes with the Text Box button and callouts with the Callout button. As with the shape tools, drag on the screen to create the item. You can format your callouts by selecting each in turn and clicking on the Format Callout button.

This action brings up the Callout Defaults dialog box (see fig. 4.22), which enables you to choose from several default patterns and to adjust the characteristics of your callouts using the controls provided.

Figure 4.22

*The Callout
Defaults dialog
box.*

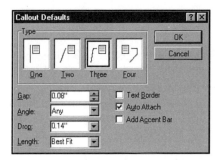

You also can place any object in front of or behind others by selecting the object and clicking on the Bring to Front or Send to Back buttons. You can place a text box over or behind a shape by performing the same procedure with the Bring in Front of Text and Send Behind Text buttons. You can create groups of objects by clicking on the Select Drawing Objects button (arrow button), selecting the objects to be in the group by dragging, and clicking on the Group button. You then can manipulate the grouped objects as a single object, and you can ungroup them by selecting the group and clicking on the Ungroup button.

The flip and rotate buttons do just as their names indicate—flipping or rotating the selected object. The Reshape button enables you to change the dimensions of any freeform object you have drawn. The Snap to Grid button aligns the objects in your drawing on a grid with the dimensions you specify in the dialog box that appears when you click the button (see fig. 4.23). Select the dimensions for the grid using the controls and then click on OK.

Figure 4.23

*The Snap to Grid
dialog box.*

Clicking on the Align Drawing Objects button brings up a dialog box, shown in figure 4.24, that enables you to place objects in particular places on the page. First select the object or objects you want to align. You then select their location using the option buttons. Clicking on OK aligns the objects.

Figure 4.24

The Align drawing objects dialog box.

Setting the location relative to the page means relative to the Word page, not relative to the current picture boundary. Bottom right relative to the page means the lower right corner of the page as it prints, as shown in figure 4.25.

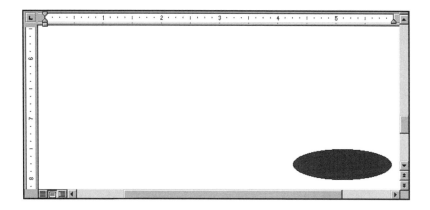

Figure 4.25

An object aligned to bottom right with respect to the page.

Setting the locations relative to each other superimposes the objects over one another with the positioning you specify. Figure 4.26 shows several objects aligned relative to each other.

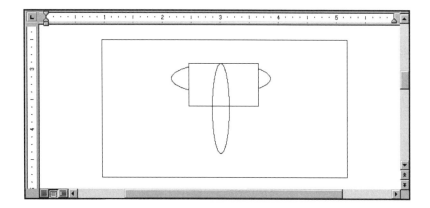

Figure 4.26

Three objects with top center alignment relative to one another.

Tip
Word's drawing capabilities enable you to create pictures of any type for use in your Word document. And you can import pictures using the **P**icture option on the **I**nsert menu.

Using WordArt

The WordArt 2.0 applet included with Word is another example of how to embed objects in documents. WordArt enables you to create special text effects and embed them into your Word documents. You access WordArt by opening the **I**nsert menu and selecting the **O**bject option. This action causes the Object dialog box to appear (see fig. 4.27). In the **O**bject Type list box on the **C**reate New tab, select Microsoft WordArt 2.0, then click on the OK button.

Figure 4.27

The Object dialog box showing the selection of WordArt 2.0.

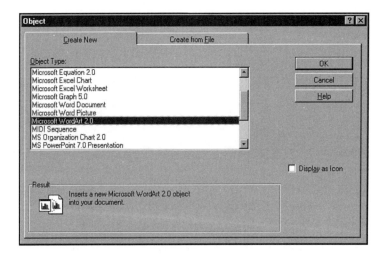

When WordArt opens it provides you with both a menu and a toolbar. Although all the effects you can create with WordArt can be accessed from the menu, the toolbar is easier and more convenient to use. WordArt also presents you with a dialog box into which you enter the text for your special effect and a representation of the text object embedded in your document, as shown in figure 4.28.

To create a special text effect, enter your text in the Enter Your Text Here dialog box. If you need to insert a symbol not readily available from your keyboard, click on the **I**nsert Symbol button to open the Insert Symbol dialog box (see fig. 4.29). You can select any symbol available in your current font for insertion into your text. Just click on the symbol and then click on OK. If you need a symbol not in your current font, select a new font from the font drop-down list box described later in this section.

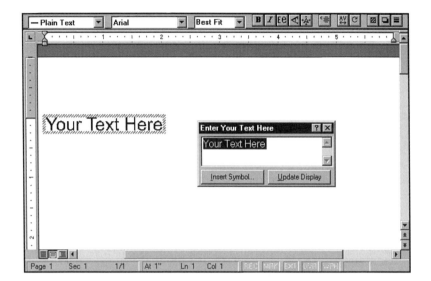

Figure 4.28

The WordArt menu, toolbar, and dialog box.

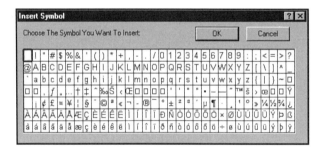

Figure 4.29

WordArt's Insert Symbol dialog box.

You can design your special effect by working with the controls on the WordArt toolbar. First, select a shape by opening the Shape drop-down list box. This action displays a grid of the preset shapes you can give to your text, as shown in figure 4.30. Just click on the shape you want.

Next, select the font and size you want to use from the Font and Size drop-down list boxes. These controls work exactly the same as those offered by Word on the Formatting toolbar. You also can apply the character styles **bold** and *italic* using the Bold and Italic buttons, exactly as you might from Word's Formatting toolbar.

Tip   Most of the time your text is updated immediately in your Word document. If you feel you need to update the text, click on the **U**pdate Display button in the Enter Your Text Here dialog box.

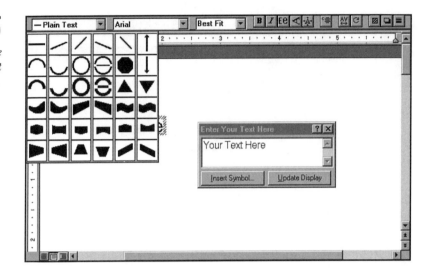

The next few buttons apply special effects to your text. You have the following options:

◆ The Even Height button causes all the characters in your text to be the same height, regardless of whether they are upper- or lowercase.

◆ The Flip button causes each character of your text to lay over on its left side, so that the text reads vertically from bottom to top.

◆ The Stretch button causes your characters to expand to fill the space allotted for your WordArt effect. To cancel the effect, click on the button again.

◆ The Align button opens a drop-down list box of alignment options, most of which should be familiar from working with Word (see fig. 4.31). The less familiar options are letter justify, stretch justify, and word justify. *Letter justify* increases the spaces between letters to justify a line. *Stretch justify* stretches the width of the characters to justify a line. *Word justify* increases the space between words to justify a line.

◆ The Spacing Between Characters button enables you to adjust the spacing between characters to achieve a more readable effect. Experiment with the options described by the option button captions, which represent the range from very close together to very far apart, until you find the option that works for you (see fig. 4.32). You also can experiment with clearing the Automatically Kern Character Pairs check box to see whether your effect benefits from turning this feature off. (Pairs of characters that present odd spacing problems are automatically *kerned*, or adjusted closer, by WordArt unless you clear this check box.)

◆ The Rotation button opens the Special Effects dialog box, as shown in figure 4.33. This contains two spin boxes that control the angle of rotation and the slider, or slant from vertical, of the rotated text. Adjust the controls so that your text effect appears the way you want it.

Figure 4.32

The Spacing Between Characters dialog box.

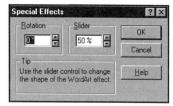

Figure 4.33

The Special Effects dialog box in WordArt.

◆ The Shading button gives you access to the Shading dialog box (see fig. 4.34). This enables you to select among various shading patterns and colors for your characters. Experiment with the controls to achieve the effect you want.

◆ The Shadow button opens a list box that offers you several choices of shadows for your characters, as shown in figure 4.35. The MORE option gives you access to the Shadow dialog box, which enables the additional option of selecting the color of the shadow. (The default color is silver, which is a good complement for most text colors.)

Figure 4.34

WordArt's Shading dialog box.

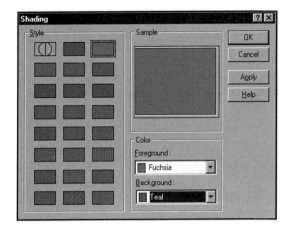

Figure 4.35

The Shadow drop-down list box.

◆ The Border button opens the Border dialog box, as shown in figure 4.36, which enables you to select the border width for the characters you use and the border color. The border referred to is the one that snakes along the edge of each character itself. Widening the border of the character reduces the area of the shading pattern you might have applied to your text effect.

Figure 4.36

The Border dialog box.

When you are finished creating your WordArt effect, click anywhere on the Word workspace to return to working on your document. This action closes WordArt and embeds the text effect in your document as an object. To return to working on your text effect, double-click on it.

Tip WordArt effects are not automatically enclosed in frames; that is, your text cannot flow around them. If you want to use a frame, select your WordArt object and select the **F**rame option from the **I**nsert menu.

Using Microsoft Graph

Microsoft Graph is yet another example of the OLE tools provided with Word, giving you the opportunity to place charts in your documents as illustrations. You can either import an Excel chart for use with your document, or you can create one using the built-in spreadsheet capabilities of Microsoft Graph. In either case, Word treats the chart in the same way.

To bring a Graph into a Word document, choose **O**bject from the Insert menu. Choose Microsoft Graph 5.0 as the Object Type. The Graph program opens, as shown in figure 4.37. The menu bar changes, adding a Data menu and eliminating the Table menu. The choices for each of the menu items change to be relevant for working on graphs. The toolbar changes to provide buttons that are useful for working on the graph and its accompanying data sheet.

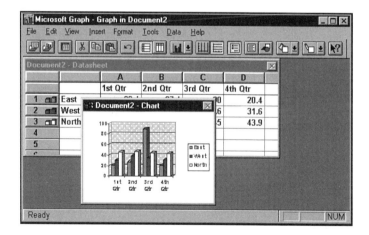

Figure 4.37

Adding a Graph to a Document.

The Graph program provides two document windows in which you build your chart. One represents the datasheet from which the chart is built, and the other represents the chart itself.

Word opens the windows with a default datasheet and chart in place. You can edit the datasheet to prepare the chart for your Word document by changing the names of the rows and columns, adding rows and columns, deleting rows or columns, or changing the character of the chart.

The sample datasheet is intended to show you the most common situation for creating a chart and to suggest possibilities for your data by example. Editing the datasheet and pressing Enter after each edit causes an automatic update of the chart.

When you finish editing the datasheet and the graph, click on any place in the document and the Word window returns to its "document state" with the graph inserted in the document. The menu items return to the familiar Word format, as do the toolbar buttons. To return to the graph and the graph-related window, double-click on the graph. If you want to edit the datasheet after the Graph menu and tool-bar are displayed, choose **V**iew, then choose **D**atasheet.

In addition to editing the example datasheet, you can import a datasheet from a spreadsheet. In the case of the Office suite of applications, this would be from Excel. To do this, select the datasheet, open the **E**dit menu in the Graph window and select the **I**mport Data option (or click the Import Data button on the toolbar. Graph displays the Import Data dialog box, shown in figure 4.38. Select the file containing the data. If you want to select only a row:cell range of data or a named range of data, select the **Ra**nge option button and enter the row:cell specification or the name of the range in the text box, then click on OK. Word issues a warning that the imported data will overwrite the existing data. Choose OK to continue importing the data.

Figure 4.38

The Import Data dialog box.

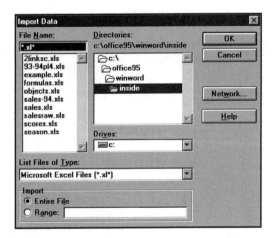

You also can import an Excel chart that you have already created using Excel. In this case, open the **E**dit menu and select the Import C**h**art option. Graph displays the Import Chart dialog box. Use the controls to navigate the directories until you find the chart you want. When you do, click on OK. Graph imports the chart and the data on which it is built.

The **E**dit menu in Graph provides you with some of the familiar options; however, there are some options that are specific to working on the datasheet and the **E**dit

menu for the datasheet is displayed by clicking the right mouse button anywhere on the datasheet (see fig. 4.39).

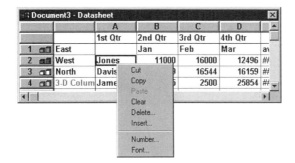

The Datasheet **E**dit menu provides the following functions:

◆ **Cut** and **Copy** place the selected cells on the clipboard.

◆ **Clear** erases data from the selected cells.

◆ **Delete** expunges a row, column, or selected cells.

◆ **Insert** adds a row or column.

◆ **Number** displays the Number Format dialog box that lets you choose formats for numerical data (see figure 4.40).

◆ **Font** displays a Font dialog box for changing the fonts in the datasheet.

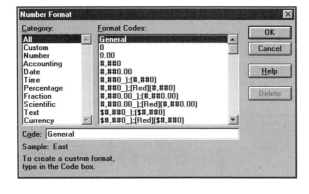

You can select the type of chart you want to present by choosing **C**hart Type from the Format menu. Choose 2-D or 3-D to see the respective choices available. Figure 4.41 shows the 2-D choices, with Columns selected as the chart type.

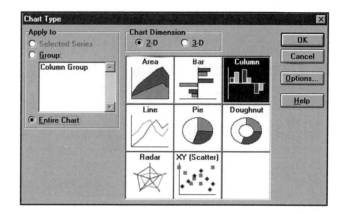

After you choose a type, select **O**ptions to choose a sub-choice and see a preview of the appearance of each selection (see fig. 4.42).

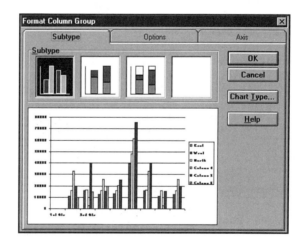

You can further customize the appearance of the chart by using the choices available with the Options tab of this dialog box; for example, specifying the gap width and overlap of the columns. The Axis tab lets you choose primary and secondary axes for the charts connected to a datasheet.

The **C**hart menu is accessed by clicking the right mouse button on the Graph (most of the items are also available on the **I**nsert menu on the menu bar). Use this menu to specify the characteristics for the type of chart you have chosen to build. Each menu option changes one of the characteristics of the chart's display. You have the following options:

◆ **Clear** removes formatting and formulas from a selected area of the graph.

◆ **Insert Titles** opens a dialog box that enables you to attach a title to one of the five items that can carry a title (see fig. 4.43). Use the option buttons to select the item that will bear the title.

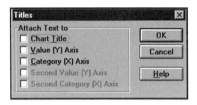

Figure 4.43

The Titles dialog box.

◆ **Insert Axis** specifies the axes that display.

◆ **Insert Gridlines** specifies the gridlines that display.

◆ The **Insert Data Labels** option brings up the Data Labels dialog box (see fig. 4.44), which enables you to attach a label to each series displayed. Use the option buttons to select the type of label appropriate for your chart.

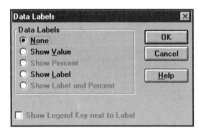

Figure 4.44

The Data Labels dialog box.

◆ Select **Format Chart Area** to customize the colors, patterns, and fonts for the graph.

◆ **Chart Type** produces the same selection dialog box discussed above.

◆ Choose **Autoformat** to reformat the graph automatically, using the specifications you've entered.

◆ If your graph is a 3-D type, you can select 3-D View to display the Format 3-D View dialog box shown in Figure 4.45. Using the specifications shown, you can change the appearance of the graph.

Figure 4.45

Change the view of a 3-D graph with the Format 3-D View dialog box.

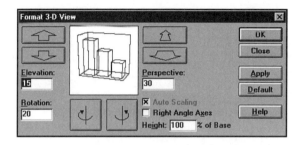

Place the pointer on the Legend and click the right mouse button to display the Legend menu.

Choose Clear to delete formatting from the selected part of the legend. Choose Format Legend to bring up the Format Legend dialog box (see fig. 4.46) where you can configure borders, colors, patterns, and fonts, as well as the placement of the Legend.

Figure 4.46

The Format Legend dialog box.

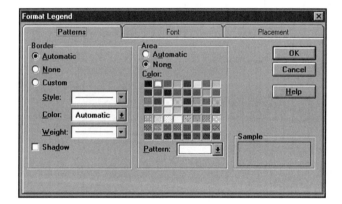

Understanding Printing and Printers

The last sections of Chapter 1 introduced you to printing with Word. In this chapter, you will learn the finer points of printing by working through realistic scenarios. The topics discussed in this chapter include the following:

- ◆ Setting up document pages

- ◆ Working with print preview

- ◆ Printing an entire document

- ◆ Printing parts of a document

- ◆ Changing printers

- ◆ Working with special-purpose printers

After you finish reading this chapter, you will know why you should follow particular printing procedures, and you will see ways in which you can extend Word's printing capabilities.

Chapter 1 covered the basic printing features of Word. Now it is time to explore these features in greater detail and see the ways in which you can fully exploit them. Printing does involve a few tricks, and thinking through what you want can save you time and paper. The guided tour of the printing controls in Chapter 1 is only an introduction to printing with Word. Working through some practical examples will help you see how you can use the printing controls effectively.

Setting Up a Document

Before you prepare a document for printing, you need to review why you are printing the document. Is the document something you need fast and that no one else really needs to see? Is it the final draft of a major presentation, something that needs to look magnificent to impress someone? Answers to questions like these help determine the way you want to set up the document for printing.

Setting Up a Template

You can set the default page setup for a document template so that it is appropriate for documents based on the template. The page setup information is stored in the document template. As a result, when you are ready to print, you don't have to modify the controls in the Page Setup dialog box to suit your document.

Creating a default page setup for a document template is easy. Follow these steps:

1. Open the document template or create a new document based on the template.

2. Open the **F**ile menu and select the Page Set**u**p menu option.

3. Adjust the controls on the tabs in the Page Setup dialog box to suit your needs.

4. Click on the **D**efault button in each tab, as shown in figure 5.1.

5. When the Confirmation dialog box appears, click on the **Y**es button.

Tip Clicking on the **D**efault button to save the default information also closes the Page Setup dialog box. If you want to adjust the defaults in another tab, you need to reopen the dialog box.

Your document template now contains the page setup information that you want to use for your documents.

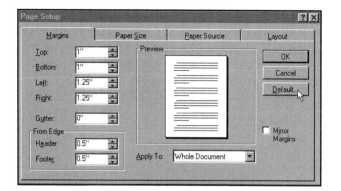

Figure 5.1

Setting the default page setup for a template by clicking on the Default button.

A practical example clarifies why you might want to make these adjustments. Suppose that each month you have to write a 10-page sales report that you present to the sales management team. Each month, the sales managers for each product line meet with the marketing vice president to review progress toward sales goals. Each division produces such a sales report, and these documents are distributed, photocopied on both sides and three-hole punched, to the sales management team. Each member of the team stores these reports in a three-ring binder for future reference.

When you set up the pages for such a document, you need to leave room for the holes that are punched along the left margin of the odd pages. You need to print using odd and even pages, opposing headers and footers, and opposing page numbers so that the document looks good in the binder. But remembering to make all these adjustments each time you print might be a hassle. You might have to make several test prints before you get a usable print.

The best solution is to create a template for these reports and store the page setup in the template. You would go through steps like these:

1. Open a document based on the template.

2. Open the **F**ile menu and select the Page Set**u**p option.

3. On the **M**argins tab, use the G**u**tter spin box to create a 0.5-inch gutter to accommodate the punched holes (see fig. 5.2).

4. Check the M**i**rror Margins check box because the completed document will be printed on both sides of the page.

5. Make sure the **A**pply To drop-down list box shows Whole Document as the selection.

Tip

If you have a selection active in your document, the Apply To drop-down list box automatically shows Selection as the current option. Always verify that this control shows the correct selection before you set the default.

6. Click on the **D**efault button and accept your changes in the confirmation dialog box.

7. Open the Page Setup dialog box again.

Figure 5.2

Adjusting the Gutter and Mirror Margins controls on the Margins tab.

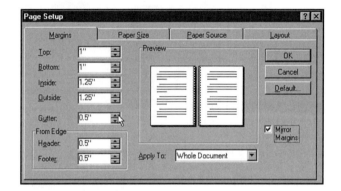

8. Click on the **L**ayout tab and check the Different **O**dd and Even Pages box in the Headers and Footers group, as shown in figure 5.3. Check the Different **F**irst Page check box to keep the first page clear of the headers and footers for the rest of the document.

Figure 5.3

Setting up opposing headers in the Layout tab.

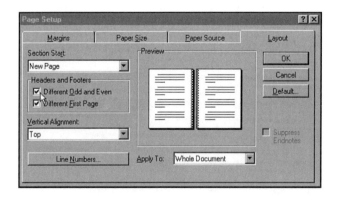

9. Make sure the **A**pply To drop-down list shows Whole Document.

10. Click on the **D**efault button and accept your modifications.

You now should print a test document to make sure you have set up the page correctly. If you see other changes that are necessary, make them as well and save them as the template defaults. After you are satisfied with the test prints, your document template is ready. Now you do not have to adjust the page setup controls every time you print.

Setting Other Printing Options

There are other printing options of which you will want to take advantage, even though you cannot store them in each template. These are the options that you set on the Print tab of the Options dialog box. You should set these controls to reflect the majority of your printing needs and adjust them only as you need to for your less frequently printed documents.

You can get to these controls in two ways. You can open the **F**ile menu, select the **P**rint option, and click on the **O**ptions button, or you can open the **T**ools menu, select the **O**ptions item, and click on the Print tab. In either case, you reach the Print tab of the Options dialog box, shown in figure 5.4.

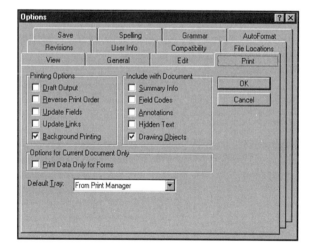

Figure 5.4

The Print tab in the Options dialog box.

The Printing Options group provides check boxes that you can use to specify the default behavior of your printer driver. You might choose to use these options for reasons such as the following:

◆ Check **D**raft Output for the fastest printout possible. The document will not look its best, but it will print quickly. This option is especially useful if you have a dot-matrix printer that slows down considerably when it does letter-quality printing and you are in a hurry.

◆ Use **R**everse Print Order if you are using a laser printer or similar printer that sorts the printed sheets in the reverse of page order to avoid curling the sheets around the printing rollers. By reversing the print order, your sheets stack in page order.

◆ Check **U**pdate Fields if you insert fields into your document that can go out of date. Suppose you use sequence numbers to number the figures in a document, then insert two new figures after the most recent print. You can easily forget to manually update the sequence fields. Checking this check box causes the sequence fields to be updated for you before each printing operation.

◆ Use Update **L**inks if your documents have automatic links to data that is updated frequently. Checking this box assures that each document has the latest data.

◆ **B**ackground Printing is checked by default because this option enables you to continue working while Word prints your document. This is the preference of most users. If you are in a hurry for your printed copy, however, uncheck this box. This forces you to wait, of course, until Word finishes printing before you can work again.

The Include with Document group provides check boxes that enable you to specify the additional information that prints with the document. You might want to use these options for reasons such as the following:

◆ Check **S**ummary Info to print the information displayed by the Summary Info dialog box. To see the Summary Info dialog box or to update its contents, open the **F**ile menu and select the Summary **I**nfo option.

◆ Use the **F**ield Codes option to print the text that makes up each field code in your document. If you are searching for a problem with the way a field is behaving, a printout of the field codes can be extremely useful.

◆ Check the **A**nnotations box if you need to see the annotations that various reviewers leave on a document. This option is most useful if you want to work on a printed copy as you revise a document.

◆ Select H**i**dden Text when you want to print characters formatted as hidden text in your document. If you have formatted notes to yourself embedded in the document as hidden text, you might want to print them if you are going to work with a printed copy as you revise.

◆ Drawing **O**bjects is checked by default to enable the embedded pictures in your document to print. If you are printing a draft on a slow printer, however, you might want to deselect this box to speed printing.

After you store your desired page setups in your document templates and set your print options to cover the majority of jobs, printing is easier. Usually you simply click on the Print button on the Standard toolbar, and Word does the rest. The only time you need to review your print options and page setup is when you encounter special circumstances.

Exploiting the Preview Feature

The print preview feature in Word can be extremely useful. After you reach the final stages before printing, you should use the previewer to examine your document. Make sure all the details are correct on-screen. To access this feature, open the File menu and select the Print Preview option.

Print preview has several handy features, including the capability to edit in preview mode. By editing in preview mode, you easily can see formatting problems in your document and make the necessary changes. Just click on the Magnifier button on the toolbar to take the magnifier out of its default activated status. You then see the insertion point flashing in your document. You can edit the document just as if you were in normal or page layout view, as shown in figure 5.5. You can even edit in a multiple page view. As a result, you do not have to jump into and out of preview mode to make changes to your document's format.

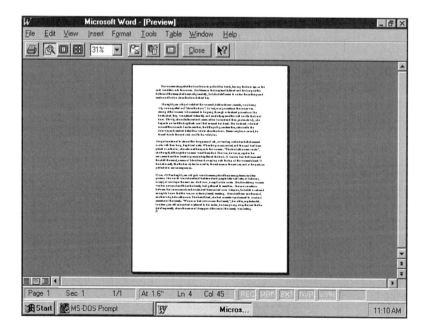

Figure 5.5

Editing a document in preview mode.

In addition to editing, you can access any of Word's menu options while you are in preview mode. If you need to set font formatting or insert a field, you can do so. (Figure 5.6 shows an example.) You must remember that some menu options are incompatible with preview mode. If you change to page layout view, you exit preview mode. In general, you can make any insertion you need to make or change any formatting while remaining in preview mode.

Figure 5.6

Changing a font format while in preview mode.

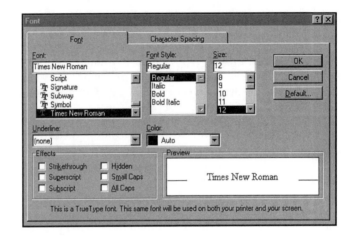

 Tip   The major exception to editing while staying in preview mode is changing the contents of the headers and footers.

Using print preview, you can carefully review your documents and get them into proper shape without doing a test print, thus saving the paper and time used on test prints.

Printing Documents

Word provides several options for printing a document. Of course, you will want to print an entire document. You might also want to print segments of a document. And you certainly need to know the way to handle printing from the master document format.

Printing an Entire Document

As Chapter 1 explained, you print an entire document by clicking on the Print button on the Standard toolbar or opening the File menu, selecting Print, and clicking on

OK. There are some tricks to printing an entire document, however, that you might be glad to know about.

If you proofread a document that has different odd and even pages, you might want to print it differently than when you print the final copy. You can open the Print drop-down list box in the Print dialog box and select Odd Pages or Even Pages (see fig. 5.7). Printing odd or even pages separately enables you to compare headers and footers, margins, gutters, and similar features to more easily ensure that they are correct. If you look only at pages that have the same layout in a single stack, you can detect errors in the layout faster because a deviation from the norm is more obvious.

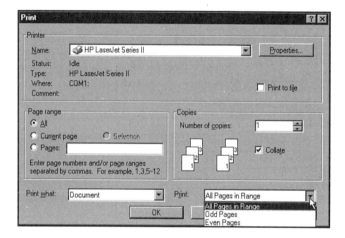

Figure 5.7

Using the Print drop-down list in the Print dialog box.

If you print multiple copies, you can collate them by checking the Collate Copies check box in the Print dialog box, shown in figure 5.7. The box is checked as the default because most people want their copies collated. If you plan to distribute a document page by page in a meeting, however, it is more convenient not to collate the copies as they print. You might readily prepare a set of one-page handouts as a single Word document, each page representing one of the handouts. Unchecking the Collate Copies box prints them as you need to distribute them. Also, if a printer has the capability to make multiple copies of the same page, you will have to unselect Collate Copies so that the printer's internal copies command will be used.

You might also find the Print to File check box useful on occasion. When you check this check box, also shown in figure 5.7, Word does not print your document to a printer. Instead, Word formats the document for the printer selected but prints the document to a disk file. You then can submit that file to the printer you have specified at a later time by using the DOS PRINT command or by dragging and dropping the file icon to Print Manager.

The capability to print to a file is most useful for preparing a document to print at a service bureau. You can install the driver for the printer type used by the service bureau, print to a file, and take the file to the service bureau. The service bureau need not use the same word processor as you; it needs only the correctly formatted file and a means of submitting the file to the printer.

This capability also is useful if you need to print a document on a printer that is not attached to your computer or LAN. You can put the document on a disk, take the disk to the appropriate computer, and print the document. You can use this technique to avoid carrying bulky loads of paper to meetings at remote locations. It is especially useful to avoid carrying lots of paper on an airline trip to one of your company's clients or one of your company's sites.

Printing Portions of a Document

As noted in Chapter 1, Word also enables you to print portions of a chapter. In fact, Word offers three methods for printing parts of a document. The method you should choose depends on your goals.

If you discover an error in a single page and you can correct the error without changing the pagination, for example, you can select the Current Page option button in the Print dialog box (see fig. 5.8) to print that single page. Scroll through your document until you reach that page. Next, make your correction. Make sure the insertion point is on the page you need to print. Then open the **F**ile menu, select **P**rint, click on the Curr**e**nt page option button, and click on OK. The problem in the printed version is corrected with a minimum of effort.

Figure 5.8

Selecting the Current page option.

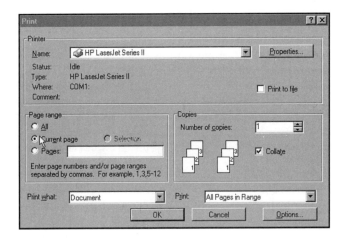

You might also use the Current page option if you need to provide a copy of a single page in a document to someone else, possibly to proofread or to provide important data for an oral presentation. At times, however, you might need to print more than a single page for such purposes. You could, of course, perform the current page procedure repeatedly, but there is an easier way.

Word permits you to print multiple pages and page ranges. To use this option, select the Pages option button in the Print dialog box, as shown in figure 5.9. Then, in the text box next to the option button, type the pages and/or page ranges you want to use. You can enter single page numbers (like 3), or page numbers indicating a range by using a hyphen (like 12–15). You can enter several pages and page ranges, as shown in figure 5.9, as long as you separate them with commas. When you click on OK, Word prints only the pages and page ranges indicated.

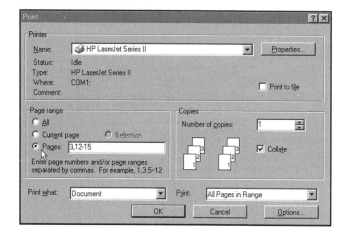

Figure 5.9

Using the Pages option in the Print dialog box.

Sometimes you need a part of a document that begins at the middle of one page and ends at the middle of another to present as a separate document. You'd like for this to start at the top of a page and to look like a stand-alone document. You can, of course, copy that part of the document to a blank document and then print the new document, but there is a simpler way. Select the section you need to print, just as if you were going to copy it. Then open the **F**ile menu, select **P**rint, and choose the **S**election option button in the Print dialog box (see fig. 5.10). When you click on OK, Word adjusts for the new page numbers and prints the section as a regular document. You save a few steps and get the same results.

Word offers printing scenarios that meet your needs. When you decide how to print just part of a document, just think about what you need the part for and how you need it to look on the page. You can achieve the results you want straight from the Print dialog box.

Figure 5.10

*Using the
Selection option
in the Print
dialog box.*

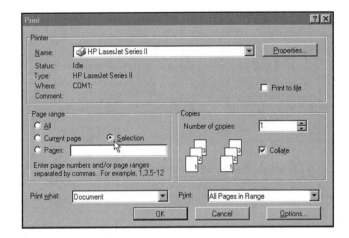

Printing Master Documents

When you organize a document as a master document, you have flexible control over printing. Master documents add one more level of control. If you display a document in master document view, as described in Chapter 2, "Understanding Word for Windows Concepts," you can select which portions of the document to print by expanding and collapsing different headings. The expanded headings print the text included under them, the collapsed ones do not. Figure 5.11 shows an example of a master document being prepared for partial printing.

Figure 5.11

*A master
document set up
for partial
printing.*

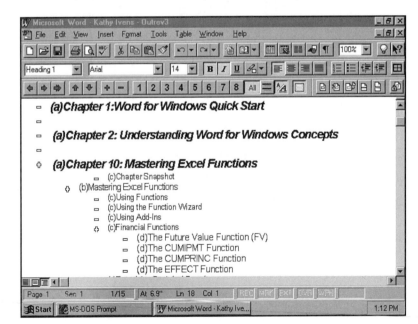

Tip You also can use the techniques described earlier in this chapter in the section "Printing Portions of a Document" when you print a master document.

To print an entire master document, display it in normal view. Print the document using the techniques described earlier in this chapter in the section "Printing an Entire Document." Your entire master document prints with the formatting you have applied.

Changing the Printer

You might work with several different printers, especially if your computer is attached to a network. Using Microsoft Office, you might have installed a Genigraphics graphics printer so that you can prepare PowerPoint slides to be printed in special image formats, such as 35mm slides, by a service bureau.

If you have cartridges (either fonts or a PostScript emulator) for a laser printer, you can install a second printer with the appropriate settings for that configuration.

 Note A printer driver is a control program that translates a Word document into instructions for your printer. You install printer drivers using the Add Printer icon in the Printer Settings Folder. Installing a printer driver and installing a printer are one and the same operation in.

Obviously, if you have more than one printer, even a phantom one, you need to know how to change printers. The process is straightforward, as shown by the following steps:

1. Open the **F**ile menu and select the **P**rint option.

2. Click on the arrow to the right of the Name box to display the available printers (see fig. 5.12).

3. Click on the **O**ptions button to verify that the printer is set up correctly for your print job. A dialog box like the one shown in figure 5.13 appears, specific to your printer. Adjust the controls as necessary and click on OK. This returns you to the Print Setup dialog box. Choose OK to close the dialog box.

Figure 5.12

*Selecting a printer
from the Print
dialog box.*

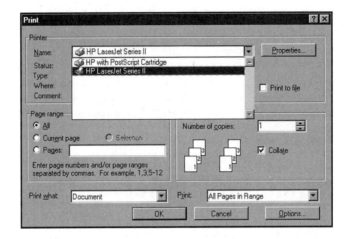

Figure 5.13

*The Options
dialog box.*

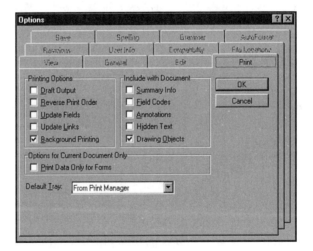

If you want to make this printer the default printer (until you change the default again), follow these steps:

1. Press the Start button on the bottom of your window (or press Ctrl+Esc) to bring up the task menu. Highlight Settings, then choose the Printer folder to see all your printers (see Figure 5.14).

2. Highlight the printer you want to make your new default printer.

3. Choose Set As Default from the File menu.

4. Close the Printer folder.

Figure 5.14

The Printer folder.

One common reason you might need to change printers is to print envelopes or labels. You might have a printer that is set up with an envelope feeder, or a specialized label printer. Or you might have a dot-matrix printer dedicated to printing checks for your company or similar special-purpose forms. You might also have a color printer on the network, as well as a black-and-white local or network printer to select from.

Changing the Printer Setup for the Print Job

After you select the printer to use, you might want to adjust its setup to reflect the printing job you have to do. You can accomplish this from the Print dialog box by choosing Properties after you have selected the printer you want to use. The choices available in the Properties dialog box are specific to the selected printer.

The Page tab (see fig. 5.15) is where you choose a paper size and type, orientation, and the paper tray.

The Graphics tab is for specifying resolution measurements, graphics printing levels, and dithering levels. You can choose the number of dots per inch you want to print by selecting an available dpi measurement from the Resolution box (see fig. 5.16). Notice that Word knows the limits of your specific printer's capability.

The Fonts section offers a choice to print TrueType fonts as graphics instead of downloading them to the printer's memory, and the Device Options section lets you specify the memory usage for printing.

Figure 5.15

*Choose a paper
size and type.*

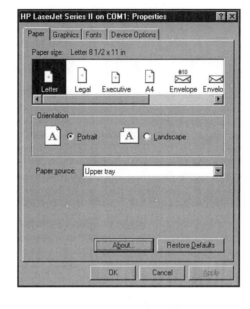

Figure 5.16

*Graphics and
Resolution choices
for the printer.*

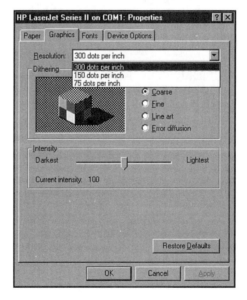

Creating a Printer with Different Properties

It is a good idea to create separate printers for the different properties. For those print jobs that use legal paper or print every page in landscape mode, for example, it's easier to select a different printer than it is to make all the Properties changes in the current printer.

To accomplish this, follow the steps to add a printer. Add a new printer, using the same driver as the existing printer. Word will add the new printer's icon to the Printer folder with the same name as the old printer, but the words "copy 2" are added.

The first thing you want to do is change the name. Select (highlight) the new printer, then choose Rename from the File menu. Type in a new name—make it specific to the properties for this printer, such as "Laser with Legal Tray."

Then set the permanent properties for this printer. Choose Properties from the File menu. Change the properties to suit the new printer. In addition to the properties mentioned earlier in this chapter, you can also set up Port and Spooler properties.

It makes sense to have multiple configurations of the same printer. The printers shown in the Printer Folder (refer to fig. 5.14) are the printers that are listed when you want to change printers in the Print dialog box.

Word's Word Basic Macros

This chapter explains how to create Word macros. You will learn how to record macros and assign them to the keyboard, menu, and toolbars. You also will learn the basics of Word Basic macro programming. More specifically, you will learn the following:

- What a macro is

- The way to record a macro

- The way to use the Customize dialog box to assign macros

- The way to prevent common macro problems

- The way to program macros

By the time you complete this chapter, you will be able to build simple macros—just by recording your actions with the menu, keyboard, toolbars, and mouse—and more complex and useful macros.

As explained in Chapter 2, "Understanding Word for Windows Concepts," Word is a word processor that is based on the concept of macros. Each command that you can execute from the menu constitutes a named block of code created by the Word programmers. When you execute a command from the menu, your menu action selects the block of code by name and has it executed. As a result, the action you wanted Word to take occurs exactly as you asked when you selected the menu option.

This chapter extends the concept of Word macros by showing you how to create your own commands, which you can attach to the menu or to toolbar buttons. You need not think that this business of creating custom commands is beyond you. Word makes the process easy—as easy as clicking a few buttons and taking the action you wanted to make with a single command. You need to know little about programming to build your own macros.

Explaining Macros

In Word, a macro is a special type of document, for two reasons. First, a macro is a document that is stored as a part of a template. In that sense, a macro bears the same relationship to a template that a subdocument bears to a master document. Second, a macro consists of only certain kinds of "sentences": the names of Word commands, the same names you saw listed in the Macro dialog box in Chapter 2.

The names of the Word commands make up Word's macro programming language, officially named Word Basic. Word Basic contains a few additional commands that do not appear on the Word menu. These commands enable you to open special-purpose files and to create dialog boxes. As a result, by using Word Basic you can make Word do anything you want it to do. You have complete control over all Word's commands, all its file-handling capabilities, and even its capability to create and display dialog boxes.

 Tip Use macros to automate your most frequently repeated actions. If you perform a multistep action repeatedly as you work, you can use a macro to do it for you.

You have two ways at your disposal to create macros. You can sit down and figure out exactly what you want Word to do. You can read through the list of Word commands and decide which ones would accomplish the task, then you can type each of the commands into a macro file in the proper order, hoping you did not make any typing mistakes. And you would have a macro that has taken you a lot of time and effort to build, even assuming that you had gotten all the commands right and the macro works correctly.

On the other hand, you can have Word record the macro for you. First, you open the Macro dialog box, click on the **R**ecord button, and fill in some information in a dialog box. You then take the action you want to have automated as a macro, performing all the menu and mouse steps exactly as if you were simply using them straight out. When you are finished, click on the Stop button. You would have a macro correctly built that does exactly what you did as you were recording. Word builds a macro file for you containing all the commands necessary, and it works exactly as you did with the mouse and keyboard. Unless you made a mistake, your macro will not take the wrong action.

Recording Macros

To show you why and how to record a macro, let's examine the case of a computer book author. When a chapter is finished and ready to send to the publisher, several tasks have to be performed. The line of text needs to be set to 6.5 inches throughout the document. The fields used to number figures and tables need to be updated. Since the publisher needs a text-only document, the links in the fields need to be broken. The document needs to be checked for spelling. The spacing between a period and the next sentence needs to be cut from two spaces to one. Finally, for some publishers, the document needs to be saved in Word for Windows 2.0 document format, the version that the publisher uses.

Tip While this example relates to only one type of document, every document has finishing steps that need to be taken once the text and layout are complete. Record these steps as a macro saved in the template for the document and you will never forget to do any of them again.

Odds are that on any given day the author of a chapter is going to forget to do one or more of those things, especially as deadlines approach and the writer tires out struggling to produce the chapters due. The writer could use a checklist, but checklists have a way of getting lost or forgotten. The best solution for the author is to record a macro that performs all these steps and save it in the template used to create the chapter. Word then is responsible for maintaining the checklist of things to be done. The writer only needs to remember to run the end-of-chapter macro, and Word takes care of all the details.

To record such a macro, follow these steps:

1. Open the **T**ools menu and select the **M**acro option, or double-click on the REC box on the status bar. (If you double-click on the REC box, continue to step 3. Word skips the Macro dialog box when you use this method.)

2. When the Macro dialog box appears, as shown in figure 6.1, click on the **R**ecord
   button; this brings up the Record Macro dialog box (see fig. 6.2).

Figure 6.1

*Starting the
macro recording
process from the
Macro dialog box.*

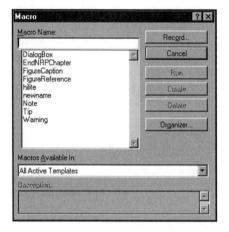

Figure 6.2

*The Record
Macro dialog box.*

3. Enter a name for the macro in the **R**ecord Macro Name text box in the Record
   Macro dialog box. You cannot use punctuation or spaces for the macro name.
   Keep it short but descriptive. You may wish to use capital letters at word begin-
   nings to make it more readable. For this example, type **EndChapter**.

4. Open the Make Macro **A**vailable To drop-down list box and select the template
   in which the macro will be stored. If you want the macro available to all documents, store it in NORMAL.DOT. If not, store it in the template for the documents that will use it. In this example, we will store the macro in
   NEWRIDE.DOT.

5. Enter a description of what the macro does, up to 255 characters, in the **D**escription text box. A description is good protection against forgetting what the macro does. While the description is optional, it appears in the **D**escription text box in the Macro dialog box and appears on the status bar when the macro is selected as a menu command or as a toolbar button. For this example, enter **Ends New Riders chapter**.

6. If you want to assign the macro to a toolbar, the menu, or the keyboard, click on the appropriate button in the Assign Macro To group. Each button opens the Customize dialog box (discussed in detail in Chapter 7, "Customizing Word for Windows") to the appropriate tab. In this example you will assign the macro to the keyboard, so click on the **K**eyboard button.

7. In the Customize dialog box (see fig. 6.3), press the key combination that you want to use to run the macro. In this example, press Ctrl+Shift+E. Word displays the keys you pressed in the Press **N**ew Shortcut Key text box. Word also warns you if the key combination is already assigned to another command or macro. (If it is and you do not want to disturb the assignment, press Backspace to clear the text box and try again.)

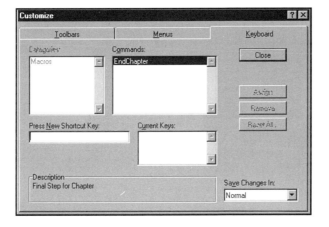

Figure 6.3

The Customize dialog box.

8. Click on the **A**ssign button, then click on the Close button. At this point, the Macro Recording toolbar will float above your Word screen and the pointer will display a cassette tape below the arrow (see fig. 6.4). You are recording your macro.

9. To record your macro, perform the following actions in sequence:

   a. Open the **E**dit menu and choose the Select A**ll** option. (You select the entire text because your next actions must affect the entire text.)

b. Drag the right margin pointer to the 6.5-inch indicator. If it is already there, click on it to set that right margin for all paragraphs.

c. Press F9 to update the figure-number fields. (Number fields are explained later in this chapter.)

d. Press Ctrl+Shift+F9 to unlink the fields. (This action converts all number fields to plain text that represents the last update of the field.)

e. Press Ctrl+Home to clear the selection and move to the beginning of the document.

f. Click on the Spelling button on the Standard toolbar and check the spelling in the document.

g. Open the **E**dit menu and select the Re**p**lace option. Enter two spaces in the Fi**n**d What box and one space in the Re**p**lace With box. Click on the Replace **A**ll button.

h. Open the **F**ile menu and select the Save **A**s option. In the Save As dialog box, open the Save As File **T**ype drop-down list box and select the Word for Windows 2 option. Click on the OK button.

Figure 6.4

The Word screen as you record a macro.

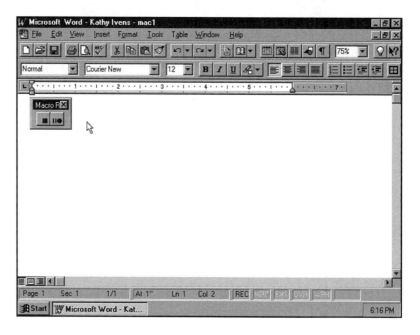

10. Click on the Stop button on the Macro Recording toolbar. Your macro has been recorded and saved.

Tip If you are unsure as to the next action to perform during your recording of the macro, you can use the Pause button on the Macro Recording toolbar to pause the recording. You then can try out the next step until you are sure how it should go. Click on the Pause button again to record your well-practiced action.

You can run your new macro in any document you create with the NEWRIDE.DOT template. However, there are two cautions to using this macro. First, do not use it in a document that does not have active fields. The unlink-fields action that you recorded has nothing to do under such circumstances and causes an error. Word presents a dialog box informing you that a command failed, and then exits the macro procedure, doing none of the rest of the work. Second, if you run your new macro on a document, it will name the document using the same name as the file with which you recorded the macro. You could accidentally overwrite a file.

Obviously your macro needs to be modified slightly before it is ready for use. The next section tells you how.

Modifying Macros

You have seen how you can record some rather complex actions as a macro very easily. However, you also have seen how some recorded macros can have unfortunate side effects. Typically, unfortunate side effects include the following:

◆ Commands that cause errors when they cannot perform the intended action. Virtually every Word command and every macro you create can have this unfortunate consequence.

◆ Commands that record specific file names or other document-specific information.

You can easily modify your macros to resolve these side effects. To make the modifications, you need to know how to edit a macro, how to test a macro, and how to debug a macro. Fortunately, these are not complex tasks. Word makes it easy to solve both of the problems associated with recording macros.

Word Basic is designed to report an error every time a command cannot carry out its action, for whatever reason. The reason Word reports the error and stops the action is that it has no other instructions. However, you can add a command to each macro you record that tells Word what to do when it encounters an error.

Word also identifies document-specific information in easy-to-spot ways. Typically, if you delete the document-specific information from the command, Word carries out the command using the defaults for the document at hand. In the case of the Save As command, if the command has no file name to use, it uses the file name for the document on which the macro is operating. You easily can scan your macro commands and remove such information.

Tip   Before you read through the next few sections, you might want to make sure that the Word Basic Help file is available on your computer. When you select the typical installation using Setup, this file is not installed. Double-click on either the Word or Office Setup icon and add the Word Basic Help file to your installation.

Editing

The procedure for editing a macro is much like the procedure for editing a document, because a macro is just a special type of document. To open a macro for editing, follow these steps:

1. Open the **T**ools menu and select the **M**acro option.

2. In the Macro dialog box, select the name of the macro to edit from the **M**acro Name combination box (see fig. 6.5). You might need to open the Macros **A**vailable In drop-down list box to select the appropriate template so that your macro shows in the list box.

Figure 6.5

Preparing to edit a macro using the Macro dialog box.

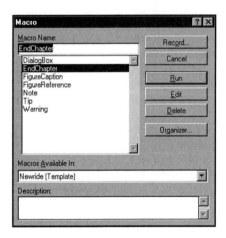

3. Click on the **E**dit button.

At this point, Word opens the macro and displays it as a document. Word also displays the Macro toolbar, which assists you in working with the macro. Figure 6.6 shows the EndChapter macro you just recorded opened for editing.

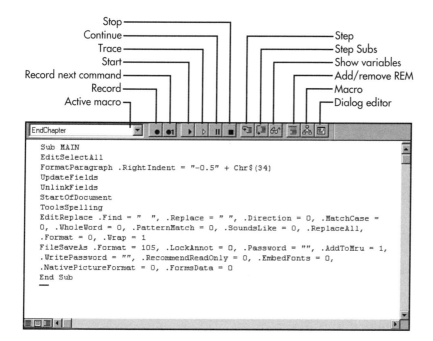

Figure 6.6

The EndChapter macro open for editing.

You edit a macro exactly as you edit a document; all the same editing actions apply. There are a couple of cautions, however. Keep each macro command in its own paragraph. Turn on paragraph marks by clicking the Show/Hide ¶ button to see how Word defines the end of each macro command with a paragraph mark. If a paragraph mark does not separate two commands, Word will display an error message indicating that it could not interpret the command.

In addition, do not add extraneous characters to a macro command, place extra characters before the command, or misspell a command keyword. Word Basic does not know how to deal with such issues except to display an error message that explains it could not understand the command. When you make changes, you want to make them with the precision of a surgical air strike. Go into the file, add or delete or change what you need to, and exit the file leaving the rest intact.

As you are editing, the macro toolbar provides a button that can be of great assistance—the Record Next Command button. If you want to add a command to your macro, you need not type the command. You can switch to a document, click on this button, and perform the action representing the command. Word adds the command to the active macro file at the current insertion point position, then stops the recording process. You do not need to type commands, and you can record and modify commands as necessary. (There are a few exceptions to this rule, as you will see, but not many.) In general, if you have the choice of recording or typing, select record. Word does not make typing errors while it records.

Tip The active macro is the one that runs when you click on the Start button on the Macro toolbar. The Active Macro drop-down list box (refer to fig. 6.6) always indicates which macro is active. If you have more than one macro open for editing and testing, you can change which one is active by selecting its name from this list.

To make the specific changes necessary in the EndChapter macro, you need to add one statement and delete a portion of another. To solve the problem of an error being generated, you need to add a statement telling Word what to do if a statement cannot carry out its action. Word Basic provides a family of three such commands, each of which gives Word different directions. In the case of this macro, you want simply for the command that cannot complete its action to give control to the next command so that the rest of the macro can run. In other words, if a command cannot be carried out, you want to ignore that command and get on with the rest of the macro.

To add this functionality to your macro, perform the following procedure:

1. Position the insertion point at the end of the Sub MAIN line.

2. Press Enter to create a new line.

3. Type On Error Resume Next.

The line you have just added tells Word that when it encounters an error to resume running the macro with the next command. No dialog box appears, and the macro keeps running until it ends. You have to type this command; it is one of the few that you cannot record.

To solve the problem of Word using the default document name inappropriately, you need to remove document-specific information. In this macro, only one element needs to be removed. If you look at the line that begins FileSaveAs, you see that it contains a specification of the file name to use. If you remove that specification, Word will use the name of the file on which the macro is running instead. To solve this problem, follow these steps:

1. Select .Name = "CHAP06FH.DOC" (include the space at the end).

2. Press Del.

Save the changes you have made in your macro by pressing the Save button on the Standard toolbar—just as you would in any other file. You can close a macro-editing window by opening the **F**ile menu and choosing the **C**lose option.

Testing

Testing your revised macro is largely a process of running the macro and verifying that it works. If it does not work, then you need to proceed to the stage of debugging. When you test your macro, you should have its editing window open to take advantage of the Macro toolbar's testing aids; however, you cannot test a macro while its editing window is the active document window. You must make a document window active and run the test from the Macro toolbar, which remains available as long as you have a macro-editing window open.

The macro toolbar offers the following buttons that can help with testing, as shown in figure 6.7:

Figure 6.7

The testing buttons on the Macro toolbar.

◆ **Start** runs the active macro, the name of which is always shown in the Active Macro drop-down list box on the left side of the toolbar. You can change the active macro if you want by selecting a new macro name from this list. Your first step in testing should be to run the macro to see what happens.

◆ **Trace** runs the active macro with a slight variation. Each command in the macro-editing window is highlighted as it runs. If you arrange your document windows so that the active document and the macro-editing windows are both visible, you can watch the actions performed and also see which lines are responsible for them. This is a variation of the testing procedure that provides more information to you about which line caused the problem, if a problem should occur. (If a problem does occur, Word highlights the command that caused it.)

◆ **Continue** restarts the running of a macro if it has stopped for some reason. You might have stopped it using the Stop or Step buttons, for instance.

◆ **Stop** halts the execution of a macro. This button is extremely useful if your macro runs away from you and continues executing after it should have stopped.

◆ **Step** causes one command in a macro to execute and then stops the macro. You can click on Step repeatedly to work through a macro line by line, or you can click on Continue to allow the remainder of the macro to run without interruption.

◆ **Step Subs** functions exactly like Step, except it does not pause after each action taken when you run a macro from within a macro. Step Subs pauses only after the commands in the active macro's editing window are completed. If the active macro were to have another macro you wrote as one of its commands, which is perfectly allowable, Step Subs does not pause after the execution of each command in the embedded macro. It pauses again when it encounters the next command after the embedded macro, whereas Step would pause after each command in the embedded macro. Step Subs is useful when you know that all the commands in the embedded macro are running properly.

Testing is a no-brainer process. You run the macro if necessary, looking for an error message or a failure of the macro to perform its action. If the macro runs correctly, you are finished with it. If it fails to run correctly, you need to proceed to the step of debugging.

Debugging

Debugging is not a no-brainer process. It can be tedious and time-consuming. That is why your first step in debugging should be to re-record the macro. If this course of action solves the problem, you do not have to proceed further. If recording again does not solve the problem, use the Step button to move through your macro line by line. You need to have both your active document and your misbehaving macro visible on your screen, and you need to follow some straightforward, common sense rules.

The first rule to follow is that Word is doing exactly what you told it to do, which is not necessarily what you want it to do. You need to look first at what you told Word to do to see if you can find the problem. If a paragraph format is not set correctly, did you set it correctly in the dialog box when you recorded the macro? If fields are not updating, did you press F9 (or was it F8) when you recorded the macro? If the file name is not correct on the save, what file name did you tell it to use? Chances are the source of the problem is something you told the macro to do that was not what you intended to say.

The second rule to follow is that Word Basic commands consist of a name and some parameters that the command might require. The name of the command invokes the action named. Most Word Basic commands are named after the menu items that you use when you take the same action by hand, as in `FileSaveAs`. Some commands take no parameters, others do. Parameters can appear as an item or list of items separated by commas in parentheses after the command name, as in `AppMaximize ("Microsoft Excel")`. Parameters also can appear as an item or list of comma-separated items following the command name, as in the following:

```
Font "Arial", 8.
```

Parameters also can appear in similar lists, but in a form wherein some begin with a period and have an equal sign followed by a value, as in this (normally single) line:

```
EditReplace .Find = " ", .Replace = " ", .Direction = 0, .MatchCase = 0,
➡.WholeWord = 0, .PatternMatch = 0, .SoundsLike = 0, .ReplaceAll, .Format = 0,
➡.Wrap = 1.
```

In this form of a Word Basic command, each item beginning with a period serves to represent the state of a dialog box control bearing a similar name. The value after the equal sign, if it is present, represents the state of that dialog box control. Violating these conventions always leads to problems.

The third rule to follow is that there are just a few things, really, that can go wrong in writing a macro. The following list describes these possibilities, along with common symptoms:

◆ **Infinite Loops.** The macro just keeps on running and will not stop unless you click on the Stop button on the Macro toolbar. The most likely cause is a command that causes the macro to execute a second command, which in turn causes the first command to be reexecuted, causing the second to reexecute, and so on. The most likely cause in a recorded macro is an incorrect On Error statement. Examine the macro carefully using the Step button on the Macro toolbar. When you have found the two statements that are calling each other, break the chain of calls in the most convenient way.

◆ **Misspelled Statements.** You receive a Syntax Error or a Label Not Found Error. Word cannot compensate for your mistakes in typing. Prevention is to record commands whenever possible. Correction is to compare what you typed, character by character, to the examples given in the Word Basic Help file, accessible from the Word Help contents by clicking on Programming with Microsoft Word.

◆ **Extra Characters.** You receive any of a variety of errors, but they will all have "incorrect" or "missing" or a similar word in their description of the problem. Word is interpreting the extra characters as a part of a command and cannot make sense of the command. The solution is to compare what is in the macro-editing window, character by character, to the example in the Word Basic Help file.

◆ **Incorrect Information.** Your macro does not do what you want it to do, but everything else seems correct. Check the values you have assigned to the parameters of your commands; one of these is probably wrong. The easiest way to correct the problem is to select the problem command, switch to an available document, and re-record the command using the Record Next Command button while paying close attention to the settings in the dialog boxes you use. If you have typed the command because you cannot record it, select the command and retype it.

A Note from the Author

The instruction to retype a problem command sounds totally stupid, but sometimes, under the most mysterious of circumstances, it works. In typing the command you did something wrong that you did not see. You might never see it. But the focused activity of retyping the command might cause you to do it correctly the second time.

Debugging a macro can be frustrating. It can be so frustrating that continuous, long efforts at it usually are unproductive. You easily can get trapped in a rut and not see the problem from a fresh perspective. Debugging is best done in short bursts with breaks in between. Stay with the procedures suggested above for the best results. Change only one thing at a time in your macro between each test run. If you change more than one command, you might fix the problem you had but introduce another one.

Tip   You can prevent a command from executing by placing the characters REM, for REMark, in front of them. To do so, place the insertion point in the line you want to remark out, or select the lines, and click on the Add/Remove REM button. This button switches the presence of the remark characters.

If all else fails, both the Word Help file and the Word manual explain how to get technical assistance from Microsoft. The good news about Word Basic, however, is that if you record when you can and type only when you have to, and if you follow these suggested procedures, you should rarely run into a problem with a macro that you cannot solve yourself very quickly.

Using Word Basic

As stressed in Chapter 2, if you use Word, you use the Word Basic macro language. Word is simply a set of Word Basic commands organized into a menu, a set of toolbars, and a set of keystrokes with which you can create documents. Once you go beyond using what Word provides to you, you have entered a new level of using Word Basic. Your involvement with Word Basic can take you to any of three levels of using the language.

The Beginning User

If you are working at the beginning level, you are recording your own macros and adding an On Error Resume Next command after the Sub MAIN line that begins your macro. You probably are assigning your macros to keystrokes so that you can conveniently use them just by pressing mnemonic keys. Your macros work well. You rarely run into errors or debugging problems. You are automating frequently repeated tasks very effectively, but you are not trying to program in Word Basic. This chapter has shown an example of the kind of macro you are likely to create.

The Intermediate User

When you break into the intermediate level, you start using more commands that cannot be recorded, and you start using commands that look as though they have to be programmed. Your macros involve some flow control and more planning. They also involve some interdependence.

As an example of a macro that an intermediate user might create, consider the problem of inserting figures into a document. Each figure has to be numbered, and you might not insert the figures into the emerging document in the correct order. As you revise, you might insert a new figure in between two existing ones, and you would very much like for the figure numbers to automatically sequence themselves. Furthermore, the information necessary in each figure caption is the same for all figures, with the exception of figure numbers and possibly chapter numbers.

Along with the figure captions, you must insert a figure reference in the text you create to indicate to readers which figure to look at as they read. If you could automate the sequencing of these numbers and coordinate their numbering with the figure captions, you certainly could save yourself lots of work.

As an intermediate user of Word Basic, you can accomplish this task. You have to learn a bit about how Word Basic describes number fields, and you have to program that description to get the kind of number field you need to use. You also have to create two macros, one to insert captions and one to insert references, and make them cooperate with one another. In fact, this process is rather easy. You just have to master the language Word Basic uses to describe sequential number fields.

The first macro you create builds the figure reference in the text. The reason this is the first macro is that it contains the key figure number. The figure caption has to stay in sequence with its reference, which occurs earlier in the text than the caption. To create this macro, perform the following procedure:

1. Double-click on the REC box on the status bar. This action initiates the process of creating a macro.

2. Enter the name **FigureRef** in the **R**ecord Macro Name text box (see fig. 6.8).

3. Enter the following description in the **D**escription text box: **Inserts a figure reference**.

4. Select NEWRIDE.DOT, your template for creating chapters containing figures, in the Make Macro **A**vailable To drop-down list box.

5. Click on the Toolbar button to assign the macro to a toolbar. This opens the Customize dialog box.

Figure 6.8

Beginning the recording of the FigureRef macro.

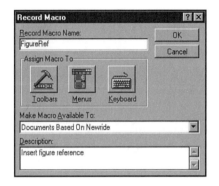

6. In the **T**oolbars tab of the Customize dialog box, drag the name of the macro from the right-hand Categories list box and drop it on an existing toolbar (see fig. 6.9). Use the Standard toolbar for the purposes of this example.

Figure 6.9

Adding the FigureRef macro to the Standard toolbar.

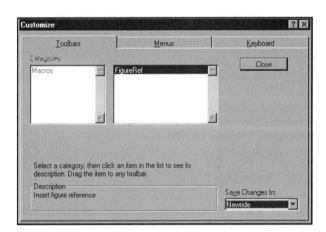

7. In the Custom Button dialog box, which appears automatically, select a button that you want to use, then click on the **A**ssign button. In this example, use a Text button. Abbreviate the name of the macro to FigRef to save space using the **T**ext Button Name text box.

8. Click on the Close button in the Customize dialog box. The recorder starts.

9. Type **figure 1.** at the keyboard.

10. Open the **I**nsert menu and select the Fi**e**ld option.

11. Select Numbering in the **C**ategories list box and Seq in the Field **N**ames list box (see fig. 6.10).

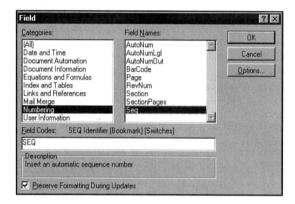

Figure 6.10

Inserting the number sequence field.

12. Now practice a bit of Word Basic programming. Enter the name **Figures** in the Field Codes text box. The field code is the Word Basic descriptor of the field. It consists of a field type and several parameters. The name parameter identifies the sequence for Word. You can use several automatic sequences of numbers in the same document as long as they have different names. You could, for instance, have one for figures and one for tables.

13. Click on the **O**ptions button.

14. In the Field Options dialog box, shown in figure 6.11, select the type of numbers you wish to use (for this example use 1 2 3) from the F**o**rmatting list box on the **G**eneral Switches tab. Click on the **A**dd to Field button. This action adds the switch \Arabic to the field code, which tells Word Basic to use Arabic numbers to create the figure reference.

15. On the Field **S**pecific Switches tab, as shown in figure 6.12, select the \n switch from the S**w**itches list box. Click on the **A**dd to Field button. This action adds the switch to the field code, which instructs Word to use the next number in the sequence.

16. Click on the OK button in the Field Options dialog box, and again in the Field dialog box.

17. Click on the Stop button to stop the recorder.

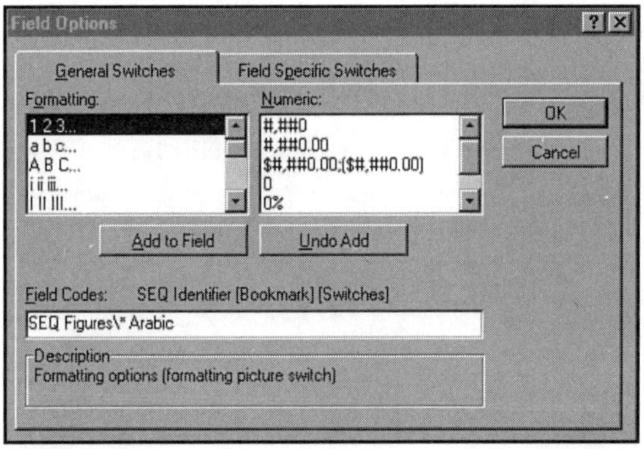

Figure 6.11

The Field Options dialog box showing the General Switches tab.

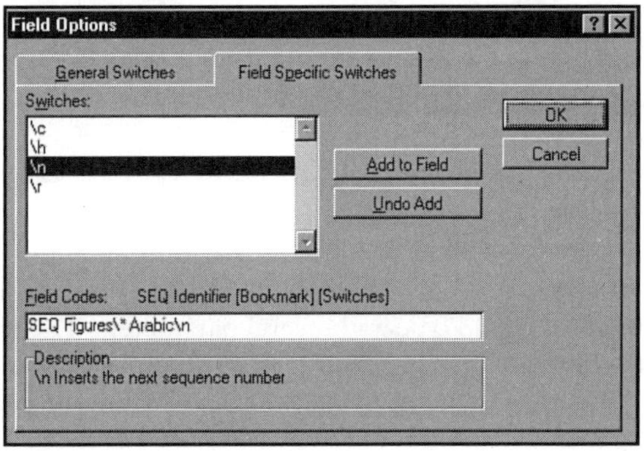

Figure 6.12

The Field Options dialog box showing the Field Specific Switches tab.

The macro you have created inserts a figure reference of the following form inside the text of your document: **figure 1.1**. Each time you insert another figure reference, the number after the period increments. If you insert a figure reference between two existing figure references, you can update the figure numbers to be in correct sequence by selecting the entire document and pressing F9. (The EndChapter macro you created earlier, in fact, includes this action as one of the things it does!) You do have to edit the macro manually to change the chapter number each time you create a new chapter. Figure 6.13 shows the code recorded for this macro.

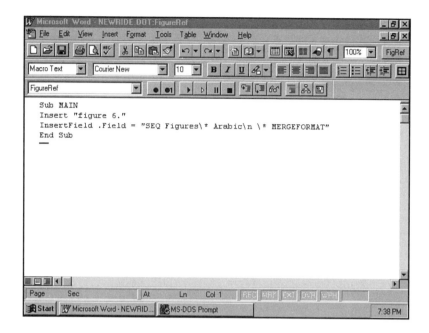

Figure 6.13

*The code for the
FigureRef macro.*

After you insert a figure in your text, you need to write a caption for it that matches
the figure reference in the figure number. Create such a macro by following this
procedure:

1. Double-click on the REC box on the status bar.

2. Enter the name **FigureCap** in the **R**ecord Macro Name text box (see fig. 6.14).

Figure 6.14

*Beginning the
recording of the
FigureCap macro.*

3. Enter the following description in the **D**escription text box: **Inserts a figure caption**.

4. Select NEWRIDE.DOT, your template for creating chapters containing figures, in the Make Macro **A**vailable To drop-down list box.

5. Click on the Toolbar button to assign the macro to a toolbar.

6. In the **T**oolbars tab of the Customize dialog box, drag the name of the macro from the right-hand Categories list box and drop it on an existing toolbar (see fig. 6.15). Use the Standard toolbar for the purposes of this example.

Figure 6.15

Adding the FigureCap macro to the Standard toolbar using the Custom Button dialog box.

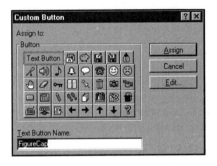

7. In the Custom Button dialog box, which appears automatically, select a button that you want to use. In this example, use a Text Button. Abbreviate the name of the macro to FigCap to save space using the **T**ext Button Name text box. Then click on the **A**ssign button to return to the Customize dialog box.

8. Click on the Close button in the Customize dialog box. The recorder starts.

9. Type **Figure 1.** at the keyboard.

10. Open the **I**nsert menu and select the Fi**e**ld option.

11. Select Numbering in the **C**ategories list box and Seq in the Field **N**ames list box (see fig. 6.16).

12. Now practice a bit of Word Basic programming. Enter the name **Figures** in the **F**ield Codes text box. This number will be in the same sequence as the figure reference.

13. Click on the **O**ptions button.

14. In the Field Options dialog box, shown in figure 6.17, select the type of numbers you want to use (for this example use 1 2 3) from the Fo**r**matting list box on the **G**eneral Switches tab. Click on the **A**dd to Field button.

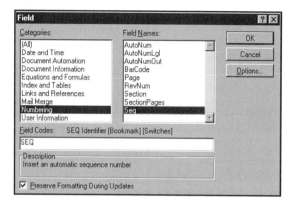

Figure 6.16

Inserting the number sequence field for the figure caption.

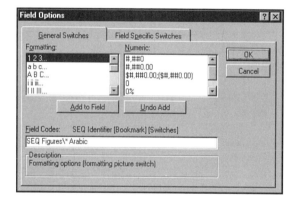

Figure 6.17

The Field Options dialog box showing the General Switches tab for the figure caption.

15. On the Field Specific Switches tab, as shown in figure 6.18, select the \c switch from the Switches list box. Click on the Add to Field button. This action adds the switch to the field code, which instructs Word to use the nearest preceding number in the sequence.

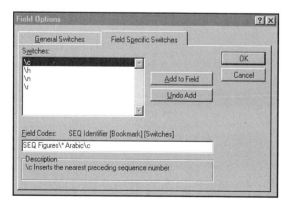

Figure 6.18

The Field Options dialog box showing the Field Specific Switches tab for the figure caption.

16. Click on the OK button in the Field Options dialog box, and again in the Field dialog box.

17. Type a colon and then press Enter.

18. Click on the Stop button to stop the recorder.

This macro inserts a figure caption of the following form:

Figure 1.1:

(blank line here)

The insertion point appears on the blank line following the figure number, ready for you to type the actual caption. The number matches that of the preceding figure reference. Insert your figure reference, then insert your figure. Finally, insert your figure caption. If you insert your figures, references, and captions out of sequence, select your entire document and press F9. The figure numbers will automatically update to the correct sequence. (You do have to edit the macro, however, to set the right chapter number.) Figure 6.19 shows the code recorded for this macro.

Figure 6.19

The code for the FigureCap macro.

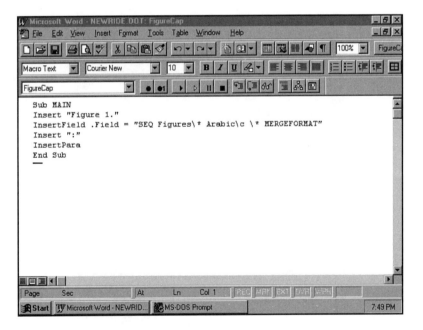

```
Sub MAIN
Insert "Figure 1."
InsertField .Field = "SEQ Figures\* Arabic\c \* MERGEFORMAT"
Insert ":"
InsertPara
End Sub
```

In this intermediate macro, you have mastered some minor aspects of Word Basic programming, mainly with the help of the Field Options dialog box. At this level, more can go wrong with a macro. When debugging, you have to pay special attention to whether all the correct switches appear in all the correct places. Your macros, however, can be very useful, much more so than at the beginning level.

The Advanced Level

At the advanced level, you actually program your macros. You are still recording as much as possible, but you are also entering nonrecordable statements. If you want to get involved with this level of macro building, you need to get the *Microsoft Word Developer's Kit* described in the Word Basic Help file. You also should look for third-party books on the subject of Word Basic. What you can do with macros at this level is absolutely astounding! The next section gives you a peek at what you can do at this level.

Creating Complex Macros

Macros can become very complex and exciting. When you reach the advanced level, you will be creating custom dialog boxes and entering nonrecordable commands. You will be working at the level of a macro programmer. But the benefits of using Word Basic at this level are definitely worth the effort. This section describes the way to create a custom dialog box to manage the macros that you have created in this chapter. It illustrates the way to create a dialog box and how to work with flow control. Your dialog box will present a list of the three macros created in this chapter from which to choose. After you select a macro from the list, clicking on OK starts that macro. The list will be displayed in a combination box.

Recording commands is not the first step in creating a macro at this level and using these features. Few of the commands used by this macro are recordable. You must type the commands instead. Start your macro by performing the following procedure:

1. Open the **T**ools menu and select the **M**acro option.

2. Enter the name DialogBox in the **M**acro Name text box (see fig. 6.20).

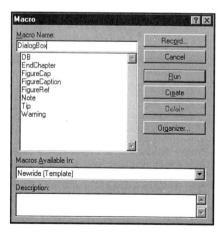

Figure 6.20

Creating the DialogBox macro using the Macro dialog box.

3. Click on the Create button.

Word opens a macro-editing window that contains only the Sub MAIN and End Sub lines, with a blank line between. You now are responsible for inserting the macro commands yourself. However, the Macro toolbar gives you some help.

To create the dialog box that you need, click on the Dialog Editor button, the last one on the right. Word's dialog-box editor starts and displays its window on your screen. You use this editor like a drawing program to create your dialog-box code. To create the dialog box for this example, follow these steps:

1. Click on the Dialog Editor button on the Macro toolbar.

2. Drag the border of the dialog box shown in the editor so that it is a convenient size.

3. Double-click on the dialog box to reveal the Dialog Information dialog box. Enter the name **My Macros** in the Text$ text box (see figure 6.21) and click on OK. The caption on the dialog box changes to "My Macros".

Figure 6.21

The Dialog Information dialog box.

Dialog Information	☒

┌─Position─────────────┐ ┌─Size──────────────────────┐
X: [ ] ☑ Auto   Width: [320] ☐ Auto
Y: [ ] ☑ Auto   Height: [144] ☐ Auto

Text$: [My Macros]   ☑ Auto Quote

.Field: [ ]

Comment: [ ]

.OptGroup [ ]

[OK]   [Cancel]

4. Open the Item menu on the Dialog Editor menu bar and select the List Box option. In the New List Box dialog box, select the Combo Box option button and click on OK (see fig. 6.22). Drag the border of the combination box inserted to make it a convenient size.

5. Open the Item menu on the Dialog Editor menu bar and select the Text option. Drag the text control until it is positioned over the combination box and aligned with the left edge of the combination box. Double-click on the text control. In the Text Information dialog box, type **Select a macro:** in the Text$ text box (see fig. 6.23), then click on the OK button. You now have the directions for using the combination box included in your dialog box.

Figure 6.22

The New List Box dialog box.

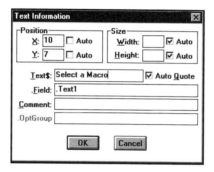

Figure 6.23

The Text Information dialog box.

6. Open the **I**tem menu and select the **B**utton option. In the New Button dialog box, select the **O**K option button and click on the OK button. Drag the button to the position you want it to have.

7. Repeat step 5, except choose the **C**ancel option. This button is automatically aligned under the OK button you just created. Your dialog box is finished. The finished dialog box is shown in figure 6.24.

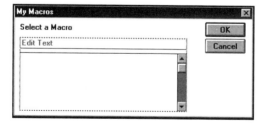

Figure 6.24

The finished dialog box.

8. Open the **F**ile menu and select the E**x**it option. Answer **Y**es when the dialog box appears asking if you want to save the dialog box to the clipboard.

9. Place the insertion point between the two commands in the DialogBox macro-editing window and paste the dialog box statements in by clicking on the Paste button on the Standard toolbar.

Examine the dialog-box code that the dialog-box editor has created for you. (The code is shown in figure 6.25. Your code might vary slightly from the code presented here.) It begins with a Begin Dialog command, which announces to Word that you are going to explain the details of how the dialog box will look on the screen. Word reads from the Begin Dialog command to the End Dialog command and learns how to present the dialog box on the screen.

Figure 6.25

The dialog box code inserted by the dialog box editor.

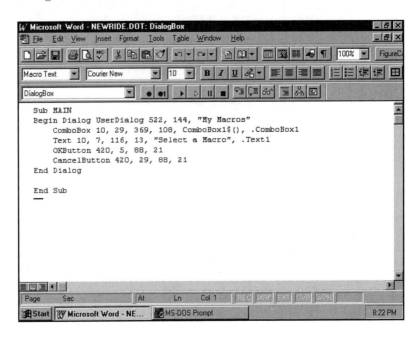

The Begin Dialog command tells Word that this is a UserDialog box (as opposed to other types Word allows), gives its width and height, and provides the caption to display in the title bar.

Each subsequent statement announces a type of control, gives its dimensions, and provides other details about it. The Text control, for example, indicates what text should be displayed within its boundaries. The ComboBox provides the name of the array containing the list of items to be displayed in the combination box, and the name of the variable that will contain the item the user selected. (Variables and arrays are explained in the next three paragraphs.)

You must now add the commands to the macro that fill the list box with options and cause the dialog box to take action when you click on the OK button. To accomplish these feats, you must learn to use both variables and arrays.

A *variable* in Word Basic is a name that refers to a block of memory in your computer. Whenever you use the name, you refer to the contents of that block of memory. You can store information in a variable and use the information you have stored there simply by referring to it by the name of the variable. In this macro, for example, you will use a variable called `Dlg.ComboBox1`. This variable refers to the place in memory where the characters in the item you select in the combination box are stored after the dialog box is gone from the screen. You can use the characters simply by using the name of the variable, as you will see.

An *array* is a set of variables that share a common name because they are related in the way they are used. Each variable in the array has a subscript number attached to it so that each variable sharing the common name can be differentiated. In this macro, you will use an array called `ComboBox1` to store the characters in the items that are displayed in the combination box in the dialog box. This array has three items, because you have three macros that you want to display for selection in the combination box. You reference each variable in the array using the name plus subscript: `ComboBox(0)`, `ComboBox(1)`, `ComboBox(2)`, and so on.

 Tip Array subscripts always begin at 0 in Word Basic.

The first code you need to add to your macro must appear before the dialog box code inserted from the dialog box editor. You need to define the array of items to be displayed in the combination box. To do so, add the following lines of code:

```
Dim ComboBox1$(3)
ComboBox1$(0) = "Figure Reference"
ComboBox1$(1) = "Figure Caption"
ComboBox1$(2) = "End Chapter"
```

The first line informs Word to create an array (or dimension it) so that the highest subscript can be 3. This dimensioning statement guarantees you room for four items in the array, because array subscripts start at 0, but it is easier for you to read as a programmer. You look at the statement and you know you have room for your three items because you know you can have at least the three subscripts indicated in the Dimension statement. The next three lines assign the characters between quotation marks to each indicated element in the array.

Now, when Word reads the dialog box code and sees that it is to use an array called `ComboBox$()` to fill the combination box, it takes the array you have just defined and fills the combination box with the items in the array.

After the code inserted from the Dialog Editor, you need to add the following lines:

```
Dim Dlg As UserDialog
Trap = Dialog(Dlg)
If Dlg.ComboBox1 = "Figure Reference" Then
     FigureRef
ElseIf Dlg.ComboBox1 = "Figure Caption" Then
     FigureCap
ElseIf Dlg.ComboBox1 = "End NRP Chapter" Then
     EndChapter
End If
```

The first line tells Word to take the dialog box that has been described to it and create it in memory. The second line displays the dialog box. You use a variable named Trap to capture the value that the Dialog command passes back to Word when it is finished, because Word will report an error every time the user clicks on the Cancel button. This error simply is normal behavior for Word. If you give Word the variable Trap to store the value that the Dialog command passes back, however, Word does not generate the error.

The remaining three lines create a test to see which item the user selected from the combination box. The variable Dlg.ComboBox1 is used in this test. This is the variable in which Word stores the item the user selected. The tests are all of the form If Dlg.ComboBox1 contains this value, then take this action. The first test uses the keyword If to create the test. If the characters stored in Dlg.ComboBox1 are "Figure Reference," then Word executes your macro FigureRef, which is named as the action to take after the Then keyword.

The remaining lines use the ElseIf keyword to initiate the test. These lines execute only if the test immediately preceding them failed. They check to see if the other possible items in the list box were selected, and run the appropriate macro if they were. The End If line simply informs Word that no more tests are following.

Save your macro exactly as you would save any other Word file. Close the file by selecting **C**lose from the **F**ile menu.

Obviously, using Word Basic at this level requires some programming skill and some programming knowledge. You have to master variables, arrays, logical tests, and similar concepts. But after you do, you can create custom dialog boxes and get Word to perform even more complex actions in an automated way. For example, you now have a dialog box that, with a little modification, can serve to manage any set of macros you would like to make available through it. You can add this dialog box to the menu, giving yourself and other users a convenient way to access macros. Figure 6.26 shows the finished dialog box running.

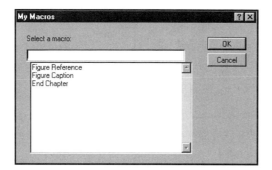

Figure 6.26

The finished My Macros dialog box.

The next chapter explains how to add the My Macro dialog box to the menu. The process is the same as if you were to assign it to the menu from the Record Macro dialog box.

Customizing Word for Windows

Customizing Word enables you to make the word processor do more of the work for you. You make Word tell you what you need to know about a document in the ways you need to know it. In this chapter, you will learn ways to perform the following customization techniques:

- ◆ Customizing toolbars

- ◆ Customizing menus

- ◆ Customizing the keyboard

- ◆ Adjusting Word's options

By the time you complete this chapter, you will be able to perform tasks that make Word for Windows do your bidding.

Microsoft advertises Word as "the world's most popular word processor." One of the reasons for that popularity is that you can customize Word to suit your needs. Migrating from an earlier version of Word? You can get your familiar toolbar back if you want it. Don't like the way the menu is organized? You can rearrange it if you like. You can make Word work your way.

Making Word Work for You

Customizing Word is a matter of working with two items found on the **T**ools menu, **C**ustomize and **O**ptions. Each of these options opens a tabbed dialog box. From the Customize dialog box, you can change the items that appear on toolbars, change key assignments, and add, rearrange, and subtract items from the menu. From the Options dialog box you can adjust many other features of Word, changing the behavior of the word processor by doing so. One other menu option, the **T**oolbars item on the **V**iew menu, also is involved in customization. Using the Toolbars dialog box that this item activates, you can create new toolbars, reset default toolbars, and select which toolbars are displayed. The following sections explain each of the customizations that you can perform to tune Word to your preferences.

 Note   Four of the tabs displayed in the Options dialog box are covered in the sections of this book that deal with using the features the folders govern. The Print tab is explained in "Printing the Document" in Chapter 1 and "Setting Up a Document" in Chapter 5. The Spelling tab is explained in "Spelling Checker" in Chapter 2. The Grammar tab is covered in "Grammar Checker" in Chapter 2. And the AutoFormat tab is covered in "Using AutoFormat" in Chapter 3. Chapter 7 covers the Customization tabs and the other Options tabs.

Customizing Toolbars

You can use as many toolbars at the same time as you want with Word. You also can create your own custom toolbars or change existing toolbars, both through the Toolbars dialog box (see fig. 7.1). You access this dialog box by opening the **V**iew menu and selecting the **T**oolbars item. If you press the right mouse button when the pointer is on any toolbar, a list of toolbars displays, and the current toolbars are checked. You can select Toolbars from this menu to see the dialog box shown in figure 7.1.

Figure 7.1

The Toolbars dialog box.

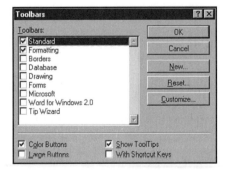

Using Multiple Toolbars

As noted before, Word enables you to use multiple toolbars. To show a toolbar on the screen, check the box next to its name in the **T**oolbars list box. To hide a toolbar from view, uncheck the check box. Using multiple toolbars gives you immediate access to most of Word's features, but displaying multiple toolbars does reduce the size of the workspace, as shown in figure 7.2.

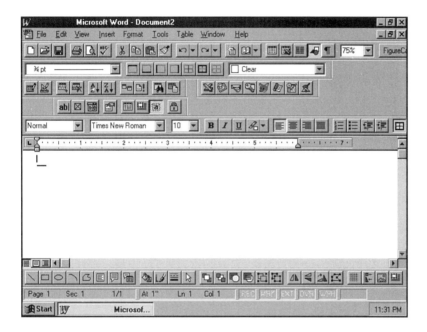

Figure 7.2

Plenty of toolbars, but little space to work in!

 Tip
The number of toolbars displayed in the **T**oolbars list box changes depending on what you are using Word to do. If you are in outline view, for example, the Outlining toolbar appears on the list, although it does not normally.

Changing the Appearance of Toolbars

You can use the check boxes along the bottom edge of the Toolbar dialog box to control the appearance of toolbars. These check boxes control the following characteristics of a toolbar:

◆ C**o**lor Buttons switches the display of color buttons. Unchecking this box causes the buttons to appear in shades of gray.

◆ **L**arge Buttons switches the size of the buttons between large and small. The large buttons are easier to see, especially if you work with one of the higher screen resolutions, like 1024×768.

◆ **S**how ToolTips governs whether ToolTips are displayed when you point the mouse pointer at a button. ToolTips can be useful, but they might become distracting or annoying once you are familiar with the toolbars you display. You can turn ToolTips off by unchecking this box.

Creating New Toolbars

To create a new toolbar, click on the **N**ew button in the Toolbars dialog box. Word displays the New Toolbar dialog box, shown in figure 7.3.

Figure 7.3

The New Toolbar dialog box.

Enter a name for the toolbar, which will be displayed in its title bar when it floats, in the **T**oolbar Name text box. Open the **M**ake Toolbar Available To drop-down list box to select the template that will contain the toolbar. Then click on the OK button.

Word creates your new toolbar as a floating toolbar and opens the Customize dialog box to the **T**oolbars tab (see fig. 7.4). You use the **T**oolbars tab to add buttons to your new toolbar.

Figure 7.4

The floating toolbar and the Customize dialog box opened to the Toolbars tab.

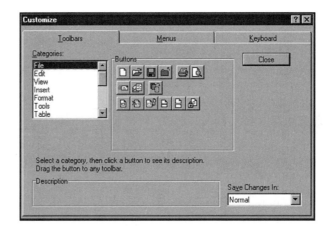

To add a button to your toolbar, follow this procedure:

1. Select a category of Word commands in the **C**ategories list box. Word shows the buttons for that category in the Buttons box.

2. Click on a button to see which function is associated with it. The function appears in the Description box.

3. Drag the appropriate button and drop it in the location you want it on the floating toolbar.

If you select one of the last four categories on the list—Macros, Fonts, AutoText, or Styles—Word displays the list of available items. Drag the item you want to the floating toolbar, which opens the Custom Button dialog box, shown in figure 7.5. This dialog box offers you a variety of graphical buttons and the option of creating a text button.

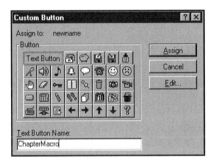

Figure 7.5

The Custom Button dialog box.

You can perform the following actions in this dialog box:

◆ If you like one of the graphical buttons provided, click on it and then click on the **A**ssign button.

◆ If you prefer to use a text button (the default), type the text that you want to appear on the face of the button in the **T**ext Button Name text box and click on the **A**ssign button.

◆ If you would like to create a custom graphical button, click on the **E**dit button. Word opens the Button Editor, shown in figure 7.6. Select a color from the Colors palette and click on any square in the grid to change the pixels represented by that box to the color you have selected. You can see your work in the Preview box. And you can move your entire painting one square on the grid in any direction by clicking on the appropriate arrow button. Using the arrows, you align your picture on the button.

Figure 7.6

*The Button
Editor.*

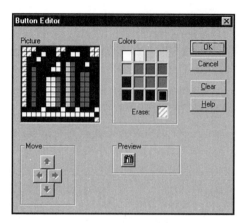

Tip   Even if you click on the Cancel button in the Custom Button dialog box, Word
places a button on your floating toolbar. To remove an unwanted button, open the
Customize dialog box by selecting the **C**ustomize option on the **T**ools menu. Select
the **T**oolbars tab, then drag the unwanted button from the toolbar and drop it on the
Toolbars tab.

Changing Existing Toolbars

You can change toolbars in several ways. To change the buttons on the toolbar, follow
these steps:

1. Open the Toolbars dialog box by selecting **T**oolbars from the **V**iew menu.

2. Select the toolbar to change in the **T**oolbars list box.

3. Click on the **C**ustomize button.

Tip   You can also open the Customize dialog box to work on a toolbar by opening the
Tools menu and selecting the **C**ustomize option, or by clicking the right mouse
button when the pointer is on any toolbar and selecting Customize.

4. Drag buttons from the Customize dialog box to the toolbar to add buttons, or
   drag buttons from the toolbar to the dialog box to delete buttons. To create
   custom buttons, follow the procedure described in the preceding section.

5. Click on the Close button when you are finished.

If you have changed one of Word's default toolbars, you can change it back to its original state easily. Follow these steps:

1. Open the Toolbars dialog box by selecting **T**oolbars from the **V**iew menu.

2. Select the toolbar to reset in the **T**oolbars list box.

3. Click on the **R**eset button.

4. Select the template to which the change applies using the drop-down list box titled Reset changes made to '*toolbar name*' for:. Then click on the OK button.

If you have created a custom toolbar and no longer want it, you can delete it by following these steps:

1. Open the Toolbars dialog box by selecting **T**oolbars from the **V**iew menu.

2. Select the toolbar to delete in the **T**oolbars list box.

3. Click on the **D**elete button. (This button replaces the Reset button after you select the toolbar.)

4. Click on the **Y**es button in the confirmation dialog box that appears.

Obviously you can create toolbars that fit your working style and manage them easily in Word. You can also do the same sorts of things with menus.

Customizing Menus

You can customize Word's menus in much the same way as you can customize toolbars. You can add an entire menu to the menu bar or remove a menu from the menu bar. You can also add items to or delete items from any of the menus. You perform these actions using the **M**enus tab in the Customize dialog box, which you access by opening the **T**ools menu and selecting **C**ustomize. Figure 7.7 shows the **M**enus tab.

 Tip Before you do any work on the menu, make sure you have selected the correct template in the Sa**v**e Changes In drop-down list box.

Figure 7.7

*The Menus tab in
the Customize
dialog box.*

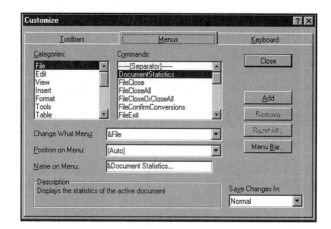

Adding and Deleting Menu Items

To add an item to a menu, follow this procedure:

1. Open the **T**ools menu, select the **C**ustomize option, and select the **M**enus tab.

2. Select the category of the item you want to add in the **C**ategories list box.

3. Select the command you want to add in the C**o**mmands list box.

4. Select the menu to which you want the command added in the Change What Men**u** drop-down list box.

5. Select the position on the menu where you want the item added using the **P**osition on Menu drop-down list box. Selecting a current item changes the **A**dd button to **A**dd Below, and the new item is placed below the current item.

6. Edit the text that will appear on the menu in the **N**ame on Menu text box. The ampersand (&) indicates that the following letter will be the hot key for the menu item. Make sure the hot key does not conflict with any other item on the menu.

7. Click on the **A**dd or **A**dd Below button.

8. When you have finished making changes, click on the Close button.

To delete a menu item, follow these steps:

1. Open the **T**ools menu, select the **C**ustomize option, and select the **M**enus tab.

2. Select the item you want to remove in the **P**osition on Menu drop-down list box.

3. Click on the **R**emove button.

4. When you have finished making changes, click on the Close button.

Adding and Deleting Menu Bar Items

To add a menu to the menu bar, follow these steps:

1. Open the **T**ools menu, select the **C**ustomize option, and select the **M**enus tab.

2. Click on the Menu **B**ar button. This action opens the Menu Bar dialog box (see fig. 7.8).

Figure 7.8

The Menu Bar dialog box.

3. Type the name of the menu you want to add in the **N**ame on Menu Bar text box. Place an ampersand (&) before the hot key, and make sure the hot key does not conflict with any other item on the menu bar.

4. Select the position where you want to add the menu using the **P**osition on Menu Bar list box. Selecting an existing menu causes the **A**dd button to become **A**dd After, and the new menu is added to the right of the existing menu.

5. Click on the **A**dd or **A**dd After button.

6. When you have finished making changes, click on the Close button to return to the Customize dialog box, then click on the Close button to end the procedure.

To rename an existing menu, follow these steps:

1. Open the **T**ools menu, select the **C**ustomize option, and select the **M**enus tab.

2. Click on the Menu **B**ar button to open the Menu Bar dialog box.

3. Type the new name for the menu in the **N**ame on Menu Bar text box. Place an ampersand (&) before the hot key, and make sure the hot key does not conflict with any other item on the menu bar.

4. Select the menu you want to rename using the **P**osition on Menu Bar list box.

5. Click on the **R**ename button.

6. When you have finished making changes, click on the Close button to return to the Customize dialog box.

Stop   Once you rename a menu, you can change it back to its original name only by retyping the original name or resetting the menu. If you have to reset the menu, you might lose other changes you have made. Keep a record of the exact name as it was before you changed it to save wasted effort fixing a mistake. The procedure for resetting the menu is the next section in this chapter.

To remove a menu from the menu bar, follow these steps:

1. Open the **T**ools menu, select the **C**ustomize option, and select the **M**enus tab.

2. Click on the Menu **B**ar button to open the Menu Bar dialog box.

3. Select the menu you want to remove using the **P**osition on Menu Bar list box.

4. Click on the **R**emove button. Click on the **Y**es button in the confirmation dialog box that appears.

5. When you have finished making changes, click on the Close button to return to the Customize dialog box.

Resetting the Menu

If you have made mistakes or want to get back to the menu that shipped with Word, follow this procedure to reset the menu.

1. Open the **T**ools menu, select the **C**ustomize option, and select the **M**enus tab.

2. Click on the Re**s**et All button.

3. Click on the Close button to return to the Customize dialog box. Click on the Close button in this dialog box to end this procedure.

Customizing the Keyboard

The Word keyboard also is completely customizable. You can assign any command, macro, style, AutoText entry, or font to a key so that when you press that key the assigned action is performed. Word is shipped with many keys preassigned, and you can reassign these if you want. If you want to return to the default Word key layout, you can reset the keyboard to its original state.

Tip   If you are wondering which keys are assigned which functions, you can always print a list of the key assignments. Open the **F**ile menu, select the **P**rint option, select Key Assignments in the **P**rint What drop-down list box, and click on the OK button.

To make a keystroke assignment, follow these steps:

1. Open the **T**ools menu and select the **C**ustomize option.

2. In the Customize dialog box, select the **K**eyboard tab (see fig. 7.9).

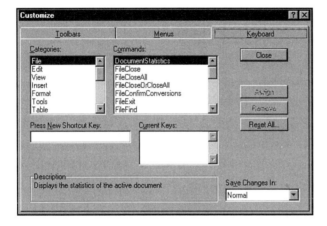

Figure 7.9

The Customize dialog box showing the Keyboard tab.

3. Select the template you want to alter in the Sa**v**e Changes In drop-down list box.

4. Select a category of commands from the **C**ategories list box, and select the exact command from the Co**m**mands list box.

5. Make sure that the Press **N**ew Shortcut Key text box has the focus. Press the key combination that you want to use to invoke the selected command. The current key assignment for the selected command appears in the C**u**rrent Keys list box and the Description box shows what the selected command does. If the keystroke you have chosen to assign is already assigned to another command, a Currently Assigned To message appears above the Description box to let you know which command your intended new keystroke already invokes.

6. Click on the **A**ssign button.

7. When you have finished making changes, click on the Close button.

To remove a keystroke assignment from a command, follow these steps:

1. Open the **T**ools menu, select the **C**ustomize option, and select the **K**eyboard tab.

2. Select the template you want to alter in the Save Changes In drop-down list box.

3. Select a category of commands from the Categories list box, and select the exact command from the Commands list box.

4. Select the key assignment to remove in the Current Keys list box.

5. Click on the Remove button.

6. When you have finished making changes, click on the Close button.

As noted, you can remove key assignments and make new assignments as often as you like. If, however, you want to return to the original key assignments, perform the following steps:

1. Open the Tools menu, select the Customize option, and select the Keyboard tab.

2. Select the template you want to alter in the Save Changes In drop-down list box.

3. Click on the Reset All button.

4. Click on the Yes button in the confirmation dialog box that appears.

You might find that you want to reassign keys so that the commands and macros you most desire to use from the keyboard are assigned to mnemonic keys. Word now is shipped with so many preassigned keys that you might find it impossible to find free keys that you can remember as representing a command. For example, you might find it convenient to assign the FigureCaption macro to the Ctrl+F keystroke, and the figure reference to the Ctrl+Shift+F keystroke, *F* being a good mnemonic key for *Figure*. However, Word already has assigned these keys, along with Alt+Shift+F and Ctrl+Alt+F, to other commands. Do not feel locked in by these assignments. Design your keyboard to meet your needs. You can always reset or change the key assignments later.

Adjusting Other Options

You can customize Word in many other ways. The Customize dialog box offers the ways to change the features most commonly involved in customization. However, the Options dialog box (see fig. 7.10) provides the capability to alter Word's behavior in many other ways. The 12 tabs in this dialog box control the way Word appears on the screen, the way Word interacts with files, and numerous other features. You should be sure to review each of the tabs to make sure that Word is taking the actions you want as it runs.

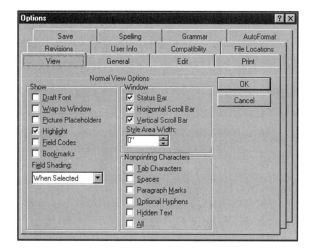

Figure 7.10

The Options dialog box.

Note   Remember, 4 of the 12 tabs are explained in relation to the processes they govern. The Print tab is explained in "Printing the Document" in Chapter 1 and "Setting Up a Document" in Chapter 5. The Spelling tab is explained in "Spelling Checker" in Chapter 2. The Grammar tab is covered in "Grammar Checker" in Chapter 2. And the AutoFormat tab is covered in "Using AutoFormat" in Chapter 3. The following sections explain the tabs that cover more general features of Word.

General

The General tab (see fig. 7.11) covers some miscellaneous features of Word, including screen appearance, help features, and measurement units.

Figure 7.11

The General tab in the Options dialog box.

The controls within the General tab are described in the following list:

◆ The **B**ackground Repagination check box governs whether Word repaginates documents as you are working. You probably want background repagination most of the time. But if you are working on a long document, the long breaks for repagination at certain working junctures might become annoying.

◆ The Help for **W**ordPerfect Users check box switches on and off special help for those migrating from WordPerfect for DOS. When you press a WordPerfect for DOS keystroke, Word displays help explaining the Word command that performs the same function.

◆ The Na**v**igation Keys for WordPerfect Users enables and disables the Word emulation of WordPerfect keystrokes involving the PgUp, PgDn, Home, End, and Esc keys. If you prefer the WordPerfect key assignments for these keys, check this box.

◆ The Bl**u**e Background, White Text check box, when checked, converts Word's workspace to the named color scheme.

◆ Beep on Error **A**ctions governs whether Word beeps when you make a mistake. Check it if you need the audible reminder, uncheck it if you prefer silence from your word processor.

◆ C**o**nfirm Conversion at Open specifies whether or not a Conversion dialog box appears to confirm conversion from another word processor when you open such a document. If you do not select this option, Word takes its best guess at the original format of the document and automatically converts it to Word.

3D **D**ialog and Display Effects governs whether the Word window and dialog boxes have a three-dimensional look. Check or uncheck this box to give Word the appearance you prefer.

◆ Update Automatic **L**inks at Open, when checked, causes automatic links to be updated when you open a file. If you would prefer to know when and which links are updating, however, uncheck this box and use the **L**inks option on the **E**dit menu to update automatic links.

◆ The Mail as A**t**tachment check box allows you to attach documents to mail messages if you have an e-mail system available to you. Check it if you have e-mail; uncheck it if you do not.

 Tip Word has special e-mail features that you can use directly from the menus. You can attach routing slips to a document that automatically send a document, either sequentially or at the same time, to the individuals who need to see it. Reviewers also can annotate a document or add revisions to a document using the **A**nnotation option on the **I**nsert menu and the **R**evisions option on the **T**ools menu.

◆ The **R**ecently Used File List check box governs whether the list of the last opened files appears on the **F**ile menu. If you check it, set the number of files to include in the list using the spin box.

◆ The Tip Wi**z**ard Active check box turns on the Tip Wizard. Deselect this option if you don't need this feature.

◆ The **M**easurement Units drop-down list box enables you to choose the unit of measurement that Word displays on its rulers and uses to calculate dimensions in most of its dialog boxes.

 Tip
Even though the Options dialog box does not offer hot keys for the tabs, you can move from one tab to another using the Ctrl+Tab key combination and the Ctrl+Shift+Tab key combination. The former cycles through the tabs to the right, the latter to the left. If a control on the tab has the focus, however, these keystrokes will cycle through all the controls on the tab before cycling through the tabs.

View

The View tab (see fig. 7.12) governs which elements of a document you see on the screen. It offers three groups of controls that control what to show in the workspace, which elements of a document window to display, and which special characters to display on-screen. The View options vary slightly depending on the view option selected from the **V**iew menu.

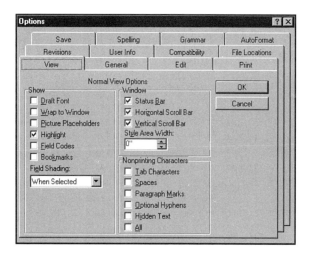

Figure 7.12

The View tab in the Options dialog box.

The Show group offers the following controls in Normal, Outline, and Master Document views.

Tip   You can select among Normal, Outline, and Master Document views using the View menu.

◆ The **D**raft Font check box controls whether formats and graphics are displayed as a part of a document. When the box is checked, character formatting appears only as bold and underlined, and graphics appear as empty boxes. Using **D**raft Font can speed your work with a draft and printing of drafts but does not give you an accurate view of your document's layout.

◆ The **W**rap to Window option, when checked, causes the text to be wrapped at the current document window border. You can use this option to avoid the annoying horizontal scroll when you are typing on a line wider than the current window can display; however, using this option does not give you an accurate view of your document's layout.

◆ The **P**icture Placeholders option, when checked, displays a box instead of a picture. Using this option speeds scrolling through a document and gives you a complete sense of the text format; however, you do not see the pictures on screen.

◆ The High**l**ight option, when checked, causes highlighted text to display on the screen. This highlight option refers to the new feature that enables you to place color highlights on text in order to draw attention to it. It does not refer to the highlight that occurs when you select text for manipulation.

◆ The **F**ield Codes option, when checked, causes fields to display as the text codes that create the field rather than as the result of those codes. In a date field, for example, you see the instructions for creating the date rather than the date itself. This option is useful if you know how to work with field codes and need to see the codes to make adjustments.

◆ The Boo**k**marks option, when checked, causes bookmarks and links to be displayed in grayed brackets. This option is useful when you want to see where bookmarks and linked information appear.

◆ The Fi**e**ld Shading drop-down list box enables you to select whether—and if so, when—Word displays nonprinting shading around fields. You can select from Never, When Selected, and Always. When Selected is the default.

When working in page layout view, the following two controls replace the Wrap to Window check box:

◆ The **O**bject Anchors check box, when checked, causes an anchor icon to appear that shows where an object is anchored to a paragraph. Using this option enables you to tell when moving a paragraph might affect an object.

◆ The Te**x**t Boundaries check box switches whether dotted lines appear to show the boundaries of paragraphs, columns, objects, and frames. Using this option enables you to see the exact placement of these items on the page.

The remaining two groups in this tab are fairly self-explanatory. The Window group offers check boxes that control whether the Status **B**ar, Hori**z**ontal Scroll Bar, and **V**ertical Scroll Bar are displayed. It also provides a spin box that enables you to set the St**y**le Area Width, which displays the style of each paragraph at the left of the workspace. The Nonprinting Characters group provides check boxes that control whether the named nonprinting characters are displayed on the screen. Use these controls to set up your display so that your workspace is comfortable and familiar.

Edit

The Edit tab (see fig. 7.13) controls how Word behaves when you use editing features, including when you edit pictures. These controls determine which keys perform certain editing functions and how drag-and-drop features work.

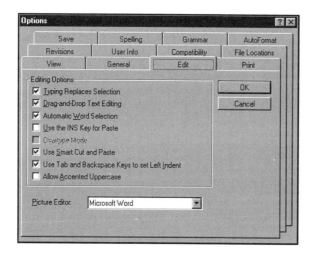

Figure 7.13

The Edit tab in the Options dialog box.

The Edit tab provides the following controls:

◆ The **T**yping Replaces Selection check box, when checked, causes a selection to be deleted when you start typing, before the characters you type appear on the screen. The net effect is that the selection appears to be replaced by what you type. When unchecked, this control causes what you type to appear, scrolling the selection to the left.

◆ When checked, the **D**rag-and-Drop Text Editing option enables you to copy and move a selection by dragging with the mouse. When this box is unchecked you must perform these operations using the **E**dit menu.

◆ When you check the Automatic **W**ord Selection check box you can select an entire word just by selecting a part of it. When this box is unchecked you select only the characters you have dragged over with the mouse.

◆ The **U**se the INS Key for Paste option enables you to paste data from the Clipboard by pressing Ins rather than Shift+Ins.

◆ **O**vertype Mode, when checked, has the same effect as pressing Ins. Each character you type replaces the character at the insertion point. Unchecking the box returns you to inserting new characters to the right of the character at the insertion point.

◆ Use **S**mart Cut and Paste deletes unnecessary spaces when you cut information from a document or paste information into a document. If you included extra spaces at the end of a sentence in the cut operation, Word removes the extra spaces (or adds more spaces, if necessary) to fit the context into which you paste.

◆ The Use Tab and Backspace Keys to set Left **I**ndent option lets you use those keys to create a Left Indent. To see how this feature works (after you have selected it in the Edit Tab selections), place your Insertion Point at the beginning of a paragraph and press the Tab key twice. This creates a first line tab for that paragraph. Then, with the cursor at the same place, press the Backspace key. The entire paragraph indents to the first tab, but this is only useful if, for some reason, you've opted to remove the Indent icon from the Formatting toolbar.

◆ **A**llow Accented Uppercase enables Change Case and the proofing tools to suggest and insert accented uppercase letters when you are working in text formatted for the French language.

◆ The **P**icture Editor drop-down list box enables you to select the graphics editor you want to use to create pictures for your Word documents. The list offers the options of Microsoft Draw, Microsoft Word, PowerPoint Presentation, and PowerPoint Slide.

Save

The Save tab (see fig. 7.14) provides controls that govern Word's behavior in saving documents. These options enable you to set up automatic saving, to embed fonts in a document, and to set passwords on documents.

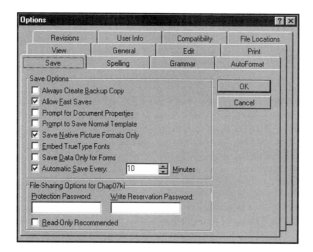

Figure 7.14

The Save tab in the Options dialog box.

The Save tab gives you the following controls:

◆ Always Create **B**ackup Copy, when checked, causes Word to copy the current version of the document to a file with a BAK extension before saving any changes. You then have two versions of the document at all times: the version you opened before making changes and the version you saved with the changes.

◆ Allow **F**ast Saves causes Word to save only the changes to a document, not the entire file. As a result, the saving process is faster.

Tip   You cannot keep a backup copy if you enable fast saves. These two options are mutually exclusive. Word enables you to check only one or the other.

◆ Checking Prompt for Document Proper**t**ies causes Word to display the Properties dialog box as you save each new document. If you used Word 6.0, this is similar to the Summary Info feature.

◆ Pr**o**mpt to Save Normal Template, when checked, causes Word to display a dialog box that asks if you want to save changes to the NORMAL.DOT template each time you close Word.

◆ Save **N**ative Picture Formats Only, when checked, causes Word to store only the Windows version of an imported graphic with the document file. This choice saves file space. If you import documents back and forth between the Macintosh and Windows platforms, however, you should uncheck this box. Unchecking this box causes Word to store both versions of the graphic, making transport back and forth across the platform barrier easier.

◆ **E**mbed TrueType Fonts, when checked, causes the TrueType fonts used in your document to be stored in its file. When others open and read the document, they can see the fonts you used even if those fonts are not installed on their computer.

◆ The Save **D**ata Only for Forms check box enables you to create special templates called forms and use them to create database records. When this box is checked, the data on your form is stored in a single record, enabling you to import the record into a database.

Note   A form is a template that you have protected using the **P**rotect Document command on the **T**ools menu. It contains tables and some special fields that you can insert using the For**m** Field command on the **I**nsert menu. When you use a form as the template for a document, you can enter information only in the table grid and controls provided. Because the form is protected you cannot change the rest of the document. You can save the entire form document, or only the data entered into the fields. The purchase order template included with Word is a sample of a form.

◆ The Automatic **S**ave Every check box causes Word to save your document on the schedule of minutes that you set using the spin box. You should select this option to guard against losing parts of your document if your computer loses power or is accidentally reset. These events happen more often than you think. If you work rapidly, three minutes might be a good choice.

The File-Sharing Options group enables you to set passwords on a document. You have the following options:

◆ Enter a **P**rotection Password in the text box to keep other users from opening a document. Unless other users enter the correct password, they cannot open the document.

◆ Enter a **W**rite Reservation Password to prevent users from saving changes to a document. Other users can open the document, but they cannot save it without entering the correct password.

◆ For a moderate level of protection, check the **R**ead-Only Recommended check box. When other users attempt to open the document, they see a message that

recommends opening the document for reading only. However, they can open the document for both reading and writing if they want.

Revisions

The Revisions tab (see fig. 7.15) gives you control over the way revisions are marked in your document. You can select the color and style for each type of revision mark. You can make these choices for text inserted into a document, text deleted from a document, and text marked as revised in the margin.

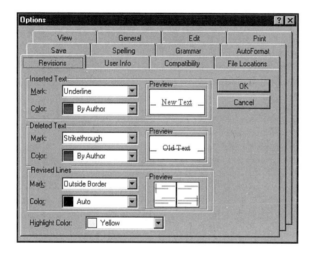

Figure 7.15

The Revisions tab in the Options dialog box.

 Note You can mark revisions to a document by opening the **T**ools menu, selecting the Re**v**isions option, checking **M**ark Revisions While Editing in the Revisions dialog box, and clicking on the OK button. All further changes you make to the document are formatted as you specify in this tab. You can use the other controls in the Revisions dialog box to accept revisions made to a document, to compare two documents, and to merge revisions from the revised version of a document into the original document.

In each of the Inserted Text, Deleted Text, and Revised Lines groups, you can select the Mark used to identify the item and the Color used to code the item using the drop-down list boxes. In the Colo**r** drop-down list boxes, you can select to code each different author as a different color or to select a single color for all revisions. In the Mar**k** drop-down list boxes, you can select from the various character styles and formats offered. The preview boxes show you the effects of the changes you have made.

The Hi**g**hlight color drop-down list box offers the color choices for highlighting text.

User Info

The User Info tab enables you to set the information for the user of the system, as shown in figure 7.16. The controls are straightforward. Enter your **N**ame, **I**nitials, and **M**ailing Address in the text boxes provided, then click on the OK button.

Figure 7.16

The User Info tab in the Options dialog box.

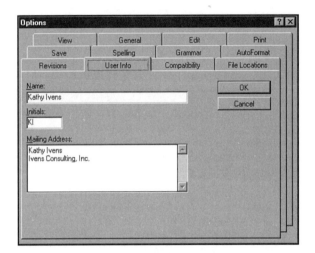

Tip

On systems used by several people, you can build an AutoExec macro that collects the user information from the current user and sets the user information before work starts.

Compatibility

The Compatibility tab (see fig. 7.17) gives you the chance to change the way Word imports files from other word processors. As a rule, you should modify the options presented here only when file conversion has not been successful. However, experimentation is relatively risk free. You can always exit the document without saving and reconvert it by opening the original file again.

If your converted document is not formatted as you want, perform the following action:

1. Open the **T**ools menu, select the **O**ptions item, and click on the Compatibility tab.

2. Review the available conversion options and make the adjustments you think necessary. When you click on OK, your document's formatting adjusts to reflect the changes you have made.

3. After you have the look you want, click on the **D**efault button to make the
   conversion options you have selected the default options applied when converting from that word processor (see fig. 7.18). Answer Yes to make your changes
   the new default for all documents converted from the word processor in
   question.

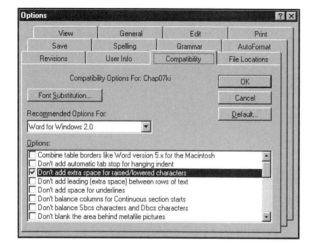

Figure 7.17

The Compatibility tab in the Options dialog box.

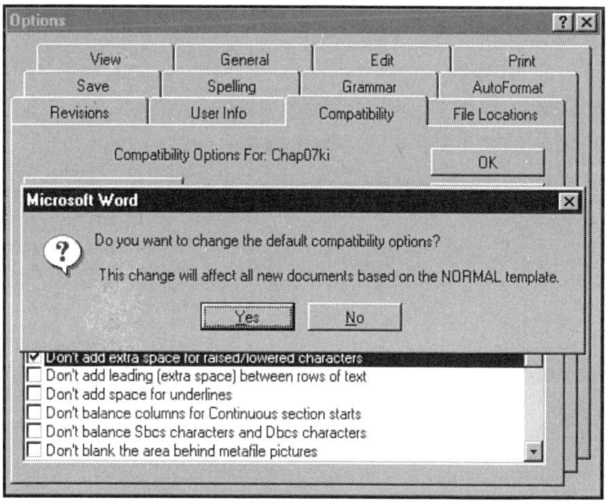

Figure 7.18

You can make the new options the default for all documents.

The specific controls offered by the Compatibility tab are as follows:

◆ The Reco**mm**ended Options For drop-down list box shows the word processor
  Word recognizes as having created the converted document. You can make a
  new selection if Word did not recognize the correct word processor.

◆ The **O**ptions list box offers 25 conversion options that Word applies in converting files. The options applied to your document are checked. To indicate that additional options should apply, check the box next to the description of the option. To prevent an option from applying, uncheck its box.

Tip If you have a question about whether an option will help, try it and click on OK. If you do not like the changes, remove it. You can easily experiment using the Compatibility tab.

◆ The Font **S**ubstitution button opens a dialog box that enables you to select fonts that substitute for fonts used in the document but not installed on your machine. If any substitution has taken place, clicking on this button brings up the Font Substitution dialog box.

Note To use the Font Substitution dialog box, click on one of the fonts listed in the **M**issing Document Font list box. Open the **S**ubstituted Font drop-down list box and select the font you want to substitute for the missing font. Click on the OK button to apply your changes. Click on the Convert **P**ermanently button to make the changes permanent for the document. (In other words, Word no longer sees the font as having been substituted.)

File Locations

The File Locations tab displays a list of the directories where Word stores eight types of files (see fig. 7.19). This tab enables you to review these locations and make changes in the directories specified. You should make such changes if you have moved the files from a previous directory to a new directory, as when consolidating all the clip art images installed by various programs on your system into a single directory that all the programs access.

Tip If you have not installed a network, you will not see a directory for workgroup templates.

To change the directory specifications, follow this procedure:

1. Select the directory to change in the **F**ile Types list box.

2. Click on the **M**odify button or double-click on the directory in the list box.

3. In the Modify Locations dialog box, either type the new location into the **L**ocation of Documents list box or use the **D**irectories and Dri**v**es controls, which

work like those in the Open dialog box, to specify the new directory. If you need to create a directory, click on the **N**ew button, type the name in the resulting Create Directory dialog box, and click on OK. Then click on OK in the Modify Locations dialog box.

4. Repeat steps 1–3 for each change you need to make.

5. Click on the Close button in the File Locations tab.

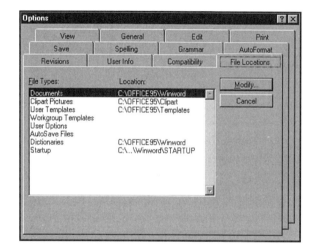

Figure 7.19

The File Locations tab in the Options dialog box.

Stop Be careful with the changes you make. Word will look for the exact directory you specify. If you make a mistake, you might experience errors which report that Word could not locate certain files, or dialog boxes that should show a list of files might be blank. If such problems occur, double-check the file locations for accuracy.

Using Macros to Customize Word

As you saw in Chapter 6, "Word's Word Basic Macros," you can customize Word using macros. When you create a macro, you create a custom command. You can attach these commands to a button, a menu, or the keyboard by using the techniques described earlier in this chapter. Besides creating custom commands, you can use special macros to customize the behavior of Word on certain actions. There are five such macros; table 7.1 identifies them and explains when they run.

TABLE 7.1
The Auto Macros in Word

Macro	Action
AutoExec	Runs when Word starts
AutoOpen	Runs when a file opens
AutoNew	Runs when a new file is created
AutoClose	Runs when a file is closed
AutoExit	Runs when Word exits

Using these macros, you can customize Word's behavior at each of these events. For example, with AutoExec, you could use Word to organize your start of work each day. Word could use the Shell command to launch the contact list you have stored in an Access database, launch Notepad and load your to-do list, and open Excel and load the worksheets you need to use during the day. Such a macro would look like this:

```
Sub MAIN
Shell "msaccess.exe contact.mdb"
Shell "notepad.exe todo.txt"
Shell "excel.exe workday.xls"
End Sub
```

Tip   The string included in the Shell command must have the name of the application's executable file and any command-line arguments, such as the name of the file to open, that you want to include.

With AutoOpen, you can build appropriate start-up routines into each document template you create. For example, for documents that are lists that have to be up-dated, such as notes on conversations that you have during the day, you could insert an EndOfDocument command in the AutoOpen macro. Then you would not have the need to scroll manually to the end of the file each time you opened it; the AutoOpen macro would do the scrolling for you. In fact, you insert the date automatically as well using an InsertDateTime command. Such a macro would look like the following:

```
Sub MAIN
EndOfDocument
InsertDateTime
End Sub
```

With AutoNew, you can automatically save each new file by prompting yourself for a file name and to save the file. This macro would need an InputBox$() command to collect the file name and a FileSaveAs command to save the new file. Such a macro would have the following lines:

```
Sub MAIN
FName$ = InputBox$("What name do you want to use for this file?",
"New File")
FileSaveAs .Name = FName$, .Format = 0
End Sub
```

With AutoClose you can automatically apply formatting to a document by using the AutoFormat feature. As a result, you would not have to be concerned about how you typed the document or whether you applied the right styles. You type, and when you close the file the right styles are applied by a FormatAutoFormat command. Such a macro would look like the following:

```
Sub MAIN
FormatAutoFormat
End Sub
```

AutoExit can easily perform the clean-up operations you would like to perform as Word exits. You could make the macro perform the reverse action of your AutoExec macro. To follow through with these examples, this macro would use the SendKeys command to send the equivalent of Alt+F+X (the equivalent of Alt+**F**ile+E**x**it) to each running application. You must follow this command with an AppActivate command to make sure each application receives the keystrokes. Such a macro would look like the following:

```
Sub MAIN
SendKeys "%fx"
AppActivate "Microsoft Access "
SendKeys "%fx"
AppActivate "Notepad - TODO.TXT"
SendKeys "%fx"
AppActivate "Microsoft Excel - WORKDAY.XLS"
End Sub
```

Tip The % sign indicates that a keystroke is an Alt+character keystroke in the SendKeys command. You must include the exact title bar title for each running application in the AppActivate command.

How would you create such macros? Follow this procedure:

1. Open the **T**ools menu and select the **M**acros option.

2. Enter the name of the macro you want to create in the **M**acro Name text box. Make sure you are storing the macro in the appropriate template by using the Macros **A**vailable In drop-down list box.

3. Click on the Cr**e**ate button.

4. After the macro editing window is open, enter the lines that make up your macro.

5. Close and save the macro file as you would any file.

Using the Auto macros, you can make Word perform some dazzling tasks when any of the Auto events occurs. You can make your work easier by using these macros to automate tasks you would otherwise perform each time one of the events occurred.

Organizing Macros

After you create macros in one template, you might want to move them to another template, delete them, or rename them. Word provides a utility for performing such operations: the macro organizer. To use this facility, perform the following steps:

1. Open the **T**ools menu and select the **M**acro option to display the Macro dialog box, shown in figure 7.20.

Figure 7.20

The Macro dialog box.

2. Click on the Organizer button to display the Organizer dialog box, then click on the **M**acros tab (see fig. 7.21).

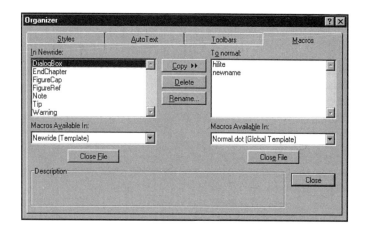

Figure 7.21

The Macros tab in the Organizer dialog box.

3. Use the Macros Available In drop-down list boxes to select the files that you want to work with. If you want to work with only one file, click on the Close File button below one of the list boxes. If a file you want is not listed on the drop-down list, use the Close File button, which then converts to an Open File button. Click on the Open File button to reveal a standard Open dialog box, and select the template for use.

4. To copy macros, select the macro or macros in the **I**n list box and click on the **C**opy button. Use the Ctrl and Shift keys with mouse clicks to select multiple macros—such as Ctrl+click for discontinuous selection and Shift+click for continuous selection—as you would in File Manager.

   The **I**n list box is always the one that has the focus, so clicking on either list box switches their names between **I**n and **T**o. The arrow on the **C**opy button changes direction depending on which list box has the focus.

5. To delete a macro, select it and click on the **D**elete key. Click on **Y**es or Yes to **A**ll in the confirmation dialog box that appears. You can make multiple selections using the Ctrl and Shift keys.

6. To rename a macro, select it in one of the list boxes and click on the **R**ename button. In the Rename dialog box, type the new macro name in the New **N**ame text box and click on OK.

7. When you are finished with the macro organizer, click on the Close button.

Part II

Excel

Excel Quick Start

Excel is one of the most popular Windows-based spreadsheets in the computer industry. This chapter jump starts you to using Excel. Specifically, you are introduced to the following Excel 7 basics:

◆ Excel for Windows 95's newest features

◆ What Excel's interface looks like and how it functions

◆ The way to create a worksheet and a chart

◆ The way to format a worksheet

◆ When and how to use formulas and functions

◆ The way to save and print your worksheets

This chapter does not go into much detail about these procedures. The remaining chapters in Part Two will cover Excel for Windows 95 much more thoroughly.

Probably the second most popular application (next to Word) in the Microsoft Office suite is Microsoft Excel. Excel is a powerful spreadsheet program that helps you collect, chart, manage, and analyze data.

This chapter provides a quick tour of Excel for Windows 95, while offering you opportunities to use functions and to create a worksheet, a chart, and formulas. This chapter will not answer all your questions about Excel. Use it as the first of many lessons toward learning and understanding Excel for Windows 95.

This chapter provides a hands-on tutorial for creating a simple example worksheet and a chart. Within this tutorial, you are presented with concepts, terms, and procedures that will help you get up and running on Excel quickly.

Looking At Excel's Features

Although Excel for Windows 95 has made it easier than ever to build spreadsheets, create charts, and integrate data from various sources, you will need to learn a great deal in order to understand all the components and functions of Excel. Before you start entering numbers and text, acquaint yourself with Excel for Windows 95's interface and its vast array of features.

What Excel for Windows 95 Offers

With the release of Excel for Windows 95, Microsoft has greatly expanded its best-selling spreadsheet to offer many features that have been available in other spreadsheet programs. These features enable novice as well as experienced users to increase their spreadsheet power. Some of the new features include the following:

◆ **More Wizards.** Among the key features in Excel for Windows 95 are Wizards, which help you create sophisticated worksheets and charts. The Answer Wizard lets you type a question in your own words, a fast track to getting exactly the help you need. Programming and Reference Language help is also available. Visual Answers demonstrate features by displaying graphical sample screens— click on a function to get more detailed help.

◆ **Spreadsheet Speed-ups.** Autocalculation is available for fast answers when you have to check a total quickly.

◆ **Easier Number Formatting.** Single-click access to number formats, and there are new formats available.

◆ **Autocorrection.** Just like Word, Excel now provides automatic correction of common typing mistakes, such as "teh" when you meant "the." DOuble CApitals are fixed, as are other common problems (sUCH aS tHIS). You can even create your own shorthand words, for example, type **2q** and tell Excel to substitute Second Quarter or 2nd Quarter automatically.

◆ **Cell Tips.** Add a note to a cell to explain where the data came from or why it's there.

◆ **Maps.** Data that includes regional or state information can be placed on auto-created maps.

Note This book is limited in the depth that it can go into with each application in the Office suite, and some of these features might not be examined in detail. For a thorough view of these and other Excel for Windows 95 features, look for other books on Excel published by New Riders Publishing.

Excel for Windows 95's Interface

The elements of the Excel screen include both basic Windows features, such as scroll bars and windows, and Excel-specific items, such as toolbars and menus. The primary document in Excel is called a *workbook*. Think of a workbook as a ledger book or binder that stores all your critical information about a project, sales report, or any other data you need to keep. Like a normal book binder, each workbook is made up of *sheets*. These sheets can be worksheets or chart sheets. You can switch between sheets by clicking on tabs at the bottom of the workbook. Figure 8.1 shows you worksheets, tabs, and a workbook.

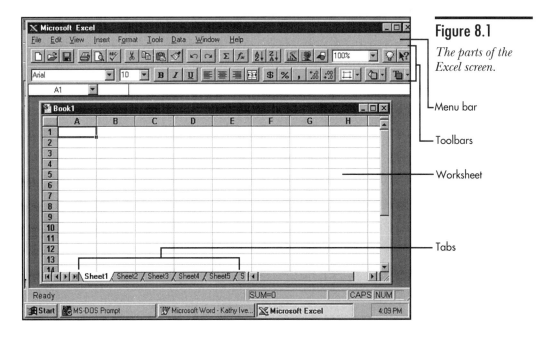

Figure 8.1

The parts of the Excel screen.

Menu bar

Toolbars

Worksheet

Tabs

Excel for Windows 95 provides a number of different toolbars. In Chapter 14, "Customizing Excel for Windows 95," you learn how to customize and change the look of these toolbars, but the following sections introduce you to some of the more common elements you will need to know as you work on your worksheets and charts.

 Note You can find the name and function of a toolbar button by moving the mouse over the button and waiting a second or two. Excel shows you the name of the button in a banner next to your pointer and displays its function in the status bar at the bottom of the screen. This feature comes in handy when you have several toolbars and various buttons on your screen.

The standard toolbar at the top the screen helps you select choices that might be buried several menus or dialog boxes deep in the Excel menu structure. From this toolbar, you can open workbooks, print and save worksheets or chart sheets, and ask for help. Table 8.1 shows the individual buttons and tells you their functions.

TABLE 8.1
Excel's Standard Toolbar

Button	Name	Function
	New Workbook	Creates a new workbook
	Open	Opens a document
	Save	Saves the active workbook
	Print	Prints the active workbook
	Print Preview	Shows the active document in print preview mode
	Speller	Checks the spelling of the document
	Cut	Cuts the selection to the Clipboard
	Copy	Copies the selection to the Clipboard

Button	Name	Function
	Paste	Places the Clipboard contents at the insertion point
	Format Painter	Copies and pastes formats for cells and objects
	Undo	Undoes the last action or command
	Repeat	Repeats the last action or command; this is the same as the redo feature in Word 6
	AutoSum	Inserts the SUM function and shows sum range
	Function Wizard	Starts the Function Wizard
	Sort Ascending	Sorts selected rows in ascending order
	Sort Descending	Sorts selected rows in descending order
	ChartWizard	Activates the ChartWizard
	Map	Creates a map of your data
	Drawing	Turns the drawing toolbar on or off
100%	Zoom Control	Sets the view of the document
	TipWizard	Turns the TipWizard toolbar on or off
	Help	Displays Help

Immediately below the standard toolbar is the formatting toolbar. This toolbar enables you to select fonts, change point sizes, add character enhancements, and customize other sheet attributes. Table 8.2 shows you each of the buttons on this toolbar.

TABLE 8.2
Excel's Formatting Toolbar

Button	Name	Function
Arial	Font	Sets the font for the selection
10	Font Size	Sets the font size for the selection
B	Bold	Boldfaces the selection
I	Italic	Italicizes the selection
U	Underline	Underlines the selection
	Align Left	Left-aligns the selection
	Center	Centers the selection
	Align Right	Right-aligns the selection
	Center Across Columns	Centers the selection across columns
$	Currency Style	Changes the selected cells to default currency style
%	Percent Style	Changes the selected cells to default percent style
,	Comma Style	Changes the selected cells to default comma style
+.0 .00	Increase Decimal	Adds one decimal place to the number format

Button	Name	Function
![Decrease Decimal button]	Decrease Decimal	Removes one decimal place from the number format
![Borders button]	Borders	Enables you to select a border for the selection
![Color button]	Color	Sets the color for the selection
![Font Color button]	Font Color	Sets the color for the selected font

Creating a New Worksheet

Now that you are familiar with some of Excel's tools and naming conventions, you can start creating your own workbook and adding worksheets to it. The rest of this chapter leads you through some simple examples for getting up to speed quickly with Excel for Windows 95 and using some of its basic charting and formatting features.

 Note   For details about worksheets, charts, functions, and other Excel components, the remaining chapters in Part Two provide more insight into these areas. Turn to those chapters when you are comfortable with the basics presented in this chapter.

Worksheet Basics: Columns, Rows, and Cells

When you start Excel, it opens up a brand-new workbook that has 16 blank worksheets. You can start working in any of these worksheets, close them, or open up an existing workbook that you have saved previously. For this example, you can just start working on the topmost worksheet, labeled Sheet1.

On the worksheet is a grid of columns and rows (see fig. 8.2). *Columns* run vertically and are labeled alphabetically, starting with *A. Rows* run horizontally and are labeled numerically (1, 2, 3, and so on).

You can tell which column you are in by looking at the top of the worksheet for the corresponding letter, such as A, B, and so on. Likewise, by looking at the left side of the worksheet, you can find the row number you are in. The intersection of a column and row is called a *cell*. Cells are where you do most of your work in Excel and are named by the column and row that make them up. This is called the *cell address* or *reference*. In figure 8.3, for example, the word Team is located at cell reference C5.

Figure 8.2

Worksheets are divided into rows and columns.

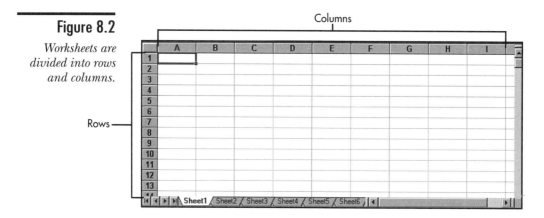

Figure 8.3

Cells and cell references are the basic components of Excel worksheets.

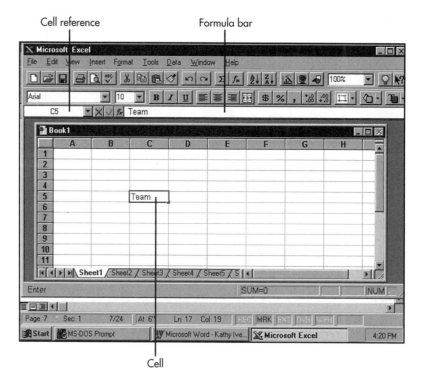

New Riders Publishing
INSIDE
SERIES

To enter data in a cell, first select it by moving the mouse pointer over the desired cell and clicking. This places the insertion point in the active cell, which is high-lighted on-screen with a bold border around it. After you select a cell, you can start entering data from your keyboard or numeric keypad. Above the worksheet, in the formula bar (see fig. 8.3), the cell reference and the text you type appear.

An Example Worksheet: Monthly Team Scores

To help you get acquainted with Excel's basic worksheet components, make sure you have Excel started and a blank worksheet on-screen. Next, follow these steps to create a worksheet of monthly points scored by a hypothetical sports league.

1. Move the mouse pointer over cell reference C5 and click. This places the insertion point at C5. Notice that the border around the selected cell is high-lighted and that the cell reference is displayed in the formula bar.

2. Type **Team** and press Enter. The insertion point moves to cell C6, and you can continue to enter data. In cell C6 enter **Lions** and press Enter. Continue adding team names using the names **Panthers**, **Eagles**, and **Tigers** until the worksheet looks like the one in figure 8.4.

Figure 8.4

Entering team names in the example worksheet.

	A	B	C	D	E	F	G	H	I
5			Team						
6			Lions						
7			Panthers						
8			Eagles						
9			Tigers						

Tip

Although using a mouse in Windows greatly increases efficiency, you might find that keyboard shortcuts help you during data entry in Excel. To move from cell to cell, use the left- and right-arrow keys to move left or right. Use Tab to move to the next cell to the right. You also can use the up- and down-arrow keys to move to the cell above or below your current cell.

3. Enter the months in which the points are scored. In this example, the season runs from January through May. Move to cell reference D5 and type **January.** Press Enter.

Note Before you continue, you should save the work you've already done on this worksheet. Click on the Save button in the standard toolbar to open the Save As dialog box. In the File **N**ame list box, type the name SCORES and click on OK or press Enter. This saves the workbook with the name SCORES, which displays on the title bar. If you check a directory listing, the actual name of the file is SCORES.XLS. All Excel workbooks have the extension .XLS. The actual worksheet is still named Sheet1 (as shown at the bottom of the worksheet), but you learn in Chapter 9, "Understanding Excel Worksheet Concepts," how to rename worksheets to fit your needs. As you continue with this exercise, be sure to save your work periodically by clicking on the Save button.

4. Enter the next four months (through May) in cells E5, F5, G5, and H5. The worksheet should now look like that in figure 8.5

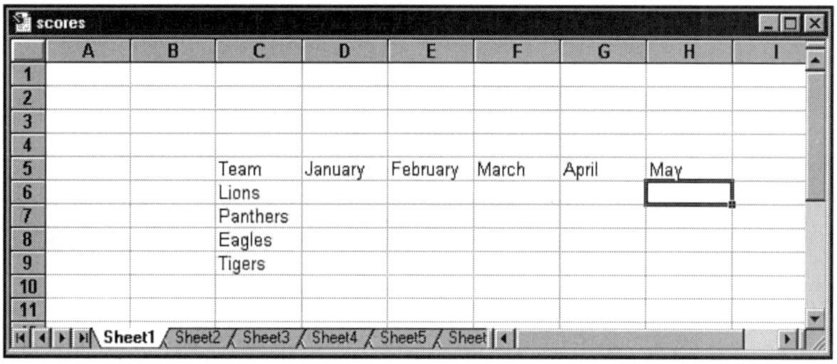

Figure 8.5

Entering the months of the season in the SCORES worksheet.

Tip You can automatically fill in certain types of data that you previously had to fill in manually. One example is the months of the year. In the preceding step, to fill in the months after January, just click on the cell containing January and move your mouse pointer to the bottom right corner of the highlighted cell. This is called the fill handle. Grab the fill handle with the mouse and drag it to the right until the mouse pointer is in cell H5 and release the mouse button. The months from February through May automatically fill the cells. This is called AutoFill, and you will learn more about this in Chapter 9.

5. Now that you have your teams and months in place, you can fill in monthly score totals for each team. This is sometimes referred to as *raw data*. Use table 8.3 as a guide.

TABLE 8.3
Monthly Team Scores

Team	January	February	March	April	May
Lions	25	85	49	18	127
Panthers	46	81	107	57	159
Eagles	17	42	23	74	28
Tigers	45	85	43	51	57

The worksheet should look like the one shown figure 8.6.

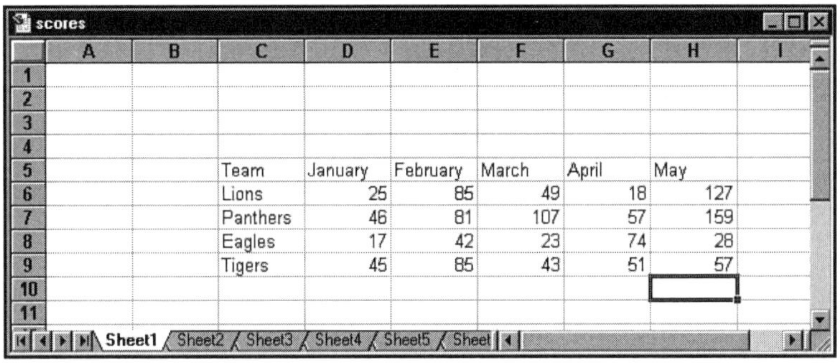

Figure 8.6

The SCORES worksheet with monthly team scores entered.

6. To help you remember which type of information you are looking at in this worksheet, place a report title in the upper left corner of the sheet. Move the insertion point to cell A1, type **American Conference**, and press Enter. Notice how the title flows into cell B1 so that you can see the entire title.

7. In cell A2, enter **Monthly Team Scores 1995** and press Enter. The worksheet should look like the one shown in figure 8.7.

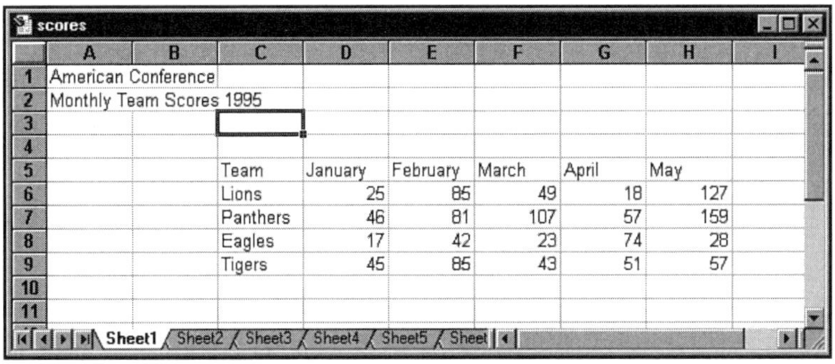

Figure 8.7

Entering the report title in SCORES.

You've now set up a worksheet with team names, months, and monthly scores. At this point, you can enhance the worksheet by providing a more friendly looking worksheet, moving things around, creating a chart, or manipulating the data in a variety of ways to suit your needs. In the next section, you total the monthly team scores to see which team has scored the most points per month.

Data Manipulation: Summing Monthly Scores

One of the main functions of a spreadsheet program like Excel is to calculate data for you automatically. These calculations can be as a simple as basic arithmetic or as complex as a probability statement. In Excel, you use *formulas* to get the results you are looking for. Because many mathematical calculations, such as adding up columns of data, never change, Excel provides you with a number of *functions;* these are predefined formulas that you can use or add to other formulas. The SUM function, for instance, is used so often that it is placed on the default standard toolbar as the AutoSum button (refer to table 8.1).

 Note Later in this chapter, you will see some examples of functions and how to use them in your workbooks. See Chapter 10, "Mastering Excel Functions," however, for more in-depth coverage of functions.

To become familiar with formulas, and particularly the SUM function, return to the SCORES worksheet and total the monthly scores for each team. Perform the following steps:

1. In cell I5, enter **Total** and press Enter. This is the column in which the total scores will be placed.

2. Make sure cell I6 is selected and click on the AutoSum button on the standard toolbar. Excel examines the data around cell I6 and assumes that you want to add up (that is, *sum*) the data in the range D6 through H6.

 Note When you select a number of cells in a worksheet, this is called a range. When you refer to a range, use the form ColumnRow:ColumnRow, such as D6:H6. This is the same as saying "D6 through H6."

3. Press Enter or click on the AutoSum button again to have Excel add up the values in cells D6:H6. The total in this example is 304. If you click on cell I6, the cell shows the sum but the formula bar shows the actual formula, =SUM(D6:H6).

4. You can use the same method to calculate the other teams' scores, or you can copy the AutoSum formula into the cells. To copy the AutoSum formula, first click and hold down the mouse button in cell I7. Next, drag the mouse to cell I9. All three cells are selected now. Click on the AutoSum button, and Excel automatically sums the total scores for the Panthers, Eagles, and Tigers.

Figure 8.8 shows the completed worksheet.

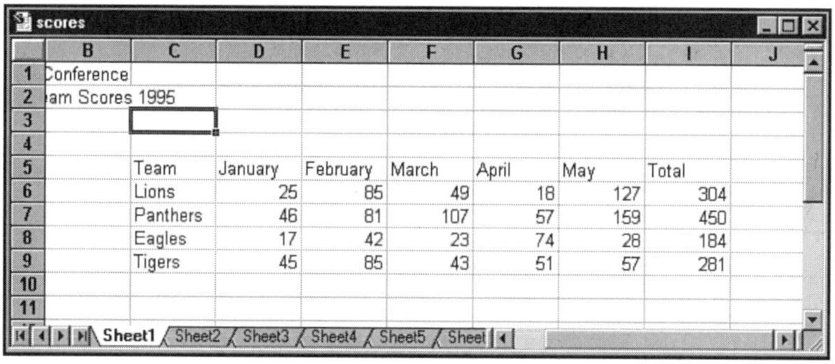

Figure 8.8

Using the AutoSum button to automatically calculate the total monthly scores.

	B	C	D	E	F	G	H	I	J
1	Conference								
2	am Scores 1995								
3									
4									
5		Team	January	February	March	April	May	Total	
6		Lions	25	85	49	18	127	304	
7		Panthers	46	81	107	57	159	450	
8		Eagles	17	42	23	74	28	184	
9		Tigers	45	85	43	51	57	281	
10									
11									

Although many of your Excel spreadsheets might be numerically based (such as sales reports, sports scores, or number of videos sold in a region), you also might have employee lists, address lists, and the like. Excel provides a variety of ways to manage and view lists.

As you look at the totals for each of the teams in this example, you might want to list them in descending order of points scored. This way you can quickly see which team has scored the most runs in the season. This is one way that you can manage lists in Excel.

To sort the scores in descending order (highest to lowest), make sure the SCORES spreadsheet is still open and perform the following steps:

1. Select cells C6:I9.

2. Choose **D**ata, **S**ort. The Sort dialog box appears (see fig. 8.9).

3. In the **S**ort By pull-down list box, choose Total. Click on **D**escending to sort the team totals from highest to lowest.

4. Press Enter or click on OK. Excel sorts your data and displays the teams in descending order, based on the total points scored during the season (see fig. 8.10).

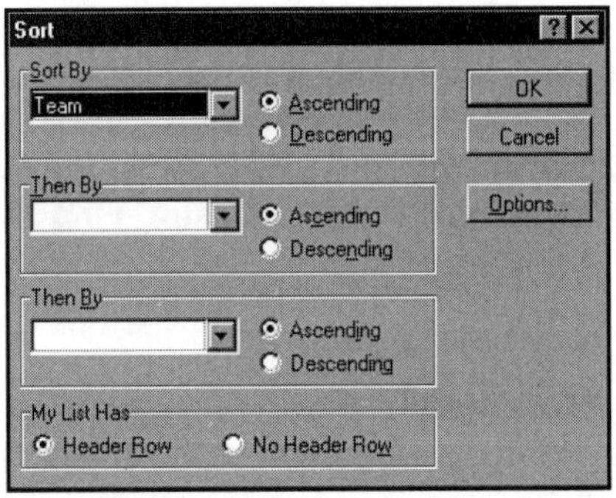

Figure 8.9

The Sort dialog box.

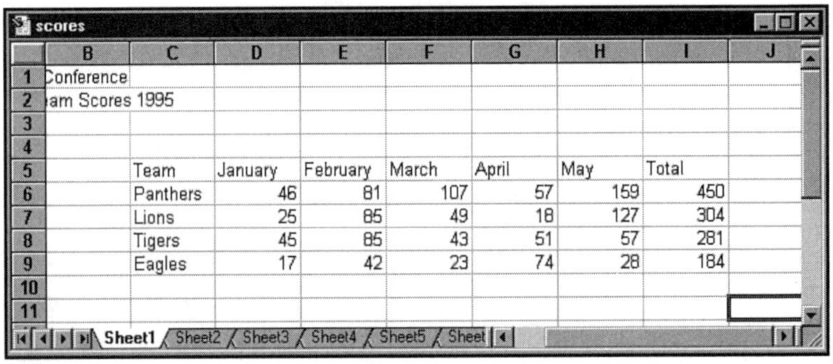

Figure 8.10

Sorting points scored during the season from highest to lowest.

Now you need to format the worksheet a little to make it more presentable and readable.

Formatting Data

When you enter data into worksheets, Excel uses the default template to format the data. Usually, this is the Normal template, which is activated when you open a new workbook. Although this format is functional, it is not always that attractive to look at.

You might, for instance, want to make the Total column bold to make it stand out, or make it a different color than the rest of the data. You might want to center the report title to make it clear what data the reader is looking at. Excel also enables you to use TrueType fonts, so you can take advantage of the TrueType font investment you might have made for your other Windows-based applications, such as CorelDRAW!, PowerPoint, or Word for Windows.

To apply different formatting features to your worksheets, you have a couple of choices. You can, for instance, use Excel's AutoFormat feature, which automatically sets up your document in a pleasing and professional-looking way. You also can manually format the worksheet. In the following examples, you will learn how to format using both methods.

The following examples show you how to autoformat the table of team scores in the SCORES worksheet.

1. In the SCORES worksheet, select the entire table—the range C5:I9.

2. Select F**o**rmat, **A**utoformat. The AutoFormat dialog box appears, in which you can select the type of formatting you want for your table. In the Table **F**ormat list, Excel provides several different choices, including Simple, Classic 1, Colorful 2, and so on.

 Note See Chapter 9 for more information about each of the **T**able Format options, including examples of what each looks like.

3. Choose the format you want to apply to your table. The Sample area in the AutoFormat dialog box shows you an example of what your table will look like. For this example, scroll down the list of formats, choose 3D Effects 1, and click on OK or press Enter. Figure 8.11 shows the formatted table.

	A	B	C	D	E	F	G	H	I	J
1	American Conference									
2	Monthly Team Scores 1995									
3										
4										
5			Team	January	February	March	April	May	Total	
6			Panthers	46	81	107	57	159	450	
7			Lions	25	85	49	18	127	304	
8			Tigers	45	85	43	51	57	281	
9			Eagles	17	42	23	74	28	184	
10										
11										

Figure 8.11

Using the 3D Effects 1 format.

Now that you have formatted the table, you can set up your title across the top of the worksheet. First, widen the columns the titles are in so that all the text fits in one column.

Move the mouse pointer between the A and B column headings at the top of the worksheet (see fig. 8.12) until the pointer changes to a double arrow, then double-click.

Figure 8.12

Changing the column width to fit the worksheet title in one column.

Double-click to change column width

	A	B	C	D	E	F	G	H	I	J	K	L	M
1	American Conference												
2	Monthly Team Scores 1995												
3													
4													
5			Team	January	February	March	April	May	Total				
6			Panthers	46	81	107	57	159	450				
7			Lions	25	85	49	18	127	304				
8			Tigers	45	85	43	51	57	281				
9			Eagles	17	42	23	74	28	184				

scores

Sheet1 / Sheet2 / Sheet3 / Sheet4 / Sheet5 / Sheet6

This changes the column width so that your titles fit in one column (the A column). The worksheet should look like the one shown in figure 8.13.

Figure 8.13

The worksheet title fitting into column A.

	A	B	C	D	E	F	G	H	I	J
1	American Conference									
2	Monthly Team Scores 1995									
3										
4										
5			Team	January	February	March	April	May	Total	
6			Panthers	46	81	107	57	159	450	
7			Lions	25	85	49	18	127	304	
8			Tigers	45	85	43	51	57	281	
9			Eagles	17	42	23	74	28	184	

scores

Sheet1 / Sheet2 / Sheet3 / Sheet4 / Sheet5 / Sheet

To help readers see the worksheet titles, you might want to add special character formatting to them, such as bold, italic, or underline. Excel makes it easy to add these effects to your data. In most cases, you can select the cell in which the character, number, word, or set of words appear and click on the appropriate formatting buttons on the formatting toolbar.

The following example uses the SCORES worksheet and formats the titles to make them easier to view and read.

1. Make sure the SCORES worksheet is open and click in cell A1. This selects the title American Conference and displays it in the formula bar.

2. Because this is to be the top title of the worksheet, you should make the typeface larger than the other characters on the page. One way to do this is to change the font and then change the font size.

For this example, choose the font named Times New Roman (you should have this font if you installed Windows 95 and all its standard fonts) from the Font list on the Format toolbar.

Note Remember, you can find the name and function of a toolbar button by moving the mouse over the button and waiting a second or two. Excel displays the name of the button in a banner next to your pointer and displays its function in the status bar at the bottom of the screen. This feature comes in handy when you have several toolbars and various buttons on your screen.

3. Next, click on the Font Size tool on the Format toolbar and choose 20. This changes the font size to 20 points, making it larger than the other characters on the worksheet.

4. Click once each on the Bold and Underline buttons on the format toolbar. This makes the title bold and underlined.

5. Now, select cell B1 and change the font size to 14 points (keep the font the same, which should be Arial in this example). Add bold italic to this title. The worksheet should look similar to the one shown in figure 8.14.

	A	B	C	D	E	F	G	H	I	J
1	**American Conference**									
2	Monthly Team Scores 1995									
3										
4										
5			Team	January	February	March	April	May	Total	
6			Panthers	46	81	107	57	159	450	
7			Lions	25	85	49	18	127	304	
8			Tigers	45	85	43	51	57	281	
9			Eagles	17	42	23	74	28	184	
10										
11										
12										

Sheet1 / Sheet2 / Sheet3 / Sheet4 / Sheet5 / Sheet

Figure 8.14

Adding character formatting to titles.

You now can center the title over the table, making the worksheet easy to read and more professional-looking.

1. Select the range A1:L2.

2. Click the Center Across Columns button on the Formatting toolbar (refer to table 8.2).

You also can choose Format, Cells and click on the Alignment tab. Choose the Center across option and press Enter or click on OK. This centers the title across the range of cells so that it is centered over the table (see fig. 8.15).

Figure 8.15

Centering the title over the table of team scores.

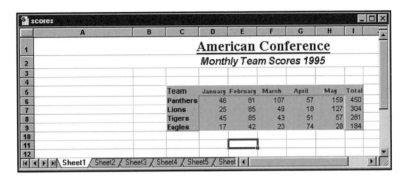

Now the worksheet is set up with its data and is formatted to make it more readable. The following sections show you how to expand the worksheet's functionality and purpose by introducing formulas, functions, and charts.

Using Excel Formulas and Functions

Formulas are the cornerstone of any spreadsheet, including Excel worksheets. You create formulas to perform the calculations that you don't want to, whether because of speed, redundancy, or accuracy. With a calculator or a pencil and pad of paper, a math or accounting whiz could perform all the same functions of an electronic spreadsheet, but why should she? Excel lets you worry about the most important part of the spreadsheet: acquiring and disseminating the data. You don't have to worry about calculating every mathematical formula just to get the results you need.

How to Use Formulas

To enter a formula in a worksheet, you first must decide what calculation you want and where you want to perform it. Earlier, you calculated the sum of the scores for each team using the AutoSum feature. In another worksheet, you might calculate the gross sales of a product during the last fiscal year. Or, you might need to find the interest gained on an invested stock.

When you enter a formula in a cell, you need to preface it with an operator, such as the equal sign (=), plus sign (+), minus sign (-), or at sign (@). (When you use any of the last three operators, Excel changes it to an equals sign.) You must also tell Excel where to find the data, whether it is in an individual cell or a range of cells. You can name these cells or point to them. When you point to cells, these cells are surrounded by a dotted line, called a *moving border*. This border helps you see which cells are selected when you create the formula.

Note See Chapter 9 for more detail about other ways to enter and use formulas in your worksheets, including how to point to a range of cells.

To create formulas in your worksheets, perform the following steps:

1. Double-click on the cell that you want to include the formula.

2. Enter an equal sign (=) or other operator. Remember that Excel changes these other operators to equal signs.

3. Enter a value, cell reference, range, or function name. You can enter a cell reference or range by typing them or by selecting them with your mouse. The cell reference or range displays in the formula.

4. If the formula is complete, press Enter.

5. If the formula is not complete, enter an operator, such as +, -, or @.

6. Repeat steps 3–5 to continue building the formula until it is complete.

One of the easiest ways to understand how to enter formulas is to enter one yourself. The following example, using the SCORES worksheet, calculates the average monthly points scored for each team.

1. Make sure the SCORES worksheet is active.

2. In cell J5, type **Average** and press Enter.

3. In cell J6, enter the formula to average the points scored for the Panthers. This formula adds up the total points scored in cells D6 through H6 and divides that number by the number of months for the season (5).

   Because you already have a Total column that adds up D6:H6, you can use this cell as the first part of your formula, as in the formula =I6/5.

   See figure 8.16 to see how this looks in the worksheet.

4. Press Enter. This calculates the average monthly points that the Panthers scored this season.

5. You now can calculate the average for each of the other teams by repeating the formulas in cells J7–J9, remembering to use the appropriate Total cell as the first cell reference (for instance, use =I7/5 for the Lions).

Figure 8.16

Entering a formula to determine the average monthly points scored.

	B	C	D	E	F	G	H	I	J	K	L	M
1			**American Conference**									
2			*Monthly Team Scores 1995*									
3												
4												
5		Team	January	February	March	April	May	Total	Average			
6		Panthers	46	81	107	57	159	450	=i6/5			
7		Lions	25	85	49	18	127	304				
8		Tigers	45	85	43	51	57	281				
9		Eagles	17	42	23	74	28	184				
10												
11												
12												

Tip To quickly create the formulas for the other three teams, you can copy the formula by double-clicking on cell J6, moving the mouse pointer to the lower right corner of the cell, and dragging the mouse down to cell J9. Release the mouse button, and the formula is copied to each of the cells; Excel automatically calculates the average points scored for each team.

The completed worksheet should look like the one shown in figure 8.17.

Figure 8.17

The average monthly points for all four teams.

	B	C	D	E	F	G	H	I	J	K	L	M
1			**American Conference**									
2			*Monthly Team Scores 1995*									
3												
4												
5		Team	January	February	March	April	May	Total	Average			
6		Panthers	46	81	107	57	159	450	90			
7		Lions	25	85	49	18	127	304	60.8			
8		Tigers	45	85	43	51	57	281	56.2			
9		Eagles	17	42	23	74	28	184	36.8			
10												
11												
12												

How to Use Functions

As you saw earlier in the chapter, you can use built-in functions to help you calculate the results of your data. These functions help you add up columns of data, calculate averages of a range of cells, or return the interest rate for a fully invested security.

Simple calculations on a number or series of numbers are performed by using formulas. Such formulas, such as adding a column of numbers, are the foundation of many functions. Other functions use a combination of several formulas. Functions can be applied in a variety of different ways.

Note For in-depth coverage of functions, see Chapter 10, "Mastering Excel Functions."

Functions are used only in formulas, even if they are the only element of a formula. When you create a formula, you must start the expression with an equal sign (=). Functions have parentheses after them; some are empty and some must include values (such as a range of cells). You must also include the function name, information about a cell or range of cells to be analyzed, and arguments about what to do with the selected range of cells (some functions need additional information). The Address function, for example, returns a value about a cell address in a worksheet. The following is the syntax for this function:

ADDRESS (**row_number,column_number**,absolute_number,a1,sheet_text).

The arguments in bold are required arguments; the remainder of the arguments are optional. Chapter 10 goes into more detail about each of these arguments.

You can incorporate up to 1,024 arguments in a function, as long as no single string of characters in the function statement exceeds 255 characters. Functions can be entered into worksheets manually, by a macro, or by using the FunctionWizard.

To help you get acquainted with using functions, use the SCORES worksheet to find the highest point total for each month.

1. Make sure SCORES is the active worksheet.

2. Select cell D10.

3. Select **I**nsert, **F**unction. The Function Wizard - Step 1 of 2 dialog box appears (see fig. 8.18).

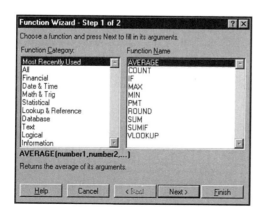

Figure 8.18

The Function Wizard - Step 1 of 2 dialog box.

4. In this dialog box, you can choose any function that Excel provides. For this example, click on Most Recently Used in the Function **C**ategory list box. This displays the functions that Excel has determined to be the most used functions in worksheets.

5. In the Function **N**ame list box, click on MAX. This tells Excel that you want to use the MAX function, which returns the maximum value in any of the cells you select (in this example, the most points scored in a month).

6. Click on the Next button to display the Function Wizard - Step 2 of 2 dialog box.

7. You now must tell Excel which arguments you want to use to determine the maximum value. To do this, you can enter the cells in the number 1 field. You also can click on cell D6 to highlight it and drag the mouse to select cells D7 through D9 (see fig. 8.19). (You might have to move the dialog box to see the worksheet better.)

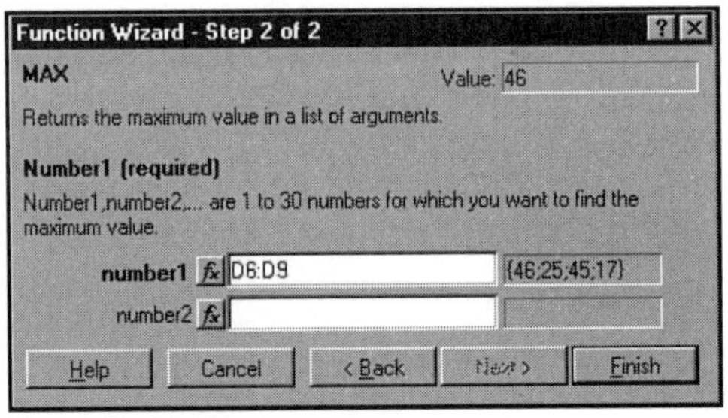

Figure 8.19

Selecting the cells to find the maximum points scored.

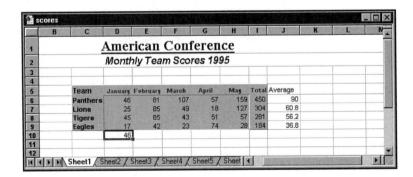

8. Notice in the number 1 field that Excel automatically places the cell references to calculate.

9. Click on the Finish button to return to the worksheet and to see the most points scored in January (see fig. 8.20).

Figure 8.20

The highest (MAX) score for the month appears.

10. Copy and paste this same function to find the most points scored for the rest of the months of the season. Figure 8.21 shows the final worksheet.

	scores												
	B	C	D	E	F	G	H	I	J	K	L	M
1			**American Conference**									
2			**Monthly Team Scores 1995**									
3												
4												
5		**Team**	**January**	**February**	**March**	**April**	**May**	**Total**	**Average**			
6		Panthers	46	81	107	57	159	450	90			
7		Lions	25	85	49	18	127	304	60.8			
8		Tigers	45	85	43	51	57	281	56.2			
9		Eagles	17	42	23	74	28	184	36.8			
10			46	85	107	74	159					
11												
12												

Sheet1 / Sheet2 / Sheet3 / Sheet4 / Sheet5 / Sheet

Figure 8.21

Calculating the highest points for each month.

Creating Excel Charts

At some point, you might have to present your data to other people. You can, of course, use your worksheets as-is in your presentation, whether you present them electronically or in printed format. On the other hand, you can present your data in charts. A *chart* is a visual representation of your worksheet data. You can use Excel to create several different types of charts, including pie charts, line charts, and 3D charts.

Note   See Chapter 12, "Excel Charts and Graphics," for more information about using and creating Excel for Windows 95 charts.

Charts help you and your audience grasp concepts and details about your data quickly and easily. Colorful charts and graphs are seen every day (as in *USA Today*, which uses charts and graphs to display interesting—and sometimes trivial—data).

Excel for Windows 95 makes creating, editing, and printing your charts a breeze. You can place the chart either in the current worksheet or on its own chart sheet. When you change the data in the worksheet, Excel automatically updates the chart associated with that data.

The following steps show you the way to create a simple chart using the data in the SCORES worksheet. For this example, you create a column chart that shows the points scored each month by the Panthers in the 1995 season. This data can be used by coaches, scouts, or the media to assess the team's performance throughout the season. (Of course, other data is important for a thorough analysis of the team's performance, such as schedule, injuries, and playing conditions.)

To chart the Panthers monthly scores, perform the following steps:

1. Make sure that the SCORES worksheet is open.

2. Select the range D5:H5. This range represents the labels for the months during the season.

3. Select the data that you want to chart. Hold down Ctrl and select the range D6:H6.

4. Click on the ChartWizard button on the standard toolbar. Notice that the mouse pointer changes to a cross hair with a chart graphic.

   You use this pointer to tell Excel where you want to place the completed chart. For this example, you will place the chart on its own chart sheet.

5. Click on the Sheet2 tab at the bottom of the screen. This displays a blank sheet on which you can place the chart (see fig. 8.22).

Figure 8.22

Switching to a new blank sheet.

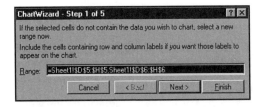

6. Drag the pointer from cell B4 to H14. The ChartWizard - Step 1 of 5 dialog box appears (see fig. 8.23).

Figure 8.23

The ChartWizard - Step 1 of 5 dialog box.

7. The ChartWizard - Step 1 of 5 dialog box asks you to select the range you want to chart. You already have done this in Step 5, so click on the Next button.

8. The ChartWizard - Step 2 of 5 dialog box appears. In this dialog box, you select the type of chart you want to use. To keep it simple, use the default selection, **C**olumn, by clicking on the Next button.

Note Chapter 12 describes each of the chart options and the formats available, as well as how to use them.

9. The ChartWizard - Step 3 of 5 dialog box appears. Choose the format of your chart. Again, select the default choice, which is number 6, by clicking on the Next button.

10. The ChartWizard - Step 4 of 5 dialog box appears. In this box, you see a sample of your chart using the data that you selected, as shown in figure 8.24. Click on the Next button.

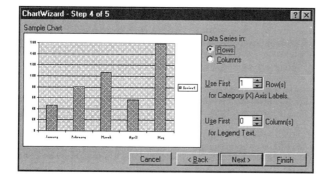

Figure 8.24

The ChartWizard previews the finished chart.

11. The ChartWizard - Step 5 of 5 dialog box appears. This dialog box gives you the option of having a legend, adding a title to your chart, and filling in the axis titles. For this example, select the **N**o option under Add a Legend? and type **Panthers 1995 Points Scored** in the **C**hart Title box (see fig. 8.25).

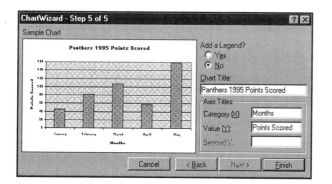

Figure 8.25

The ChartWizard - Step 5 of 5 dialog box.

12. In the Category (**X**) box, type **Months**. In the Value (**Y**) box, type **Points Scored**. Click on the **F**inish button.

The chart appears on Sheet2 in the area you selected in Step 6. The chart should look like the one in figure 8.26.

Figure 8.26

The finished chart.

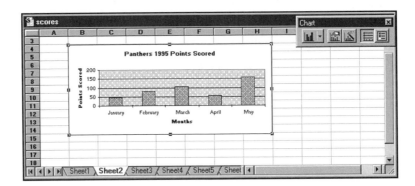

Saving and Printing Your Work

At some point, you will need to save and print your workbooks. By saving your workbooks, you can use them over and over again, without having to enter the data again or create a chart over and over. When you print your work, you can use the hard copy for reports or as handouts for presentations. This section shows you the way to save and print your workbooks.

Saving Your Workbook

As you work through your worksheets and chart sheets, you will want to save them periodically. When you use the **F**ile, **S**ave option in Excel for Windows 95, you save the active workbook, which contains the sheets you are working in. If it is the first time that you save your workbook, Excel displays the Save As dialog box. The name you enter in the File **N**ame text box appears at the top of the workbook. Try to use file names that help you remember the contents of the workbook.

Tip

Another way to quickly save your work is to click on the Save button on the standard toolbar. You also can press Ctrl+S.

Save your work often. Too many hours and data have been lost due to system crashes, power glitches, or children experimenting with Reset buttons on computers. Make it a habit to save your work after you make a substantial change to your workbook, enter data into several cells, create a chart, write a macro, or when you think you will be away from your desk for awhile.

New Riders Publishing
INSIDE
SERIES

If you want to rename a workbook that already has been saved with another name, select File, Save As. This displays the Save As dialog box, enabling you to enter a new name and optionally save the file in a different subdirectory. The original file remains saved under the old name.

The following steps show you how to save the SCORES worksheet by another name—SEASON:

1. Make sure the SCORES worksheet is active.

2. Select File, Save As to display the Save As dialog box.

3. In the File Name text box, type **SEASON**.

4. To change the path to a different drive or subdirectory, use the Directories and Drives lists (this is optional).

5. Press Enter or click on OK. If the Prompt for File Properties option is selected, Excel displays the File Properties dialog box; you can enter the information for the workbook if you want.

 Note   See Chapter 14, "Customizing Excel for Windows 95," for information about customizing Excel and selecting different options, such as File Properties.

6. Press Enter or click on OK.

Printing Your Worksheet and Chart Sheet

Now that your worksheets and charts are saved for posterity and future work, you can print a copy of one to see how it looks on paper. Excel provides several choices when you are ready to print your workbooks. You can, for instance, add a header and footer to your pages, add page numbers, or insert the name of the workbook on the printout.

Previewing Your Work

One of the handiest tools that Excel provides is the Print Preview command. Print Preview enables you to see exactly how your worksheets or chart sheets will appear when printed. This saves time, paper, and printer toner by showing you what you need to change or modify before you send your print job to the printer. Sometimes, for instance, a chart or worksheet may look fine when you are entering and editing data, but when you print it, the chart or worksheet is too large or too small, or you lose rows and columns from the worksheet. Print Preview can help you prevent some of these problems.

To preview your print job in Excel, select **F**ile, Print Pre**v**iew. Your screen displays a facsimile of the final, printed worksheet or chart. As you can see in figure 8.27, you might not be able to read or see all (or any!) of the details in your sheets. This is because Excel is trying to fit an electronic piece of paper (usually 8 1/2 by 11 inches) on your screen. Still, you can get an idea of the information that will printed. (As you see in the following example, you can magnify this view to get a closer, more readable view.)

Figure 8.27

Using Print Preview to view the worksheet before it is printed.

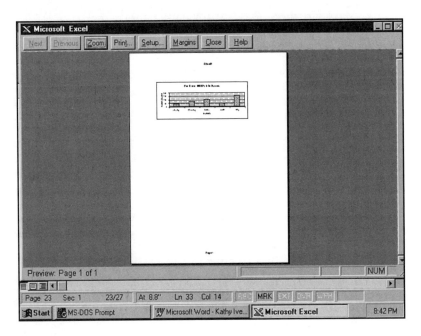

The preview window has the following controls and buttons:

◆ **Next.** When highlighted, this button enables you to view the next sheet in your workbook.

◆ **Previous.** When highlighted, this button enables you to view the previous sheet in your workbook.

◆ **Zoom.** The **Z**oom button enables you to change the magnification of the print preview. Click on this button to view the sheet in full size.

◆ **Print.** When you press the Prin**t** button, Excel returns you to the normal editing window and displays the Print dialog box.

◆ **Setup.** This button displays the Setup dialog box, in which you can change page setup options. This dialog box is discussed later in this chapter and again in Chapter 9.

◆ **Margins.** Use this button to activate or deactivate the margin option, which enables you to view and change the margins of the worksheet. The Margin option is discussed in Chapter 9.

◆ **Close.** Use this button to close Print Preview mode and return to the worksheet.

◆ **Help.** If you have a question about any of these options or any other Excel feature, click on the **H**elp button.

 Note   See Chapter 9, "Understanding Excel Worksheet Concepts," for information on adjusting the size of the columns and rows in your worksheets.

Use the following steps to view the SEASON worksheet in Print Preview mode.

1. Make sure that SEASON.XLS is active.

2. Select **F**ile, Print Pre**v**iew, or click on the Print Preview button on the standard toolbar. The worksheet appears on-screen in the preview window (refer to figure 8.27).

3. As you move the pointer over the worksheet, notice how it changes to a magnifying glass. This enables you to click on the worksheet to zoom in on any part of the worksheet you want to see in more detail. You might have to zoom in on different cells to see if everything fits as you want it to. If a cell displays number signs (#####) instead of actual values or figures, for example, you need to widen the columns before you print the worksheet.

4. Everything should look okay in the SEASON print preview, so click again to zoom out and click on the **C**lose button. This returns you to the normal worksheet screen.

Printing the Worksheet

Now that you have previewed the worksheet, you are ready to print it. Perform the following steps to learn how to use some of the print options that Excel offers.

1. Make sure you have the SEASON worksheet active.

2. Select **F**ile, Page Set**u**p to display the Page Setup dialog box.

3. Click on the Page tab and make sure the **L**andscape button is clicked. Next, click on the Margins tab to switch to the margins options.

4. In the Center on Page area, click on Hori**z**ontally to center the worksheet on the page (see fig. 8.28). Notice how the Preview area in the middle of the dialog box reflects how the worksheet will be set up on the page.

Figure 8.28

Selecting the Horizontally option in the Center on Page area.

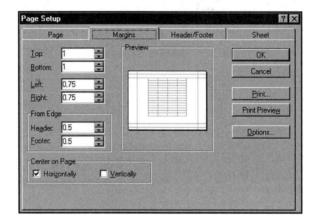

5. Click on the Sheet tab. In the Print area, clear the **G**ridlines check box to turn of the gridlines.

Note As you will learn in Chapter 9, gridlines are the horizontal and vertical lines that help you locate and set up cells on your worksheets. Usually, you keep gridlines on while you enter and edit your data; you usually turn off gridlines when you want to present your worksheets in a clean, professional way.

6. Click on OK.

   Now you are ready to print the worksheet. If you want to take another quick look at your sheet before you print, use the Print Preview feature, as you did in the preceding section.

7. Select **F**ile, **P**rint, to display the Print dialog box (see fig. 8.29). In the Print What area, make sure the Selecte**d** Sheet(s) option is checked. This tells Excel to print only the selected worksheet(s) or chart sheet(s).

8. Click on OK. The worksheet should start printing.

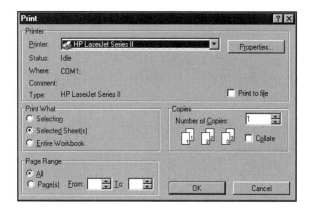

Figure 8.29

The Print dialog box.

If you want, click on the Sheet2 tab and preview and print the Panther Season 1995 chart. You can use any or all of the same options you used for the preceding example.

Understanding Excel Worksheet Concepts

Worksheets are the primary elements that you work on when you use Microsoft Excel. Worksheets can be simple or complex, depending on your needs. To fully develop your worksheets, you need to understand all their rules, nuances, and features. This chapter gives you this understanding by presenting the following topics:

◆ Using workbooks, worksheets, and data

◆ Entering text, numbers, and figures

◆ Formatting your worksheets

◆ Mastering borders, patterns, and colors

When you finish this chapter, you will be well on your way to building more spectacular and dynamic worksheets.

Look around your desk. How many piles of papers or notebooks do you have? Do you have key data placed in these piles, such as budgets, sales reports, or invoice statements? Are some of the piles vital to the success of your business, job, or home budget planning? Would you like a better way to manage some of this mess? If you answer "Yes" to these questions, you are a prime candidate for a spreadsheet program such as Excel for Windows 95.

Examining Worksheets

As you saw in Chapter 8, "Excel Quick Start," Excel workbooks contain worksheets, which are like the ledger sheets you might have used in high school accounting class. Along the left side of the sheets are rows numbered 1, 2, 3, and so on, and along the top of the sheets are columns lettered A, B, C, and so on. The intersection of these rows and columns are *cells*. Worksheets contain 256 columns and 16,384 rows.

The data that you place in worksheets can be text, formulas, or numbers. Usually, *text* entries are labels, such as American Conference or December Sales Results. You also might use text entries when you have numbers and text combined, such as account codes. *Number* entries might be points scored, dollars earned, taxes paid, interest rates, or any other number that you need to store. *Formula* entries are calculations based on values that you specify, such as cells or ranges.

Selecting and Viewing Sheets

Not surprisingly, each type of data that you can enter in Excel has its own rules and features. The basic means of getting the data into the worksheets, however, is the same: You select the sheet and cell in which you want the data placed, and you type the information.

Before you enter the data, make sure that you are working in the correct workbook and worksheet. When Excel starts, a blank workbook with 16 blank sheets opens. Along the bottom of the workbook are tabs that enable you to select the sheet on which you want to work. These tabs are numbered Sheet1, Sheet2, and so on. If you do not want to start a new worksheet, you also can enter data in a workbook that you have saved previously by selecting **F**ile, **O**pen and opening the desired file. You then click on the tab to change to the sheet in which you want to enter the data and select the cell to contain the data.

If you have more than one workbook open, you can move between workbooks by selecting **W**indow and choosing the workbook that you want to make active. This is handy if you are cutting and pasting data from one workbook to another. You also can arrange the workbooks on your screen to make them easier to switch between by using the **W**indow, **A**rrange option. When you select this option, the Arrange Windows dialog box appears (see fig. 9.1).

Figure 9.1

Use the Arrange Windows dialog box to keep your workbooks organized on-screen.

This dialog box enables you to arrange your workbooks so that they are placed vertically or horizontally (by using the **V**ertical and H**o**rizontal options), tiled (by using the **T**iled option), or cascaded (by using the **C**ascade option). You also can arrange only the windows of the active workbook by clicking in the **W**indows of Active Workbook check box. This puts the active workbook in the foreground and the inactive ones in the background.

Tip

As with any other Windows application, you can move individual Excel workbook windows around by using the mouse and grabbing the title bar. The Arrange Windows dialog box is useful in some cases when you just cannot seem to set up the interface to suit your needs and you want a more automatic way of doing so.

Hiding Workbooks

As your worksheets get more complex, or if you have several workbooks open at once, you might find it irritating to have your workplace so cluttered. You can keep it clean by hiding workbooks or worksheets.

Note

As you will see throughout Part II, you might need to have workbooks open even though you are not working in them. You might, for instance, have a workbook linked to another workbook, but not be using the former one for data-intensive work.

To hide a workbook, select the workbook that you want to hide and choose **W**indow, **H**ide. The workbook disappears immediately from your screen. To unhide any windows that are hidden, perform the following steps:

1. Select **W**indow, **U**nhide. This displays the Unhide dialog box with a list of the hidden windows (see fig. 9.2).

2. In the **U**nhide Workbook list box, click on the window you want to unhide.

3. Choose OK or press Enter. The window you want to unhide reappears on-screen in its previous size and position.

Figure 9.2

*The Unhide
dialog box keeps a
list of hidden
windows.*

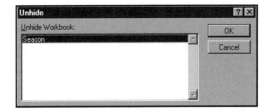

Hiding Worksheets

What if you want to hide all those other worksheets in a workbook that you are not using? To do this, you cannot use the **W**indows, **H**ide command. You have to use the F**o**rmat, **S**heet command, as follows:

1. Switch to the sheet you want to hide.

2. Select F**o**rmat, **S**heet. A submenu pops out to the side of the pull-down menu.

3. Choose **H**ide. The sheet instantly disappears.

To unhide the worksheet, select F**o**rmat, **S**heet, **U**nhide to display the Unhide dialog box. Click on the sheet you want to unhide and choose OK or press Enter. The sheet reappears on-screen.

Locking Workbooks

You might want to keep all the windows in place, or you might want to keep other people from moving windows around if they are using your workbooks. To lock a window after you have it in place, select **T**ools, **P**rotection, Protect **W**orkbook to display the Protect Workbook dialog box (see fig. 9.3). In this dialog box, you can enter a password in the **P**assword (optional) text box so that users will need a pass-word to move the windows or modify the structure of the workbook (such as hide, unhide, delete, or move it). Click in the **W**indows check box so that the position of the windows cannot be changed. Click in the **S**tructure check box to protect the structure of the workbook.

Figure 9.3

*The Protect
Workbook dialog
box.*

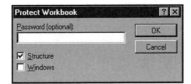

Tip   Remember your password. If you forget it, you cannot unprotect your workbook.

Moving Around in Workbooks and Worksheets

From Chapter 8, "Excel Quick Start," you already know that you can click on the sheet tab of your choice to switch to that sheet. Excel offers a few other navigational tools to help you move around in your workbooks. You can, for instance, use scroll bars to move around. You also can type a cell reference to switch to that cell.

Tab scrolling arrows appear at the bottom of workbooks to enable you to move through the worksheet names in a workbook. You cannot switch to a different sheet by using the tab scrolling arrows, but you can view the names of the sheets and then click on the sheet tab that you want to activate. Each workbook has four tab scrolling arrows. The far left and far right arrows move to the first and last sheets in the workbook, respectively. The middle two arrows move one sheet to the left or right in the workbook. See figure 9.4 for the placement of these scrolling arrows.

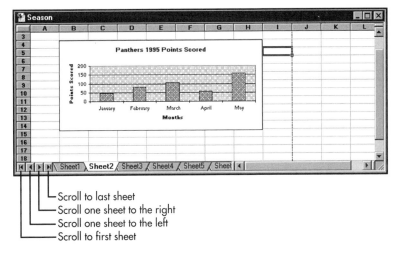

Scroll to last sheet
Scroll one sheet to the right
Scroll one sheet to the left
Scroll to first sheet

Figure 9.4

Tab scrolling arrows help you identify sheets in your workbook.

Selecting More than One Worksheet

You might have to select several worksheets (say, if you have a reference to multiple, noncontiguous workbooks) in a workbook that are not side by side—Sheet2, Sheet4, Sheet 11, and Sheet13, for example. To do this, perform the following steps:

1. Click on the tab scrolling arrows to show the first sheet that you want to select, such as Sheet2.

2. Click on that tab (in this example, Sheet2).

3. Click on the tab scrolling arrows to show the next sheet in the group that you want to select, such as Sheet4.

4. Click on that tab while pressing Ctrl (in this example, Sheet4).

5. Continue scrolling to the next sheet tab, using Ctrl+click, until all the sheets are selected.

As you select the sheets, the tabs change color to signify that you have selected them.

In other situations, you might need to select several sheets that are in order, such as Sheet3 through Sheet8. Follow these steps:

1. Click on the tab scrolling arrows to show the first sheet you want to select, such as Sheet3.

2. Click on that tab (in this example, Sheet3).

3. Click on the tab scrolling arrows to show the last sheet in the group that you want to select, such as Sheet8.

4. Click on the last sheet name while pressing Shift. This selects all the sheets between the first and last sheets on which you clicked. Again, the tabs change color to show that they have been selected.

Using the Go To Command

If you want to move to a specific sheet in an open workbook, but you don't want to scroll through all the sheets and you know exactly the sheet and cell reference, perform the following steps:

1. Select **E**dit, **G**o To (or press F5 or Ctrl+G). The Go To dialog box appears.

2. In the **R**eference text box, enter the name and cell of the sheet to which you want to switch. You have to separate the name and cell with an exclamation point, such as in the following example:

   SCORES!H6

   In this example, you are telling Excel to jump to cell H6 in the SCORES worksheet.

3. Choose OK or press Enter.

Understanding Excel's Three Types of Data

You might have stacks of papers on your desk and loose invoices jammed in your filing cabinet. These numbers, dates, products, inventory lists, dollars spent and received, phone numbers, addresses, and other miscellaneous words and numbers are forms of data. You need to find a way to administer all this data so that you can use it quickly and efficiently. Now that you know how to move among workbooks and worksheets, you can start entering all this wealth of information that you have been putting off for months (or years!).

When you finally break down all the data and see what you have, you can begin to formulate how you want it to look in your worksheets. Phone numbers and addresses, for instance, can comprise a Black Book worksheet. Sales data for the entire midwestern sales force can be put into a Midwest Sales worksheet. You even can start thinking about creating sophisticated workbooks that rely on macro or Visual Basic for Applications front ends.

Tip One way to get ideas on the types of workbooks and worksheets that you can build in Excel is to view the sample files that come with Excel for Windows 95. These files are usually stored in the \EXAMPLE subdirectory in which you have Excel stored. Open these files and see how Excel enables you to present data in several different ways.

Using Text as Data

You can include text entries that are alphabetical characters, numbers, symbols, and spaces. Usually, text entries, which can be up to 255 characters long in a cell, are used to label worksheets and to help readers understand the contents of the workbooks. You also can enter numbers and have them treated as text, such as in the case of addresses, numbers used as labels, and numbers that begin with 0. When you enter a number that has a leading zero, Excel deletes the 0. You can, however, retain the 0 by leading the entry with an apostrophe ('), which tells Excel that the entry is to be accepted as text. (The apostrophe does not appear in the cell.)

Tip Another way to enter a number as text is to select F**o**rmat, **C**ells. This displays the Format Cell dialog box. Click on the Number tab and select the Text option in the **C**ategory list. Click on OK or press Enter. This returns you to the active worksheet where you can enter the number, and it is accepted as text.

Excel places text in a cell by aligning it on the left side of the cell. Numbers, on the other hand, are right-aligned. If your text entry is too large to be viewed in the default cell size, you need to resize the cell by using the formatting features explained later in this chapter.

To enter text in a worksheet, select a cell and type the text. In the following example, you enter some text and some numbers as text. Notice how text aligns on the left side of the cell.

The following exercise uses a new worksheet that you can open by choosing **F**ile, **N**ew:

1. Select **F**ile, **N**ew or click the New button on the toolbar, to create a new work-book. A new workbook with blank worksheets appears.

2. Click in the cell in which you will enter the text—for example, cell B4.

3. Type the text you want—for example, **Sales**. Notice how the text aligns on the left side of the cell.

4. Enter some numbers that you want to appear as text, such as the current year. To do this, add an apostrophe (') before the number: **'1995**. Excel interprets this data as text and does not think it is a number entry. (You learn about number entries in the next section.)

Another way to enter text (or any other data) is to use the formula bar on the formatting toolbar. To make this your default choice, turn off the in-cell editing feature. This method is nice if you don't want to see your entries made directly in the cell until you are finished entering them.

To turn off in-cell editing, use these steps:

1. Select **T**ools, **O**ptions. The Options dialog box appears.

2. Click on the Edit tab to display the Edit dialog box (see fig. 9.5).

3. Click on the **E**dit Directly in Cell check box to turn it off.

4. Click on OK or press Enter.

Now, when you click or double-click on a cell to edit the contents, your insertion point appears on the formula bar instead of within the cell. The characters are still displayed in the cell as you type. Some people find it easier to work this way.

Regardless of the location of your insertion point, when you begin entering charac-ters, the formula bar displays four buttons (see fig. 9.6).

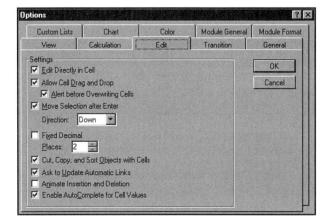

Figure 9.5

The Edit tab of the Options dialog box.

Figure 9.6

The buttons on the formula bar give you mouse-click access to data entry functions.

◆ The Name box on the formula bar shows you the cell reference for the selected cell. You can press the arrow to the right of the box and enter a cell reference in order to move to that cell quickly.

◆ The Cancel button enables you to undo what you have typed before entering the data. You also can press Esc to do the same thing.

◆ The Enter button is used to place the entry into the selected cell, or you can press the Enter key.

◆ The Function Wizard button activates the Function Wizard to help you build formulas that contain functions. (You learn more about the Function Wizard in Chapter 10, "Mastering Excel Functions.")

Text entries may become lengthy and run too long for the cell in which they are contained. To avoid having text flow into other cells, you can use text wrapping to display the entry in multiple lines in one cell.

To see how the feature works, enter a lengthy string of some data in a cell. Next, select **F**ormat, **C**ells and click on the Alignment tab. Choose the **W**rap Text check box and press Enter or click on OK. The cell (along with the row) grows higher to accommodate all the data.

Using Numbers as Data

For the most part, your worksheets will contain numbers. The primary function of a spreadsheet is to help you calculate, store, manipulate, and present numbers. These numbers might be dollar amounts, percentages, dates, or other values. Excel lets you enter these characters as number data: 1 2 3 4 5 6 7 8 9 0 E e . % - + / . (Later in this chapter, you are shown how to change the formatting of numbers.)

Numbers are entered the same way text is: select the cell, type the number, and then press Enter or click on the Enter box on the formula bar. Excel right-aligns the numbers in the cells. If you want to enter fractions, type an integer (such as 1 or 0), a space, the numerator, a slash (/), and the denominator: **3 1/2** or **0 5/16**. The first fraction in these examples reads as *three and one-half*, and the second fraction reads as *five-sixteenths*. If you do not use an integer before the fraction, Excel thinks you are entering a date. The second example without the zero (5/16) would be read as *May 16*.

Some other forms of numbers that you might need to enter are negative numbers, dollar amounts, decimals, and very large or small numbers. Negative numbers are placed inside of parentheses—**(45)** for negative 45, for example. Dollar amounts are entered with the dollar sign, then the number: **$34.90**. Decimal values are entered with the decimal point: **432.89**. If you deal with large numbers, such as scientific notations, you use the form **84.3992 E+3**. (*E* is the symbol that represents scientific notation.)

Tip

To enter a number that has thousands and uses one or more commas in it, you have to place the comma in the correct place or Excel will think it is a text entry. The number 34,45 is not the same as 3,445 to Excel. The first is interpreted as text and the second is interpreted as a number.

The easiest way to see whether an entry is interpreted as a number or text is to see whether Excel aligns it on the left side or the right side of the cell when you enter it. If it is aligned on the right side, it's a number. On the left, it's text.

When you enter a number that does not fit in a cell, Excel displays a series of ####s to indicate that the column is not wide enough (see fig. 9.7). To change the ####s to the actual numbers, you can widen the columns or change the numeric format (such as changing the font or point size of the number). To change the numeric format, you might need to change a long number to scientific notation. (Later in this chapter, you are shown how to widen columns.)

	Sales											_ □ ×
	L	M	N	O	P	Q	R	S	T	U	V	V
1												
2												
3												
4	#######		#######		#######							
5	#######		#######		#######							
6	#######		#######		#######							
7	#######		#######		#######							
8	#######		#######		#######							
9	#######		#######		#######							
10	#######		#######		#######							
11	#######		#######		#######							
12	#######		#######		#######							
13	#######		#######		#######							
14	#######		#######		#######							
15	#######		#######		#######							
16	#######		#######		#######							
17												

Figure 9.7

When an entry is too long to fit in a cell, you see a series of ####s.

Entering Dates and Times

You might need to place actual dates and times into your worksheets, such as February 1, 1995, or 5:13 p.m. When you enter dates and times, Excel stores this data as a serial number. *Serial numbers* represent starting points that are programmed into Excel. A date serial number is computed from the starting point of December 31, 1899. A time serial number is computed using fractions of the 24-hour clock.

If you enter the date December 31, 1993, for example, the serial number is 34,334. This means that 34,334 days have passed between December 31, 1899, and December 31, 1993. If you enter a time of 12:00 noon, Excel saves it as the serial number 0.50; 5:00 p.m. is 0.70833. This means that when it is noon, half the day has passed; when it is 5:00 p.m., you have only about three-tenths of the day left.

Note Why are serial numbers used by Excel? Serial numbers make it easy to calculate dates and times you might need in your results, such as delivery times and dates or account payable data. All you need to think about, however, is entering dates and times the way Excel accepts them, which is in a number of different formats. You do not need to enter serial numbers, even though you can if you want; Excel handles the conversion itself.

The secret to entering and displaying dates and times correctly is to use Excel's date and time formats (see table 9.1). These formats are found by selecting F**o**rmat, **C**ell and clicking on the Number tab (see fig. 9.8). In the **C**ategory list box, you can choose the type of number, including Date and Time, that you want to format. The format appears in the **F**ormat Codes box.

Figure 9.8

Use the Number tab to format dates and times.

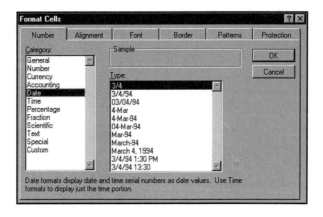

TABLE 9.1
Date and Time Formats

Date or Time	Format
1/12/94	m/d/yy
12-Jan-94	d-mmm-yy
12-Jan	d-mmm
Jan-94	mmm-yy
1/12/94 11:15	m/d/yy h:mm
11:15 a.m.	h:mm AM/PM
11:15:34 a.m.	h:mm:ss AM/PM
11:15	h:mm
11:15:34	h:mm:ss
1/12/94/ 11:15	m/d/yy/h:mm

The way a time or date is displayed in your worksheet depends on the number format applied to the cell. When you type a date or time in a format that Excel recognizes, the cell's format changes from the General number format to a built-in date or time format. The specified format is applied to your entry (unless you change the format for that cell). Figure 9.9 shows a worksheet in which the formula bar displays the way the date was entered, but the cell displays the data according to the formatting assigned.

One of the most useful shortcuts when you are entering data is to enter the current date and time automatically in a cell. Press Ctrl+; to enter the current date, and press Ctrl+: to enter the current time.

New Riders Publishing
INSIDE
SERIES

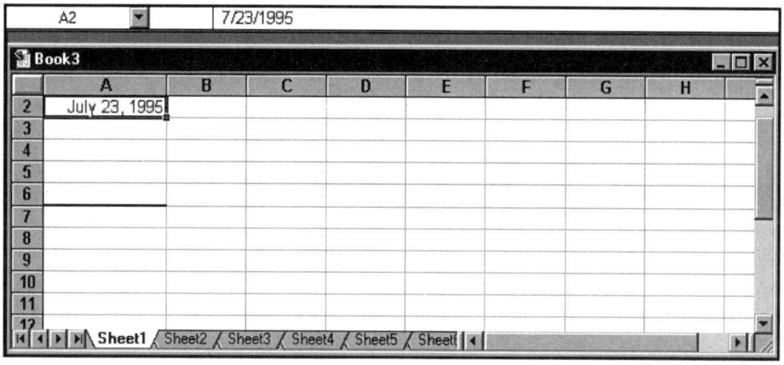

Figure 9.9

Excel reformats date displays to match your settings.

Using Formulas as Data

The third type of data that you can enter in Excel is formulas. Formulas are simple to understand. They calculate results based on values. In Chapter 8, for example, you entered a few formulas to help you calculate totals, averages, and highest points scored in each month. You can use numbers, cell references, text, or functions in formulas.

To enter formulas in your worksheets, perform the following general steps:

1. Double-click on the cell in which you want to include the formula.

2. Enter an equal sign (=) or other operator. Remember that Excel changes these other operators to equal signs.

3. Enter a value, cell reference, range, or function name by typing it or selecting it with your mouse. The cell reference or range appears in the formula.

4. If the formula is complete, press Enter.

5. If the formula is not complete, enter an operator, such as +, -, or @.

6. Go back to Step 3 and continue building the formula until it is complete.

Most of the time, you use Excel formulas to calculate results of numbers. These types of formulas are called *arithmetic formulas.* Generally, arithmetic formulas calculate results by using numbers, function results, and cell addresses with one or more of the following mathematical operators:

$$= - * / \% \wedge$$

The caret ($\wedge$) operator denotes an *exponentiation operator.* An example of exponentiation is raising a number to a certain power. The formula $=5\wedge2$ means *5 raised to the second power,* or 25.

Calculating by Order of Precedence

When you enter a formula that contains operators, you need to keep in mind the order by which Excel calculates the formula. This is called *order of precedence,* and is used by Excel to determine which part of the formula to calculate first, second, and so on.

If you have the formula =5*3^2, for example, it is not clear which part of the formula should be calculated first. Excel's order of precedence first calculates the exponentiation part (3^2=9) and then the multiplication part (5*9). The result of this total formula is 45.

If you calculate the parts in the opposite order, the results are quite different (5*3=15; 15^2=225), so it is important to understand Excel's order of precedence when you create your formulas. Table 9.2 shows the order in which Excel calculates formulas and the operators associated with certain operations. (Some of the operations in the table are covered in more detail in Chapter 10, "Mastering Excel Functions," and later in this chapter in the section discussing ranges.)

TABLE 9.2
Order of Precedence in Formulas

Order	Operation	Operator
1	Range	:
2	Intersection	Space
3	Union	,
4	Negation (such as –9)	-
5	Percent	%
6	Exponentiation	^
7	Division and multiplication	/ and *
8	Addition and subtraction	+ and -
9	Concatenation	&
10	Comparison	= < > <= >= <>

You might want to create formulas that do not follow the natural order of precedence. You might, for instance, want to add two numbers together and *then* multiply the sum by another number. In the order of precedence, however, Excel multiplies first, then adds. To overcome this in your formula, use parentheses to surround the numbers that you want Excel to calculate first.

If, in the preceding example, you want to add 5 and 3 and then multiply the sum by 10, set up the formula as the following:

=(5+3)*10

When you have more complicated formulas, you might have parentheses inside of parentheses. This is called *nesting*. Keep in mind that Excel calculates what is inside of parentheses first, and the formulas within the inner parentheses are calculated before those within the outer ones.

The following example provides some sample formulas that you can enter in a new worksheet to help you get acquainted with entering formulas.

1. In cell B4, enter =**2+2** and press Enter.

2. In cell B6, enter =**2*2** and press Enter.

3. In cell B8, enter =**2/2** and press Enter.

4. In cell B10, enter =**2-2** and press Enter.

5. In cell B12, enter =**2^2** and press Enter.

6. In cell B14, enter =**2*(2^5)** and press Enter.

Figure 9.10 shows the results of these formulas and how your worksheet should look. (A worksheet title, called "Entering Formulas," has been added to cell B2 in this figure.)

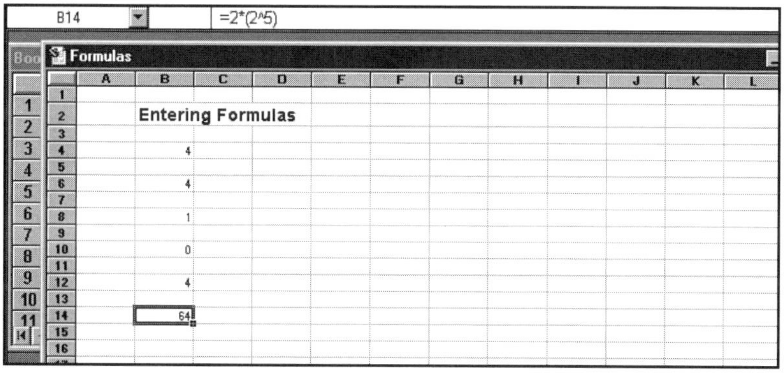

Figure 9.10

Entering formulas.

Tip

Remember to type the equal sign to start the formula. If you forget to do this and press Enter, Excel interprets your entries as text and does not calculate the formula. To edit the cell after you have entered the formula, double-click on the cell (to edit directly in the cell), or click on the cell and move your pointer to the formula bar and edit the entry there. Press Enter to have Excel evaluate the formula.

Copying and Moving Formulas

Recall that you learned in Chapter 8 how to copy formulas from one cell to another. You can click on the cell that contains the formula and select **E**dit, **C**opy from the menu bar, then move the insertion point to the new cell and select **E**dit, **P**aste. The results of the calculation appear in the cell.

Tip

A quicker way to copy a formula to an adjacent cell (one that is above, below, to the right, or to the left) is to use the mouse. Click on the cell that contains the formula and move the mouse pointer to the lower right corner of the cell border. Grab the cell handle that appears and move the selection into the cells where you want to copy the formula. Then release the mouse button.

When you copy a formula, you usually have a number of calculations to perform in a worksheet that use the same formula but have different cell references. The worksheet shown in figure 9.11, for example, has the monthly sales earnings for January through June. Cell H4 shows the total earnings for Janet Wiedmann through June. The formula to calculate this result is the following, as displayed in the formula bar:

=SUM(B4:G4)

Figure 9.11

Creating a formula that can be copied.

H4	▼	=SUM(B4:G4)					

Sales-94

	A	B	C	D	E	F	G	H
1	Sales Results Jan–Jun 1994							
2								
3	Employee Name	Jan-94	Feb-94	Mar-94	Apr-94	May-94	Jun-94	Employee Total
4	Janet Wiedmann	4161	3745	4173	4667	4266	4755	$25,767
5	Jody Hudson	5115	4801	6111	5824	6310	6811	
6	Paula Plager	3203	2753	3332	3428	3729	3919	
7	Kevin Merrick	1712	2104	2312	2535	2727	3105	
8	Pam Mahoney	2387	1947	2582	2274	2845	2242	
9	Lisa Williams	1663	1366	1962	2171	1984	2081	
10	Bob Snyder	1735	1355	2398	1798	1806	1812	

Ready   SUM=$25,767   NUM

Now that you have this formula written, you can use it to add the totals for the other salespeople. When you copy the formula into another cell, Excel assumes that you want to use the same general formula, but the cell references are to be changed. That is, to calculate Jody Hudson's total, you want to use cell references B5:G5, not B4:G4 as in the original formula. The other salespeople also have their own data that needs to be calculated.

How does Excel know which cell references to use? This is known as *relative reference format* in Excel. When you create a formula that asks Excel to "add the contents of cells B4:G4," Excel interprets this as "adding the contents of the cell six rows to the left (cell B4), to the contents of the cell five rows to the left (cell C4), to the contents of the cell four rows to the left (cell D4), to the contents . . ." until all are added and displayed in H4.

When you copy this formula to H5 to add Jody Hudson's sales numbers, Excel automatically adjusts the cell references but interprets the formula the same. In this case, Excel interprets the formula as "add the contents of the cell six rows to the left (cell B5), to the contents of the cell five rows to the left (cell C5), to the contents of the cell four rows to the left (cell D5), to the contents . . ." until all are added and displayed in H5.

Sometimes, however, you cannot just copy a formula from one cell to another and get the correct results. This occurs when you have some references that change in a formula *(relative references)* and some that do not. Those that do not are called *absolute references*. When you use absolute references in a formula, Excel uses the specific cell reference that you enter, regardless of where you copy the formula.

You might, for example, want to add another formula to the worksheet shown in figure 9.11 that determines the total sales quota for the next six months for each salesperson, and the quota is two-and-one-half times the total amount they produced in the first six months. This quota index is placed on the worksheet in cell C18 as 2.5. The formula is =H4*C18 and is created in J4 for Janet Wiedmann.

When you copy the formula to another cell using the techniques you have learned, Excel assumes it is working with a relative reference format and you get $0 in the cells, which obviously is the wrong sales quota (see fig. 9.12). You get this result because Excel interpreted your copied formula to mean "multiply the number that is 2 columns to the left by the number that is 14 rows down and 7 columns to the left." When you copy the formula to Jody Hudson's row (J5), Excel cannot find a value that is "14 rows down and 7 columns to the left," so it multiplies the number 2 columns to the left (in this case, $34,972) by 0.

Figure 9.12

Using relative references does not always work when copying formulas.

	A	B	C	D	E	F	G	H
1	Sales Results Jan–Jun 1994							
2								
3	Employee Name	Jan-94	Feb-94	Mar-94	Apr-94	May-94	Jun-94	Employee Total
4	Janet Wiedmann	4161	3745	4173	4667	4266	4755	$25,767
5	Jody Hudson	5115	4801	6111	5824	6310	6811	0.00
6	Paula Plager	3203	2753	3332	3428	3729	3919	0.00
7	Kevin Merrick	1712	2104	2312	2535	2727	3105	0.00
8	Pam Mahoney	2387	1947	2582	2274	2845	2242	0.00
9	Lisa Williams	1663	1366	1962	2171	1984	2081	0.00

To get the correct results, use Excel's absolute reference format to anchor the number that you want to use in all the formulas. The anchored value is the cell reference that does not change, regardless of where you copy or move a formula. In the example shown in figure 9.12, you need to anchor the quota index number (2.5) so that each salesperson's total value can be multiplied by this value. To distinguish between absolute and relative references in a formula, use a dollar sign ($) before the row and column of the cell address that you want to anchor—$C$18, for example.

The following steps show the way to set up the example worksheet by using absolute references and then copying the formula to other cells. For this example, the figures and formulas entered in figure 9.11 are already in the worksheet:

1. Use the numbers shown in figure 9.11 (or enter your own, but it is easier to follow along if you simulate the example we use).

2. In cell J4, type the formula **=H5*$C$18** and press Enter. The result of the calculation is $64,417.50.

 Tip Use Shift+F4 to switch between absolute and relative references.

3. Copy the formula into cells J5:J13 to calculate the new quotas for the rest of the sales force. To do this, click on cell J4 and grab the handle at the bottom right side of the cell border.

4. Drag the selection down to cell J13 and release the mouse button. The new values appear in the selected cells, showing the sales quota for the rest of the staff (see fig. 9.13).

 Tip You can use absolute references to anchor part of a cell reference. You can, for example, anchor just the column part or row part of the reference. To do this, place the dollar sign in front of the column address or the row address, depending on which part you want to anchor. You might want to do this if the column you refer to in a formula stays the same but the row changes with each calculation.

Sales-94										
A	**B**	**C**	**D**	**E**	**F**	**G**	**H**	**I**	**J**	**K**
2										
3 **Employee Name**	**Jan-94**	**Feb-94**	**Mar-94**	**Apr-94**	**May-94**	**Jun-94**	**Employee Total**		**New Quota**	
4 Janet Wiedmann	4161	3745	4173	4667	4266	4755	$25,767		$64,417.50	
5 Jody Hudson	5115	4801	6111	5824	6310	6811	$34,972		$87,430.00	
6 Paula Plager	3203	2753	3332	3428	3729	3919	$20,364		$50,908.75	
7 Kevin Merrick	1712	2104	2312	2535	2727	3105	$14,495		$36,237.50	
8 Pam Mahoney	2387	1947	2582	2274	2845	2242	$14,277		$35,692.50	
9 Lisa Williams	1663	1366	1962	2171	1984	2081	$11,227		$28,067.50	
10 Bob Snyder	1735	1355	2398	1798	1806	1812	$10,904		$27,260.00	
11 Glen Kaufman	1766	1570	2278	1904	1742	2183	$11,443		$28,607.50	
12 Beth Hooper	1681	1403	1707	1853	1921	2123	$10,688		$26,720.00	
13 Peter Owens	1569	1755	1828	1935	1714	1720	$10,521		$26,302.50	
14										
15 Monthly Totals	$24,992	$22,799	$28,683	$28,389	$29,044	$30,751	$164,658			

Figure 9.13

Copying the quota formula using Excels absolute reference format.

Referencing Another Worksheet in a Formula

If you have a lot of data and you create many worksheets to store this data, you might have occasions when a formula in one worksheet needs to use data from another sheet. These *sheet references* are handy so that you do not have to create redundant data in numerous sheets.

To refer to another cell in another sheet, place an exclamation mark between the sheet name and cell name. You might, for instance, write a formula in cell A9 in Sheet1 that needs to reference cell B5 in Sheet2. This reference looks like SHEET2!B5. (Use the sheet name in place of SHEET2 if you have named the sheet.)

Tip   When the sheet name contains spaces, such as Sales 94, you need to place single quotation marks around it when you are making sheet references.

If you are not sure of the cell reference in another sheet, you can start writing your formula and switch to the sheet that you want to reference when you get to that part of the formula. Then use your mouse and click on the cell or range of cells that you want in your formula. The cell or range reference appears automatically in your formula. You then can finish your formula and press Enter to calculate it.

Using 3D References

What if you have a formula that needs to reference a cell range that has two or more sheets in a workbook? This might happen if you have identical worksheets for different sales teams, regions, or states. You also might have several different worksheets that have totals calculated and entered in identical cell addresses. You then can add all these totals to get a grand total by referencing all the sheets and cell addresses in one formula.

When you have cell ranges such as this, Excel refers to them as *3D references.* A 3D reference is set up by including a *sheet range,* which names the beginning and ending sheets, and a *cell range,* which names the cells to which you are referring. A formula that uses a 3D reference that includes Sheet1 through Sheet10 and the cells A5:A10 might look something like the following:

=SUM(SHEET1:SHEET10!A5:A10)

Another way to include 3D references in your formulas is to use the mouse and click on the worksheets that you want to include in your formula. To do this, start your formula in the cell where you want the results. When you come to the point where you need to use the 3D reference, click on the first worksheet tab that you want to include in your reference, hold down Shift, click on the last worksheet that you want to include, and select the cells you want to reference. When you finish writing your formula, press Enter.

Calculating a Formula

As soon as you enter a formula (that is, type it and press Enter), Excel automatically calculates it. You might not want Excel to do this all the time, however, if you have created a complex, time-consuming calculation that you don't want to do right away. Or, you might want to write a formula before you get all the data in the worksheet.

To tell Excel not to calculate a formula automatically, perform the following steps:

1. Select **T**ool, **O**ptions. This displays the Options dialog box.

2. Click on the Calculation tab to display the calculations options (see fig. 9.14).

Figure 9.14

The Calculation tab in the Options dialog box.

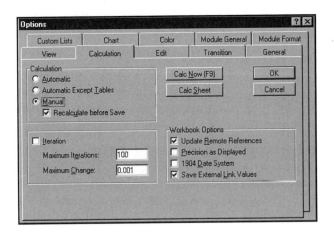

3. Click on the **M**anual option. You also can set up Excel to calculate the worksheet automatically, except items in a table, which you can calculate manually by clicking on the Automatic Except **T**ables option.

The Calc **N**ow (F9) button can be used to calculate all your open worksheets. Or, you can use the Calc **S**heet button to calculate only the active worksheet. You can press F9 while you are working in the worksheet to calculate all open worksheets; you do not have to open this dialog box every time you want to calculate your worksheet. Press Shift+F9 to calculate the active worksheet.

4. When you choose the **M**anual option, you then can decide whether to have Excel calculate before you save the worksheet by clicking the Recalc**u**late before Save option.

5. Press Enter or click on OK.

Viewing Worksheet Formulas

As you learned in Chapter 8, Excel displays the formula for a selected cell in the formula bar and the results of the calculation in the cell. You might, however, find this inconvenient if you want to view all your formulas at once. To see the formula in a single cell, select the cell and press Ctrl+'. To see all the cells displayed as formulas, perform the following steps:

1. Select **T**ools, **O**ptions.

2. Click on the View tab to display the View options (see fig. 9.15).

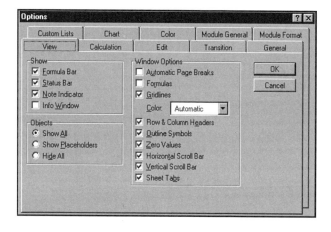

Figure 9.15

The View tab of the Options dialog box.

3. Click on the Fo**r**mulas check box in the Window Options group. This tells Excel to display formulas instead of values.

4. Press Enter or click on OK.

Using Arrays in Formulas

In the worksheet in the preceding examples, notice how there are several areas that use the same formulas but have different cell references. The Employee Total column, for example, uses the same SUM formula to calculate each of the employees' sales numbers.

When you have situations such as this, you can save system memory and time by using an *array formula,* a rectangular range of formulas that is treated as one group. Excel denotes array formulas by placing braces ({}) around them. Excel automatically places these braces; you do not have to place them yourself.

To enter an array formula, perform the following steps:

1. Select the range that you want to contain the array formula.

2. Enter the formula and use the range coordinates for the area you want to include in the array formula. You also can use the mouse to select this area.

3. Finish the formula.

4. Press Shift+Ctrl+Enter to tell Excel to make this formula an array formula. Excel places braces around the formula.

Tip   You cannot insert cells or rows within an array, edit a single cell in an array, or delete part of an array. You can edit an array by double-clicking on the array range. Edit the array formula and press Shift+Ctrl+Enter.

Formatting Your Worksheet

Once you enter your data and set up some formulas, your worksheet is functional, but it might not look very appealing. You might, for instance, want to highlight certain columns in your sheet, use color-coded cells, change fonts, or format dates, numbers, and times to improve the appearance of your worksheet.

Alignment

When you enter data into a cell, it aligns automatically to Excel's default. For text, this alignment is left-justified. For numbers, this alignment is right-justified. However, you might want to center the text or align the numbers along the left side of the cell. Excel enables you to align data in a number of different ways by using the Alignment tab in the Format Cells dialog box (see fig. 9.16). To use this option, select Format, Cells and click on the Alignment tab.

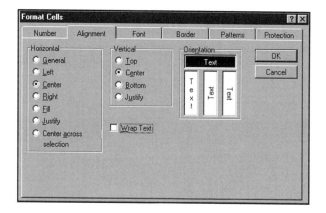

Figure 9.16
*Use the Alignment
tab to customize
the way data
aligns in the cells.*

These are the options that you can choose:

◆ **General.** Displays the data in the default alignment.

◆ **Left.** Left-aligns the data in the cell.

◆ **Center.** Centers the data in the cell.

◆ **Right.** Right-aligns the data in the cell.

◆ **Fill.** Repeats the data in the cell until the cell is full.

◆ **Justify.** Aligns the data in the cell with the left and right edges of the cell when you have more than one line of text in the cell.

◆ **Center across selection.** Centers the data in the cell across the range you select.

 Tip   The Formatting toolbar contains buttons for aligning text, including the Left, Center, and Right Align buttons. You also can center text across cells by using the Center Text in Selection button.

When you use the Center across selection option, you can set up titles in your worksheets easily. In Chapter 8, for instance, you centered the title "American Conference" over your data.

Later in this chapter you are shown how to modify the height and width of rows and columns. When you do, you can change the way the cell contents are aligned vertically by using the options in the Vertical section of the Alignment tab. You can, for instance, align the data at the top of the cell with the **T**op option. Use the C**e**nter option to align the data in the center of the cell. The **B**ottom option is used to place the data at the bottom of the cell. **Ju**stify is used to justify the data in the cell vertically.

Another problem that you can overcome easily with the alignment options is a long text entry. In figure 9.17, for instance, the text in cell B4 overlaps several neighboring cells. To correct this problem, click in the **W**rap Text check box on the Alignment tab to have Excel automatically adjust the height of the cell to accommodate several lines of text. Notice in figure 9.17 how cell D6 is large enough to contain all its text, making it easier to read.

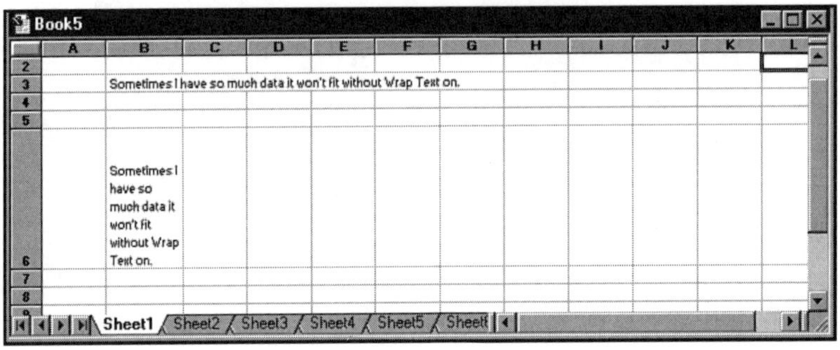

Figure 9.17

The Wrap Text option enables you to place several lines of text in a cell.

You might want to have text displayed in several different ways. This is handled by the Orie**n**tation section of the Alignment tab. The default selection is horizontal. You can choose the vertical option so that the text reads from top to bottom. Or, you might want to read the text sideways, reading top to bottom with the text rotated 90 degrees counterclockwise or 90 degrees clockwise. These latter options are handy when you need vertical titles for reports or charts. (See Chapter 12, "Excel Charts and Graphics," for more information regarding creating and formatting charts.)

Tabs and Carriage Returns

Most computer users are comfortable using a word processor to type text and do elementary tasks such as tabbing and starting new paragraphs. In most word processing applications, you press Tab to tab over or press Enter to start a new paragraph. In Excel, however, these tasks are not as intuitive.

If you press Enter while you are typing text, Excel interprets this as the end of your entry and enters the contents into the cell. Similarly, when you type text and then press Tab, Excel enters what you have typed and moves over to the next cell. To place a carriage return in a cell entry, press Alt+Enter. To place a tab in a cell entry, press Alt+Ctrl+Tab. By using tabs and carriage returns in your cell entries, you have more control over how your final worksheet looks.

Tip You can delete Tab and carriage returns as you do any other character in a cell. First select the cell, press F2 for editing, and press Del to delete the Tab or return.

Fonts

The numbers, letters, and other characters that appear on your screen all belong to a certain font. A *font* is the typeface, type size, and type style of a certain character. With Windows 95, you can use TrueType fonts, a specially designed font that you can resize and print with semiprecision. That is, what you see on-screen in your worksheet will be what you should see when it is printed (or a close resemblance to it).

The size, type, and variations of fonts you use help make your worksheet stand out among other reports. Keep in mind that when you format your worksheets you ultimately intend to have someone (maybe just you) look over it. For this reason, make your worksheets easy to use, to the point, and functional. A functional worksheet does not have to be drab in appearance or intimidating.

You might, for instance, change the point size from the default 12 points to a larger 14- or 16-point size. You can make the text bold, italic, or underlined. Along with centering titles or justifying text, you can add these subtle formatting changes to make your text pop off the page. Compare the worksheets in figures 9.18 and 9.19. Both contain the same data and text. Which one are you more likely to read?

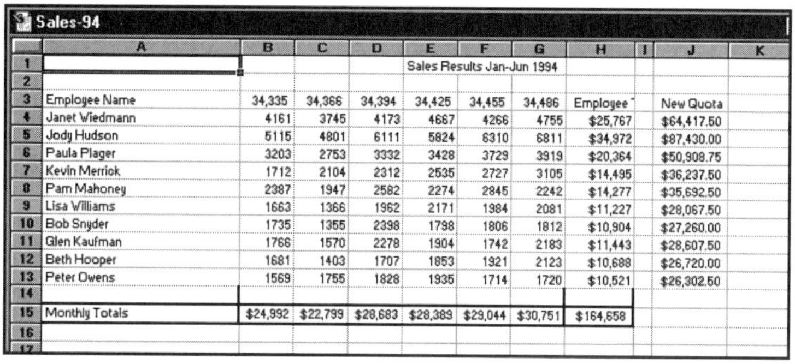

Figure 9.18

A worksheet without formatting enhancements.

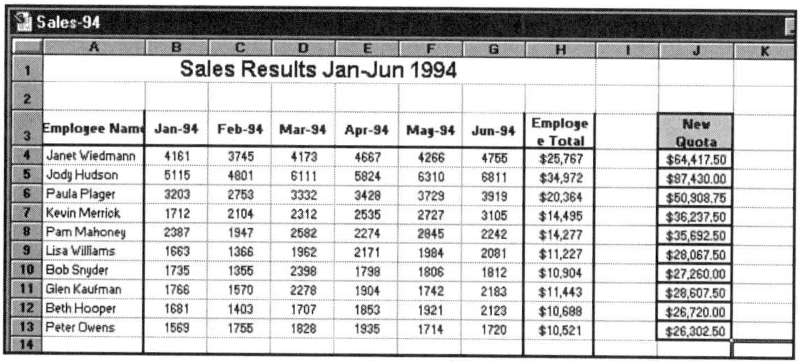

	A	B	C	D	E	F	G	H	I	J	K
1						Sales Results Jan-Jun 1994					
2											
3	Employee Name	34,335	34,366	34,394	34,425	34,455	34,486	Employee		New Quota	
4	Janet Wiedmann	4161	3745	4173	4667	4266	4755	$25,767		$64,417.50	
5	Jody Hudson	5115	4801	6111	5824	6310	6811	$34,972		$87,430.00	
6	Paula Plager	3203	2753	3332	3428	3729	3919	$20,364		$50,908.75	
7	Kevin Merriok	1712	2104	2312	2535	2727	3105	$14,495		$36,237.50	
8	Pam Mahoney	2387	1947	2582	2274	2845	2242	$14,277		$35,692.50	
9	Lisa Williams	1663	1366	1962	2171	1984	2081	$11,227		$28,067.50	
10	Bob Snyder	1735	1355	2398	1798	1806	1812	$10,904		$27,260.00	
11	Glen Kaufman	1766	1570	2278	1904	1742	2183	$11,443		$28,607.50	
12	Beth Hooper	1681	1403	1707	1853	1921	2123	$10,688		$26,720.00	
13	Peter Owens	1569	1755	1828	1935	1714	1720	$10,521		$26,302.50	
14											
15	Monthly Totals		$24,992	$22,799	$28,683	$28,389	$29,044	$30,751	$164,658		
16											
17											

Figure 9.19

The same worksheet with font enhancements.

	A	B	C	D	E	F	G	H	I	J	K
1			Sales Results Jan-Jun 1994								
2											
3	Employee Name	Jan-94	Feb-94	Mar-94	Apr-94	May-94	Jun-94	Employee Total		New Quota	
4	Janet Wiedmann	4161	3745	4173	4667	4266	4755	$25,767		$64,417.50	
5	Jody Hudson	5115	4801	6111	5824	6310	6811	$34,972		$87,430.00	
6	Paula Plager	3203	2753	3332	3428	3729	3919	$20,364		$50,908.75	
7	Kevin Merriok	1712	2104	2312	2535	2727	3105	$14,495		$36,237.50	
8	Pam Mahoney	2387	1947	2582	2274	2845	2242	$14,277		$35,692.50	
9	Lisa Williams	1663	1366	1962	2171	1984	2081	$11,227		$28,067.50	
10	Bob Snyder	1735	1355	2398	1798	1806	1812	$10,904		$27,260.00	
11	Glen Kaufman	1766	1570	2278	1904	1742	2183	$11,443		$28,607.50	
12	Beth Hooper	1681	1403	1707	1853	1921	2123	$10,688		$26,720.00	
13	Peter Owens	1569	1755	1828	1935	1714	1720	$10,521		$26,302.50	
14											

Some of the most common character enhancing options are available on the default formatting toolbar. You probably will use this toolbar throughout the time you create your worksheets and enter data. The options available to help you change your font characteristics include the following (see fig. 9.20):

Figure 9.20

Character formatting options on the formatting toolbar.

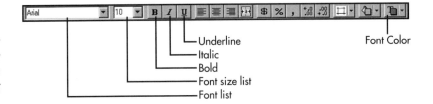

◆ **Font drop-down list.** Use this list to choose the font for the selection.

◆ **Font Size list.** Use this list to change the point size of the selected entry.

◆ **Bold, Italic, Underline buttons.** These buttons enable you to add bold, italic, and underline font styles to your selection.

◆ **Font Color.** Add a little color to your entries by changing the color of the selection from black to a number of different colors. You might, for instance, use red to denote late payments.

If you want to use a dialog box interface to change the selected character(s), select Format, Cells and click on the Font tab. This displays the Font tab options (see fig. 9.21):

Figure 9.21

The Font tab options.

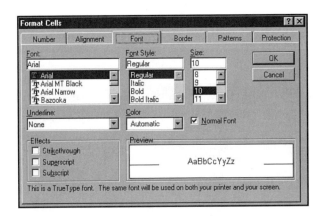

◆ **Font.** This option enables you to choose the font for the selection. TrueType fonts appear with a double-T logo next to them. Printer fonts appear with a printer icon next to them.

◆ **Font Style.** Use this list to add character enhancements, such as regular (also know as *roman*), italic, bold, and bold italic.

◆ **Size.** This option enables you to select a different point size for your selection.

◆ **Underline.** This drop-down list enables you to select the type of underlining you want for your selection, such as None, Single, Double, and Single or Double Accounting. Accounting underlines only the numbers in a cell, not the entire cell.

◆ **Color.** Use this list to select a color for your selection. You might want to experiment with the way different colors print. Use Automatic for black-and-white printers if you do not want to take any chances.

◆ **Normal Font.** This check box enables you to select Excel's default font. Chapter 14, "Customizing Excel for Windows 95," discusses changing Excel's default settings.

◆ **Effects.** This area enables you to add Strikethrough, Superscript, and Subscript characteristics to your selection.

The Preview window in the lower right corner of the tab screen lets you view what the changes will do to your selection.

Tip

A printer font is used to print your worksheets and charts from preinstalled fonts in your printer or in cartridges you can plug into the printer. PostScript fonts, for example, are printer fonts. You also can download fonts from your computer to the printer's memory.

When you use a printer font, another font is used to display the characters on your screen. These screen fonts usually are installed when you install your printer in Windows 95. You might see some differences between what is on-screen and what actually prints, because the screen fonts might not always have the same font size and styles that the printer font has. You usually will use TrueType fonts when working with worksheets, but you can invest in some professional-quality printer fonts that will add much more to your final presentation.

Numeric Formats

In Chapter 8 you were introduced to the different types of numeric formats that Excel offers. Because spreadsheet applications are designed around conveying numeric data, the format your numbers are in is probably the most crucial part of your worksheet. The way you format your numeric data is up to you, but you should be consistent in the way you handle numbers from worksheet to worksheet in each workbook.

The following are ways that you might want to handle numeric data: make all negative numbers a different color, such as red or blue; use commas for thousands separators.

Excel provides several built-in number formats (see table 9.3), and also enables you to create your own number formats. (For more information on creating your own number formats, pick up a copy of *Inside Excel for Windows 95,* published by New Riders Publishing.)

TABLE 9.3
Excel's Built-In Number Formats

Format Category	Format Setting	Examples Positive	Negative
All	General	4500.75	–4500.75
Custom	Lists custom formats (if any)		
Number	0	4501	–4501
	0.00	4500.75	–4500.75
	#,##0	4,501	–4,501
	#,##0.00	4,500.75	–4,500.75
	#,##0_);(#,##0)	4,501	(4,501)
	#,##0_);[Red](##,##0)	4,501	(4501)*
	#,##0.00);(#,##0.00)	4,500.75	(4,500.75)
	#,##0.00_);[Red](#,##0.00)	4,500.75	(4,500.75)*
Accounting	_(*#,##0_);_(#,##0);_(*"-"_);_(@_)	4,500	(4,500)
	_(*#,##0.00_);_(*(#,##0.00);_(*"-"??_);_(@_)	4,500.75	(4,500.75)
	_($*#,##0_);_($*(#,##0):_($*"-"_);_(@_)	$4,500	$(4,500)
	_($*#,##0.00_);_($(#,##0.00);_($*"_"??);_(@_)	$4,500.75	$(4,500.75)
Percentage	0%	45%	–45%
	0.00%	45.75%	–45.75%
Fraction	#?/?	45 3/4	–45 3/4
	#??/??	45 31/42	–45 31/42
Scientific	0.00E+00	4.5E+04	–4.5E+04

Format Category	Format Setting	Examples Positive	Negative
Text	@ (Text placeholder)		
Currency	$#,##0_);($#,##0)	$4,501	($4,501)
	$#,##0_);[Red]($#,##0)	$4,501	($4,501)*
	$#,##0.00_);($#,##0.00)	$4,500.75	($4,500.75)
	$#,##0.00_);[Red]($#,##0.00)	$4,500.75	($4,500.75)*

*Denotes red numbers when a negative value appears

To apply a format to an individual cell or range, select that cell or range and perform the following steps:

1. Select **F**ormat, C**e**lls to display the Format Cells dialog box.

2. Click on the Number tab to activate it (see fig. 9.22).

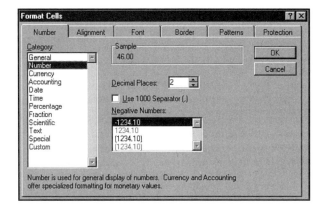

Figure 9.22

Use the Number tab to select number formatting.

3. In the **C**ategory list box, click on the type of number that you want to format, such as General, Number, or Percentage. When you select a category, the choices available for that category are shown. For example, for Numbers you can choose the number of decimal places, the Thousands separator, and a format for negative numbers. If the selected cell has data, the Sample section will display that data in the highlighted format.

4. For more choices, choose Custom in the Category list, and the list in the Type box changes to show the format settings listed in table 9.3.

5. Press Enter or click on OK.

If you want a quicker way to apply common number formats, you can use keyboard shortcuts. The following list shows the key combination and the format code that is applied:

Key Combination	Format Code
Ctrl+Shift+~	General
Ctrl+Shift+!	0.00
Ctrl+Shift+$	$#,##0.00;($#,##0.00)
Ctrl+Shift+%	0%
Ctrl+Shift+^	0.00E+00

When you enter your numeric data, you can specify the type of format you want applied to the number by adding certain characters, such as the dollar sign ($) and percentage sign (%). To enter a dollar amount, begin your entry with a dollar sign, enter the numeric data, and press Enter. Excel interprets your entry as a Currency format. To enter a percent, type the number, then add a percent sign (%) after it. Excel interprets this as the Percentage format and enters it as such.

Tip A quick way to display the Number dialog box is to select the cell that you want to format, click the right mouse button, and select Format Cells from the pop-up menu. This immediately displays the Format Cells dialog box, enabling you to add or change number formats.

Modifying Columns

One of the common problems you run into with any spreadsheet application, including Excel, is the default size of the cells. They usually are too small to hold all the data you want to place in them. Excel for Windows 95 makes it easier to resize the rows and columns of your worksheets.

Recall that when you enter a number, or after a calculation is evaluated, you might have cells that contain #### characters. These characters tell you that the cell is not large enough to display the number. You need to widen the column to display the number.

You can change one or several columns by performing the following steps:

1. Select the cells in the column that you want to widen. Select a cell in each column that you want to adjust if you are resizing multiple columns.

2. Select Format, Column to display the pop-out menu shown in figure 9.23.

Figure 9.23

Formatting columns.

The Column options provide you with the following choices:

◆ **Width.** This option enables you to modify the selected columns to a width based on the Normal font. When you select this option, the Column Width dialog box appears (see fig. 9.24). You can enter a specific width in the **C**olumn Width field box.

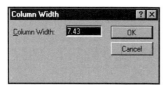

Figure 9.24

Use the Column Width dialog box to enter a specific column width.

◆ **AutoFit Selection.** This option probably is the most convenient option to use because it modifies the column widths to accommodate the widest cell contents in your selection. When you choose this option, Excel automatically increases or decreases the size of the selected columns to best fit your entries.

◆ **Hide.** You can hide specific columns to keep sensitive data secure. You learn more about this option later in this chapter.

◆ **Unhide.** Use this option to unhide hidden columns. This option is discussed in more detail later.

◆ **Standard Width.** This option enables you to select the default standard column width for the selected columns. When you select this option, the Standard Width dialog box appears (see fig. 9.25). You can press Enter or click on OK to accept the default width. Or, you can change the default column width by changing the value in the **S**tandard Column Width field box. The standard column width is 8.43 characters, the number of characters that can be displayed in the cell in the normal font.

3. Press Enter or click on OK to accept your choice.

Figure 9.25

*You can change
the standard
column width in
the Standard
Width dialog box.*

Tip
To change columns quickly, use your mouse. Select the columns you want to modify and move the pointer onto the column separator directly to the right of the column heading (see fig. 9.26). Drag the column left or right until the column is the width that you want. Release the mouse button.

Figure 9.26

*Move the mouse
pointer to the
column separator
in the column
heading to modify
column widths.*

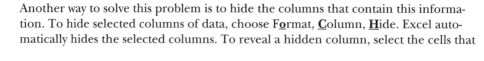

	A	B	C	D	E	F	G	H
2								
3	Employee Name	Jan-94	Feb-94	Mar-94	Apr-94	May-94	Jun-94	Employee Total
4	Janet Wiedmann	4161	3745	4173	4667	4266	4755	$25,767
5	Jody Hudson	5115	4801	6111	5824	6310	6811	$34,972
6	Paula Plager	3203	2753	3332	3428	3729	3919	$20,364
7	Kevin Merrick	1712	2104	2312	2535	2727	3105	$14,495
8	Pam Mahoney	2387	1947	2582	2274	2845	2242	$14,277
9	Lisa Williams	1663	1366	1962	2171	1984	2081	$11,227
10	Bob Snyder	1735	1355	2398	1798	1806	1812	$10,904
11	Glen Kaufman	1766	1570	2278	1904	1742	2183	$11,443
12	Beth Hooper	1681	1403	1707	1853	1921	2123	$10,688

Sheet1 / Sheet2 / Sheet3 / Sheet4 / Sheet5 / Sheet6 /

Ready | SUM=329315 | NUM

Tip
If you want to fit the column to the widest cell entry, move your mouse pointer to the column heading and double-click on the column separator. This automatically modifies the selected column to fit the widest entry.

Hiding Columns

If you have a budget worksheet, some of the information will be shared with your management and staff, but some, such as management salaries, should not be available to all readers. To get around this problem, you can create two separate worksheets—one with salaries and one without. This, however, separates key data that you need to include in your total budget expectation.

Another way to solve this problem is to hide the columns that contain this information. To hide selected columns of data, choose F**o**rmat, **C**olumn, **H**ide. Excel automatically hides the selected columns. To reveal a hidden column, select the cells that

New Riders Publishing
INSIDE
SERIES

span the hidden column and choose F**o**rmat, **C**olumn, **U**nhide. The hidden column appears.

Tip

To hide a column using the mouse, move the mouse pointer over the column separator that is to the right of the column heading you want to hide. When the pointer changes to a two-headed pointer, drag the column separator left until it is past the separator on its left.

Reverse the process to unhide the column. Move the pointer until it touches the column separator on the right of a hidden column. The pointer then changes to a two-headed pointer with space between the two heads. Move the pointer so that its left tip touches the column separator, and drag the separator to the right. Release the mouse button, and the column is revealed.

Modifying Rows

Row size also might be a problem for the type of data you use. The standard row height, for example, usually is not large enough to display readable text or make large enough worksheet titles. You also might want to add more space between different types of numbers, such as monthly and annual totals.

You can adjust the height of rows much the same way you can columns. The standard row height is 12.75 points, enabling it to fit the default Excel font, Arial 10 point.

Tip

If you change the point size of a font, to 20 points, for example, Excel automatically resizes the row height to fit the new font size. You do not need to adjust the row height manually.

To change the row height of selected rows, perform the following steps:

1. Select the rows you want to resize.

2. Select F**o**rmat, **R**ow to display the pop-out menu shown in figure 9.27.

Figure 9.27

Use the Row option to change the appearance of selected rows.

The Row options provide you with the following choices:

◆ **Height.** Use this option to enter a specific height for the selected rows. When you select this option, the Row Height dialog box appears (see fig. 9.28). Fill in the desired height in the **R**ow Height field box.

Figure 9.28

Use the Height option to specify row heights precisely.

◆ **AutoFit.** Use this option to change the row height quickly to accommodate the best fit for the row. This option is nice if you don't want to mess around with changing row heights manually.

◆ **Hide.** This option enables you to hide selected rows. You learn more about this later in this chapter.

◆ **Unhide.** This option enables you to unhide selected rows. You learn more about this later.

3. Press Enter or choose OK when you specify the row height in the **R**ow Height field box.

Tip

To change row heights quickly, use your mouse. Select the line under the row header you want to modify and drag the pointer up or down until the row height is what you want. Release the mouse button.

If you want to change the row to fit the tallest entries in a cell, move your mouse pointer to the row heading and double-click on the row separator. This automatically modifies the selected row to fit the tallest entry.

Hiding Rows

If you have data entered in certain rows in your worksheets that you want to hide, select those rows and choose Format, **R**ow, **H**ide. You then can reveal the rows by selecting the cells that span the hidden rows, as you learned earlier in this chapter.

Tip

To hide a row using the mouse, move the mouse pointer over the row separator that is below the row heading you want to hide. When the pointer changes to a two-headed pointer, drag the row separator up until it is past the separator above it.

Reverse the process to unhide the row. Move the pointer over the row number that is under the hidden row until it changes to a two-headed pointer with space between the two heads. Drag the line down to reveal the row.

Mastering Borders, Patterns, and Colors

Pick up your favorite magazine and notice how the layout adds to the readability of the information. Most of the design features that professional designers employ are subtle, yet effective: colors, borders, shading, and patterns. Excel for Windows 95 enables you to improve the presentation of your worksheets with these same tools.

Borders

One of the easiest ways to enhance the appearance of your worksheets is to add borders to cells or ranges of data. You can, for instance, add a border around a table of data, use borders to highlight totals, or place a border to call attention to data-entry areas on your worksheets. Excel gives you a number of different borders, as shown in figure 9.29.

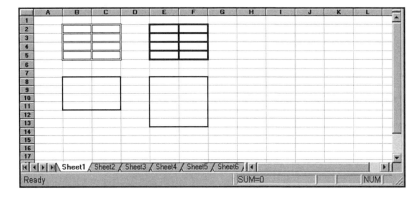

Figure 9.29

Use borders to enhance your worksheets.

The quickest way to add a border to a selected cell or range of cells is to use the Border button on the Formatting toolbar:

1. Select the cell or range of cells that you want to enclose in a border.

2. Click on the down arrow on the Border button to display the borders list box (see fig. 9.30).

Figure 9.30

Click on the down arrow on the Borders button to display the borders choices.

3. Pick the border style you want to use and click on it. This places the selected border around your selection.

Tip

One of the features of Excel is the use of tear-off menus and tools. If you plan to use the Border button several times in succession, you can "tear" it off the toolbar and let it float on your desktop. To do this, click on the down arrow on the Border button, grab the border list with your mouse, and drag it to someplace convenient on your desktop. When you release the mouse button, the border list floats on your worksheet, waiting for you to use it.

Another way to select borders for your worksheets is to use the Border tab in the Format Cells dialog box. To access this dialog box, select F**o**rmat, **C**ell, and click on the Border tab (see fig. 9.31).

Figure 9.31

Use the Border tab to select borders.

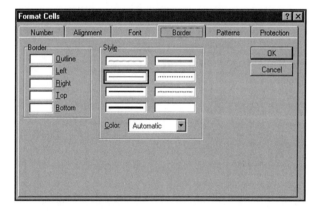

The Border tab contains the following options:

◆ **Outline.** Use this option when you want to add a border to the outside edges of your selection.

◆ **Left.** This option applies a border to the left edge of the selection.

◆ **Right.** This option applies a border to the right edge of the selection.

◆ **Top.** This option applies a border to the top edge of the selection.

◆ **Bottom.** This option applies a border to the bottom edge of the selection.

◆ **Style.** This option shows the eight different border styles you can choose, including double lines, dashed lines, thin lines, and so on.

◆ **Color.** Use this pull-down list box to apply different colors to your borders. Keep in mind that these colors do not print if you have a black-and-white printer. You can, however, achieve high-quality and easier-to-read worksheets using various color schemes with your borders.

Patterns

Another effective tool for formatting your worksheets is the use of patterns. Excel enables you to use patterns to add background effects to your lists, tables, and other entries. The patterns can be used for your printouts and for your on-screen or visual presentations. You can, for example, output your worksheet to Microsoft PowerPoint and use it in an overhead presentation. To make your worksheets more powerful, experiment with the patterns until you find ones that do not overpower the information in your sheets, but add to its effectiveness.

To apply patterns to your worksheets, use the Pattern tab in the Format Cells dialog box. Excel gives you many different types of patterns to choose from. To add a pattern to your selection, select F**o**rmat, **C**ells, and click on the Patterns tab (see fig. 9.32).

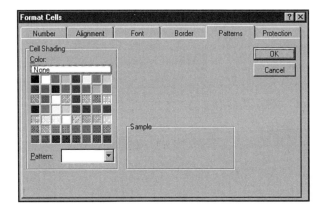

Figure 9.32

Apply patterns and shading to your worksheets with the Patterns tab.

Click on the **P**attern pull-down list box and examine the various types of patterns available to you. You can see an example of each one by clicking on it and looking at the Sample area of the dialog box. When you decide on a pattern, press Enter or click on OK. The pattern is applied to the worksheet selections.

Tip   You might want to set off a row, column, or specific cells that should not contain any data. To help you and others keep from entering data into these cells, use a pattern, such as a diagonal pattern, that makes it impossible to read the data.

Colors

As you have seen, Excel enables you to apply several different formatting enhancements to your worksheets. Probably the most effective and underused feature is color. You can brighten your on-screen presentations by effectively using color to point out areas of interest, key data points, or data-entry areas.

Stop   Although you should use as much color and shading as you can to enhance your worksheets, you should keep in mind your printing limitations. If you have a black-and-white printer, you cannot, of course, print color images.

Many times, these colors are converted to gray-scale images when you try to print them. If you have key data separated by color, such as a light blue and a yellow, these colors usually print as similar gray tones, making it nearly impossible to distinguish them from each other. The best way to determine what works best for your individual situation is to experiment with different shading and colors.

To apply colors to your cells or range of cells, perform the following steps:

1. Select the cell or range to which you want to add color.

2. Select Format, Cells.

3. If you want to add color to your border, click on the Border tab and, using the Color drop-down list box, choose the color you want.

   If you want to add color to your pattern, click on the Patterns tab and choose the color you want from the Color area. If you want a foreground color, click on the Pattern drop-down list box and select a color.

4. Press Enter or click on OK to apply the color to your selection.

Tip   You also can click on the Color button on the Formatting toolbar to add color to a cell. Click on the down arrow on the button and choose the color of your choice.

If you plan to use the Color button several times, remember to tear it off the toolbar and let it float on your workspace. To do this, click on the down arrow on the Color button to display the color list. Then, grab the color list with the mouse and drag it off the toolbar. When you release the mouse button, the color list floats on your desktop, enabling you to use it over and over.

Examining Advanced Printing Options

You learned in Chapter 8 how to use some of Excel for Windows 95's printing options and how to print your worksheets. This section adds to that discussion and shows you how to perform more sophisticated printing operations.

Setting Print Ranges

When you print a worksheet, Excel prints the entire worksheet by default. You can, however, adjust the print range to include only those cells or portions of worksheets that you want to print. To do this, use the **F**ile, Prin**t** Area command.

To set up a print area, perform the following steps:

1. Select **F**ile, Prin**t** Area, to display the choices (see fig. 9.33).

Figure 9.33

Choosing the portion of a worksheet for printing.

2. Choose **S**et Print Area.

3. Move your mouse pointer back to the area of your worksheet that you want to print and select the cells you want to print.

4. Choose **F**ile, **P**rint to display the Print dialog box (see figure 9.34). In the Print What section, choose Selectio**n**.

Figure 9.34

The Print dialog box configured to print a selected portion of the worksheet.

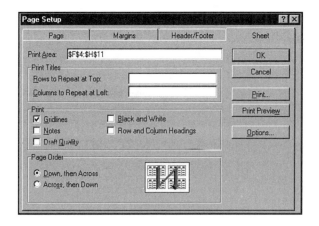

To remove the print range from Excel's memory, select **F**ile, Prin**t** Area, **C**lear Print Area.

You can edit the Print Area or select it by using the Sheet page of the Page Setup dialog box:

1. Choose **F**ile, Page Set**u**p to display the Page Setup dialog box.

2. Click the Sheet tab, then click in the Print **A**rea box.

3. To specify the print area, move your mouse pointer onto the worksheet and select the cells you want to print. If you have already selected the print area with the Print Area menu choice, but want to change it without re-selecting, edit the appropriate cell addresses that appear in the Print area box (see fig. 9.35).

Figure 9.35

The Sheet tab with Print Area options determining the printing selection.

Controlling Page Breaks

After you select the print range, you might want to modify a few of the print settings to make sure that what you want to print fits on a page. One such option inserts a page break to reposition an automatic page break that Excel has added to your worksheet.

When you insert manual page breaks, Excel inserts them above and to the left of where you have the insertion point (or the active cell). Another feature of Excel is that the manual page breaks appear as longer and darker dashed lines than automatic page breaks. If you cannot see the page breaks very well, turn off the gridlines. This helps automatic and manual page breaks stand out better.

Perform the following steps to insert manual page breaks:

1. Select the cell below and to the right of the place where you want a manual page break to be inserted.

Tip   To select a vertical page break, move the insertion point to row 1 of where you want the vertical break to be. If, for instance, you want a vertical page break to occur between columns D and E, move the insertion point to cell E1.

2. Choose **I**nsert, Page **B**reak. Excel places a manual page break at the point you specify.

To remove the manual page break, select the cell below and to the right of the page break. Choose **I**nsert, Remove Page **B**reak, which appears on the menu only when you select a manual page break to remove. If the menu item does not appear, you have not selected the correct cell in the worksheet. Try again.

If you want to remove all manual page breaks in your worksheets, select the entire worksheet and choose **I**nsert, Remove Page **B**reak. This clears all the manual page breaks. It does not, however, clear automatic page breaks, which cannot be removed. You can reposition them by inserting manual page breaks, as prescribed in the preceding steps.

Resizing Margins

Sometimes you create worksheets that contain a ton of data, but you do not want to print out pages and pages. You want to print out the fewest number of pages possible to get all your data on hardcopy reports. One way to do this is to reset page margins so that you can squeeze as much onto a page as possible.

Tip Check your individual printer to see what the minimum margin can be on your documents. Some printers must have at least a 1/4-inch margin on the paper's edge. This means, of course, that your worksheet margins must be at least 1/4 inch.

If you cannot fit everything on the page even by modifying the margins, try different fonts and font sizes until you find one that can fit everything you want on a page or a few pages. Keep in mind, too, that you need to be able to read the data, so don't choose a point size that is too small, such as 6 point. You would need to carry around a magnifying glass just to read your worksheets.

To change the margins in your worksheets, change to Print Preview mode first. This way you can see the entire page and resize the margins. To do this, choose <u>F</u>ile, Print Pre<u>v</u>iew, then perform the following steps:

1. Click on the <u>M</u>argins button in the Print Preview toolbar.

2. Move the mouse pointer to the margin or column you want to change. The pointer changes to a two-sided arrow indicating that you can drag the handle. Look in the status bar to see the margin size or column width of your selection.

3. Hold down the mouse button and drag the handle until it is placed where you want the new margin or column. Continue Steps 2 and 3 until your worksheet is set up as you want it.

Selecting Printers

If you have more than one printer set up under Windows, you might want to use more than one to print your worksheet, depending on the type of paper or other options available for a specific need. You might, for instance, choose to print out all your rough drafts on a dot-matrix printer to conserve laser printer resources. Or, you might have a color printer set up for your finished worksheets.

To select a printer that is not the default printer, select <u>F</u>ile, <u>P</u>rint, then click on the arrow to the right of the Printer box to see a list of printers (see fig. 9.36). Click on the printer of your choice. You also can click on the P<u>r</u>operties button to modify the printer's options.

Tip One way to dress up your printouts is to include titles on your worksheets. To do this, select <u>F</u>ile, Page Set<u>u</u>p and click on the Sheet tab. Click in the <u>R</u>ows to Repeat at Top text box or the <u>C</u>olumns to Repeat at Left text box to specify where you want the title to appear. Choose the rows or columns (they must be adjacent rows and columns) that you want to have printed on each page. Press Enter or click on OK.

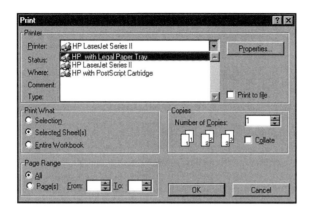

Figure 9.36

Choosing a different printer with the Print dialog box.

Mastering Excel Functions

This chapter introduces you to Excel for Windows 95 functions. *Functions* are tools you can use to analyze data and get information in the form of values. These values result from a calculation or group of calculations on information from your worksheets. Put another way, functions help give you answers to questions for evaluation, examination, and projections in your business. In this chapter, you will learn about the following:

- ◆ Using functions

- ◆ Using the Function Wizard

- ◆ Using add-ins

- ◆ Various mathematical and text functions

- ◆ Troubleshooting Excel functions

- ◆ Linking functions

If you are new to functions, you will find the first part of this chapter most helpful. If you are experienced with functions, you might want to go directly to the section containing the functions that you want to apply to your workbooks.

This chapter begins with a discussion of what functions are and the concepts behind them. Throughout this section you will use sample worksheets and workbooks and have an opportunity to practice using several popular functions. Each function has a step-by-step explanation of its use, purpose, and syntax.

For many of the function categories available in Excel, you will learn about several functions and see examples of how to use them. The following functions are covered in this chapter:

◆ **Financial.** FV is the future value. CUMIPMT is the cumulative interest payment. CUMPRINC is the cumulative principal payment. EFFECT is the effective annual interest rate. AMORDEGRC is the depreciation that prorates assets for accounting periods. AMORLINC is the depreciation that calculates on the life of assets for accounting periods.

◆ **Statistical.** AVERAGE averages a group of values. SUM adds a group of values. MAX returns the largest number in a group. MIN returns the smallest number in a group. RANK ranks values from largest to smallest, or vice versa.

◆ **Math and Trigonometry.** MEDIAN returns the median in a group of values. ABS returns an absolute value for a number or range of numbers. COUNTIF counts the number of cells in a range, if they are not blank and if certain conditions are satisfied. EVEN and ODD round numbers to the nearest integer as even or odd. MOD returns the remainder of a division calculation. PI returns the value of pi. ROMAN converts Arabic numerals to roman numerals. ROUND rounds numbers to specific levels. ROUNDDOWN rounds numbers down. ROUNDUP rounds numbers up. SUMIF adds cells based on given criteria. POWER raises a number to a specific power. PRODUCT sums a group of numbers.

◆ **Text.** CONCATENATE merges text from multiple locations into one item. DOLLAR formats numbers as text, with the currency format. FIXED formats numbers with a fixed number of decimal places. LEFT and RIGHT extract a certain number of characters from the left or right of a string of characters. UPPER, LOWER, and PROPER change the case for the display of text. UPPER displays in all uppercase, LOWER displays in all lowercase, and PROPER displays the first character of each word capitalized. TRIM removes spaces from strings of text.

◆ **Lookup and Reference.** ADDRESS returns information about the cell address of a reference. AREAS returns a value about an area in a reference. CHOOSE returns a value based on an index number and a list of values.

MATCH returns the location of a string in an array. HLOOKUP returns a value for an indicated cell from the top row of an array. VLOOKUP returns a value from the leftmost column of an array.

◆ **Information.** CELL returns information about a cell and its contents. COUNTBLANK counts blank cells in a range or array. INFO returns information about your system, environment, and setup. ISEVEN and ISODD return values of TRUE or FALSE based on whether a value is even or odd. N converts numbers to other formats for use in other spreadsheet programs. TYPE returns a numeric value based on the type of information contained in a cell.

◆ **Logical.** AND and IF return TRUE or FALSE values about a statement or calculation. AND needs all arguments to be true to return a TRUE value. NOT reverses the logic of an argument; true arguments become false, and vice versa. OR returns a TRUE value if any statement in a set of statements separated by OR is true (otherwise FALSE is returned). TRUE and FALSE return TRUE and FALSE as values.

◆ **Database and List.** SQLREQUEST enables connection with an outside data source and runs a query from Excel, returning the result as an array done without macros. SUBTOTAL returns subtotals from lists or databases.

◆ **Date and Time.** DAYS360 returns the number of days between two dates in a 360-day year (if your accounting year is based on 12 30-day months). WEEKDAY converts a serial number to a day of the week. YEARFRAC returns a fraction figured on the number of days between two dates.

Using Functions

Simple calculations, such as adding or subtracting, on a number or series of numbers are executed by using simple formulas. The simple formula SUM(A1..A5), for instance, inserts the sum of the numbers contained in the range A1..A5 into the cell containing the formula. These formulas are the foundation of many functions. Other functions use a combination of several formulas or procedures to achieve a desired result.

Functions, like formulas, all follow the same basic format:

◆ They must begin with an equal sign (=).

◆ The function name must be entered.

◆ Information about a cell or range of cells to be analyzed must be included.

◆ Arguments about what to do with the selected range of cells are entered last.

Some functions need additional information, and those examples will be discussed as they arise. For example, the following is the syntax for the ADDRESS function, which returns a value about a cell address in a worksheet:

ADDRESS (row_number,column_number,absolute_number,a1,sheet_text)

The arguments row_number and column_number are required arguments, and the remainder of the arguments are optional.

Some functions permit a variable number of arguments; for instance, use as many arguments in the SUM function as necessary. You can incorporate up to 1,024 arguments in a function, as long as no single string of characters in the function statement exceeds 255 characters.

Functions can be entered into worksheets manually, with a macro, or by using the Function Wizard.

Using the Function Wizard

One of the most exciting tools Excel has is the Function Wizard. It makes functions easier to use and understand by organizing them into logical categories by type, and by prompting you to complete the arguments required to make the function return a correct value.

Starting the Function Wizard can be done several ways. Clicking on the Function Wizard button on the Standard toolbar (see fig. 10.1) invokes the Wizard's first screen, which indicates that you are working on the first of two steps. The same button also appears on the formula bar when you double-click on a specific cell in your worksheet. This button works the same way that the Standard toolbar button does.

Figure 10.1

The Standard toolbar, showing the Function Wizard button.

You also can start the Function Wizard from the menu selections in the title bar, by selecting Function from the Insert menu. A keyboard shortcut for starting the Function Wizard is Shift+F3. Yet another way to start the Wizard is to enter the name of the function in a cell and press Ctrl+A.

Clicking on either of the Function Wizard buttons, using the pull-down menu, and using the keyboard method all produce the same result—the first of two dialog boxes. In the Function Wizard dialog box title, the status of the function insertion process is displayed as Step 1 of 2. You select which function you want to use by function category and function name. The function categories are listed on the left side of the box, and the associated functions are listed on the right.

The most recently used category of functions also appears in the Category window. This is useful especially if you use a particular group of functions regularly (the list changes and maintains the last 10 functions used). When a function is highlighted, its name, a brief description, and its arguments are displayed below the category list.

After the function is chosen, clicking on the Next button advances you to the second step: entering arguments or instructions for calculation.

If you invoke the Wizard by typing an equal sign, the name of the function, and pressing Shift+F3, typing the name in lowercase provides a validation of the function name. If the name is entered correctly, Excel will convert it to uppercase automatically. If the entered name is incorrect or invalid, Excel will insert a plus sign and leave the invalid name in lowercase.

In this second step, the name, description of the function, and arguments appear along with boxes showing the values of each argument. The resultant value of the function is shown in the top right corner of the box.

 Note Using the manual name entry method, the Wizard skips to the Step 2 of 2 dialog box (entering arguments) because you have already selected the function you wish to use.

Arguments that require cell addresses or range information can be entered by keyboard or mouse. Other arguments that are not associated with specific cells on the worksheet must be entered manually. Some arguments are required for a value to be returned, and some are optional. Arguments that are required appear in bold and (required) appears above the edit boxes when the field is selected. Optional arguments appear in regular typeface, with (optional) next to the name (see fig. 10.2).

Note that to the left of each function edit box is a Function Wizard button. Use this if you need to incorporate additional calculations or functions as arguments, a process known as *nesting functions*. Excel enables nesting of up to seven levels. When you nest functions, another Function Wizard box appears, and the dialog box title indicates that you are editing function 1 of 2. When you click on the Next button, that function is entered into the current function, and editing of the second function is enabled. You will have a chance to practice nesting functions and editing functions later in this section.

Figure 10.2

*Required
and optional
arguments in the
Function Wizard.*

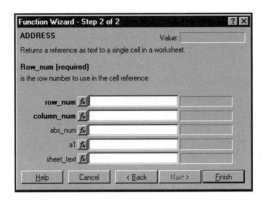

Tip When you want to edit a function using the Function Wizard, click on the cell containing the function to edit and press Shift+F3. This invokes the Function Wizard and takes you directly to the Step 2 of 2 dialog box, with all the arguments in the edit boxes.

The buttons at the bottom of the first screen in the Function Wizard are **H**elp, Cancel, **B**ack, Next, and **F**inish. If you get stuck on a particular function, click on the **H**elp button. A help session will begin for the topic or formula highlighted. Cancel closes the Function Wizard completely, unless you are nesting a function. If so, it cancels only the function you are nesting. **B**ack is activated when the Step 2 of 2 dialog box is active, and it takes you back to the Step 1 of 2 dialog box so that, if needed, you can select a new function type or name. The Next button takes you from the Step 1 of 2 to the Step 2 of 2 dialog box, and **F**inish completes the Function Wizard and places the function statement in the cell that was activated when the Function Wizard was invoked.

Using Add-Ins

Some functions require add-ins to work. An *add-in* is a file that can be installed from the T**o**ols menu, enabling additional commands and functions. The following are add-ins that come with Excel:

◆ Analysis ToolPak is used for financial and engineering functions and provides additional tools for statistical and engineering applications.

◆ AutoSave performs timed saves to disk while you work.

◆ MS Query is used to query external programs for data.

◆ ODBC (Open Data Base Connectivity) Query is a collection of worksheet and macro functions for retrieving data from external database files using Microsoft Query.

◆ Report Manager prints reports based on views and scenarios.

◆ Solver is installed at setup, enabling you to analyze what-if scenarios based on changing information.

◆ Template Utilities let you manipulate and work with Excel templates.

◆ Template Wizard with Data Tracking provides a Template Wizard that accesses and tracks data.

◆ View Manager saves the current window display as a view and enables you to look at worksheets in varying ways.

 Tip   Add-ins are located in the Excel LIBRARY directory or one of its subdirectories. If an add-in does not appear in the Tools, Add-Ins menu selection, using Microsoft Excel Setup will enable you to install it.

See Chapter 11, "Advanced Worksheet Capabilities," for a more detailed explanation of add-ins.

Financial Functions

Excel has over 50 financial functions prewritten and available for use in worksheets. Many of them require the use of add-ins. If a function does not appear, you may need to check which add-ins are installed in the Tools, Add-Ins menu selection. A good example of financial functions is the Future Value function.

The Future Value Function (FV)

FV, the Future Value function, calculates the future value of an investment. The syntax used for this function is the following:

```
=FV(rate, nper, pmt, pv, type)
```

The required arguments are rate (the current percentage rate fixed for the term of the investment), nper (the number of periods of payment), and pmt (the payment amount per period). In the optional arguments, pv is the present value of a lump sum of future payments, and type is 0 or 1 depending on whether payments are due at the beginning or end of a period.

Figure 10.3 shows the process of finding the future value of a monthly $100.00 payment into an annuity that yields 10 percent over a five-year period, with payments at the end of each period.

Figure 10.3

Using the Function Wizard to find the future value of an annuity.

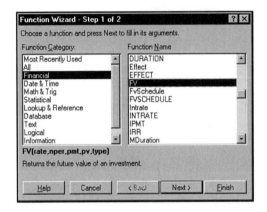

One technique you can use to organize your worksheets in a workbook is to name the sheets with unique identifiers, as you will see in many of the figures throughout this chapter. To name a worksheet, double-click on its tab to display the Rename Sheet dialog box. Type the new name and click on OK. The new name will appear on the tab.

Using the same function with worksheet cell addresses rather than values enables you to change numbers and see the effect of different interest rates, payment amounts, or terms, without having to reenter the entire function or go through all the Wizard's steps.

Enter the following in B8:

```
=FV(B1/B2,B2*B3,-B4,B5,B6)
```

This enables you to enter all the pertinent information into your equation and see immediate results. Try performing the function using the manual typing method (use lowercase letters for function validation), and then do the same thing using the Function Wizard.

Manually typing the functions usually is more time-consuming and cumbersome than using the Function Wizard. Shorter, more frequently used functions can be faster and easier to enter using the keyboard, though. Experimenting with both methods will allow you to find the most effective way to use your software.

Notice in the formula entry that the payment and present values have a negative value. This is important to several financial functions because the functions return negative values, which can be confusing. Adding the negatives to the function cell references enables you to enter positive numbers, which for many people might make more sense. If you are setting up a worksheet for another person to use who is not familiar with functions or financial analysis, this can be very helpful. The negative references can be entered either from the keyboard or prior to cell selection using the Function Wizard.

The rate for a five-year annuity at 10 percent should be entered as **10%/12**, and the number of periods of payment as **12*5**. The payment amount should be entered as a negative value.

Using the Function Wizard, you can enter the values used for the calculation in a similar way. Click on the Function Wizard button on the Standard toolbar to display the Step 1 of 2 dialog box. Select Financial Functions from the Category of functions list on the left side of the box. On the right, select FV, either by clicking once and then clicking below on the Next button, or by double-clicking on FV.

Tip   In the Function Wizard Step 1 of 2 dialog box, you can press Alt+C to choose Function **N**ames, and by typing the first letter of the desired function, the highlight bar will advance to the first function that begins with that letter. The same applies to Function **C**ategory.

This takes you to the Step 2 of 2 dialog box, in which arguments are completed. To complete this function, and return the future value, type the values directly into the edit boxes (**10%/12** for 10 percent over a 12-month period). For each value entered, an adjacent value for calculation purposes is displayed at the right side of the edit box (see fig. 10.4).

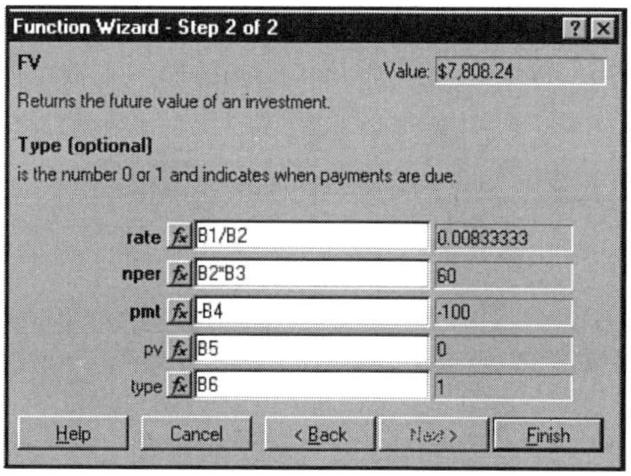

Figure 10.4

The completed Function Wizard dialog box, ready to be inserted into the worksheet.

Upon completion of argument entry, the value of the FV function is displayed in the Value box at the top right of the dialog box. Clicking on the **F**inish button returns you to the cell in your worksheet where the function will go. Press Enter to complete the insertion of the function into the sheet.

You also can use the Function Wizard to enter values as cell references by opening and choosing the type of function and specific function name, and then proceeding to the Step 2 of 2 dialog box. Once there, instead of entering numeric values into the sheet, use the mouse to click on cells in the worksheet where values are located.

In the sample worksheet, interest rate is in cell B1, number of payments per year is in B2, number of years in annuity is in B3, payment amount is in B4, present value is in B5, and time of payment (`Beg=0 End=1`) is in B6.

For entry of the rate, click on cell B1, type /, and click on cell B2. This yields the rate, divided by the number of months in a year. Tab to `nper`, and click on cell B3. Type * and click on B2 again. This yields the total number of payments, or number of years multiplied by the number of months per year. Tab again. Be sure when you click on the payment and present value arguments to give the cell reference that preceded it a minus value, or your ending value will be negative.

In the process of evaluation, if you enter a number in the present value cell and later remove it, you need to replace it with a 0, or the `#value!` message will appear in the FV cell B16. When the function is first entered, if there is no value, FV assumes 0. After it is cleared, the formula sees the cell as text-formatted and empty. This produces the error message.

Figure 10.5 shows the finished product, inserted into the worksheet with the function syntax in the formula bar.

Figure 10.5

*The completed
future value
calculation.*

	A	B	C	D	E	F	G	H	
1	Rate	10%							
2	Months	12							
3	Years	5							
4	Payment	100							
5	Present Value	0							
6	Beg=0 End=1	1							
7									
8	Future Value	$7,808.24							
9									
10									
11									
12									
13									

Sheet1 / Sheet2 / Sheet3 / Sheet4 / Sheet5 / Sheet6 /

The CUMIPMT Function

The CUMIPMT function returns a value that represents the cumulative interest paid between two periods. It is one of the functions that requires the Analysis ToolPak add-in.

If you borrowed $1,000.00 from the bank at a 13.5 percent interest rate for a term of two years beginning on March 1, and you want to know how much interest you have paid for a calendar year, this function does the job.

The syntax of CUMIPMT is the following:

```
=CUMIPMT(rate,nper,pv,start_period,end_period,type)
```

All the arguments are required for this function: `rate` is the interest rate, `nper` is the number of payments per period, `pv` is the present value, `start_period` is the number of the first period to calculate from, `end_period` is the number of the period to complete the calculation, and `type` is either 0 or 1 based on whether payment is made at the beginning or the end of each period.

To compose the function, enter the following:

```
=cumipmt(13.5%/12,12*2,1000,1,10,1)
```

The resultant value (shown as a negative number) is the cumulative amount of interest in the 10-month period between March and December that you paid on your $1,000.00 loan: $81.27799685.

 Stop As you enter formulas and function statements, pay close attention to spacing in the formula bar. An added space or missed comma can result in errors in the results or in not having the command executed.

You can use the Function Wizard to create your own interest payment evaluation function. Then you can determine what the benefits of borrowing money over certain periods of time at various interest rates might have on your corporate or personal finances.

Using the worksheet shown in figure 10.6, you can enter values for the arguments in the cells and see the results of different loan calculations. Begin by typing the cell labels in column A, row 4. The first value label should be **Interest Rate:**. Press Enter, which drops the active cell to A5, and type **Payments per Year:**. Complete the cell labels as shown in figure 10.6.

Figure 10.6

The worksheet format for the CUMIPMT formula.

	A	B	C	D	E	F	G
1							
2							
3							
4	Interest Rate	13.50%					
5	Payments Per Year	12					
6	Years of Loan	2					
7	Value of Loan	1,000					
8	Starting Period to Evaluate	1					
9	Ending Period to Evaluate	10					
10							
11	Cumulative Interest Payment						
12							
13							

CUMIPMT / Sheet2 / Sheet3 / Sheet4 / Sheet5 / Shee

Now, enter the values for the loan interest calculation so that your screen looks like the following:

```
Interest Rate:              13.50%
Payments Per Year:             12
Years of Loan:                  2
Value of Loan:              1,000
Starting Period to Evaluate:    1
Ending Period to Evaluate:     10
```

Double-click on cell B11, and click on the Function Wizard button on the formula bar. In the first dialog box, select Financial in Function **C**ategory, select CUMIPMT from the Function **N**ame list, and click on the Next button, or press Enter. The dialog box changes to Step 2 of 2 and the arguments in the form of cell references or values can now be entered.

For the rate, click on the worksheet cell B4, type /, and click on cell B5, which shows a value for that argument of 0.01125. Tab to the next argument, nper. Click on B6, type *, and click on B5. The resulting value to the right of the nper edit box shows 24. The value box at the upper right corner of the sheet does not show a value because all the required arguments are not complete yet. Tab to the pv edit box and click on B7. The value shows 1,000 to the right of the edit box. Tab to the start_period field, click on B8, tab to end_period, click on B9, tab to type (you will have to press the down arrow on the scroll bar to see the type field), and click on B10. The B10 cell is blank and returns a value of 0 until it is cleared manually. Actually, because it is blank, you should enter the number **1** in the type field. If you want to evaluate the difference between paying at the beginning or the end of a period, which is an optional argument, add a cell for Beg=1 End=0 in A10, and the value 0 or 1 in B10. The calculations should now equal -81.27799685 (see fig. 10.7).

Click on the **F**inish button, and the function, complete with arguments, is ready to be entered into the sheet. Pressing Enter or clicking on the check mark in the formula bar inserts the calculation and shows the result. On the workbook where the value is

returned, with that cell highlighted, click on the $ button on the Standard toolbar. The result is formatted as currency with two decimal places and is rounded to $81.28.

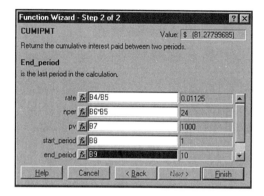

Figure 10.7

The Function Wizard displaying the variables for CUMIPMT.

The CUMPRINC Function

The CUMPRINC function takes the CUMIPMT function one step further. It returns the value of the principal paid on a loan during a period of time. The two functions can be used together on one sheet because they share the same arguments and structure. Use the previous loan example and type the following:

```
=CUMPRINC(13.5%/12,2*12,1000,1,10,0)
```

This returns a value of 391.18 total principal paid in the 10-month period between March and December. Click on the cell, and click on the $ button in the Formatting toolbar to display the value as currency.

The worksheet now looks like figure 10.8, formatted with dollar values in the cells that contain the CUMIPMT and CUMPRINC functions.

	A	B	C	D	E	F	G
1							
2							
3							
4	Interest Rate	13.50%					
5	Payments Per Year	12					
6	Years of Loan	2					
7	Value of Loan	1,000					
8	Starting Period to Evaluate	1					
9	Ending Period to Evaluate	10					
10							
11	Cumulative Interest Payment	-$81.28					
12	Cumulative Principal Payment	-$391.18					
13							

CUMIPMT / Sheet2 / Sheet3 / Sheet4 / Sheet5 / Shee

Figure 10.8

The values from both the CUMIPMT and CUMPRINC functions.

The EFFECT Function

The EFFECT function returns the effective annual interest rate, given the nominal interest rate and the number of compounding periods per year. For an annual interest rate of 18.25 percent that is compounded four times per year, the syntax is the following:

```
=EFFECT(18.25%,4)
```

With this function, the effective interest rate is 19.54 percent.

Examining Statistical Functions

Statistical functions frequently return values about arrays of data or groups of numbers. The example here provides you with a foundation of how statistical functions can help you look at data in interesting ways.

The AVERAGE Function

The AVERAGE function returns the arithmetic mean of a group of numbers. This function can have up to 30 arguments, and arguments can be names of cell ranges or individual cells.

 Tip   Blank cells in an array to be averaged are counted and figured into the average, unless the cell has been designated as empty. Empty cells are not counted. To check or change the zero values options, select Options, **T**ools. In the View tab, check or clear the **Z**ero values box.

For this example, you will create a worksheet with information about a group of salespeople. The example in figure 10.9 shows the basic information that you will build on to learn about statistical functions.

There are four salespeople, with three columns of information adjacent to each name. Each column represents one month's sales. To place headers on the worksheet, type **Jan** in cell B2. Click once with the mouse on that cell, and, using the AutoFill handle, drag it across the other columns from B to D to fill in **Feb** and **Mar**. If the result is ####s across your cell, double-click on the right edge of the column header to adjust the width of the columns.

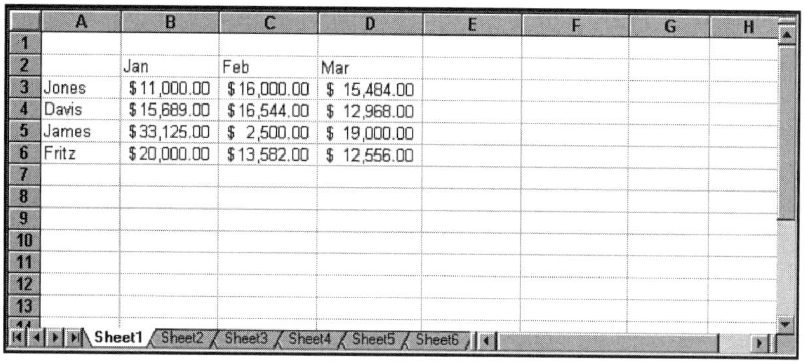

Figure 10.9
The sales worksheet.

To continue the formatting of this sheet, highlight cells B3 to H13. This is the range of cells you will use for the statistical analysis, where currency format is important. On the Standard toolbar, click on the $ button. See table 10.1 for the data for the sales worksheet.

TABLE 10.1
Data for Sales Worksheet

Salesperson	Jan	Feb	Mar
Jones	11,000	16,000	15,484
Davis	15,689	16,544	12,968
James	33,125	2,500	19,000
Fritz	20,000	13,582	12,556

The SUM Function

In analyzing sales performance, sales totals are critical. You can add quarterly and monthly totals to your worksheet quickly by using one of Excel's most popular functions, the SUM function. It even has its own button on the Standard toolbar. In your worksheet, below the names in column A, skip one row and type **Total:** in cell A8. Then, in the column to the right of the Averages Column, in cell F2, enter **Quarterly Total** as the heading of the new column. Position the mouse on cell F3, and, holding down the left mouse button, highlight the cells to cell F6. Then move the cursor over to cell B8, hold down the Ctrl key on the keyboard, and highlight the cells from B8 to F8. You now should have two separate ranges of cells highlighted (see fig. 10.10).

Figure 10.10

The cells prior to pressing the SUM button.

	A	B	C	D	E	F	G	H
1								
2		Jan	Feb	Mar	Averages	Quarter Total		
3	Jones	$ 11,000.00	$ 16,000.00	$ 15,484.00				
4	Davis	$ 15,689.00	$ 16,544.00	$ 12,968.00				
5	James	$ 33,125.00	$ 2,500.00	$ 19,000.00				
6	Fritz	$ 20,000.00	$ 13,582.00	$ 12,556.00				
7								
8	Total							
9								
10								
11								
12								
13								

Sheet1 / Sheet2 / Sheet3 / Sheet4 / Sheet5 / Sheet6 /

Once you have your ranges highlighted, on the Standard toolbar, click on Σ, the Greek letter (sigma) that represents the SUM function. Excel automatically totals the number in the rows and columns you have selected, and returns the values. The SUM button on the toolbar can save a lot of time in arriving at totals for large worksheets and projects.

The AVERAGE Function

For this example, you will find out what the average sales amount is for each representative. To do this, click on the cell in the first empty column of data, on the same row as salesperson Jones. This is cell E3. On the Standard toolbar, click on the Function Wizard. Choose function category Statistical and function name AVERAGE, and click on the Next button. For the Step 2 of 2 dialog box, hold down the mouse button on cell B3 and drag to cell D3. The keyboard entry is **=AVERAGE(B3:D3)**. The value returned by the formula is the sum of cells B3 through D3, divided by the number of entries in the range: $14,161.33.

You can complete the averages for the rest of the salespeople by using the AutoFill feature. To do this, click on E3, the cell for the average of the first person, and position the cursor over the fill handle in the lower right corner of the cell. Then, hold down the left mouse button, and drag the pointer down to cells E4, E5, and E6. The averages automatically fill in for the remainder of the sales force (see fig. 10.11).

The next step is to determine what the high sales month was for each salesperson.

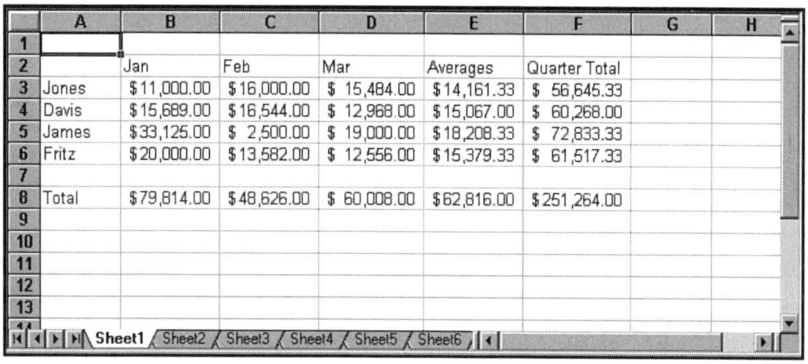

	A	B	C	D	E	F	G	H
1								
2		Jan	Feb	Mar	Averages	Quarter Total		
3	Jones	$11,000.00	$16,000.00	$ 15,484.00	$14,161.33	$ 56,645.33		
4	Davis	$15,689.00	$16,544.00	$ 12,968.00	$15,067.00	$ 60,268.00		
5	James	$33,125.00	$ 2,500.00	$ 19,000.00	$18,208.33	$ 72,833.33		
6	Fritz	$20,000.00	$13,582.00	$ 12,556.00	$15,379.33	$ 61,517.33		
7								
8	Total	$79,814.00	$48,626.00	$ 60,008.00	$62,816.00	$251,264.00		
9								
10								
11								
12								
13								

Sheet1 / Sheet2 / Sheet3 / Sheet4 / Sheet5 / Sheet6

Figure 10.11

The sales worksheet showing totals and averages.

The MAX Function

Of course, it is easy to look at the sheet and determine what the current high number is for each person, but you might want to monitor these figures over a period of months or years to determine the top month of each one. (There also is a formula to look at the lowest month.) The MAX function is the answer.

In cell G2, type the Heading **High** and press Enter. The active cell is now G3. On the Standard toolbar, click on the Function Wizard button.

Select function category Statistical and function name MAX, and click on the Next button. The Wizard prompts you for the first argument entry, which is Column B3 through D3. Position the pointer on B3, hold down the left mouse button, and drag to cell D3. Now, in the Function Wizard box, click on the Finish button. Pressing Enter inserts the function in the sheet and returns the value $16,000.00. This represents the highest value in the range for salesperson Jones.

You can use the AutoFill feature again to complete the rest of the sales staff's MAX months and provide a new entry for the MAX month for the company's total sales. Position the mouse on cell G3, click once to make G3 the active cell, and position the pointer to the lower right corner of the cell until the pointer changes to a small, black +. While holding down the left mouse button, drag the pointer down to cell G8. This action AutoFills the MAX function in all the highlighted cells, returning the maximum values for each representative and the company. Figure 10.12 shows the result of the MAX function.

You can accomplish the same result with the keyboard. With cell H3 active, type **=max(B3:D3)** and press Enter. The function returns the maximum value found for cells B3, C3, and D3. Using the AutoFill, you then can fill in the rest of the cells by dragging the AutoFill handle to the appropriate cells.

Figure 10.12

The MAX results.

	A	B	C	D	E	F	G	H
1								
2		Jan	Feb	Mar	Averages	Quarter Total	High	
3	Jones	$11,000.00	$16,000.00	$ 15,484.00	$14,161.33	$ 56,645.33	$16,000.00	
4	Davis	$15,689.00	$16,544.00	$ 12,968.00	$15,067.00	$ 60,268.00	$16,544.00	
5	James	$33,125.00	$ 2,500.00	$ 19,000.00	$18,208.33	$ 72,833.33	$33,125.00	
6	Fritz	$20,000.00	$13,582.00	$ 12,556.00	$15,379.33	$ 61,517.33	$20,000.00	
7							$ -	
8	Total	$79,814.00	$48,626.00	$ 60,008.00	$62,816.00	$251,264.00	$79,814.00	
9								
10								
11								
12								
13								

Sheet1 / Sheet2 / Sheet3 / Sheet4 / Sheet5 / Sheet6 /

The MIN Function

The MIN function is the opposite of MAX; it returns the smallest numeric value found in a range of cells. MIN uses the same arguments and syntax.

In cell H2, type **Low** and press Enter. Your active cell is now H3. Type **=min(B3:D3)** and press Enter. The dollar amount for salesperson Jones is returned, and the active cell is now H4. Click again on cell H3, and, from the lower right corner, AutoFill the rest of the salespeople and company information with the MIN function. The MAX and MIN function columns for sales are now complete.

The RANK Function

Now that you have calculated what the highs and lows are for the salespeople and the company, you can use the RANK function to assign a numeric rank to each person, based on their sales. Click on cell A2, making it active. Type the header for that column, **First Quarter Rank**, and press Enter. In cell A3, invoke the Function Wizard from the Standard toolbar. Statistical Functions still should be active, if that was the last function category used. From the function name box, select RANK, and click on the Next button.

The Step 2 of 2 dialog box is now active, and the first argument is the number you want to rank. Because our heading was First Quarter Rank, you should choose the First Quarter Total Cell for Jones, which is in cell F3. Click once on F3, and press Tab to move to the next argument. The next argument is called ref, which indicates the numbers to compare to the first argument, or the total for the quarter.

With the ref edit box active, highlight cell F3, and, holding down the left mouse button, drag the pointer to cell F6. This creates the reference for the first representative's monthly total compared to all other salespeople. Press Tab to move to the last edit box in the Function Wizard, and type **0**. Note that the value in the upper right of the Wizard dialog box is now filled in.

Note In the order edit box, Excel ranks in ascending order for nonzero characters, descending order for zero characters.

In order to rank the remainder of the salespeople, we can use the AutoFill feature to drag the function to the remaining cells. However, this operation will return incorrect results because the cells referenced will change. In other words, our goal is to move the function to analyze a new number, but compare it to the same original arguments chosen in the Jones ranking. In order to have RANK look to the same cells for each comparison, you need to make the cells referenced in the function absolute cell references. This means that regardless of the location of the function, or where it might later be moved, it still will rank the number we wish to compare to the first quarter totals, located in cells F3:F6.

The following example illustrates the effect of absolute and regular cell references on a simple array of numbers:

			Totals	
			Normal Cell Reference:	Absolute Reference:
Jan	Feb	Mar	B8:D8	$D$10:$F$10
1	1	1	3	3
2	2	2	6	3
3	3	3	9	3
6	6	6	18	3

The example shows normal referencing in the next-to-the-last column. To input this total, type **=sum(B8:D8)** and press Enter in the D10 cell. Then AutoFill down to E10 and F10. Each time the formula or function is moved, its cell pointers adjust accordingly.

The formula in D14 now reads =SUM(D10:F10), which returns the correct sum for that row. The last column uses absolute cell references, which point only to D10:F10. When the function is moved or copied to another location, it still returns a value associated with that original range of cells.

This example uses absolute cell references to return an incorrect set of values for three of the four entries. With the RANK function, use of absolute cell references is essential to producing accurate results.

Tip You can make cell references absolute from Excel's Formula bar as formulas and functions are entered, or when editing an existing one. To do this, select the cell with the function or formula you want to make absolute, click on the cell reference,

continues

and press the F4 key. The row and column references cycle through the levels of reference type each time you press the F4 key. Using this method, you can choose to make both row and column absolute, or just one or the other.

The MEDIAN Function

The median value returned by the MEDIAN function represents the number in the middle of a set of values. In other words, half the numbers in the set have values that are higher than the median, and half have values that are lower. This is similar to averages, yet the median is not representative of a calculation on a value or values in a worksheet. It is simply the middle value from a group.

To add the MEDIAN function to our sales analysis spreadsheet, click once on cell I2. Type the heading for this column, **Median Month**. Press Enter, moving the active cell to I3. Try invoking the Function Wizard by pressing the keyboard key combination shortcut, Shift+F3. From the function category, select Statistical, and from the function name window, select MEDIAN. Pressing Enter or clicking on the Next button moves you to the next step.

The first edit box shows the caption Number1. Position the mouse pointer on cell B3, and drag the pointer to D3. The first argument is the only one required for this function, so you can click on the **F**inish button to return the value to your worksheet. For this function, because you do not need absolute cell references, use the AutoFill feature to complete the MEDIAN function for the remainder of the salespeople. Figure 10.13 shows what the finished sheet should look like.

Figure 10.13

The Sales worksheet showing the MEDIAN function results.

	A	B	C	D	E	F	G	H	I	J
1										
2		Jan	Feb	Mar	Averages	Quarter Total	High	Low	Median	
3	Jones	$ 11,000.00	$ 16,000.00	$ 15,484.00	$ 14,161.33	$ 56,645.33	$ 16,000.00	$ 11,000.00	$ 15,484.00	
4	Davis	$ 15,689.00	$ 16,544.00	$ 12,368.00	$ 15,067.00	$ 60,268.00	$ 16,544.00	$ 12,368.00	$ 15,689.00	
5	James	$ 33,125.00	$ 2,500.00	$ 19,000.00	$ 18,208.33	$ 72,833.33	$ 33,125.00	$ 2,500.00	$ 19,000.00	
6	Fritz	$ 20,000.00	$ 13,582.00	$ 12,556.00	$ 15,379.33	$ 61,517.33	$ 20,000.00	$ 12,556.00	$ 13,582.00	
7										
8	Total	$ 79,814.00	$ 48,626.00	$ 60,008.00	$ 62,816.00	$ 251,264.00	$ 79,814.00	$ 48,626.00	$ 60,008.00	

Math and Trigonometry Functions

Excel has nearly 60 different mathematical and trigonometric functions available for use in worksheet analysis. Several of these are discussed in the following sections.

The ABS Function

The ABS function returns the absolute value of a number; that is, the number without its sign. This function can be used in calculations that require positive numbers in order to work properly, such as the CUMIPMT example.

Earlier in this chapter, you were able to display the resulting value from CUMIPMT by placing a negative value in the argument edit box for present value. For this example, you use that CUMIPMT function with the same numbers, and nest the ABS function so that the result is a positive value.

Recall the syntax of the original CUMIPMT function formula:

```
=CUMIPMT(rate,nper,pv,start_period,end_period,type)
```

The result is a negative number. Using cell address arguments in the formula and placing a minus before the cell containing present value enables a positive number as the result. Another way to accomplish this is to nest the ABS function with CUMIPMT.

Tip You can use ABS by itself to change the contents of a cell from a negative number to a positive number, and if the cell already contains a positive value, no changes are made to the contents.

If you already have put your formula in place and it returns a negative value, and you want to change it to a positive one, you can accomplish this quickly. Click on the cell that contains the negative value and press F2. This displays the value in the cell and displays the formula in the formula bar, located near the center of the screen. Figure 10.14 shows the result of this action.

Click on the formula bar, and you then can edit the formula.

Tip The cursor will go where the pointer is at the time of the click on the bar. Once there, the End, Home, and left- and right-arrow keys on the keyboard can help you move to the spot at which you need to make additions or corrections.

Figure 10.14

The display of the formula in the formula bar.

Formula bar

B11		=Cumipmt(B4/B5,B5*B6,B7,B8,B9,1)					
	A	B	C	D	E	F	G
1							
2							
3							
4	Rate	13.50%					
5	Payments Per Year	12					
6	Years of Loan	2					
7	Value of Loan	1000					
8	Starting Period to Evaluate	1					
9	Ending Period to Evaluate	10					
10							
11	Cumulative Interest Payment	($81.28)					
12							
13							

Highlighted cell

Sheet1 / Sheet2 / Sheet3 / Sheet4 / Sheet5 / Sheet6

Press the Home key, which moves you to the first character in the formula, and press the right-arrow key. This action takes you inside the = where you can insert the ABS function to return a positive value always. Type **abs(**, then press the End key and type **)**.

The original formula was the following:

=CUMIPMT(D22/D23,D24*D23,D25,D26,D27,1)

and the resultant value was ($81.27). This is the new formula:

=ABS(CUMIPMT(D22/D23,D24*D23,D25,D26,D27,1))

and its value is $81.27. Using ABS changes the negative value returned by CUMIPMT to a positive one so that it can be used in other calculations with the desired sign.

Nesting the ABS function with the keyboard is fast, and using the Function Wizard to either edit an existing function or nest a function as it is created is fast as well.

To use the Function Wizard to create a new CUMIPMT that returns an absolute number, select the cell where the value is to be returned to the worksheet, and invoke the Function Wizard. First, select Math & Trig Functions from the function category list and ABS from the function name list.

When you click on the Next button, to the right of the edit box there is another Function Wizard button, which facilitates nesting. Click once on that button, and the Function Wizard Step 1 of 2 (Nested) dialog box appears. Select Financial **C**ategory CUMIPMT from the function category list, and proceed to the next dialog box, Step 2 of 2 (Nested), by pressing Enter or the Next button.

At this point, enter the arguments that are needed to return the cumulative interest payment value. As the arguments for CUMIPMT are completed, the value displayed in the Function Wizard value box is a negative value. Click on **F**inish, and the original function Step 2 of 2 dialog box appears, with the CUMIPMT information highlighted and entered in the ABS argument. Note here that the resulting value in the Wizard shows as a positive number. Clicking on the **F**inish button completes the nesting process and returns the calculation to your worksheet (see fig. 10.15).

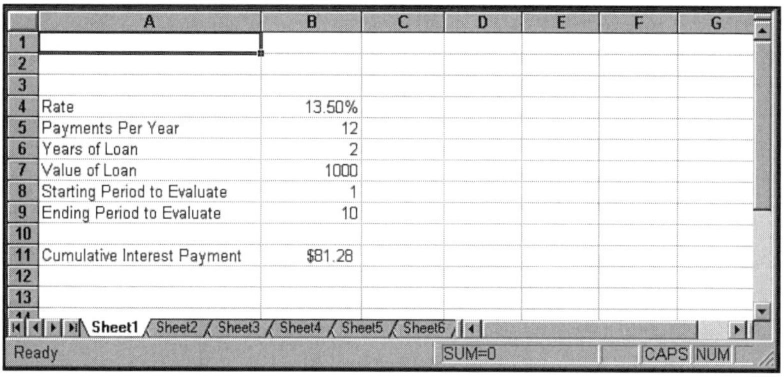

Figure 10.15

The CUMIPMT results entered in the ABS argument.

The ABS function is a good example of a simple function that has immediate results. It is relatively easy to add to an existing formula, either from the keyboard or the Function Wizard.

The COUNTIF Function

The COUNTIF function examines a range of nonblank cells and counts the number of cells that match certain criteria. In the sales worksheet example, if each salesperson had to sell $10,000 every month to reach quota, and you wanted to have a column in your sheet that indicates how many months they reach their goals in a certain time period, COUNTIF is the perfect function to use.

To add this entry to your sheet, make cell J2 active by clicking on it. Then type the heading **# Mths. over Quota** and press Enter. Next, invoke the Function Wizard in J3. Select the Math & Trig **C**ategory, the COUNTIF function, and click on the Next button. In the first edit box (range), position the mouse pointer on cell B3, hold down the left mouse button, and drag the pointer to cell D3. Tab to the next edit box (criteria), type **>10000**, and press the **F**inish button.

The result is the number of months that Jones finished above quota, or with sales over $10,000. Using AutoFill, position the mouse pointer on the lower right corner of cell J3 until the cursor becomes a plus sign. Holding down the left mouse button, drag the highlight box down to cells J4, J5, and J6. The resulting calculations appear.

The keyboard entry for this function is **=COUNTIF(B3:D3,">10000")**. A salesperson who sells exactly $10,000.00 for a given month does not get credit for having achieved quota based on this calculation. If the goal is $10,000 or greater, the operand in the formula should be changed from > to >= (greater than or equal to). Figure 10.16 illustrates the results. (For clarity, the High, Low, and Median columns in figure 10.16 have been hidden with the **H**ide command under the **C**olumn option in the F**o**rmat menu.)

Figure 10.16

The Sales worksheeting showing COUNTIF results.

	A	B	C	D	E	F	J	K	L	M
1										
2		Jan	Feb	Mar	Averages	Quarter Total	# Mths. over Quota			
3	Jones	$ 11,000.00	$ 16,000.00	$ 15,484.00	$ 14,161.33	$ 56,645.33	3			
4	Davis	$ 15,689.00	$ 16,544.00	$ 12,968.00	$ 15,067.00	$ 60,268.00	3			
5	James	$ 33,125.00	$ 2,500.00	$ 19,000.00	$ 18,208.33	$ 72,833.33	2			
6	Fritz	$ 20,000.00	$ 13,582.00	$ 12,556.00	$ 15,379.33	$ 61,517.33	3			
7										
8	Total	$ 79,814.00	$ 48,626.00	$ 60,008.00	$ 62,816.00	$ 251,264.00				
9										
10										
11										
12										
13										
14										
15										
16										
17										
18										

Sheet1 / Sheet2 / Sheet3 / Sheet4 / Sheet5 / Sheet6

The EVEN and ODD Functions

The EVEN and ODD functions are simple and useful for certain applications. The keyboard entry is about as fast if not faster than using the Wizard; the syntax is the following:

```
=even(number)
```

or

```
=odd(number)
```

The EVEN function takes a number, or extracts a number from a cell reference, and rounds it up to the nearest whole even number. The ODD function does the same, to the nearest odd whole number.

An application for which this function can be useful is an inventory/ordering worksheet in which particular stock items are shipped in quantities of two only. A customer ordering one could be notified upon order entry that this was the case. You can accomplish this by having the quantity ordered in one column, and the shipping quantity (with the function performed on its contents) drawn from the quantity ordered cell.

The MOD Function

MOD is a function that returns the remainder from division of a number. This calculation can be used in figuring a check digit for an account number for security purposes. An example of this might be a formula that takes a customer's telephone number, divides it by a constant number, and adds the remainder to the end of the phone number as a verification.

The syntax for MOD is the following:

=mod(number,divisor).

Using the previous example, if a customer's phone number is 555-1212, and you chose 8 as your special divisor, the formula =mod(5551212,8) returns a value of 4. The customer account number would be 55512124. The worksheet uses the MOD function and the CONCATENATE function from the Text function category. The former returns the remainder, and the latter returns the value needed for displaying the account number as one complete number. (The CONCATENATE function is discussed in more detail later in this chapter.)

First, set up a column for phone numbers (in the example, column A, cell 3), a column for the remainder (column B, cell 3), and a column for the new account number (column C, cell 3). When the phone number is entered in the first cell, the function automatically figures the remainder and joins, in the third column, the original number with the remainder.

To set up the MOD function using the Function Wizard, click on cell B3 and invoke the Wizard. From the Function **C**ategory list, choose Math & Trig, and select MOD from the Function **N**ame list. Press Enter, or click on the Next button, and the arguments section appears. Click on the cell containing the number, or cell A3. Tab to the Divisor field, and type the number **8** (a number chosen at random). Press Enter, or click on the **F**inish button, and the MOD is placed in the remainder column. Then, move to cell C3, the account number column.

Invoke the Wizard again, and select Text as the type and CONCATENATE as the function to be used. When you click on the Next button, the arguments required are to select the text items you wish to join together. Select A3 for the first item and B3 for the second. When you press Finish, the 55512124 account number, complete with check digit, is returned as the value.

The PI Function

PI is one of the few function selections that does not require any arguments. It can be used in formulas or calculations to return special values. The geometric equation for figuring the circumference of a circle is π (pi) × (radius)^2. The syntax for this calculation is the following:

```
=pi()*(12^2)
```

Where the value 12 is the radius of the circle whose circumference you wish to obtain.

The ROMAN Function

The ROMAN function takes numeric values and converts them to Roman numerals, and it can display the numerals in one of five different formats. The ROMAN function can convert numbers only up to a maximum of 3,999, and it can convert only positive values. Negative values, and those exceeding 3,999, return the #value! error message.

The syntax for using the ROMAN function is the following:

```
=roman(number,style)
```

where number is the numeric value you wish to convert, and style is a number from 0 to 4. The help information about ROMAN says that style 0 is the Classic Roman style, and 1 through 4 are More Concise.

To use the Function Wizard to enter the ROMAN function, highlight the cell in which to display the value, and invoke the Wizard. From the Function **C**ategory list, choose Math & Trig, and from the Function **N**ames window, select ROMAN. Clicking on the Next button enables argument entry, where you can preview the conversions by entering a number and style, or enter a cell address for the numeric value and 0–4 for the style.

Note You also can enter TRUE and FALSE for style arguments, where TRUE is Classic format, or 0, and FALSE is More Concise, such as style 4.

The ROUND Function

ROUND is a straightforward function that takes a number and rounds it to a specified number of decimal places. The rounding feature is important for many calculations because the values that come from calculations might be different from the rounded number. Figure 10.17 illustrates how rounding can affect one number used in a simple calculation.

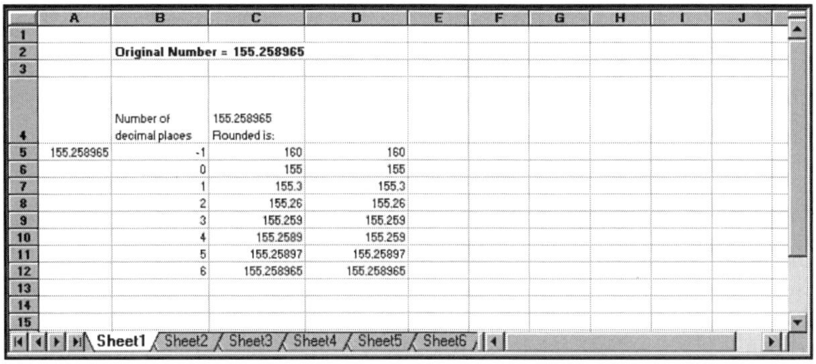

Figure 10.17

The effects of rounding and decimal places.

The syntax for the ROUND function is the following:

```
=round(number,num_digits)
```

If `num_digits` is less than 0, the number is rounded to the left of the decimal. If it is 0, the number is rounded to the nearest integer. If it is greater than 0, it is rounded to that number of decimal places.

Using the Function Wizard, after selecting the category and function name, the argument selection uses cell addresses. The number to be rounded has an absolute address ($A$5) and the num_digits argument is variable (B5). When the formula is AutoFilled to adjacent cells, the rounding takes place on the same number each time because of the absolute cell address.

The POWER Function

The POWER function returns the result of a number raised to a power. If you want to take the number 10 to the second power, for example, the keyboard entry to your selected cell is **=power(10,2)**, and the result is 100. You can accomplish the same result in Excel by typing **=10^2**.

The SUMIF Function (with PRODUCT)

The SUMIF function adds values from a list of numeric values, provided certain criteria are met. This is an interesting function and has many potential uses. Revisiting the sales worksheet used earlier in this chapter, if your company has a bonus program for salespeople that is calculated as a percentage of total sales over quota, the SUMIF function can help you calculate the bonuses automatically.

If you pay a quarterly bonus of 1/2 percent of total sales for those salespeople who exceed their quota of $10,000.00 for a given month, the SUMIF syntax is the following:

=PRODUCT(SUMIF(B3:D3,">=10000"),0.5%)

In the example, SUMIF is nested within PRODUCT, which is a function that multiplies its arguments. The result of this function yields a number that includes only those months' sales that are greater than or equal to quota (10000), and multiplies that number by 0.5%, which is the bonus.

To use the Function Wizard with SUMIF, choose the PRODUCT function from the Math & Trig category, and when the first argument edit box is on screen, press the Function Wizard box next to it. This brings up the nested Function Wizard box. Then highlight the cells and the criteria added as an argument to the SUMIF function. Upon completion, enter the multiplier for the PRODUCT function; the returned value is displayed (see fig. 10.18).

Figure 10.18

The worksheet showing PRODUCT, with SUMIF nested, resulting in the Bonus Column.

	A	B	C	D	E	F	J	K	L	M
1										
2		Jan	Feb	Mar	Averages	Quarter Total	# Mths. over Quota	Bonus		
3	Jones	$ 11,000.00	$ 16,000.00	$ 15,484.00	$ 14,161.33	$ 56,645.33	3	212.42		
4	Davis	$ 15,689.00	$ 16,544.00	$ 12,968.00	$ 15,067.00	$ 60,268.00	3	226.005		
5	James	$ 33,125.00	$ 2,500.00	$ 19,000.00	$ 18,208.33	$ 72,833.33	2	260.625		
6	Fritz	$ 20,000.00	$ 13,582.00	$ 12,556.00	$ 15,379.33	$ 61,517.33	3	230.69		
7										
8	Total	$ 79,814.00	$ 48,626.00	$ 60,008.00	$ 62,816.00	$ 251,264.00				
9										
10										
11										
12										
13										
14										
15										
16										
17										
18										

Sheet1 / Sheet2 / Sheet3 / Sheet4 / Sheet5 / Sheet6

Using Database Functions

There are two types of database functions: those that do calculations on worksheet databases and those that can be used to retrieve external data. The worksheet commands have counterparts as statistical functions. The only difference between them is that the database functions perform their calculations on database worksheets, and statistical functions perform theirs on lists in worksheets.

Working with Text Functions

Text functions, unlike many of the other function types, manipulate numbers and characters for formatting, sorting, display, and computation.

The CONCATENATE Function

The CONCATENATE function can be used in a variety of different ways to extract information from worksheets. Text can be joined to form sentences about values located in your worksheet. For example, the following text:

```
Salesperson Jones averaged 14112 for the first quarter
and exceeded quota 3 times for a bonus amount of
$211.68!
```

was extracted directly from the sales worksheet using the CONCATENATE function with this syntax:

```
=CONCATENATE("Salesperson ",$B$3," averaged ",$F$3," for the first
quarter "," and exceeded quota ",$K$3," times"," for a bonus amount
of ",$M$3,"!")
```

The cell references are absolute, so the function formula can be moved anywhere in the workbook and maintain integrity. The example was formulated using the Function Wizard, but can be done from the keyboard as well.

Tip When joining entered text and cell references, make sure to enter the two items in separate edit boxes in the Function Wizard. This is important because the Wizard places quotation marks around entered text. If you have the text `"Salesperson"` and the cell reference in the same edit box, the result will be `Salesperson $B$3`, not Salesperson Jones.

The DOLLAR Function

The DOLLAR function converts numbers into text and formats the value as currency, with any number of decimal places. The difference between using DOLLAR and formatting numeric values as currency is that Excel converts DOLLAR formatted cells to text. The results still can be used in formulas and calculations, because Excel also converts them to numbers when it calculates.

Figure 10.19 shows the difference in appearance between cells formatted using DOLLAR and those using the $ button from the toolbar.

	A	B	C	D	E	F	G	H
1	Using Tool Bar		Using DOLLAR()					
2								
3	$ 1,100.00		$1,100.00					
4	$ 159.00		$159.00					
5	$ 3,125.00		$3,125.00					
6	$ 22,251.00		$22,251.00					
7								
8								
9								
10								
11								
12								
13								

Sheet1 / Sheet2 / Sheet3 / Sheet4 / Sheet5 / Sheet6

The FIXED Function

FIXED is a text function that formats numeric values as text with a given number of decimal places. The FIXED function also can insert commas for formatting appearance. The syntax for FIXED is the following:

```
=fixed(number,decimals,no_commas)
```

and is similar to the DOLLAR function because of its text-to-numeric conversion for calculation purposes.

To use the Function Wizard with FIXED, select text from the Category Function window, and FIXED from the Function **N**ame window. Click on the Next button, and arguments can be entered.

The LEFT and RIGHT Functions

The LEFT and RIGHT functions extract a certain number of characters from the left or right of a string of text. If the word MICROSOFT is in cell L23, for example, and you enter the function **=left(L23,5)**, the resulting value is MICRO. If you then enter the function **=right(L23,4)**, the value is SOFT. This could be used as an account identifier, in a similar fashion to the prior example in the function MOD.

The UPPER, LOWER, and PROPER Functions

The UPPER, LOWER, and PROPER functions change the case of text strings in a worksheet. UPPER and LOWER modify the entire text string. Entering **=lower(MICROSOFT CORP)** yields microsoft corp as its value, and entering **=upper(microsoft corp)** yields MICROSOFT CORP as its value. Either all upper- or lowercase text using PROPER capitalizes the first letter of each word and converts, if necessary, the remaining characters in the string to lowercase.

The TRIM Function

The TRIM function removes spaces from text. This function is handy if your worksheet has received data from an external source that has added too many spaces between words in a string. Figure 10.20 illustrates how TRIM can be effective.

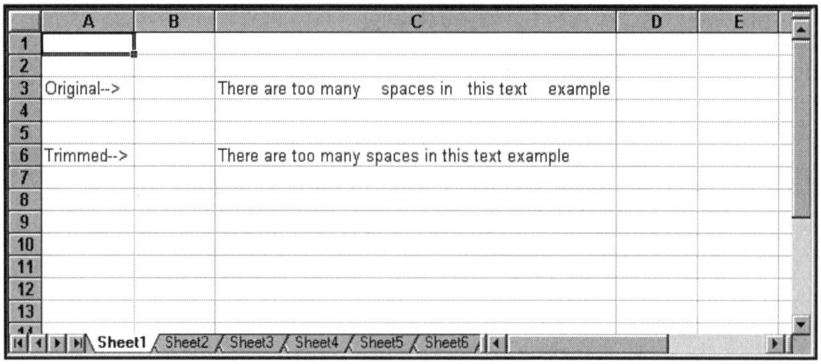

Figure 10.20

Trimming a cell of spaces.

Functions related to TRIM include the following:

◆ **CLEAN** removes all nonprintable characters from a text string.

◆ **MID** returns a specific number of characters from a string.

◆ **REPLACE** replaces characters within a string.

◆ **SUBSTITUTE** replaces certain characters with new ones.

Using Lookup and Reference Functions

Lookup and reference functions are functions that return values about locations of rows, cells, columns, and data in worksheets. They also can extract information from a table.

The ADDRESS Function

The ADDRESS function returns the location of a cell, given the row and column numbers, as text. The syntax used for this function is the following:

```
=address(row_num,col_num,abs_num,a1,sheet_text)
```

row_num is the number of the row, col_num is the number of the column, abs_num is a value from 1 to 4 (referring to the type of reference), a1 is a logical value that determines if the returned value is in A1 or R1C1 format, and sheet_text is the name of the worksheet from which to return the value.

The abs_num argument's values are the following:

1=Absolute value, such as $A$1

2=Absolute Row, Relative Column, such as $A1

3=Relative Row, Absolute Column, A$1

4=Relative reference, A1

An example of the Address function is **=address(1,1,1,1)**, which returns the value $A$1. To use the Function Wizard to enter this formula, select the category and name, then type the argument entry.

If you use a mouse to select a cell for the row and column, the cell addresses are inserted rather than only the row and column identifiers. The end result is a #value! error. Additionally, clicking on the row or column names at the top of each respective worksheet inserts the value C:C if you click on the C column. This insertion also returns an error.

The AREAS Function

The AREAS function returns a value for the number of areas in a reference. An *area* is a range of contiguous cells or a single cell or both.

Tip   If you want to include several references in a single argument, you need to include an extra set of parentheses so that Excel will not interpret the comma separator as a field separator.

The syntax for AREAS is the following:

=areas(reference)

A multireference entry example is =areas((B3:G3,A4,C5:H5)). This function as entered returns the value 3.

The MATCH Function

The MATCH function returns the relative location of a value in an array of text. If you enter **=MATCH("davis",A1:A4,1)**, the function searches the text in the range C5

though C8 to find the string davis. The value it returns is 1, and the text davis appears as the first match in the array.

If the data array is resorted alphabetically in descending order, the new position returned by MATCH is 4. Figure 10.21 shows examples of how MATCH can work in the worksheet.

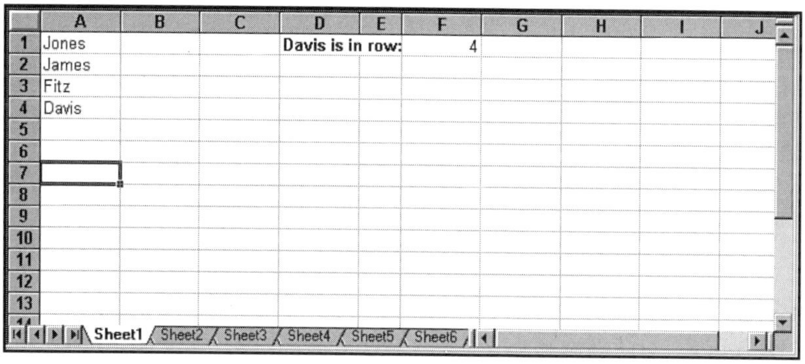

Figure 10.21

The worksheet showing MATCH results.

Working with Information Functions

Information functions return values based on how a cell is formatted or what it contains.

The CELL Function

CELL returns specific information about all types of numeric formats and date formats, about whether a cell is blank or contains a label or value, or even what or where that value is. If you need to determine what the width is for cell A3, type this formula: **=cell(width,A3)**. It can give this information by individual row and column. CELL is used for compatibility with other spreadsheet programs.

The COUNTBLANK Function

The COUNTBLANK function returns a value based on how many empty or blank cells it locates in a given array. This function is especially handy in the Function Wizard (see fig. 10.22). If you need to find out how many entries in a particular array contain no entry, highlight that entry with the mouse after you have selected the function from Step 1.

Figure 10.22

*The number of
blank cells in the
highlighted range
of cells.*

	A	B	C	D	E	F	G	H	I	J
1	Jones			Davis is in row:		4				
2	James									
3	Fitz									
4	Davis									
5										
6										
7	18									
8										
9										
10										
11										
12										
13										

Sheet1 / Sheet2 / Sheet3 / Sheet4 / Sheet5 / Sheet6

Note The COUNTBLANK function does not count blank text cells that contain quotation
marks as true blank cells. Value cells that have 0 are counted, however.

The ISEVEN and ISODD Functions

The ISEVEN and ISODD functions return the values TRUE or FALSE. ISEVEN
returns TRUE if a number is even and FALSE if the number is odd. ISODD, naturally,
returns FALSE if a number is even and TRUE if odd.

Note ISEVEN and ISODD return a #value! message if run on a cell that contains a non-
numeric value. If a number is a decimal, the ISEVEN and ISODD functions test only
the integer, not the value to the right of the decimal point.

The N Function

The N function is like the CELL function in that it is included with Excel for compatibility with other spreadsheet programs. The syntax for N is the following:

`=N(number)`

Where number is the value you want to convert. If N encounters a number, that
number is returned. If N sees a date, it converts that to a serial number. If N sees
TRUE, it converts it to a 1, and everything else N sees returns the value 0.

The TYPE Function

The TYPE function is like the INFO function, except that TYPE returns values 1, 2, 4,
8, 16, and 64 only. If a selection is a number, the value is 1. If it is text, the value is 2.

If it is a formula, the value is 8; if it is an error, the value is 16; and if it is an array, the value is 64. TYPE has a simple syntax:

```
=type(value)
```

The argument value can be a cell or array reference, or a direct value entered.

Logical Functions

Logical functions return values based on whether certain values in a worksheet are met.

The AND and IF Functions

The AND function returns a TRUE or FALSE value, based on worksheet values. This can be useful if you want to display information about a number or numbers in a sheet. AND enables up to thirty arguments. The syntax is the following:

```
=AND(logical1)
```

Figure 10.23 shows two examples of the AND function. The first is the function by itself, and the second is nested with another logical function, IF, and returns a different value based on similar criteria.

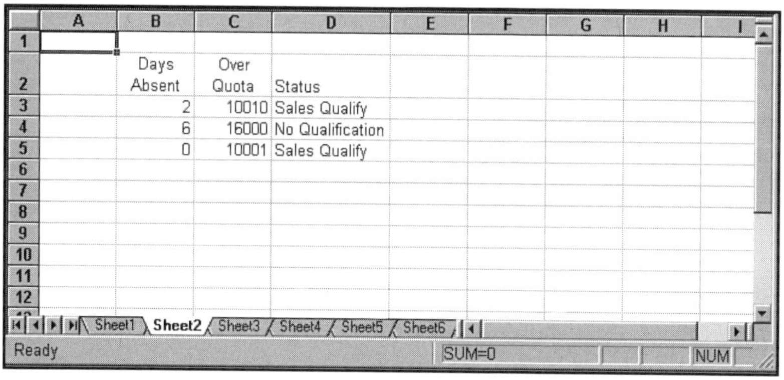

Figure 10.23

IF and AND nested together.

The problem solved in figure 10.23 is to determine whether salespeople qualify for a contest. The criteria for qualification are less than five days absent from work and sales greater than $10,000.00. If those two criteria are met, the salesperson qualifies. The functions used are IF, to satisfy the criteria examination, and AND, to return a value based on IF's determination of TRUE or FALSE, based on the criteria. The syntax is the following:

```
=IF(AND(B8>10000,A8<5),"Sales Qualify","No Qualification.")
```

The NOT Function

The NOT function is a simple one: it reverses the logic of an equation or argument. For example, in the formula **=not(10=11)**, the returned value is TRUE. The numbers, of course, are *not* equal. The NOT function reports FALSE for the formula **=not(10=10)**.

The OR Function

The OR function, like AND, returns a TRUE or FALSE value based on its argument. Unlike AND, however, OR returns a TRUE value if *any* argument is true, whereas AND returns a TRUE only if *all* arguments are true. If you change the qualification rules for the example in the AND and IF discussion—either less than five days of absenteeism or greater than $10,000.00 in sales—the OR statement returns `Sales Qualify` for all the arguments in figure 10.23.

The TRUE and FALSE Functions

The TRUE and FALSE functions are among the easiest to use of all the Excel functions because they do not require any arguments at all. They simply return the values TRUE or FALSE when entered. You can use these functions through the Function Wizard or they can be typed directly into a worksheet.

Troubleshooting Excel Functions

The process of troubleshooting functions has improved drastically over previous releases of Excel because of the Function Wizard. The Wizard enables immediate feedback and prompting through each step of the function, which can be invaluable.

 Note As you gain more comfort with Excel functions and formulas, you might find that function entry is faster from the keyboard than through the Wizard. It makes little sense to use some simple functions, such as TRUE and FALSE, with the Wizard. However, the Function Wizard and some of Excel's built-in features make most function entries easier and more accurate, and error recognition faster.

When you are troubleshooting functions, the Function Wizard can do all the formatting, typing, and arranging of function statements for you. If you invoke the Wizard and choose the function name you want to use, the entry in the formula bar is made for you before any arguments are entered. After clicking on the Next button, the arguments are displayed, and after all the required functions are completed (and prior to clicking on **F**inish), the value is displayed in the upper right corner of the Step 2 of 2 dialog box. You can see the results prior to actual entry into your sheet.

If your function returns #value!, #name!, or another error message, you can change values by moving back to your arguments to determine what the cause of the problem is. For newer users of Excel, the Help button also is a good way to work through problems.

As you enter functions and determine which ones you will need to analyze your worksheets and workbooks adequately and completely, the Help button brings up specific syntax notes, tips, and, in many cases, examples of ways in which functions can be used. Often, mistakes in value entry can be spotted by looking at Help's examples and working back through the arguments to determine the root of the problem.

 Tip   You might want to use the Bookmark/Define feature in online help if you are going back and forth on different kinds of function questions or varying types of examples. The bookmark takes you to the spot you last were and saves time and keystroking or mouse clicking.

As you become more comfortable with functions, entering them from the keyboard can become more effective. If you get in the habit of entering the formula, Excel converts lowercase entries to all uppercase—if they are typed correctly and are function names Excel recognizes.

Using this method, you can skip the first dialog box with the Wizard as well, by first typing the equal sign, then typing the function name in lowercase with an opening parenthesis, then pressing Shift+F3. This action brings up the Step 2 of 2 dialog box, in which you then can enter arguments, using the mouse for cell or array references or the keyboard.

Another way of editing function statements is to position the mouse pointer on the cell that contains the statement and press F2. This brings up the formula and makes it available for editing in the cell in which it is written. It also brings up a copy in the formula bar, but you must click on the formula bar to edit the function there. When the formula is opened for editing, the arrow keys can move you one space at a time through the statement so that you can make any necessary changes. Pressing Enter ends the editing session and returns the value of the function.

While the statement is open for editing, whenever the cursor is on a cell reference, you can press the F4 key to modify the cell reference's type from absolute row or column to relative row or column, or vice versa. This is helpful when moving functions or when copying them with AutoFill or copy/paste and cut/paste features. Figure 10.24 shows a function that is being edited and the mouse pointer clicked on the formula bar for easier editing.

Figure 10.24

Absolute references changed using the F4 key (note the formula bar).

D3	▼	=IF(AND($C$3>10000,B2<5),"Sales Qualify", "No Qualification")

	A	B	C	D	E	F	G	H	I
1									
2		Days Absent	Over Quota	Status					
3		2	10010	No Qualification					
4		6	16000	No Qualification					
5		0	10001	Sales Qualify					
6									
7									
8									
9									
10									
11									
12									

Sheet1 \ **Sheet2** \ Sheet3 \ Sheet4 \ Sheet5 \ Sheet6

Ready   SUM=0   NUM

Linking Functions

Data from one sheet in a workbook can be linked to cells located in another worksheet, another workbook, or even an external source such as a database or another spreadsheet program. Sharing information between sheets can be accomplished in a variety of ways, depending on your specific needs and application.

If you have a workbook with information related to a separate workbook, and you want to use information from the first one, the first workbook is called the *source workbook*. The sheet that receives the information from this source is called the *dependent worksheet* (or *workbook*). An *external link* refers to another Excel cell or range of cells or specific named region.

To create a link between workbooks, highlight the cells that you want to link in the source workbook. From the toolbar or the **E**dit menu, select Copy, which places a flashing dotted line around the cells that you have selected. Click on the **W**indow menu. Select the workbook to which you want to take the selected referenced cells, and make it the active window. (You also can have both books open at one time on a single screen.)

In the dependent sheet, or the one you want to receive the cell references, choose Paste Special from the **E**dit menu. In the resulting dialog box, you can choose to copy all information about the selected cells—such as formulas, formats, values, and notes—and you can perform operations on the data. If you check **A**ll and select Paste **L**ink in the Paste Special dialog box, the entire cell group, along with its entire contents, are copied to the new worksheet. Now, any time items are changed on the original or source workbook, those changes are passed along to the dependent reference. Figure 10.25 displays an example of this procedure.

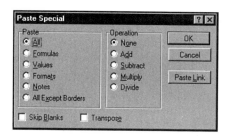

Figure 10.25

The Paste Special dialog box.

Tip

There is a shortcut to this paste process. Highlight the cells to which you want to copy the references and click the right mouse button. This brings up a cell menu that includes Cut, Copy, Paste, Paste Special, Insert, Delete, Clear Contents, and Format Cells. Move to your dependent worksheet, click on a cell to receive the information, and click the right mouse button again. Choose Paste Special to complete the process.

When you link workbooks in this manner, Excel creates absolute references in the formulas that are transferred so that if you move the information in the workbooks, the references to the source remain intact. Movement in either the source or dependent workbooks is protected.

Linked formulas use this syntax:

```
{='[WORKBK.LXS]Worksheet_Name'!abs_cell_ref}
```

For example, the formula `{='[SALES.XLS]Sales Report'!$C$4:$D$8}` in the SAMPLE1.XLS workbook is dependent on `SALES.XLS` workbook, `Sales Report` worksheet, and cells C4 to D8. At the point when those cells are updated on the source link, the dependent links will be updated automatically as well.

Excel also will update dynamically any charts or related information you are using that are linked to your source reference.

Note

Excel includes visual auditing capability. For a detailed discussion, see Chapter 11, "Advanced Worksheet Capabilities."

Example Application

The following example uses many of the formulas and concepts outlined in this chapter.

Creating an application requires some forethought and planning to be effective. Key issues to a successful application include what data to use, where it comes from, what level of sensitivity it carries, what format it is in, and who needs to use it.

Other important issues include what new data will be entered into a worksheet and what will be calculated. How will updates be made, and by whom? What level of experience does the person doing the updates have? What portions of the data are meaningful for some, but not for others?

Often, you will find that changes need to be made and documentation needs to be done. Excel has some great tools and methods for these tasks, as described in the section "Using Excel's Auditing Functions" in Chapter 11, "Advanced Worksheet Capabilities."

Because several different people will need the sales information generated from this example application, three separate workbooks will be created. The first is MASTER.XLS, the second is SLSRES.XLS, and the third is SALACCT.XLS. The MASTER workbook is the source for much of the data that the other two workbooks will receive, so the amount of work needed to maintain current information in all of them is minimized because of the links created.

MASTER.XLS contains raw sales numbers, received from the billing department, about each salesperson. The data can be extracted from a monthly billing analysis report generated by accounts receivable, an external source (see Chapter 13, "Excel Data Management"). For this example, data will be entered manually from customer billing analysis reports by a sales support person.

SLSRES.XLS contains a recap of the sales reports by region and by salesperson. Information in this workbook is distributed to regional sales managers, and can be used to track performance by region, by person, and by product.

SALACCT.XLS is the sales accounting workbook. This data is used in payroll, where bonuses, contests, and commissions are calculated and checks are written.

The MASTER.XLS workbook has four active worksheets, one for each region of the company. Each region has two salespeople, and the MASTER workbook is the source for a portion of all the worksheets. The columns that list sales by product type for each month of the year are totaled, with running year-to-date sums for each category and one grand total.

Most of the SLSRES workbook is extracted from the MASTER. The sales totals by product category and region are calculated and presented on this sheet. In addition, an average sales figure by salesperson, by product category, and by month is listed. The sheet also includes a range of cells that represent the percentage of sales for the company by product type and by representative.

The SALACCT workbook also is linked to the source MASTER workbook. In this workbook, the totals are calculated and profits are figured from cost data. The profit report is broken out into profits by line of business, salesperson, and region. Sales managers are paid a bonus for profit growth and increased revenue.

Salespeople in this organization are paid a percentage of profits of their quarterly sales for hardware. They are paid a straight percentage of revenue for software and service. They also get bonuses for each month that their quota is exceeded, and the bonus is figured on quarterly dollars.

The information from these workbooks is distributed to different locations and people throughout the company.

In the MASTER.XLS workbook, each worksheet has a new name to assist with organization. To rename a worksheet, double-click on the worksheet tab at the bottom of the screen. This brings up a dialog box in which you can enter the new name. Clicking on OK changes the name in the tab.

 Note When you name a worksheet in a source workbook and change the worksheet name later, the formulas in the dependent workbooks are updated automatically.

Because the base values for this example come from sales data about each representative in the company, the best place to begin is with the salesperson sales data (see fig. 10.26). The basic information about the people, territories, and regions are the headers for the sheet. In the data range, the column headings are product categories, and the row headings are months of the year.

	A	B	C	D	E	F	G	H	I	J	K	L
1	Sales Person	Anderson, Kate			YTD TOTAL	Hardware	Software	Service				
2	Territory:	R1850				98000	12000	24000				
3	Region:	1										
4	Quota:	10000										
5												
6												
7		Hardware	Software	Service	Total							
8	January	10000	1000	2000	13000							
9	February	8000	1000	1	9101							
10	March	8000	1000	2000	11000							
11	April	8000	1000	2000	11000							
12	May	8000	1000	2000	11000							
13	June	8000	1000	2000	11000							
14	July	8000	1000	2000	11000							
15	August	8000	1000	2000	11000							
16	September	8000	1000	2000	11000							
17	October	8000	1000	2000	11000							
18	November	8000	1000	2000	11000							
19	December	8000	1000	2000	11000							

Anderson,KT. / Sheet2 / Sheet3 / Sheet4 / Sheet5 / S

Figure 10.26

The base format for the MASTER worksheet.

The three product headings are Hardware, Software, and Service. The fourth column heading is for monthly totals. There is a number at the bottom of each column representing year-to-date (YTD) totals—by product category—and summary information at the top of the sheet using the same totals as cell references. The totals are copied from the bottom of the columns and pasted as links for the YTD totals at the top. This automatically creates absolute references to the totals numbers.

The SLSRES.XLS sheets use the values from MASTER for many of the calculations. To create the SLSRES workbook, select **N**ew from the **F**ile menu. Rename the first worksheet tab Region 1. From the **W**indow menu, click on **A**rrange. Select **T**ile in the dialog box, and click on OK. This displays both the MASTER and SLSRES workbooks on-screen, which makes creating the link between the two easier.

Make the MASTER workbook and the Anderson, K. worksheets active by clicking on them. Highlight the range of cells from A1:H4 and click the right mouse button. Choose Copy from the Cell menu, and move to the SLSRES workbook. In the worksheet Region 1, click on cell A1 and click the right mouse button. Select Paste Special from the menu, and click on the Paste **L**ink button in the dialog box. This action copies the cell references from MASTER to SLSRES and completes the link between the two. Now, each time data is updated for a salesperson, the changes will be updated in the dependent worksheets.

The Paste Special command can copy cells a number of different ways. You can paste all the attributes of a cell, or formats, formulas, values, or nothing. You also can perform operations during the copy. You can copy the cells, or you can add, subtract, multiply, or divide the target values with the cells you have chosen to copy.

The SLSRES workbook has three active worksheets. The first two are the sales recap sheets for the salespeople in each region. Each salesperson has a group of cells that contains her year-to-date sales in each of the product categories. In addition, the summary shows the last active month entered. This number is calculated by using the HLOOKUP function. The function is written in SLSRES as the following:

```
=hlookup(IF***) CG: fill in the formula to do the lookup if
sales>1.and return the value of the month.**
```

This updates the regional managers with the values for the current month's sales.

The third worksheet in the SLSRES workbook is the company totals and rankings worksheet. It shows the total sales for each salesperson, followed by that person's respective ranks for Hardware, Software, and Service. It also shows the percentage of total sales for each product category, as well as percentage of total sales for the region. The last area of the sheet shows the values that reflect the averages by region for all salespeople in all categories.

The last workbook in the series, SLSACCT, is the sales accounting workbook. This group has three sheets in it as well. The first is the Quota % worksheet. In this sheet, the quota performance is calculated for each salesperson, and for each region. These numbers are all drawn from the MASTER workbook. The salespeople again are ranked, but this time by percentage of quota achievement, and the number of months over quota is listed as well.

The second worksheet in this book is Bonus $, or the place where the bonuses are figured. This sheet figures its values from the individual sales recap sheets in MASTER. The bonuses are paid if the salesperson is over quota for the month, and paid on the dollars sold during the current quarter. Quarterly totals are figured here, and the bonuses are figured on those numbers.

The third sheet in the book is Commission $, which figures the commissions paid to each person, along with the tax information for each check and for the year. The profits for hardware are figured here from the fourth sheet, Costs. Because the salespeople are paid for hardware on percentage of profit, the values are linked together, and the commissions are calculated from that. In addition, the sales manager's bonus is figured from these calculations. The growth for each region is figured here, too.

The last worksheet in this application is the Performance Recap. The recap shows the total sales, the total commissions, and rank for overall sales for each region and each salesperson. Each person also has a cell for contest bonus points and for performance against quota. The total dollars are graphed for distribution to all offices to post so that salespeople can see how they are doing in relation to the rest of the group.

Advanced Worksheet Capabilities

Microsoft Excel for Windows 95 has some powerful capabilities. This chapter will introduce these capabilities to you so that you can learn to use them in your applications. The advanced capabilities covered in this section include an in-depth discussion of several of the add-ins and advanced features that are part of Excel. In this chapter, you will learn about the following:

◆ Excel add-ins

◆ Installing and removing add-ins

◆ Using Excel's auditing features

◆ Changing the appearance of your worksheet

◆ Using outlining

After you finish this chapter, you will know how to install add-ins, use advanced features, and apply them in applications. You also get a chance to use some of Excel's advanced tools, such as Auditing, Report Manager, and Pivot tables.

Add-ins in Excel are worksheet tools that bring advanced power to your desktop. The add-ins included with Excel that are covered in this chapter are AutoSave, Analysis ToolPak, Goal Seek, Solver, Scenario Manager, View Manager, and Report Manager. A brief description of each follows:

◆ **AutoSave.** Automatically saves your work at specified intervals.

◆ **Analysis ToolPak.** Provides a number of worksheet functions and macro functions that help with data analysis in the workbook, the Function Wizard, and the Tools menu.

◆ **Goal Seek.** Enables you to find values to complete questions based on a specific outcome.

◆ **Solver.** Enables you to determine answers to complex what-if questions by analyzing cells and determining the optimum value adjustments to arrive at a desired result.

◆ **Scenario Manager.** Enables you to create and analyze results from various groups of changing cells. The scenario manager enables you to define custom assumptions and to answer complex what-if questions.

◆ **View Manager.** Helps you arrange and look at your information in a variety of ways.

◆ **Report Manager.** Enables you to format your information contained within workbooks and worksheets and scenarios in an organized, uniform report output format.

Installing and Removing Add-Ins

The add-in files are located in the \EXCEL\LIBRARY subdirectory. To look at the available add-ins, choose Add-Ins from the **T**ools menu. A list of the available add-ins appears; add-ins that are installed have their check boxes selected. You install the add-in you want by clicking on the check box to the left of the description of the add-in. Removal is just as simple. To remove an add-in that is already installed, just click on the appropriate check box.

Many add-ins bring with them menu choices. When you install an add-in, the menu options are made available; when you remove an add-in, the options are made inactive. Additionally, with Analysis ToolPak you can choose from 50+ more functions than without it activated.

Selecting Add-Ins from the Tools menu displays the Add-Ins dialog box (see fig. 11.1). Note which add-ins are currently selected. For examination, click in the check boxes currently marked with an X so that all add-ins are deselected. After you do this, close the Add-Ins dialog box by clicking on the OK button. This removes the add-ins from Excel, and changes the functions, selections, and menu selections that you can access throughout the various menu choices on the main toolbar, from the pull-down menus, and through several of the Wizards, such as the Function Wizard.

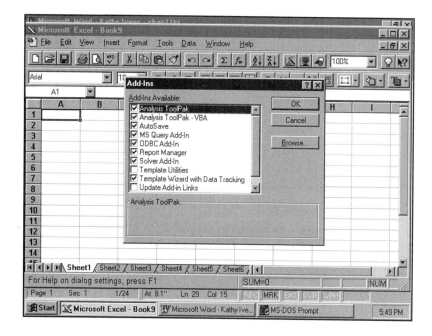

Figure 11.1

The Add-Ins dialog box.

Even after you remove all the add-ins from Excel, several of them remain available from pull-down menus, such as Solver, Goal Seek, and Scenario Manager. When they are invoked under the **T**ools pull-down menu, they are resubmitted to the add-ins list that Excel uses to track what is automatically loaded when starting up the software, so that the next time you use the program, the same tools are available.

Note Using all add-ins with Excel changes the time required to load the program and may slow down other operations such as Cut and Paste because of the extra demands on system memory and resources.

Using the Add-Ins

The following sections describe the features of the Excel add-ins and get you up to speed in working with them.

AutoSave

AutoSave is one of the easiest add-ins to use, and offers one of the greatest benefits: it saves your work for you in specified intervals.

To activate AutoSave, choose Add-**I**ns from the **T**ools menu. When the Add-Ins dialog box appears, click in the AutoSave check box.

Configuring the AutoSave add-in is straightforward. Again click on the **T**ools menu, and if you have properly installed the add-in, AutoSave appears in the drop-down menu with a check mark next to it. Click on AutoSave, and the AutoSave dialog box appears with several options you can use to modify the add-in (see fig. 11.2). The default values are to autosave every 10 minutes, to save the active workbook only, and to prompt the user before saving. You also can configure AutoSave to save workbooks or workspaces automatically, with or without user intervention.

Figure 11.2

The AutoSave dialog box.

If the **P**rompt Before Saving check box is selected, you can save the current workbook, skip the save, cancel the operation, or get help.

If you have AutoSave activated under the default settings and you switch to another Windows application while working on an Excel Workbook, the Excel title bar beneath whatever application you are running flashes, indicating that user input is required. When you switch back to Excel, the AutoSave dialog box is in the foreground of the workbook, and the Excel title bar stops flashing.

If you want to change the interval of time between saves, or save all open workbooks instead of just the active workbook, change the options from within the AutoSave dialog box. You can disable AutoSave, change the Automatic **S**ave Every setting, choose Save Active **W**orkbook Only or Save **A**ll Open Workbooks, and decide whether to check Prompt Before Saving. If you are working on a new workbook and have not

previously saved your work, AutoSave takes you through the normal steps required to save a workbook, such as assigning a name and location for storing the workbook.

Analysis ToolPak

After you install the Analysis ToolPak, a new option appears on the **T**ools menu—**D**ata Analysis, which lists the Analysis tools available in Excel.

Before you use the Analysis ToolPak, you need to organize your worksheet data as an input range, and select an output range in which to place results. The contents of the output vary, depending on which tool you use. Excel assists you by providing labels for cells in an output range if you do not supply them.

The tools available in the ToolPak are shown in table 11.1.

TABLE 11.1
Tools Available in the Analysis ToolPak

Tool Name	Description
Anova: Single Factor	Performs simple variance analysis based on rows or columns of data
Anova: Two Factor with Replication	An extension of the single factor Anova, which includes more than one sample for each group of data
Anova: Two Factor without Replication	Performs two sample Anova, which does not include more than one sampling per group
Correlation	Finds a correlation coefficient for a group of numbers
Covariance	Averages the deviations of two ranges of data from their respective means
Descriptive Statistics	Reports on the variability and central tendencies of data
Exponential Smoothing	Returns a value based on a prior forecast, using a constant that determines the magnitude of how strongly forecasts respond to numbers in a forecast
F-Test Two-Sample for Variance	Compares two population groups for variance
Fourier Analysis	Solves problems in linear systems analyzing periodic data

continues

TABLE 11.1, CONTINUED
Tools Available in the Analysis ToolPak

Tool Name	Description
Histogram	Calculates individual and cumulative frequencies for ranges of cell data and bins, and generates the number of occurrences of a value in a set
Moving Average	Projects values based on previous periods, such as sales or inventory
Random Number Generation	Fills cells with random numbers for a variety of different statistical uses
Rank and Percentile	Provides the percentage rank of each value in a data set
Regression	Using the "least Squares" method, analyzes a set of observations about an event to enable forecasting of other events
Sampling	Creates a sample of data from an existing sample or population
t-Test: Paired Two-Sample means	Compares whether two Sample for means are distinct
t-Test: Two-Sample, equal variances	Determines whether two sets' means are equal, assuming equal variances
t-Test: Two-Sample, unequal variances	Determines whether two sets' means are equal, assuming unequal variances
z-Test: Two Sample	Tests the difference between two population means

Each of the Analysis ToolPak functions has similar requirements to return values, like regular worksheet functions. All require *input values*, cells or ranges that Excel assigns as absolute values using the ROWCOLUMN reference type. In addition, you are prompted for arguments specific to the type of analysis required so that a meaningful number or report is returned as you use the functions.

The information for most Data Analysis tools can be output to a range of cells, a new worksheet ply, or its own workbook. A *worksheet ply* is simply another worksheet in your existing workbook, which you can name in the dialog box under output options, as shown in figure 11.3.

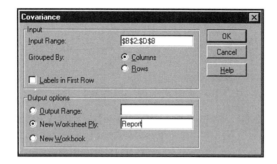

Figure 11.3

Outputting in the Covariance dialog box to a New Worksheet Ply, with new name Report.

Many of the Data Analysis tools are specific for exact specific analysis, and extensive help is available in the user's guides, and through online help. When you want more specific information about one of the Data Analysis tools, highlight it with the mouse and press F1 or click on the Help button.

The results generated by many of the Data Analysis tools are extensive, as typified by an Anova: Single Factor, for example. Taking a simple sample of six numbers, in two worksheet cells, selecting the input range as two columns by three rows, and output range as a new worksheet ply called Anova, the resulting report is extensive, showing the count, sum, average, variance, and an analysis of the variance in detail.

The Analysis ToolPak was developed by GreyMatter and KRISTECH companies.

Goal Seek

Goal Seek is a handy tool that you can use to achieve a certain value in a cell that has a formula, by adjusting the value of another cell that has a direct effect on that cell. Suppose that the salespeople's totals for the month were 70,000, and that result was obtained by adding the individual's numbers for each month and displaying it in a cell below the column. You can use Goal Seek to see how much your top representative needs to sell to make the monthly total 80,000.

Goal Seek is invoked by choosing **T**ools, Goal Seek. The dialog box prompts you to select the cell that has the formula whose result you want to alter, then enter the value you want to reach. The final step in Goal Seek is to select the cell whose value you want to modify to reach the goal or target specified in the first step.

Figure 11.4 shows the Goal Seek dialog box.

Figure 11.4

The Goal Seek dialog box.

After you choose the options you want to use with Goal Seek, the Goal Seek Status dialog box appears with several options: stepping through an operation, pausing operations, and seeking additional help. This dialog box also displays the cell information, the target value, and the current value, so that as Goal Seek works, you can see the result and step through, pause, or alter it as you go. Clicking on the **P**ause button changes the choices to **S**top and **C**ontinue.

When you click on OK in the Goal Seek Status dialog box, Goal Seek places the value found into the specified cell. If you find that this is not what you want, you can restore the values by choosing **U**ndo Goal Seek from the **E**dit menu on the main menu bar. If you really can't decide what to do, choose **E**dit, then Redo Goal Seek, to recalculate the goal seek you just undid.

You can use Goal Seek with data tables to answer what-if questions about multiple variables against a single formula or single variables against multiple formulas. A *data table* is an array or group of cells that shows the effects of different variables on a formula. There are two types of data tables, single-input and two-input tables. A *single-input table* takes a single variable in a formula and displays multiple values in the data table.

If you want to see the results of a varying interest rate on a loan in table format, for example, you would use a single-input data table. Figure 11.5 shows the format for a column-oriented table, and you can do the same thing in a row format. To make a data table, begin by entering a column of the values for which you want to see results. From the first entry in the column, go right one cell and up one cell. At this location, input the formula that contains the target cell where you want your table variables inserted—in this case, interest rates. Now, using the right mouse button, select the area that contains the variables, the formula you entered to the right and up one row, and from the **D**ata menu, select table.

Figure 11.5

The format for a column-oriented table, showing multiple interest rates and payments.

	A	B	C	D	E	F	G	H	I
7		Payment	903.54						
8		22							
9									
10		Rates							
11		33	903.54						
12		100%	8333.33	0	0				
13		200%	16666.67	0	0				
14		9%	804.62	0	0				
15		10%	877.57	0	0				
16		15%	1264.44	0	0				
17		20%	1671.02	0	0				
18		0.25	2084.578636	0	0				
19		0.14							
20									

Sheet1 / Sheet2 / Sheet3 / Sheet4 / Sheet5 / Sheet6

The Table dialog box appears, and you can choose **R**ow Input Cell or **C**olumn Input Cell. In a single-input table, you can fill in only one value (in a two-input table, you

must input values for both). Your input cell, because this example uses a columnar format, is the second choice, **C**olumn Input Cell. The *input cell* is the cell whose value you want to change in the representative table of variables.

To make a two-input table, take the same column of figures and move the formula entered earlier to the cell directly above the first entry in the column. Then, directly to the right of that, enter your second variable—the length of time on a loan. Next, highlight the entire area, including the variables and formulas, as shown in figure 11.6.

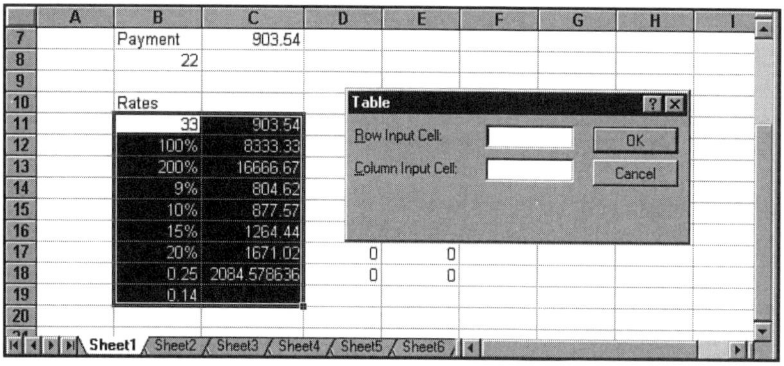

Figure 11.6

The two-input table example and the Table dialog box.

Again, choose **D**ata, Table. For the row input cell, choose the time frame from the main portion of the worksheet. Press Tab, or click on the next field—the Column Input Cell. Click on the percentage rate from the main area, and click on the Done button. Goal Seek fills in the values for each corresponding time frame, at each interest rate. At this point, perform the following steps:

1. Choose **D**ata, Table.

2. For the row input, choose the time frame from the main portion of the worksheet.

3. Tab to the column input box and click on the value for percentage rate.

4. Click on OK.

Any changes you make to the interest rate column or the time row are reflected automatically as you enter the numbers, which can be a valuable way to answer what-if questions.

A *two-input table* takes two variables in a formula and returns the values as shown in figure 11.7.

Goal Seek can save time in doing tedious what-if type analysis by offering quick solutions to questions that might take a long time using trial and error.

Figure 11.7

Example of a two-input data table.

	A	B	C	D	E	F	G	H	I
13									
14	Rates	877.57	10	15	20	30			
15		9%	$1,266.76	$1,014.27	$ 899.73	$ 804.62			
16		10%	$1,321.51	$1,074.61	$ 965.02	$ 877.57			
17		15%	$1,613.35	$1,316.79	$1,316.79	$1,264.44			
18		20%	$1,932.56	$1,756.30	$1,698.82	$1,671.02			
19		25%	$2,774.93	$2,135.53	$2,098.72	$2,084.58			
20		14%	$1,552.66	$1,331.74	$1,243.52	$1,184.87			
21									
22									
23									
24									
25									
26									

Sheet1 \ **Sheet2** \ Sheet3 \ Sheet4 \ Sheet5 \ Sheet6

Solver

Solver calculates answers to what-if scenarios by using adjustable cells, and even minimizing or maximizing specific cells in order to attain the desired result.

Solver is useful for three types of problems:

◆ **Integer problems.** Problems that require a yes or no answer (0 or 1), or problems in which no decimal places are required. Integer problems can greatly increase the amount of time Solver needs to reach a solution.

◆ **Linear problems.** Problems that involve functions or operations such as addition and subtraction, or some of the built-in functions such as FORECAST.

◆ **Nonlinear problems.** Problems that use any algorithms, pairs of changing cells that are multiplied or divided by one another, or exponents. Growth and SQRT are two functions that might be present in a nonlinear problem.

Solver is similar to Goal Seek; however, it has more options, and can answer questions of greater complexity. In addition, after Solver answers the questions you pose, you can have it generate reports based on the changes you make to your worksheets.

To start Solver, choose **T**ools, Solver. The Solver Parameters dialog box appears (see fig. 11.8), in which you enter the information it needs. The first item Solver needs is a *target cell*, a cell that contains a formula that you want to find a value for by altering other dependent parts of your worksheet or workbook. To select a target cell, click on the cell you want to change. If you highlight the cell you intend to change and then invoke Solver, that cell address is automatically entered in the S**e**t Target Cell edit box.

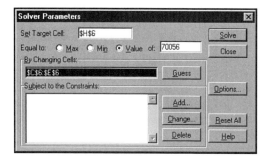

Figure 11.8

The Solver Parameters dialog box.

Next, you select an Equal to parameter, **M**ax, Mi**n**, or **V**alue of. There is an entry box to enter the specific value, which is activated if you check the **V**alue of selection. After you complete these two steps, you need to tell Solver which cells to change to arrive at the desired result, and you can use the **G**uess button if you need help for this. Clicking on **G**uess highlights the cells on the worksheet and displays the absolute values of the cells in the box beneath the **B**y Changing Cells text box. **G**uess selects all nonformula cells referred to by the formula in the **B**y Changing Cells text box, which can save you some time.

To further customize your problem setup, you can add constraints to the equations by clicking on the **A**dd button and choosing limits or ranges for the cells to be modified. Suppose you want to see which numbers would need to be modified for each of your salespeople to reach 80,000 sales for a month. The current sales are 55,600, but you want the values for a particular person to remain at or below a certain dollar value. You can, in the S**u**bject to the Constraints box, add the cell reference to the person whose number you want to keep at or below the value, and indicate the Less than or equal to sign and the value.

You can add multiple constraints to the equation to reach the desired goal. If you have multiple constraints and you want to change, edit, or delete them, the buttons to the right of the Constraints window enables these functions. Clicking on the **A**dd button brings up an empty dialog box in which you fill in the appropriate cell, limit, and operator. **C**hange brings up the same box, but with all the values filled in for editing. **D**elete prompts you to confirm the deletion of a particular constraint from the problem.

If you plan on running a similar problem against other worksheets, you can save your model problem and modify those parameters for the new problem. The **O**ptions button in the Solver dialog box presents the following options:

◆ **Max Time.** Limits the amount of time spent in solving the problem by limiting the number of interim calculations. The default value is 100 seconds, and the maximum is 32,767. The default is adequate for most small problems. This value must be a positive integer.

◆ **Iterations.** Limits the amount of time Solver uses to process your problem. Again, the default is 100, which is adequate for most simple problems, and this option has the same maximum value and rules as Max Time.

◆ **Precision.** Determines whether the constraint cell value matches the target value or is within the upper or lower value ranges you specified. The default is 0.000001, and the number you use must be a fraction. The lower the number, the higher the precision, and therefore, the longer Solver takes to reach the solution.

◆ **Tolerance.** Deals with changing cells that are restricted to integers. The *tolerance* is a percentage of error allowed in a calculation in which an integer is used. A higher tolerance level increases solution speed, and this setting has no effect if there are not integer limits placed on the cells to change.

◆ **Assume Linear Process.** Speeds the solution if all the specified relationships are linear.

◆ **Show Iteration Results.** Stops Solver after each iteration and shows the results, which can be useful if you are examining a problem or troubleshooting a scenario.

◆ **Use Automatic Scaling.** Handy when the changing cells and the target have large scale differences. The Estimates box specifies whether you should use Tangent or Quadratic methods to estimate target and changing cells. The Default is Tangent, but Quadratic can improve results in nonlinear problems. Derivative's choices of Forward (the default) and Central are useful if the graphical representations are not smooth and continuous. The Central method also might be useful if Solver gives you a message that it could not improve the solution.

◆ **Search.** Defines whether the Newton or Conjugate gradient method of searching is used. This tells Solver which algorithm to use, and which direction to search after each iteration. The Newton method requires more memory, but results in less iteration. The Conjugate method is useful with larger problems, if memory is a problem, and can be used to step through a problem.

The Load and Save Model buttons each bring up their own dialog boxes, and can assist you in saving additional models, or bringing them into use in other worksheets. The First Solver model is automatically saved with your work.

Solver calculations can stop for three reasons:

◆ The maximum time limit based on the value in the Options section for Max Time is reached.

◆ The maximum number of iterations or trials is reached.

◆ Solver solves the questions satisfactorily or runs into a problem. If Solver runs into a problem, you receive a message that Solver was unable to adequately solve your problem.

The amount of time Solver needs to operate is affected by two factors:

◆ The number of changing cells

◆ The complexity of the problem

Scenario Manager

Scenario Manager is a tool that enables you to evaluate changes made to worksheets by changing information in a select set of cells. Scenario Manager tracks and maintains the input values you choose, and plugs them into the cells you request. Scenario Manager is a powerful tool for what-if analysis in a worksheet, across multiple sheets in a workbook, or across multiple workbooks.

You can activate Scenario Manager from the Workgroup toolbar or through the Tools menu. Once input, each scenario has a unique name, and its own set of changing cell information.

You can merge scenarios from sheets with other sheets to form consolidation sheets. Suppose you need to borrow money. You have a monthly payment you know you can afford, but you are not sure of how much you should borrow to meet the payment. Furthermore, competing financial programs offer varying interest rates over varying terms. You can set up a model of the loan structure you want to evaluate and use Scenario Manager to evaluate for the best loan structure for your situation. If you use different scenarios to plug in different interest rates available from different banks, the Scenario Manager shows you at a glance what each program offers in terms of the final outcome. Figure 11.9 shows the model, using First in the Scenario Name field.

To create the scenario, choose Scenarios from the Tools menu. The Scenario Manager dialog box appears, and any scenarios associated with the current worksheet are shown in the Scenarios list box. If there are no existing scenarios, click on the Add button to display the Add Scenario dialog box. Scenarios do not require much information, but the results can be very useful.

The scenario needs a name that can offer an indication of its purpose. The example shown previously is called First. The next box of information Scenario Manager needs is the Changing Cells box. This is the area where the variables appear on your worksheet so that Scenario Manager can provide what-if analysis.

Figure 11.9

The Add Scenario dialog box.

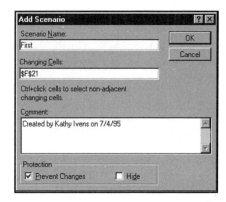

Select the cells you want to change. If there are cells outside the contiguous range you want to include in the changing cells, use Shift+click to include them. Insurance cells can be included by pressing Ctrl+click.

The next information box in this step is the user C**o**mment box, which indicates the registered user's name and the date that the scenario was created or modified. Scenario Manager uses this information to track names and maintain order in the Merge function.

The last field on the Scenario Manager dialog box gives you the option of protecting the scenario by preventing any changes to it or by hiding it.

After you have filled in the fields, choose OK. The Scenario Values dialog box appears (see fig. 11.10), and you can fill in the values for the cells you want to change. When you have finished, choose OK.

Figure 11.10

The Scenario Values dialog box.

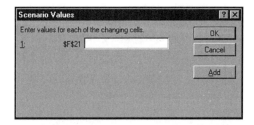

You return to the main Scenario Manager dialog box, in which you should see the name of the scenario you just entered. Several buttons are available along the right side of the box:

◆ **Show.** Enters the results of your variables.

◆ **Close.** Closes the Scenario Manager.

◆ **Add.** Displays the Add Scenario dialog box, which you use to create a scenario.

◆ **Delete.** Removes scenarios.

◆ **Edit.** Enables you to change or modify the elements of a scenario.

◆ **Merge.** Displays the Merge dialog box, which enables you to select the workbook, sheet, and scenario you want to merge.

◆ **Summary.** Provides a new worksheet with a complete formatted summary of the variable changes

The Summary button does some interesting things. It provides a formatted report on its own worksheet of the values that were changed and the results of the scenario. The Scenario Summary dialog box appears, and you have a choice of two different types of reports. The first is the scenario summary, which is a report on its own worksheet, showing the complete details of the scenario.

You also can put the results into a pivot table. A *pivot table* is an interactive worksheet table that you can use to organize and analyze data in a variety of ways. After you create a pivot table, you can rearrange data by dragging fields and items.

View Manager

View manager can change the way your worksheets and workbooks appear on-screen and eventually on paper without saving a separate workbook. Because Excel has a vast number of formatting options that can change the appearance of a worksheet, you might want to use View Manager to add additional enhancements to the way your work appears.

The view that you save reflects current window size, in addition to many of the settings in the Options dialog box. Because each view is saved across a complete workbook, it can be helpful to use the name of the worksheet as well as a brief description.

To invoke View Manager, choose **V**iew, **V**iew Manager. The option at the bottom of the menu choices should indicate View Manager; if it does not, you should reinstall this add-in through the **T**ools menu.

When you choose View Manager from the **V**iew menu, the View Manager dialog box appears (see fig. 11.11). From this dialog box, you can select existing views of your worksheet if available. You can **A**dd a new view, **S**how the effect of the view, Close the View Manager, or **D**elete a view.

Figure 11.11

The View Manager dialog box.

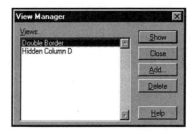

Views save the print settings and displays settings for a worksheet as well as hidden column or row information. You have the option of changing these settings when you create the view in the Add View dialog box. This is done at the same time as you assign a name to the view.

To set up a view, first create the look you want to use by changing the settings, zoom factors, and print settings, and hiding any columns or rows that you want to exclude from the view. After your sheet looks that way you want, choose View from the main menu and invoke the View Manager. Choose Add and name your view. Indicate whether you want to save print settings and hidden columns or rows in the Add Views dialog box, and click on OK to save the view of that sheet.

Note If you do not have any print settings made for a particular sheet, the entire worksheet prints.

Report Manager

The Report Manager provides detailed reports of your workbooks in a variety of ways. You can create customized reports from your information using the Report Manager tools.

Reports can include different views and scenarios, and a report can automatically switch between scenarios and views and print them in a specific order.

To create a report, choose View Report Manager from the View menu. The main Print Report dialog box appears, in which you can print, close, add, edit, delete, or get help.

The first step is to name the report, followed by creating a section. To do this from the Print Report dialog box, choose Add, then name your report and tab to the section area of the Add Report dialog box. A *section* of the report is defined by simply choosing which worksheet from the workbook you want to use and whether you want to use any predefined views or scenarios from the sheets in your reports.

After you name the report, the default values for **S**heet, **V**iew, and Sce**n**ario are marked in the Section to Add group. The sheet name is the same name as the sheet that was active when you launched Report Manager. The drop-down boxes for **V**iew and Sce**n**ario are used to select available variables and representations of your workbook.

After you define a particular addition to the Report Manager, click on the **A**dd button, and it will show up on the Print Report dialog box as well as in the S**e**ctions of this Report area.

If you want to keep an original report to show a history of a particular sheet, for example, you can choose **A**dd in the Report Manager dialog box, and define a new report that uses your new views or scenarios.

Figure 11.12 shows Report Manager's Add Report dialog box.

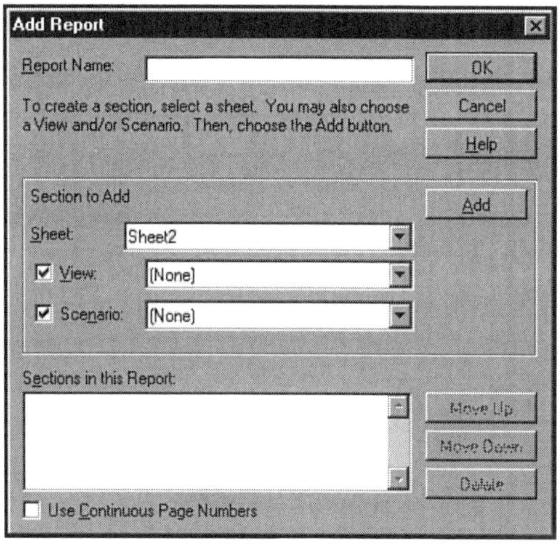

Figure 11.12

Report Manager's Add Report dialog box.

When you add a new report, if you do not want to use views or scenarios in printing, you can keep the default values or uncheck the boxes to the left of the choices. Unchecking the boxes grays the selections available from the drop-down menus for each selection.

With each report you design, you can have multiple sections. In the initial stages of report design, you can update the S**e**ctions in this Report section of the dialog box, after you click on the **A**dd button next to the Section to Add group.

You might want to use different sections in a report to illustrate projected changes in business trends. If you incorporate all the selections into one report when you print, all are included together. If, on the other hand, you want to have the flexibility to print all the information but do not want to have all the reports print together, set up separate reports that reflect the same values.

The Add Report dialog box is also where you change the position of sections in your report, such as in what order your sections fall. If you want the report to be one large report, you should select the Use **C**ontinuous Page Numbers check box. This option prints the page numbers across multiple sections. Unselecting this box resets the page number at each section.

Note   After you define the information in the section that you want to incorporate in your report, you must click on the **A**dd button in the S**e**ction to Add area. If you do not, an error message appears, indicating that you cannot have a report that does not have designed sections. It becomes even more important if you add sections, however, because if you define a new section and forget to add it to the report, Report manager discards all your changes.

After adding a section and clicking on OK, the Print Report dialog box is activated. To print a report, select the title of the report you want and click on the **P**rint button. Your screen changes to each sheet, view, and scenario as it generates the report, and a standard dialog box that indicates print status appears after Excel generates the information. Upon completion your original view, scenario, and worksheet are restored so that you can continue work.

Using Report Manager, you can set up one report to print each scenario you create, with the view options you designate for each scenario, in the order you want the reports to appear.

Using Excel's Auditing Features

Excel has auditing tools that you can use to illustrate how values are arrived at and to figure out where problems have occurred.

The Auditing toolbar provides a quick way to use some of Excel's features—using visual tools called tracers. *Tracers* are graphic displays, such as arrows, that show visually where formulas get their values. To display the Auditing toolbar, choose Auditing from the **T**ools menu. The last selection on the menu is Show Auditing Toolbar, and if it is already active, there is a check mark next to the selection. If you do not want the toolbar to be displayed, simply click in the Show Auditing Toolbar check box.

You also can display the toolbar by choosing Toolbars from the **V**iew menu. The dialog box that appears shows all available Excel and add-in toolbars. If the toolbar

you want is not on the list, return to the **T**ools menu and choose Add-**I**ns to make sure that the add-in you want is loaded. This displays the Add-Ins dialog box so that you can make the selection.

From the Auditing toolbar, you can select and remove tracers of different types: precedents and dependents. You also can add notes, trace errors, and show an information window.

Tracers are graphic representations that display a relationship between cells. Tracers can illustrate two types of relationships: precedent and dependent. Precedent cells are cells that are referred to directly by a formula. Dependent cells, conversely, are cells that contain formulas that refer to other cells.

Another way to describe the relationships is with the terms direct and indirect. A *direct precedent* is a cell that is referred to by the formula in the active cell. An *indirect precedent* is referred to by a formula in a direct precedent cell or another indirect cell.

A *direct dependent* is a cell that contains a formula that refers to the active cell, and an *indirect dependent* is a cell that contains a direct dependent cell or another indirect dependent cell

In the worksheet in figure 11.13, for example, the formula for `Total` in cell C6 is directly dependent on cells C2:C4. The average formula in C8 is directly dependent on the formulas in cells C6 and C7, but indirectly dependent on the values in C2:C4. The cells C2:C4 are direct precedents of the formula in cell C6. They are also indirect precedents of the formula in C8.

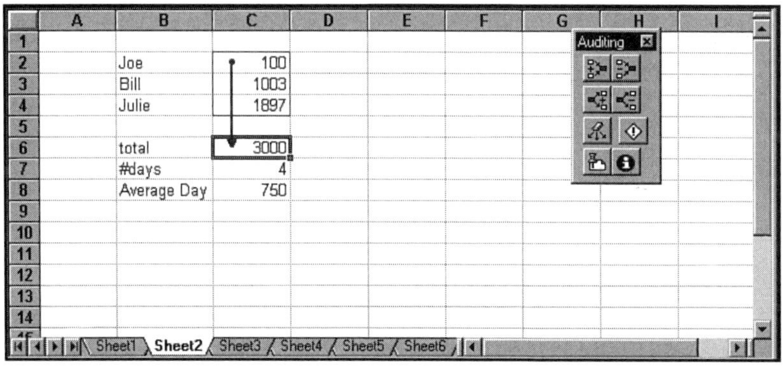

Figure 11.13

Samples of precedent and dependent cells.

Using Auditing tools can help understand, visualize, and troubleshoot these concepts and the data associated with them. In the worksheet in figure 11.13, to trace the precedents of cell C8, make C8 the active cell by clicking on it. Then, on the Auditing toolbar, click on the Trace Precedents button. A box is drawn around cells C3:C6, and a solid line is drawn from the boxed cells to the formula in C8. Then, by clicking on the Trace Dependents button while C8 is still active, a similar line is drawn from C6 to C8, indicating that C8 is directly dependent on C6. This action shows what the relationships are between the cells.

Another way to show this relationship is to make C8 the active cell, and click on the Trace Precedents button. The line is drawn to C6, pointing in the same direction. Click on the Trace Dependents button again to draw the box again on C2:C4, and put the arrow there as well (see fig. 11.14).

Figure 11.14

Tracing precedents from C8, direct and indirect.

	A	B	C	D	E	F	G	H	I
1								Auditing ☒	
2		Joe	100						
3		Bill	1003						
4		Julie	1897						
5									
6		total	3000						
7		#days	4						
8		Average Day	750						
9									
10									
11									
12									
13									
14									

Sheet1 \ **Sheet2** \ Sheet3 \ Sheet4 \ Sheet5 \ Sheet6

To find out which cells are dependent on which values, select cell C2. Click on the Trace Dependents button, and the arrow points to the cell that contains the formula that is directly dependent on the value in that cell. Click on the Trace Dependents button again to draw the line to the next cell, C8, that is indirectly dependent on C2.

Auditing also can be useful in tracking errors in worksheets. If you have a formula that returns an error message, making the errant cell active and clicking on the Trace Errors button shows where the problem lies in the formula.

Tip

You can move along a trace line by placing the mouse pointer on the line and double-clicking. This action moves the active cell to the location to which the trace points. Clicking again returns you to the origin point.

Excel shows tracers in three ways. The first is by a solid blue line. The destination point is indicated by an arrowhead on the end of the line. On a monochrome screen, the line appears black. Errors are traced by a solid red line, or by a dotted line on a monochrome monitor. The error tracer also has an arrowhead point. The third type of tracer is a dashed black line that has an icon, and is the same in both color and monochrome. This tracer refers to an external reference in another worksheet. Figure 11.15 illustrates all three types of lines.

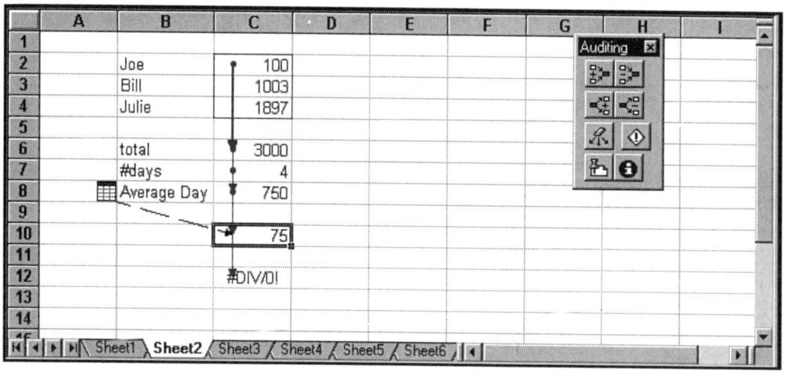

Figure 11.15

*Examples of the
three types of
tracer lines.*

You can remove tracer arrows as easily as you can produce them. Press the Remove Precedent Arrows button to undo the most recent trace precedent function; the Remove Dependent Arrows button works exactly the same way.

If when tracing you press the Trace button numerous times to step through a progression of relationships, each set of arrows is removed one at time. You can remove all the arrows on a sheet by clicking on the Remove All Arrows button

Using the Auditing features, you can add comments to your worksheets. Adding comments is useful if you are going to share your work with others and some explanation is necessary to make certain portions of the worksheet or workbook clear. It also is helpful if you are using complex formulas and references to track your work and trace your footsteps. Users—whether the actual users or just receivers—of larger worksheets can benefit from annotations and explanations of information as well.

Notes

Adding notes or sounds to worksheets is done through the Auditing toolbar. The icon of a pushpin and paper is the Add Notes button. You can type the note, or a note can be a sound that you import. You can even record your own messages if your computer has the appropriate recording hardware and software.

Choosing Note from the **I**nsert menu brings up the Cell Note dialog box, as shown in figure 11.16. The cell that is active when you press the Attach Notes button is where the note indicator is placed, and it is indicated by a small red square in the upper right corner of the cell. If you have multiple cells highlighted when you enter your note, it will be placed in the last cell clicked on.

To play or read a note from anywhere on a worksheet, click on the Attach Note button to bring up the Cell Notes dialog box, and the notes in the worksheet are listed in the Notes in **S**heet list box. Click once on a note to make it active and display the contents of the written note in **T**ext Note edit box in the center of the dialog box. If there is a sound file attached, the **P**lay button at the bottom is activated. If the note is text only, the **P**lay button is disabled.

Figure 11.16

The Cell Note dialog box.

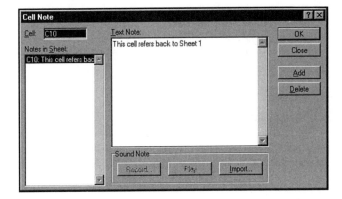

You can check the spelling of notes just like worksheets. Just click on the Check Spelling button on the main toolbar, or choose **T**ools, **S**pelling. Alternatively, you can press F7.

You also can print text notes. From the **F**ile menu, choose Page Set**u**p. On the Sheet tab in the Page Setup dialog box, click on the **N**otes check box. If you want the row and column references to print as well, click in the Row and Column References check box.

You also can choose not to display notes indicators. Choose **O**ptions from the **T**ools menu. Choose the **V**iew tab, and you can select or deselect the **N**ote Indicator check box in the Options dialog box. When the note display indicator is not activated, you can still read, play, and print notes.

To copy the notes from cells to other cells, select the cell that has the note you want to copy. Click the right mouse button or press Shift+F10 to bring up the Cell menu. Select Copy and move the mouse to the destination cell. Click the right mouse button again and choose Paste Special. The Paste Special dialog box appears. Click in the Note check box at the bottom of the box to copy the contents of the note to the new cell. You also can use the pull-down menus to copy notes.

Information Window

The last button on the Auditing toolbar is the Information Window. The Information Window shows detailed information about a cell. You can customize the information you want to display about cells.

To display the Information Window, click on the Show Info Window button on the Auditing toolbar or choose **O**ptions from the **T**ools menu and click in the check box next to Information Window in the View tab.

To specify the information you want to display, click on the **I**nfo menu item when you are in the Information Window. You can choose to display the following information:

◆ **Cell Address.** Displays the value of the cell location in Row and Column.

◆ **Formula.** Displays the contents of the formula in the cell.

◆ **Value.** Displays the contents in general format.

◆ **Format.** Displays the formatting of the cell.

◆ **Protection.** Displays the protection status.

◆ **Names.** Displays the names that refer to the cell.

◆ **Precedents.** Brings up the Precedents dialog box with options of either displaying all levels of precedents or just direct ones.

◆ **Dependents.** Brings up the Dependents dialog box with options of displaying either All Levels or just Direct.

◆ **Note.** Displays the contents of typed notes, and shows whether sound is attached to the file

You can switch between the worksheet and the Information Window by pressing Ctrl+F2. This command works only if the Information Window box is activated.

You can use the Information Window to print information about a range of cells as well. To do this, highlight the cells you want to print information about and switch to the Information Window. From the **F**ile menu choose **P**rint, or for a shortcut, click on the **P**rint button on the standard toolbar.

Go To Special

The Go To Special command helps find notes, constants, formulas that meet a particular criteria, blank cells, cells in the current region or array, cells that do not fit a pattern in a row or column, precedents or dependents (direct or all levels), the last active cell in your sheet, visible cells, or objects. The Go To Special dialog box can be accessed by pressing **F5** (or by selecting **E**dit, **G**o) and then clicking on the **S**pecial button. Figure 11.17 shows the Go To Special dialog box.

Figure 11.17

The Go To Special dialog box.

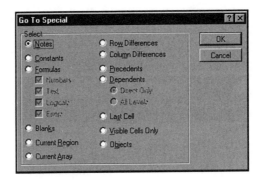

The **N**otes option selects all cells that contain notes (you also can press Ctrl+Shift+?). *Constants* are cells whose contents are deemed not to be a formula, so those cells whose values do not begin with an equal sign are considered to be constants, whether they are numbers or text.

The **F**ormulas option selects cells that meet the selection criteria of values returned as numbers, text, logical, or errors. Using the Current **R**egion option selects a range of cells as the active cell and all adjacent cells surrounded by any combination of blank rows or columns.

You can select the current array to which a cell belongs by checking the Current **A**rray radio button, or by pressing Ctrl+/. To find cells that do not fit a pattern in a row or column based on the value in the active cell, press Ctrl+\ for rows or Ctrl+Shift+| for columns. This feature finds all the cells in a column or row that differ from the active cell at the time you select the Go To Special command.

You also can use Go To Special to find cells referred to by specific formulas (precedents) or cells with formulas that refer to selected cells (dependents). With the Go To Special dialog box options of selecting just the direct cells or all levels, you can find for precedents:

◆ All cells that are directly or indirectly referred to by a formula and for dependents

◆ All cells that contain formulas that directly or indirectly relate to cells

Figure 11.18 shows the dependents at all levels that relate to a specific cell.

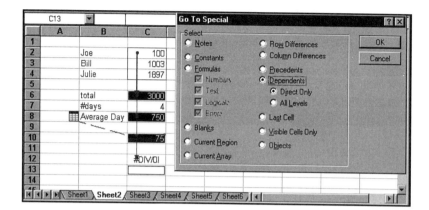

Figure 11.18

Dependent Cells with Direct Only selected in the Go To Special dialog box.

Changing the Appearance of Your Worksheet

You can modify the appearance of worksheets in several ways, and you can modify how they can be used in the new ways. You can split worksheets and freeze titles, which is a great way in large worksheets to move to various cells or scroll through the worksheet but still keep the column or row labels visible.

One of the easiest ways to begin to change the way your worksheet looks without changing the original is to choose **N**ew from the **W**indow menu. This operation makes a second window of the original worksheet, so you can modify, split, format cells, and vary the appearance in many ways without affecting your original document. Splitting worksheets is a useful tool for viewing different parts of a worksheet, even in drastically different sections on the same screen (see fig. 11.19).

The splitting done to the worksheet in figure 11.19 was performed by positioning the active cell at C1 and choosing **S**plit from the **W**indow menu. The position of the active cell at the time you select **S**plit will affect the way Excel performs the command. In figure 11.19, the active cell was in the first row of the sheet, near the middle of the active screen. Excel splits the sheet across the middle, horizontally. Using the mouse, you can move from one side of the split to the next to modify or examine data.

If the active cell had been C15, Excel would have split the worksheet into four separate areas. If you position the active cell in column A, no matter what row, Excel splits the worksheet vertically. In essence, Excel splits the window into panes at the active cell. Excel splits horizontally above the selected cell, and vertically to the right of the selected cell.

Figure 11.19

Splitting a worksheet and viewing different sections on the same screen.

calc3:2									
	A	B	C	D	E	F	G	H	I
1									
2		Joe	100						
3		Bill	1003						
4		Julie	1897						
5									
22		total	0						
23		#days	4						
24		Average Day	0						
25									
26									
27									

Sheet1 **Sheet2** Sheet3 Sheet4 Sheet5 Sheet6

Another way you can create a split is to drag the split box to the position you want. One split box is located above the scroll bar, to the far right side of the screen, just above the up arrow. Another is located on the horizontal scroll bar, toward the right end. They appear as small black separations, and when you position the cursor on the box, the pointer changes from the regular arrow to the split pointer, enabling you to drag down to create the split. You can create horizontal or vertical splits using split boxes.

After you finish with either the horizontal or vertical splits, you can drag the bar back to the bottom or side of the worksheet where it originated, and it removes that portion of the split.

After you split sheets, you can position the pointer on any of the split bars to reposition them for ease of viewing.

Regardless of how you split a worksheet, or whether you split it into two or four panes, you can undo the effect of the split by choosing the Remove **S**plit option from the **W**indow menu.

After you split worksheets, you can freeze panes from the same menu. Freezing panes automatically freezes or prevents scrolling of the upper or left pane. This keeps information visible in the upper or left pane, while allowing freedom of movement or change of view in any other section of the worksheet

The Zoom command on the standard toolbar enables you to reduce or enlarge the size of the cells so that you can see more or less. Excel sets some common useful zoom factors but also enables you to set your own. To use Zoom, click on the drop-down arrow in the edit box on the standard toolbar or choose **V**iew, **Z**oom. This displays the Zoom dialog box. You get a range of choices from 200% to 25% in the drop-down menu, and **S**election. You can even select an entire worksheet by clicking on the box at the upper left corner of the worksheet, above the column numbers, and

to the left of the row numbers, click on Zoom, choose Selection, and see zoom at its smallest possible size. Experimenting with some of the choices provides you with a clear understanding of how you can use zoom.

Perhaps a more practical use of Zoom is to select a range of cells that you want to get a better look at, and **Z**oom Selection on the selected cells. They can be used in this manner for a Slide Show or to view as well. Zoom can help display slightly larger portions of your sheet for easier data entry or analysis. If 100%, or normal viewing, does not enable you to see all your worksheet by just a few columns or rows, using zoom to shrink your worksheet by a small percentage can save a great deal of time scrolling back and forth.

Another way to change the way a worksheet appears is to hide rows or columns of information. Excel has the capability of hiding and unhiding so that you can view or print just what you want. In a worksheet that has a column for each month of the year and a grand total column at the end, for example, you might want to hide the month columns and display only the labels and grand totals.

Additionally, you might want to hide the rows for individual salespeople, and just display region totals for the summary view or printed report. Hiding rows and columns does not affect formulas or delete information—it only keeps them from the display.

To hide a column or row, choose either **C**olumn or **R**ow from the F**o**rmat menu. The **H**ide command becomes available in a submenu.

Using Outlining

Outlining is a method of creating summary reports that enables you to hide or display as much information as you want. An outline can have up to eight levels of groups, both on the horizontal axis and the vertical axis. One worksheet can have only one outline.

Excel can outline automatically or manually. To create an outline, first highlight or select the data you want to outline. Then choose Group and Outline from the **D**ata menu. If your data is in a format that you can easily outline, select Auto Outline. Figure 11.20 shows the effect of automatic outlining on the sales worksheet.

The result is a grouping of related items in row and column orientation that you can then hide, expand, or change based on the way your data is formatted. If, for example, you want to show selective portions, just click on the minus signs above the lines that indicate which areas to eliminate from view in the worksheet (see fig. 11.21).

Figure 11.20

*The Auto Outline
of a worksheet.*

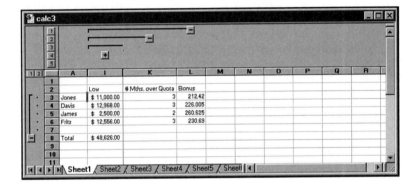

Figure 11.21

*Hiding some of
the detail by
eliminating an
outline level.*

As you experiment with hiding and displaying different levels within your outline, Shift-clicking on the outline levels shows what will be hidden if you reduce the outline area.

If your data is not organized in a way that makes sense to automatically outline, you can use the manual method. From the **D**ata menu, choose Group and Outline, then S**e**ttings. The Outline dialog box appears prompting you for information about the location of summary information—whether row summaries are to be located below the detail and if column summaries are located right of the detail. You can choose to have **A**utomatic Styles, **C**reate the outline, or apply **S**tyles.

CHAPTER

12

Excel Charts and Graphics

After you have entered your data into a worksheet, you can use Excel's powerful charting and graphics capabilities to display your data in different ways. Excel can display data from cells—called *data points*—in a worksheet as bar graphs, pie graphs, line charts, or in relation to other data points from other worksheets. Showing information graphically makes the understanding, comparison, and evaluation of data easier.

In this chapter you will learn about the following:

◆ Using Excel's ChartWizard

◆ Different types of charts

◆ How data organization affects your charts and graphs

◆ Options for setting up charts and graphs

◆ Building Chart Axes

◆ Customizing your chart by adding text

◆ Updating your chart by adding a new data series

◆ Modifying an existing chart

◆ Changing between chart types

◆ Changing the appearance of the chart you have created

Excel's charting and graphics capability goes far beyond simply showing values or data points in a graph. Using the ChartWizard, you can create presentations that can be incorporated into documents, embedded in workbooks, or even placed into a slide show. And because your data was linked to your charts at their creation, the charts are automatically updated when data in the worksheet is changed.

Charts and graphs can be very simple, or they can be created to display complex relationships among data. Through the use of Excel's ChartWizard, the creation and display of a chart is made simple. Like the other Excel Wizards, the ChartWizard is a series of dialog boxes that take you step-by-step through the chart-making process, providing various options to make it quick and easy. After you have generated a chart, it can be changed to appear exactly as you want.

Using the Excel ChartWizard

The ChartWizard button, located on the Standard toolbar, prompts you to select a location, such as a new or existing worksheet, for your chart to appear. The instruction "Drag in document to create chart" appears in the status window at the bottom of the screen. Simultaneously, the cursor changes from the regular mouse pointer to a cross with an icon of a chart attached to it.

The area you select can be as small as a single cell or as large as you want your chart to be.

Note After you have chosen an area for your chart, you can later change its size, depending on the amount of data points selected and the chart's type. Experimenting with area size to find a chart's optimum size is discussed later in this chapter.

For the chart you will create in this exercise, first create a worksheet like the one used in previous chapters (or retrieve it if you saved it). It lists salesperson names, monthly totals for three months, and other related data.

To expedite the charting process, highlight the cells you want to represent in the graph before starting the Wizard. The ChartWizard presumes the data points you want to use in your graph have been highlighted.

1. With the first sheet active, click on the ChartWizard button, then move your pointer to the worksheet and drag the mouse to select a range of cells below the data that is five cells wide and five rows deep, starting at A10. This area represents the display area in which ChartWizard will place the graphic representation you will create. When you release the mouse button, the ChartWizard dialog box displays, as shown in figure 12.1.

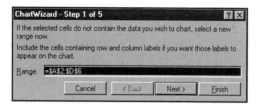

Figure 12.1

The ChartWizard's main dialog box with a range of cells selected.

Note When you select a range of data points to include in your graph, be sure to include the column and row headers, as they can be used for descriptors in the graphic.

2. If you began the process by selecting only one cell, use the mouse to select cells A1..D6. The range indicated in the ChartWizard dialog box is automatically updated with the new range information. Click on Next to move to the next step.

3. Now you must choose a chart type. There are 15 different Excel chart types, and each one has a variety of options available to it. Select the column chart type from the ChartWizard - Step 2 of 5 dialog box (it is highlighted as the default choice) and click on the Next button. The ChartWizard - Step 3 of 5 dialog box displays all 10 different column chart types from which to choose (see fig. 12.2).

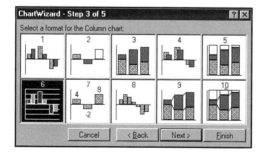

Figure 12.2

The 10 types of column charts available in the ChartWizard - Step 3 of 5 dialog box.

4. Click on the Next button to accept the default column chart type (type 6). The ChartWizard then takes you to a dialog box that gives a preview of the chart selected with the data you have chosen.

At this point, you can change the orientation of your graph by clicking on one of the Data series choices to change from **R**ow orientation to **C**olumn orientation, and you can specify (if necessary) from where ChartWizard will obtain the data labels used in the graph.

Note   A series in an Excel chart is a set of data that will be graphed as a single entity on the chart. When charting the performance of a group of salespeople, for instance, each person's monthly sales for the year 1994 will be a series on the chart.

Using the **R**ow orientation, the Wizard picks the axis labels from the first row of data by default. Use this option when the first row of data contains labels or other information you intend to use as the X-axis label. You can change this default to be either the first row by itself, or multiple rows.

For the chart's legend (which is descriptive text across the top of the chart), the same operation can be performed by clicking on the arrow buttons to use the first column, or multiple column information for legend labels.

5. Click on the **F**inish button, and the ChartWizard places the final graph in the area that was selected. The graph is displayed as shown in figure 12.3.

Figure 12.3

The final sales graph display.

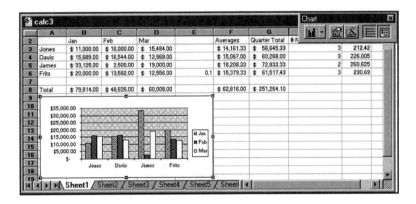

As you noticed when you stepped through the options in ChartWizard, there are numerous choices that you can pick to make your graph appear the way you want. One of the choices that makes the biggest difference in the appearance of your graph is chart type.

Understanding Chart Types

Excel has 15 chart types to choose from to display your graphics in documents or worksheets. Choosing a particular chart type is an important step in making your presentation effective and clear. The chart types are the following:

- ◆ Area chart
- ◆ Bar chart
- ◆ Column chart
- ◆ Line chart
- ◆ Pie chart
- ◆ Doughnut chart
- ◆ Radar chart
- ◆ XY (scatter) chart
- ◆ Combination chart
- ◆ 3-D area chart
- ◆ 3-D bar chart
- ◆ 3-D column chart
- ◆ 3-D line chart
- ◆ 3-D pie Chart
- ◆ 3-D surface Chart

Area Charts

Area charts show the relative change of values over a period of time. Figure 12.4 illustrates an area chart.

Figure 12.4

*An example of an
area chart.*

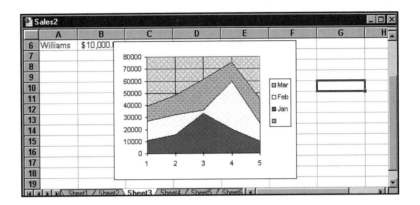

Bar Charts

Bar charts illustrate relationships among items. Use stacked bar charts to show the relationship between specific items and the rest of the data set used to build the chart. Bar charts are organized and displayed horizontally to emphasize differences in values, as shown in figure 12.5.

Figure 12.5

*A bar chart
example.*

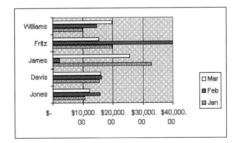

Column Charts

Column charts are similar to bar charts, except their orientation is vertical instead of horizontal (see fig. 12.6). This shifts emphasis from a comparison of difference in values to an emphasis on a change over a certain period of time.

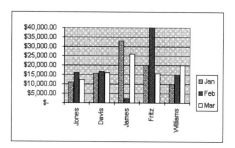

Figure 12.6

A column chart example.

Line Charts

Line charts are great for showing trends in data over a period of time. This type of graph is similar to an area chart, but emphasizes the change of data over time in a somewhat different manner, as figure 12.7 illustrates.

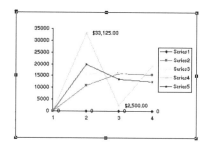

Figure 12.7

A line chart example.

Pie Charts

Pie charts show how data points relate to a whole set of data. The pie contains only one data series, even if you have selected more than one. Figure 12.8 shows an example of the pie chart. In this pie chart, the relationship of each salesperson to the whole group is displayed in percentage figures.

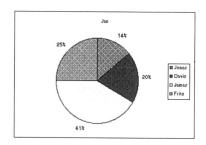

Figure 12.8

A pie chart example.

Doughnut Charts

A doughnut chart is similar to the pie, but can be used to display more than one data series at a time. Each concentric ring of a doughnut chart contains the data from a different series in the data set (see fig. 12.9).

Figure 12.9

A doughnut chart example.

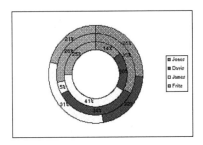

Radar Charts

The radar chart shows changes in data relative to a central point and individual data points. The value categories are scattered around the center point of the graph with lines connecting the values, as shown in figure 12.10.

Figure 12.10

A radar chart.

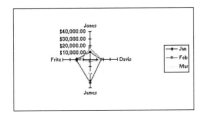

XY or Scatter Charts

XY or scatter charts show the relationships among data points by plotting dots on a graph relative to two or more groups of numbers as a series. The XY chart clearly shows data clusters, and is commonly used in scientific data analysis. Figure 12.11 is an example of a scatter chart.

Figure 12.11

The XY or scatter chart.

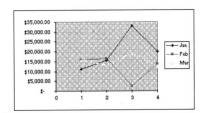

Note You can use a line to connect the points in an XY chart by selecting the correct autoformat choice when creating the chart. Or, to connect the lines in an existing XY chart, double-click on the data series, which displays the Format Data Series dialog box, and choose a line in the **P**atterns tab.

Combination Charts

Combination charts combine chart types to display data in different ways (see fig. 12.12). This is useful if you want to show two different series of data in a chart.

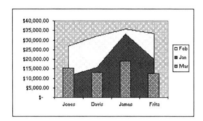

Figure 12.12

A combination chart.

3-D Area Charts

You can create a number of three-dimensional charts using Excel and the ChartWizard. The 3-D area chart is good for showing totals and illustrating the differences among the series, as shown in figure 12.13.

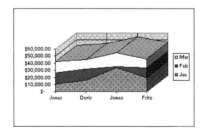

Figure 12.13

A 3-D area chart.

3-D Bar Charts

Another type of 3-D chart is the 3-D bar chart, seen in figure 12.14. This type shows data and draws a graphic relationship between items or series of data. You also can use the stacked 3-D bar to show relationships to a whole with a different twist.

Figure 12.14

The 3-D bar chart.

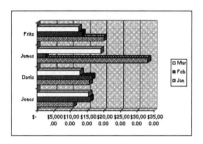

3-D Column Charts

3-D column charts can be used to display relationships in two different ways. The simple 3-D column chart shows columns along the X axis. The perspective column chart compares the data along the X and Y axes. In both instances, data is plotted along the Z axis.

The 3-D perspective column chart (see fig. 12.15) often is used to display "three-dimensional" data. An example of three-dimensional data would be the total sales figures for all the salespeople in a company over a number of years. There are three dimensions to this data: an individual salesperson's total sales, the sales totals of all the salespeople for the previous year, and the sales totals of all salespeople for all previous years.

Figure 12.15

The 3-D perspective column chart.

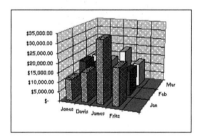

3-D Pie Charts

You also can make pie charts appear three-dimensional. Figure 12.16 shows a single data series, just like the standard pie chart. To show more than one data series, the two-dimensional doughnut chart should be used.

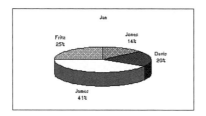

Figure 12.16

A 3-D pie chart.

3-D Line Charts

The 3-D line chart shows data trends so that they look like ribbons, as shown in figure 12.17.

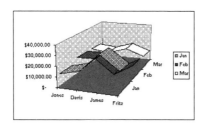

Figure 12.17

A 3-D line chart.

3-D Surface Charts

Finally, the 3-D surface chart shows a "flexible" continuum for data display (see fig. 12.18). This type of chart is useful for showing relationships among large amounts of data.

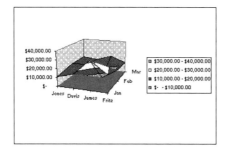

Figure 12.18

A 3-D surface chart.

Understanding Data Organization

Because you have used the same worksheet data across all the different chart types, data points appear in a graph with specific relation to other data points or data series. The horizontal and vertical lines along which data are displayed are called the chart *axes*.

A two-dimensional graph shows data along two separate axes, the X axis and the Y axis. The X axis typically is horizontal and the Y is vertical.

3-D charts can have two or three axes. The third axis, perpendicular to both the X and Y axes, is the Z axis, and it is present only in 3-D charts. While there is no such thing as a three-dimensional screen (or printout), imagine that the Z axis is sticking out towards you.

The value axis is usually the Y axis, and the category axis is the X axis. In a two-dimensional graph, you can change the orientation of a chart from X to Y by double-clicking on the chart, and then double-clicking on a portion of the data range. This brings up the Format Data Series dialog box. Selecting the Axis tab, you can plot the data on the primary or secondary axes, changing the appearance of the data completely (see fig. 12.19).

Figure 12.19

Changing a chart's orientation in the Axis tab of the Format Data Series dialog box.

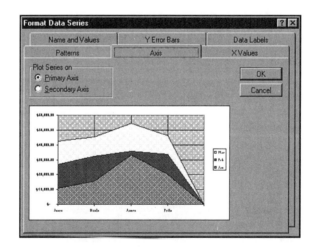

Exploring Chart Options

Using the ChartWizard, you can add a number of options while you are building your chart. After your chart has been completed, it can be modified using methods discussed later in this chapter.

The first choice you have when building your chart is its location on your Excel worksheet. You can select for a chart's location a single cell, a specific area (high-lighted with the mouse), or an individual sheet.

The next step is selecting the range of data you want to display graphically. If you selected a range of data prior to invoking the ChartWizard, the information appears in the range window of the dialog box. If you did not select a data series to chart, or if you want to modify your selection, highlighting a range of worksheet data by clicking and dragging with the mouse will update the range box.

After these two choices have been made, you will need to choose a chart type. The prompt for this appears in the Step 2 of 5 dialog box. Because there are several types available, you must think about how your data would best be displayed and choose a chart type accordingly. The Step 4 of 5 dialog box in the Wizard displays a sample of the chart based on the chart type, data, and format you have chosen.

At this point, you can choose to have your data series appear in row or column orientation. In figure 12.20, for example, a data series is shown in row orientation. This places the X axis values as Dollars and Y axis values as Months. Changing to column orientation places the Months as the X axis data, and the Representatives as Y axis. Figure 12.21 shows the change.

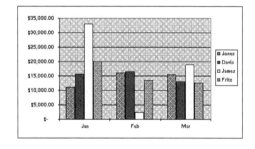

Figure 12.20

The sales graph with row orientation for the data series.

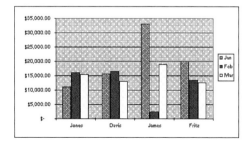

Figure 12.21

The sales graph with column orientation for the data series.

Additionally, select the data labels for your graph. In the ChartWizard - Step 4 of 5 dialog box, you can select the contents of the first 0, 1, 2, 3, or 4 rows to appear as labels for the X axis labels. In addition, you have the same options for the Legend.

The effect that choosing the labels has on the appearance of the chart is interesting. Choosing more labels in this example reduces the number of data points on the graph. Similarly, choosing additional legend columns reduces the number of data series across the X axis.

Specify the title of your graph and the labels of your axes in the last dialog box of the ChartWizard. This box also enables you to decide whether you want to include a legend. Clicking on the **F**inish button closes the ChartWizard and creates the graph on your workbook.

Adding Text to Your Chart

You can add text to your charts in a number of ways. If you decided not to include a legend in your chart, you can add one later. Legends are especially useful on large, complex graphs where they help the reader keep track of what is going on.

The first method to add text to an existing chart is to activate it by double-clicking on the chart. Sizing handles will appear in the corners and along the sides of the chart. Right-click anywhere on the chart to open the shortcut menu. From this menu you can add titles, edit titles, and make changes to existing text in these areas.

You can also add text boxes to your graphs. A *text box* clarifies a graphic representation, emphasizes a particular point, or simply annotates some detail on your graphs.

The Excel drawing toolbar contains the Text box button. A text box can be placed next to a graph or directly within the chart.

Note If you add a text box on or next to a graph while the graph is not activated, the box will not move with the graph when it is moved. If, however, the graph is activated, the box and graph become one object. Then, if you want, the box still can be moved around within the graph.

Adding a New Series to Your Chart

After you have defined a chart and have it displayed on a worksheet, Excel will automatically update the chart as the data displayed within it changes. If you want to add a data point or an entirely new data series, however, you can modify the structure of your chart by following a few simple steps.

If you add a new person to your staff, you will need to update the chart with that person's sales figures. To include this series of figures in this chapter's example chart, add a new row with the new person's data to the worksheet. For this example, the person's name is Williams, and his sales totals for January, February, and March are 10,000, 15,000 and 20,000, respectively.

After you have entered that information into your worksheet and have formatted the numbers appropriately, select the range (including the name) with the mouse. Then, using the shortcut menu (brought up with the right mouse button), choose Copy.

Next, choose the graph to which you want to add the data series. Click on the graph to highlight it, then bring up the shortcut menu again and choose Paste. The new data series will be added to the graph (see fig. 12.22). If the results are what you expected, your graph is complete. If something did not transfer as you wanted, you can undo the paste by choosing **U**ndo from the **E**dit menu.

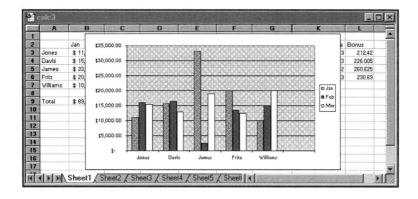

Figure 12.22

The new data series pasted into an existing graph.

You also can copy-and-paste highlighted worksheet data by using toolbars or pull-down menus.

To add new data to a chart using a pull-down menu, double-click on the chart, then select the **N**ew Data option from the **I**nsert menu to display the New Data dialog box. This dialog box walks you through the steps necessary to add a new range of data to your chart. The New Data dialog box enables you to specify the location of the new data and how you want it displayed on the chart.

Modifying Charts

After your chart is in place in a given location, there are options available that affect the appearance of the data.

Activating a Chart

Before trying to change its appearance, you first must activate a chart by double-clicking on it. To indicate that it is ready for modification, an activated chart is shown with a wide border.

The first way to modify an area of a graph is to double-click on the area of the chart (legend, labels, text boxes, and so on) to be changed. Separate format options are available for each area. If you want to modify the plot or type area, bring up the formatting shortcut menu by clicking on the background of the chart and then the right mouse button (see fig. 12.23).

Figure 12.23

The shortcut menu after clicking on the plot area.

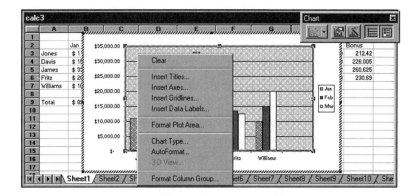

 Note   When you activate a chart, the choices in the Excel menu bar become chart- and graph-specific. The F**o**rmat choices with an active graph are different from those available when a cell or range of cells is active, for example.

Double-clicking on the plot area of the graph invokes the Format Plot Area dialog box, which is one of the options available on the shortcut menu.

Making Text Changes

The Insert Titles dialog box enables you to insert titles on charts, value axes (y axis), and category axes (X axis). If your graph has secondary value or category titles, these options can be used, too.

The Insert Axes menu enables you to add or remove axes from your graph's display. This can change the way your data appears by either bringing in a new axis to view data or by removing one.

The Insert Gridlines shortcut menu selection adds X or Y lines in major or minor categories. This means that you can show background lines to make your data easier to view across a graph. Figure 12.24 shows all gridlines enabled.

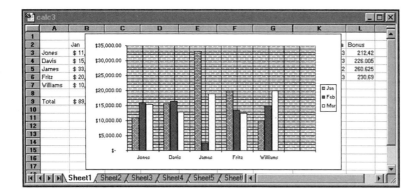

Figure 12.24

The sales graph with all gridlines enabled.

The Insert Data Labels dialog box provides options for viewing data labels. You can decide to show data labels as values, percentages, labels, or labels and percentages. There also are options to show the legend key beside the label or even to not show labels at all.

Changing the Chart Type

The Format Chart Area dialog box (invoked by double-clicking on the chart area itself) is used to change borders, lines, and colors that display on the graph that is active.

The Chart Type dialog box selected from the shortcut menu enables you to actually switch from a column graph to the other types of Excel graphs, such as doughnuts, pie, area, and so on. Here, you can select two or three dimensions. Furthermore, after a graph type is selected, you can choose the subtype of graph from the options dialog box (opened with the options button). From there, you can modify sort orders within your selected data series, vary colors, change the axes, and so on.

Using AutoFormat

The AutoFormat selection (again, from the shortcut menu) combines many of the formatting options available by using galleries of different chart and subchart types. With AutoFormat, you can select from any of the available chart types in Excel, as well as some of the popular subtypes. In addition, you can define and save your own customized chart types and formats, adding uniformity and customization to a worksheet or presentation.

The Format Column Group selection from the shortcut menu contains many of the same options. You can change chart types in the Options tab. Choices also are given to change colors, to modify the overlap of columns or data shapes on your graph, to change the series order that the chart has, and even to change the subtype of the graph.

If you need to modify the appearance of a column or group of columns, double-clicking anywhere on them will open the Format Data Series dialog box.

To open the shortcut menu for modifying a single series on the chart, click on an individual column or line in a data series area, then right-click on the highlighted column or line. The options on this menu are the following:

◆ Clear

◆ Insert Data Labels

◆ Insert Trendline

◆ Insert Error Bars

◆ Format Data Series

◆ Chart Type

◆ AutoFormat

◆ 3-D view

◆ Format Column (or Line) Group

Some of the options on this menu overlap those on other formatting menus. Others, however, are new additions that can be performed only on the data series and cannot be done from the plot area as previously described. Specifically, you can add trendlines and error bars to your graph.

Adding Trendlines

Trendlines show trends in the data by drawing lines across data points. The line represents and displays the movement of a data point over time.

There are several ways to format trendlines. There are six different types to choose from and numerous ways to format each. Format types include the display of linear trends, logarithmic, polynomial, power, exponential, and moving average. The type of trendline you choose for your information is determined by the type of information your chart contains.

After you have inserted a trendline, you can change its pattern or type of line. Activate the line by clicking on it once, then double-click on any of the blocks on the line or column.

Formatting Axes

You can change the formatting of the X or Y axis. Double-clicking on the axis information opens the Format Axis dialog box. Here, you are presented with tabbed choices for formatting the pattern of the axis, the scale, font selection for number displays, and alignment of text on the axis.

The Format Axis dialog box provides flexibility for formatting the graph's axes. Formatting options include changing the text font on titles, data labels, and legends. The scale of the graph—the way that the data points are plotted—relative to the Y axis values is automatically calculated based on the values displayed in the range of data. You can modify the value if you want your axis values to be different than the values shown on the default selection.

You can directly modify sheet data by moving information on a chart. To do this, click on the border of a particular data point to place an "active" box around the data point. The values in the worksheet actually change to represent the new graphic label, relative to where a data shape is as you drag it.

Graph axes are delimited by *tick marks,* variable indicators of where data labels are located in relation to the data points graphed. In the Format Axis dialog box (see fig. 12.25), you can change tick mark location and appearance, as well as where axis labels will appear in relation to their tick marks. Tick marks can be *major,* meaning that each axis label value has only one mark, or *minor,* meaning that each label has numerous marks to indicate many small steps in value before the next label is reached.

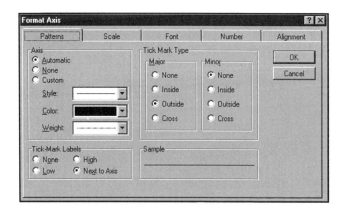

Figure 12.25

The Format Axis dialog box.

Excel Map

New in Excel for Windows 95, Map lets you create graphics for regional comparisons, showing the geographic locations named in your worksheet on a map. To use this feature, create a worksheet that includes geographic data such as country names, state names or zip codes. Figure 12.26 shows a worksheet with state names.

Figure 12.26

A worksheet showing figures by state.

	A	B	C	D	E
1					
2					
3					
4		Total Sales	Jan	Feb	Mar
5	Pennsylvania	$45,110.00	$12,000.00	$17,225.00	$15,885.00
6	Colorado	$70,038.00	$22,485.00	$26,999.00	$20,554.00
7	Washington	$31,911.00	$12,355.00	$9,554.00	$10,002.00
8	California	$27,429.00	$11,544.00	$6,880.00	$9,005.00

Note There are some conventions to follow for creating a map. The geographic data should be in a column, not a row; ZIP codes must be in cells formatted for text.

Select the cells you want to include in your map, making sure to include the column that contains the geographic data, then click on the Map button, which is on the Standard toolbar to the right of the ChartWizard.

Click the mouse pointer on the worksheet where you want the map to display and drag it until you have a box of the proper size for your map. Excel checks the data and, when it finds a map that matches the names in the worksheet, it displays it.

In this case, there are multiple maps that match the data, the Multiple Maps Available dialog box appears, and you should choose the map you want to use (see fig. 12.27).

Figure 12.27

Choose a map of the U.S. or a map of North America from the Multiple Maps Available dialog box.

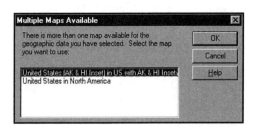

When the map displays (see fig. 12.28), the locations named in your worksheet are highlighted with patterns. A legend accompanies the map, displaying data from the worksheet.

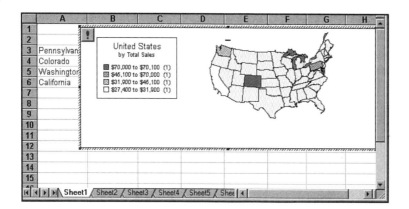

Figure 12.28

Geographic locations are highlighted with individual patterns.

You can edit and configure the map by double-clicking on it to enter Edit mode. Your Excel window displays the Map Toolbar (see fig. 12.29), which has the following icons:

◆ **Select Map Objects**, which lets you select specific objects in the Map area.

◆ **Zoom In**

◆ **Zoom Out**

◆ **Grabber**, to grab and move the map

◆ **Map Lables**, to edit the data labels

◆ **Add Text**

◆ **Custom Pin Map**, to add custom labels to any part of the map

◆ **Display the Entire Map**

◆ **Redraw**

◆ **Show/Hide Data Map Controls**

You can also change the way the map displays the country or continent. Click on the map with the right mouse button to bring up the Map Menu, then choose Features. As shown in figure 12.30, you can add or eliminate parts of the display.

Figure 12.29

The Map toolbar above the worksheet helps you manipulate maps.

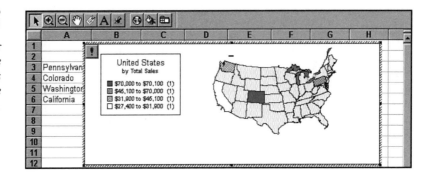

Figure 12.30

You can make parts of your map visible or invisible by checking the box next to each of the map's elements.

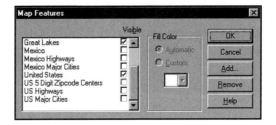

Excel Data Management

Many people find that they don't need the full power (and complexity) of a database program like Access to manage most of their information. Instead, Excel's list management features fulfill the vast majority of most people's needs. There are two components to managing data in Excel. First, unless you plan on typing your data into Excel, you must be able to automatically bring in your data from whatever source currently holds it. Second, when you have the data in Excel, you will need to work with it in a variety of ways.

In this chapter, you learn about the following:

◆ Using Microsoft Query to Query and Import Data

◆ Importing ASCII Data

◆ Sharing data in MS Query

◆ Sorting and subtotaling your data

◆ Using AutoFilter to examine parts of your data

◆ Improving the appearance of your data with AutoFormat

◆ Using pivot tables to summarize lists

Not only does Excel let you move all or selected data records from one data source into a worksheet, it lets you work with the data in a variety of ways.

Being able to import and export data can lead to more effective use of office staff and increased productivity, as well as increased accuracy. It also means added power in terms of the type of information you can have in a worksheet and the steps for getting it there.

Excel uses Microsoft Query to perform a number of data import and export tasks. In this chapter, you have a chance to learn about MS Query, how it works, and what it can do for you when used with Excel Worksheets and on its own. In addition, you can learn how Excel shares data with other applications—in other words, how you can send information from your workbooks to other applications or coworkers for additional analysis and use.

Because Excel and MS Query are very flexible, you have a chance to evaluate a number of different ways to harness the power of data import and export to and from your applications.

Using Microsoft Query

Microsoft Query is a tool that enables you to retrieve and sort data from a wide range of sources. Some of these sources include the following:

- ◆ Microsoft Excel

- ◆ Microsoft Access

- ◆ Microsoft FoxPro

- ◆ Microsoft SQL Server

- ◆ ASCII Text

- ◆ dBASE

- ◆ Paradox

- ◆ Btrieve

You need to install Query with the drivers to access these different data sources, and drivers for some of these sources come with MS Query. After you use MS Query to access the data source that you need, you can use it to sort, filter, and display information that you need, and then send it to an application that you choose, such as Excel.

Note   If you do not have drivers for the source you need, contact Microsoft.

In MS Query, you can perform several functions that manipulate data. The most common operation is called a query. A *query* is a question about a group of data, for example, "For which customers do we have information?" or "How many customers do we have in the 12345 ZIP Code?" MS Query translates your questions into a format that your computer can understand, and returns the answer in the form of a table.

A *table* is a group of information in rows and columns. An example of a table is an Excel worksheet. Tables usually are organized by topic or related item, such as customers, parts numbers, or the like. The rows and columns equate to records and fields from the database perspective. A *field* is one portion of a record. Name, Address, and ZIP Code are examples of fields. A *record* is a row of related fields. A *customer record* might be a collection of 10 fields of data, all relating to one customer.

You can start MS Query from its own program icon as a stand-alone application, or you can invoke it from within Excel, Word, or Access. After you start MS Query, you can use it in a number of ways.

One way to start MS Query is to choose **D**ata, Get E**x**ternal Data. If the Get External Data option is not available on your **T**ools menu, select Add-ins to see whether the Query Add-in is installed. Odds are, it isn't, in which case, you can use the Excel Setup program to configure it for your system.

You also can use certain other external data retrieval functions to launch MS Query, such as pivot tables, which are explored in greater detail in "Using Pivot Tables" later in this chapter

For this example, start MS Query by choosing the **D**ata menu and then choosing the Get E**x**ternal Data command. The Microsoft Query window opens along with MS Query Cue Cards. If you do not want Cue Cards to appear with Query in the opening screen, you can click in the lower check box titled "Don't display this card on startup."

Before using MS Query, you must select the type of data source you'll be working with. The Select Data Source dialog box (see fig. 13.1) lists dBASE files as an option. You can choose additional data sources by clicking on the **O**ther button, which brings up the dialog box shown in figure 13.2.

For now, close all of these dialog boxes to go to the main MS Query screen. You should review the MS Query screen and its toolbar. Table 13.1 describes the toolbar's buttons.

Figure 13.1

The Select Data Source dialog box.

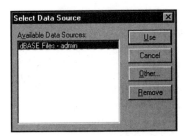

Figure 13.2

The Other button opens this dialog box.

TABLE 13.1
The Microsoft Query Toolbar Buttons

Icon	Name	Description
	New Query	Enables you to define a new question or questions about a group of data.
	Open Query	Starts a query that has already been defined and saved.
	Save Query	Enables you to keep the query you designed in the New Query Steps for future use.
	Return Data	Closes MS Query, returning the data you found to the active Excel sheet automatically.
	View SQL	Enables you to look at the Structured Query Language associated with a query of a data source.

New Riders Publishing
INSIDE
SERIES

Icon	Name	Description
	Show/Hide Tables	Enables you to look at or suppress view of tables.
	Show/Hide Criteria	Enables you to look at or suppress certain information.
	Add Tables	Enables you to add tables to a query or data set.
	Criteria Equals	Selects all records that have the same value as the current cell.
	Cycle Through Totals	Provides a quick total for the current column.
	Sort Ascending	Sorts the selected tables in ascending order.
	Sort Descending	Sorts tables in descending order.
	Query Now	When Automatic Query is deactivated, click this button to force the query to update manually.
	Automatic Query	Automatically performs any query.
	Help	Enables you to access Cue Cards or regular MS Query help screens.

Importing Data from External Data Sources

To start a query, click on the New Query button on the toolbar. The Select Data Source dialog box appears. Available Data Sources might be empty, so click on the Other button. The ODBC dialog box appears. *ODBC* is an acronym for Open Database Connectivity. Any previously defined data source appears in the ODBC box, and you can create your own data source. Click on the name of the data source you want, or type it in the selection box.

Click on dBASE Files, click on the OK button, and dBASE Files appears in the Select Data Source dialog. You can now select dBASE Files and click the <u>U</u>se button, which causes the Query1 window to appear in the background and the Add Tables dialog box to appear in the foreground.

The Add Tables dialog box lists the files that are compatible with the data source you chose in the previous steps. Because you chose dBASE files, all files in the current directory that have a DBF extension appear as choices. To begin, select the sample data file called CUSTOMER.DBF (it's located in your \WINDOWS\MSAPPS\MSQUERY directory) and click on the Add button. Then close the window. Now the Query1 window is active, and the Customer table or data file is shown in the upper portion of the window.

The Query1 window is divided into two sections called *panes*. The upper pane is referred to as the *table pane* and the lower pane is the *data pane*. The tables or data sources you select appear in the table pane, and any fields and records you select appear in the data pane.

Several ways are possible for selecting fields from a table or data source to appear in the data pane. You can select a field by double-clicking on the name, which places the field in the data pane, or you can drag-and-drop a name from the table pane to the data pane.

Figure 13.3 shows the result of double-clicking on the CUSTMR_ID field and COMPANY field, and dragging the ADDRESS field to the data pane.

Figure 13.3

The results of adding fields from the table pane to the data pane (note the Auto Query button is on).

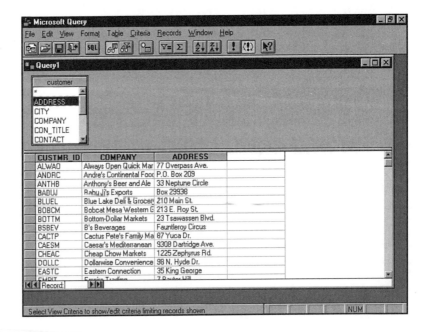

Note The Auto Query button defaults to On, which means that when you add a field from the table pane to the data pane, the corresponding data from the table is displayed. If you click on the Auto Query button, it no longer appears recessed, and the resulting data associated with the fields is no longer displayed. If you want the data to be displayed with each entry of a field, leave the Auto Query button on at all times. You also can activate Auto Query from the **R**ecords menu. Figure 13.4 shows the difference between Auto Query on and Auto Query off.

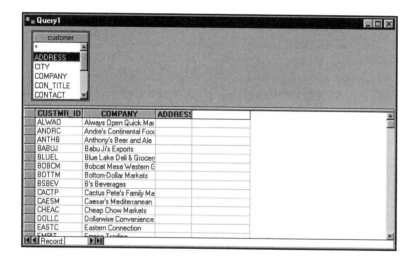

Figure 13.4

When Auto Query is off, adding new fields does not display their data. Click Query Now to see the data.

After the fields from the selected table appear in the data pane, you can manipulate your information, add fields, edit fields, or select data that you want to move into other applications.

Thus far, you have learned how to select tables or databases, select fields, and display them. The section that follows concentrates on the MS Query toolbar and the file functions that you can perform. In addition, because you can format and display your information in numerous ways, you get a chance to move and manipulate the windows or panes within MS Query.

If you want to insert a field from the table pane into the data pane, you have a couple different avenues to take. You might want to insert a field from the table pane to the data pane to rearrange existing fields or to insert a field where you had already chosen another. To insert a field, choose the field from the table list, and drag it down to the data pane. Position the field just above the label of the column where you want to insert it. MS Query automatically moves the existing field to the right, and inserts the new one at the point you choose.

If you need to rearrange the order of your data fields in the data pane, you can select an entire data column and move it. To select an entire column, click on the column label at the top of the column or press Ctrl+spacebar with any field in that column active (see fig. 13.5). After you select the column, you can drag it to a new location and drop it into place, similar to the insert operation described earlier.

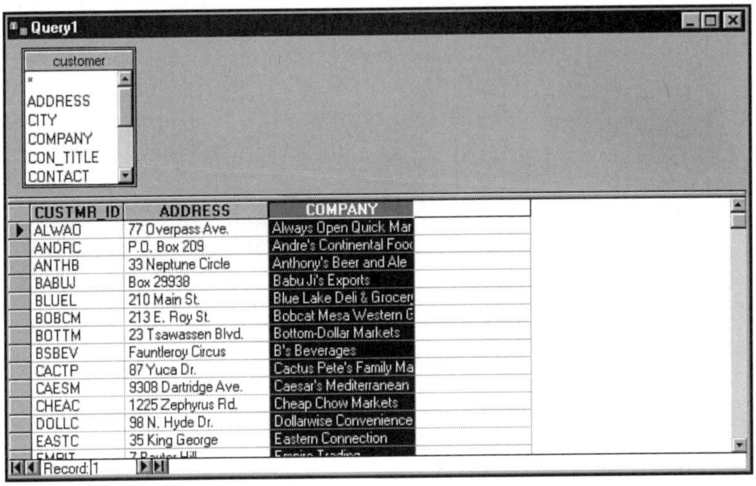

Figure 13.5

Selecting an entire data column.

CUSTMR_ID	ADDRESS	COMPANY	
ALWAO	77 Overpass Ave.	Always Open Quick Mar	
ANDRC	P.O. Box 209	Andre's Continental Fool	
ANTHB	33 Neptune Circle	Anthony's Beer and Ale	
BABUJ	Box 29938	Babu Ji's Exports	
BLUEL	210 Main St.	Blue Lake Deli & Grocer	
BOBCM	213 E. Roy St.	Bobcat Mesa Western G	
BOTTM	23 Tsawassen Blvd.	Bottom-Dollar Markets	
BSBEV	Fauntleroy Circus	B's Beverages	
CACTP	87 Yuca Dr.	Cactus Pete's Family Ma	
CAESM	9308 Dartridge Ave.	Caesar's Mediterranean	
CHEAC	1225 Zephyrus Rd.	Cheap Chow Markets	
DOLLC	98 N. Hyde Dr.	Dollarwise Convenience	
EASTC	35 King George	Eastern Connection	

You also can use the **R**ecords menu to insert a column. Begin by selecting the column directly to the left of the column that you want to insert. After that column appears in reverse video, select Insert **C**olumns from the **R**ecords menu. The Insert Column dialog box appears. Choose the field name from the active table, and select the field you want. Select the asterisk (*) if you want to select all fields in the table.

You can type your own column headings with the Column **H**eading field. Also, you can determine whether totals are displayed at the bottom of each column with the **T**otal drop-down list box. You can use the **T**otal drop-down list box to choose sum, average, minimum, or maximum. Figure 13.6 shows the Insert Column dialog box.

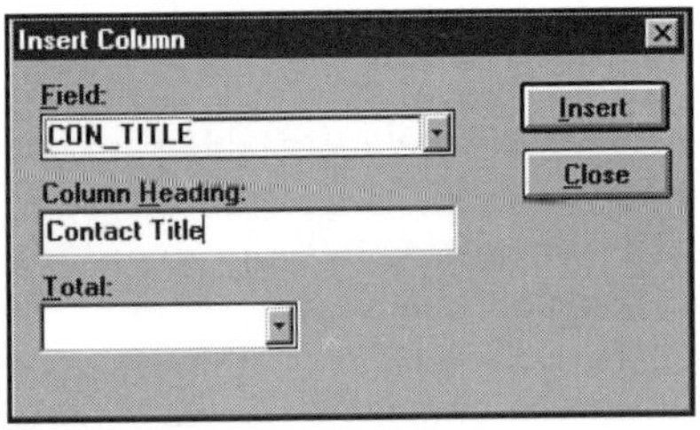

Figure 13.6

The Insert Column dialog box.

If you want to edit the columns you drop into the data pane, double-click on the top bar of the column. The Edit Column dialog box appears. You can replace the field with another field, or you can change the column header. You also can add or remove a total to or from the pane.

You can use the Insert Column dialog box to insert more than one field at a time. To do so, hold down the Ctrl key as you click on the field in the **F**ield drop-down list box, or click on the * (asterisk) to insert all the fields into the data pane. Yet another way is to double-click on the title bar of the table whose fields you want to add, and hold the Ctrl key, click on the fields you want to deselect, and drag them down.

If you want to remove a field from a table, select the field in the data pane section and press the Del key. When you delete the field, the data actually is not removed from the table, only from view on the data pane. To remove a field using the menu system, select **R**emove column from the **R**ecords menu.

 Stop   If you delete a row, unlike a field, it is deleted from the data table. This is a very important distinction, and you should deal with it carefully.

 Note   You cannot remove or delete a blank column from the data pane.

After you select the fields that you want from the data pane, you can save that particular "request" as a query. To do so, click on the Save Query button, or select **S**ave Query from the **F**ile menu. The Save **A**s dialog box appears the first time you save a query. After you name the query, click on OK.

If you modify a query and you want to save it along with the original query, select the Save **A**s option from the **F**ile menu. Rename the query, and click on the OK button. Your modified query is saved under the new name, and the original is still the same. You can use the Save button on the toolbar to save your query for the first time, and to save modifications if you do not want to maintain a copy of the original.

Changing the Appearance of Data in MS Query

You can alter the appearance of selected fields in the data pane when the fields are displayed. You might, for instance, want to change the size of a row or column, move columns, sort the data in a particular order, hide or display columns, or change the font. MS Query lets you do any of these actions.

If you want to change the width of a column so that you can see more or less of the field, you can do so in either of the following ways:

◆ Place the mouse pointer on the right side of the column heading and drag it. There's a trick to this; wait until the pointer changes to a two-headed arrow, then click and drag.

◆ Click anywhere on the column, and then select the <u>C</u>olumn Width option from the Forma<u>t</u> menu. Enter the value for the width of the column in the Column Width dialog box.

To restore the original size of the column, select the <u>S</u>tandard Width checkbox in the Column Width dialog box.

If necessary, you can change the width of several columns at the same time. Drag across the headings of several columns at one time to select those columns. Then position the mouse on the right side of the far right column. When the pointer changes to a double arrow, change the size of the width displayed, which modifies all the selected columns.

 Note   To make the width of a column the same as the maximum width of your largest data field, double-click on the right side of the column header, just as you would in Excel—a very quick and easy way to make an optimum adjustment.

To change the height of the rows of data shown in the data pane, position the mouse pointer above the row number on any row. When the pointer turns into a double arrow, resize the row. If you increase the height of a row, information in the row might word wrap. If you reduce the height so that the display font is too large to fit, the font is reduced. MS Query attempts to make the adjustment for you. Changing the height of one row modifies all rows in a query.

Another way to modify row height is to select <u>R</u>ow Height from the Forma<u>t</u> menu. The value is displayed in points in the Row Height dialog box. One point is equivalent to 1/72 inch. All rows change to the value you specify. Select the <u>S</u>tandard Height checkbox in the Row Height dialog to restore the rows to the default value.

To hide, but not delete, a column of information, click on the column you want to hide, then select <u>H</u>ide Columns from the Forma<u>t</u> menu. The column disappears from view. To unhide a hidden column, follow the same procedure used to hide a column, only select the <u>S</u>how Columns option from Forma<u>t</u> menu. Show Columns is the multipurpose display manager for MS Query. The Show Columns dialog box provides a list of columns. You can select column names, and hide or show them, depending on the current status of the column.

 Tip   You can select multiple columns to hide by clicking the left-most and then right-most column header while holding down the Shift key.

MS Query enables you to sort data in the data pane. Select the fields you want to sort, and choose **S**ort from the **R**ecords menu. The Sort dialog box appears, as shown in figure 13.7.

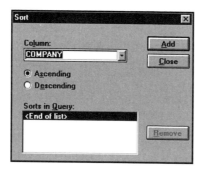

Figure 13.7

The Sort dialog box lets you control how a particular column sorts.

 Tip
The Sort Ascending and Sort Descending buttons on the toolbar are good for quick sorting tasks. Select a column that you want to sort, and click on the appropriate button. MS Query returns the results immediately.

The Sort dialog box has the following options:

◆ **Col_umn.** Initially, all of the column titles available in the data pane appear. After you select the column you want to sort and select the order, click on the **A**dd button. Two things happen:

   ◆ The requested sort of the data in the result set is performed

   ◆ The Sort command is added to the list of sorts available in the query

After you select a column for sorting in the query, that column no longer appears in the list of columns. If you want to resort the data in a different order, or at a different time in relation to other sorts, highlight it in the Sorts in **Q**uery list box and click on the **R**emove button. Then resubmit the data using the same steps.

◆ **A_scending and D_escending radio buttons.** Use these to change the order in which a sort is performed. Before you click on the **A**dd button, high-light the sort in the Sorts in **Q**uery list box just after where you want the new sort to be added. Then, when you add the new sort, it is inserted preceding the one you specify.

◆ **Sorts in Q_uery list box.** This provides a list of the sorts in the query.

After you sort the data, click on the **C**lose button to close the dialog box.

Changing Column Headings

MS Query uses the field name from selected data tables for the title of the column that is displayed. If you want a more meaningful name, double-click on the heading bar at the top of the column where the name appears. The Edit Column dialog box appears (see fig. 13.8). This dialog box has three boxes:

◆ **Field.** Use to select a column (it uses the one you click on as the default).

◆ **Column Heading.** Use to change the column header.

◆ **Total.** Use for totals.

If your data table has a column named CON_TITLE, you might want to change the heading to read Contact Title for aesthetic, or even proper identification, purposes.

You can accomplish the same result if you click anywhere in the column and then select **E**dit Column from the **R**ecords menu to display the Edit Column dialog box (see fig. 13.8).

Figure 13.8

*The Edit Column
dialog box.*

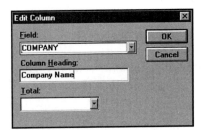

Editing or Adding Data

When your data is displayed in the data pane, MS Query enables you to manipulate your data in several ways, including sorting, which you just reviewed. You also can edit, change, copy, and delete information or records.

Note   Before you can change or delete information, you must check **A**llow Editing in the **R**ecords menu.

If you need to make a change to a field within a record, highlight the contents of the cell by clicking on the field cell. Enter information while the cell is highlighted to overwrite the existing contents. If you only need to make a modification, just click on the field. One click selects the entire cell, two clicks selects the text in the active cell, and three clicks gives you the individual edit cursor. At this point, you can scroll

through the field to the where you need to do your editing. If a cell is highlighted, you can press F2 to get into Edit mode. The cursor is positioned at the end of the field, and you can use the Home, End, and arrow keys to move through the cell to edit the part that you need to change.

Note   If the entire cell contents are highlighted, the arrow keys move from cell to cell rather than from character to character.

Before you attempt to edit a record, you should be aware of a few other rules. You must enter the correct type of information into the cell. For example, you cannot enter alpha characters in a date field. You also have a limited amount of space, depending on how the field is set up in the source database. In addition, you must follow any other rules defined by the source database.

Any permitted changes to a record or field are automatically saved when you leave that record. If you make a mistake while editing a field, press Esc to revert the contents of a cell to its original state. While in Edit mode, a pencil appears in the row box to the left (see fig. 13.9), indicating that the changes being made are penciled in and not yet permanently saved to disk.

CUSTMR_ID	ADDRESS	Company Name	Contact Title
ALWAO	77 Overpass Ave.	Always Open Quick Mar	Sales Representative
ANDRC	P.O. Box 209	Andre's Continental Foo	Sales Representative
ANTHB	33 Neptune Circle	Anthony's Beer and Ale	Assistant Sales Agen
BSBEV	Fauntleroy Circus	B's Beverages	Sales Representative
BABUJ	Box 29938	Babu Ji's Exports	Owner
BLUEL	210 Main St.	Blue Lake Deli & Grocer	President
BOBCM	213 E. Roy St.	Bobcat Mesa Western G	Marketing Manager
BOTTM	23 Tsawassen Blvd.	Bottom-Dollar Markets	Accounting Manager
CACTP	87 Yuca Dr.	Cactus Pete's Family Ma	Sales Agent
CAESM	9308 Dartridge Ave.	Caesar's Mediterranean	Marketing Manager
CHEAC	1225 Zephyrus Rd.	Cheap Chow Markets	Sales Representative
DOLLC	98 N. Hyde Dr.	Dollarwise Convenience	Assistant Sales Agen
EASTC	35 King George	Eastern Connection	Sales Agent

Record: 6

Figure 13.9

Changes are "penciled in" while in Edit mode.

Adding records to your database is easy in MS Query. Navigate to the bottom of the result set where there is a blank record. Position the pointer in the first cell, and make an entry. After you complete the entry for that cell, press Enter to move to the next cell to the right, or use the arrow keys. As you enter data, the row indicator changes from the active row triangle to the pencil, indicating that you are making unsaved changes. After you press Enter on the last cell in the set, the pencil disappears, and your new record is saved.

If you need to delete a cell, highlight the information in the cell, and press the Del key. If you have deleted the contents of a cell, but haven't yet left it, you can still press Esc to abort the deletion. If you leave the cell, but make no other changes, you can still undo your deletion by selecting <u>U</u>ndo Current Record from the <u>E</u>dit menu. But as soon as you make any changes after leaving the cell, you cannot undo the deletion.

Before you can manipulate multiple rows or columns of information, you must select the data you want to manipulate. To select an entire column, click on the title bar, or click anywhere in the column, then press Ctrl+spacebar. To highlight an entire row, click on the corresponding row button or press Shift+spacebar.

When you delete a row, you actually are deleting data from your database. And unlike individual cell deletion, which you can undo, you cannot undo row or record deletion.

Times do arise when you cannot delete or add information to a result set. These times depend on the application, the rules associated with specific data fields, and the setup of the query.

For instance, you cannot edit data in queries that use more than one data table. You cannot edit data in fields whose totals are calculated. Some applications can lock records or fields, and these prohibit changes and deletions. Some applications require unique entries in certain fields. If you get the Duplicate Key error, the value you entered is already in the data file, and you cannot have multiple copies of that value.

Sharing Data in MS Query

To share data from one cell in a result set to another, highlight the cell you want to share, and from the <u>E</u>dit menu, choose Cu<u>t</u> if you want to move the data permanently, or <u>C</u>opy if you want to copy it to another cell. Then place the mouse pointer where you want the data, and select <u>P</u>aste from the <u>E</u>dit menu. Your data is moved or copied to the destination.

Tip The Cut (Ctrl+X), Copy (Ctrl+C), and Paste (Ctrl+V) shortcut keys work when editing data in MS Query.

Sharing data with other applications also is possible. You can share two different types of data, and MS Query provides two different ways to copy the information.

The two data types that exist in databases and tables are referred to as static and dynamic. *Static data* are constant, unchanging groups of fields and records. When you make updates with static data, copied information does not reflect changes. The copy

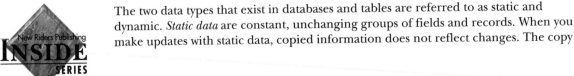

is an exact duplicate of the original, unconnected after the copy is made. *Dynamic data*, on the other hand, is linked to the source. With dynamic data, when you make changes to the source data, the changes are passed on dynamically to the copy, and the updates are kept current with the original records. If you dynamically copy information from a dBASE file to an Excel workbook, for instance, whenever changes are made to the dBASE file, the changes are passed along so that the data in the Excel workbook is always current.

To copy data from MS Query to another application, select the data that you want to copy in the result set. Then choose **E**dit, **C**opy, or press Ctrl+C. If you want to copy the headings and row numbers as well as the information, choose the Copy **S**pecial option. The Copy Special dialog box appears in which you can choose whether to include column headings and row numbers. Make your selection (the default is Column Headings), and click on OK. Then switch to the destination application, or start it if it is not already running. Open the file that you want to receive the data, and place the cursor in the upper left corner.

If you want a static copy of the data, choose **P**aste from the **E**dit menu in the other application. The information is placed in the area of the application you choose, and the data is an exact, unchanging representation of the original. If you want to make a dynamic copy, choose **E**dit, Paste Link. The information and the update link are pasted to the source application.

After you finish with the file you have pasted information to and saved it to disk, the next time you open the application, you can reestablish the link and update any changes to your data. Figure 13.10 illustrates a static copy of selected information from MS Query to Excel.

In Excel, data are placed into respective columns as in the original format. You can paste the same information by clicking on the Paste button in the standard toolbar. You can paste data as many times as needed and to multiple applications, until new data is entered into the Clipboard.

The Paste Special dialog box enables you to paste data as text, or to paste a link to the data. If choose Paste Link, you also can paste the link as an icon. If you paste the link as an icon, Excel pastes the icon of the MS Query application into the worksheet rather than the data. The link, however, remains so that when you double-click on the icon from your worksheet, it launches or switches to MS Query and brings up the file to which the link points.

To illustrate the way a dynamic link differs, edit one of the fields in the source application. Go to MS Query, and edit the title of one of the pasted records. For this example, you add the title President to G.K. Chattergee's record. Save the information in MS Query simply by moving the cursor to another record. Then switch back to Excel. Your data might still be the same as it was prior to the switch. Save the workbook, then close it. From the **F**ile menu in Excel, reopen the file and see what happens.

Figure 13.10

*Copying selected
data from MS
Query.*

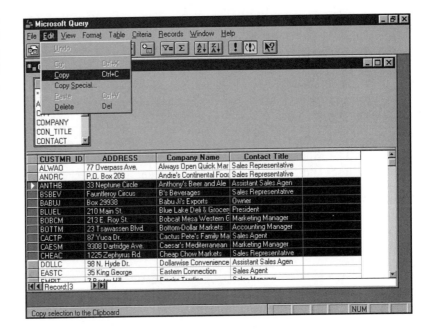

First, a dialog box appears that tells you this sheet contains links to other applications.
You can reestablish those links by clicking on the Yes button. As the worksheet opens,
the values in the sheet go to #N/A errors for a few seconds, and then the data
reappears along with the changes made from MS Query.

Take special note of the format of the cells on the dynamic paste. The static copy of
information treated everything as text only, and the dynamic copy treated blank fields
in the FAX number column as 0. Also, each cell has the following information in the
formula bar and cell.

```
=MSQuery.exe¦FISRST.QRY!'R4:R12'
```

The preceding line includes the name of the application (MSQUERY.EXE), the
associated query file from the dynamically linked application (FISRST.QRY), and the
positions of the file, in this case from row 4 to row 12.

Keeping the preceding line in mind, return to MS Query, and choose **S**ort from the
Records menu. Select Contact as the column, A**s**cending, add the sort, and close. The
order of the data changes.

Now, switch back to Excel. Click on the Save button, and observe the changes that
result after the save. The data in rows 4 through 12 in the source application changes,
and so do the values linked to the worksheet.

You can further maximize this powerful tool by using the additional features that MS Query has available for asking specific questions about data, and selecting only data that meets your criteria.

Another pane you can use to filter the records display in MS Query is the *criteria pane*. To display the criteria pane, click on View, and select <u>C</u>riteria. You also can find this command on the toolbar, called View Criteria. The criteria pane appears between the table and data panes.

You can create a typical example of a simple criteria entry by double-clicking on the CITY field in the table pane, which adds the CITY column to the data pane. Then drag the CITY label to the CRITERIA field cell in the criteria pane. Press Enter to move the cursor to the value cell directly below the CRITERIA field cell. Type **Auburn** and press Enter. This represents the question "Display all the customers whose CITY is Auburn."

If the field that contains Auburn is displayed, you can click on the cell, which makes it active, then click on the Criteria Equals button. This runs the query in exactly the same way.

Query automatically displays all matching records from the table or database. There is one entry for this query, and it is displayed alone.

Note   Query uses Structured Query Language, or SQL, to "ask" questions. The questions you enter in plain language are automatically converted to the format MS Query needs to execute properly.

You can adjust the size of the criteria pane by using the horizontal bar and dragging, just like the other panes. To take your question further, for example, "Display all customers whose CITY is Auburn or London," press Enter again, then move one box down to the OR field in the criteria pane and type **London**. Press Enter to get the answer to your question. Although simple questions like this are helpful, MS Query can do much more complex tasks with ease.

You can perform the same function with the mouse for all entries. Clear all criteria from the criteria pane. Click the down arrow in the Criteria field box. Select CITY. Move down to the Value box, and double-click on the empty box. The Edit Criteria dialog box appears. Here, you can select different operators, and different values from the table to match the question you need to ask.

The operators that you can use are as follows:

◆ Equals

◆ Does not equal

◆ Is greater than

◆ Is greater than or equal to

◆ Is less than

◆ Is less than or equal to

◆ Is one of

◆ Is not one of

◆ Is between

◆ Is not between

◆ Begins with

◆ Does not begin with

◆ Ends with

◆ Does not end with

◆ Contains

◆ Does not contain

◆ Is like

◆ Is not like

◆ Is null

◆ Is not null

Some operators obviously are more useful for certain data types than others. For instance, it might make sense if you're looking for a letter or character string to look in a text field, but not in a numeric or date field.

After you select a field and an operator, click on the Values button to bring up a list of the values in your table in that field. You can select any of the values from the list of available values, and look for that value, or edit the value once in the edit box. For instance, if you want to search for a city that begins with "Aust," rather than type that, you can select Austin from the values list and delete the last two letters from the result displayed in the box. Closing the dialog box puts the query in motion (as long as the Auto Query button on the toolbar is pressed) and returns the result set.

To ask a more complex question, click on the Criteria menu and select **R**emove All Criteria. This clears the prior question. Click again on Criteria, and select **A**dd Criteria. The Add Criteria dialog box appears, which enables you to ask new types of questions.

For instance, to identify people in your customer base who are in Sales or Marketing for a mass marketing campaign, select Add Criteria, and click the down arrow in the **F**ield box. Then select the CON_TITLE field. Tab down to the Operator's box, press the down arrow, and choose the operator "contains." Enter Sales in the Value box, then click on the **A**dd button. The dialog box stays active, but the query is executed in the background. Click on the **O**r button at the top of the box, and delete the word Sales and type **Marketing** in the Values box. Click again on the **A**dd button, and close the dialog box. Your list now includes those contacts whose title has either the word Sales or Marketing in them (see fig. 13.11).

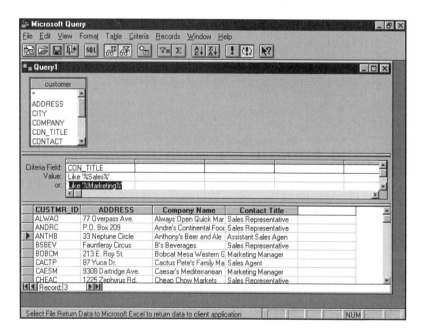

Figure 13.11

You can combine criteria in powerful ways to get the data you want. Here, the Contact Title field will only show titles that contain either the word "Sales" or "Marketing."

Note The search is case-sensitive. The same search for sales and marketing (in all lowercase letters) would return nothing.

Another way you can use this criteria is to track records. If you want to test the completeness of your contacts database and find out, for instance, for which customers you lack fax numbers, MS Query can fulfill your needs easily.

Click on the Criteria Field box, and select FAX. Then, from the Value box, double-click on Is Null from the operators list. Close the box, and you have your answer. All those customers need to be contacted so that the records can be completed.

You can clear criteria in much the same way as you delete columns from view. If you click on the top of the column of cells in the criteria pane, the entire group of cells is selected, and pressing the Del key removes them.

Note   The criteria on which you perform your queries can belong to fields that you can't see in the data pane. For instance, if you want to search on *REGION equal to IL,* but do not include it in the data pane, select REGION in the criteria pane only. If you do want it in the data pane, you can always hide the column later if you want to display it for some users only.

Selecting Records

You can use expressions to evaluate criteria in the criteria pane. For instance, to see a list of customers whose orders averaged $500.00 or more, you need to add an expression to your criteria search.

To illustrate this example in MS Query, click on the New Query button on the toolbar. Follow the steps to bring up a new database from dBASE files, called orders.

First, select a data source. dBASE files should be highlighted, and click on Use. Then, in the Add Tables dialog box, double-click on ORDERS.DBF (found in your \WINDOWS\MSAPPS\MSQUERY directory). Close the box, and you are returned to your query screen.

Select the fields to appear in the data pane by double-clicking on the labels in the table box. Choose CUSTMR_ID, SHIP_NAME, and ORDER_AMT. Then from the toolbar, choose the Show/Hide Criteria button, which displays the criteria pane. Double-click on the Criteria Field box in the criteria pane, and the Edit Criteria box opens. Choose the down arrow in the **T**otal box. The values Sum, Avg, Count, Min, and Max appear as choices. Select AVG, and tab to the **F**ield choice. Select ORDER_AMT, and click on OK.

Double-click on the Value field, and select the operator "is greater than," tab to Values, and enter 500. Close this box, and your result set will be a set of the customers who have orders greater than $500.00.

Calculating Your Data in MS Query

MS Query can perform calculations on your data, too. You can perform calculations on all records in a table or selected records in a group, and you can use the five most common operators—Sum, Avg, Count, Min, and Max—or create your own.

To create your own operators, use the same orders database and clear the data pane of all fields except ORDER_AMT. Then click on the Cycle Through Totals button. The sum of all orders is displayed first, then the average, the minimum, the maximum, and the count (see fig. 13.12).

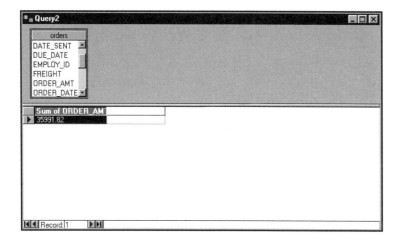

Fig. 13.12

Click on Cycle Through Totals to see, successively, the sum, average, minimum, maximum, or count for the values in the field.

For each type of total, there are some qualifiers that must be met, as follows:

◆ **Sum.** Sums the values in a field; works on numeric fields only.

◆ **Avg.** Calculates the average value of a numeric field.

◆ **Count.** Returns the number of entries in a field, except blank or null records.

◆ **Min.** Returns the lowest value of the field (for Text fields, A is the lowest); it also works with numbers, dates, times, and logical fields (yes or no).

◆ **Max.** Returns the highest value in the field; (for Text fields, Z is the highest); it also works on numbers, date and time fields, and logical fields.

To create a report of all the totals, select the ORDER_AMT field five times for your data pane. One-by-one, double-click on each column head bringing up the Edit Column edit box. Select each total for each column and the For Each in the fifth ORDER_AMT column. The totals for each category are displayed, as well as the individual order values in the last column. Figure 13.13 shows the end result.

Figure 13.13

The end results of the order totals report.

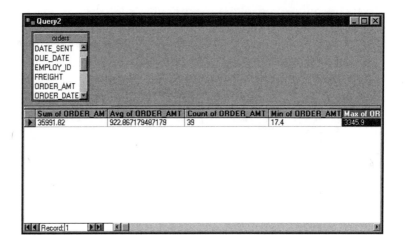

Before you can perform a calculation on a group of records in a table, you must determine what field you want to total, how you want the total to appear, and how to organize the group.

Calculating on Groups in MS Query

In this example, you find the sum of the ORDER_AMT field for each SHIP_CITY in the database. First, clear the data pane of all fields, and resubmit the ORDER_AMT and SHIP_CITY fields. Next, edit the column for ORDER_AMT by double-clicking on the column header, or by selecting the column and choosing **R**ecords, **E**dit Column from the pull-down menu.

Then, in the Edit Column dialog box for ORDER_AMT, select SUM as the total. Click on OK. The total of the orders for each city are combined and shown in the Sum of ORDER_AMT column.

Note   Click on the Cycle Totals button on the toolbar to show each category of totals for the group. To see the other values, continue to click through the cycle.

In MS Query you can change the order and the type of records you display by changing the query criteria. For instance, if you want to display the sum of the orders for

cities that have two or more orders, select the same setup as in the previous example. Using the ORDER_AMT column, set with the Sum for the total and the SHIP_CITY column in the criteria pane, add the information for the criteria field of Count as the total, ORDER_AMT, and the value as Greater than or equal to 2. This displays the total order values for those cities that generated two or more orders.

Taking that one additional step, if you want to see which of those cities that had two or more orders averaging over $1,000, add another criteria column. Choose for field the ORDER_AMT field, the Total of AVG, and for values, choose greater than or equal to 1,000. The list now is smaller and more defined than before.

To change the display to show the average order for those cities that had two or more orders and averaged over 1,000, select the ORDER_AMT Column in the data pane, and click on the Cycle Totals button until the Average ORDER_AMT heading appears.

You can cycle through all the values and get an idea of the power of this type of lookup. Figure 13.14 shows an example of such a search.

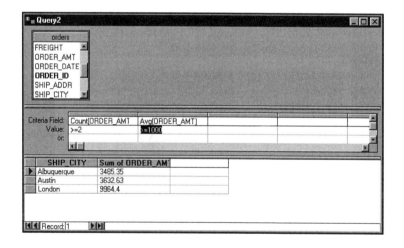

Figure 13.14

Cities that had more than two orders, which averaged more than $1,000.00 per order, shown with total sales.

You have a great amount of flexibility in how you can set up your queries to obtain a desired result set. You can select the records you want first, then calculate totals, or you can calculate first, then display records based on the calculations. The best method for a particular application varies, yet having the capability to adjust and modify can produce some powerful and specific results.

There are additional calculations that you can perform on your data other than the five most popular functions offered by MS Query. Adding your own calculations is easy and straightforward.

In the data pane, select the column heading where you want to put your calculation. If you want to project what orders for a time period might be based on current orders, you can take the order amount field and multiply it by a value to result in a new set of data in the result set. If your data displayed is for one month, and you want to multiply that month by 12 to determine year totals, type (ORDER_AMT)*12 in the column header box and press Enter.

The information that results is the projection, with new numbers. By adding a new label to the column header, your custom calculation is complete. Figure 13.15 shows the annual projections.

Figure 13.15

The annual projections.

SHIP_CITY	ORDER_AMT	Annual Projection	
Eugene	135	1620	
East Vancouver	1316.95	15803.4	
Walla Walla	731.8	8781.6	
Helena	498.18	5978.16	
Austin	3194.2	38330.4	
Buffalo	173.4	2080.8	
Bellingham	87.2	1046.4	
Helena	1405	16860	
Phoenix	1171	14052	
London	1530	18360	
Helena	470	5640	
Sevenoaks	589.05	7068.6	

Record: 1

Joining Tables

So far, you have experimented only with single table queries. MS Query can use multiple tables to build specific result sets. You get a chance later in this chapter to evaluate multiple table queries and see the difference between that and single table queries, and to link tables by using joins.

The biggest operational difference between single table and multiple table joins is that when you use multiple table queries you cannot edit the data in your result table. Also, field names appear differently, with the table name first, followed by a period, and then the field name.

To make a relationship between tables, MS Query performs a join between one field in each table if possible. Before a meaningful join can occur, the fields must be similar in some way. The most common way to create a join is to use a primary index from one data table to the next.

To illustrate this concept, click on the New Query button. Then choose dBASE Files again as your data source, click once on CUSTOMER.DBF, choose the **A**dd button, and select ORDERS.DBF. Close the dialog box, and look at the table pane. Notice that the two tables have a line drawn between them, going from CUSTMR_ID in the CUSTOMER.DBF to CUSTMR_ID in the ORDERS.DBF (see fig. 13.16). This line represents the join between these tables. Because the data fields in each file share the same name and have the same type of data, Query automatically makes the join and draws the line to illustrate the relationship.

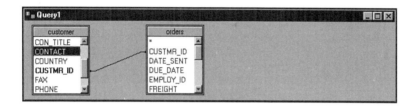

Figure 13.16

The join between CUSTOMER.DBF and ORDERS.DBF on CUSTMR_ID.

Now that your data is joined, you can perform queries based on criteria in either or both tables, and your result set displays the result set of the query. To set up your data pane, choose COMPANY and CONTACT from CUSTOMER.DBF, and choose DATE_SENT, SHIP_CITY, and ORDER_AMT from ORDERS.DBF. The resulting data displays records only for those customers who have placed orders because there has to be a customer ID in both the customer and orders data files.

If you want to produce a result set of customers who have been shipped orders between two dates, select **C**riteria from the **V**iew menu. The criteria pane appears, and in the first selection box, choose the field ORDERS.DATE_SENT. As indicated by the pull-down choices, the fields now are preceded by the table name so that query can track the data source.

Double-click in the Values field to access the Edit Criteria dialog box and choose Is Between as the operator. Then, click on the Va**l**ues button. From the Values box, choose the two values of 1989-05-17 and 1989-07-15. Click on OK. The orders sent between those two dates for customers whose CUSTMR_ID matches in CUSTOMER.DBF and ORDER.DBF, and who shipped orders within the selected date range, appear.

You can sort your new result set by any of the columns displayed. If you want to see who had the largest order in that time frame, select the ORDER_AMT column, and click on the Sort D**e**scending button. The result set should look like figure 13.17.

Figure 13.17

A joined multitable query, sorted by order value.

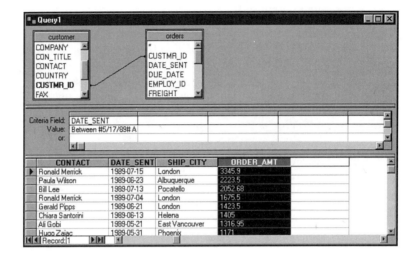

Understanding Joins

This type of join is called an *inner join,* and the default is that the values in the two joined fields (CUSTMR_ID) must contain the same value for data from either table to be displayed. If MS Query does not create the join automatically, you can use the Joins command from the **T**able menu to modify or create joins.

You also can delete joins. To illustrate how this works, first click on the line that joins the two tables you have selected in the query. Press the Del key, and the line and join disappear. Also, press the Auto Query button on the toolbar so that the result set is not updated for each change. Choose **R**emove All Criteria from the **C**riteria menu so that the result set will be complete.

The fastest way to create (or re-create) a join between two tables is to drag the name of the first field to the second. To re-create the join you just removed, click on CUSTMR_ID in CUSTOMER.DBF, and drag it over to CUSTMR_ID in ORDERS.DBF.

To evaluate further the way the inner join works, click on the join line between the tables, and select **J**oins from the **T**able menu. Click on the line prior to choosing Joins to ensure that you are editing the existing join and not creating a new one. As you can see, you can harness the power of joining information from multiple tables in a number of ways.

The top of the Joins dialog box shows the field from the first table that is joined, and its relationship to the field from the second table. In this case, an *equi-join,* a join involving two fields whose values equal one another, is used, and the result is a display of only records from the two tables whose values are equal. This is called an inner join.

The Joins Include section of the Joins dialog box enables you to choose an outer join instead of an inner join. An *outer join* is one that selects all records from one table, and only records from the second table that have equal joined values.

In the example, this process shows all customers who have IDs that are equal in both tables, and it displays all the records from the orders table and shows blank cells where the fields cannot be matched. This can show you missing information and help track down errors.

You also can display the opposite of the previous example by choosing the last Join includes option, which takes all values from Orders and only those from customers whose IDs are equal.

 Note   Outer joins cannot be performed with more than two tables in a query.

Another type of join, known as the *self-join*, compares values within a single table by adding two copies of the same table in a query.

Click on the New Query button, select data sources as dBASE Files, and select the EMPLOYEE.DBF twice. Query informs you that the table is already in the query one time, so you need to confirm that you do want another copy. Choose OK to close the dialog box, and return to the query.

Query gives the second copy of the table a new name that has the extension _1 for differentiation. To create a list of employees and their managers, delete the join that exists between the two tables if MS Query joins them automatically. Drag the name REPORTS_TO from the first table to EMPLY_ID in the second table. Add the fields of First Name, Last Name, and EMP_TITLE to the data pane from the first table, and add LAST_NAME from the second table.

The self-join returns a list of employees and their managers. The REPORTS_TO and EMPLY_ID fields are the same data type. When the tables are joined by this link, the information from the first table appears along with the information of each employee's boss. The link displays the name of the manager (REPORTS_TO) for each EMPLY_ID.

Adding Tables

You can use MS Query to add new tables to provide new information in addition to just looking at existing data. Select **T**able Definition from the **F**ile menu after you select a data source. The Select Table dialog box appears. Click on **N**ew. The New Table Definition dialog box appears.

To define a new table, name it, and tab to the field section of the dialog box. From here, you must give each field a name, data type, and length. After you define each field, click on the **A**dd button, and the field appears in the lower section of the window.

You can specify whether the field is required. After you define the table you want to add, click on Create and the table appears on the list of available data sources. You also can use the Table feature to view the definition of other existing data sources or tables in MS Query.

Note You cannot change fields after a data table has been created. The best way to add or modify tables is to bring up the existing definition, use the Add and Remove features to get the table in the correct format, and save it under a new name. You then can use MS Query to transfer all the information from the old table to the new corrected one.

The types of fields and lengths available vary with different ODBC Driver types.

You also can use **T**able Definition from the **F**ile menu to delete a table you no longer need. Select the file from the Available Sources list and click on **R**emove

Another way to create a new table is to use a result set from a query. This is a powerful way to transfer information from one format to another and create meaningful new data files.

To do this, run the query you want, and display the result set in the data pane. Select Save **A**s from the **F**ile menu. You then can select the data source you want to use. You can save your query as a query file, or as a new database table. In the window for available data sources, the list might not include all the different types of data files you might want to use. If it doesn't, click on **O**ther, and a new ODBC Sources box appears.

If you have chosen to define new files or sources, they appear in the ODBC Sources box. To create a new data source category, click on the New button. The following list shows some of the ODBC Driver data types that are available from MS Query.

◆ Microsoft Access Files

◆ Btrieve Files

◆ dBASE Files

◆ Excel Files

◆ FoxPro Files

◆ Oracle

◆ Paradox

◆ SQL Server

◆ Text Files (*.TXT, *.CSV)

You can transport your result set to a wide variety of popular formats. This is extremely important for several reasons. Because information sometimes needs to be shared between applications, computers or even companies, having the capability to deliver data in a format that others can use can save time and money. In addition, being capable of accepting data in all these formats and porting it to the format you want to use is very powerful.

For instance, if you have a client that has a dBASE application that he has been using for some time, and you need to use some of his data for a project, but your company uses Access as a database, you can use MS Query to read his dBASE file, filter out what you don't need, and create a new Access file directly from his information. The original data is unchanged, you have the information you need to use (in the right format), and it was accomplished with a minimum of time, hassle, and money spent.

Understanding SQL

MS Query performs its tasks by using a special language called SQL (pronounced "sequel"). Each time MS Query examines, retrieves, updates or does any function with a database, a SQL statement controls the way the process runs.

When MS Query builds a query, the software composes a SQL statement that begins with the SELECT command. Figure 13.18 shows a simple SELECT statement after choosing three fields from CUSTOMER.DBF for display in the data pane.

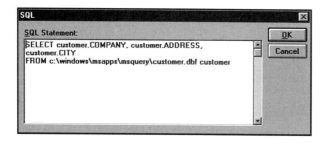

Figure 13.18

Clicking on the SQL button shows you the underlying language of your queries.

The view in the preceding figure is displayed by clicking on the SQL button on the toolbar. It also can be displayed by choosing <u>V</u>iew, <u>S</u>QL from the pull-down menus.

When the SQL box is active, you can edit or customize your statement. Using the toolbar, pull-downs, and tools that you have learned about in this chapter, MS Query translates that into SQL terminology. You can also type it directly. Figure 13.19 shows what a more complex join with criteria looks like in SQL.

Fig. 13.19

A more complex join with criteria in the SQL language.

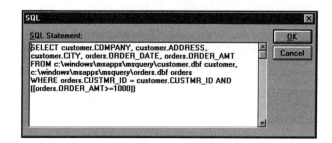

Some of the SQL statements that you use, either by entering them directly into the SQL box or by using the graphical interface provided by MS Query include the following:

- ◆ **From.** Specifies tables added to the table pane, where Select gets its fields.

- ◆ **Outer Join, Left or Right.** Joins tables and changes the way the join is set up.

- ◆ **AND.** Use for inclusive evaluation of more than one criteria.

- ◆ **OR.** Use for exclusive evaluation of more than one criteria.

- ◆ **DISTINCT.** Use if the Unique Values Only box in Query Properties is used.

- ◆ **ORDER BY.** Use on selected fields for sorting.

- ◆ **GROUP BY.** Use to display records together.

- ◆ **WHERE.** Use to evaluate or change criteria in a calculated field; joins tables using equi-join.

- ◆ **HAVING.** Use when working with an untotaled field in a set that contains totals.

Some types of queries cannot be created using the Query window, which involves granting of privileges, modifying tables, or creating indexes on data. You can use the Execute SQL dialog box to define and create custom statements.

Retrieving External Data from Excel

You can launch the power of MS Query from within Excel to bring data to your workbooks.

Earlier you learned how to select and copy data either in a static, unchanging mode, or dynamically, from Query to other applications. Now, you will learn how to retrieve external data from Query, and the external sources available to it from within Excel 7.

To begin, load Excel, and have a blank workbook on screen. Select Get External Data from the **D**ata menu. If the menu option is not available, make sure that the XLQuery and ODBC add-ins are activated in the Add-in dialog box.

Selecting Get External Data launches MS Query, and prompts you to select a data source, choose a table, and complete the basics of retrieving the data you want. You can create a new query, run an existing one, or change queries as you learned earlier in this chapter. After the result set displays what you request, select **R**eturn Data to Excel from the **F**ile menu.

An options dialog box appears in Excel asking you to specify whether to keep Query References (default is yes), Include Field Names (default is yes), Include Row Numbers (default is no), and destination for the data in the workbook. The default destination is the cell that was active when you invoked the Get External Command. You can change it to be specific for the sheet and cell range you need.

Clicking on OK brings the data from Query into Excel, places each column in an Excel column, and adjusts the width of the cells that receive the information.

Your data is now copied and ready use in the worksheet however you want (see fig. 13.20).

 Note   If you need to return to the data source and edit the information, you can double-click on the worksheet data, and the data is brought up from the source. This is a feature that can come in quite handy. Using the Query and Pivot toolbar accomplishes this as well. Click on the Get External Data button to launch or switch to MS Query.

Fig. 13.20

Data brought into Excel from MS Query.

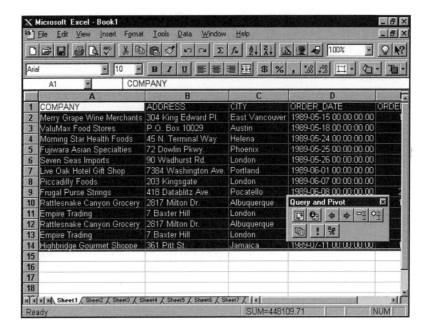

Importing ASCII Data

Many times you will need to import data that exists in ASCII—or text—format. This usually happens when you have another program that exports its data in this format, such as an accounting system of some sort. Excel uses its Text Import Wizard to help you to bring in data that isn't formatted for Excel.

To start importing data from an ASCII file, simply open it using the **O**pen command in the **F**ile menu. Excel will recognize that the file is ASCII based, and starts the Text Import Wizard automatically to walk you through the process of identifying the data for Excel, as shown in figure 13.21.

In Step 1 of 3 (see fig 13.21), you identify these two pieces of information for Excel:

◆ Choose between **D**elimited and Fixed **W**idth. A delimited file is one in which some character—such as a comma, space, or tab—separates each field. A fixed width file is one in which all the fields are in exactly the same position on each line (and sometimes are all together, such that it is hard to see where each field begins and ends).

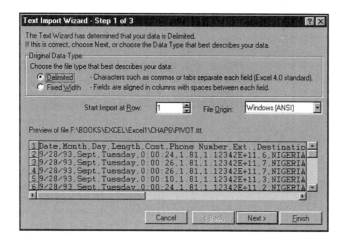

Figure 13.21

Opening an ASCII file automatically starts the Text Import Wizard.

◆ If the file contains heading information (look in the Preview window to see what the file actually contains), set the Start Import at **R**ow field to the number of lines that Excel should skip. For instance, if you're importing an accounting report, the first several lines may just contain report heading information that you really don't want in your spreadsheet.

Click on the Next button to move to Step 2 of 3, shown in figure 13.22.

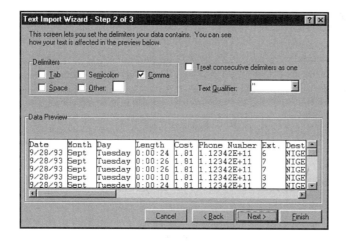

Figure 13.22

In Step 2 of 3, you tell Excel how the file is layed out. This step will be different for delimited or fixed width files.

For Step 2 of 3 with delimited files, set these options:

◆ In the Delimiters area, choose the appropriate character that separates each field. A comma is a common delimiter character, and is used in figure 13.22. You can choose multiple delimiters if your file uses them.

◆ The check box T**r**eat consecutive delimiters as one elimites any empty fields from your data input. Often, a null field will simply show up with, say, two commas right next to each other. Selecting this check box causes Excel to skip over those blank fields. However, choosing this check box will leave you with data that is not aligned in the same column in the final spreadsheet.

◆ Many ASCII files make a special point of distinguishing text fields by enclosing the text with quotation marks or some other character. This lets Excel know which fields are text and which are simply numbers. If your file uses a special extra delimiter for text fields, choose that character in the Text **Q**ualifier drop-down list.

Click on Next to move to Step 3 of 3, shown in figure 13.23.

Figure 13.23

In the final step (3 of 3) of the Text Import Wizard, you identify how Excel should format each column of data.

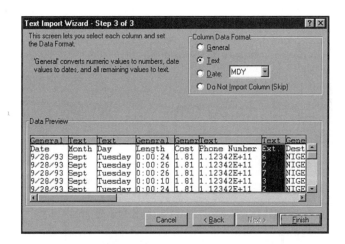

Select each column of data in Step 3 of 3 and then choose the appropriate Column Data Format for each column. By default, each one will be formatted for General. However, there is a danger in letting this choice remain for some types of fields. Sometimes numeric data should be treated as text. For instance, an inventory listing might contain part numbers that lead with zeroes. If you import that column as General, the values will be entered into Excel as numbers and so any leading zeroes will be lost. Prevent this problem by forcing Excel to treat such a column as text.

After you've completed all three steps and clicked on the **F**inish button, your data is opened into a sheet, as shown in figure 13.24 with some call accounting data.

X Microsoft Excel - Pivot.xls								
File Edit View Insert Format Tools Data Window Help								

	A	B	C	D	E	F	G	H	I
1	Date	Month	Day	Length	Cost	Phone Number	Ext.	Destination	Type
2	09/28/93	Sept	Tuesday	0:00:24	1.81	0112341844716	3	NIGERIA	International
3	09/28/93	Sept	Tuesday	0:00:26	1.81	0112341844716	5	NIGERIA	International
4	09/28/93	Sept	Tuesday	0:00:26	1.81	0112341844716	5	NIGERIA	International
5	09/28/93	Sept	Tuesday	0:00:10	1.81	0112341844716	4	NIGERIA	International
6	09/28/93	Sept	Tuesday	0:00:24	1.81	0112341844716	8	NIGERIA	International
7	09/28/93	Sept	Tuesday	0:00:18	1.81	0112341844716	7	NIGERIA	International
8	09/28/93	Sept	Tuesday	0:00:24	1.81	0112341844716	2	NIGERIA	International
9	09/28/93	Sept	Tuesday	0:00:28	1.81	0112341844716	7	NIGERIA	International
10	09/28/93	Sept	Tuesday	0:00:58	1.81	0112341844716	7	NIGERIA	International
11	09/28/93	Sept	Tuesday	0:00:24	1.81	0112341844716	4	NIGERIA	International
12	09/28/93	Sept	Tuesday	0:00:24	1.81	0112341844716	9	NIGERIA	International
13	09/28/93	Sept	Tuesday	0:00:34	1.81	0112341844716	8	NIGERIA	International
14	09/28/93	Sept	Tuesday	0:00:08	1.81	0112341844716	7	NIGERIA	International
15	09/28/93	Sept	Tuesday	0:00:34	1.81	0112341844716	2	NIGERIA	International
16	09/28/93	Sept	Tuesday	0:00:24	1.81	0112341844716	1	NIGERIA	International
17	09/28/93	Sept	Tuesday	0:00:28	1.81	0112341844716	4	NIGERIA	International
18	09/28/93	Sept	Tuesday	0:41:18	44.45	0112341844716	10	NIGERIA	International

Figure 13.24

Here, data captured from a telephone call accounting system is imported with Excel's Text Import Wizard.

Filtering Your Data

Excel contains a tool called AutoFilter that helps you to make sense of long lists of data. AutoFilter lets you quickly and easily restrict a list to show only a subset of your data.

To use AutoFilter, start with a worksheet that contains a lot of data, such as the one imported in figure 13.24. Make sure your active cell is within the data you want to filter, then pull down the **D**ata menu and choose **F**ilter. This displays a submenu in which you can find the Auto**F**ilter command (see figure 13.25).

Figure 13.25

The Data menu contains the AutoFilter command.

Note The Auto**F**ilter command is a checked command. In other words, when you select it you turn AutoFilter on; select it again and AutoFilter is turned off.

Activating AutoFilter displays arrows next to your headings. Clicking on these drop-down arrows displays lists of all the valid choices for that column (see figure 13.26).

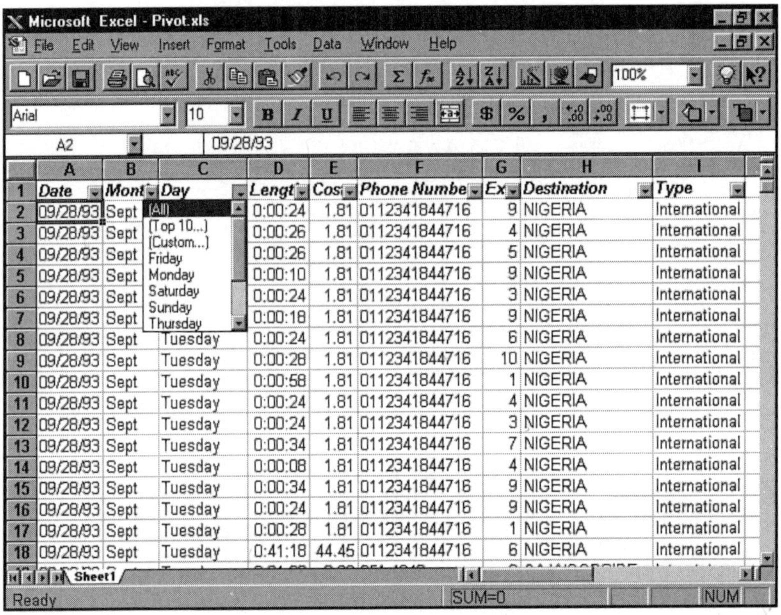

Figure 13.26

Each heading has a drop-down list arrow that lets you choose from all the valid choices for that column.

When you choose to AutoFilter a column, only the lines that contain the choice you made are displayed. You can restrict what you see by combining columns in whatever way you want. In this case, for example, you could show only the calls made to Nigeria, and then further restrict the listing to calls made on Tuesday.

To return to seeing all of your data, activate the columns that you filtered and choose (All) from their lists.

More Complex Filtering

AutoFilter also lets you ask additional questions. For one thing, each column drop-down list contains a choice called (Top 10) that displays all the rows that contain the 10 most frequent choices for that column. For example, if you choose (Top 10) in the Detination field in this example, you would see a list that only showed the records for

the top 10 calling destinations. Or, you could find the Extension field that shows what phone in the company placed the call, and restrict the list to the 10 extensions that made the most calls. Doing this helps you to focus your analysis efforts.

You can also choose custom AutoFilter choices. For any column, choose the (Custom) choice. This brings up the dialog box shown in figure 13.27.

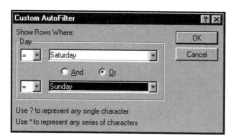

Figure 13.27

Use the (Custom) choice to define complex criteria.

The (Custom) choice lets you define more complex criteria. In this example, you could see all calls made on weekends. Another choice would be to restrict the Cost field to amounts greater than $10.00, to see only those calls.

Totaling and Subtotaling Lists

Excel also lets you quickly total and subtotal your lists of data. To do this, make sure your active cell is within your data, pull down the **D**ata menu and choose Su**b**totals. This displays the Subtotal dialog box shown in figure 13.28.

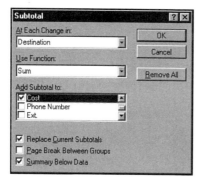

Figure 13.28

The Subtotal dialog box lets you choose how you want your data subtotaled.

In this example, when the subtotals are applied, you will see a subtotal every time the destination changes (thereby subtotaling for each different destination), and the subtotal shown will be a Sum of the values in the Cost field.

Note Be sure to sort your data (see the next section) by the column that you want to use as your *break group* before performing the subtotal. The break group is the one in which you will be inserting subtotals. In this example, it is the Destination column.

After filling in this dialog box, click the OK button to insert the subtotals. The results are shown in figure 13.29.

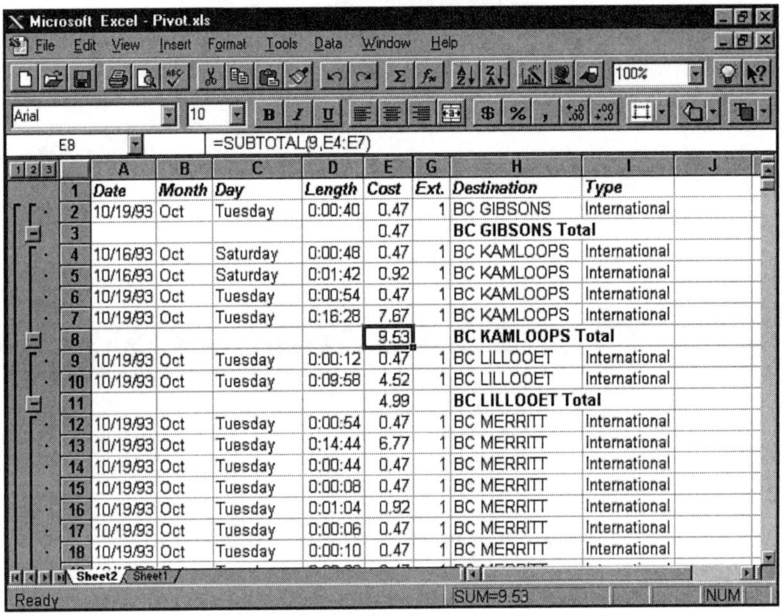

Figure 13.29

The inserted subtotals.

Subtotals are inserted as outline levels. If you choose, you can collapse the outline levels (by clicking on the minus buttons) to hide the detail, leaving only the subtotals.

Note To remove the subtotals, reaccess the Subtotal command and click on the Remove All button.

Sorting Your Data

Excel can quickly and painlessly sort your data in a variety of ways. To access the sort feature, make sure your active cell is within your data, activate the **D**ata menu and choose the **S**ort command. You see the dialog box shown in figure 13.30.

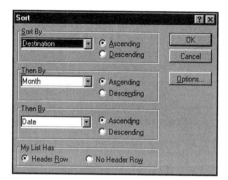

Figure 13.30

Use the Sort dialog box to resort your data in whatever order you want.

Note If your data has column heading descriptions (and it should to make things easier) you can choose to sort by those names. If, on the other hand, you do not have column headings, the Sort dialog box only displays column letters.

Using Pivot Tables

Pivot tables are tools used in Excel to summarize large lists, databases, worksheets, workbooks, or other collections of data. They are called pivot tables because you can move fields with the mouse to provide different types of summary listings, that is, the tables can change, or pivot.

Pivot tables can get their source information from a number of different sources. For this discussion, you extract data for the pivot table from external sources using MS Query.

Begin with a blank worksheet. The first part of creating a pivot table is to invoke the Pivot Table Wizard. This is the first button on the Query and Pivot toolbar. You also can use the **P**ivot Table command in the **D**ata menu. The first screen of the Pivot Table Wizard is the data source selection step. You have the following choices:

◆ Microsoft Excel List or Database

◆ External Data Source

◆ Multiple Consolidation Ranges

◆ Another Pivot Table

Choose External Data Sources and click on **N**ext. The Step 2 of 4 dialog box appears. Click on the Get Data button, which has the notation *no data retrieved.* MS Query is launched.

Follow the steps involved in choosing a data source, choosing a table, and setting up a result set. You can, if you have not already done so, retrieve a saved query. After the result set is the information you want to summarize in the pivot table, select Return Data to Microsoft Excel from the **F**ile menu and click on **N**ext.

The Data is then sent to Excel through the Clipboard. The Pivot Table Wizard - Step 3 of 4 dialog box appears. Figure 13.31 shows the Pivot Table setup screen.

Figure 13.31

Setting up the pivot table involves dragging the field buttons to positions in this dialog box.

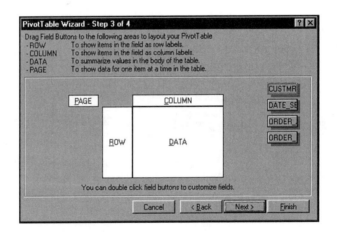

The fields that you select in your result set show along the right side of the dialog box. The areas of the pivot table you work with are Row information, Column information, Data, and Page. You can drag the selected fields into these separate areas for table formatting.

In the query, for example, the ORDERS.DBF file was chosen. The fields selected were: Customer Id, Order Id, Ship City, Ship Date, and Order Amount. If you want to create a summary table of this information, you might want to see it as a breakdown by customer and city, with the orders totaled, but listed separately by customer ID and order ID. The pivot table can easily provide you with this information.

Because a separate breakdown by City is desired, drag the City field over to the PAGE section of the Pivot Table setup, Step 3 of 4 dialog box. This means that for each city, you can see a separate page of data, or a recap of the sales in that city. Next, take the Order Amount field, and drag it into the data area. That information is summarized and totaled in the table. For row, take the Ship Date field. Drag it over and your table provides a row breakdown in date order. The column information is the Customer ID and Order ID fields. The final setup appears as shown in figure 13.32.

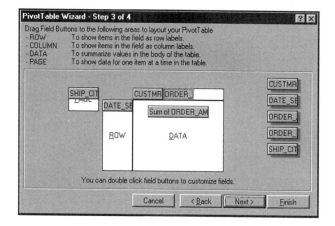

Figure 13.32

The completed Pivot Table setup.

Click on Next, then click on **F**inish. The resulting pivot table is shown in figure 13.33.

Figure 13.33

The resulting pivot table.

	A	B	C	D	E	F	G	
1	SHIP_CITY	(All)						
2								
3	Sum of ORDER_AMT	CUSTMR_ID	ORDER_AMT					
4		ANTHB	ANTHB Total	BLUMG	BLUMG Total	BOBCM	BOBCM Total	CA
5	DATE_SENT	970		1148		94.88		35
6	5/17/89		0	0	0	0	0	
7	5/19/89		0	0	0	0	0	
8	5/21/89		0	0	0	0	0	
9	5/26/89		0	0	0	0	0	
10	5/31/89		0	0	0	0	0	
11	6/1/89		0	0	0	0	0	
12	6/5/89		0	0	0	0	0	
13	6/9/89		0	0	0	0	0	
14	6/12/89		0	1148	1148	0	0	
15	6/13/89		0	0	0	0	0	
16	6/14/89		0	0	0	0	0	
17	6/21/89		0	0	0	0	0	
18	6/23/89		0	0	0	0	0	

The resulting pivot table looks somewhat ominous at this point because it shows all the information for all facets of the data. In the Ship City box at the top of the table, there is a drop-down arrow. Click on the arrow to bring out a list of each city in the data. Click on the city whose sales numbers you want to see. When you select an individual value for the page criteria, such as London, the table automatically recalculates and displays the recap of sales, complete with grand totals at the bottom and to the right, for total sales by date for that city, and total sales by customer for that city.

The pivot table is a very powerful analysis tool. You can summarize a vast amount of information in a friendly, informative, interactive worksheet table.

You cannot edit information in a pivot table because it maintains a link to the source data, but updating the source file does pass any new or changed information to the table. In this example, for instance, any new orders for customers show up on the pivot table if they are entered into the source database. When the table is retrieved, on the Query and Pivot toolbar, the Exclamation Point button is the Refresh Data tool. Clicking on this button performs the original query and returns any new or changed information to your table.

If you decide you want to change the orientation of the table, you can change it dynamically by dragging the field identifiers to the location you want them. As an example, if you want to see the Customer ID information in a row instead of a column, click and drag the field name for Customer ID from the its present column to the Row area. The pivot table automatically reformats itself with the new information.

Another way to modify your table is to click anywhere on the table and then click on the Pivot Table Wizard button on the Query and Pivot toolbar, or the **P**ivot Table command in the **D**ata menu. This process takes you directly to Step 3 of 4, the set up, where you can drag row, page, column, or data information around to format the table the way you want.

You also can double-click on a field name to customize it. The customization can change where it is located, row, column or data, and how it is totaled, if at all. You also can choose to hide items if you want. For instance, if you drag the Order ID field from column to row, you get a detail breakdown by Order ID of order total, and by date (the other row identifier) for each customer within each city.

The totals that show on the table are figured for each subcategory in the row and for the column. When you add an additional row field, the pivot table provides a new subtotal field on the row. The same occurs with column information. The information in every row and every column is totaled. There is a grand total field for the table.

After you create your table, you can change the way it displays information in addition to dragging row and column and page fields to new locations. By highlighting a range of cells in the detail section of the table, and selecting Group from the toolbar, the pivot table combines the information into a combined section. Then, using the Hide Detail button, you can just display the totals. Another way to use this is to highlight the information under the Date Sent field, and click on the Hide Detail button. This suppresses the display of the subtotals for each Order ID for each date, but still shows the dates and the grand total.

You can also hide the detail on a row-by-row or column-by-column basis.

Highlighting an entire column of information, such as the row data, which is the Date Sent field, and clicking on the Group button makes an interesting display. You then can view or hide the detail on an entire group of cells by double-clicking on the cell that contains the Group label—Group 1, in this case.

To obtain a great amount of detail about a pivot table, you can output each sheet of the table to its own worksheet if necessary. You can do this to allow further individual data manipulation or calculation. Just click on the **S**how Pages button on the Query and Pivot toolbar to take each page from the table and create a worksheet for each one.

If you combine this with large collections of data, minus proper organization, a great deal of space and time can be required. In this example, Show Pages creates a recap of sales for each city.

Now, with each city on its own sheet, in its own pivot table, you can drag and move information around to create the views you want, and if you do not like the way your result looks, you can use the **E**dit menu to undo your pivot changes and revert back to the original design

Another way to reformat your pivot table is to click once on the field you want to alter, and from the Query and Pivot toolbar, click on Pivot Table Field. The Edit Field dialog box appears, where you can change the orientation, from page, to row or to column, you can modify the type of subtotal that is applied to the information, such as SUM, COUNT, AVERAGE, MAX, MIN PRODUCT, Standard Deviations, and so on. And, if you want to suppress the display of information, you can hide items on the list of values for the field.

If you want to suppress the display of certain cities in the table, you can selectively click on the values you do not want to show, and they remain hidden until you go back and tell the pivot table edit field criteria to redisplay them.

Double-clicking on any of the field names brings up the Edit Field dialog box.

When you double-click on the Totals fields, the information that is used to calculate that total is copied into an additional worksheet tab within the workbook. For instance, if you select all from the Ship City Page selection, to bring up all the information in the table, and go to the end of the table to the last grand total, double-clicking copies the summary into its own worksheet, which you can then manipulate, edit, and work with separate from the pivot table.

You can change the way your data appears by moving fields around from different orientations. You also can change how the sheet looks. You change a pivot table by selecting AutoFormat from the Format menu, because the changes made to individual cells or ranges are not passed along to the other worksheets.

AutoFormat provides a consistent look across the sheet. Using AutoFormat, you can choose from many varying styles of background colors, styles, column and row display changes, from simple to complex.

Automatically Formatting Your Tables

Often you want to format your tables to make them more pleasing to look at. Perhaps you want to print them out and make them easier to read, or perhaps you need to present the data to someone else. In any case, Excel provides an AutoFormat function that gives you lots of pre-designed choices from which to choose.

Start with your active cell within the table you want to format, pull down the Format menu and choose **A**utoFormat. This displays the AutoFormat dialog box shown in figure 13.34.

Figure 13.34

The AutoFormat dialog box makes formatting your data quick and painless.

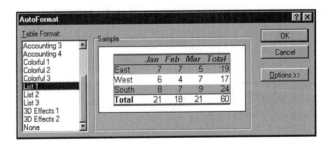

Select each different **T**able Format to see a preview of how the formatting will appear. When you've found one that you want, select it and click on the OK button. Your table will be formatted using the same guidelines as the preview.

Note Some printers may not correctly handle the shading for some of the pre-defined table formats. If you're working with a large amount of data, try printing just one page to make sure your printer gives you results that come out the way you want them. Then, either choose a different table format and try again or print the entire set of data.

C H A P T E R

14

Customizing Excel for Windows 95

Now that you are a little more comfortable using Excel, you might want to add a little of yourself to the way Excel works and looks. Excel for Windows 95 gives you great flexibility in deciding the types of toolbars you want to display, the menu items you want available, and where you want toolbars to be placed. This chapter shows you the way to take advantage of these customization features and provides the following insights into Excel:

◆ How to set up menus for the way you work

◆ How to place a Visual Basic subroutine or macro on a toolbar

◆ How to create new buttons for the toolbar

◆ How toolbars can be torn off and made to float

Although this chapter contains more advanced features, even beginners can take advantage of Excel for Windows 95's customization routines.

Have you ever pulled down a menu or looked at the standard toolbars and thought, "Why do I have to rummage through all these options I never use to choose the Options command?" Although the Excel interface is easy to use, it also is packed with dozens of commands and options you might never use. You can eliminate, add, move around, and create your own menus, dialog boxes, toolbars, and toolbar buttons to make Excel work the way you work.

Exploring Excel's Customizable Menus

One of the unique features of Excel is the Menu Editor. The Menu Editor enables you to customize the menu system, giving you the capability of creating your own menus. You can use this feature when you build macros or Visual Basic applications to create your own worksheet applications.

To use the Menu Editor, you first must activate a Visual Basic module or create a new one. Perform the following steps to start and use the Menu Editor:

1. Activate a Visual Basic module, or select **I**nsert, **M**acro, **M**odule to start a new one. The Visual Basic toolbar appears on-screen.

2. Select **T**ools, Menu E**d**itor to display the Menu Editor dialog box (see fig. 14.1).

Tip You also can click on the Menu Editor button on the Visual Basic toolbar to start the Menu Editor. This button is the second button from the left and looks like a pull-down menu.

Figure 14.1

The Menu Editor dialog box enables you to customize your menus.

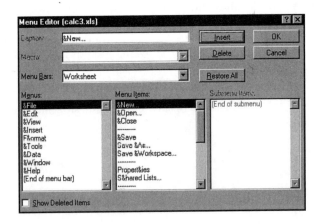

At this point, you need to use some of your knowledge about Windows applications. Most Windows applications, for instance, have standard menus that are on a menu bar, such as File, Edit, Window, and Help. Standard menus also have standard elements, including menu items (commands), separator bars, submenu items, and the ellipsis (if the menu item activates a dialog box). For the most part, you take these elements for granted when you learn to use a Windows application.

Another feature that usually is taken for granted when you use Windows applications is how menu bars change depending on what you are doing. Notice, for instance, that when you performed the previous Step 1, the menu bar changed, giving you new menus with different menu items. This enabled you to select commands that are specific to the Visual Basic module. The menu bar that is activated when you choose this module is called the Visual Basic Module menu bar.

Excel has seven types of menu bars from which you can choose when you create or modify menus. You can choose these menu bars from the Menu **B**ars drop-down list box in the Menu Editor dialog box. The following are descriptions of the menu bars:

- ◆ **Worksheet.** This is the standard menu bar that you see when you work with worksheets.

- ◆ **Chart.** This menu bar is active when you have a chart active.

- ◆ **No Documents Open.** You see this menu bar when there are no open workbooks. This menu bar contains only **F**ile and **H**elp.

- ◆ **Visual Basic Module.** This menu bar appears when you have a Visual Basic module active.

- ◆ **Shortcut Menus 1.** This is the menu that appears when you right-click on a toolbar, row or column header, window title bar, tool, cell, desktop, or workbook tab.

- ◆ **Shortcut Menus 2.** You see this menu when you right-click on a drawing object, button, or text box.

- ◆ **Shortcut Menus 3.** This is the menu that appears when you right-click on parts of a chart, including data series, text, arrow, plot area, gridline, floor, and legend. You also see this menu when you click on the whole chart.

In the Menu Editor dialog box, the **M**enus, Menu I**t**ems, and S**u**bmenu Items lists contain the actual menu names and commands (items) for each menu bar. You work from these lists to determine which menus and menu items you want to include in each customized menu bar.

Adding Menus to a Menu Bar

Although creating your own menus requires you to know a different language of sorts, you already are familiar with most of it just by using Windows applications on a regular basis. The menu bar that you use can be one of the seven Excel menu bars or one that you create from scratch. The following steps show you the way to add your own menu to a menu bar:

1. In the Menu **B**ars drop-down list box in the Menu Editor dialog box, select the menu bar you want to customize. You might, for instance, want to add a menu to the Worksheet menu bar. If so, click on Worksheet.

2. You now need to tell Excel where you want to place the new menu on the selected menu bar. To indicate this, select from the M**e**nus list box the menu that is immediately left of where you want the new menu to appear.

   Suppose, for example, that you want to add a menu named Fiscal and place it to the left of the Data menu. To do this, click on &Data in the M**e**nus list box.

Note The ampersand (&) is an instruction that tells Excel to underline the next character. This underlined character denotes the accelerator key, or hot key, in the menu name.

3. Click on the **I**nsert button, telling Excel that you want to insert a new menu. This activates the Caption field box in the Menu Editor dialog box (refer to fig. 14.1).

4. In the Caption field box, type the name of the new menu: **Fi&scal**, for example. You can place the ampersand to the left of any other character to denote a hot key. Just be sure that the hot key does not conflict with other hot keys that already are set up on the menu bar.

5. Return to Step 1 to add more menus. Press Enter or choose OK when you finish adding menus.

This returns you to the Visual Basic module. If you created a new menu on the module, you will see it displayed on the menu bar. If you created a menu on another menu bar—the Worksheet menu bar, for example—click on a sheet tab to switch to a worksheet. You can see your new menu on the menu bar. In figure 14.2, for example, the Fiscal menu appears on the menu bar.

Figure 14.2

Adding the Fiscal menu to the Worksheet menu bar.

Adding Items to a Menu

If you click on a newly created menu, nothing happens. This is because you have just created the menu and not any menu items under it. The following steps show you the way to create menu items and place them on your new menu:

1. Be sure you switch back to the Visual Basic module, and select **T**ools, Menu E**d**itor to display the Menu Editor dialog box.

2. In the Menu **B**ars drop-down list box, select the menu bar that includes your new menu; Worksheet, for example.

3. In the M**e**nus list box, click on the menu that you want to add items to; Fi&scal, for example.

4. In the Menu I**t**ems list box, select the menu item before which you want your menu item to appear. If this is a new menu (as in the Fiscal example), the only option is (End of menu), as shown in figure 14.3. Click on (End of menu) if this is the only option or if you want the item to be at the bottom of the menu.

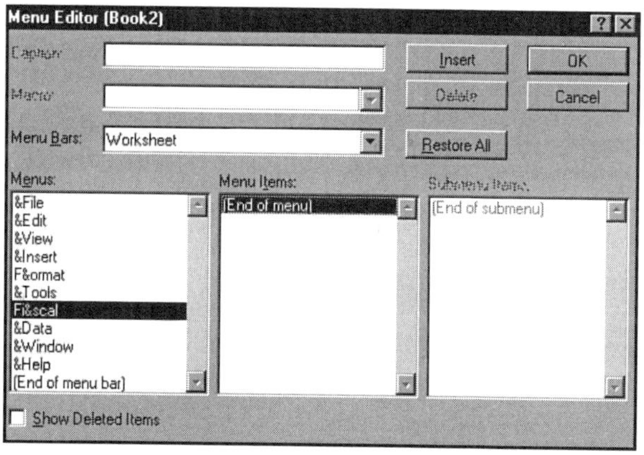

Figure 14.3

The Menu Items list includes all the menu commands for the selected menu.

5. Click on **I**nsert. This activates the **C**aption field box.

6. Type the name of the menu item you want to add to the menu; **&Budget**, for example. If you want to include a separator bar, use a hyphen (-) instead of a name.

Tip Some menus use separator bars to group different types of commands or items. In the **F**ile menu, for example, the printing commands are grouped and separated from the other commands by two separator bars. Try to use separator bars to group similar items. The separator bar is created by using a hyphen (-) when you include a caption name.

7. To add another menu item, return to the Menu I**t**ems list box and click on the menu item before which you want your menu item to appear. Do not click on OK or press Enter yet; this would return you to the Visual Basic module.

8. Repeat steps 4–7 until you finish adding all the menu items. Click on OK or press Enter when you finish.

You can see your new menu structure by returning to the menu bar that contains the new menu, such as a worksheet. You now are ready to add some functionality to your menu items so that they do more than just sit on a menu.

Tip You also can add submenu items to menu items by following the preceding steps, but selecting the item before which you want your submenu item to appear in the S**u**bmenu Items list box.

If, for example, you want to include a submenu item called Equipment to the &Budget menu item, click on &Budget in the Menu I**t**ems list box and then click on (End of submenu) in the S**u**bmenu Items list box. Click on Insert and fill in the Caption field box with &Equipment.

Adding Functionality to Menu Items

When you create new menu items and customize them, you have to assign a command or procedure to them. In other words, you must attach a macro or Visual Basic subroutine to them. If, for example, you create a Visual Basic subroutine that runs a budget analysis worksheet, you can attach this routine to the &Budget menu item in the preceding examples.

The following steps show you the way to attach a macro or subroutine to a menu item:

1. Make sure the Menu Editor dialog box is active by returning to a Visual Basic module and selecting **T**ools, Menu **E**ditor.

2. Select the menu item or submenu item to which you want to attach the macro or subroutine. Select &Budget in the Menu I**t**ems list box, for example, to attach a macro or subroutine to it.

3. In the **M**acro pull-down list box, select the macro or subroutine name you want to attach to the menu item (see fig. 14.4).

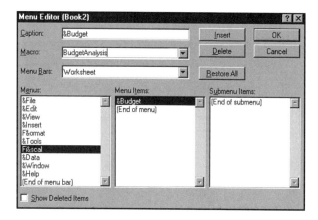

Figure 14.4

Attaching a macro or subroutine to a menu item using the Macro pulldown list box.

4. Return to Step 2 to continue adding macros and subroutines to menu items.

5. Press Enter or click on OK when you finish.

You now can return to the menu bar that you customized and use the new menu and menu item(s).

Tip

When you want to delete a menu, menu item, or submenu item, start the Menu Editor, select the item you want to delete, and click on the **D**elete button. Use the **R**estore All button to return the menus to their original, built-in state.

Customizing Toolbars

Excel makes it very easy—too easy, in fact—to customize the toolbars that appear on your screen. They are so easy to customize that you might overdo adding new icons and macros to your toolbar. This clutter slows down your system. On the other hand, you can add or delete tools that you use a lot or never at all.

If, for example, you use the double-underline formatting feature often, you might get tired of navigating menus, tabs, and dialog boxes to insert a double-underline to a word or phrase. To speed up this process, you can add the double-underline tool to the Formatting (or any other) toolbar. Excel includes several predefined tools that you can add to your desktop, including the double-underline tool, making it easy to customize the look and functionality of your toolbars. You also can add your own macros and Visual Basic subroutines to toolbar buttons.

Understanding Toolbar Options

When you first install and start Excel for Windows 95, you are shown the default toolbars and tool buttons. These include the Standard and Formatting toolbars. Unbeknownst to new users, there are several other toolbars that you can display, including the Query and Pivot toolbar, Chart toolbar, and Forms toolbar. To display these toolbars, use the following steps:

1. Select **V**iew, **T**oolbars to display the Toolbars dialog box, as shown in figure 14.5.

Figure 14.5

*The Toolbars
dialog box
displays the
available
toolbars.*

2. Click in the check boxes to display the toolbars of your choice. If you want to deactivate one, be sure its check box is empty.

3. Along the bottom of the dialog box, you can tell Excel to show color in the toolbars (the C**o**lor Toolbars option), display large buttons (the **L**arge Buttons option), or show the tool button names (the **S**how ToolTips option).

Tip   Use the **L**arge Buttons option if you use a high resolution video display, such as 1024×768. This makes the buttons a little larger, helping you to see and use them better.

4. If you want to add specific buttons to (or delete them from) a toolbar, click on the **C**ustomize button. This displays the Customize dialog box (see fig. 14.6).

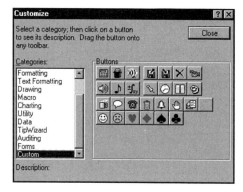

Figure 14.6

Add buttons to a toolbar using the Customize dialog box.

5. In the **C**ategories list box, click on the category that contains the button you want to add. The Buttons area changes to display the buttons included in the selected category.

   You might, for instance, want to add the double-underline button to the Formatting toolbar. To do so, click on Text Formatting in the **C**ategories list box.

6. To see the button's function, click on the button in the Buttons area. A brief description of the button's function appears at the bottom of the dialog box.

7. Grab the button you want to add to the toolbar and drag the button to where you want it. If, for example, you want to place the double-underline button between the italic (I) and the underline (U) buttons on the Formatting toolbar, drag the double-underline button there and release the mouse button.

Cleaning Up a Crowded Toolbar

If you get carried away or your display is not large (you might be using standard VGA display or a laptop display, for instance), your toolbars might get too crowded or disappear off the right side of the screen. If this happens, you need to clean up your toolbar and move around or remove some toolbar buttons. You also can resize the width of a pull-down list box—the Font pull-down list box, for example.

To remove or move a button, perform the following steps:

1. Select **V**iew, **T**oolbars, **C**ustomize to display the Customize dialog box.

2. To remove a button, drag the button you want to remove off the toolbar and drop it onto the worksheet area. This automatically removes the button from the interface.

3. To move a button, drag the button that you want to move and drop it in its new place on the toolbar. You should drag it so that its center is placed between the buttons where you want it.

4. Click on Close in the Customize dialog box when you are finished reorganizing your toolbars.

Customizing a Button with a Macro

You might create a macro that you want to assign to a button on a toolbar. You can assign it to a built-in button or create your own button. You might, for instance, create a macro that assigns various formatting features to a selected cell or range of cells. You then can create a toolbar button using the Button Editor and assign the macro to it.

To assign a macro to a built-in or custom button, perform the following steps:

1. Make sure the toolbar that contains the button you want to modify is on your screen.

2. Select **V**iew, **T**oolbars. This displays the Toolbars dialog box. Click on **C**ustomize to bring up the Customize dialog box.

3. Select the button you want to assign the macro to and drag it to the toolbar. If you want to use a custom button and place it on the Formatting toolbar, for example, click on Custom in the **C**ategories list, pick one of the buttons, and drag it to the Formatting toolbar.

4. Select **T**ools, Assi**g**n Macro from the menu bar. The Assign Macro dialog box appears, as shown in figure 14.7. If you are assigning a macro to a Custom button, the Assign Macro dialog box displays automatically.

Figure 14.7

Assigning a macro to a toolbar button with the Assign Macro dialog box.

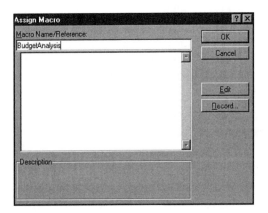

5. Click on the macro name you want to assign in the **M**acro Name/Reference list.

6. Press Enter or click on OK to return to the Customize dialog box. Click on Close or press Enter. This displays the active worksheet.

Designing Your Own Toolbar

Suppose, for example, that you don't want to use any of the built-in toolbars that Excel provides. This might be the case if you have several customized buttons that you created (see the following section on creating your own buttons) or you just want to group certain buttons together.

To design your own toolbar, perform the following steps:

1. Select **V**iew, **T**oolbars to bring up the Toolbars dialog box.

2. In the Tool**b**ar Name field box, type the name of the new toolbar you want to create, such as **Quick Tools** (see fig. 14.8). Use as many characters and spaces as you like in the name.

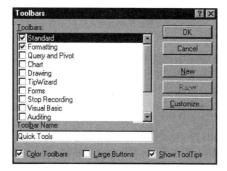

Figure 14.8

Naming the new toolbar in the Toolbar Name field box.

3. Click on the **N**ew button, which places the toolbar on the screen.

4. The Customize dialog box appears, with a toolbar large enough to fit one button on it. From the Buttons group, drag any buttons you want onto the new toolbar.

5. After you place all the buttons, click on Close. The new toolbar displays, with the buttons available for use.

Figure 14.9 shows an example of a custom toolbar with several buttons added to it.

Figure 14.9

Adding buttons to a custom toolbar.

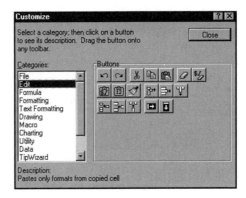

Designing Your Own Buttons

Excel enables you to draw your own toolbar buttons or modify existing ones using the Button Editor. If you have ever used an icon editor, you'll feel at home with the Button Editor.

The following steps show you how to use the Button Editor:

1. If you want to modify a button, make sure its toolbar is displayed.

2. Select **V**iew, **T**oolbars to display the Toolbars dialog box.

3. Right-click on the button (on the toolbar) you want to edit and choose Edit Button Image from the menu. This displays the Button Editor dialog box (see fig. 14.10).

Figure 14.10

Use the Button Editor to create or change a button face.

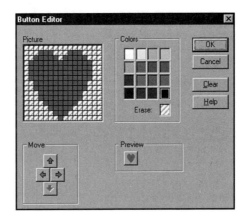

If you want to create a new button, click on the **C**lear button in the Button Editor dialog box.

4. In the Colors area, click on a color. Next, click on the boxes in the Picture area to create the picture that you want to appear on the button. Use the Preview area to see what the actual button looks like.

5. Continue clicking on the colors you want to finish the drawing. Press Enter or click on OK to place the finished button on the toolbar.

Assigning Toolbars to Workbooks

Let's say you want to assign a toolbar to a specific workbook. Or, you want to trade toolbars with a friend or co-worker. To execute both of these tasks, you must attach the toolbar to a workbook. Perform the following steps:

1. Open the workbook file to which you want to attach the toolbar.

2. Activate the Visual Basic module by switching to a Visual Basic module or selecting **I**nsert, **M**acro, **M**odule.

3. Select **T**ools, Attach **T**oolbars to display the Attach Toolbars dialog box (see fig. 14.11).

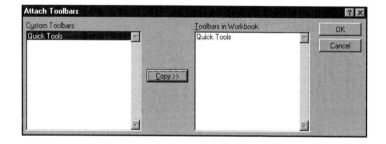

Figure 14.11

Attaching custom toolbars to workbooks using the Attach Toolbars dialog box.

4. Click on the toolbars you want to attach in the **C**ustom Toolbars list box.

5. Select **C**opy. Excel places the name(s) in the **T**oolbars in Workbook list box.

6. When you finish adding names to the **T**oolbars in Workbook list box, press Enter or click on OK.

7. Save the workbook.

Floating Toolbars

Excel enables you to reposition toolbars to fit your editing needs. You might, for instance, like to have certain toolbars handier than others. One way to keep them close at hand is to tear them off the top of the screen and let them float on your desktop.

To tear off a toolbar, move the mouse pointer to a blank area on the toolbar, grab the toolbar, and drag it onto the worksheet area. Release the mouse. The toolbar becomes a floating "toolbox" that stays visible on your screen as you enter and edit data. You can grab the title bar of the toolbar and move it around as you do any other Windows window. See figure 14.12 for examples of floating toolbars.

Figure 14.12

Floating toolbars, carried to an extreme.

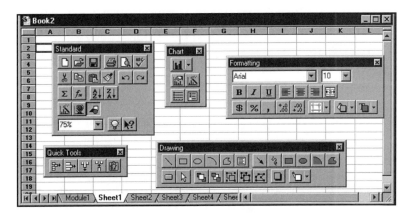

To place the floating toolbar back on top of the screen, grab the toolbar, drag it to the top of the screen where you want to place it (it must be above the worksheet area), and drop it. The toolbar elongates into a rectangular object to help you get an idea of where it will be placed when you release the mouse button.

Part III

PowerPoint

PowerPoint Quick Start

PowerPoint is a presentation software program that helps you quickly and easily create professional-quality presentations. Your presentations can be transferred onto plain paper, color or black-and-white overheads, or 35mm slides, or they can be shown on a video screen or computer monitor. To complete your presentation package, PowerPoint's printing options include formats ranging from audience handouts to speaker's notes.

This chapter discusses the following topics:

- ◆ Using the PowerPoint AutoContent Wizard

- ◆ Entering presentation text in the outline

- ◆ Viewing slides

- ◆ Applying a PowerPoint template to a presentation

- ◆ Adding a shape with text inside to a presentation

- ◆ Inserting a new slide and clip art into a presentation

- ◆ Printing and saving a PowerPoint presentation

This chapter will get you up to speed and comfortable with PowerPoint in a short period of time. The explanation behind many exercises is brief; the remaining chapters in Part Three discuss PowerPoint's features in more detail.

Many PowerPoint design and formatting tools are identical to those in Microsoft Word and Microsoft Excel. If you know how to use these applications, you already know how to use many functions in PowerPoint.

PowerPoint automates many layouts and formatting functions to take the fear out of using presentation software—even if you are not a professional designer. Preformatted templates and color schemes eliminate the need for time-consuming formatting. PowerPoint Wizards (the AutoContent Wizard and the Pick a Look Wizard) guide first-time presenters through creating first-rate presentations and speed experienced presenters through the building stages. Also, extensive customization enables you to use presentation formats over and over. As you will see, the endless presentation enhancements let you professionalize your work without a lot of hassle.

PowerPoint presentations can be *data-driven*. That is, graphs and charts in PowerPoint presentations can derive, for example, from data in Excel spreadsheets or contain text from Word documents.

Whether you are producing slides, color overheads, black-and-white overheads, plain-paper printouts, or any other format, PowerPoint uses the word *slide* to refer to each individual screen of information in your presentation. Each PowerPoint presentation is a series of slides, each of which contains a graphic or text.

To get started quickly, you will work through creating a 35mm slide presentation about the Shipshape Cruise Lines training program. This training program focuses on handling passenger complaints.

If you haven't already, double-click on the PowerPoint icon to start PowerPoint. PowerPoint opens with the Tip of the Day (see fig. 15.1).

These helpful tips offer suggestions about PowerPoint functions, shortcuts, and slide design. These tips help you quickly learn how to use PowerPoint, and you can access them through the **H**elp menu anytime PowerPoint is open. To see another tip, click on the Next Tip button in the Tip of the Day dialog box. Click on the More Tips button to take you to the Help Index. To keep the Tip of the Day dialog box from appearing each time you open PowerPoint, click on the check box in front of Show Tips at Startup at the bottom of the Tip of the Day dialog box to deselect it. When you are done viewing the tips, click on OK.

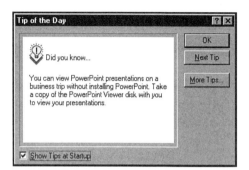

Figure 15.1

PowerPoint's Tip of the Day.

Choosing a Presentation Format and Entering Presentation Text

The purpose of your presentations can range from discussing strategy to selling a product to delivering bad news. PowerPoint's flexibility enables you to present any kind of information and customize a presentation format. PowerPoint also includes preformatted outlines to help you determine the ideal content of a specific type of presentation. If you are delivering bad news to a group of employees, for example, PowerPoint suggests ways to organize the presentation material to ease the blow.

Using the PowerPoint AutoContent Wizard

After the Tip of the Day, the PowerPoint dialog box appears and presents many paths through which you can begin creating a new PowerPoint presentation (see fig. 15.2).

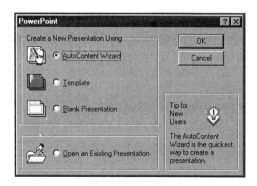

Figure 15.2

PowerPoint offers many paths to help you create a new presentation.

This dialog box appears every time you open PowerPoint, but you can turn it off through the **T**ools menu. Sometimes when you open PowerPoint, you might want to begin working with a favorite template or go directly to a blank presentation. Or, you can choose to open an existing presentation.

Each of these options will be discussed in later chapters. For this exercise, select **A**utoContent Wizard and click on OK.

The PowerPoint AutoContent Wizard opens and explains that the wizard will help you to begin creating a presentation (see fig. 15.3).

Figure 15.3

The AutoContent Wizard opens to begin creating a presentation.

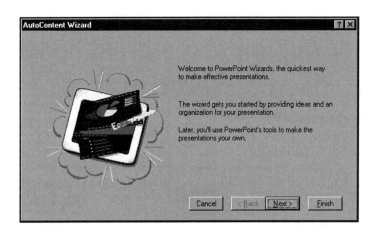

The PowerPoint AutoContent Wizard helps you to organize your thoughts and makes suggestions about the content of a presentation based on the type of material you want to cover.

To continue, click on **N**ext.

The AutoContent Wizard automatically begins by gathering the information needed to create the title slide for a presentation.

The AutoContent Wizard asks, "What is your name?" This box might already be filled in with your name or a department name because this data comes from the PowerPoint setup information. Type **Shipshape Cruise Lines** to overwrite the high-lighted text. Press Tab to proceed to the second text box. The AutoContent Wizard asks, "What are you going to talk about?" A flashing cursor waits for you to enter the presentation title. Type **Handling Passenger Complaints**, then press Tab to go to the next text box.

With the current information highlighted, type **Become part of the crew!**. After filling in all three fields, your screen should look like the one in figure 15.4.

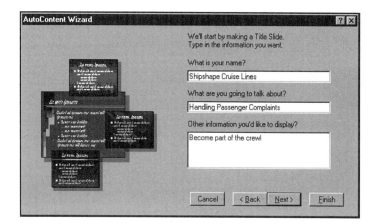

Figure 15.4

Filling in the title slide information.

If you want to return to a previous box to change information, press Shift+Tab to highlight the text and type new information. After you have filled in the information, click on **N**ext.

Note   If you want to go back a step at any time in the AutoContent Wizard, click on **B**ack.

Next, the AutoContent Wizard asks you to choose the type of presentation you are going to give (see fig. 15.5).

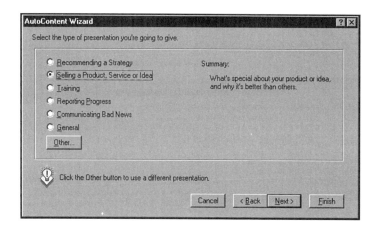

Figure 15.5

Select the type of presentation.

The skilled presenter knows that, depending on the presentation type, key information should be delivered to an audience in a certain order. The PowerPoint AutoContent Wizard guides you through building an effective presentation by offering content outlines designed for a particular type of presentation.

The AutoContent Wizard offers six presentation types for you to use:

◆ **R**ecommending a Strategy

◆ **S**elling a Product, Service or Idea

◆ **T**raining

◆ Reporting **P**rogress

◆ **C**ommunicating Bad News

◆ **G**eneral

If you want to design your own presentation type, you can click on **O**ther. For this exercise, select the presentation type **T**raining, and click on **N**ext to see the AutoContent Wizard dialog box shown in figure 15.6.

Figure 15.6

Choose the parameters for the presentation style and time frame.

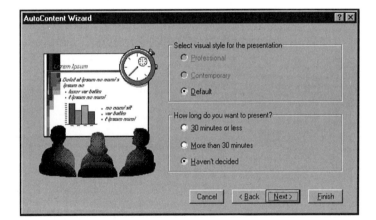

Choose a visual style for the presentation. You can also set a time duration for the presentation or indicate that you haven't yet decided on the length.

Click on **N**ext to move to the dialog box seen in figure 15.7, which holds information about the type of output. The choices are as follows:

◆ Black and **w**hite overheads

◆ **C**olor overheads

◆ On-**s**creen presentation

◆ **3**5mm slides

You also can decide whether or not you want to have printed material available for your audience.

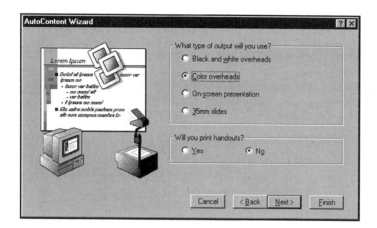

Figure 15.7

Designing the output of the presentation.

For this example, we've chosen **C**olor Overheads and elected not to have handouts for the audience.

Choose **N**ext to see the last AutoContent Wizard dialog box (see fig. 15.8). At this point, you can also elect to go **B**ack if you want to make any changes to the configuration. If you are ready to enter text and build the presentation, choose **F**inish.

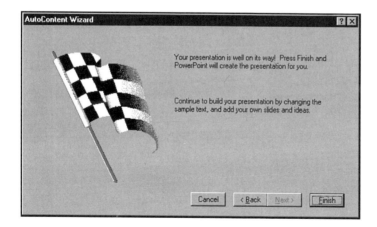

Figure 15.8

The last AutoContent Wizard dialog box.

Now, by changing the sample text in the Outline view and adding new slides, the Shipshape Cruise Lines training presentation will unfold.

To continue, click on **F**inish. PowerPoint takes a moment to prepare the outline, and then presents the title slide.

Entering and Editing Slide Text in the Outline View

PowerPoint's Outline view helps you to organize your thoughts. Think of the PowerPoint Outline view as an outline in Microsoft Word. Many of the word processing functions are identical. Using the word processing functions, you replace the existing content suggestions with information pertaining to the Shipshape Cruise Lines training program.

 Note PowerPoint provides many ways for you to delete text and replace it with new information in the outline. You can highlight the text and overwrite it with new information by simply typing. You also can highlight the text, press Del, and type the new information. Or, you can highlight the text and press the Cut button on the toolbar. In this chapter, you will have a chance to try each method.

By working through the PowerPoint AutoContent Wizard, you already have the title slide text completed (see fig. 15.9) and need only to input text for the additional slides.

Figure 15.9

The title slide for the presentation.

The presentation is in Slide View, which means that you see the slides and the text for the slides in a graphical fashion. You can use the arrows on the vertical scroll bar to move through the slides.

It's faster (and easier to edit) the slides if you work in Outline mode. To do so, select **O**utline from the **V**iew Menu. Figure 15.10 shows the title slide in Outline view.

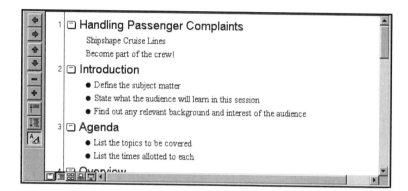

Figure 15.10

The presentation in Outline view.

Each slide in a presentation usually has a slide title. In the Outline view, text on the same line as the slide number and Slide icon is the slide title; for example, the current slide title for Slide 2 is Introduction.

To replace the title with a more appropriate title for this specific presentation, type **How To Handle Complaints** and delete Introduction.

The PowerPoint AutoContent Wizard suggests that you should next define the subject matter. Highlight the words *Define the subject matter* using the I-beam cursor and click on the Cut button on the toolbar. Type **The standard procedures for handling passenger complaints on Shipshape Cruise Lines**. Then, in the second bullet point, type **Become a certified member of the Shipshape crew**, replacing the existing text. For this example, you can delete the third bullet point (see fig. 15.11).

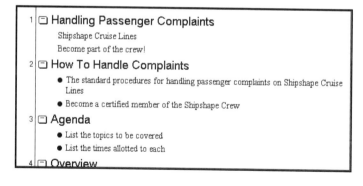

Figure 15.11

Completing the bullet points on Slide 2.

The PowerPoint AutoContent Wizard suggests that you discuss the agenda next. Leave the slide title Agenda, but replace *List the topics to be covered* with **Shipshape Complaint Compliance**.

Suppose you want another blank bullet point on Slide 3 to present an additional topic to be covered in the Shipshape Cruise Lines presentation. To add another bullet point, click at the end of the first bullet point and press Enter (see fig. 15.12).

Figure 15.12

Adding a blank bullet point on Slide 3.

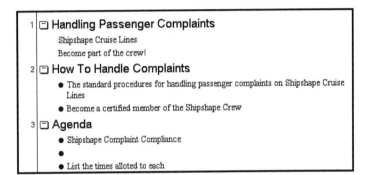

Another blank bullet point appears with the cursor flashing, waiting for you to type. Type **Complimentary Lunch**. Then, replace the text in the third bullet point with **Role Playing**. The bullet points in Slide 3 now are completed, as shown in figure 15.13.

Figure 15.13

The finished bullet points for Slide 3.

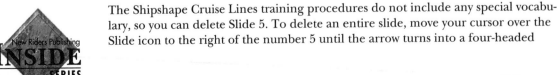

In Slide 4, leave the slide title as Overview but replace the content suggestions with the following text:

◆ Replace *Give the big picture* with **Keep the passengers happy.**

◆ Replace *Explain how all the individual topics fit together* with **Learn the techniques then practice for perfection.**

The Shipshape Cruise Lines training procedures do not include any special vocabulary, so you can delete Slide 5. To delete an entire slide, move your cursor over the Slide icon to the right of the number 5 until the arrow turns into a four-headed arrow. Click once with the left mouse button. Notice that all the slide text including bullet points is selected (see fig. 15.14)

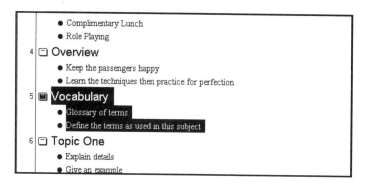

Figure 15.14

Selecting an entire slide.

Click on the Cut button on the toolbar; the slides are automatically renumbered. The slide titled Topic One becomes Slide 5.

The first topic to discuss in the Shipshape Cruise Lines training program is Shipshape complaint compliance. Replace the content suggestions in Slide 5 with the following text:

◆ Replace *Topic One* with **Shipshape complaint compliance.**

◆ Replace *Explain details* with **Follow the manual.**

◆ Replace *Give an example* with **If a passenger wants a towel, get him a towel.**

◆ Replace *Exercise to re-enforce learning* with **Role playing.**

The text for Slide 5 is complete (see fig. 15.15).

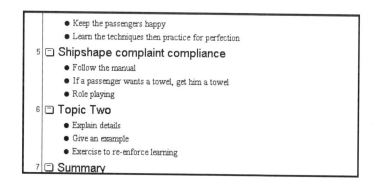

Figure 15.15

The outline with replaced text in Slide 5.

You can continue to replace the content recommendations with presentation text using these same word processing steps. Replace the content suggestions in Slide 6 with the following text:

◆ Replace *Topic Two* with **Role playing.**

◆ Replace *Explain details* with **Talking to a passenger with a complaint**.

◆ Replace *Give an example* with **A passenger does not like his room**.

The last bullet point is not required for topic two, so you can delete it.

To move forward in this section, delete Slides 7 and 8. To delete these slides, move the mouse pointer over Slide 7's Slide icon until it turns to a four-headed arrow, and click to highlight the entire Slide. Move the mouse pointer over Slide 8's Slide icon, hold down the Shift key, and click the left mouse button (see fig. 15.16). Click on the Cut button on the toolbar or press Del to remove these slides.

Figure 15.16

Selecting multiple slides.

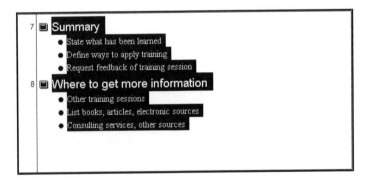

Congratulations! You have a slide presentation with six slides. Before moving to the next step, click on the Slide icon before the Title Slide to select it. Use the vertical scroll bar if necessary to move to the top of the outline.

Viewing Slides and Adding a PowerPoint Template

Now that you have organized your thoughts using the AutoContent Wizard and revised the outline using the Outline view, you can view the slides you have created by changing to the Slide view.

Look at the group of five buttons at the bottom left corner of the workspace. The first four buttons are called *View buttons* (see fig. 15.17).

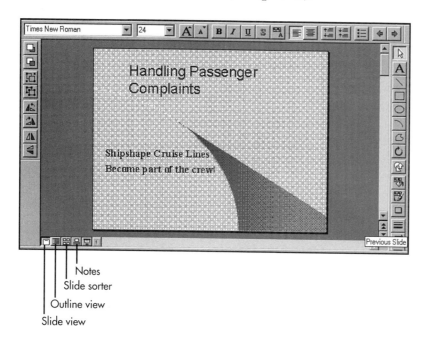

Figure 15.17

The View buttons.

These buttons manipulate the PowerPoint views and enable you to see a presentation in other formats such as a Slide view, Slide Sorter view, or Notes view. The currently pressed button with the picture of an outline indicates that you are in Outline view. These views will be discussed in depth in Chapters 16, "PowerPoint Tools and Concepts," and 17, "Enhancing PowerPoint Presentations."

To view the Shipshape Cruise Lines presentation in Slide view, click on the Slide view button at the bottom of the workspace. This button has the Slide icon on it.

The title slide appears in the workspace in 8-by-11-inch landscape mode. Use the down arrow on the vertical scroll bar to look at your text changes as they appear in the slides (see fig. 15.18). PowerPoint has applied some formatting and graphics that you will alter later in this chapter.

Using the PowerPoint Slide Changer

The vertical scroll bar at the right moves you through the PowerPoint presentation to look at other slides.

Click on the vertical scroll bar handle and drag it slowly down. PowerPoint shows you which slide will appear when you release the left mouse button.

You also can move from slide to slide by clicking on either the Previous Slide or Next Slide buttons, which look like double arrows and are located at the bottom of the scroll bar (see fig. 15.19). The Next Slide button moves you forward one slide; the Previous Slide button moves back one slide.

Figure 15.18

Looking at the changed text in Slide view.

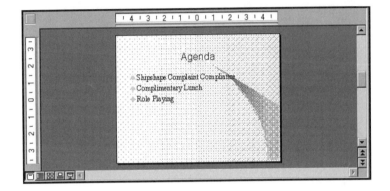

Figure 15.19

Using the vertical scroll bar to move through the slides.

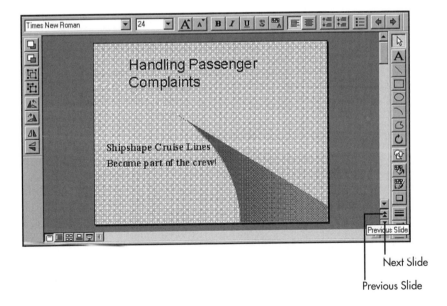

Next Slide

Previous Slide

Tip

For presentations with multiple slides, using the handle method enables you to move more quickly to the specific slide you want to view. You also can press PgUp or PgDn on the keyboard to move through presentations, or click in the scroll bar above or below the scroll box to move forward or back.

Keep in mind that you can see the entire slide in the workspace. The vertical scroll bar works differently when you view slides at reduced views. Scaled views will be discussed in depth in Chapter 16, "PowerPoint Tools and Concepts."

Applying a PowerPoint Design Template

Applying a PowerPoint design template transforms the look of every slide in a presentation with graphics, color, and text formatting. Altering these preformatted templates enables you to further customize your work. You can apply a template to a presentation at any time.

To apply a template to a presentation, click on the Template button on the Standard toolbar. This displays the Apply Design Template dialog box, as shown in figure 15.20.

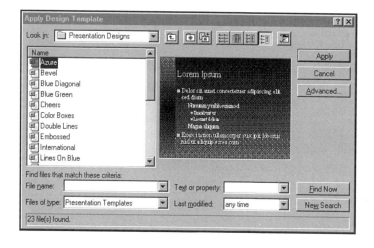

Figure 15.20

The Apply Design Template dialog box.

As you click on each design template, a thumbnail sketch of the template appears, enabling you to roughly preview the template's colors, graphics, and text formatting. For the Shipshape Cruise Lines presentation, the Tropical template is most complimentary. Scroll down the file list and highlight Tropical. Notice the preview, seen in figure 15.21, then click on A**p**ply.

All the slides in the presentation assume the Tropical design formatting; an example is shown in figure 15.22.

Figure 15.21

Previewing the Tropical design template.

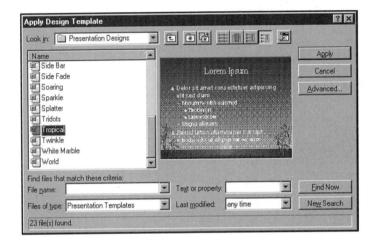

Figure 15.22

The Tropical design template format is applied to the presentation.

PowerPoint templates specify the font, style, placement, and color of the title on every slide in the presentation. Even the placement of the body text and the bullet style used for each slide subpoint are stored in the template. Using templates greatly reduces the amount of work you have to do to prepare PowerPoint presentations. Modifying and creating templates is discussed in Chapters 16, "PowerPoint Tools and Concepts," and 17, "Enhancing PowerPoint Presentations."

Adding an Object Containing Text on Every Slide

Shipshape Cruise Lines requests that its name appear on each slide. Carefully adding the word SHIPSHAPE in exactly the same place on each individual slide would be time-consuming.

The PowerPoint Slide Master solves this problem; any object on the Slide Master appears on every slide in a presentation. Rather than place SHIPSHAPE on every slide, you can place it once on the Slide Master.

Opening the Slide Master

To access the Slide Master, open the View menu and choose **M**aster. Masters are available for other PowerPoint formats, including Outline, Handout, and Notes. So, a cascading menu appears for you to select the Master you want—in this case, the Slide Master.

Tip   To open the Slide Master, you also can hold down the Shift key and click on the Slide view button at the bottom of the workspace. This shortcut works to open any other master corresponding to a view.

The tropics.ppt template Slide Master contains the following elements (see fig. 15.23):

◆ The Title Area for AutoLayouts box

◆ The Subtitle Area for AutoLayouts box

◆ The Footer Area associated with the template

Figure 15.23

The Slide Master for the Tropical template.

Notice that the text *Click to edit Master title style* in the Title Area box includes character formatting such as the font, font size, and alignment. This Title Area text shows the formatting of the Slide Titles on every slide except the Title Slide. To change the look of the Slide Titles throughout a presentation, make those changes here in the Slide Master to save time.

The text in the Object Area also is formatted. Everything from the bullet styles to the indentation of the subpoints is retained in the Slide Master.

Drawing an Object and Adding Text

To add a rectangle containing the word SHIPSHAPE to every slide in the presentation, first click on the Rectangle button on the tool palette, as shown in figure 15.24.

Figure 15.24

Selecting the Rectangle drawing tool.

When you move the mouse cursor onto the slide, the pointer changes to a cross hair. In the upper right corner of the slide, click and drag the cursor to the right to draw the box. Don't worry if the rectangle overlaps the Title Area for AutoLayouts box. Release the left mouse button when the box is the size you want; the box displays square resizing handles in each corner and on the top, bottom, and sides (see fig. 15.25). These handles indicate that the shape is selected and that you can resize the object at this time.

Figure 15.25

The box displays square resizing handles.

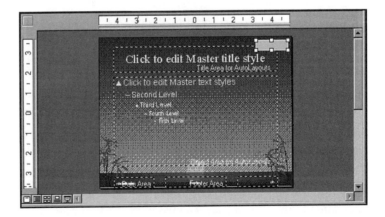

With the handles still showing, type the word **SHIPSHAPE** (see fig. 15.26).

Notice that when you begin typing, the square handles disappear and a crosshatched frame appears. This crosshatched frame indicates that the shape is selected and currently in text-edit mode.

Figure 15.26

Typing text inside the rectangle.

PowerPoint center-aligns the word and positions it in the middle of the rectangle automatically. Changing this alignment and positioning within shapes is discussed in Chapters 16 and 17.

If the rectangle you have drawn is not large enough to accommodate the entire word, you need to make the rectangle larger. To enlarge the rectangle, you must first get the square resizing handles to reappear. Currently, a text cursor is flashing at the end of the word SHIPSHAPE (although it might be difficult to see).

To make the square handles reappear, click on the crosshatched frame of the rectangle. This click takes you back to Object edit mode, and the square handles reappear.

Move the cursor over one of the square handles; notice that the cursor changes to black arrows.

These arrows show you which direction you can resize the object. Grab the bottom left resizing handle in the rectangle's corner by clicking on the handle and holding down the left mouse button. Drag the outline of the rectangle to the left to make the rectangle wider. The cursor changes to a cross hair as you enlarge the rectangle, and a dotted outline of the rectangular shape shows the rectangle's new size. Make the rectangle large enough to hold the text (see fig. 15.27).

After you have made the rectangle the size you want, open the **V**iew menu and choose **S**lides or click on the Slide view button to return to Slide view (see fig. 15.28).

Figure 15.27

Changing the size by dragging the rectangle.

Figure 15.27

Changing the size by dragging the rectangle.

Figure 15.28

Clicking on the Slide View button to return to the Slide view.

Move through the slides using the vertical scroll bar; notice that the rectangle containing SHIPSHAPE is on every slide in the location where you drew it on the Slide Master (see fig. 15.29).

Figure 15.29

SHIPSHAPE appears on every slide, including the Title slide.

Note   The PowerPoint Tropical design template assigns the rectangle's text and fill color automatically. These colors can be changed, so don't worry if they are not to your liking.

Adding a New Slide with Clip Art

You often will want to insert a new slide within a presentation even after you have finished entering text in the Outline view. Also, adding graphics or pictures to individual slides adds interest to presentations and helps to effectively communicate to your audience.

PowerPoint provides a quick and easy way to add a new slide with clip art using preformatted AutoLayouts. The PowerPoint Clip Art library offers a vast selection of images so that you can select just the right picture for a presentation.

Before the Agenda slide, Shipshape Cruise Lines wants a slide that shows what its average cruiser looks like.

Adding a New Slide and Choosing a Layout

PowerPoint inserts a new slide after the current slide you are viewing in Slide view or the highlighted slide in Outline or Slide Sorter view.

You want to insert a Slide before the slide titled Agenda. Using the vertical scroll bar, move to Slide 2. Ensure that the Agenda slide is Slide 3 by scrolling down one slide; then return to Slide 2.

To add a new slide, click on the New Slide button. The New Slide dialog box appears, enabling you to select the AutoLayout for the new slide (see fig. 15.30).

 Note   To bypass the AutoLayout dialog box and insert a new slide with the same layout as the slide before it, press Shift while clicking on the New Slide button.

The AutoLayout box includes 24 layouts, ranging from a title slide to a blank slide. Click once on an AutoLayout with the cursor and notice the layout description that appears on the right. For example, click on the layout that has a text block and columns, and notice the description says Text & Graph (see fig. 15.31). The one next to it, with the block and columns reversed on the slide, is Graph & Text.

Figure 15.30

Selecting an AutoLayout in the New Slide dialog box.

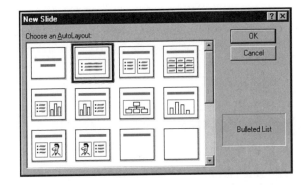

Figure 15.31

The layout description for a selected AutoLayout.

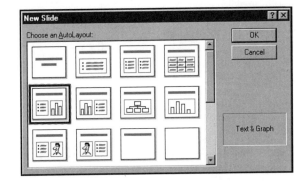

PowerPoint enables you to add one or a combination of the following to a slide:

◆ Bulleted text

◆ A graph

◆ An organizational chart

◆ Clip art

◆ A table

◆ Other objects, such as media clips or Word Art

Use the vertical scroll bar within the dialog box to view the additional AutoLayouts beyond those shown in the box.

For the new slide in the Shipshape Cruise Lines presentation, find the AutoLayout described as Text & Clip Art (see fig. 15.32).

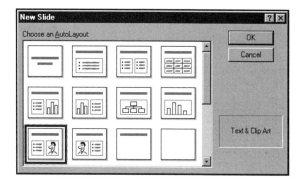

Figure 15.32

Selecting the Text & Clip Art AutoLayout.

Click on this AutoLayout and click on OK in the New Slide dialog box, or double-click on the AutoLayout. The new slide appears with a slide title box, a bulleted text box, and a clip art box, as shown in figure 15.33.

Figure 15.33

The new slide with the AutoLayout.

Adding Slide Text and Clip Art

You can add slide text directly to the slide as well as in the Outline view. PowerPoint leads you through placing and aligning text to save you time.

Click inside the box labeled Click to add a title. A flashing cursor appears in the crosshatched frame for you to type the title; type **A Shipshape Cruiser**. Next, click inside the bulleted text box labeled Click to add text; a flashing cursor appears after the bullet. Type **Take a vacation on a Shipshape Cruise!** (see fig. 15.34).

Now you're ready to add clip art. Double-click inside the box labeled Double-click to add clip art. The Microsoft ClipArt Gallery appears, as shown in figure 15.35.

Figure 15.34

Adding a title and text to the slide.

Figure 15.35

The Microsoft ClipArt Gallery.

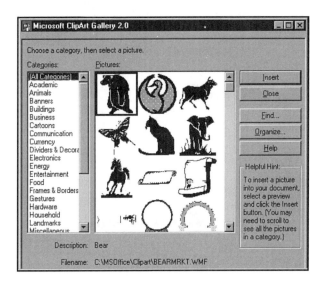

 Stop The first time you add clip art to a slide, PowerPoint loads all the graphics into the ClipArt Gallery. This might take some time. Do not interrupt this process—all the images might not transfer into the gallery.

PowerPoint arranges the individual pieces of clip art by different categories; clip art featuring modes of transportation are in the Transportation category, for example. The Microsoft ClipArt Gallery opens showing all categories of clip art.

Looking at the categories, both Transportation and Travel seem likely candidates for providing a useful graphic. To move quickly to various categories, use the vertical scroll bar in the box displaying the categories to scroll down. Click on Transportation to select it, then look in Travel. Among the various clip art images available, you can choose something like the ship's wheel shown in figure 15.36.

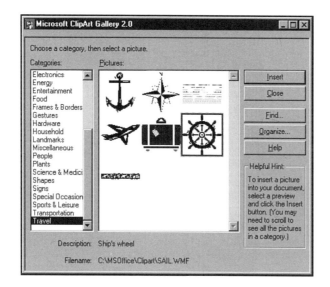

Figure 15.36

Scrolling to find suitable clip art.

Note   If you forget how to use the Microsoft ClipArt Gallery, a Helpful Hint at the bottom right of the dialog box walks you through inserting clip art into a document.

After clicking on OK, the Microsoft ClipArt Gallery closes, returns you to the presentation, and inserts the clip art in the designated area (see fig. 15.37).

Figure 15.37

Inserting the clip art into the slide.

Moving Clip Art

You need to place the clip art in a spot that doesn't interfere with the title or text. Square resizing handles surround the picture of the ship's wheel showing that the picture is selected. To move the picture, place the cursor over the picture. Click and hold the left mouse button to grab the clip art. Now, drag the picture up and to the left, away from the palm trees (see fig. 15.38).

Figure 15.38

Moving and positioning the clip art.

When the picture is positioned where you would like it, release the left mouse button.

You can insert clip art on a slide without working through the AutoLayout, and you can paste multiple pictures on one slide. Sizing and altering clip art is discussed in Chapter 17.

Previewing, Printing, and Saving the Presentation

This final step helps you to preview the Shipshape Cruise Lines presentation before printing, and shows you the way to print and save your work.

Using PowerPoint Slide Show

PowerPoint Slide Show enables you to view a presentation without the menus, toolbar, tool palette, or scroll bars. This feature lets you see how the presentation would look on slides, overheads, or a video screen without the PowerPoint workspace.

Before beginning the Slide Show, make sure you are viewing the first slide in the presentation. The Slide Show starts on the current slide seen in the workspace, instead of automatically beginning on Slide 1.

To begin the Slide Show, click once on the Slide Show button, which is the fifth button on the bottom left of the workspace. This button shows a picture of a slide screen on a stand (see fig. 15.39).

A black screen appears moments before showing the first slide. Don't worry—you haven't lost your work! The first slide eventually comes into view on-screen without showing the Slide workspace, as shown in figure 15.40.

Figure 15.39

Selecting the Slide Show feature.

Figure 15.40

Viewing the first slide of the presentation using the PowerPoint Slide Show.

PowerPoint provides some tools that let you interact with the slide show. Suppose you want to emphasize "Become part of the crew!" on the title slide by drawing a circle around it as you talk about it. With the pointer anywhere on the slide, click the right mouse button to display the menu shown in figure 15.41.

Choose Pen from the menu and you will see that your pointer changes to a pencil.

Move the pencil somewhere near the words *Become part of the crew!*. Click and drag with the left mouse button to draw a circle around the text (see fig. 15.42).

Figure 15.41

Choosing a tool to use with the slide show.

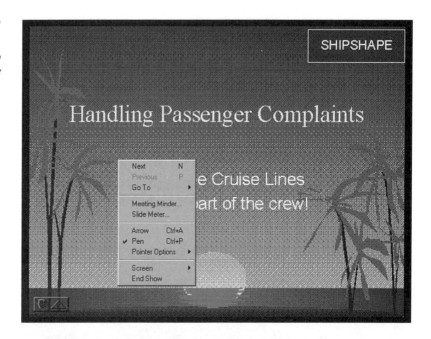

Figure 15.42

Drawing a circle using the Pen.

You can continue to draw on the slide by holding down the left mouse button. To turn off the drawing tool, press Esc.

Press E on the keyboard at any time to erase the freehand drawing on a slide. Otherwise, the drawing appears until you move to the next slide. When you return to the slide, the drawing is gone.

The left mouse button works like a slide projector button, moving you through the slides with a single click. You can also press N on the keyboard for the **N**ext slide. Press P on the keyboard to back up to the **P**revious slide.

Move through the presentation until you see the final slide. Press Esc to return to the PowerPoint Slide view with the workspace.

Printing a Presentation

Even if you intend to transfer a presentation to slides or overheads, printing the slides on plain paper can save time and money because you can preview your work. Printed presentations can be routed among many people and allow for written comments or corrections. You will not be able to check the colors, but you can preview the overall look, proof spelling, and so on. PowerPoint includes a spelling checker tool that is discussed in Chapter 16, "PowerPoint Tools and Concepts."

To print the PowerPoint presentation, open the **F**ile menu and choose **P**rint, or click on the Print button on the toolbar (see fig. 15.43).

Figure 15.43

Clicking on the Print button.

The Print dialog box appears, showing PowerPoint's default print settings. PowerPoint is set to print one copy of all the slides in the presentation (see fig. 15.44).

You also can choose to print the current slide on-screen or only a few specific slides. Additional printing options will be discussed later in Chapter 16.

Stop Be aware that printing times can vary depending on how many graphics are on a slide, so be sure to allow adequate time for your printout. It's probably not a good idea to start printing a presentation five minutes before you are scheduled to present it!

To begin printing, click on OK to print all the slides.

Figure 15.44

The Print dialog box.

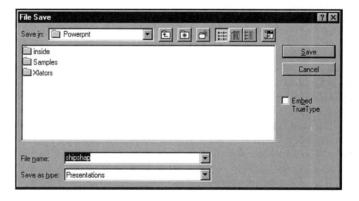

Saving Your Work

As shown in the PowerPoint title bar, PowerPoint labels the file "[Presentation]" until you give it a permanent name. You must save the presentation to access it at a later time. All PowerPoint presentations have the file extension .ppt.

To save the presentation, open the **F**ile menu and choose **S**ave, or click on the Save button on the toolbar.

The File Save dialog box appears and prompts you to name your presentation file (see fig. 15.45).

Figure 15.45

The File Save dialog box.

The file type is preselected for a PowerPoint presentation so that PowerPoint will automatically add the .ppt extension. Type the name **shipshap** in the File **n**ame box. Select the directory and path where you would like to save your file and click on OK. The file name now appears in the PowerPoint title bar.

CHAPTER

16

PowerPoint Tools and Concepts

U nderstanding PowerPoint concepts such as the PowerPoint toolbars or the Slide Master means smarter and faster presentation construction. For example, the PowerPoint Slide Master holds, for every slide in a presentation, formatting details that you can use to reduce design time and eliminate potential frustration.

This chapter explains many PowerPoint design tools in detail by discussing the following topics:

◆ Beginning a new presentation

◆ Using PowerPoint views

◆ Manipulating PowerPoint toolbars

◆ Using toolbar functions

◆ Using the Text tool

◆ Working with shapes

◆ Using alignment tools

◆ Understanding the masters

To help illustrate some of the PowerPoint concepts and tools in this chapter, we will return to the Shipshape Cruise Lines training presentation you created in Chapter 15.

As you saw in Chapter 15, "PowerPoint Quick Start," PowerPoint supplies many tools to help you quickly create a professional presentation. PowerPoint templates provide preformatted slide layouts, but you can implement your own creative presentation designs using the additional tools and Wizards that PowerPoint offers.

Beginning a New Presentation When You Open PowerPoint

Many times you will open PowerPoint to access an existing presentation. Sometimes you will open PowerPoint knowing exactly what kind of file you want to create—a one-page handout or flyer, for example. In both cases, you would not necessarily want to utilize PowerPoint's AutoContent Wizard or AutoLayouts.

PowerPoint lets you decide how you want to begin every time you open the application by offering options in the PowerPoint dialog box (see fig. 16.1). At this point, you can choose from the existing options and click on OK, or click on Cancel to bypass this dialog box.

Figure 16.1

PowerPoint's initial dialog box offers many options.

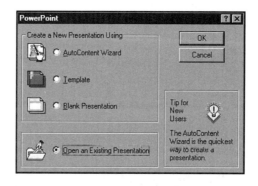

You can choose to not have this dialog box appear when PowerPoint first opens. To keep this dialog box from appearing, open the **T**ools menu and select **O**ptions. The Options dialog box appears and presents many options to customize the way PowerPoint works. The General section includes the option Show Startup **D**ialog. To turn this feature off, click on the check box. For now, however, leave the setting on.

The following sections discuss the options offered in the PowerPoint dialog box and where each one takes you. By understanding these various paths when starting out, you can make the best choice for your particular task.

AutoContent Wizard

The PowerPoint AutoContent Wizard provides suggestions about the kind of information you might include in a presentation, depending on the type of presentation you are creating. To use the AutoContent Wizard, select **A**utoContent Wizard and click on OK. See Chapter 15, "PowerPoint Quick Start," for more information.

Template

When beginning a new presentation, you might simply want to select the slide template and add the slides as you work using the AutoLayouts. If this is the case, choose **T**emplate from the PowerPoint dialog box when it first opens. PowerPoint takes you directly to the template directory for you to make a template selection. To find out more about previewing templates and opening directories that utilize your presentation format, see Chapter 15.

Blank Presentation

You might want to begin creating a new presentation by selecting an AutoLayout for the first slide and working from there. You can always select a template, add objects, or choose to print outputs during or after you have finished entering slide text. When you select **B**lank Presentation from the initial PowerPoint dialog box, PowerPoint takes you to the AutoLayouts and asks you to make a selection. Continue to click on the New Slide button and choose an AutoLayout to build a presentation.

Open an Existing Presentation

To access an existing presentation, select **O**pen an Existing Presentation from the initial PowerPoint dialog box. The Open dialog box appears for you to choose a file. Click on OK to open the file.

Establishing Slide Setup

At times you might create a presentation on custom-sized paper or need the slides to be in a certain orientation. In PowerPoint, slide setup includes slide size, numbering, and orientation for slides, notes, handouts, and outlines.

Changing the slide size or orientation after you have completed a presentation results in graphics or text on the slides adjusting proportionally in size to accommodate the new slide size. However, these changes can result in distortions of clip art, text, or other graphics, so it is important to make these changes at the beginning if your presentation requires an unusual setup.

 Note Remember that whatever presentation type you ultimately choose, a PowerPoint presentation is a series of slides.

When you begin creating a new presentation, the basic PowerPoint slide appears in the landscape position and is sized for letter paper (10 inches wide by 7.5 inches tall). PowerPoint allows some margin space to accommodate slide and overhead holders. To make changes to the slide setup, choose Slide Setup from the File menu. The Slide Setup dialog box appears (see fig. 16.2), enabling you to change the slide size, numbering, and orientation.

Figure 16.2

The Slide Setup dialog box.

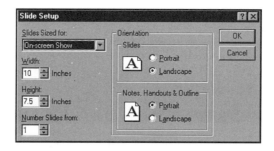

Slide Size

PowerPoint offers five slide-size formats to accommodate various presentation types. Open the Slides Sized for list box to show the following sizes (see fig. 16.3):

Figure 16.3

The slide-size list box options.

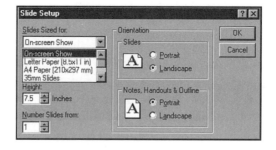

◆ On-screen Show is used for video-screen or computer-monitor presentations.

◆ Letter Paper is used for presentations on 8 1/2-by-11-inch paper.

◆ A4 Paper is used for presentations on 210-by-297mm or 10.83-by-7.5-inch paper. This paper is an international size.

◆ 35mm Slides is used for presentations on 35mm slides.

◆ Overhead is used for transparencies that are the size of letter paper.

◆ Custom is used for presentations on materials with a special, custom size.

To adjust the slide height or width, click on the up- or down-arrow buttons, or select the numbers using the I-beam cursor and enter the slide size. Notice when you click on the up- or down-arrow buttons or enter numbers that the slide size automatically changes to Custom.

Slide Numbering

PowerPoint numbers slides automatically, beginning with Slide 1. However, a presentation can begin with any number. You might, for example, create a presentation that is the second half of a 100-slide presentation. The slides should begin with Slide 51 to keep the order exact.

To change the beginning slide number, click on the up or down arrows or select the number using the I-beam cursor and enter a number.

Slide Orientation

At times you might want to create and print PowerPoint slides for use in a booklet or binder that already includes portrait-oriented pages. To keep the orientation uniform, you can change the slide setup orientation to portrait. To change the slide orientation, click on the button before **P**ortrait or **L**andscape in the Slide Setup dialog box.

The small sheet of paper with an *A* will adjust to show which orientation you have chosen. These same orientation changes also can be made to notes, handouts, and outline pages. Click on OK when you are finished making your selections.

Using PowerPoint Views

PowerPoint offers four views in which you can work on one presentation: Slide view, Outline view, Slide Sorter view, and Notes view. These views play a role in organizing an impressive presentation package. You can switch smoothly between these views while working on a presentation by using the four view buttons at the bottom of the workspace (the fifth button is for previewing a slide show), or selecting them from the View menu (see fig. 16.4). The Status bar indicates which view you are in.

Figure 16.4

The four View buttons and the Status bar.

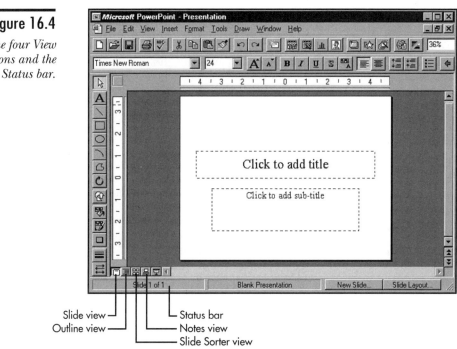

Many views share toolbars. However, the Outline and Slide Sorter views each have a toolbar that offers functions particularly useful in that view. For example, the slide transition tools appear on the Slide Sorter view toolbar because you can apply transitions only in this view.

Slide View

To select the Slide view, click on the view button with the slide icon on it or choose **S**lides from the **V**iew menu. The Slide view is the basic PowerPoint view (see fig. 16.5). Most of the slide formatting and design work is done in the Slide view. PowerPoint includes many default settings in the Slide view that you can change so they appear automatically when you begin PowerPoint.

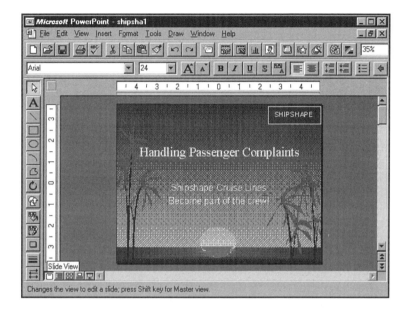

Figure 16.5

The PowerPoint Slide view.

To see which toolbars are available in the Slide view, open the **V**iew menu and choose **T**oolbars. The Toolbars dialog box lists the toolbars available in the Slide view (see fig. 16.6).

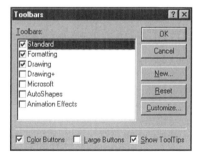

Figure 16.6

The toolbars available in the Slide view.

The Standard, Formatting, and Drawing toolbars are checked, indicating that they are currently in use. For a discussion of manipulating and customizing toolbars, see the section "Manipulating PowerPoint Toolbars" later in this chapter. To exit the Toolbars dialog box and return to the Slide view, click on OK.

Outline View

To select the Outline view, click on the Outline view button or choose **O**utline from the **V**iew menu. The Outline view shows the slide titles and text (see fig. 16.7). As shown in Chapter 15, the Outline view enables you to organize your thoughts when creating a presentation. You can insert additional text in the Outline view, create a new slide, and rearrange text or slide order.

Figure 16.7

The PowerPoint Outline view.

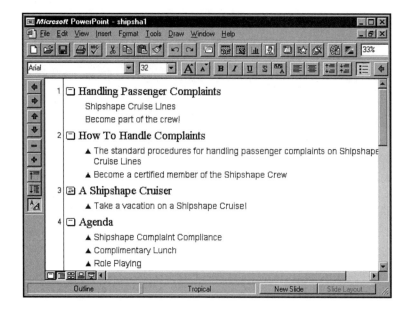

The Slide icon before each slide title indicates whether the slide contains clip art or objects not shown on the Outline. In figure 16.7, Slide 3 has shapes inside its Slide icon, but the other slide icons do not. The clip art accounts for the shapes inside Slide 3's icon.

The Outlining toolbar appears on the left when you select the Outline view. The functions of each button will be discussed later in this chapter, and refer to Chapter 15 to review entering text in the Outline view. From the **V**iew menu, choose **T**oolbars to view the toolbars available in the Outline view (see fig. 16.8). Notice that some of the toolbars available in Slide view do not appear as choices in the Outline view, but there is a toolbar named Outlining. Click on OK to continue.

Figure 16.8

Toolbars available in the Outline view.

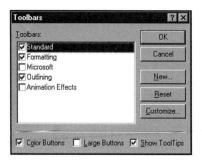

Slide Sorter View

To select the Slide Sorter view, click on the Slide Sorter view button or choose Slide Sorter from the **V**iew menu. The Slide Sorter view shows each slide, numbered (see fig. 16.9). The Slide Sorter view enables you to rearrange a presentation's slide order; delete, copy, or add new slides; and assign slide transitions to each slide. Slide transitions are discussed in Chapter 17, "Enhancing PowerPoint Presentations."

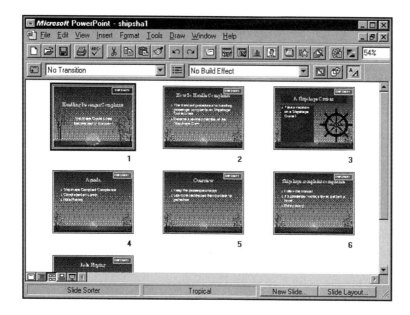

Figure 16.9

The PowerPoint Slide Sorter view.

A dark box surrounds the first slide, meaning that it is selected and can be moved, deleted, copied, or assigned a slide transition. To move a slide, place the mouse pointer on the selected slide. Click and hold the left mouse button, then drag the mouse pointer between Slide 2 and Slide 3 and release the left mouse button (see fig. 16.10). The mouse pointer changes to a slide icon with an arrow pointing down when you move it. Notice that the first slide moved and the slide numbering automatically adjusted.

To select more than one slide in the Slide Sorter view, hold down the Shift key and click on the slides you want to select. To move multiple slides, follow the same steps outlined for moving one slide.

Deleting one or more slides is as easy as selecting the slide or slides and pressing Del. Alternatively, you can select the slide, open the **E**dit menu and choose **D**elete Slide. To copy a slide, select the slide and click on the Copy button. Click the mouse where you want the copied slide to appear and click on the Paste button.

Figure 16.10

*Rearranging the
slide order.*

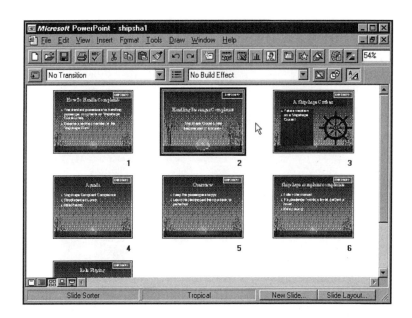

To add a new slide, click on the spot at which you want the new slide to appear. If you
want a new slide between the second and third slide, for example, click in the space
between these slides. A large flashing cursor appears where you clicked the mouse
pointer. Click on the New Slide button in the bottom right corner of the workspace.
When the cursor is flashing, you also can open the Insert menu and choose New Slide
or press Ctrl+M. PowerPoint asks you to choose an AutoLayout for the new slide, then
inserts the new slide with the same color scheme and format as the other slides in the
presentation.

Open the View menu and choose Toolbars to see which toolbars are available in the
Slide Sorter view. Notice that there is a Slide Sorter toolbar (see fig. 16.11). Click on
OK. *For a discussion of the Slide Sorter toolbar, see Chapter 17.*

Figure 16.11

*The toolbars
available in the
Slide Sorter view.*

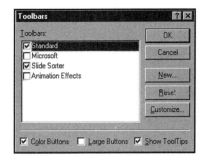

Notes View

To select the Notes view, click on the Notes view button, or open the <u>V</u>iew menu and choose <u>N</u>otes. The Notes view shows a small picture of a slide with a text box below it (see fig. 16.12).

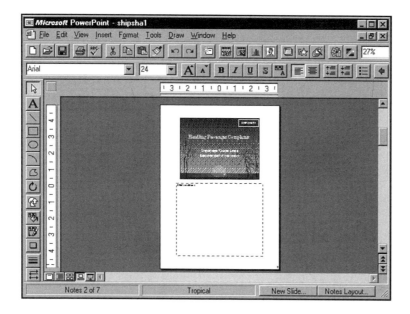

Figure 16.12

The PowerPoint Notes view.

The Notes format is ideal for speaker's notes or for creating audience handouts with speaker's comments about each slide. The box beneath the slide works like a word processing box in which you can type comments or additional information. Words wrap just as in word processing software. To add text in that box, click inside the box and begin typing.

Note   Any text inside this box in the Notes view will not appear in the Outline view.

The same toolbars available in the Slide view also are available in the Notes view.

Manipulating PowerPoint Toolbars

Located initially across the top and down the left side of the workspace, PowerPoint toolbars provide easy access to frequently used PowerPoint functions. The toolbar buttons work just like the toolbar buttons in Microsoft Word and Microsoft Excel, requiring one press to execute the function.

PowerPoint includes Tool Tips to let you know the button name and the button function. When you activate a Tool Tip, a button name appears next to the button and a button function description appears in the status bar in the lower left corner of the workspace (see fig. 16.13). To activate the Tool Tips, move the mouse pointer over a button and wait a moment. These tips help you learn and recall the functions of these toolbar buttons.

Figure 16.13

Activating PowerPoint Tool Tips.

As you work more and more in PowerPoint, you will begin to recognize functions you are performing regularly. You can customize PowerPoint toolbars just like in Microsoft Word and Microsoft Excel. Customization can help you work more quickly and efficiently. The way to customize toolbars is discussed in "Customizing Toolbars," later in this section.

As in Microsoft Word and Microsoft Excel, PowerPoint requires that you select the text or numbers you want to change before performing a function. However, depending on the PowerPoint formatting function, you can select text or numbers in many time-saving ways. If you want to boldface a single word in a sentence, for example, you simply can place the flashing cursor within the word and click on the Bold button on the Formatting toolbar.

Floating Toolbars

When you first open PowerPoint, some toolbars are docked at the top and down the left side of the workspace. By double-clicking in the gray area in between toolbar buttons, you can float the toolbars in the workspace and move them where you like.

Move the mouse pointer between the Spell Check and Cut buttons on the top toolbar. Double-click, and watch the toolbar pop out into the slide area (see fig. 16.14). Following these steps, you can float any toolbar in the workspace. Notice the toolbar name is at the top of the window and the control menu icon in the upper left corner of the window. You can float as many toolbars at one time as you would like.

Figure 16.14

The Standard toolbar is floating.

Move the mouse pointer in the gray area around the buttons. Click and drag the window anywhere in the slide area. An outline of the window moves to show you where the toolbar will land when you release the left mouse button.

To remove a floating toolbar from view, click once on the X in the upper right corner of the toolbar window. To make the toolbar reappear, open the **V**iew menu and choose **T**oolbars. Click on the check box in front of the appropriate toolbar and click on OK (see fig. 16.15).

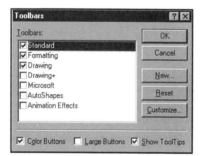

Figure 16.15

Choosing to show a toolbar.

The toolbar reappears floating in the workspace because you removed it while it was floating. To dock a toolbar, double-click on the gray space around the buttons and watch the toolbar snap into position.

Moving Toolbars

PowerPoint enables you to manipulate toolbars by dragging them out into the workspace. Move the mouse pointer in a gray space between the Spell Check and Cut buttons. Click and drag the toolbar down into the workspace. The toolbar outline shows you where the toolbar is moving. After the toolbar is well into the workspace, it changes into a square shape. When you move the toolbar down to the bottom of the workspace, it changes back to a long rectangle (see fig. 16.16).

Figure 16.16

*The toolbar
flattens out to
clear the
workspace view.*

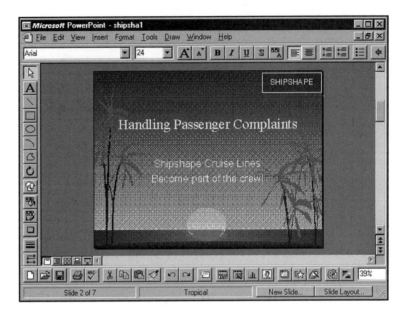

Viewing Additional Toolbars

To view additional PowerPoint toolbars, open the Toolbars dialog box by choosing **T**oolbars from the **V**iew menu. The Toolbars dialog box shows you which toolbars currently are showing and the toolbars that are available to open while in the current view. To remove a toolbar, remove the check in front of the toolbar name by clicking inside the check box. To make a toolbar appear, click in the check box.

In the Toolbars dialog box, you also can choose to have color in the toolbar buttons, use large buttons, or hide the Tool Tips. Click to add or remove the checks in the boxes (see fig. 16.17). To implement your changes, click on OK. Toolbars might appear floating at first. You can move them or dock them at the top by double-clicking in the gray area around the toolbar buttons.

Figure 16.17

*Selecting options
for toolbars.*

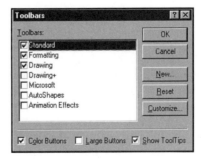

PowerPoint offers a shortcut to hiding or showing toolbars. To access this shortcut, move the mouse pointer over any visible toolbar and click the right mouse button. A pop-up menu appears showing the toolbars that are available in the current view; current toolbars have a check mark next to the toolbar name (see fig. 16.18). To make a toolbar appear, click on the toolbar name to make the check appear. You also can access the Toolbars dialog box through this shortcut menu by choosing Toolbars.

Figure 16.18

Click the right mouse button to access a shortcut menu.

Customizing Toolbars

PowerPoint enables you to customize toolbars to expedite regularly used functions. Notice that PowerPoint provides extra space to the right of horizontal toolbars and at the bottom of the vertical toolbars. This extra space enables you to add toolbar buttons. To customize a toolbar, select **C**ustomize from the **T**ools menu to display the Customize Toolbars dialog box, as shown in figure 16.19.

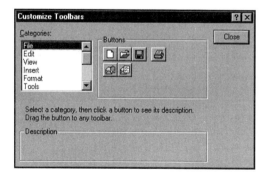

Figure 16.19

The Customize Toolbars dialog box.

Tip   You can access the Customize Toolbars dialog box through the shortcut menu by placing the mouse pointer over any current toolbar and clicking the right mouse button. Select Customize.

The Customize Toolbars dialog box displays categories of tools from which you can choose. The toolbar buttons available in those categories appear in the Buttons box. To see the buttons available in the Edit category, for example, click on Edit in the **C**ategories list box (see fig. 16.20).

Figure 16.20

Selecting a category to view the available buttons.

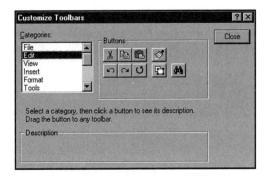

Tool Tips are available on the buttons in the Customize Toolbars dialog box. Move the mouse pointer over a button in the Buttons box and wait a moment. A Tool Tip eventually appears, showing you the name of the button. To see a full description of the button's function, click on the button and view the description in the Description box (see fig. 16.21). To confirm the button description you are viewing, a dotted outline forms around the button to indicate that it is selected. All these steps are outlined in the Customize Toolbars dialog box for your information.

Figure 16.21

Viewing a button's description.

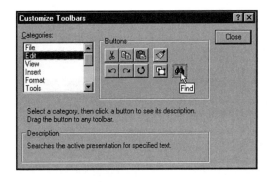

To place buttons on the toolbars already showing in the workspace, click and hold down the left mouse button with the mouse pointer over a button. Notice that when you click and hold the left mouse button, a small plus sign (+) appears on the button.

Drag the button off the Customize Toolbars dialog box and onto the toolbar where you would like it positioned, placing the plus sign on the exact spot. Release the left mouse button and watch the button take its place where you positioned it (see fig. 16.22).

The button retains its dotted outline to let you know that you still can move the button to another location. To move the button again, click on the button, drag it to where you want to position it, and release the left mouse button.

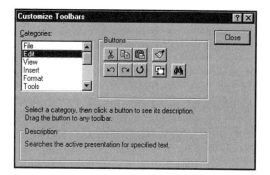

Figure 16.22

Placing the button on a toolbar.

You can rearrange other buttons on current toolbars while the Customize Toolbars dialog box is open. Click on any button, then drag the button to another location (see fig. 16.23). The other buttons on the toolbar reposition themselves to accommodate the button.

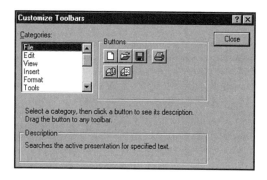

Figure 16.23

Repositioning a button on a toolbar.

In addition to adding buttons, you can remove buttons from a toolbar with the Customize Toolbars dialog box open. To remove a button, click on the button, then drag it off the toolbar and into the workspace.

If the Customize Toolbars dialog box is not open, you can hold down the Alt key and drag a button off the toolbar to remove it. If you've been following along, drag the Find button off the toolbar using these steps. To copy a button from one toolbar to another, press Ctrl+Alt and drag the button to a new position. When you are done customizing toolbars, click on Close in the Customize Toolbars dialog box.

Using Toolbar Functions

As you can see, PowerPoint toolbars are flexible and designed to help you work in an efficient, comfortable manner. Now that you know how to manipulate the toolbars, you are ready to learn the functions of the buttons on four toolbars. You will recognize many of the functions because they are identical in Word and Excel. Tool Tips can help you to review the button names and functions if you forget.

As in Word and Excel, you must select text or objects before you perform the function. PowerPoint AutoSelect is designed to select entire words rather than individual characters, so selecting text to format is easier than ever.

Button functions that are common across Microsoft Office applications are only briefly explained in the following section. This section will focus on buttons that carry functions unique to PowerPoint. To demonstrate the toolbar functions, return to the Shipshape Cruise Lines training presentation you created in Chapter 15.

The Standard Toolbar

The Standard toolbar (see fig. 16.24) is available in every PowerPoint view. The buttons on the Standard toolbar cover the basic functions such as Save, Cut, Copy, and Paste.

Figure 16.24

The PowerPoint Standard toolbar.

Common Standard Toolbar Buttons

The first eight buttons on the PowerPoint Standard toolbar are basic tools found also in Word and Excel. If you know how to use these tools in these other applications, you already know how to use them in PowerPoint.

When you are in PowerPoint and want to begin a new presentation while an existing presentation currently is on-screen, press the New button on the Standard toolbar. The New Presentation dialog box appears, presenting the same options as the dialog box that appears when you first open PowerPoint, and one new option: Current Presentation Format, which opens a new presentation with the same presentation format as the presentation currently on-screen.

The Open button brings up the Open dialog box, from which you can select a presentation file to open. The Save button quickly saves a presentation that already is named; if you have not named the presentation, the Save As dialog box appears and enables you to name your file. The Print button brings up the Print dialog box, enabling you to print either a presentation or specific slides in that presentation. The Spelling button begins a spelling check on the current slide or a selected slide if you are in Slide Sorter view. The Spelling dialog box works the same way as in Word and Excel.

The Cut, Copy, and Paste buttons also work just as they do in Word and Excel. In PowerPoint you need to select text or objects by clicking on them before you perform one of these functions.

The Format Painter

The Format Painter button (the button showing a paintbrush) enables you to copy the format of a selected object and apply that same format to another object. This function expedites formatting and saves you time. Suppose you want to make Slide 1's title bold and italic, then decided you wanted the title on Slide 3 in the same format. The Format Painter is ideal for this situation because it copies entire formatting instructions.

Note This simple exercise is meant as an example to show how the Format Painter works. Changing to Slide 3 and clicking on the Bold and Italic buttons would work, too. However, think of how much time the Format Painter could save when copying an extensively formatted object.

First, select Slide 1's title by clicking on *Handling*, then dragging the I-beam over *Passenger Complaints* (see fig. 16.25). Open the Format menu and choose Font. In the Font dialog box, choose Bold Italic, then click on OK.

Figure 16.25

Selecting the title slide's title.

With the text still selected, click on the Format Painter button. Move the pointer out to the workspace and notice that it has changed to a paintbrush and I-beam. Use the vertical scroll bar to move to Slide 3. When Slide 3 appears, move the mouse pointer out to the workspace. Notice that the paintbrush and I-beam still appear.

Select the title *A Shipshape Cruiser* using the I-beam. Notice that the Format Painter automatically applies the format, including color, of Slide 1's title (see fig. 16.26). By double-clicking on the Format Painter button, you can repeatedly format text.

Suppose you want all the text on the title slide formatted the same as the title. Return to Slide 1 and select the title again using the I-beam cursor.

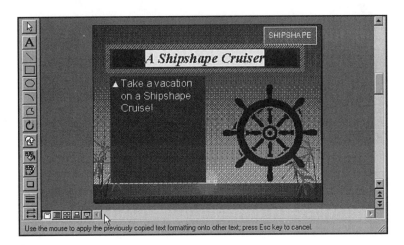

Double-click on the Format Painter button and move the paintbrush and I-beam over *Shipshape Cruise Lines* (see fig. 16.27). Next, move the paintbrush and I-beam over the words *Become part of the crew!* and watch the Format Painter apply formatting to this text. Press Esc to remove the paintbrush and I-beam and return to the mouse pointer.

You also can use the Format Painter to transfer slide color schemes from one slide to another in the Slide Sorter view.

The Undo Button

The Undo button reverses the last edit made to a slide. If you delete an object by mistake, for example, simply click on the Undo button to retrieve the object and place it back where it originally was.

The Report It Tool

The Report It tool quickly transfers the outline text from an open PowerPoint presentation into Word for use in a word processing document. Suppose you want to use the Shipshape training presentation text in an employee manual. Instead of retyping all the text, you can click on the Report It button (second from the right on the toolbar) to transfer the text into Word to get you started quickly.

Adding Objects to a Slide

The following four buttons are used to insert objects on a blank slide. These buttons work in the same way: click on the button and watch the rectangle with square resizing handles appear on the slide to show you where the object will appear after it is created.

The objects you add to a slide using the Insert Microsoft Word Table and Insert Microsoft Excel Spreadsheet buttons are OLE/DDE objects, meaning that when the object is selected, you have access to all the editing and creating tools and menus you would have in the corresponding applications. If, for example, you insert an Excel spreadsheet on a PowerPoint slide and select it by clicking on it, you instantly have access to Excel toolbars and menus. These tools appear where the PowerPoint toolbars are; you do not temporarily exit PowerPoint and work within Excel, then return to PowerPoint.

◆ The Insert Microsoft Word Table button enables you to add a table to a slide conveniently. Click on the button and select the number of columns and rows you want included in the table. When you release the left mouse button, the table appears on the slide.

◆ The Insert Microsoft Excel Spreadsheet button opens a grid, just like the Insert Microsoft Word Table button. Select the columns and rows you want in the spreadsheet and release the left mouse button. The spreadsheet appears for you to add numbers and formulas.

◆ The Insert Graph button enables you to place a graph on a slide. To insert a graph, click on the Insert Graph button on the toolbar and see PowerPoint place a rectangular outline on the slide to show you where the graph will be placed. You can alter the size of the graph after you create it using the square resizing handles. PowerPoint also offers an AutoLayout in which you can insert a graph by double-clicking in a designated area. For more information about using Microsoft Graph, see Chapter 17, "Enhancing PowerPoint Presentations."

◆ The Insert Clip Art button enables you to insert clip art on a PowerPoint slide. Just as a rectangle with black resizing handles appears when you click on the Insert Graph or Insert Organizational Chart button, this same rectangle appears when you click on the Insert Clip Art button. PowerPoint then takes you to the Microsoft ClipArt Gallery. For more information about using the Clip Art Gallery to select an image, see "Adding a New Slide with Clip Art" in Chapter 15, "PowerPoint Quick Start."

Using Zoom Control

PowerPoint Zoom Control adjusts the distance at which you view and work on slides, notes, and outlines. Zoom Control appears on each of the four toolbars and helps you get a closer or more distant look while you work. When altering clip art or drawing graphics in the Slide view, for example, the closer views at 66% and 100% enable you to work with more precision. To assess the overall look of the slides, you might want to step back from the slides to a 33% or 25% view.

To access the preset magnification levels, click on the down arrow to the right of the percentage (see fig. 16.28).

Figure 16.28

Opening the drop-down list of present magnification levels.

The magnification levels available vary from view to view:

◆ The Slide, Slide Sorter, and Notes views have the following magnification levels: 25%, 33%, 50%, 66%, 75%, 100%, 150%, 200%, 300%, and 400%.

◆ The magnification levels offered in the Outline view include 25%, 33%, 50%, 66%, 75%, and 100%.

You also can select any of these magnification levels by choosing **Z**oom from the **V**iew menu. The Zoom dialog box appears (see fig. 16.29) and presents some preset magnification levels, but it also enables you to select a specific magnification percentage. To increase the magnification level, move the mouse pointer over the up arrow

and click to increase the magnification by one-percent increments. To decrease the magnification level, click on the down arrow with the mouse pointer. You also can select the percentage with the I-beam cursor and enter the magnification you would like. Click on OK to activate the view you have chosen.

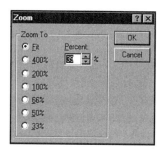

Figure 16.29

The Zoom dialog box.

Using Context-Sensitive Help

The Help button enables you to find out more information about a toolbar button function or any menu command. To utilize the Help function, click on the button and move the mouse pointer into the workspace; the mouse pointer appears with a question mark. At this point, you can move the pointer to the area anywhere on the screen where you need more information and click. A Help window appears and provides more information. Open the Help window **F**ile menu and choose E**x**it to return to the presentation.

The Formatting Toolbar

The Formatting toolbar provides functions to help you with formatting operations, such as changing fonts or italicizing text (see fig. 16.30).

Figure 16.30

The Formatting toolbar.

Choosing and Formatting Fonts

The Font list box works like the list box in Microsoft Word. Simply select the text and click on the down arrow to view the font choices (see fig. 16.31). Notice the font located above the double line. PowerPoint places the fonts you used last at the top of the font list for easier accessibility as you work. Only three fonts remain at the top of the list at one time.

Figure 16.31

The Font list box.

You also can change the font by opening the **Fo**rmat menu and choosing **F**ont. The Font dialog box opens and enables you to choose the font, font style, and size (see fig. 16.32). Click on OK to exit the Font dialog box.

Figure 16.32

The Font dialog box.

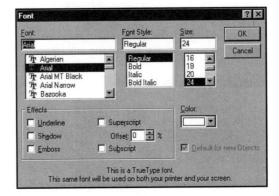

The **S**ize list box drops down so that you can choose the font size you want. These font sizes are preset (for example, 12, 14, 18, 24). You also can select the current font size with the I-beam cursor and type an exact font size.

The Increase Font Size and Decrease Font Size buttons in the Formatting toolbar enable you to quickly change selected text's font size by various increments.

The Bold, Italic, Underline, and Text Shadow buttons on the toolbar perform these character changes on selected text. PowerPoint's Bold, Italic, and Underline buttons work just like in Word. Simply select the text and click on the style you want to apply to the text.

The Text Shadow button enables you to add a shadow to slide text only, not to shapes or other objects. This style is especially effective in slide titles or to emphasize text. To add a shadow to text, select the text and click on the Text Shadow button.

Because you can output your presentation to color slides or overheads, color text is particularly effective. When you click on the Text Color button, a color palette appears with the eight colors you used most recently (see fig. 16.33).

Figure 16.33

The Text Color palette.

Click on a color block to change the color of the selected text. If you do not see a color you like, click on Other Color for more choices. The Colors dialog box opens, showing the Standard tab (see fig. 16.34).

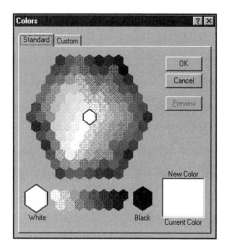

Figure 16.34

Choosing another color.

You even can create your own color by selecting the Custom tab in the Colors dialog box to display the custom color design dialog box (see fig. 16.35). Move the black marker on the color waves to the shade of color you want. Then click on the triangular pointer along the color band and drag it up or down to select the color intensity. When you have chosen a color, click on OK and then OK again to close the Other Color dialog box. This custom color shows on the color palette that appears for you to use later when you click on the Text Color button.

Figure 16.35

Creating your own color.

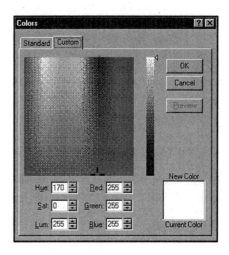

Aligning Text

The Align Left and Align Center buttons work exactly as they do in Word. Simply select the text and click on the alignment you would like. You also can access text alignment by opening the F**o**rmat menu and choosing **A**lignment (see fig. 16.36). A cascading menu offers you four choices: left, right, center, and justify. Choose the alignment by clicking on it.

Figure 16.36

Aligning text through the Format menu.

Bullets

PowerPoint can automatically add bullets to lists added in the slide body text box on slides other than the title slide. Notice that if you select this text, the bullet button on the Formatting toolbar is pressed. To bullet text, select the text and click on the bullet button.

You are not limited to a simple dot for your bullets. To access other bullet styles, select the text, open the F**o**rmat menu and select **B**ullet. When the Bullet dialog box appears (see fig. 16.37), click on the bullet you would like. You can select the bullet color by opening the list box under Special **C**olor (see fig. 16.38). Notice that if you created a custom color earlier, it also appears on this palette. Click on OK to implement any bullet formatting.

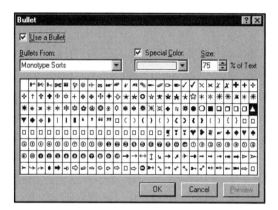

Figure 16.37

Selecting a style for a bullet.

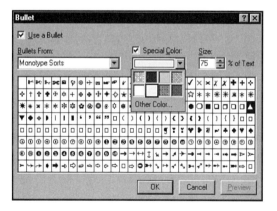

Figure 16.38

Selecting a bullet color.

 Note As a shortcut to adding a bullet to a line of text, simply place the flashing cursor within the line and click on the bullet button.

Promoting and Demoting Bullet Points

The left- and right-arrow buttons on the Formatting toolbar are the Promote and Demote buttons, respectively. These buttons enable you to create a hierarchy of text using subpoints. Suppose that on Slide 2 you wanted to move the second bullet point under the first bullet point to make it a subpoint. Click the I-beam cursor anywhere in the text, then click on the Demote button on the Formatting toolbar (see fig. 16.39).

Figure 16.39

Demoting a bullet point.

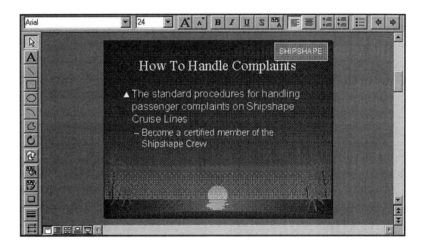

Notice how the second bullet indents and assumes another style of bullet. This bullet format is defined in the Slide Master. The Promote and Demote buttons are particularly useful in the Outline view to manipulate text and organize your thoughts.

The Outline Toolbar

The Outline toolbar is available only in the Outline view. Change to the Outline view by pressing the Outline view button in the bottom left corner of the workspace. The Outline toolbar automatically appears vertically down the left side of the workspace (see fig. 16.40).

Figure 16.40

The Outline toolbar.

Moving Text or Slides Up and Down

The Move Up and Move Down buttons rearrange text vertically one line to eliminate cutting and pasting. Suppose you want Complimentary Lunch to be the last point on the Agenda slide. To rearrange text, select the bullet point using the four-headed arrow, then click on the Move Down button (see fig. 16.41).

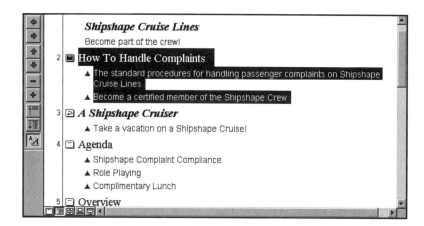

Figure 16.41

Moving text down the outline.

These buttons also can be used to rearrange entire slides. To move Slide 2 into Slide 3's position, select Slide 2 by placing the mouse pointer over the slide icon until it turns to a four-headed arrow, then click.

Click on the Move Down button once and watch the slide begin its descent (see fig. 16.42). Click on the Move Down button again to position all the highlighted text completely into the Slide 3 position. The slides automatically renumber. You also can use these buttons to move multiple slides.

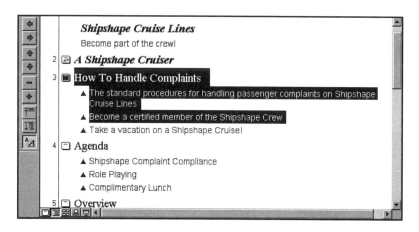

Figure 16.42

Slide 2 moves one level with a click of the Move Down button.

Collapsing and Expanding Selections

The Collapse Selection and Expand Selection buttons work like the Collapse and Expand buttons on Microsoft Word outlines. For example, you currently are viewing all slide titles and subpoints. To view only the title of a slide, select the entire slide and click on the Collapse Selection button. Watch the subpoints hide (see fig. 16.43). Click on the Expand Selection button to expand the slide text.

Figure 16.43

Collapsing a section of the outline.

The Show Titles and Show All buttons enable you to see only the slide titles in the Outline view. No text needs to be selected. Click on the Show Titles button (see fig. 16.44). If you move a title when Show Titles is pressed, all the subpoints under the title also move. This is especially helpful when organizing long presentations. To see all the presentation text, click on the Show All button.

Figure 16.44

Viewing only the slide titles using the Show Titles button.

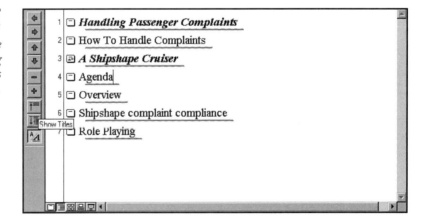

Showing and Hiding Text Formatting

The Show Formatting button changes the outline text to reflect the font and font size as they appear on the slides. To revert to a default font and font size while working in the Outline view, click once on the Show Formatting button (see fig. 16.45). This default text formatting enables you to see more of the outline text at one time. To change back to viewing the actual fonts and font styles, click on the Show Formatting button once again. Change to the Slide view to continue.

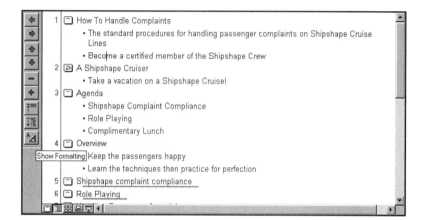

Figure 16.45

Viewing Outline text in a default font and font size.

The Microsoft Toolbar

The Microsoft toolbar (see fig. 16.46) is available in all four views and enables you to switch instantly between other Microsoft applications. You are able to access these applications, however, only if they currently are available on your computer or through a network.

Figure 16.46

The Microsoft toolbar.

To make the Microsoft toolbar appear, display the Toolbars dialog box by selecting Toolbars from the **V**iew menu, then check the box next to Microsoft. Or, as a short-cut, you can move the mouse pointer on any current toolbar and press the right mouse button. When the pop-up menu appears, click on Microsoft. The Microsoft toolbar appears floating in the workspace. Double-click in the area around the toolbar buttons to dock the toolbar at the top of the workspace. As you move the mouse pointer over each button, a Tool Tip shows you which button accesses what application.

The Custom Toolbar

The Custom toolbar is a blank toolbar that is available for you to customize with buttons that you frequently use. To open the Custom toolbar using the right mouse button shortcut, move the mouse pointer on any current toolbar and press the right mouse button. Select Custom from the pop-up menu.

The Custom toolbar appears floating and initially is very small because there are no buttons on it. The toolbar will enlarge as customized buttons are placed on it by using the Customize Toolbars dialog box. Or, you can hold down the Alt key and move buttons from any current toolbars to the Custom toolbar. You also can use Ctrl+Alt to copy buttons from a current toolbar to the Custom toolbar.

Using Drawing Toolbars

Three of PowerPoint's toolbars pertain to drawing and manipulating shapes: the Drawing toolbar, the Drawing Plus toolbar, and the AutoShapes toolbar. You can manipulate all three drawing toolbars just as you can the others. You can dock them on either side of the workspace or at the top and bottom of the workspace (see fig. 16.47). You also can customize these toolbars using the same customization techniques discussed earlier in this chapter.

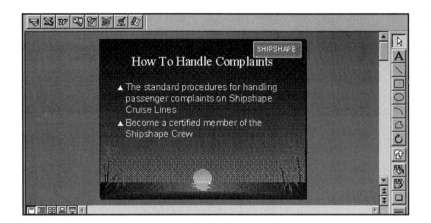

Figure 16.47

Docking the Drawing toolbar on the right side of the workspace.

The Drawing Toolbar

The PowerPoint Drawing toolbar offers many basic drawing and object-formatting tools for you to enhance your presentations.

The Selection Tool

The Selection tool is used to select objects using the mouse pointer. All objects need to be selected to apply formatting. You also use the Selection tool when you want to move objects. PowerPoint reverts to the Selection tool when you finish performing a function, so sometimes it is unnecessary to click on the Selection tool button to activate it. After you draw a rectangle, for example, the mouse pointer automatically changes from a cross hair back to the Selection tool. To select multiple objects, select the first object, hold down the Shift key, and click once on the other objects you want to select.

The Text Tool

Using the Text tool, you can add to a slide text that is separate from the text typed in the Outline. Often single words or phrases showcased on a slide add interest and help communicate a thought or process. Also, a company name included on slides—such as *SHIPSHAPE* on the Shipshape Cruise Lines training presentation—creates recognition and promotes awareness.

The two options for adding text with the Text tool are a text label and a word processing box. Text doesn't automatically wrap in a text label. Text labels are ideal for single words or phrases that you want to place on a slide.

To create a text label, first move to Slide 3 in the Shipshape Cruise Lines presentation. Then click on the Text tool button on the Drawing toolbar and move the mouse pointer onto the slide. Notice that the mouse pointer turns to a text cursor. Click on the slide where you want to place the text label, and a flashing cursor appears inside a crosshatch frame. Type **Service!**. The cursor remains flashing at the end of the text label. Move the mouse pointer off the slide and click.

After typing the text label, you might want to move it somewhere else on the slide. To move the text label after you have typed it, click once on the word or words to select it. A crosshatch frame appears, letting you know you have selected the label and that the text can be edited (see fig. 16.48).

Figure 16.48

Selecting the text label.

Place the mouse pointer on the crosshatch frame and click again; the edit-object frame appears with square resizing handles (see fig. 16.49). Click directly on the edit object frame but not on the square resizing handles. Then, click and drag the label to another location on the slide. The label's dotted outline shows the size of the label as you move it. Release the left mouse button when the label is where you would like it. From this point, you can make text-formatting changes by selecting the text label and making style selections, such as enlarging the font size or changing the text color.

Figure 16.49

The edit-object frame.

Use these same steps to move other text labels, word processing boxes, or clip art. You can move objects one pixel at a time using the arrow keys on the keyboard while the object is selected.

Text wraps inside the boundaries of a word processing box. If you plan to type a long sentence or more than one sentence, use a word processing box. To create a word processing box, click on the Text Tool button and move the text cursor over the slide. Click and drag the text cursor down to the right to draw a box. Notice that the text cursor turns into a cross hair when you begin to drag the cursor to draw the word processing box.

After you draw the box, a flashing cursor appears inside a crosshatch frame and waits for you to begin typing. Type **Shipshape Cruise Lines wants you to be a well-trained crew member.** Move the mouse pointer off the slide and click. To move the word processing box, follow the same steps outlined for moving a text label.

The Line, Rectangle, Ellipse, and Arc Tools

The Line, Rectangle, Ellipse, and Arc tools all work the same way. To obtain a clean palette to draw objects, move to the end of the presentation and insert a blank slide. Click on the New Slide button and choose Blank from the AutoLayouts. Click once on the rectangle button and move the mouse pointer onto the slide. Notice that the cursor turns into a cross hair. Click and drag the cross-hair cursor down and to the right or left, depending on where you want the object on the slide. Release the left mouse button when the rectangle is the size you want.

Tip   As noted in the status bar, you can hold down the Shift key to constrain the angle when drawing a line, to draw a square when using the Rectangle tool, to draw a circle when using the Ellipse tool, or to draw a circular arc when using the Arc tool.

The cross hair immediately returns to the mouse pointer. Also, PowerPoint instantly attaches an object frame to the shape and provides square resizing handles for you to alter the shape.

Tip   If you double-click on a drawing-tool button, you can draw shapes one after another. After drawing the first object, the cross hair remains instead of reverting to the mouse pointer, enabling you to draw another object. Press Esc to remove the cross hair.

The following procedure resizes any PowerPoint object. Move the mouse pointer over the bottom right square resizing handle. Notice that the mouse pointer turns to arrows, showing you which way you can resize the rectangle. Grab the square resizing handle, and click and drag the mouse in the direction you want to alter the rectangle.

PowerPoint shows you an outline of the object as it is being resized to let you judge how big or small you want the object. Release the left mouse button when the object is the size you would like.

Sometimes when you resize an object, it becomes difficult to keep the object proportional; a circle can become elliptical, for example, or a square rectangular. To resize an object around the center so it maintains its proportionality, hold down the Ctrl key as you drag the resizing handle. The status box also gives you this information.

 Tip If you accidentally alter the object's size too drastically and want to restore the object to its original proportions, press Ctrl and double-click on any square resizing handle.

The Freeform Tool

The Freeform tool enables you to draw objects with freeform lines and straight lines. To use the Freeform tool, click on the Freeform tool button and move the mouse pointer onto the slide. Just as with the other tools, the mouse pointer turns into a cross hair when you move it into the workspace. Now, hold down the left mouse button and watch the cross hair turn into a pencil. Still holding down the left mouse button, move the mouse to draw in freeform (see fig. 16.50). Release the left mouse button, and the pencil returns to a cross hair. Move the mouse down to draw a line. Press and hold the left mouse button to return to the freeform drawing using the pencil. When you are done drawing, double-click the left mouse button. The object immediately acquires the square resizing handles and can be altered using the same steps discussed earlier in this section.

Figure 16.50

Drawing in freeform.

You can use the Freeform tool to draw polygons, too. Click on the Freeform tool and move the cursor into the workspace. Using the cross hair, click the left mouse button once but do not hold it down. Now, move the mouse to draw a line. Click the left

mouse button once again to end that line, and drag the mouse to draw another line. The status bar tells you to continue clicking for each point of the polygon and to double-click to end your drawing.

The Free Rotate Tool

The Free Rotate tool enables you to rotate any object; even text will rotate within an object. Suppose you want to rotate the rectangle you drew. Select it by clicking on it, then click on the Free Rotate tool button and move the cursor onto the slide. The cursor changes to a circular shape with a plus sign (+) in the middle. The status bar tells you to position the cursor over any square resizing handle. When you have done this, hold down the left mouse button and drag the object to rotate it, as shown in figure 16.51.

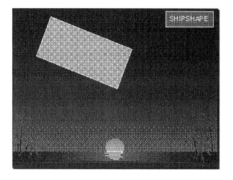

Figure 16.51

Rotating the object.

To rotate an object on restricted angles such as 45 or 90 degrees, hold down the Shift key while you rotate the object. The status bar informs you of this information if you forget. Release the mouse button when you are finished rotating the object, then press Esc to exit the object-rotating mode.

The AutoShapes Button

Click on the AutoShapes button to display a choice of shapes you can add to a slide (see fig. 16.52). Click on the shape you want to use, then drag the mouse on the part of the slide that will receive this shape. You can combine AutoShape objects with freeform drawing to have some fun with your presentation (see fig. 16.53).

Figure 16.52

The AutoShapes dialog box.

Figure 16.53

Using AutoShape objects along with freeform drawing in a slide.

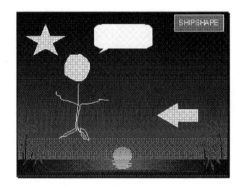

The Fill Color Button

The Fill Color button shows a paint can filling up a square. To access the button, you must have selected an object on the slide, then you can click on the Fill Color button to change the object's color (see fig. 16.54).

Figure 16.54

The Fill Color choices.

To select another fill color, click on one of the eight color blocks. To remove the fill, select No Fill. To make the fill the same color as the slide background, choose Background. PowerPoint also enables you to create a shaded fill that adds interest to any shape. To add a shaded fill, select Shaded. The Shaded Fill dialog box opens, displaying the various shading patterns.

The shading styles direct the shading within the shape. PowerPoint provides a number of patterns with which to spice up a shape's fill. Click through the various Shade Styles and watch the examples appear in miniature in the dialog box. Select the shading style you like and click on OK.

You also can add a colored pattern inside an object. Choose Pattern to display the Pattern Fill dialog box, which presents many patterns from which you can choose. Click on the pattern you would like and click on OK.

You can also use the Fill Color button to select a textured fill.

Any of those choices brings up a dialog box such as the one shown in figure 16.55.

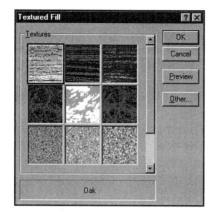

Figure 16.55

Choosing a textured fill for an object.

You can also change an object's fill color by choosing Colors and **L**ines from the F**o**rmat menu. The Colors and Lines dialog box displays, as shown in figure 16.56. In the Colors and Lines dialog box, you can change an object's fill color, line color, and line style, including dashed lines and arrowheads.

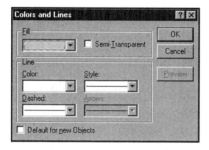

Figure 16.56

The Color and Lines dialog box.

The Line Color Button

The Line Color button lets you change a line's color. With an object selected, click on the button to see the color choices (which are the same as the colors available for fill). Choose Other to custom-design your own color for the object's lines.

You can also format lines by opening the Color and Lines dialog box through the F**o**rmat menu and following the same steps as changing an object's fill color. The Color and Lines dialog box also enables you to change the line's thickness in the Line **S**tyles box.

The Shadow On/Off Button

The Shadow On/Off button, showing a rectangle with a black shadow, switches on or off to apply a shadow to an object. To shadow an object, select the object and click on the button (see fig. 16.57).

Figure 16.57

An object with a shadow.

To change the shadow's color, open the F<u>o</u>rmat menu, choose S<u>h</u>adow, and select the color you would like from the Shadow dialog box. In the Shadow dialog box you can adjust the shadow's offset direction and thickness. To increase the thickness of the shadow going up or down, click on the up or down arrow (see fig. 16.58).

Figure 16.58

The Shadow dialog box.

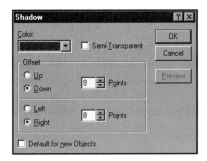

The Line Style Button

Use the Line Style button to change the width or style of a line, choosing from several thicknesses of single lines as well as double and triple combinations of lines.

The Arrowhead Button

The Arrowhead button applies only when you draw a line or an arc and want to place an arrowhead at one end or another, or both. Click on the Line button, for example, and draw a line on the slide. With the line still selected, click on the Arrowhead button, then click on the arrowhead style you want to apply to the line.

The Drawing Plus Toolbar

The Drawing+ toolbar is used to manipulate the objects on your slides. It appears in figure 16.59 on the left side of the workspace.

Figure 16.59

The Drawing+ toolbar.

The Bring Forward and Send Backward buttons work in tandem and help you arrange multiple objects. The following steps illustrate how these buttons work. First, insert a blank slide by choosing New Slide, then another using AutoLayout. Then draw a line, a rectangle, and an ellipse on the blank slide using the techniques described earlier in this chapter. Move the objects so that they are overlapping each other as shown in figure 16.60.

Figure 16.60

Overlapping the objects.

Select the ellipse by clicking on it. You will know it is selected when the square resizing handles appear. To move the ellipse behind the rectangle, click on the Send Backward button on the Drawing Plus toolbar (see fig. 16.61).

Grouping Objects

Right now, the three objects are separate. You can select each one individually by
clicking on it. To move these objects, you would have to move them one at a time.
Sometimes you will want to group objects in order to move them or ungroup objects
to edit them separately. Ungrouping objects is especially useful when altering clip art,
as shown in Chapter 17, "Enhancing PowerPoint Presentations."

To group the line, rectangle, and ellipse, you must select all of them at one time.
Remember, you can select one object, hold down the Shift key, and select the rest;
however, PowerPoint provides a shortcut. You can drag a selection box around the
objects using the cursor. To drag this selection box, place the cursor in the area to
the upper left of the objects. Press and hold the left mouse button until the cursor
changes to a cross hair.

Drag the cross hair so that you drag a box around the three objects. A dashed outline
of the box shows you whether you have surrounded all the objects. Release the left
mouse button. All the objects acquire square resizing handles, which let you know
they are selected (see fig. 16.62).

Figure 16.62

*All objects are
selected.*

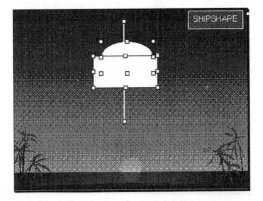

Click on the Group button on the Drawing Plus toolbar and notice that the square resizing handles encompass all the objects (see fig. 16.63). At this point, you can move or resize all the objects at one time. For example, click in the center of the rectangle and drag the mouse pointer over to the left. Notice that all the objects move together. Place the mouse pointer over a square resizing handle, grab the handle by clicking the left mouse button, and hold. Now, drag the handle the way that it will let you move. Notice that all the objects either increase or decrease in size, depending on which way you move the mouse.

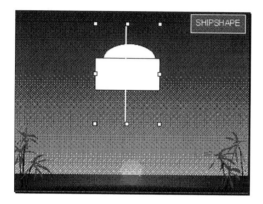

Figure 16.63

Grouping the three objects.

Flipping Objects

The next four buttons rotate and flip objects both horizontally and vertically. To flip or rotate a shape, select the shape using the Select tool and select the rotation or flip direction. Experiment with the objects you have just drawn. You can rotate or flip any object including clip art. When you are finished experimenting with objects, select them and click on the Cut button on the Standard toolbar or press Del to remove them from the slide.

Working with Text within Shapes

Adding text to shapes enables you to highlight words in an interesting way. Text inside shapes can be edited just like other slide text; however, PowerPoint enables you to anchor and align text within shapes in creative ways.

Adding Text inside Shapes

To add text within a shape, open the AutoShapes toolbar if it is not already open and click on the up arrow. Draw the shape on the blank slide (see fig. 16.64). While the arrow is still selected, type **Arrow**. Notice that the word automatically appears centered in the middle of the arrow in the default font (see fig. 16.65). To add text inside a shape that has already been drawn, select the shape and begin typing.

Figure 16.64

Forming an arrow on the slide.

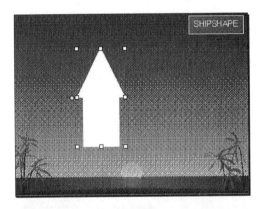

Figure 16.65

The text appears in the arrow.

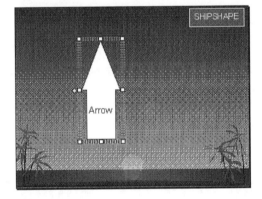

Understanding Text Anchor

Text anchor refers to where text is located within shapes. PowerPoint defaults to the Middle anchor point, but you can change this anchor to better suit your needs. With the arrow shape selected, select **T**ext Anchor from the F**o**rmat menu to display the Text Anchor dialog box (see fig. 16.66). Within the Text Anchor dialog box you can change the **A**nchor Point. Open the list box by clicking on the down arrow; you can choose from Top, Middle, Bottom, Top Centered, Middle Centered, and Bottom Centered. Select Bottom Centered and click on OK. Notice how the word *Arrow* moves to the bottom of the shape.

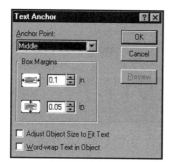

Figure 16.66

*The Text Anchor
dialog box.*

Adjusting Text within Shapes

Text does not wrap automatically within shapes. To illustrate this, click the I-beam
cursor at the end of the word *Arrow* so the cursor is flashing. Then, press the space
bar and type **Facing Up** (see fig. 16.67).

Figure 16.67

*Adding text that
is wider than the
object.*

Notice that the words extend beyond the outline of the shape and do not wrap.
However, you can choose to have text wrap or to have the object adjust automatically
to accommodate the text. With the arrow selected, open the Text Anchor dialog box
by selecting **T**ext Anchor from the F**o**rmat menu. At the bottom of the Text Anchor
dialog box there are two options: Adjust Object Size to **F**it Text and **W**ord-wrap Text
in Object. To make the text word-wrap within the arrow, check the box in front of
Word-wrap Text in Object, then click on OK. The words *Arrow Facing Up* now wrap
within the shape (see fig. 16.68).

Suppose you want the shape to automatically adjust its size to accommodate the
amount of text. In this case, there is more than enough room inside the arrow to
accommodate the text, so you can draw another shape. Choose the Ellipse tool and
draw a small ellipse on the slide. With the shape still selected, type **Adding text inside
an ellipse** (see fig. 16.69).

Figure 16.68

The text wraps inside the shape.

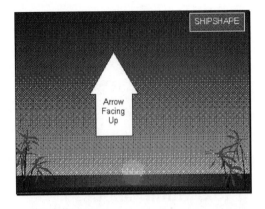

Figure 16.69

Adding text inside a small ellipse.

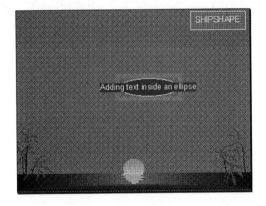

Open the **F**ormat menu and choose **T**ext Anchor. Click on the Adjust Object size to **F**it Text check box and click on OK. Notice that the ellipse adjusted its size to accommodate the words (see fig. 16.70). If you type more text inside the ellipse, it will continue to adjust in size.

Figure 16.70

The ellipse adjusted to fit the text.

If you have been following along, delete the objects and hide the AutoShapes toolbar to continue.

Using Alignment Tools

PowerPoint makes precisely aligning and positioning shapes or objects easy by providing tools to help. When you have many objects on a slide, adjusting each object individually to line up with other objects can be time-consuming. This section discusses the ways in which you easily can make these adjustments.

Ruler

The PowerPoint Ruler is similar to the Microsoft Word ruler. You can add tabs and define text margins within text labels or word processing boxes or shapes. To turn on the PowerPoint Ruler, open the **V**iew menu and choose **R**uler. The Ruler is available only in the Slide and Notes views and extends only as wide and tall as the slide size in the Slide view and the page size in the Notes view.

The PowerPoint Ruler shows you where the cursor is positioned on the slide or notes page with dotted lines that move as you move the mouse. The ruler is in inches. On each axis, the ruler places the 0-inch mark in the center of the slide or notes page. So, if the dotted marks on each axis are on 0, the mouse pointer is positioned in the middle of the slide or notes page (see fig. 16.71).

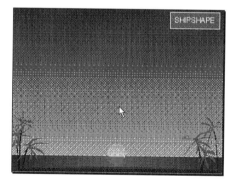

Figure 16.71

The mouse pointer is positioned in the middle of the slide.

The ruler is ideal for helping you draw sizes with specific dimensions. If you want to draw a 2-by-2-inch rectangle, for example, click on the rectangle tool and position the cross hair so that you begin to draw at 0.

Click and drag the cross hair down to the right. Make sure the dotted marks line up on 2 on both axes (see fig. 16.72). Release the mouse button when you have lined up the dotted marks.

Figure 16.72

Drawing a 3-by-2-inch rectangle.

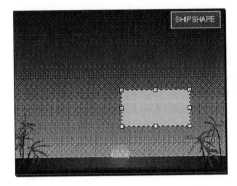

To remove the Ruler from view, open the **V**iew menu and click on **R**uler to remove the check mark.

Guides

PowerPoint guides help you to align one object or multiple objects to a straight edge. To turn the guides on, open the **V**iew menu and select **G**uides. Horizontal and vertical dotted lines appear on the slide. Any shapes that you draw and move near these guides will snap to the guides.

The guides first appear intersecting at the center point of the slide. You can move the guides separately and reposition them to help you align objects. To move the guides, move the cursor on the dotted line and hold down the left mouse button. Notice the box that appears when you hold down the mouse button, showing the current location of the guide in inches. Move the horizontal guide up or down and the vertical guide left or right; the guide location adjusts as you move the guide. To remove the guides from view, open the **V**iew menu and select **G**uides to remove the check mark.

Snap to Grid

PowerPoint's Snap to Grid option helps you to precisely align objects by providing an invisible grid of lines on the slide. To turn this grid on, open the **D**raw menu and select **S**nap to Grid.

To get a feel for working with the grid, draw a rectangle on the slide. Place the cursor inside the rectangle and hold down the left mouse button. Move the rectangle slowly down the slide. Notice how the rectangle seems to jump as it moves; this is the rectangle adhering to the invisible gridlines. You can temporarily override the grid by holding down the Alt key as you move the object. To turn off the Snap to Grid, open the **D**raw menu and select **S**nap to Grid to remove the check mark.

Understanding the Masters

PowerPoint Masters are powerful because they enable you to make formatting changes that apply to all the slides, outline pages, audience handout pages, and notes pages included in your presentation package. By making changes or additions in one place, you do not have to take the time to make changes on each individual slide or page.

PowerPoint provides masters for Slides, Outlines, Handouts, and Notes. Handouts are paper printouts that show two or six slides on a page. Sometimes you want to pass a printout of the presentation slides to audience members for their information. Handouts provide an easy, automatic way to prepare these pages.

Often you will want the date or a page number to appear on audience handouts or slides. The Masters are a perfect place to add these objects and automate them for even more time savings. This section discusses each of the four PowerPoint Masters and which objects can be inserted on the Master. A basic understanding of the PowerPoint Masters can help you save formatting time.

The Slide Master

The PowerPoint Slide Master contains formatting information that is applied to every slide in a presentation. The Slide Master enables you to conveniently change slide characteristics, such as the slide title position, the body text position, slide background colors, text formatting, and bullet formatting. By making changes in one place, you do not have to take the time to make changes on each individual slide. For example, in the Shipshape Cruise Lines training presentation, when you placed the word *SHIPSHAPE* on the Slide Master, you placed it on every slide in the presentation.

To view the Slide Master, open the **V**iew menu and select **M**aster, then choose **S**lide Master. Or hold down the Shift key as you click on the Slide View button. The Status bar reads Slide Master. Notice that the toolbars do not change when changing views from the PowerPoint Slide view to the Slide Master. At this point, you can make any text-formatting changes or add objects that you want to appear on every slide. You work in the Slide Master just as you would in the Slide view; the difference is that additions or changes affect every slide in the presentation.

To change text formats, select the text and make changes using the toolbar buttons or the menus. If you want every slide title to be underlined, for example, select *Click to edit Master title style* and click on the Underline button on the Formatting toolbar (see fig. 16.73).

Figure 16.73

Formatting the slide titles throughout a presentation.

Suppose you wanted to change the bullet color from yellow to pink on every slide. Click on the words *Click to edit Master text styles*. Open the F**o**rmat menu and choose **B**ullet to display the Bullet dialog box. Open the Special **C**olor list box and click on the pink color block. Click on OK and notice the bullet turns to pink. You can change the bullet colors and styles on any level of text by following these same steps. To view these changes in the presentation, click on the Slide View button.

The Handout Master

To view the Handout Master, open the **V**iew menu and choose **M**aster, then select Han**d**out Master from the cascaded list. The Handout Master outlines where slides appear if you print handouts with two or six slides (see fig. 16.74).

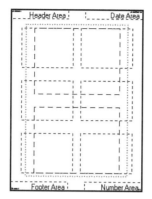

Figure 16.74

The Handout Master.

The Notes Master

To view the Notes Master, open the **V**iew menu and choose **M**aster. Then, from the cascaded list, select **N**otes Master. The Notes Master shows a small Slide Master and a box labeled Notes Area for AutoLayouts (see fig. 16.75). You are able to type in this box any notes that you want to appear on every note printout. Commonly, however, you will not want to type any text here because the notes will differ from slide to slide. You might want to add a logo or page numbers.

Figure 16.75

The Notes Master.

Inserting Items on the Masters

Many times you will want the date, time, or page numbers to appear on every slide, notes page, handout page, or outline page. PowerPoint Masters are the perfect place to add these items. PowerPoint even takes this process a step further by using items similar to field codes in Microsoft Word. These items automatically keep track of dates, times, and page numbers so you don't have to.

To place the date on every handout page, for example, open the **V**iew menu and choose **M**aster. Then choose Han**d**out Master. Select the Date area in the upper right corner. Open the **I**nsert menu and choose D**a**te and Time. From the dialog box (see fig. 16.76), choose the date format you want and select the **U**pdate Automatically (Insert as Field) box. The actual date will not appear until you print the handout pages.

Figure 16.76

The Date and Time dialog box.

To move the date to the lower left corner of the Handout Master, place the cursor on the gray border of the box. Click and drag the box down into the left corner. Release the left mouse button when the box is positioned where you want it.

You can format text by making selections from toolbars. Follow these same steps to insert the time or page numbers on other PowerPoint Masters. Notice the other items you can add on the Masters. All these other items come into the Masters in the same way as the date did. In many cases, however, you have to decrease or increase the size of the objects.

Enhancing PowerPoint Presentations

PowerPoint provides a number of tools to help you enhance your presentations, such as adding color schemes and slide transitions. PowerPoint also provides tools to help you become a more effective and polished presenter, including Drill Down and hidden slides containing information you can retrieve during a presentation to answer difficult audience questions. PowerPoint automates creating graphs and organizational charts to make developing these objects easy and quick, while keeping them professional-looking. Customizing existing clip art helps to further enhance your presentations and make them look as though you hired a professional designer.

This chapter discusses the following topics:

- ◆ Using color schemes

- ◆ Using Microsoft Graph

- ◆ Using the Organizational Chart software

◆ Adding and editing clip art

◆ Working with the Slide Sorter toolbar

◆ Showing presentations on the road

Most importantly, PowerPoint provides continuous help when executing most common tasks while creating a presentation.

To begin this chapter, assume you are beginning a new presentation about learning PowerPoint. Open PowerPoint and select a blank presentation from the PowerPoint dialog box. If you currently are in PowerPoint, click on New on the Standard toolbar and select Blank Presentation. From the selection of AutoLayouts, choose Title Slide. This first slide in the Blank Presentation assumes PowerPoint's default template, which includes a white slide background and black text (see fig. 17.1).

Figure 17.1

The first slide assumes the default template.

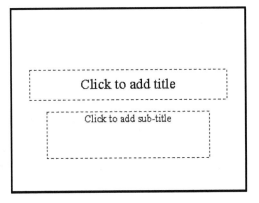

Type **Learning PowerPoint** for the title and **Making presentations easy!** for the subtitle (see fig. 17.2).

Figure 17.2

Adding title slide text.

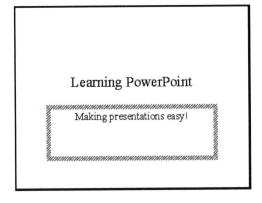

Using Color Schemes

PowerPoint guides you through choosing a presentation color scheme by offering colors based on the slide background color. PowerPoint uses color combinations that work well together so that you don't have to worry about getting into a color nightmare. You can change the color scheme for an individual slide or an entire presentation using the same techniques.

 Tip Shading a slide background can be particularly effective if you want to add a professional touch to a presentation. Making the top half of a slide dark can highlight a slide title. Leaving the bottom half light can make slide text pop off the screen.

Selecting a Color Scheme

Before you select a slide background, you need to think about the conditions under which you will deliver the information. If you will be in a dark room that seats many people, for example, slides with a dark background and lightly colored text will be easy to read for audience members in the back of the room.

PowerPoint enables you to select different color schemes for slides and notes. Normally, however, you will want to keep the background for notes white so that you do not detract from the slide image or text (not to mention use a lot of printer toner).

To begin constructing a color scheme, open the F**o**rmat menu and choose Slide **C**olor Scheme.

 Note Because you currently are in the Slide view, the Format menu offers only options that affect slides. If you were in the Notes view, the Format menu option would read Notes Color Scheme.

The Slide Color Scheme dialog box appears and displays seven choices for schemes. The current presentation color scheme is displayed with a box around it (see fig. 17.3). Click on any of the schemes to make it the active scheme. The color scheme includes the slide background color, text and lines color, object shadow color, title text color, object fill color, and three accent colors. A slide preview shows you where each color is used. As seen in the slide preview, the accent colors appear in objects such as graphs.

Figure 17.3

The Slide Color Scheme dialog box.

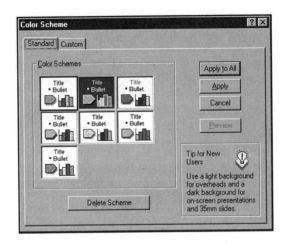

If you want to change a single color after you have picked a scheme, click on the Custom tab and choose the color of the feature you want to change (see fig 17.4). Click on Change Color. A color palette appears for the feature you've selected (see fig 17.5); make a color selection and click on OK.

Figure 17.4

The Custom tab of the Slide Color Scheme dialog box.

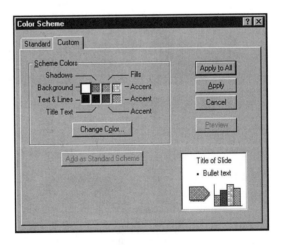

To create a new color, click on the Custom tab of the Color dialog box. Drag the crosshair to select a color, drag the scroll bar up or down to adjust the brightness, then click OK.

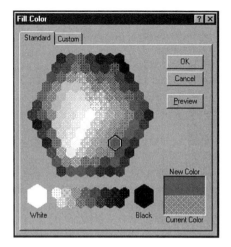

Figure 17.5

The Standard tab of the Fill Color dialog box.

Shading

Shading can add interest to an ordinary slide background. PowerPoint lets you choose from various shading directions to highlight certain areas of the slides depending on the slide background color you chose. To access the shading options, choose Custom Background from the Format menu to display the Custom Background dialog box seen in figure 17.6.

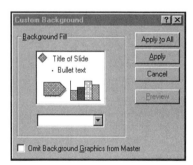

Figure 17.6

The Custom Background dialog box.

Currently there is no shade style for the slide background. Click on the arrow to the right of the empty text box to see the choices for backgrounds that are available. Choose Shaded to see the Shaded Fill dialog box shown in figure 17.7.

Figure 17.7

*The Shaded Fill
dialog box.*

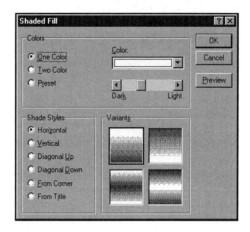

You can also use the Custom Background dialog box to create patterns or textures for the background and you can change the color if you want.

Click on **A**pply to change the shading style on an individual slide. To implement the shading on every slide in a presentation, choose Appl**y** to All. To see how the shading looks on your slide, choose a shading style and variant and click on **A**pply (because you currently have a single title slide).

If you want to add shading to the background of Notes pages, change to the Notes view by clicking on the Notes View button. Then, open the F**o**rmat menu and select Notes **B**ackground. Experiment with a few shading styles and variants to change the background on the Notes page. You probably will want to keep the Notes background white to keep the focus on the slide and notes.

Using Microsoft Graph

On the second slide in this presentation, you want to present a graph showing how many new PowerPoint users there will be in the next three months. PowerPoint makes creating a graph easy with Microsoft Graph. Insert Slide 2 by clicking on the New Slide button. From the AutoLayouts, select one of the Graph layouts (see fig. 17.8).

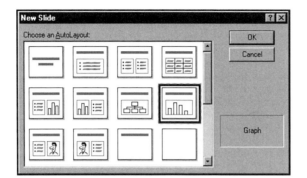

Figure 17.8

Select a layout for a Graph.

The new slide is inserted in your presentation, as seen in figure 17.9.

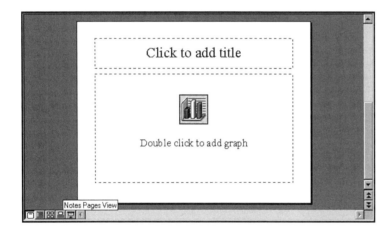

Figure 17.9

The new slide, ready to receive a graph.

Click on the title area and type **New PowerPoint Users** for the title. Double-click where it says to add a graph to access Microsoft Graph.

Microsoft Graph Datasheet

Microsoft Graph opens over the PowerPoint presentation and uses a datasheet to capture data to drive the chart. The datasheet appears on top of the chart with data already in some of the datasheet cells (see fig. 17.10). The menu bar now includes drop-down menus with commands pertaining to Microsoft Graph. Microsoft Graph uses its own Standard toolbar, which appears docked at the top of the workspace. Under the datasheet is the current slide and how the graph appears on the slide. You can edit this chart directly when the datasheet is not showing using Microsoft Graph functions discussed in this section. Clicking on the slide will take you back to PowerPoint.

Figure 17.10

A Microsoft Graph datasheet.

		A	B	C	D
		1st Qtr	2nd Qtr	3rd Qtr	4th Qtr
1	East	20.4	27.4	90	20.4
2	West	30.6	38.6	34.6	31.6
3	North	45.9	46.9	45	43.9
4					

> **Tip**
>
> If at any time you accidentally click on the slide and return to your presentation, double-click on the chart to take you back to Microsoft Graph.

The Microsoft Graph datasheet looks like a Microsoft Excel spreadsheet with rows, columns, and cells; however, the datasheet does not use formulas. You can import Microsoft Excel spreadsheet information into a datasheet or cut and paste it into the datasheet to save time. Also, you can export datasheet information.

To change data in the cells, double-click on a cell. A flashing cursor appears, waiting for you to enter data. The mouse pointer also changes to an I-beam, enabling you to select, delete, and reenter information. Just as you can select multiple cells in Excel spreadsheets, you also can select multiple cells in the datasheet. You can edit information using the Cut, Copy, and Paste buttons on the Standard toolbar, just as you edit data in Excel spreadsheets. Click on the Cut button on the standard toolbar to remove the data.

To clear the current information in the datasheet, select all the cells by clicking on the button where the column and row headings intersect (see fig. 17.11) and press Del. The datasheet now is clear for you to input new PowerPoint users information. Click on the cell under column A and type **January**.

Press the right-arrow key once and enter **February** under column B. Under column C, enter **March**. Click in row 1 and type **# of Users**. If the text does not fit in the column, open the Format menu and choose Column **W**idth. Enter a larger number to widen the column. In the datasheet, in row 1, column A, type **50**. In row 1, column B, type **75**. In row 1, column C, type **100** (see fig. 17.12).

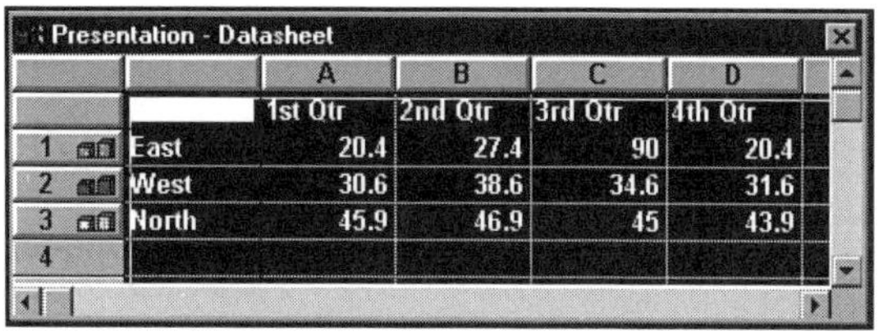

		A	B	C	D
		1st Qtr	2nd Qtr	3rd Qtr	4th Qtr
1	East	20.4	27.4	90	20.4
2	West	30.6	38.6	34.6	31.6
3	North	45.9	46.9	45	43.9
4					

Presentation - Datasheet

Figure 17.11

Selecting all the cells in the datasheet.

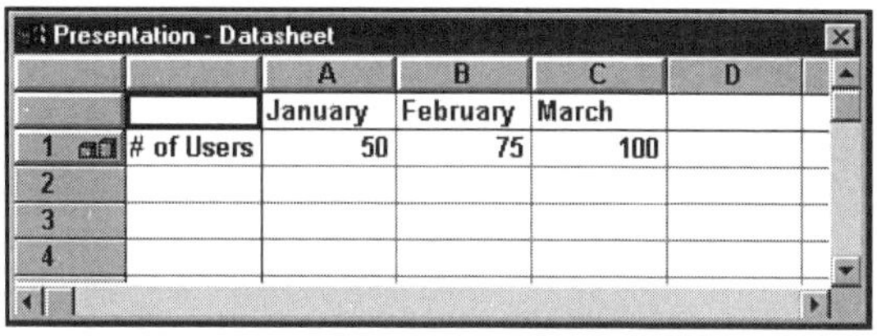

		A	B	C	D
		January	February	March	
1	# of Users	50	75	100	
2					
3					
4					

Presentation - Datasheet

Figure 17.12

Entering data in the datasheet.

To become quickly proficient with Microsoft Graph, a discussion of the Microsoft Graph Standard toolbar functions will be helpful.

The Standard Toolbar in Microsoft Graph

The Standard toolbar in Microsoft Graph enables you to quickly perform many Microsoft Graph functions (see fig. 17.13). The Standard toolbar in Microsoft Graph cannot be customized like the toolbars in PowerPoint. It can, however, be moved and floated in the workspace.

Figure 17.13

The Microsoft Graph Standard toolbar.

The Import Data Button

The Import Data button enables you to bring in data from an entire spreadsheet or a range of cells. When you click on the Import Data button, the Import Data dialog box opens and enables you to select the file from which you want to obtain the data (see fig. 17.14). To change the type of file you want to find, open the List Files of **T**ype list box. To select only a range of data, enter the range in the space provided. When you have typed the file name or range, click on OK. Another dialog box might open and ask if you want to overwrite the current data in the datasheet. Click on OK or Cancel depending on your situation.

Figure 17.14

The Import Data dialog box.

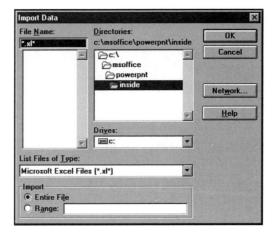

The Import Chart Button

Microsoft Graph enables you to import a chart using the Import Chart button. This button works the same way as the Import Data button. Clicking on the Import Chart button takes you to an Open Chart dialog box from which you can select a chart.

The Datasheet Button

The Datasheet button currently is pressed because the datasheet is showing. To remove the datasheet from view, click on the Datasheet button or choose **D**atasheet from the **V**iew menu. Removing the check mark removes the Datasheet from view. For now, however, click on the Datasheet button again to show the Datasheet.

The Editing Buttons

The Cut, Copy, Paste, and Undo buttons work just as they do on the Standard toolbar in PowerPoint. Select the text or object, then perform the function.

Viewing Data by Row or Column

Currently the new data is shown in rows. This is why the By Row button on the Standard toolbar is pressed. Click on the By Column button and see what happens (see fig. 17.15). Microsoft Graph assumes that you want the data to be read by columns and have the different months represent individual series of data. Click on the By Row button to change # of Users back to the data series. You also can make this change through the **D**ata menu by selecting either Series in **R**ows or Series in **C**olumns. To remove the datasheet from view to see the chart, click on the Datasheet button on the Standard toolbar.

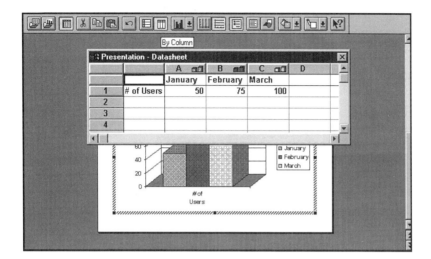

Figure 17.15

Clicking on the By Column button.

Choosing a Chart Type

Currently the information is shown in a column chart. The Chart Type button on the Standard toolbar enables you to revert quickly to a default column chart or change the type of chart through which the data is shown. Click on the down arrow next to the Chart Type button to access the types of charts Microsoft Graph offers (see fig. 17.16).

Figure 17.16

Viewing the other types of charts offered.

The first column of chart types are two-dimensional. The second column shows three-dimensional charts. The types of charts available include the following:

◆ Area charts

◆ Bar charts

◆ Column charts

◆ Line charts

◆ Pie charts

◆ Donut charts (two dimensional only)

◆ Radar charts (two dimensional only)

◆ XY Scatter charts (two dimensional only)

◆ Surface charts (three dimensional only)

You also can access the chart types by opening the F**o**rmat menu and choosing Chart Type. The Chart Type dialog box opens and ask you to choose either a two-dimensional or three-dimensional chart. The chart options will change depending on the dimension you select. Choose 3-D bar chart as an example. Click on the chart type with the mouse pointer and click on OK. Now you are viewing the new information in a 3-D bar chart.

Formatting a Chart

The Horizontal Gridline button is pressed in the Standard toolbar because these gridlines appear on the chart (although they appear vertically on the bar chart). The Legend button is pressed because a legend is currently showing. You can move the legend anywhere within the chart. The chart size might adjust to accommodate the legend. Move the cursor over the legend. Click and hold the mouse button and move the legend off the bar on the chart.

The legend has black, square resizing handles. Move the cursor over the bottom middle handle; notice the black arrows show you in which direction you can adjust the size. Grab the handle and make the legend larger by dragging the mouse down (see fig. 17.17). To remove the legend, click on the Legend button.

Figure 17.17

Enlarging the legend.

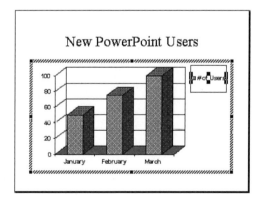

To insert a text box in the graph, click on the Text Box button and move the cursor over the chart. You cannot draw a text box anywhere outside the parameters of the chart. The mouse pointer changes to a crosshair. Drag a rectangle just as you would in PowerPoint, by holding down the left mouse button and dragging the mouse. Type the sentence **Many people will want to learn PowerPoint in the future** (see fig. 17.18).

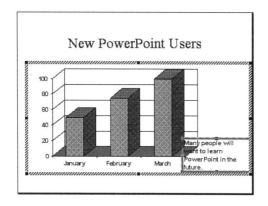

Figure 17.18

Adding a text box to the chart.

The text size is very small. With the Text Box selected, open the **Fo**rmat menu and choose **F**ont. The Format Object dialog box opens. Enlarge the text size and click on OK (see fig. 17.19).

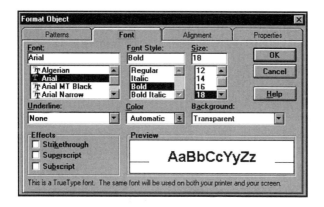

Figure 17.19

Enlarging the text size in the Format Object dialog box.

The Graph Drawing Toolbar

Microsoft Graph features a Drawing toolbar that is similar to the Drawing and Drawing Plus toolbars in PowerPoint. Click on the Drawing button to show the Drawing toolbar, as shown in figure 17.20. You can manipulate and move the Drawing toolbar just like other toolbars. Move the toolbar off the chart by dragging the title bar with the cursor (see fig. 17.21).

Figure 17.20

*The Drawing
toolbar in
Microsoft Graph.*

Figure 17.21

*Moving the
Drawing toolbar
off the chart.*

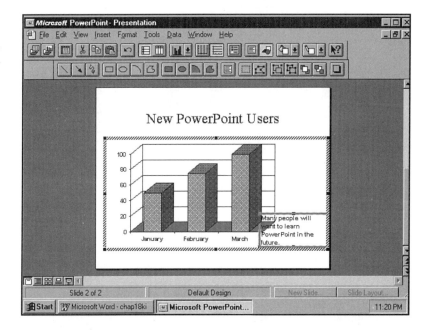

The toolbar buttons show which objects you can draw, using the same techniques as for the PowerPoint Drawing toolbar. Many buttons even look the same. To find out which buttons draw which objects, move the cursor over the button to activate the Tool Tip. To draw an object, click on the button, then move the crosshair within the chart area. Click and hold down the left mouse button, then move the mouse to draw the object.

Unlike the Freeform tool in PowerPoint, the Freehand tool remains in freehand mode and never reverts to drawing straight lines like the Freeform tool. The Selection tool enables you to drag a selection box around a number of objects or to select them at one time. This feature also is available in PowerPoint on the Drawing toolbar, but pictures a white arrow rather than a dashed outline of a rectangle.

Use the Reshape button to alter the vertices of a polygon. When the polygon is selected, click on the Reshape button to apply square resizing handles to each vertex of the polygon. You can grab these handles to reshape the polygon. Click on the Reshape button again to remove the square handles from the vertices and return to having the entire object selected.

The Group Objects, Ungroup Objects, Send to Back, Bring to Front, and Shadow buttons on the Microsoft Graph Drawing toolbar work just as they do in PowerPoint. Leave the Drawing toolbar open for the next exercise.

The Color and Pattern buttons on Microsoft Graph's Standard toolbar function to fill objects that you have drawn on the chart. To show how these buttons work, draw a filled ellipse on the chart (see fig. 17.22) using the Ellipse button on the Drawing toolbar.

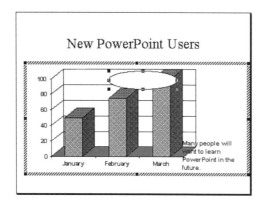

Figure 17.22

Drawing an ellipse on the chart.

The Color button shows a tipped paint can and a block of color. If you want the ellipse to be filled with this color, click on the button. If you want to select another fill color, click on the down arrow next to the Color button to display a palette of colors (see fig. 17.23). Click on the fill color you want and watch the ellipse fill with that color. If you want the ellipse to have no fill, click on None in the color palette.

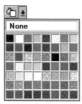

Figure 17.23

Opening the fill color options.

The Pattern button pictures a pencil drawing and a block with no pattern inside. If you want the object to have no pattern, click on the Pattern button. If you want to select a pattern, click on the down arrow and select a pattern from the choices presented on the pattern palette.

To continue following along with the examples, remove the filled ellipse and the text box by selecting each and clicking on Cut on the Standard toolbar or pressing Del.

Editing the Chart

Microsoft Graph makes editing a chart's formatting easy with AutoFormat. To use
AutoFormat, make sure the chart is selected and select **A**utoFormat from the F**o**rmat
menu. The AutoFormat dialog box opens and presents many possible formats for the
current chart (see fig. 17.24).

Figure 17.24

*The AutoFormat
dialog box.*

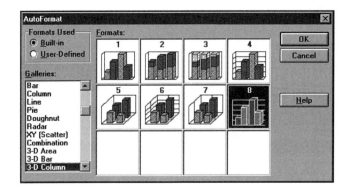

You can change the chart type in this dialog box by making a selection in the **G**aller-
ies box which lists two-dimensional and three-dimensional chart types. Click on 3-D
Column and choose Format 4, then click on OK.

Microsoft Graph enables you to change the 3-D view of a chart. Open the F**o**rmat
menu and select 3-D View. The Format 3-D View dialog box opens and shows a
wireframe of the current chart (see fig. 17.25). To change the elevation at which you
view the chart, click on the up- or down-arrow buttons; the wireframe of the chart
reflects these changes (see fig. 17.26). To change the chart's rotation, click on the
rotate right or left buttons; the outlined chart also reflects these changes. When the
view is where you want it, click on OK. If you want to return to the original view, click
on **D**efault.

Figure 17.25

*The Format 3-D
View dialog box.*

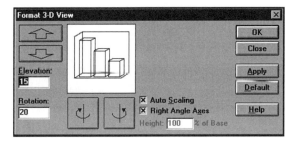

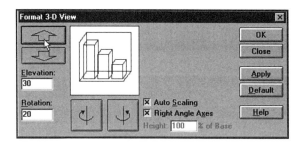

Figure 17.26

Figure 17.26

Changing the chart's elevation.

Microsoft Graph enables you to quickly make many changes to the chart in one dialog box. Suppose you want to change the font and font size for January, February, and March. Click on January on the chart and notice that the axis on which these labels fall acquires black handles. You now can make changes to the text that falls on this axis and changes to the axis itself.

Open the Format menu and choose Font. The Format Axis dialog box opens with the Font tab in front (see fig. 17.27). Notice the tabs running along the top of the dialog box labeled Patterns, Scale, Font, Number, and Alignment. Think of these as tabbed cards that you can pull forward depending on the formatting changes you want to make. You can make changes to all these chart aspects in one dialog box.

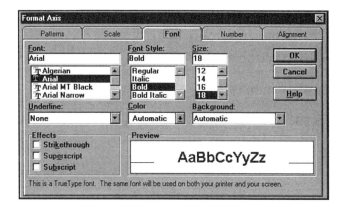

Figure 17.27

The Format Axis dialog box with the Font tab in front.

Tip The Format Object dialog box in PowerPoint uses these same tabs, enabling you to make multiple formatting changes to a selected object in one dialog box.

Make the text bold, then click on the tab labeled Alignment to move the Alignment tab to the front. Select the vertical text facing down (see fig. 17.28). Click on OK to see how the text changes orientation. With the axis still selected, click the right mouse button to access a shortcut menu (see fig. 17.29). You can select Format Axis to open the dialog box again and make changes.

Figure 17.28

Changing the direction of the text.

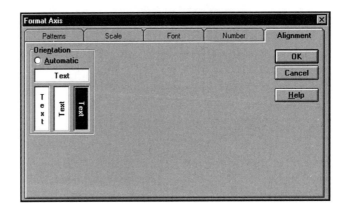

Figure 17.29

Accessing the right-mouse-button shortcut menu.

Tip   Microsoft Graph provides many shortcut menus that open and present options that relate to the selected chart objects. Experiment by selecting chart objects and pressing the right mouse button to see the options on the shortcut menu that appears.

Remove the Drawing toolbar by clicking on the Drawing button on the Standard toolbar. Click on the Datasheet button to show the datasheet.

Changing Graph Colors

PowerPoint shows pictorially on the datasheet which color represents which row or column of information; for example, any information in row 1 is shown by a blue bar on the column chart. To better illustrate this, change the chart type to a 3-D pie by opening the Format menu and selecting AutoFormat. Select 3-D Pie in the Galleries listing and select Format 5 (see fig. 17.30). Notice on the datasheet that a different color pie slice is next to A, B, and C.

New Riders Publishing
INSIDE
SERIES

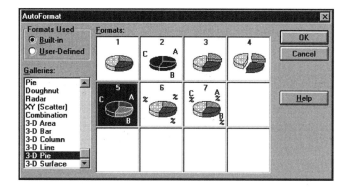

Figure 17.30

Selecting a 3-D Pie chart format.

Remove the datasheet so that you can view the chart. To change the color of an individual pie slice, click directly on the pie slice labeled February to select it (see fig. 17.31). Square handles indicate that the slice is selected. With the cursor on the slice, click the right mouse button to open a shortcut menu.

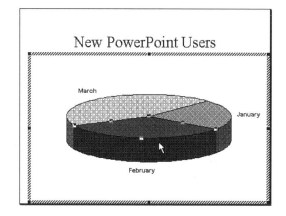

Figure 17.31

Clicking directly on the pie slice to select it.

 Note   You also can access the Format Point dialog box by double-clicking on the pie slice.

From the shortcut menu, select Format Data Point. The Format Data Point dialog box opens and shows the Patterns tab in front (see fig. 17.32). Select a color from the Area color palette. Next, click on the Data Labels tab to bring it forward. On the Data Labels tab, you can choose to show values or percentages on the chart. Leave the current selections and click on OK. The pie slice changes to the new fill color.

Figure 17.32

The Patterns tab in the Format Data Point dialog box.

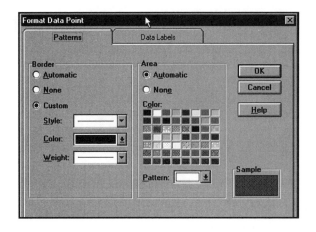

PowerPoint lets you draw attention to a pie slice by pulling the slice out from the pie. With the pie slice still selected, place the cursor in the center of the slice. Hold down the left mouse button, drag the slice down and out from the pie, and release the left mouse button (see fig. 17.33). You can move the pie slice back in by clicking and dragging it back in place.

Figure 17.33

Separating a pie slice to draw attention to it.

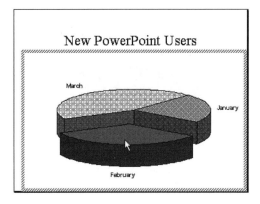

When you are done making any formatting or data changes to the chart, click on the slide outside the chart to return to the PowerPoint presentation. The chart positions itself on the slide. If you want to access Microsoft Graph again to make changes, double-click on the graph. To enlarge the chart once it is on the slide, grab a black resizing handle and adjust the size just as you would for an object.

Using Microsoft Organizational Chart

The next slide in the presentation will include an organizational chart. Making an organizational chart is easy with Microsoft Organizational Chart. Instead of tediously drawing rectangles and lines and adding text, the chart appears before you, waiting for you to fill in names, titles, or comments.

Click on New Slide. From the AutoLayouts select Org Chart (see fig. 17.34). Click to add a title and type **Potential PowerPoint Users**. Double-click where it says *Double click to add org chart* and wait for the application to open over your PowerPoint presentation. It might take some time, so don't be alarmed. When Microsoft Organization Chart opens, the beginnings of a chart already appear in the workspace just as data appears in the Microsoft Graph datasheet. This chart helps to get you started. To work through making a chart, you will select text and retype the information for your presentation.

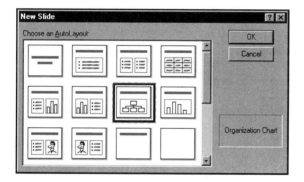

Figure 17.34

Selecting the AutoLayout featuring an organizational chart.

Changing Information

To change the organizational chart title, select the words *Chart Title* with the I-beam cursor and type **Our department structure** (see fig. 17.35). You replace the text in the organizational chart boxes in the same way. Select the top box by clicking on it, then select *Type name here* with the mouse I-beam and replace it with the name **Kelly** (see fig. 17.36).

Figure 17.35

*Replacing the
existing text with
your own.*

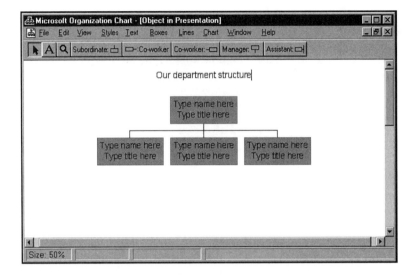

Figure 17.36

*Replacing the text
in the top box.*

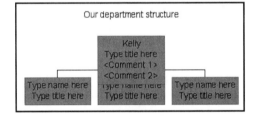

Notice that when you select the text, two lines of text labeled Comment 1 and
Comment 2 appear. You can replace these comments with job functions or any
comments pertaining to the position. Press the down-arrow key to select the next line
of text. Replace *Type title here* with **Department Manager**. Replace *Comment 1* with
Oversees department activity.

When you are done filling in information in the top box, click anywhere outside the
box. The box resizes itself and the label *Comment 2* disappears. Fill in the information
in the other boxes the same way, using the following text for examples:

◆ In the right box at the second level type **Craig**; then type **Section Manager**.

◆ In the left box at the second level type **Carol**; then type **Section Manager**.

To edit text in a box, select the box and click the mouse I-beam inside the box. Make
any edits and click outside the box to implement the changes.

Suppose there were only two people directly reporting to the department manager, so you need to remove one of the three boxes. Click the mouse pointer inside the middle box and press Del. This removes the box while the remaining boxes reposition themselves.

Adding a Box

The buttons at the top of the workspace show which level each box represents. You can tell Kelly is in a Manager position, for example, because his box is identical to the picture on the Manager button.

Kelly has an assistant who needs to be placed on the organizational chart. To add this box, click on the Assistant button and move the mouse pointer into the workspace. Notice the mouse pointer assumes a miniature of the new box to be added on the chart. Because the Assistant reports to Kelly, click the mouse inside Kelly's box. Another box appears as an Assistant (see fig. 17.37). Initially there is no text in the new box. However, click the mouse pointer inside the box to make text appear. Select *Name* and type **Jeff**. Replace *Title* with **Assistant**. Then click outside the box. You can add other boxes to the organization chart in Subordinate, Co-worker, or Manager capacities in the same way you added the Assistant box.

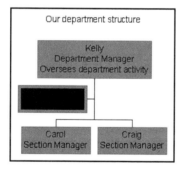

Figure 17.37

The Assistant box appears on the chart under Kelly.

Editing the Chart Style

Fonts or text colors often are used to identify levels of employees on an organizational chart. To change the characteristics of multiple boxes, you must first select them. To select more than one box, click on one box, then hold down the Shift key and click on the other boxes you want to select.

Often, however, there are many boxes with many levels of employees on an organizational chart. Selecting each box individually would be time-consuming. Microsoft Organizational Chart provides a speedy way to select multiple boxes at different levels. Suppose you wanted to select all the boxes except for the Department Manager's. Open the **E**dit menu and choose **S**elect; a number of choices appear (see fig. 17.38). Because you want to select everyone except for the department manager (who is in a Manager box), choose All Non-Managers (see fig. 17.39). At this point, you can make any formatting changes you would like to the selected boxes. Then, click outside the boxes to deselect them.

Figure 17.38

The choices under Select.

Figure 17.39

Selecting all the people under the Department Manager.

Microsoft Organizational Chart enables you to change the format of the boxes at each level. Currently, the bottom two boxes are side by side with lines coming out of the tops of the boxes. To change this format, select the two boxes by holding down the Shift key; then open the **S**tyles menu to display a palette of chart styles (see fig. 17.40). Under Group styles, a button is pressed showing the current style. Click on the button under Group styles showing the boxes lined up vertically to change the group style.

Figure 17.40

The chart styles available.

Now, suppose you want to change the text color and font size for these boxes. With the two boxes selected, open the **T**ext menu and select **C**olor. Choose a color, then click outside the boxes to deselect them and see the text assume that color. To change the font size, select the boxes and select **F**ont from the **T**ext menu. The Font dialog box appears for you to make changes to the text. To change the alignment of the text inside boxes, select the box. Open the **T**ext menu and select the alignment: **L**eft, **R**ight, or **C**enter.

You can stylize any box even further with various borders, colors, or shadows. To make these changes, select a box or boxes and open the **B**oxes menu; a number of choices appear. The first three options pertain to boxes. To change a box border, select Box **B**order and make a selection from the palette of borders. The remaining options work the same way.

To change the chart's background color, open the **C**hart menu and select **B**ackground Color. A palette of colors appears from which you can choose. Remember that this color appears on the slide and might clash with your color scheme.

Changing the Zoom Level

Microsoft Organizational Chart enables you to view the chart at four magnification levels and provides shortcuts to access these levels:

Magnification Level	Shortcut Key
Size to Window	F9
50% of Actual	F10
Actual Size	F11
200% of Actual	F12

You also can access these views through the **C**hart menu. Use the button picturing a magnifying glass on the toolbar to quickly zoom in to the 200% of Actual view. Click on the Zoom button and place the magnifying glass anywhere on the chart. Click the left mouse button to zoom in. When you zoom in, the Zoom button on the toolbar changes to a button picturing an organizational chart (see fig. 17.41). Click on this button and click anywhere on the chart to see the entire chart in the window.

Figure 17.41

The zoomed-in chart. Note that the Zoom button changes to a button with an organizational chart.

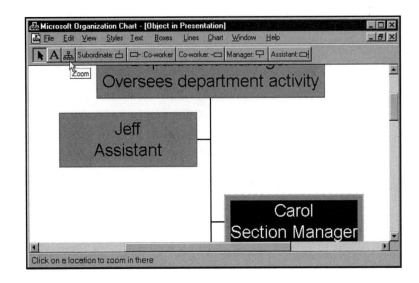

Drawing Tools

Microsoft Organizational Chart provides drawing tools to help you highlight certain areas of the chart. To show the drawing tools on the toolbar, open the **V**iew menu and select Show **D**raw Tools. The four tools appear as the last buttons on the toolbar, as shown in figure 17.42.

Figure 17.42

The Microsoft Organizational Chart drawing tools.

The first drawing tool shows a crosshair and enables you to draw only vertical or horizontal lines. To draw a vertical or horizontal line, click on the button and move the cursor into the workspace; the cursor changes to a crosshair. Hold down the left mouse button and drag the mouse vertically to draw a vertical line, or horizontally to draw a horizontal line. The second drawing tool is used to draw lines, and works just as it does in PowerPoint. Simply click on the button, move the cursor into the workspace to change the cursor to a crosshair, and click and drag the mouse. To change the thickness, style, or color of any line drawn on the organizational chart, select it and then open the **B**oxes menu. The line formatting choices appear at the bottom of the drop-down menu.

Sometimes on an organizational chart, some boxes need to connect to other boxes to show additional relationships. Suppose one of the section managers occasionally reports directly to the department manager; you would want to draw a dotted line to show this unconventional channel of reporting. Microsoft Organizational Chart provides a drawing tool to help you draw these lines without having to draw multiple straight lines. To demonstrate this, click on the dotted line drawing button on the toolbar.

Move the crosshair inside the department manager's box. Click and hold the left mouse button and move the crosshair into one of the section managers' boxes. Notice that the faint outline of a line appears. Release the left mouse button to show the new dotted line (see fig. 17.43). This line shows the additional reporting path.

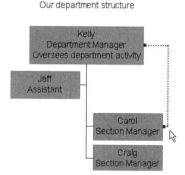

Figure 17.43

Automatically drawing a new dotted line.

You can add a rectangle to the chart by clicking on the Rectangle button and using drawing techniques outlined in Chapter 16, "PowerPoint Tools and Concepts."

The Text Tool button just to the right of the Selection Tool button enables you to add a text label to the chart outside of a chart box. This tool works just like the Text tool in PowerPoint. Simply click on the button and move the mouse I-beam near the chart. Click the left mouse button to anchor a flashing cursor and begin typing.

After you have created and formatted the organizational chart, open the **F**ile menu and choose E**x**it and Return to Presentation to close Microsoft Organizational Chart and return to PowerPoint. The organizational chart appears on the slide, and you can resize it using the square resizing handles.

Adding Clip Art

The images from the Microsoft ClipArt Gallery enable you to enhance a presentation or emphasize a key point. You can rotate or flip clip art like any other object and cut, copy, and paste it. Most of the time, clip art comes into the presentation either too large or in colors that do not compliment a color scheme. PowerPoint enables you to modify clip art extensively to make it work for your presentation. This section discusses resizing clip art and manipulating it to fit your needs.

Recategorizing Clip Art

To begin, add a new slide to your presentation by clicking on New Slide. From the AutoLayouts, select Text & Clip Art. For the title, type **PowerPoint Presentations**. Double-click on the box to access the Microsoft ClipArt Gallery.

The Microsoft ClipArt Gallery opens and presents images in All Categories. Scroll through the categories looking for images you might want to use. Suppose you wanted to use the first image, Professor, from the Academic category in your PowerPoint presentation. You also think this image would work well in future presentations about sales techniques. In fact, moving through all the clip art, you notice that there are a number of images in different categories that would work well in those presentations. Microsoft ClipArt Gallery enables you to recategorize clip art into categories that you specify.

Select the image of the professor by clicking on it; a blue box shows that the image is selected (see fig. 17.44).

Figure 17.44

Choosing clip art.

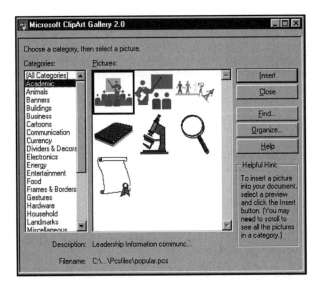

Click on Organize to display the Organize ClipArt dialog box shown in figure 17.45.

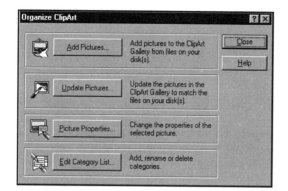

Figure 17.45

The Organize ClipArt dialog box.

Click on **E**dit Category list. This button takes you to the Edit Category List dialog box (see fig. 17.46). In this dialog box you can create a new category and reassign the selected clip art into this category. Click on **N**ew Category. The dialog box asks you to type a name for the new category; type **Sales Presentation**, then click on OK.

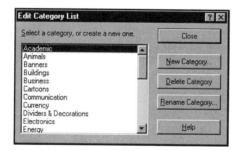

Figure 17.46

The Edit Category List dialog box lets you create a new category.

The new category appears in the category list. Now that it exists, images from any other category can be added to this new category. Close the dialog box and return to the Microsoft ClipArt Gallery dialog box.

Highlight the Academic category and click on the image of the professor that you want to use. After it's selected, click on the image with the right mouse button to see the clip art menu. Choose Picture Properties to display the Picture Properties dialog box (see fig. 17.47). Scroll through the category list to find Sales Presentations and select it to add the picture to that category. Notice that you can place images in multiple categories. Click on the Description text box and type **Man Presenting**. This description will be attached to the image in all the categories in which it exists.

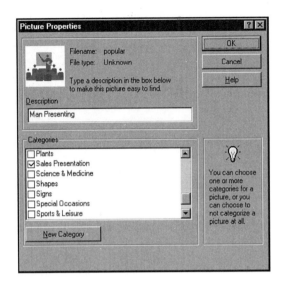

Close the Picture Properties dialog box and return to the ClipArt dialog box. Scroll down to the Sales Presentation category and double-click on the Man Presenting image to bring it into the presentation.

Resizing and Moving Clip Art

When the clip art is selected (a dotted line with sizing handles surrounds the image) you can use the sizing handles to change the size and proportion of the image. Move the pointer over a sizing handle until the pointer turns into a double-arrow. Drag the handle to change the size. To move the image, place the pointer anywhere in the selected image and drag the entire image to a new location.

Recoloring Clip Art

PowerPoint enables you to change the colors incorporated in clip art. Suppose you wanted to change the members of the audience who are green to another color. Select the image by clicking on it, then open the **T**ools menu and select **R**ecolor. The Recolor Picture dialog box opens and presents the original colors and the new colors (see fig. 17.48).

You can choose to change the colors in the picture or change only the fill colors and not the line colors. The Description box tells you this information when you choose either choice in the Change box. Leave the option at **C**olors for this exercise.

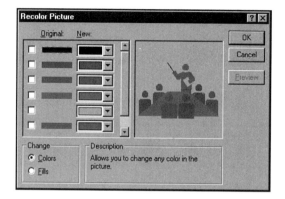

Figure 17.48

The Recolor Picture dialog box.

From the miniature of the image in the dialog box, you can see the green people. Find the matching green color in the **O**riginal column of colors, using the vertical scroll bar if you have to. Open the color palette of the green in the New column by clicking once on the down arrow (see fig. 17.49). Select a new color. The preview box makes the changes so you can see how they look. Press OK when you are finished.

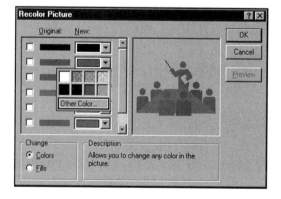

Figure 17.49

Opening the new color options for this color change.

If you don't see a color you like, choose Other Color, which brings up a Color dialog box where you can choose from the entire spectrum of available colors.

Cropping Clip Art

At times you will want to crop an image for a presentation. You could, for example, crop the image to eliminate the audience members if you wanted to make more room on the slide. To crop clip art, select the image, then open the **T**ools menu and choose Crop **P**icture. Move the cursor over the slide and notice that the cursor changes to a cropping pointer. The status bar tells you to move the cropping pointer over a square resizing handle. Move the cropping pointer over the bottom right square resizing handle.

Now, click and drag the pointer up to the man's waist to crop the bottom of the picture (see fig. 17.50). Release the left mouse button to see the cropping. To remove the cropping and return the picture to its full size, drag the bottom right handle back down using the cropping pointer. The cropping pointer will not move any farther down when the picture is at its full size. To turn the cropping pointer off, press Esc.

 Tip A shortcut for cropping is to click the right mouse button over the picture, then choose Crop Picture.

Figure 17.50

Cropping the bottom of the picture.

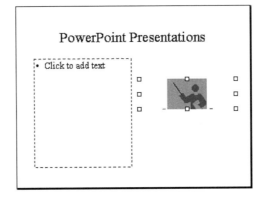

Editing Clip Art

PowerPoint clip art is composed of multiple shapes with different fill colors and shading grouped together. The clip art you bring in from the ClipArt Gallery, however, needs to be converted to PowerPoint clip art to be edited. To illustrate, select the Man Presenting image by clicking on it with the cursor. The image acquires square resizing handles to indicate that it is selected.

From the **D**raw menu, select **U**ngroup. An information box appears, explaining that the image is not a group of objects and will be converted to a PowerPoint object (see fig. 17.51). Doing this, however, will eradicate any linking or embedding information associated with the image. If you did not want to change these associations, you could press Cancel. Click on OK, however, to ungroup the image for editing purposes.

 Stop After you ungroup an image, you cannot use the Recolor or Crop Picture commands through the Tools menu. Do any recoloring or cropping before you begin ungrouping the image.

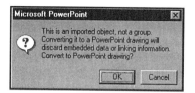

Figure 17.51

The imported object information box.

Notice now that the image has several sets of square resizing handles, one around each item in the image (see fig. 17.52). Click off the slide to remove the resizing handles. Then, click once directly on the two audience members at the foot of the table to select that piece. Move that piece away by clicking and dragging it off to the side. Notice that the table that was hidden by this piece is solid and complete (see fig. 17.53). You can separate all clip art in this way and use it as separate pieces—you now have even more pieces of the clip art than you originally saw in the Clip Art Gallery. Delete the portion of art you pulled off by selecting it and clicking on Cut on the Standard toolbar or pressing Del.

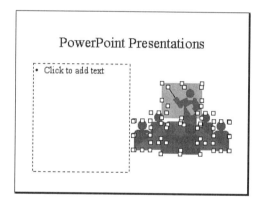

Figure 17.52

Square resizing handles appear around each element of the clip art.

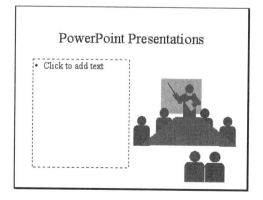

Figure 17.53

Moving one of the elements out of the image.

With some clip art, depending upon the elements in each group, you could ungroup further levels down. Just follow the same procedures.

If you make a mistake and delete part of an image that you didn't want to, you can select **U**ndo from the **E**dit menu or click on the Undo button on the Standard toolbar.

After you've created a smaller image by using the ungroup function, you want to regroup the entire remaining image so that you don't mistakenly move a piece out of place. Grouping the image makes moving it easier. To make sure you select all the images associated with the man, use the Selection tool to drag a selection box around the new image. To drag this box, move the cursor somewhere above the image but not in the title window. If you click in the title window, you will select the title box (which is not associated with the image). Click and drag the mouse to draw an invisible box around the entire image. Release the left mouse button to select all the pieces of the image (see fig. 17.54). Now, open the **D**raw menu and choose **G**roup. The square resizing handles show that the image is now just one piece.

Figure 17.54

Selecting and grouping all the pieces associated with the image you want to use.

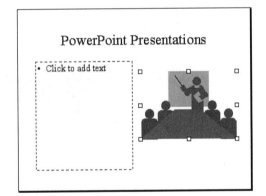

Exploring Further Text Editing

PowerPoint provides many text editing tools that make formatting presentation text quick and easy. Many times you can select multiple lines of text and apply formatting at one time to save time.

For the following exercise, click in the box that reads Click to add text and type the following in a bulleted list:

     ◆   Designer templates

     ◆   Decorator color schemes

     ◆   Professional clip art

This section will show you ways to further manipulate text in presentations.

Moving Text

PowerPoint supports drag and drop. You can use drag and drop to reposition text just as you do in Microsoft Word. In PowerPoint, text can be moved using drag and drop on slides, in the Outline, or on a Notes page. Select the text, then hold down the left mouse button until the drag and drop cursor appears. Drag the text to the new location and release the left mouse button.

You can use the four-headed arrows to move entire lines of text directly on a slide. Suppose you want *Professional clip art* to be the first bullet point. Move the cursor over the bullet in front of *Professional clip art* until it changes to a four-headed arrow. Hold down the left mouse button and slowly move the four-headed arrow up. Do not release the left mouse button.

Notice that the four-headed arrow turns into a two-headed arrow and a horizontal line moves in between the bullet points. This horizontal line shows to where the selected text will reposition when you release the left mouse button. Release the left mouse button when the vertical line is at the top of the bulleted list and watch this bullet point assume the top position. You can demote text using the same techniques, except that you move the four-headed arrow to the right. Select the second bullet point and move the four-headed arrow to the right (see fig. 17.55).

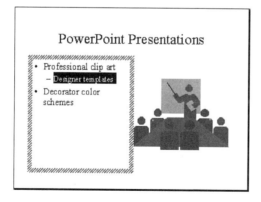

Figure 17.55

Demoting a bullet point.

The subpoint assumes the formatting that is defined in the slide master. You also can use the Promote and Demote buttons on the Formatting toolbar to indent text. With the subpoint still selected, promote the subpoint by clicking on the Promote button on the Formatting toolbar (see fig. 17.56).

Figure 17.56

*Promoting a
bullet item.*

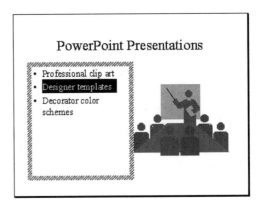

Spacing Lines

PowerPoint automatically uses single line spacing for text. You can override this spacing using the Line **S**pacing command from the F**o**rmat menu. Select all the bullet points in the text box by moving the cursor over the first bullet until it changes to a four-headed arrow. Click the left mouse button to select the line of text. Move the cursor over the third bullet until it turns to a four-headed arrow, then hold down the Shift key and click the left mouse button to select all three bullet points. With these bullet points selected, select Line **S**pacing from the F**o**rmat menu to display the Line Spacing dialog box (see fig. 17.57).

Figure 17.57

*The Line Spacing
dialog box.*

You can choose to change the line spacing or the spacing before or after paragraphs. To change the line spacing to 1.5 lines between paragraphs, click the up arrow in the line spacing box until 1.5 shows or simply type **1.5**. To see a preview of the spacing, click on **P**review. You might need to move the Line Spacing dialog box off the text box to view the preview. Click on OK to implement the new line spacing. Adjusting interparagraph spacing is particularly effective when you want very little text to fill a lot of slide space.

Changing Case

PowerPoint enables you to switch through different cases to save formatting time. This function works the same way as in Microsoft Word. With the three bullet points still selected, open the Format menu and choose Change Case. The Change Case dialog box appears and provides five options (see fig. 17.58).

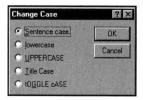

Figure 17.58

The Change Case dialog box offers five choices.

These options are shown in the dialog box just as they will appear on the slide. Select lowercase, for example, and click on OK; the slide text adjusts to reflect this choice. PowerPoint enables you to toggle through Sentence case, lowercase, and UPPER-CASE using Shift+F3, just as in Microsoft Word. With the text currently selected, press Shift+F3 until the text turns to UPPERCASE. Using the Change Case function is especially helpful when you have a lot of text that needs to be changed.

Adding and Removing Periods

PowerPoint helps you to add or remove periods on multiple lines of text with one click. With the three bullet points selected, open the Format menu and choose Periods. The Periods dialog box opens and asks whether you would like to Add Periods or Remove Periods (see fig. 17.59). Click on Add Periods and click on OK. Periods appear at the end of every bullet point. Click anywhere off the slide to deselect the text. To continue, use the vertical scroll bar to move back to the title slide.

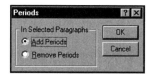

Figure 17.59

The Periods dialog box.

Using the Slide Sorter Toolbar

After you have created slides for a presentation, PowerPoint supplies tools to help you add even more features to the delivery. Also, PowerPoint enables you to hide slides that supply information to answer audience questions or provide backup information to clarify a key point.

The Slide Sorter view conveniently helps you to view all the slides in a presentation with slide numbers and to insert, delete, or rearrange slides. You also can copy and paste slides. The Slide Sorter toolbar supplies the additional tools you need to apply slide transitions, create build slides, and hide slides. You can customize and move this toolbar like the other PowerPoint toolbars.

Change to Slide Sorter view by clicking on the Slide Sorter View button in the bottom left corner of the workspace to continue.

Slide Transitions

PowerPoint slide transitions add excitement during a slide show and interest to a presentation. Instead of simply clicking through the slides, you can make a slide enter the screen from the left side or fade out when moving to the next slide. To add a slide transition to a slide, select the slide by clicking on it. A black box indicates that the slide is selected. Click on the Transition button on the Slide Sorter toolbar (see fig. 17.60).

Figure 17.60

The Slide Sorter toolbar.

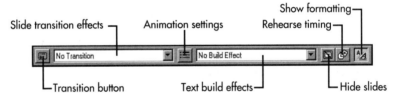

The Transition dialog box appears and shows that there currently is no transition selected for this slide. To view the effects available for the selected slide, open the **E**ffect list box by clicking the cursor on the down arrow (see fig. 17.61). Use the vertical scroll bar to view additional effects. When you get ready to make a selection, watch the picture of the dog in the bottom right corner of the dialog box. This picture illustrates the transition so that you can get a preview. Select Checkerboard Across and watch the picture. You can regulate the speed of the transition in the Transition box: choose Slow, Medium, or Fast. The picture will preview the speed combined with the selected transition.

The Transition dialog box also enables you to decide if you want to move through a slide show using the mouse buttons or if you want the slides to change after a certain number of seconds. You can type directly into the box. When you have made your selections, click on OK.

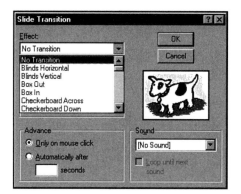

Figure 17.61

The list of available effects for slide transitions.

A transition icon appears under the slide to show you that there is a transition assigned to the slide (see fig 17.62). The Transition Effects box on the Slide Sorter toolbar shows you that Checkerboard Across is the current transition. If you want to change the transition, you can access the Transition Effects list box on the toolbar and make another selection. The selected slide will show you what the transition looks like when you make a selection.

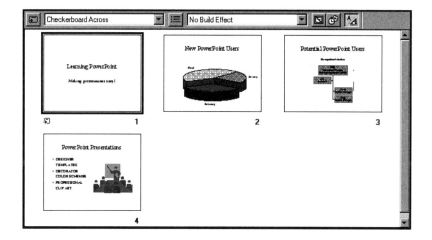

Figure 17.62

The Transition Effects box means a transition has been assigned to the slide.

Build Slides

Build slides help the audience to focus on one slide point at a time. Bullet points appear on the slide one by one, and only the most current point is shown in the default text color. The other bullet points are dimmed to focus the audience's attention. You can change any slide with bulleted text to a build slide.

Select Slide 4 and put your pointer on the **B**uild Slide Text item on the **T**ools menu to see the cascaded list shown in figure 17.63. To access additional choices, choose Other (see fig 17.64).

Figure 17.63

The Build Slide Text choices.

Figure 17.64

Choosing a text slide animation effect.

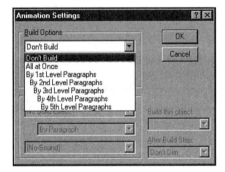

To see how the build slide looks, select it and click on the Slide Show button at the bottom left corner of the workspace. Remember that the screen momentarily goes black, but the first selected slide will eventually appear with the slide transition, if it has one (see fig. 17.65).

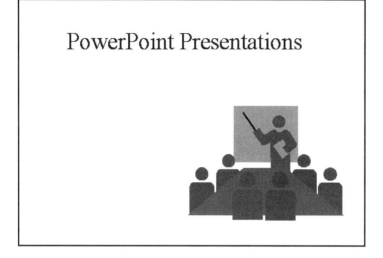

Figure 17.65

The selected slide before any text is flown in from the left.

Click (or press N) to make the first bullet point appear. Notice that it appears as defined by the Build Effects selection. Click again to evoke the second bullet point and watch the first point dim. Continue to click through all the bullet points until you return to the Slide Sorter view.

To remove the Build Slide settings on a slide, select the slide and click on the Build button on the Slide Sorter toolbar. In the Build dialog box, remove the check mark in front of **B**uild Body Text and click on OK.

 Note   Slide transitions and build slides can be used only for an on-screen show on a computer monitor or video screen.

Hide Slide

At times you might want to hide a slide during a slide show. For example, you might decide you don't want to share the information, but want to hold on to the slide for now. Instead of quickly clicking through the slide, which looks unprofessional and risks the audience reading the information, PowerPoint enables you to hide slides.

To hide a slide, select the slide and click on the Hide Slide button on the Slide Sorter toolbar. Notice that a slash mark appears over the slide number to indicate that this slide is hidden. To remove the Hide Slide instructions, select the hidden slide and click on the Hide Slide button again.

Show Formatting

Sometimes in the Slide Sorter view, you simply want to add transitions or create build slides. You cannot edit the information on the slides in this view. If a presentation includes many slides with a lot of clip art, working in the Slide Sorter view can become tedious and slow. PowerPoint enables you to remove the slide formatting so that you do not slow down. Click on the Show Formatting button on the Slide Sorter toolbar to remove the formatting.

Notice that the slide titles remain in the default font, so that you can identify the slides. You now can perform any Slide Sorter toolbar function more rapidly. To return to a formatted view, click on the Show Formatting button again; this feature switches on and off.

Using PowerPoint Presentation Help

PowerPoint provides many tools to help you perfect your delivery and to supply backup information if you get stuck. PowerPoint can track the length of a slide discussion, for example, or access files containing supportive data during a presentation.

Rehearse New Timings

Often you do not know how long it will take to show an individual slide until you are actually making the presentation. This inaccuracy can lead to rushing through the last few slides in a presentation or completely skipping over information. As you rehearse a presentation, PowerPoint can keep track of how much time you take to cover the information on a slide.

To use Rehearse New Timings, select Slide **S**how from the **V**iew menu to display the Slide Show dialog box (see fig. 17.66). In this dialog box, you can choose to show all the slides or only specific slides. You also can select how to advance through slides; choose **M**anual Advance if you want to use the mouse buttons or keyboard. After you have rehearsed the timing on each slide, you can choose to use those times to control the slide advancement if you do not want to use the mouse or keyboard.

Figure 17.66

The Slide Show dialog box.

To rehearse new timings, select **R**ehearse New Timings and click on **S**how; the Slide Show begins immediately. A timer appears in the bottom right corner of the first slide and begins timing as soon as the slide appears (see fig. 17.67).

Figure 17.67

The timer begins as soon as the first slide appears.

Talk through the slide just as you would during a presentation. When you are done covering a slide, advance to the next one.

When you have worked through all the slides, a dialog box tells you the total time for the presentation (see fig. 17.68). The dialog box also asks if you want to go to the Slide Sorter view and see the timing for each slide. Click on **Y**es. In the Slide Sorter view, the times appear below the slides for your reference (see fig. 17.69).

Figure 17.68

A dialog box tells you the length of your presentation.

Figure 17.69

The times for each slide are displayed.

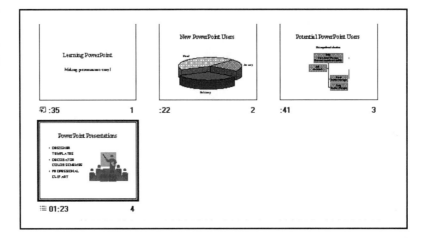

Drill Down

PowerPoint utilizes a *multiple document interface,* meaning that it enables you to access other files while it is currently running. Often, as a presenter you would like to have critical information at your disposal when an audience member asks a question or a concept is not understood. Drill Down enables you to access information directly from a slide in a presentation without closing PowerPoint and opening another application.

If someone asks what formula was used to calculate a number that is graphed on Slide 2, for example, you can open the spreadsheet from which you pulled the information. To add a Drill Down file, select Slide 2 and change to the Slide view. Select **O**bject from the **I**nsert menu to display the Insert Object dialog box. Select Create from **F**ile (see fig. 17.70).

Figure 17.70

Using Create from File in the Insert Object dialog box.

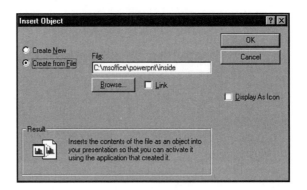

In the Fil**e** box, enter the path and file name of the file you want to be able to access from the slide. Click on **B**rowse if you want to find the file using the Browse dialog box (see fig. 17.71).

Figure 17.71

Using the Browse dialog box to select a file.

Select **D**isplay as Icon in the Insert Object dialog box because you want only an icon displayed on the slide, not the entire file. The default icon appears in the bottom right corner of the Insert Object dialog box. If you do not care for this icon, select Change Icon in the Insert Object dialog box to view other choices. Click on OK in the Insert Object dialog box. The icon appears on the slide.

To move the icon to a more inconspicuous place, move the cursor over the icon. Click and drag the icon to the bottom left corner of the slide. To access the drill down file during a presentation, double-click on the icon. You can have multiple drill down files on one slide.

Branching Presentations

PowerPoint enables you to branch to another presentation during a Slide Show to access other slides. You can choose to branch to a presentation when you click on an object or to go immediately to the other presentation.

To branch presentations during a slide show, move to the slide from which you want to branch. Open the additional presentation by clicking on the Open button on the Standard toolbar. When the other presentation opens, select the slides you want to show and click on the Copy button on the Standard toolbar. Open the **F**ile menu and select **C**lose to leave the presentation. When you return to the first presentation, open the **E**dit menu and select Paste **S**pecial. From the Paste Special dialog box (see fig.

17.72), select PowerPoint Presentation Object, then click on OK. On the current slide, a miniature of the first slide from the branched presentation appears (see fig. 17.73).

Figure 17.72

The Paste Special dialog box.

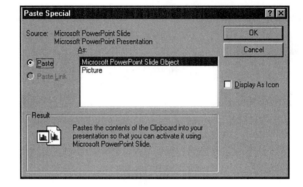

Figure 17.73

A slide from the branched presentation appears.

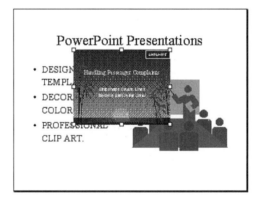

You can resize the miniature slide using the square resizing handles, or move it anywhere on the current slide. This picture appears on the slide during a slide show (see fig. 17.74). To branch to the other presentation, click on the picture. After all the slides from the branched presentation are shown, you return to the original presentation and can continue.

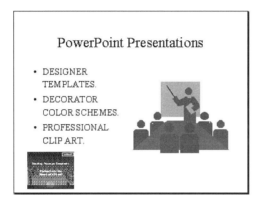

Figure 17.74

The current presentation slide with the branched presentation slide in the corner.

Pack and Go

Pack and Go lets you show a PowerPoint presentation without loading all the PowerPoint application files on a computer. Suppose you want to take a presentation on a sales call to show on a computer monitor. You don't have room to take a computer but know there is a computer and color monitor where the sales call is taking place. You also know that the location does not have the PowerPoint software.

PowerPoint Viewer software files fit on a single disk. You can take the software and your presentation file and load both on the on-site computer. Don't worry if the fonts you use in a presentation are not on the computer you intend to use. PowerPoint temporarily installs the fonts used in a presentation on the computer then removes them after you are finished presenting.

To pack up your presentation and take it on the road, choose Pack and Go from the **F**ile menu. The program is a Wizard, which walks you through all the steps you'll need. It begins with the opening screen seen in figure 17.75.

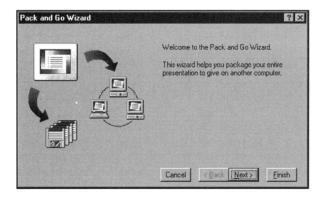

Figure 17.75

The Pack and Go Wizard begins.

Press Next to move to the next step, which is to pick the presentation you want to take. If there is a presentation loaded in PowerPoint, the dialog box defaults to it (see fig. 17.76). You can also follow the instructions to pack up multiple presentations. (If you have branched slides and you don't pack up the presentation to which they're attached, you will not be able to branch when you present your show on the road.) Press **N**ext when you have finished.

Figure 17.76

Pick a presentation.

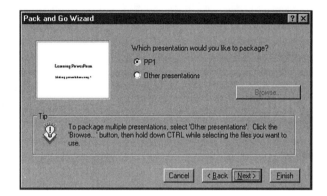

Now you have to decide where to put the files that you will need to port the presentation to another computer (see fig. 17.77). Eventually, in order to move the files, they will have to be on a disk, but you might want to put them on your hard drive in a directory you've pre-made (so you can copy the directory to a disk whenever you're travelling with your presentation). For now, choose drive A and press Next.

Figure 17.77

Picking a target for the files.

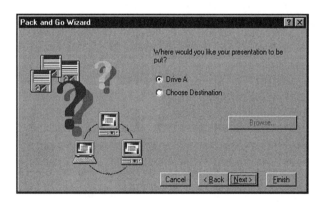

The next Wizard dialog box asks if you want to include linked files and fonts with the presentation or embed the fonts. If you include the fonts, you don't have to worry whether the computer you'll use has those fonts. If you embed the fonts, those fonts have to be available (but the files are smaller). It's safer to include the linked files and fonts. Press **N**ext when you have made your choice.

The next Wizard page asks whether you want to include the PowerPoint Viewer with your portable presentation (see fig. 17.78). If you do, your presentation must be run on a computer that operates with Windows NT or Windows 95. If you are going to run your presentation on a computer that is running Windows 3.1, you will have to provide the Viewer program from that system. Press **N**ext to move on.

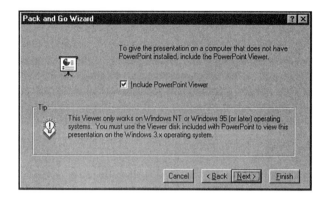

Figure 17.78

Deciding on packing up the Viewer.

The last screen displays, explaining that your presentation files will be compressed and moved to drive A (see fig. 17.79). Press **F**inish to begin the transfer.

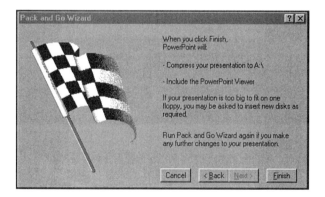

Figure 17.79

Getting ready to create the disk.

If you make changes to your presentation, remember to run Pack and Go again.

Part IV

Schedule+

Schedule+ Quick Start

Microsoft Office includes a comprehensive program that lets you get control of your personal information, such as contacts, appointments, tasks, projects, and meetings. Through Schedule+, one of the Office applications, you can run your life instead of letting it run you. In this chapter you'll learn how to get going with Schedule+ quickly:

◆ Create your Schedule+ database

◆ Add and modify information, such as your contact list

◆ Set appointments

◆ Create projects and events

◆ View your schedule in a variety of ways

◆ Print the information in Schedule+

There are many different Personal Information Managers (PIMs) on the market from which you can choose. However, none combine the power of Schedule+ along with its unparalleled integration with the rest of your application suite, Microsoft Office.

Software that manages your personal information—so-called Personal Information Managers (PIMs)—are a very popular software category. They combine the utility of the traditional paper-based calendar with the power of your computer, and you end up with a tool that is much more powerful and useful than paper-based systems. Some examples of how they're better than paper-based systems include:

◆ View your schedule in many different ways, looking at your daily schedule, weekly, monthly, or in a to-do format. And you don't need to reenter your information in order to see these different views as you would in a paper system; the software does it for you automatically.

◆ Maintain a list of your contacts, and use that list for mailings, address labels, or envelopes with Word's mail merge feature.

◆ Assign contacts to projects, and track the status of projects.

◆ Integrate the creation of meetings in Schedule+ with Microsoft Exchange to automatically schedule meetings with others in your organization.

◆ Use Schedule+ on a network, letting others see information that you make available, or letting an assistant manage your schedule while still having complete access to it yourself.

◆ Print your information, contacts, appointments, project status, in many different formats.

◆ Easily exchange your information with Personal Digital Assistants (PDAs) such as the Hewlett-Packard 95LX or the Sharp Wizard. You can even download your information into a special wristwatch made by Timex in partership with Microsoft!

And these are just a few of the advantages to computer-based personal information management. However, if you're used to a paper-based system it will take a commitment on your part in learning the transition to using a computer-based tool. You'll find, though, that the effort involved is worth it.

In this chapter, you learn the basics of Schedule+ so that you can get to work with it right away.

Understanding Schedule+ Databases

Schedule+ stores all of your information in special database files. These files use the extension SCD. When you start Schedule+ for the first time, you are asked to log on to the program, as shown in figure 18.1.

Figure 18.1

The Schedule+ Logon dialog box.

When you log on to Schedule+, it uses your name to locate your schedule file and, if necessary, get your password before giving you access to the file.

If this is your first time using Schedule+, it brings up a dialog box after you log on in which you can choose the name to store your new schedule database, shown in figure 18.2. Accept the default name, which is based on your login name, and click on the **O**pen button to create your new database.

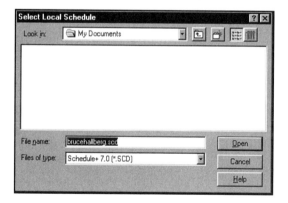

Figure 18.2

Use the Select Local Schedule dialog box to open an existing schedule database or create a new one.

After creating your database, Schedule+ opens and shows you the Daily tab. Figure 18.3 shows you the main parts of the Schedule+ screen.

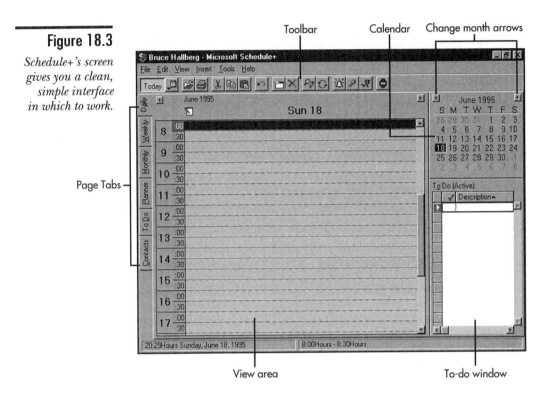

Figure 18.3

Schedule+'s screen gives you a clean, simple interface in which to work.

Toolbar   Calendar   Change month arrows

Page Tabs

View area   To-do window

You use the tabs on the left side of the screen to choose what information you see. Click on each tab to see that page of information. You can also add or remove tabs, so that the tabs you do see reflect the way you work.

The calendar has several uses. First, it displays a small overview of the dates in the current month. But you also use it to change the month that the tabbed pages display. Click on the arrows above the calendar to move forward and backward by a month, and right-click on the calendar to enter a specific date to which to jump. Take a minute to review the Schedule+ toolbar, detailed in table 18.1.

TABLE 18.1
Schedule+ Toolbar

Icon	Name	Function
Today	Select Today	Immediately jumps your current view to today's date.
📅	Go To Date	Brings up a calendar display in which you can choose a new date to view.

Icon	Name	Function
	Open	Opens a new Schedule+ database.
	Print	Activates the Print dialog box.
	Cut	Cuts selected data onto the clipboard.
	Copy	Copies selected data onto the clipboard.
	Paste	Pastes the clipboard data to your cursor location.
	Undo	Reverses your last action.
	Insert Item	Creates a new item. Depending on the view you're looking at, this button creates a new appointment, task, or contact.
	Delete	Deletes the highlighted entry.
	Edit	Edits the highlighted entry.
	Recurring	Creates a recurring appointment.
	Reminder	Sets a reminder for the selected entry.
	Private	If using a network, makes the selected information private so others don't see it.
	Tentative	Makes the current entry tentative.
	Timex Watch Wizard	Walks you through the process of downloading information to a special Timex watch.

Note You can purchase a special Timex-built digital watch that can accept data downloaded from Schedule+. These watches are available at Timex dealers and most computer software stores. With them, you can download phone numbers or appointments that you need to keep handy during the day. Then, during the day, the watch will remind you of appointments or display needed phone numbers.

Adding, Editing, and Deleting Items

Now that you know the basics of the Schedule+ interface, it's time to get busy and add some of your information to the program. There are 5 basic types of entries that you create:

◆ **Appointments.** These are specific commitments by date and by time. They have a duration that you select and also can be made recurring where Schedule+ automatically shows them for repeating intervals that you select (for example, weekly, every other week, every Monday, and so forth). Schedule+ can also pop up reminder messages to keep you on track with your appointments.

◆ **Tasks.** Most people would call Schedule+'s task entries "to-do" items. They are not tied to specific times and days, although you can set beginning and ending days if you wish. Schedule+ helps you keep track of the percentage each task is complete, and lets you mark completed items. Think of Schedule+ tasks as a virtual To-Do pad that you keep on your computer instead of the paper-based one that most people use.

◆ **Projects.** These are very simple entries that consist of just a name and priority. Projects are used (if you wish) to group your tasks together.

◆ **Contacts.** Here, you enter the information (phone numbers, addresses, etc.) on the people you know and work with. Space is also provided to track personal information like spouse name, birthday, and so forth, on top of the business information you want to keep.

◆ **Events.** You use event entries for things that are date-specific, but not time-specific. For instance, if you are scheduled to be at a trade show for a week, you would create a 5 day event to cover this. Similarly, create your vacations as events. Schedule+ also lets you create annual events that automatically repeat each year.

Note Schedule+ has some different menu options and screen displays depending on whether you are using it in stand-alone mode on a single computer or in network mode. This chapter and the one that follows assume stand-alone mode, while Chapter 20 shows you the additional features available in network mode.

Adding Appointments

There are lots of ways to enter new appointments into Schedule+. The most obvious is to activate the **I**nsert menu and choose **A**ppointment. You can also click on the Insert button in the toolbar if you're looking at a schedule display, such as the daily view. Finally, you can double-click on a time slot in any of the appointment views. In any event, choosing any of these methods displays the Appointment dialog box shown in figure 18.4.

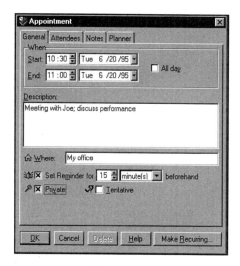

Figure 18.4

Use the Appointment dialog box to create new appointments. Each tabbed screen lets you add different types of information.

Use the drop-down lists and arrows to select the beginning and ending time for the appointment, and type the description of the appointment into the **D**escription field. If necessary, you'll want to type in the location for the appointment in the **W**here field.

If you set the Set Re**m**inder for check box, Schedule+ will let you choose how long before the appointment it will remind you about it with a message box.

Stop If you are using Schedule+ on a network and others can see your schedule for the purposes of scheduling meetings with you, be sure to check the Pri**v**ate check box on items that you would prefer they not see.

The Attendees tab of the Appointment dialog box does not function in stand-alone mode. Its features are covered in Chapter 20.

The Notes tab lets you type in any detailed notes about the appointment.

Finally, the Planner tab lets you get a quick overview of your schedule surrounding the appointment, as shown in figure 18.5.

Figure 18.5

Use the Planner tab to see other commitments that are near this appointment.

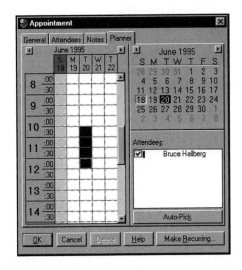

The Planner tab also lets you easily reschedule the appointment with your mouse. Simply drag your mouse over displayed time slots to change the appointment time, as shown in figure 18.5.

Adding Tasks

Tasks are added much the same way as appointments. You can use the Insert menu and activate the Tasks command or you can double-click on a row in the To Do window. When you do either, you see the Task dialog box shown in figure 18.6.

Most of the information you enter for tasks is not used by Schedule+. Instead, most fields are provided for you to keep key information on the task at your fingertips. In the Task dialog box, you enter the following information:

◆ An ending date for the task. You also can specify how long before the ending date the task should begin.

◆ If you select the Mark as done after end date check box, then the task will be automatically marked as completed once the end date passes. Be careful with this option, as it might prematurely mark an item as being done when in reality it is not.

◆ Type a description for the task in the **D**escription field.

◆ If you have defined projects, you can select the associated project using the Project drop-down list.

◆ The Pri**o**rity field lets you set your priority for the project. You can select from 1–9 and A–Z. Schedule+ doesn't use this information; it's for your purposes.

◆ Choose to set a reminder with the Set re**m**inder check box.

◆ If this task will repeat in regular intervals, click on the Make **R**ecurring button to define the intervals.

Schedule+ also lets you keep status information on the task on the Status tab, shown in figure 18.7.

Figure 18.6

Use the Task dialog box to create a new task.

While it might appear that the fields in the Status tab function in some way in Schedule+, most do not. Instead, you can type whatever values you need in order to keep track of the task. The exception to this is the **C**ontact field, in which you choose one of your defined contacts to associate with the task. Schedule+ lets you see tasks sorted by associated contact. This can be a valuable tool for a manager to keep track of projects being carried out by their direct reports.

Figure 18.7

Use the Status tab of the Task dialog box to track information about your project.

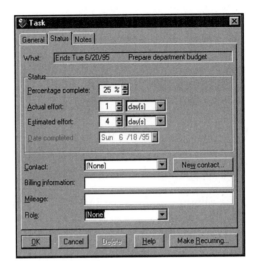

Tip When viewing tasks in Schedule+, you can right-click on a task and choose Appt. from Task on the pop-up menu to conveniently create an appointment based on the task.

Contacts

If your desk is like mine, you have business cards and scribbled notes scattered all over the place, most of which contain crucial and important information about the people you do business with or work with. Or maybe your Rolodex is crammed with cards and notes that you never seem to get caught up on.

Even if you do stay organized, it probably takes you more time than you would like to track down a phone number or address for someone. Schedule+ can help you with this with its contact management features.

Create a contact by accessing the **I**nsert menu and choose **C**ontact. Or, if you're viewing your contact list, click on the Insert button on the toolbar. You see the dialog box shown in figure 18.8.

In these connected times, your contacts will have many different phone numbers that you'll need to track on the Phone page of the Contact dialog box.

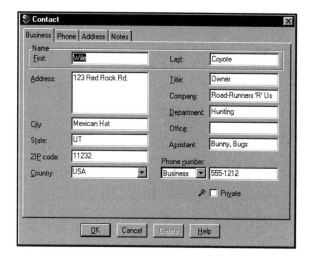

Figure 18.8

Enter all the crucial information about your contacts using the Contact dialog box. Here, you see the Business page.

Successful salespeople keep track of personal information about people they work with. Remembering that spouse's name can really help out sometimes. Alternately, if you are using Schedule+ to keep track of people you know at home, you'll want to use it to keep track of birthdays and other personal information. You do all this on the Address page of the Contact dialog, as well as the Notes page for items not included in the Address page. You can see the Address page in figure 18.9.

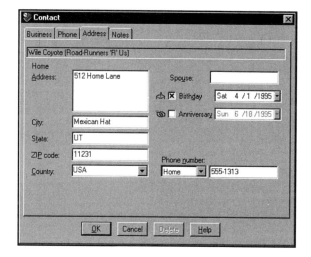

Figure 18.9

Use the Address page to keep track of personal information about your contacts.

Projects

Projects are very simple entries in Schedule+. They are merely categories with which you organize your tasks. You create new projects by accessing the **I**nsert menu and choosing **P**roject. You then see the dialog box shown in figure 18.10.

Figure 18.10

Create projects to organize all of your tasks.

 Note If you designate a project as Pri**v**ate, all associated tasks will also be made private.

Events

Events are day-specific entries that do not have an associated time. You use them to block out things like trips, vacations, all-day conferences, and the like. Create new events by choosing **E**vents in the **I**nsert menu. This activates the Event dialog box shown in figure 18.11.

Figure 18.11

Events let you block out entire days. They appear in your different calendar views of your data, usually at the top of the page.

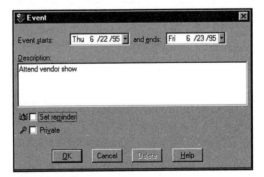

Editing Items

All of the items you enter can be edited easily using one of two methods:

◆ Select the item, click the right mouse button to activate the pop-up menu, and choose Edit Item.

◆ Select the item, access the **E**dit menu and then choose **E**dit Item or press the shortcut key, Ctrl+E.

Using either method, the original dialog box for the item is displayed in which you can change the information about the item.

Deleting Items

Deleting any item is much the same as editing it. You can select the item and click the right mouse button on it, choosing Delete Item from the pop-up menu. You also can select the item and click on the Delete button in the toolbar (it's the button that looks like a red "X" mark).

Tip   If you accidentally delete an item, you can click on the Undo button to restore it. However, only one deletion or change can be undone, so make sure you undo an accidental deletion immediately.

Printing Items

It might not be convenient for you to travel with a computer that's running Schedule+ in order to access your itinerary or appointment book. Or, perhaps you're an assistant who needs to print out appointment data for your boss. Or maybe you want to print out a telephone listing to keep handy near the phone. In any event, you will often need to commit your information to paper.

Schedule+'s printing function is remarkably comprehensive and allows you much flexibility in choosing your printed output. Select **P**rint from the **F**ile menu or press Ctrl+P to access the Print dialog box shown in figure 18.12.

There are a number of pre-defined forms you can print by selecting any of those listed in the Print la**y**out window. You can also choose from several paper forms that are specially designed to hold scheduling information and insert into a variety of schedule binders; choose your form in the Paper Fo**r**mat drop-down list.

After you've made your printing choices, click on **O**K to print or Preview to see what the result will look like.

Figure 18.12

You have lots of choices when printing the data contained in Schedule+.

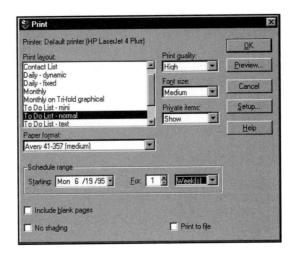

Learning Schedule+

Building on the core skills and concepts you learned in Chapter 18, you now learn to take advantage of some of Schedule+'s more advanced features, such as the following:

◆ Controlling Schedule+'s settings to work the way you do

◆ Changing the tabs that show you different views of your information

◆ Mastering the various views of your data

◆ Exchanging your data with other PIMs and PDAs

◆ Doing a mail merge using your Schedule+ contact list and Word

◆ Archiving your Schedule+ data

Schedule+ is a rich application with many features and flexibilities to help keep your schedule on track. Despite its power, however, it is easy to use once you understand what is possible and how it works. You learn about these capabilities in this chapter.

Setting Up Schedule+

Before really diving into Schedule+, you'll want to spend some time changing its settings so that it accommodates your preferences, rather than the other way around. Doing so will make your transition to a computer-based PIM easier and more efficient.

Note The features and screens in this chapter assume that you're using Schedule+ in stand-alone mode. Differences that occur when running in network mode are covered in Chapter 20, "Networking Schedule+."

You access Schedule+'s settings by pulling down the **T**ools menu and choosing the **O**ptions command. This displays the Options notebook shown in figure 19.1.

Figure 19.1

Use the Options notebook to control how Schedule+ works.

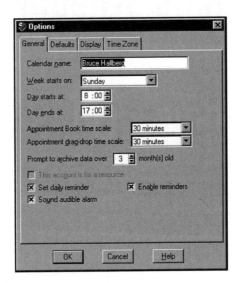

Table 19.1 reviews the settings on the General screen.

TABLE 19.1
Options Notebook—General Page

Option name	What it does
Calendar **n**ame	Stores the name of this calendar.

Option name	What it does
Week starts on	You can choose any day of the week to start the calendar on. This choice determines the left-most date in the layout of most calendar views, such as the Date Navigator.
D**a**y starts at	Enter the beginning time for your appoint-ments. Earlier times are grayed out in most views, but can still be used.
Day **e**nds at	Enter the last time for your appointments. Later times are grayed, but you can still use them.
A**p**pointment Book time scale	Here, you can choose the most appropriate time scale for your appointment book views. For instance, if you bill your time in 1/10th hour increments, you can choose a 6 minute time scale so that your calendar matches your billing method.
Appointment **d**rag-drop time scale	This choice controls in what increments you can drag the handles for an appointment to change its start or end time. You can choose 10, 15, or 30 minute increments.
Prompt to **a**rchive data over *x* months old	Schedule+ can automatically remind you to archive old data so that your disk space require ments do not grow too large. See the section on archiving later in this chapter for details.
Set dail**y** reminder	Selecting this check box causes a reminder to automatically appear when you start Schedule+ that shows you your tasks for the day.
Ena**b**le reminders	If you want Schedule+ to remind you of appoint-ments with a pop-up message or alarm sound, this check box must be selected.
So**u**nd audible alarm	If you would like a sound along with a pop-up reminder, select this check box.

The next page in the Options notebook, Defaults, lets you control the assumptions Schedule+ makes when you create appointments, tasks, and projects. Figure 19.2 shows you the Defaults page. The choices you make on this page are automatically filled in for you when you create the items mentioned in each setting. For instance, setting a Default task **p**riority of 3 will cause 3 to be selected for you when you create new tasks, which you are then free to change on an item-by-item basis.

Figure 19.2

The Defaults page controls the assumptions Schedule+ makes when you create new items.

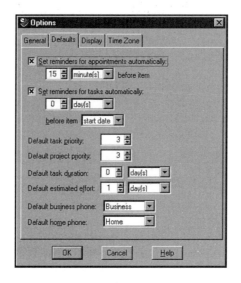

The third page in the Options notebook (see fig. 19.3), Display, controls the appearance of Schedule+. Use the drop-down list boxes to choose colors for your display. Other options on this page are detailed in table 19.2.

Figure 19.3

Use the Display page to change how Schedule+ appears on your screen.

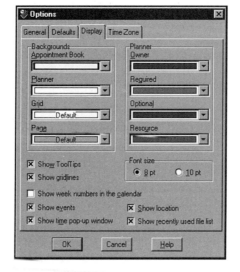

TABLE 19.2
Options Notebook—General Page

Option name	What it does
Show ToolTips	When selected, Schedule+ will show you the names of buttons in the toolbar when you leave your mouse pointer on them for a couple of seconds.
Show gridlines	This setting controls the lines that separate entries in some views. You can fit more information on your screen by turning this option off, but your display might not be as readable.
Font size	Here, the tradeoff is between readability with 10-pt text and fitting more information on your screen with 8-pt text.
Show week numbers in the calendar	If selected, the week number will appear to the left of each week in the calendar. Weeks are numbered from 1–52 starting on January 1.
Show events	Recall that events are not time-specific and therefore do not show up in your appointment calendars. Selecting this option causes events to display above or in your calendar views.
Show time pop-up window	When selected, and you click in an appointment view, the time will pop up near the mouse pointer to show you what you've selected.
Show location	You can always enter locations for appointments, but choosing this check box will show that information in your schedule views. If you don't need to see in your schedule views, turning this option off lets you see more data.
Show recently used file list	If you frequently open different Schedule+ files, perhaps to work with different people's schedules, turning on this option will make opening up files easier by displaying the recently used files in the File menu for easy access.

The final page of the Options notebook, Time Zone, is shown in figure 19.4. Select your primary time zone in the field provided. If you frequently work with people in a different time zone, select the Secondary time zone check box and choose the time zone in the drop-down list. Doing so causes both times to appear side-by-side in your appointment book. If you do this, type in a three letter designation in the two fields provided to make it easier to identify the time zone on your display. For instance, figure 19.4 shows the primary time zone abbreviated as PAC and the secondary as HK. Figure 19.5 shows you the result of this change.

Figure 19.4

The final page of the Options notebook—Time Zone—lets you choose your local and one remote time zone.

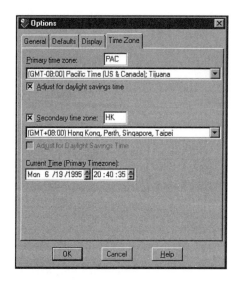

Figure 19.5

Here, you see the display effect of setting up a secondary time zone.

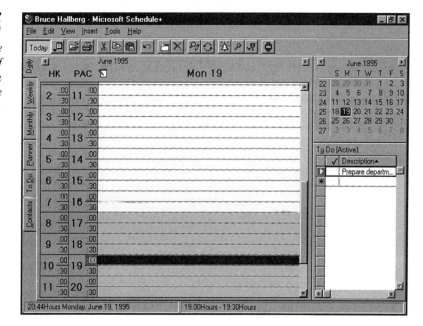

Note If you have defined a secondary time zone, you can quickly toggle its appearance in your views by accessing the Second Time **Z**one command in the **V**iew menu. Each selection of that menu command turns its appearance on and off.

Controlling the Tabs

The next major area of customization that you'll want to control in Schedule+ is the Tab Gallery, which lets you control the tabs that you use to switch views and that appear along the left side of the screen.

To access the Tab Gallery, right-click on any of the tabs and choose Tab Gallery. You see the dialog box shown in figure 19.6.

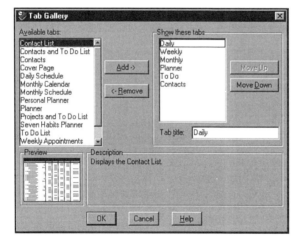

Figure 19.6

Use the Tab Gallery dialog box to control the tabs that appear in your Schedule+ desktop.

In all cases, you select a tab name in the A**v**ailable tabs listing. You will see a preview of how the tab page appears in the Preview window and a description of the tab in the Description field.

Most tab names make it obvious what they show when selected, and the Description field will offer additional information, but there are two tabs that deserve special note:

◆ The **Cover Page** tab lets you go quickly to a picture by clicking on its tab. This can make it much faster to hide your confidential information if someone comes into your office while you're working with your schedule. Just click on the tab and your work is hidden!

◆ The **Seven Habits Planner** is modeled after the principles contained in Stephen R. Covey's book, *The 7 Habits of Highly Effective People.*

Tip If you are using the Cover Page tab and want to change its picture, select it, right click in the picture area, and choose Select Cover Page from the pop-up menu. You can use any graphics file that uses the BMP format.

Reordering and Naming Tabs

You can easily reorder the tabs in your notebook with the Tab Gallery. Select a tab in the Sh<u>o</u>w these tabs box and click on the Move <u>U</u>p and Move <u>D</u>own buttons until the tab is positioned where you want it.

You can also change a tab's name without changing its contents. Select the tab in the Sh<u>o</u>w these tabs box and then edit the Tab <u>t</u>itle field.

Mastering Schedule+ Views

The tabs in Schedule+ give you many choices about how you view and work with your data. So far, in the previous chapter and in this one, you've learned how to create new entries, edit them, and delete them, and you've learned how to control how Schedule+ works. There are, however, tricks contained in various views that you should know in order to make the best use of the program. This section will walk you through the main views and show you ways to make the best use of them.

To Do List

The To Do list (see fig. 19.7) helps you keep track of your tasks and projects. It displays your task information sorted by project, and then subsorted any way you like. Click on any of the column headings to sort the display by that field. Select an entire task or group of tasks by clicking on the row buttons. Hold down the Ctrl key to select multiple tasks. Once selected, you can drag a task to another project by dragging its row button. Overdue tasks are highlighted in red with an exclamation mark. Click in the checkmark field to designate a task as done. It is crossed out, and its % Completion is changed to 100 percent. Use the horizontal scroll bar to see other columns.

Editing items in the To Do list is easy. Simply click on the item to edit, or the field you want to change, click your right mouse button, and choose Edit Item from the pop-up list. You can also press the F2 key when you have any field highlighted to change its data.

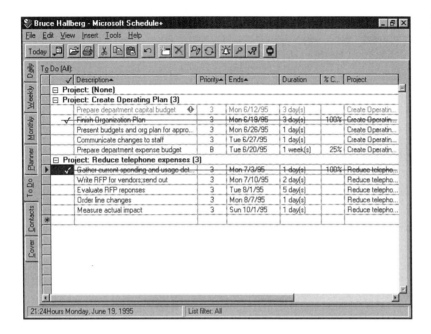

Figure 19.7

The To Do list tracks your tasks and projects.

You can control which columns are visible in the To Do list. Open the **V**iew menu and choose **C**olumns. A submenu appears that lets you choose **C**ustom, **A**ll, **T**ypical, **F**ew, and **D**escription Only. Choosing **C**ustom brings up the Columns dialog box shown in figure 19.8. You use it much like the Tab Gallery you saw earlier, where you choose the column labels and **A**dd or **R**emove them. You can also select column labels in the Sh**o**w these columns box and then click on the Move **U**p and Move **D**own buttons to reposition their order of appearance.

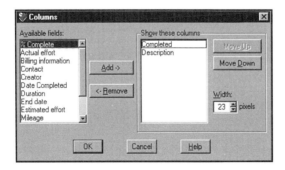

Figure 19.8

Use the Columns dialog box to choose exactly what columns appear in the To Do list.

By default your tasks are organized by project with no other sorting. You can change the grouping order with the **G**roup By command in the **V**iew menu, which shows you the Group by dialog box displayed in figure 19.9. Choose the appropriate column names in the drop-down list boxes in the Group by dialog box to change the order in which your tasks appear.

Figure 19.9

Change the grouping of your tasks with the Group by dialog box.

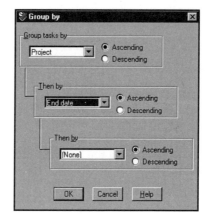

Similarly, you can control the sort order more precisely with the Sort dialog box found in the **S**ort command of the **V**iew menu (see fig. 19.10). It functions the same way as the Group by dialog box.

Figure 19.10

Exercise more control over how your To Do tasks are sorted with the Sort dialog box.

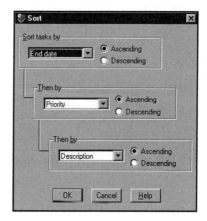

Tip Choose the A**u**toSort command in the **V**iew menu to cause Schedule+ to always keep your display sorted. Otherwise, new items won't be sorted until you choose the Sort **N**ow command, also in the **V**iew menu.

As your task list grows, you may have need to filter the items so that you only see a certain subset of them. To do this, choose the **F**ilter command in the **V**iew menu, shown in figure 19.11. Choosing a particular filter category immediately shows you only those items.

Figure 19.11

Filter large amounts of data with the Filter command.

Contact List

You use the Contact list (see fig. 19.12) to view and find your contacts quickly and easily. In general, the Contact list functions like the To Do list, with these exceptions:

◆ You cannot filter contacts.

◆ There is a quick-find feature. Type a portion of a person's last name in the **G**o to field to jump immediately to that person.

◆ You have easy access to the details on any of the contacts in the list. Use the tabs and arrow buttons in the right half of the screen to view any associated details on a particular contact.

Figure 19.12

The Contact list lets you quickly locate one of your contacts.

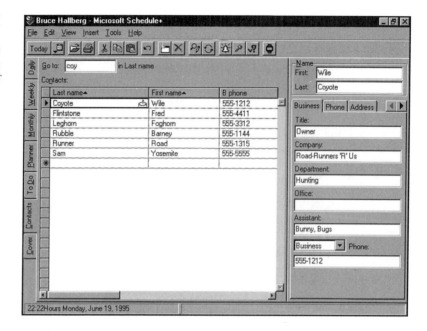

Planner

Sometimes you need to view the big picture of your schedule. Perhaps you need to look for blocks of time, or maybe you just want to get a feel for the week. You do this with the Planner page, shown in figure 19.13.

The lines that you see in the time blocks are current appointments. To see the detail on any of them without changing to a different page, right-click on the bar.

Tip   Much of the Planner's power comes into play when you use Schedule+ on a network. In those cases, you can compare different people's schedule with your own, with each person's commitments appearing in a different color.

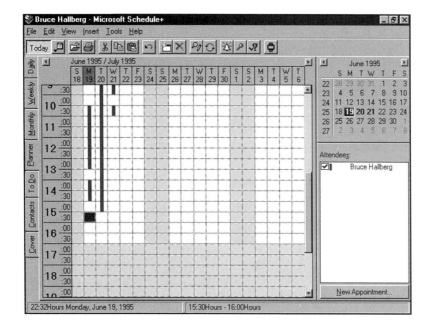

Figure 19.13

The Planner page gives you an overview of your schedule.

Daily, Weekly, and Monthly View

The "time views" let you see your detailed schedule in one of several familiar formats. Figure 19.14, for example, shows you the Weekly view. You can reschedule any appointment by dragging the bar to the left of an appointment. Carefully position your pointer over a border, and you can drag the appointment to change its start or end time. The triangle with ellipses symbol means that there is appointment information that you must scroll up to see.

Tip   You can easily schedule and create an appointment at the same time. Drag your mouse over a range of time periods, and then right-click inside the highlighted area. Choose New Appointment from the pop-up menu to create an appointment with those highlighted times.

Figure 19.14

*The Weekly view
shows you lots of
information in a
compact amount
of screen space.*

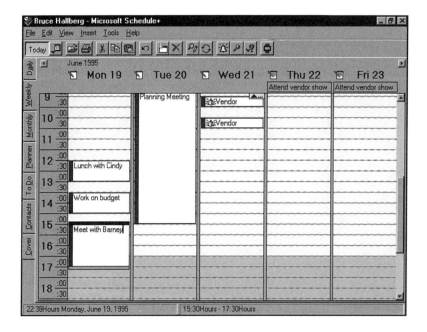

Exchanging Data

You will have many occasions where you'll want to export or import your PIM data to
other systems, and Schedule+ contains many abilities to help you do so. You can
export data in these ways:

◆ **Schedule+ Interchange**, which lets you transfer data to another computer
running Schedule+, such as a home computer or notebook computer.

◆ **Text**, where you can create ASCII text files of your PIM information. This can
be a prelude to loading the data into another system. For instance, you could
export your contact list into a different program that uses the data, but that
cannot otherwise read Schedule+ databases.

◆ **Timex Watch.** Timex sells a watch that can hold some of your appointments
and contacts. Schedule+ includes the software to download selected information
into those watches.

◆ **Other System.** There are many Personal Digital Assistants (PDAs) on the
market, and many people like to travel with them or keep them handy. Sched-
ule+ can export your information into a variety of such systems, such as the HP
95LX or many of the Sharp PDAs.

Schedule+ can also import data from a variety of systems:

◆ **Schedule+ Interchange**, when you want to load a file created by Schedule+ running on a different computer.

◆ **Text files.** Using this option you can add information to your Schedule+ database that exists in a system that can't directly communicate with Schedule+.

◆ **Other System** lets you import your PIM data from not only many PDAs, but from competing PIM software. Programs supported include ACT!, ECCO, Lotus Organizer, and the Windows Cardfile and Calendar applets.

In this section you will learn about performing these data exchange tasks.

Schedule+ Interchange

Most people use PIMs in at least two locations: work and home. Assuming you use Schedule+ in both places, you'll occasionally want to update one system with new information contained in the other. The Schedule+ Interchange export and import let you accomplish that.

Export files by accessing the **F**ile menu and choosing **E**xport. You see a submenu in which you can choose **S**chedule+ Interchange. Selecting this choice displays the dialog box shown in figure 19.15.

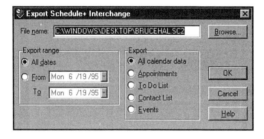

Figure 19.15

When you export data to the Schedule+ Interchange format, you see this dialog box.

Fill in the Export Schedule+ Interchange dialog box, choosing a location for the file, a date range, and the classes of information you want to transfer. Click on the OK button to create the export file.

Tip

Creating the file in your \WINDOWS\DESKTOP directory makes it automatically appear on your desktop, where it can be easily dragged to a floppy disk or attached to an e-mail message.

You might also want to directly export the file to the A:\ directory, placing it immediately on a disk that you carry to another location.

Importing Schedule+ Interchange files is even easier than exporting the data. Open the **F**ile menu and choose **I**mport. Select Schedule+ Interchange from the submenu that appears. You will see a standard File Open dialog box, such as the example shown in figure 19.16. Locate the file you want to import and click on the **O**pen button to bring the data into your current system.

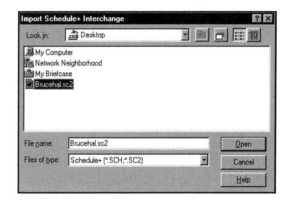

Note Schedule+ Interchange files always add to your existing information. If duplicate information is in your current database and the Schedule+ Interchange file, you will not end up with two copies of it. Instead, the data is merged.

Text Files

Schedule+ includes the ability to export and import files into a text-based format, which you can usually use as an intermediate format for exchanging data with systems that otherwise won't use Schedule+ databases. For example, you could export your contact list into a text file and import that contact list into virtually any database program.

Export begins by choosing the **E**xport command in the **F**ile menu, and then choosing **T**ext in the submenu. You see the Text Export Wizard shown in figure 19.17.

On the first screen of the Text Export Wizard, select the type of data you want to export. Here, you'll see contact information exported. Click on the **N**ext button to move to the next step, shown in figure 19.18.

Most systems will handle files in which the fields are separated by commas, and the text fields have quote marks around them. This formatting results in so-called Comma Separated Value (CSV) files, which most applications that import data can handle. If your program has other needs, though, you can make alternate choices in the screen shown in figure 19.18. When done, click on the **N**ext button to move to the third step.

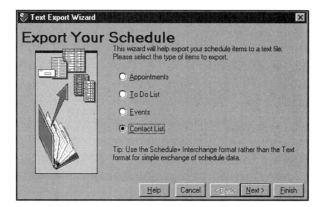

Figure 19.17

The Text Export Wizard walks you through exporting your data.

Figure 19.18

In the second screen of the Wizard, you choose how the fields will be separated in the resulting file.

The third step of the Wizard asks two questions that concern the layout of your export file (see fig. 19.19). First, you're asked how carriage returns (enter keys) that are part of fields should be handled. In most cases, you're safest answering No to that question. The second question asks whether or not column headings should be in the file in the first row. Your answer to this depends on the application that will be receiving the data. If it can use the first row for column headings, then it's fine to answer Yes to the second question.

The final screen of the Text Export Wizard (see fig. 19.20) lets you choose what fields you want to export. You must select each field you want in the list and click on the **A**dd button to move it to the E**x**port fields list. After selecting all the fields you want in this way, use the Move **U**p and Move **D**own buttons to control the order of the fields in the export file.

When done, click on the **N**ext button to move to the final screen of the Text Export Wizard, in which you specify the file name for the resulting export. Type the file name in the field provided and click on the **F**inish button to create the file.

Figure 19.19

The third step asks some questions about the layout of the export file.

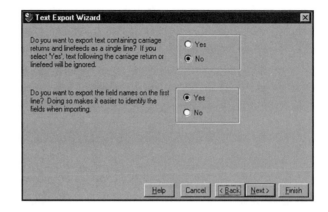

Figure 19.20

Choose the fields to export in the final screen of the Text Export Wizard.

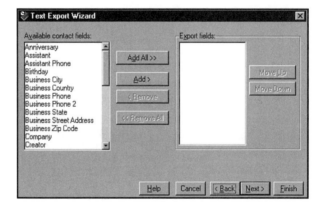

Importing records is also somewhat complex. First, access the Import Text Wizard by choosing the **I**mport command in the **F**ile menu, and then choose **T**ext. You see the Wizard shown in figure 19.21.

Before importing records into Schedule+ using the Text Import Wizard, make a copy of your Schedule+ database. If you make a mistake during the import process, you could end up with a bunch of records that are worthless. Making a copy beforehand means you can instantly reverse a mistaken import by simply using the backup file.

Type in the name of the file to import or click on the **B**rowse button to locate it. Click on the **N**ext button to move to the second screen, shown in figure 19.22.

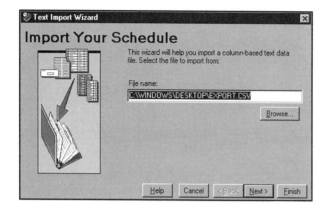

Figure 19.21

The Text Import Wizard starts by specifying the file name to use.

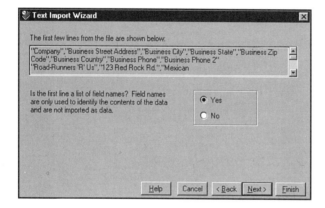

Figure 19.22

In the second screen, you answer one question about field names.

The second screen of the Text Import Wizard shows you what the file looks like, and asks you to answer a single question: does the first line of the file contain field names, or data? Answer Yes if it has field names, which causes that first line to be skipped during the import process. Click on the **N**ext button to move to the third screen.

Use the third screen (see fig. 19.23) to tell Schedule+ how the fields are separated in the file. Since you can see a preview of the import file in the top window, you can see how the fields are designated. Choose the appropriate radio buttons and the text designator, and click on the **N**ext button to move to the fourth step.

Next, the fourth screen asks you what type of data is being imported. You can only import one type of data at a time. Choose the appropriate category in the fourth screen (see fig. 19.24) and click on the **N**ext button to move to the fifth step.

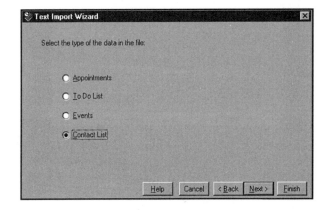

Finally, you move to the fifth and most important screen of the Text Import Wizard. Here, you tell Schedule+ which fields in the import file match up with which fields in your Schedule+ database. If the import file has labels in its first row, you will see those labels in the left half of the screen. The right half shows the Schedule+ field names into which to the data will be placed. (See fig. 19.25). Click on each line where it initially says "IGNORE THIS FIELD." You then see a drop-down list button. Choosing that button reveals a list of possible field names in Schedule+. Choose the appropriate field names for each of the fields you want to import, as shown in figure 19.25. When you're done designating all the fields, click on the Finish button to import the data.

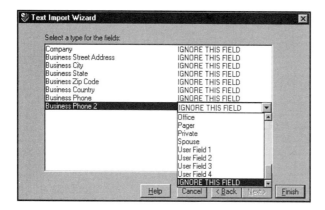

Figure 19.25

*The most
important screen
of the Text Import
Wizard, in which
you define the
field relationships
of your import.*

Other Systems

You can export your Schedule+ information to a number of different PDAs, including the following:

◆ Hewlett-Packard 95LX

◆ Sharp 5000/7000/7200

◆ Sharp 7600/7620

◆ Sharp 8000/8200

◆ Sharp 8600/YO-610

◆ Sharp 9600

Note If your PDA isn't on the list, and you cannot exchange data using the more generic Text export, a company sells translation modules that you can purchase. Call IntelliLink at (603) 888-0666 for information on their translation products.

Figure 19.26 shows you the dialog box that appears when you choose **E**xport and then **O**ther systems. Each system export procedure works a little differently.

Figure 19.26

You can export your Schedule+ data to these PDAs using built-in tools.

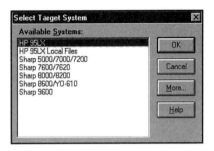

Importing from other systems works much the same way, except that in addition to importing from PDAs, you can import data from other PIM software, such as the following:

◆ ACT! for Windows

◆ ECCO

◆ Lotus Organizer

◆ PackRat Rev 4.1+

◆ Windows Cardfile and Calendar

Using either these specific tools or the more generic text import and export, you can exchange your Schedule+ data with virtually any system that handles similar types of information.

Mail Merge with Schedule+ and Word

You can use the contacts that you have stored in Schedule+ for mail merge operations with Microsoft Word. Since both are part of the Microsoft Office package, doing so is easy.

Access the Mail Merge command in the Tools menu. In the resulting dialog box, select the Create button to select the type of document you'll generate. Then, pull down the Get Data drop-down list box and choose Use Address Book, as shown in figure 19.27.

After choosing to use an address book, you'll see the Use Address Book dialog box. Select Schedule+ Contact List and click on the OK button.

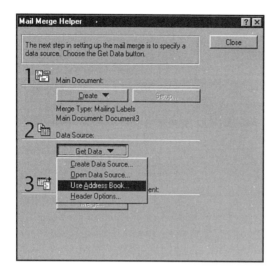

Figure 19.27

When using your Schedule+ address book, select Use Address Book in the Mail Merge dialog box.

After choosing to use the Schedule+ address book, you can edit the document to insert the appropriate merge codes for the fields in your contact list, and can complete the mail merge normally.

Archiving Your Data

Schedule+ databases can grow quite large. They can consume a lot of disk space, and slow down the operation of the program somewhat as they grow. To avoid this, you can archive your schedule information at regular intervals. This copies your information to an archive file and removes it from your main Schedule+ database. Normally, Schedule+ will remind you every three months (or in whatever interval you set in the Options dialog box). However, you can also archive your data at-will.

To create an archive, access the **F**ile menu and choose the **A**rchive option. You'll see the dialog box shown in figure 19.28.

After choosing your archive date (the date before which all information is archived), click on the OK button to create the archive file. Store the archive file in a safe place in case you ever need to access it.

Note   You might want to consult your tax advisor or attorney about the importance of your schedule archive files. They could conceivably be crucial documents with which you will want to exercise considerable care. If that's the case, make sure to keep multiple copies on separate backup tapes or disks to minimize the risk of loss.

Figure 19.28

It's a good idea to archive your schedule information every three months or so with the archiving feature built into Schedule+.

To view an archived data set, simply double-click on the file, or open it with the **O**pen command in Schedule+'s **F**ile menu. Schedule+ will load the data in the archive and will display it for you. If you need to move the data back into your normal database, use the Schedule+ Interchange Export to export it from the archive database, and then the Schedule+ Interchange Import to read it into your main database.

The 7 Habits of Highly Effective People

Schedule+ includes several tools that help you incorporate the principles contained in Stephen Covey's book, *The 7 Habits of Highly Effective People.* Access the **T**ools menu and choose Seven Habits **T**ools. This begins a lengthy Wizard that asks you to develop goals, priorities, and a mission statement for your life, and incorporates your answers into Schedule+'s planning screens. After you've completed the Wizard, use the Seven Habits tab in your planner to stay on track with your personal mission.

CHAPTER 20

Networking Schedule+

sing Schedule+ on a network that uses a compatible e-mail program, such as Microsoft Mail or Microsoft Exchange, opens up a whole new world to you. When you use Schedule+ this way, you get these added capabilities:

◆ You can use the Meeting Wizard to schedule meetings with other Schedule+ users on the network, automatically inserting your proposed meeting into their schedule and sending them a query through e-mail.

◆ You can grant another user access to your schedule as a delegate, in which they have control over your schedule and can manage it for you. This is perfect if you have an assistant that works with your schedule, or if you are an assistant that needs to manage your boss's schedule.

◆ You can both access others' schedules over the network, as well as grant access to your own schedule. This makes setting up meetings much easier. (And, of course, Schedule+ lets you mark some things as being private so others don't see them.)

◆ You can create schedule databases for resources, such as conference rooms, slide projectors, overheads, and the like. Everyone who uses Schedule+ on the network can reserve these resources over the network.

On its own, Schedule+ is a powerful tool for your own productivity. On a network, it's a tool for your entire company's productivity. In this chapter you'll learn about how to use these exciting networking features.

When PCs first started appearing, they made a big difference in individual peoples' productivity. Now that more and more PCs are being networked, a new type of productivity gain is possible: company-wide productivity. In this new model, the very fact that all the PCs in your company are networked enables new types of software to emerge, commonly called *groupware*.

Schedule+ implements this groupware concept, in that it seamlessly integrates with Microsoft Mail, as well as other e-mail systems, to let you work in a "group-enabled" mode. It also lets you access others' schedules, and lets others access yours. In this new networking mode, the program offers you new choices that you didn't see in the previous chapters, and new capabilities.

Understanding Schedule+ Networking

Your computer support people will have already configured Schedule+ to work in network mode. In fact, if you are using Schedule+ this way, the previous chapters' screen-shots might have looked a little different to you because some network-based options aren't shown when it runs in stand-alone mode.

There are two key components to using Schedule+ on a network:

◆ Shared access to all the schedules on the network, with appropriate tools to control access and preserve privacy

◆ Integration with an e-mail system that complements Schedule+

In this chapter you learn how these two core elements translate into some new possibilities within Schedule+.

Setting Schedule+ Networking Options

Consider figure 20.1, which shows the Options dialog in Schedule+. If you compare it to figure 20.1 in the previous chapter, you'll see some key differences:

◆ **This account is for a resource**

Choose this option when you are working with a Schedule+ database that controls a common resource, like a conference room or overhead projector.

◆ Automatically accept m̲eeting requests

When selected, all meeting requests sent over the network are automatically accepted. Schedule+ removes the request e-mail message, if one accompanied it, and adds any notes sent to the Notes tab of the appointment's notebook.

◆ Automatically remove c̲anceled meetings

Meetings can be both set and canceled over the network. If a meeting cancellation message is received by Schedule+, it automatically removes the appointment and removes it from your schedule when this option is selected.

◆ Send meeting requests only to my delegate

If you've chosen someone as a delegate for your schedule, this option is available. When selected, all meeting requests sent to you are automatically forwarded to your delegate.

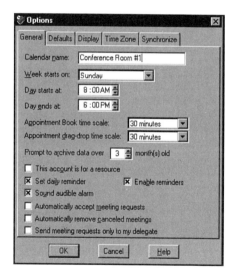

Figure 20.1

The Schedule+ Options dialog box displays some new choices when networked.

The Options dialog box also has a new tab when you work on a network, called Synchronize. This tab is shown in figure 20.2.

The Synchronize tab has the following options:

◆ S̲ynchronize every x minutes

Schedule+ keeps a copy of your schedule on both your computer and the network. This setting controls how often the two files are brought into syncronization.

◆ **Always synchronize upon exit**

When exiting Schedule+, this setting ensures that the network copy of your schedule is updated with your latest changes.

◆ **Work primarily from local file**

When selected, the network copy of your schedule is not updated on a regular basis. It will be updated when you exit Schedule+ (if you have the **A**lways synchronize upon exit check box selected) or when you click on the Synchronize **N**ow button

Figure 20.2

When using Schedule+ on a network, you have a new Synchronize tab in the Options notebook.

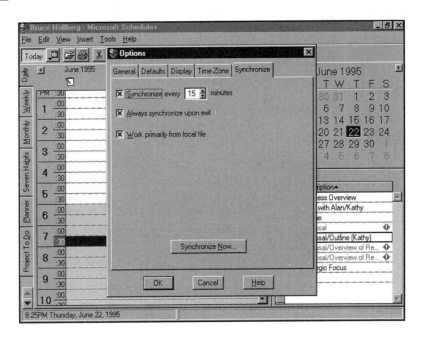

Controlling Access to Your Information

Another dialog box that changes with a network (and by quite a lot) is the Access Permissions dialog box (see fig. 20.3), accessed through the Set Access Permissions command in the **T**ools menu.

Here, you control the default access to your schedule file, as well as grant custom access to specified users on the network. The User page of the dialog box contains these options:

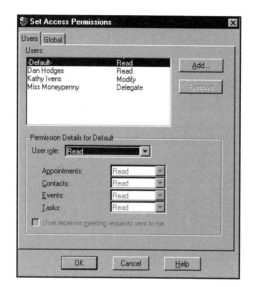

Figure 20.3

Use the Set Access Permissions dialog box to control who has access to your schedule, and to what extent.

◆ **Users**

Here, you see all the people you've granted specific access rights, as well as your Default access rights. You add a new user by clicking on the **A**dd button.

◆ **Permission Details**

This window shows you the detailed access permissions for the selected user.

◆ **User role**

This drop-down list box lets you choose from several pre-defined roles for the selected user:

None. User has no access to your schedule items.

Read. User can look at your schedule items, but cannot modify or delete items. User also cannot see private items.

Create. User can read and create new items, except for private items.

Modify. User can read and modify items, but not private ones.

Delegate. User can read and modify items, including private items.

Owner. User can read and modify all items, including private ones. They can also grant access permissions for other users.

Delegate Owner. User can read and modify items, including private ones. Further, this type of user can set access permissions and send meeting requests in your name.

Custom. Here, you set each specific permission in the four drop-down list boxes below the User role box.

When you choose a Custom user role, you can further control their access to different types of items in your Schedule+ database. For each type of item (Appointments, Contacts, Events, and Tasks) you control the level of access. You have four choices for each type of item: None, Read, Modify, and Create.

The final check box, User receives **m**eeting requests sent to me, means that any meeting requests will automatically be forwarded to that particular user's e-mail inbox.

The Global page (also in the Set Access Permissions dialog box, and shown in figure 20.4) also contains some useful options:

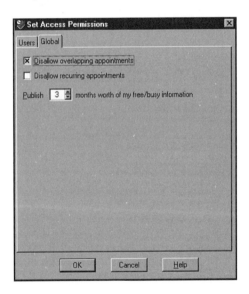

Figure 20.4

The Global page of the Set Access Permissions notebook controls some more of your meeting preferences.

◆ **Disallow overlapping appointments**

When selected, your system will not allow anyone to create an appointment that overlaps an existing one.

◆ **Disallow recurring appointments**

If you choose this check box, nobody can create automatically recurring appointments in your schedule.

◆ **Publish x months worth of my free/busy information**

The number of months you input in this field controls how much of a time span others can see of your schedule

Using Meeting Features

Have you ever hassled with trying to set up a meeting with a bunch of people, trying to find an acceptable time that works for all of them? Anytime you have more than 2 people to schedule, this quickly becomes a nightmare. Usually, you end up giving up on finding a good meeting time and just live with the fact that one person or another can't make it, and work around it. It doesn't have to be this way!

When you're using Schedule+ on a network with a compatible e-mail system, one of its nicest features is the one in which it can automatically set up meetings with others, finding time slots in which all are available. It even sends them e-mail messages to confirm their attendance! In this section you learn how to create a new meeting using Schedule+, how to reschedule one, and how to cancel one.

Using the Meeting Wizard

Meetings are most easily created using the Meeting Wizard, which goes through a number of steps to gather information from you about your needs for the meeting. You can access the Meeting Wizard by pulling down the **T**ools menu and picking the **M**ake Meeting command. You see the dialog box shown in figure 20.5.

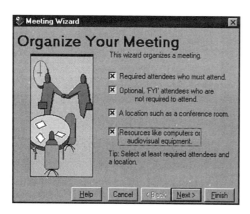

Figure 20.5

The first screen of the Meeting Wizard.

The Meeting Wizard starts by asking you about what elements you will need for your meeting. You can choose Required Attendees, Optional Attendees, a location, and any resources you need for your meeting. Choose the appropriate check boxes and click on the **N**ext button to move to the next step, shown in figure 20.6.

Figure 20.6

In this second screen of the Meeting Wizard, you choose the first element that you selected in the previous screen.

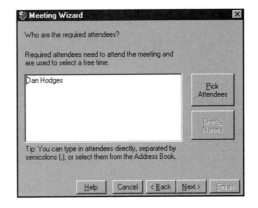

Your second Meeting Wizard screen will typically involve choosing the required attendees for your meeting. This is shown in figure 20.6, while the screen you see when you click on the **P**ick Attendees button is shown in figure 20.7.

Figure 20.7

When you click on Pick Attendees, you see this selection screen that displays the available users on your network.

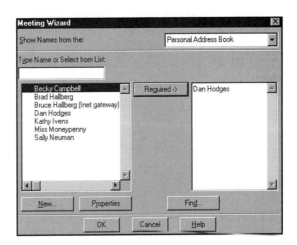

After selecting the required attendees and clicking on the **N**ext button in the Meeting Wizard, you move to the next elements. These screens will involve optional attendees, the location, and any resources. All of those screens work the same as the two you just saw in figures 20.6 and 20.7.

After choosing your attendees and resources, you see the screen shown in figure 20.8, which lets you set some meeting parameters, including the length of the meeting and how much travel time to the meeting will be required (this factor has to be taken into account with others' schedules, so that there is not overlap in the travel time).

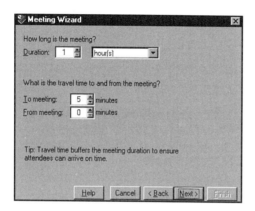

Figure 20.8

Here, you tell the Meeting Wizard how long your meeting will be, and how long it will take people to travel to and from the meeting.

Next, you move to the Meeting Wizard screen in which you specify your preferred times and days for the meeting, shown in figure 20.9.

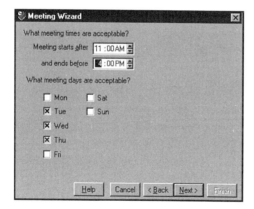

Figure 20.9

Here, select the times and days that are appropriate for your meeting.

The reason you specify the times and days for the meeting in figure 20.9 is so that Schedule+ can automatically check all of the attendees' schedules and find a time where nobody has a conflicting engagement. Your first choice involves whether you want Schedule+ to also check for available times in the optional attendees' schedules (assuming you invited any). This is done in the following screen in the Meeting Wizard, shown in figure 20.10.

Figure 20.10

*Use this screen
to tell Schedule+
whether you
want it to
automatically
check optional
attendees'
schedules for
available times.*

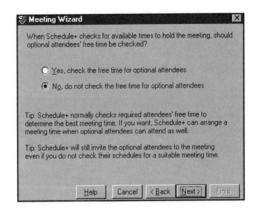

Schedule+ finally goes to the network and checks everyone's schedule for the first
available time for everyone and then displays the result in figure 20.11.

Figure 20.11

*Instead of
wasting a lot of
time, let
Schedule+ find
available time
slots!*

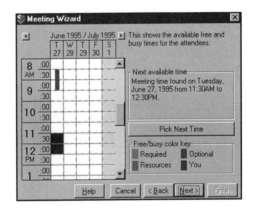

If the time automatically chosen doesn't agree with you, click on the Pick Next Time
button to find the next possibility.

Finally, the Meeting Wizard finishes and shows you its final dialog box, in which you
click on the **F**inish button. If you're using a compatible e-mail program, it automatically starts when you select **F**inish and lets you type a note to all the invited attendees
explaining the meeting, as shown in figure 20.12.

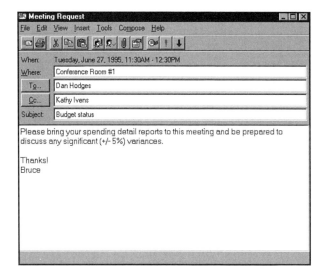

Figure 20.12

Use your e-mail software, automatically started by Schedule+, to tell the invitees about your meeting.

Rescheduling and Canceling Meetings

Just because Schedule+ lets you set up meetings in which everyone has time in their calendar doesn't mean you won't ever have to reschedule again! Fortunately, Schedule+ makes it easy to reschedule meetings over the network.

When you reschedule an appointment in any of the accepted ways (dragging it to a new time is the easiest), Schedule+ knows that you have remote users attending and shows you the dialog box in figure 20.13 automatically.

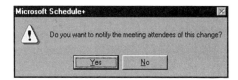

Figure 20.13

When you move a meeting that has networked attendees, Schedule+ pops up this dialog box automatically.

Clicking on **Y**es in the reschedule dialog box starts your e-mail with the original invitation and lets you add any new text, such as an explanation for the change in time.

Canceling meetings works in exactly the same way. Delete an appointment that has networked attendees and Schedule+ will ask you if you want to send them a cancellation message. Choosing **Y**es will start your e-mail letting you add whatever explanation is necessary.

Part V

Data Sharing and Integration

C H A P T E R

21

Examining Dynamic Data Exchange

Dynamic data exchange (DDE) is an internal communications protocol Windows uses to enable one application to "talk to" or exchange data with another application. Normally used to transfer information between applications, DDE can also be used within an application.

This chapter covers the following topics:

- ◆ Examining DDE links

- ◆ Using DDE links

- ◆ Creating links with menu commands

- ◆ Hot links and internal links

- ◆ Using macros to control DDE

DDE enables you not only to share information between applications, but also to send commands from one application to another to control the behavior of the receiving application. Thus, DDE is a tool that implements the Windows standard for both integration and interoperability.

DDE creates a *link*—a communication channel, rather like an open telephone line, through which data is sent. When DDE links are live, both the sending (server) and receiving (client) applications are open. While the server data is being edited, you can see the data being transferred in real time: as data in the server document changes, the hourglass flashes briefly as the other application is updated automatically through the link. You can size the application windows so that, with the two documents side by side, you can watch the entire process.

Examining DDE Links and the Way to Use Them

Windows offers two ways to implement dynamic data exchange. The first is through the application's regular interface; you execute directly, from the application's menus, any commands to create and edit links between one application and another. In the second method, you write code in an application's macro language; only through the macro programming construct can you send instructions that control another application's behavior. This chapter teaches you how to create links with each method.

Typically, you use DDE to perform the following kinds of automated data transfers:

◆ Query the data in one application from inside another, and return a result. The query can produce a one-time (static) return of data, or can be set to update the data in the destination document when the query is run again.

◆ Convey a stream of data into an application in real time, such as sending stock market quotes into a spreadsheet.

◆ Link information contained in a compound document to the information's source so that the destination document is updated automatically whenever the source data is changed. Examples of this type of link, sometimes called a *persistent link,* are discussed throughout the chapter.

A Practical Example of Using an Automatic Link

Suppose, for example, that you regularly prepare a summary sales report and send it, at specific intervals, to company managers: once a week to sales managers, twice a month to department heads, and once a month to the chief financial officer. These reports are based on sales figures that you track and total every day in Microsoft Excel. You can create in Microsoft Word a boilerplate report for each manager, including in each report a link to the range (in your Excel worksheet) that shows the running sales total.

As you update the figures in Excel every day, the updated total is sent automatically through the DDE link to the report documents. Whenever you open the Word documents to print and send them to the appropriate managers, the documents reflect the latest data from the Excel worksheet.

 Note A DDE link creates a pointer to the source data. The link is document-to-document (another way of saying file-to-file) rather than document-to-application, as is the case with OLE-embedded data. Chapter 22, "Exploring Object Linking and Embedding," discusses OLE in more detail.

After you establish a DDE link, you normally do not need to take any further action to maintain it. But when the source file is moved elsewhere on the system, or its name is changed, you must edit the link manually to tell the destination document the source's new location or name. You learn more about editing links later in this chapter (see the "Managing Links" section).

Different Flavors of DDE

Not all Windows applications support DDE. Some, such as screen savers and font managers, do not need DDE capability. DDE support generally is found in high-end word processors, spreadsheet programs, database applications, fax-generating applications, desktop-publishing programs, and electronic-mail packages.

Windows applications that support DDE can do so as a client, a server, or both. A *client application* requests or receives information from another application. A *server application* supplies information to another application.

Most applications that support DDE do so in a way that is readily accessible to the user, using commands on the application's menus and the familiar Clipboard copy-and-paste metaphor. You can think of this as *end-user DDE*. Other applications require that you access their information through macros written in a programming language. To do this you must understand the inner workings of their DDE implementation. You can think of this method of creating DDE links as *programmed links*.

Microsoft Word, Excel, Lotus WordPro, and WordPerfect are examples of applications that have their own macro languages and can access other applications through programmed DDE.

How to Discover Whether an Application Supports DDE

To find out whether the Windows application you use (such as Microsoft Word, Lotus WordPro, WordPerfect, Excel, or PowerPoint) supports end-user DDE, pull down the menus and look for commands such as Paste **L**ink, Paste **S**pecial, or **L**inks. These commands usually are on the **F**ile or **E**dit menus. The presence of these commands indicates that the application supports DDE, using the Clipboard to create the links.

 Note One advantage to using a software suite, such as Microsoft Office, is that they all tend to function very similarly with regard to features such as DDE links. Other applications will generally interface just fine with Office applications, but their implementations might work somewhat differently, depending on the programmers and designers of the other applications.

The way these clues to DDE support are expressed varies from one application to another, as you will see from the first few figures in this chapter.

Selecting the Paste **S**pecial command from Microsoft Word's **E**dit menu (see fig. 21.1) brings up the Paste Special dialog box (see fig. 21.2). In this dialog box, you can select a data type and click on the Paste **L**ink button. If the data type you choose cannot be linked, the Paste Link button is grayed out.

Figure 21.1

The Paste Special command in Word.

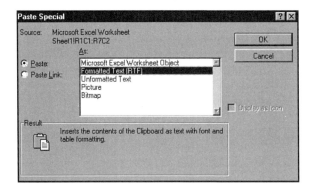

Figure 21.2

Word's Paste Special dialog box.

The Paste **S**pecial command in Microsoft Excel works in two different ways, depending on the source of data on the Clipboard. When you copy cells from the Excel worksheet to the Clipboard, the Paste **S**pecial command invokes a dialog box (see fig. 21.3) that enables you to paste the data back into the worksheet in several Excel-specific ways.

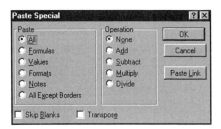

Figure 21.3

Excel's internal Paste Special dialog box.

When the data on the Clipboard is from an external source, however, Excel's Paste **S**pecial command works the way it does in Word, offering you various linking options (see fig. 21.4).

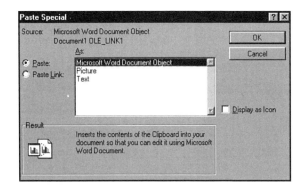

Figure 21.4

Excel's external Paste Special dialog box.

Note If your application has a macro language, the DDE commands should be documented in either the language command reference or the online help. If you do not see menu commands that refer to linking, and your program does not have a macro language, consult the documentation or the vendor to find out whether and in what form DDE is supported.

These minor inconsistencies between applications can make DDE seem too complicated or too obscure to use. The obstacle to creating DDE links disappears, however, when you remember that because end-user DDE is a Clipboard function, a reference to links appears on one or more menus—usually **F**ile and **E**dit—in applications in which end-user DDE is available.

Parsing a DDE Link

Whether you create a DDE link through the menu commands or in a macro, the link always has three parts. To keep track of where the linked information is located and what it refers to, the system needs to know the following three elements:

◆ Application

◆ Topic (sometimes called *file name*)

◆ Item

Application is Windows' alias for the program (WinWord, for example, when Word for Windows is the server). *Topic* typically is the file name of the source document, and *item* is the information in that document to which the link points. In the case of a spreadsheet, the item is the range, expressed either by a row-and-column address or, if you have named the range, by a name. In the case of a word processor such as Word or WordPro, the item is a bookmark name that the application assigns automatically or that you create. In addition to telling the client document where to look for updated source data, these placeholders enable you to "jump" from the destination document to the linked information in the source document, if your application permits.

Using Menu Commands to Create Links

Although you probably would not want to link text from a document created in one word processing application to a document created in another very often, the following example shows you the linking process in action. This example shows you how yet another program implements its DDE-related menu commands.

To copy a block of text from a Word document to the Clipboard, highlight the text and select **C**opy from the **E**dit menu (see fig. 21.5).

Figure 21.5

Copying data from Word.

Open Microsoft Exchange, start a new e-mail message, then pull down its **E**dit menu, choosing the Paste **S**pecial command.

Note When nothing is on the Clipboard, the Paste commands are grayed out to indicate that they are not available or applicable.

When you choose the Paste **S**pecial command and choose the Paste **l**ink option in the dialog box, the text is pasted into the Exchange message, and a link that points to the original text in Word is established. You can verify the link by selecting the box that contains the linked text, then using the Lin**k**s command in Exchange's **E**dit menu. This displays the Links dialog box that displays the current link information, as shown in figure 21.6.

Note Because each open DDE channel requires system memory, the number of links that can be maintained in any document is limited. Factors governing the limit include how much memory is installed on the system and the claims made upon that memory by other resources currently active in the Windows session.

Name and save a server document before you create a link. Otherwise, you have to edit the link later with the source document's name.

Figure 21.6

*Exchange's Links
dialog box
displays the
current link.*

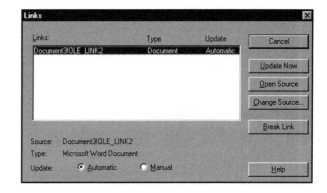

Managing Links

Can you tell, just from looking at a document, whether it contains links and if it does, where they are? Sometimes yes, sometimes no—and sometimes you must do a bit of sleuthing.

Word enables you to explore the links for which it is acting as server. As other applications do, Word creates a bookmark for each server link (these are DDE items). But because Word lists these items as bookmarks in the document, you can use the **B**ookmark command in the **E**dit menu to go to them (see fig. 21.7). Word names the bookmarks OLE_LINK*n* (*n* is an automatically incremented number). When you go to a bookmark, Word highlights the block of text to which the bookmark refers. Note that if you delete links, Word does not renumber the remaining bookmarks.

Tip To ensure that Excel's DDE links behave as you want them to, choose **O**ptions in the **T**ools menu and make sure that the **I**gnore Other Applications check box (on the General tab) is cleared. To choose whether to have all links in an individual worksheet updated automatically, select the Calculation tab in the **O**ptions dialog box and then check or clear the Update **R**emote References check box.

Figure 21.7

*Finding Links in
Word using the
Bookmark dialog
box.*

In Excel, the formula that describes the link appears in the formula bar when you select the linked object or cell that contains the object (see fig. 21.8).

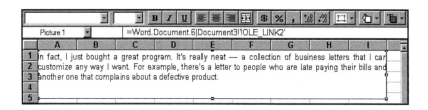

Figure 21.8

Excel displays link information in the formula bar.

No matter how programs display links, you can always access the links in the document through a menu command. In Office applications, look for the Li**nk**s command on the **E**dit menu. Other programs will use slightly different methods.

Each of these commands opens a dialog box that lists the document's links and their attributes. In this dialog box you can update individual links, change their status from automatic (active) to manual (inactive) and back again, cancel or unlink them (leaving the latest result in the document as static text), and edit them. Figure 21.9 displays Word's Links dialog box. The figure clearly shows the three parts of a DDE link: the application, the file name (usually called the topic), and the item.

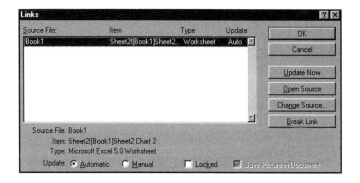

Figure 21.9

Word's Links dialog box.

In this example, you use the Links dialog box to edit the file name (topic) after you name and save the worksheet.

 Note Word not only provides the usual options, but also enables you to jump directly to the source of the link. You can do this by choosing **O**pen Source from the Links dialog box or by selecting the command (named, for example, Linked Worksheet **O**bject) that appears under the Li**nk**s command on the **E**dit menu when a linked object is selected. The best way to edit a link, in general, is to use the Cha**n**ge Source button in the Links dialog box.

continues

With Excel, you can edit the link directly in the formula bar. Just be sure to press Ctrl+Shift+Enter to save the revised link as an array formula.

Understanding Hot Links

Not only does the terminology and placement of DDE-related menu commands vary from program to program, but discrepancies also exist in the way programs respond to DDE messages. Although DDE links ordinarily are well-behaved, you need to be aware of some problems you might encounter.

A *hot* (or automatic) link is one that automatically updates the destination document after the linked information in the source document is changed. A *warm* (or manual) link is one in which the user must manually update the link when the source information is changed. A warm link is sometimes referred to as a *manual link* or an *inactive link*; a hot link is also called an *automatic link* or an *active link*.

Normally, links are hot when you first create them. But because their status can change under certain circumstances—sometimes without the user being aware that what was once a hot link is now a warm one that must be updated manually—you might need to experiment to determine just how your applications operate in this regard.

Not surprisingly, the most reliable DDE integration is between Microsoft Excel as the server and Microsoft Word as the client—the relationship with the longest history. With an Excel worksheet range paste-linked to a Word document, you can expect the following when you open the destination document during a subsequent session:

◆ If both Excel and the source document are open, the link updates automatically.

◆ If Excel is open but the source document is not, the link updates automatically.

◆ If Excel is not open, the link updates automatically.

This is DDE linking at its most efficient.

But what happens when you link Word and Excel in the other direction, with Word as the server? Excel displays a dialog box (see fig. 21.10) asking you if you want Excel to update the links to the unopened document. Clicking on the **Y**es button will update the link to the stored document.

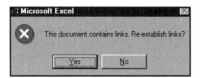

Figure 21.10

Excel's update link message.

To see how this works in reverse, paste-link some Word text into an Excel worksheet (remember to name and save the source document before you create the link). Close the Excel worksheet. Before you close Word, alter the text so that you can verify the update in Excel. Close Word and then reopen the worksheet. When you answer **Y**es to the message shown in figure 21.10, Excel automatically updates the link. In other words, Excel can find and update the link even though both the application and the Word source document are closed.

Even the most reliable end-user DDE (the one you create when you paste-link ranges from Excel into Word) has one small problem. Start with both applications closed. Open Word first. It correctly reads the changed Excel source data from the disk and automatically updates the link. Then launch Excel and open the linked worksheet. Make changes in the source data.

Word does not update the link automatically. You have to update the link manually, either through the menu and dialog box commands, or by placing the cursor anywhere in the linked data and pressing F9, which is Word's Update Fields key. The link becomes a manual link (even though it still is flagged as automatic in the Links dialog box displayed when you select Lin**k**s on Word's **E**dit menu).

To make sure that the link remains truly automatic, open the linked Excel worksheet and modify it *before* you open the Word document.

Despite the peculiarities mentioned in this section, DDE links are a powerful way to share data between Windows applications, and are indispensable to certain kinds of real-time data transfers.

Working with Internal Links

Word and Excel enable you to create internal links. In Word, an internal link is actually a reference to a bookmark.

If you copy Word text to the Clipboard and then use Paste **S**pecial to place it somewhere else in the same document, Word automatically assigns a bookmark name to the text block, as it does when Word is the server for a regular DDE link. In the case of an internal link, the bookmark name is OLE_LINKn; the number n increments each time you create an internal link.

Internal links are not hot—they are not updated automatically. You can update the links in either of two ways. You can select the field(s) by putting the cursor anywhere in the text (if **V**iew Field Codes is off) or anywhere in the field (if **V**iew Field Codes is on) and pressing F9, the Update Fields key. Or you can choose **L**inks from the **E**dit menu and then, in the Links dialog box, select the link(s) to be updated and press the **U**pdate Now push button.

In Excel, you can **C**opy and Paste **L**ink a cell or range of cells to different part of the worksheet or to another worksheet. (Note that if you copy a range, the range is pasted as an array.) In this way, you create a reference to the row-and-column or named-range address of the original cell(s). This internal link updates automatically when the source data is changed.

Using Macros to Control DDE

Now that you have explored the nature of DDE links and how to create and manage them by using menu commands, the next step is to understand how macros can perform many of these tasks for you, truly automating the integration and inter-operability of Windows applications.

Looking At DDE Commands: Examples from Excel and Word

Although the exact form of a DDE command can vary from one macro language to another, similarities exist. Table 21.1 lists the most commonly used DDE commands and their meanings in Excel, Word, and WordPro. To find the exact commands for your application, including the Office suite, check the online programming reference.

TABLE 21.1
Common DDE Commands

Common Command Name	Application	Action
DDEInitiate	All three	Starts DDE conversation with another application
DDEExecute	All three	Sends a command to another application with which you initiated conversation

Common Command Name	Application	Action
DDEPoke	All three	Sends data to another application with which you initiated conversation
DDERequest	All three	Requests data from application with which you initiated conversation
DDETerminate	All three	Terminates conversation with other application
DDETerminateAll	All three	Terminates all conversations with other applications

Using Macros

Frequently, of course, you do not have to create a persistent link because you do not need an ongoing flow of data from one application to another.

The following Word Basic macro queries an Excel worksheet for a particular piece of data. The macro also illustrates how you can control the behavior of one application from inside another. A more sophisticated macro might exercise even more precise control by sending extensive formatting instructions, instructions for the sizing and placement of open windows, and so on.

Using RequestFromExcel

The Word Basic macro RequestFromExcel easily can be created in Word. To see how the macro operates, create a new Word document, pull down the **T**ools menu, and select **M**acro. On the Macro dialog box, type **RequestFromExcel** into the **M**acro Name field, and then click on the Cr**e**ate button. In the window that appears, type the following program code. Normally, the Word Basic macro's lines are not numbered. Line numbers are included here to help you follow the explanation of the code that follows.

```
1.   Sub MAIN
2.   On Error Goto Bye
3.   DDETerminateAll
4.   ChanNum = DDEInitiate("Excel", "System")

5.   TopicsAvail$ = DDERequest$(ChanNum, "Topics")
```

```
 6.  If InStr(TopicsAvail$, "GETSTUFF.XLS") = 0 Then
     DDEExecute ChanNum, "[OPEN(" + Chr$(34) +
     "C:\EXCEL\GETSTUFF.XLS" + Chr$(34) + ")]"

 7.  NewChanNum = DDEInitiate("Excel", "GETSTUFF.XLS")
 8.  Name$ = DDERequest$(NewChanNum, "R2C1")
 9.  EditGoTo .Destination = "PutNameHere"
10.  Insert Name$
11.  Bye:
12.  DDETerminateAll
13.  End Sub
```

The macro does the following:

◆ Launches Excel. (A more refined version would check first to see whether Excel were running, and if it were not, would run it automatically.)

◆ Asks which files are open. Open files include the global macro sheet and any other macro sheets and add-ons in the XLSTART subdirectory.

◆ Sees whether the worksheet you want is open; if it is not, instructs Excel to open it.

◆ Requests information from the worksheet.

◆ Inserts the requested information into the Word document.

◆ Ends by closing the DDE channels, which are no longer necessary.

In the following explanation of RequestFromExcel's code, each number refers to the corresponding line of code in the macro:

1. Word Basic's standard opening line.

2. If executing any part of the macro is a problem, the macro branches to the label Bye: (see line 11) so that the command on line 12 (DDETerminateAll) is executed.

3. Closes any stray DDE channels that might be open. For the purpose of this macro, other open channels could cause interference.

4. Launches Excel at its system level, and returns the number of the DDE channel thus opened to the numeric variable ChanNum.

5. Asks which topics (open files) are available and puts the answer in the string variable TopicsAvail$.

6. Looks for the string GETSTUFF.XLS (the file on which subsequent commands are to operate) in the string contained in the variable TopicsAvail$. If the string is not there (that is, if GETSTUFF.XLS is not among the files loaded when Excel is launched by the command in line 4), it sends Excel a command to open that file.

   The syntax, which is complex, must be followed exactly. The command enclosed in square brackets (in this case, the OPEN command) is transmitted to Excel in the style of and with the punctuation required by its own macro commands. Chr$(34) tells Excel that the quotation marks that enclose the text are literal quotes.

7. Now that Excel has opened the required file, a new DDE channel must be opened to communicate with it. In this line, the macro is communicating with the file, not the application.

8. Asks for the item and places it in the string variable Name$. (If you are giving a cell or range address as the item, you must use R1C1 style rather than $A$1 notation. If you have named the cell or range you can use the name as the item.

9. Places the cursor at the PutNameHere bookmark.

10. Inserts the contents of the variable Name$ at the cursor.

11. The branching label specified in line 2.

12. Closes the DDE channels.

13. Word Basic's standard closing line.

CHAPTER

22

Exploring Object Linking and Embedding

In this chapter, you learn what object linking and embedding is and how it is different from dynamic data exchange (DDE). You learn step-by-step the way to create and edit OLE objects. You will learn about the following topics:

- ◆ Understanding the terminology

- ◆ Creating and editing OLE objects

- ◆ Understanding Object Packager

- ◆ Using Object Packager

- ◆ Examining multimedia and OLE

You do not need programming skills to take full advantage of OLE's capabilities. OLE is easy to use yet enormously powerful. In fact, you do not need to know anything at all about its complex underpinnings to enjoy its benefits.

With the advent of object linking and embedding (OLE, pronounced "oh-LAY"), the ideal of giving the user an effortless way to integrate Windows applications is a reality. OLE goes beyond just data sharing; it enables one application to share another application's tools as well.

Excel and Word support a version of OLE called OLE 2. This version of OLE improves the way in which different applications interact in order to create and work with compound documents (the definition of a "compound document" is discussed shortly).

Understanding the Terminology

The following three terms are important to your understanding of the workings of OLE:

- ◆ **Compound Document.** A single document made up of parts created in more than one application.

- ◆ **Container Document.** A document containing either embedded or linked data (such as objects).

- ◆ **Object.** Any piece of data that can be manipulated as a single entity, such as a picture, chart, or section of text.

A compound document is made up of parts created in more than one application. This document is a container for those different parts, which are called objects. Note that the container document is always the client in OLE transactions.

Understanding the Compound Document

As you learned in Chapter 21, "Examining Dynamic Data Exchange," to create a DDE link you first must open the server application and the source document, copy information to the Clipboard, and use the Paste Link command to paste it to the destination document. You also can program the DDE communication with a macro. Although you don't usually have to worry about the link after it is established, you might face difficulties if you want to access, edit, and update the source data. If you move or rename the source document (or, in some cases, move or rename *items*, such as spreadsheet cells or ranges), you must edit the information that Windows needs to maintain the link.

You can perform most of the tasks required to integrate information from one Windows application into another application from within the container document. You might need to leave the container document, however, to edit the linked information at its source. The source information is external to the container document.

Not so with OLE! OLE permits your work to be truly document-centered. You do not need to leave the container document to edit an embedded object. In fact, under most circumstances, you never have to leave it at all. You can initiate an OLE operation directly from within the container document. You just need to know the type of object you want to embed.

If your application can act as an OLE client, you can access a list of available object types from the menu bar. You might need to use a different procedure for each application, though. Look for an Insert menu, and a command on that menu called Object; or you might need to choose the Insert Object command from an application's File or Edit menu, for example. A list of available objects will be displayed, such as in the Word Object dialog box shown in figure 22.1.

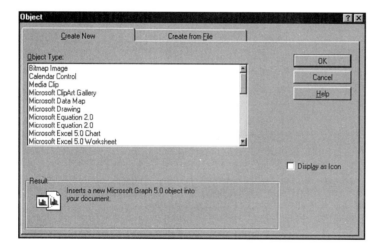

Figure 22.1

Word's Object dialog box and the list of object types you can embed.

Understanding OLE Servers and Clients

To describe the utility of OLE, Microsoft adopted the phrase, "The right tool for the right job." You create text in a word processing program, develop numeric data in a spreadsheet, chart that data in a charting program, and create bit maps in a paint program or illustrations in a drawing program. Each application is optimized for the kind of tasks you ask it to perform. After you create an object in any of these applications, you can embed the object in a container document created in another application.

Note   Modifying a drawing, changing numbers in a spreadsheet, and reformatting text all are forms of editing for which OLE can be used.

In the [embedding] section of WIN.INI, you can see a list of the object types available on your system, along with the application Windows uses to edit those objects (see fig. 22.2). Keep in mind, however, that Windows 95 relies on its new registry files instead of the settings in WIN.INI, and newer applications will only store their settings in the registry. WIN.INI still exists for compatibility purposes with applications not yet fully upgraded to use Windows 95's newer features.

Note   DDE links point to a source outside the current document. OLE objects reside within the current document.

To use OLE, you do not need to know what Windows is doing behind the scenes. You do not need to know which application will create the object (the server application), nor which application will be used to edit it. To edit an embedded object, just double-click on the object or choose an edit command from the menu. Windows then opens the server application, in which it places a copy of the embedded object and brings it to the foreground on top of the container document. You now can edit this copy of the object. After you finish, Windows asks whether you want to update the original in the container document. After you click on OK, the object is updated and the server application closes.

Figure 22.2

The [embedding] section of WIN.INI.

```
Win.ini - Notepad                                             _ 6 X
File  Edit  Search  Help

[embedding]
MSDraw=Microsoft Drawing,Microsoft Drawing,C:\WINDOWS\MSAPPS\msdraw\msdraw.exe
MSGraph=Microsoft Graph,Microsoft Graph,C:\WINDOWS\MSAPPS\MSGRAPH\GRAPH.EXE, p
WordArt=MS WordArt,Microsoft WordArt 1.0,C:\WINDOWS\MSAPPS\wordart\wordart.exe
SoundRec=Sound,Wave Sound,C:\WINDOWS\sndrec32.exe,picture
Package=Package,Package,packager.exe,picture
PBrush=Paintbrush Picture,Paintbrush Picture,C:\Progra~1\Access~1\MSPAINT.EXE,
PocketMix=Pocket Mixer Settings,Pocket Mixer Settings,C:\WINDOWS\PMIX.EXE,pict
PocketRec=Pocket Recorder Wave,Pocket Recorder Wave,C:\WINDOWS\PREC.EXE,pictur
PocketCD=Pocket CD Playlist,Pocket CD Playlist,C:\CDPCXL\PKCD.EXE,picture
Word.Document.6=Microsoft Word 6.0 Document,Microsoft Word 6.0 Document,D:\OFF
Word.Picture.6=Microsoft Word 6.0 Picture,Microsoft Word 6.0 Picture,D:\OFFICE
MSEquation.2=Microsoft Equation 2.0,Microsoft Equation 2.0,C:\WINDOWS\MSAPPS\E
MSWordArt.2=Microsoft WordArt 2.0,Microsoft WordArt 2.0,C:\WINDOWS\MSAPPS\WORD
Equation.2=Microsoft Equation 2.0,Microsoft Equation 2.0,C:\WINDOWS\MSAPPS\EQU
ExcelMacrosheet=Microsoft Excel Macrosheet,Microsoft Excel Macrosheet,C:\EXCEL
WordDocument=Word Document,Microsoft Word 2.0 Document,C:\WINWORD\WINWORD.EXE,
ExcelChart=Microsoft Excel Chart,Microsoft Excel Chart,C:\EXCEL4\EXCEL.EXE,pic
ExcelWorksheet=Microsoft Excel Worksheet,Microsoft Excel Worksheet,C:\EXCEL4\E
Excel.Chart.5=Microsoft Excel 5.0 Chart,Microsoft Excel 5.0 Chart,C:\EXCEL\EXC
Excel.Sheet.5=Microsoft Excel 5.0 Worksheet,Microsoft Excel 5.0 Worksheet,C:\E
Dialer10CallingCard=Shortcut to The Microsoft Network,Shortcut to The Microsof
midfile=MIDI Sequence,MIDI Sequence,C:\WINDOWS\mplayer.exe,picture
avifile=Video Clip,Video Clip,C:\WINDOWS\mplayer.exe,picture
mplayer=Media Clip,Media Clip,C:\WINDOWS\mplayer.exe,picture
Paint.Picture=Bitmap Image,Bitmap Image,C:\Progra~1\Access~1\MSPAINT.EXE,pictu
Wordpad.Document.1=WordPad Document,WordPad Document,C:\Progra~1\Access~1\WORD
```

New Riders Publishing
INSIDE
SERIES

Many new Windows applications and revisions of older applications incorporate OLE technology. Because user demand is high, *OLE-compliant* is a phrase that sells software. CorelDRAW!, PowerPoint, Word for Windows, and Excel are examples of high-end applications that can act as both OLE server and client.

In addition to stand-alone applications that have OLE server capabilities, a number of Windows' mini-applications (sometimes called *applets*) are designed to be used exclusively as OLE servers. Note that you can use the applets only from within an OLE client, not as independent programs. Examples of such applets are Microsoft's Note-It, WordArt, MS Graph, and MS Draw. If you try to run an OLE server applet as if it were a stand-alone program (by clicking on the name of the EXE file in File Manager, for example), you receive a message such as, "Sorry, Microsoft Draw can only run from within a destination application."

You might want to take data you developed independently in a stand-alone application and embed it in another application. To do so, follow the same copy, paste, and link procedure you use to create DDE links, with one exception: choose Embedded Object from the Paste Link (or Paste Special) dialog box. The data remains an entity in the original file, but has no link to the embedded object in your container document. Editing the original data does not update the embedded object. You can, however, edit the embedded object directly from within the container document.

Figure 22.3 compares the actions you take to create and edit links against the actions you take to create and edit embedded objects. You will find that working with embedded objects is simpler than working with links. Note that you can initiate the embedding procedure in one of two ways. You can create the object in the server application and paste it into the container document. Or, you can choose a command from the container document's menu that gives you direct access to the server application.

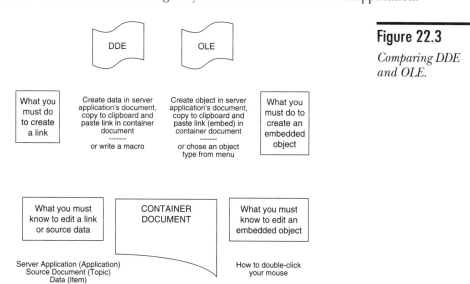

Figure 22.3

Comparing DDE and OLE.

Because an embedded object does not have an independent life—it is not stored in any external file—you must consider when to embed an object and when to link one. In general, you link an object if the server data needs to be shared with more than one client, and you embed an object when the object is to be used in only one container (client) document.

Creating and Editing OLE Objects

This section teaches you step-by-step the way to create and edit OLE objects. The first example uses two of the accessory applications that come with Windows—Paintbrush and Cardfile. The second and third examples use Word and Excel, and the fourth uses only Word.

Embedding a Paintbrush Object in Cardfile

The first OLE example uses two of the accessory applications that come with Windows—Paintbrush and Cardfile.

To create the embedded Paintbrush object on Card 1 in the file OLE.CRD, perform the following steps:

1. Choose Pictur**e** from the Cardfile **E**dit menu, and then pull down the menu again to choose **In**sert Object (see fig. 22.4). If Pictur**e** is not checked, you cannot select **In**sert Object.

Figure 22.4

Inserting an object into Cardfile.

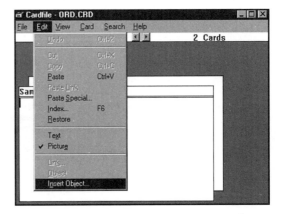

2. Selecting I**n**sert Object displays the Insert New Object dialog box. Choose Paintbrush Picture from the **O**bject Type list (see fig. 22.5).

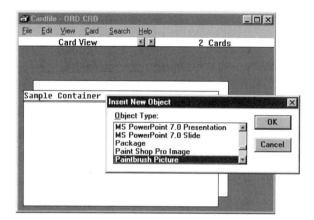

Figure 22.5

Choosing Paintbrush Picture from the Object Type list box.

Windows launches Paintbrush. As figure 22.6 shows, you can look at the title bar and see that this is not a separate file, but a "Paintbrush Picture in ORD.CRD"— an embedded object.

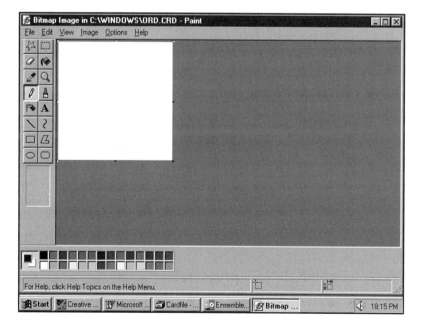

Figure 22.6

Paintbrush is now an OLE server.

3. Create your drawing and then open the **F**ile menu. This menu contains two OLE-specific commands: **U**pdate and E**x**it & Return (see fig. 22.7).

Figure 22.7

The File menu now shows OLE-related commands.

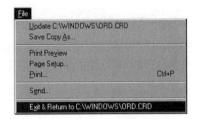

Note After you create or edit an object, remember to choose **U**pdate before you choose **E**xit & Return (although some programs automatically do this when you choose to Exit and Return).

4. After you update the Paintbrush drawing and exit from Paintbrush, you see the drawing object embedded in Cardfile (see fig. 22.8).

Figure 22.8

The drawing embedded in Cardfile.

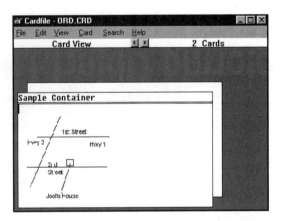

5. To modify the drawing, make sure that a check mark appears next to the Pictur**e** option in the **E**dit menu; then place the mouse pointer anywhere on the object and double-click. You also can click once to select the object, and then choose Edit Paintbrush Picture **O**bject from the **E**dit menu (see fig. 22.9).

As figure 22.10 shows, either action brings Paintbrush to the foreground so that you can use its tools to modify the object.

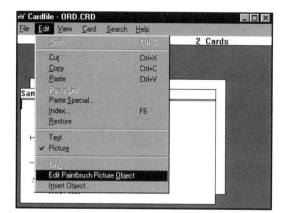

Figure 22.9

You can choose a menu command to edit the object.

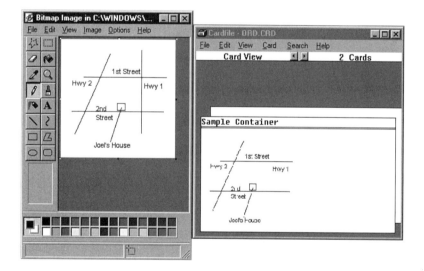

Figure 22.10

Modifying the object in the server application.

6. From the **E**dit menu, select **U**pdate and then E**x**it & Return. You see any modifications reflected in the embedded object (see fig. 22.11).

The procedure is that simple. All applications that support OLE do so in a similar manner. In all cases, the system does for you the work of choosing the editing tools and loading the object. You do not have to leave the container document. Document-centered computing is a reality thanks to OLE.

Figure 22.11

The modified object embedded in Cardfile.

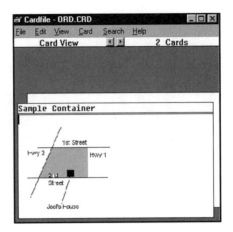

Embedding New Excel Data as an Object in Word

To create an Excel worksheet object directly from within a Word document (the container document), perform the steps in the following example. First, make sure that you have Word running, and then begin a new document by selecting **F**ile and choosing the **N**ew command.

1. From the new document in Word, select **O**bject from the **I**nsert menu (see fig. 22.12) to display the Object dialog box.

Figure 22.12

Word's Insert menu.

2. Make sure the **C**reate New tab is open. From the **O**bject Type list, choose Microsoft Excel 5.0 Worksheet (see fig. 22.13).

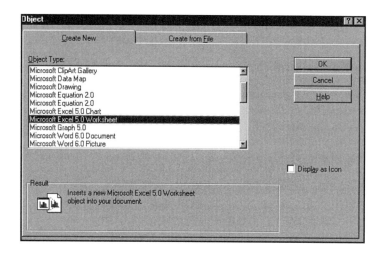

Figure 22.13

Choosing an Excel Worksheet object to embed.

ote   The list of Object Types in the various Insert Object dialog boxes illustrated in this section might not look like the list you see when you follow these examples on your own system. Remember that when you install an application that can act as an OLE server, Windows places the appropriate information about that application in the Registry Database and includes the application in the [embedding] section of your WIN.INI file. When you are working on your computer, the Object Types list will reflect the OLE servers you have installed.

You can use the worksheet and Excel's tools as you usually do (see fig. 22.14). This capability is evident if you look at the formula bar. The highlighted cell shows the result of summing the two values above it.

ote   An Excel worksheet object gives you access to all the tools and attributes of "native" Excel.

3. To return to working in "native" Word, click outside the embedded Excel sheet. You will see Word's menus and toolbar return, as shown in figure 22.15.

Figure 22.14

The embedded worksheet gives you access to "native" Excel.

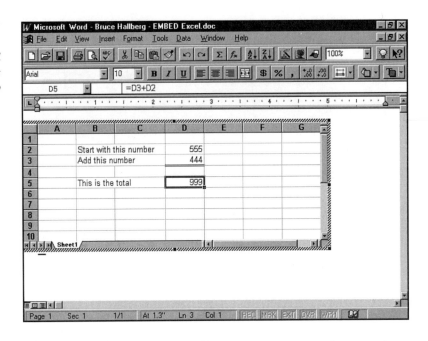

Figure 22.14

The embedded worksheet gives you access to "native" Excel.

Figure 22.15

Clicking outside the embedded object returns you to the container document.

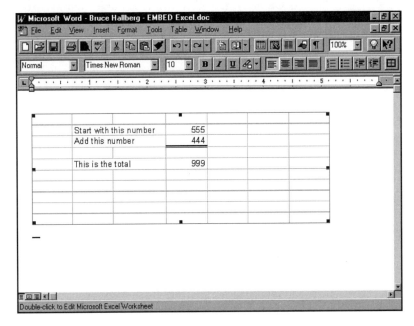

Embedding Word Text in Another Word Document

This example shows you what happens if you embed Word text in a Word document. Why would you want to do this? Perhaps you want to annotate a document, but find Word's annotations too small and difficult to read (or their placement in the footnote position too limiting) and revision markings too cumbersome.

Annotating with embedded text has the advantage of making highly visible to the reader the place at which the annotations occur, as you can see in figure 22.16. To see this effect, double-click on each of the icons. When you want to return to the main document, choose **C**lose from the **E**dit menu.

You can create these embedded text objects by using one of two procedures from within the container document. You can copy text from another document and choose Microsoft Word Object from the Paste Special dialog box (you also have to select the Display as Icon check box). You also can choose **O**bject from the **I**nsert menu, and from the **O**bject Type list box choose Word Document.

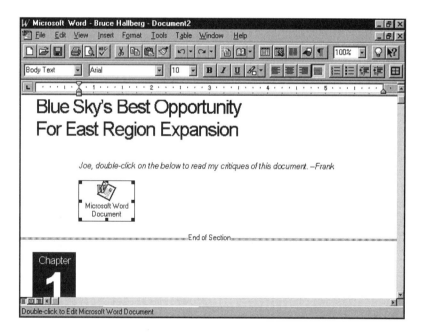

Figure 22.16

Icons represent embedded text from another Word document.

Understanding Object Packager

As is apparent from the preceding discussion, the number of OLE-compliant Windows applications is growing. What do you do if you want to embed in a container document information from an application that does not talk OLE's language? What if you need to access a DOS application while you are working in a Windows document? Windows provides a means to accomplish this task through the use of the Object Packager.

Object Packager, which is OLE-compliant, wraps itself around another application that is not OLE-compliant. Object Packager then contains information about the source that the source itself cannot provide. You then embed this "package" into your container document. Object Packager can wrap itself around Windows applications that are not otherwise OLE servers and even can act as a mechanism for embedding DOS applications, DOS commands, and batch files.

To see how Object Packager works, suppose that you manage a small office in which everybody has a computer that runs Windows, but the computers are not networked. You need to find out what each PC has in its CONFIG.SYS file.

So, you decide to put a memo on a floppy disk that is distributed to each user. The memo on the disk asks the users to access their CONFIG.SYS file by double-clicking on the icon in the memo (which represents an object packaged in the memo). When they double-click on the embedded icon, their CONFIG.SYS file is automatically opened for them. They then copy into the Word document the contents of the file by simply using copy and paste commands (which they all know how to use). After each user adds the information to the document and returns the disks to you, you will have a complete record of all the computer's CONFIG.SYS files. The users had to do little more than load the Word document to provide you the information you requested.

Using Object Packager

The following example shows you the way to create a Word document into which you embed access to Notepad, which is not an OLE-compliant application. You use Object Packager and have it load your CONFIG.SYS file. Object Packager enables you to represent a Windows or non-Windows object as an icon in your compound document.

Creating a Packaged Object

The first thing you must do to use the Object Packager is to open or create a container document. Then, to create a packaged object from within the container document, perform the following steps:

1. Begin by creating a new document in Word. From the **I**nsert menu, choose **O**bject to display the Object dialog box. From the **O**bject Type list box in the **C**reate New tab, choose Package. Figure 22.17 shows the Object Packager in the Word document.

   The Object Packager is divided into two windows, placed side by side. You specify the content of the package in the right window and the appearance of the package in the left window. The content window of the package usually displays a brief description of the package contents. The appearance window displays the icon to be used to represent the package after it is embedded in a document.

2. You can choose the object to be packaged by using several methods. This example uses the command-line method, where you specify an actual command to be executed when the object is opened. Choose Co**m**mand from the **E**dit menu to display the dialog box in figure 22.18.

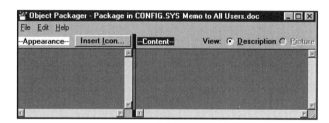

Figure 22.17

The Object Packager dialog box.

Figure 22.18

Packaging a command line in Object Packager.

The following command will load NOTEPAD with the CONFIG.SYS file:

```
C:\WINDOWS\NOTEPAD.EXE C:\CONFIG.SYS
```

 Note   If you choose a simple file name to use with the Object Packager, that file name must be associated with an application in order for the object to function correctly. So, if you were to embed, say, CONFIG.SYS, and *.SYS isn't associated with an application on your system, you will get an error when trying to open the final embedded package.

Object Packager does not know which icon to associate with CONFIG.SYS. You can choose any icon on your system, whether it resides in an EXE file, a DLL library, or independently as an icon, which is a file with an ICO extension.

3. To choose an icon, click on the Insert **I**con button in the Appearance window of Object Packager. The child window shows you the default for the object you have chosen (or Windows makes its best guess). Use the scroll bar to choose an icon from Windows' standard collection or click on the **B**rowse button to load another file that contains an icon. The Insert Icon dialog is shown in figure 22.19.

Figure 22.19

Windows includes a standard collection of icons that you can use for Object Packages.

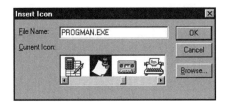

ote The appearance of an OLE package is the icon that you want inserted in the document. The content is the command or the file name of the application that is to be packaged.

4. Figure 22.20 shows you how the packaged object appears in your document and the contents of the package.

Figure 22.20

The Appearance and Content windows of the Object Packager.

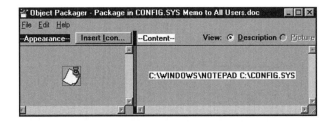

5. After you have chosen an icon, you can choose E**x**it from the Object Packager's **F**ile menu. Then, click on OK when asked if you want to update the object. Figure 22.21 shows the packaged object embedded in the completed document. It is, in fact, a picture of the icon and the label. You can select it and then format it in any way to set it off.

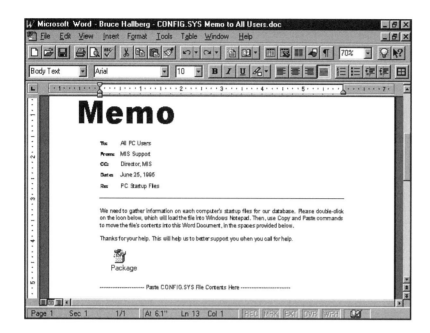

Figure 22.21

The completed document with the labeled object embedded.

Double-clicking on the icon activates the package. (In this example, it opens the CONFIG.SYS file with Notepad.) If you want to edit the package's content or appearance, you must select the icon with a single mouse click and choose Package Object from Word's **E**dit menu (see fig. 22.22).

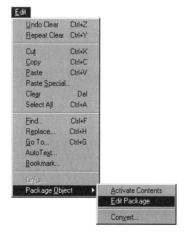

Figure 22.22

Editing the package's content or appearance with Word's Edit menu.

Choosing the Content of a Package

In the previous example, you told Object Packager which object to package by typing a command line. Alternatively, you can choose Import from Object Packager's File menu. This opens a drive and directory window, and from here you can choose a file to embed. This can be an executable file or a document file. If it is a document file, when you choose the icon embedded in your container document, Windows launches the application and loads the file. You also can drag a file from File Manager and drop it into the Content pane of the Object Packager dialog box.

DOS programs, of course, are not OLE-compliant, but thanks to Object Packager you can access a DOS program directly from within your Windows application container document. If you run that DOS program in a window, you can even copy information from it and paste the data directly into the container document.

Examining Multimedia and OLE

A new category of applications that rely heavily on OLE have exciting potential for Windows users—*multimedia.* By using the Windows operating system's multimedia extensions, developers of hardware and software that display sound, video, and animation images on-screen now have the software connections to bring these capabilities to Windows.

You must, however, have additional hardware to use parts of multimedia technology, such as sound and video boards, CD-ROM players, and so on. Windows comes with an OLE server for sound bites, for example, but you must have a sound board installed in your system (and external speakers that connect to it) to play back the files that Sound Recorder knows how to embed.

You also can plug a microphone into the sound board to record voice or other sounds, and you can create and play back MIDI synthesizer music. With the appropriate hardware, you can embed video clips from a tape or feed real-time, live video directly from a television set.

Even with relatively simple and inexpensive sound hardware you can reap some benefits from linking sound to your documents via OLE. For instance, figure 22.23 shows a letter that has both an embedded graph as well as an embedded recording of a message from the chairman. The reader of this document has only to double-click on the graph icon in order to view the graph using its native application, or to double-click on the microphone icon to hear the recorded comments from the chairman. Using these technologies can enliven documents and make them more powerful. But, of course, these benefits will not be widely available until more PCs have such hardware built in.

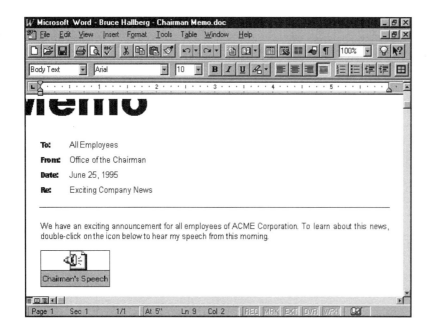

Figure 22.23

Enlivening Windows applications with embedded voice messages.

Understanding Automation with Macros and Templates

Chapters 21 and 22 introduced you to dynamic data exchange and object linking and embedding, two advanced methods by which applications can share data. The purpose of this chapter is to build on your knowledge of these concepts by showing you ways to use them to solve a problem within the context of your work environment. In doing so, this chapter covers the following points:

◆ Understanding and creating macros

◆ Understanding and creating document templates

◆ Understanding and creating compound documents

◆ Linking and embedding objects in a compound document

◆ Automating document tasks with macros

The goal is to help you to think about these concepts as problem-solving tools that you can use now, not as something you might get to later when you have more time. The trick to using macros, templates, DDE, and OLE to solve problems is to learn to see the problem and the tools in the right way.

Often computer users look at a tool such as macros and ask, "What can I use a macro to do today?" Although this question shows that the person is thinking about how to use macros, it probably will not illuminate as many possible uses from which the user might potentially benefit.

A better question for exploring the use of the integration and automation tools provided by the Windows environment is, "What tasks or problems do I have that integration tools might simplify or solve?" If you begin your exploration of macros, templates, DDE, and OLE from the task and problem end, you are more likely to include possibilities than you are if you begin your exploration from the tool end. To help you explore this task- and problem-oriented focus, this chapter considers a problem faced by anyone who writes correspondence with a word processor: the need to have stationery or letterhead that explains who the correspondence is from and how to return contact. Word for Windows serves as the example word processor, although any full-featured Windows word processor will provide these facilities.

In order to meet the need for letterhead, you could propose several solutions. You could have it printed, but then you would have to insert sheets of it strategically in your printer's feed tray if you wanted to print multiple copies of a multipage letter. A more useful solution would be to have your computer print the information on the first page for you. The question, then, is how macros, templates, DDE, and OLE might help you do that.

Learning to Think about Macros

Macros are ways of automating the keystrokes and menu commands in your application. As you examine a task or problem, looking for ways to use macros, think in terms of what you would need to do at the keyboard. What would you ordinarily have to type each time you prepare a letter? What menu actions would you have to take before you are ready to write? These are the parts of the task that macros can help you to accomplish.

How to Create Macros

In general, there are two ways to create macros. First, you can turn on a recording feature of your application and record a series of keystrokes; these are later played back to the application at your command as if you were typing the keystrokes at playback time. Alternately, you can write a set of directions and store these directions in a file; these directions are played back at your command and instruct the application to carry out the tasks you have described. The language you use for describing what the application should do is called a *macro language.*

Note Macro languages often look like programming languages. The Word for Windows macro language is in fact derived from the BASIC programming language and is called Word Basic. An explanation of each of the Word Basic statements and commands can be found in the Word for Windows help files, as well as in *Inside Word for Windows 95*, available from New Riders Publishing. If you do not feel comfortable with programming, you should not feel excluded from the capability to use macros. The macro recording facility in Word for Windows enables you to accomplish almost anything you can accomplish by writing a macro in WordBasic.

Word for Windows supports both methods of creating a macro. Recording a macro is by far the easiest. You might, for instance, have noticed that Word does not provide a means of creating bold strikethrough characters on the formatting ribbon. If you want to use the bold strikethrough format as a part of your normal writing, you could create a macro to set the bold strikethrough format. The first step, as shown in figure 23.1, is to select the **M**acro item from Word's **T**ools menu.

Figure 23.1

Starting the macro recording process.

When the Macro dialog box appears, type a name for the macro in the text box and then choose the Rec**o**rd button, which then brings up the Record Macro dialog box. Figure 23.2 shows the results of these steps.

Stop You should not assign a macro you have recorded or written to the same key as another macro. You will not erase any of the macros by doing so, but you might lose track of a macro you need if you reassign its keystroke to another macro.

Clicking on the **K**eyboard button in the Record Macro dialog box displays the Customize dialog box. By selecting the **K**eyboard tab, you can assign the recorded macro to a keystroke. Place the cursor in the Press **N**ew Shortcut Key field, then type the keystroke you want to use to execute the macro after you are done. The example in figure 23.3 shows this with the Alt+Ctrl+K combination.

Figure 23.2

Filling in the Record Macro dialog box.

Figure 23.3

Assigning the shortcut key.

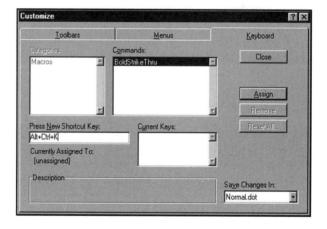

Tip

After you type the key combination, Word shows you if that key combination is already assigned to any other function, in the section of the dialog box labeled Currently Assigned To. If you want to override the current assignment and replace it with your new macro, click on the **A**ssign button; the old assignment will be overwritten.

After you have chosen the key assignment and clicked on the **A**ssign button and then the Close button, the macro will start recording, and you will see the small macro toolbar that contains the Stop and Pause buttons.

Next, type the keystrokes (or perform the mouse clicks) that will turn on the bold strikethrough character format. Hold down the Shift key and press the right-arrow key to select the character to the right of the insertion point. Then select F**o**rmat, **F**ont to bring up the Font dialog box. Click on Bold in the F**o**nt style box and the check box labeled Stri**k**ethrough, as shown in figure 23.4. Finally, click on OK.

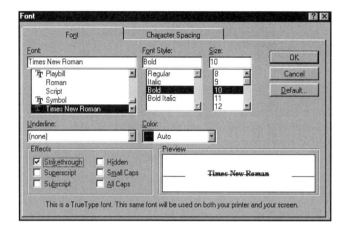

Figure 23.4

Setting the character styles in the Font dialog box.

You now have completed all the keystrokes and mouse clicks necessary for your BoldStrikeThru macro. Click on the Stop button on the Macro toolbar (see fig. 23.5) to end the recording process. Now, whenever you need to create a bold strikethrough character, simply type the text in normal format, place the insertion point to the left of the character that should become bold strikethrough, and press the key combination to which you assigned the macro. If you need to make a string of bold strikethrough characters, type the string in normal format, place the insertion point to the left of the first character, and press the macro key repeatedly until all the characters have been assigned the bold strikethrough format.

Figure 23.5

End the macro recording process by clicking on the Stop button.

Word for Windows also enables you to create a macro by writing statements in its macro language, Word Basic. To create a macro this way, select the **M**acro option on the T**o**ols menu. When the Macro dialog box appears, type a name for the macro in the text box, as shown in figure 23.6 and click on the **E**dit or Rec**o**rd button.

Word then opens a document window that has a special toolbar, enabling you to test and debug your Word Basic statements. Enter the Word Basic statements that will accomplish the task you have in mind, then close the document window just as you would close any other document window in Word. Your macro will then be ready to use. Figure 23.7 shows the statements for the BoldStrikeThru macro being entered in the special document window.

Figure 23.6

Creating a macro using the Macro dialog box.

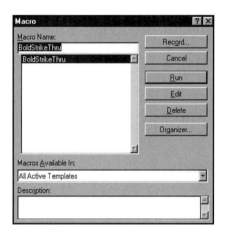

Figure 23.7

Writing the BoldStrikeThru macro in Word Basic.

```
Sub MAIN
CharRight 2, 1
FormatFont .Points = "10", .Underline = 0, .Color = 0, .Strikethrough =
1, .Superscript = 0, .Subscript = 0, .Hidden = 0, .SmallCaps = 0,
.AllCaps = 0, .Spacing = "0 pt", .Position = "0 pt", .Kerning = 0,
.KerningMin = "", .Tab = "0", .Font = "Times New Roman", .Bold = 1,
.Italic = 0, .Outline = 0, .Shadow = 0
End Sub
```

Tip

You can record a macro and then edit it afterward by selecting the **M**acro option in the T**o**ols menu. Click on the name of the macro you recorded in the Macro dialog box's list box, then click on the **E**dit button. Word will open the Word Basic file that it built during the recording process and enable you to edit the Word Basic statements.

What Macros Can Do for You

You can accomplish more with macros than change character formats. If you want to insert a date into your letters automatically, a macro can do that. If you want a dialog box to prompt you for the information in the inside address, a macro can do that. If you want to insert several lines of boilerplate text at several points in a document, a macro can do that also. Any process that you can perform manually from the keyboard, no matter how complex, can be automated as a macro. You need only to identify the tasks and processes you repeat often. They are the candidates for automation as macros.

Tip Word for Windows enables you to include dialog boxes in your macros. You can choose from several predefined dialog boxes, or you can create your own using the dialog editor in Word. In order to use dialog boxes effectively to collect information from a user, you must master the rudiments of the Word Basic language. You must write Word Basic statements to display the dialog box, collect the information, and place the information collected into your document. To master these topics, see *Inside Word for Windows 95*, also from New Riders Publishing.

Learning to Think about Document Templates

Because document templates are patterns that you use to create new documents, as you examine a task or problem looking for ways to use document templates, think in terms of how the document should look on the page. How wide will the margins be? Where will graphics appear? Should tables all have the same basic look? These are factors that a document template can automate for you.

Note Document templates, no matter what the software package, look strangely like documents themselves. In fact, they usually are documents. Word for Windows, for example, stores document templates in files much as it stores a document, except that a document template file has a DOT extension. When Word uses a document template, it inserts all the features of the template into the new Word document. Then Word turns the new document over to you to modify as you wish.

How to Create a Document Template

To create a document template in Word for Windows, select the **N**ew option on the **F**ile menu to display the New dialog box (see fig. 23.8). Select the **T**emplate option and choose from the list box the template you want to use as your starting point. (The usual choice is NORMAL, the default template, if you have no more specific template from which you want to start.) Then click on OK.

Figure 23.8

*Creating a new
document
template using
the New dialog
box.*

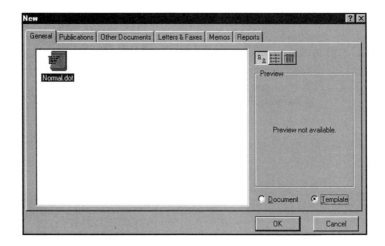

Word displays a new document window with the title Template 1 (or a higher number
if this is not the first template you have created during your Word session). You can
modify this window any way you want to define the attributes of the document you
want to use. You can set the character format, the paragraph format, or the column
format, for instance. You can create a special toolbar or menu using the **T**ools,
Options menu option. Or you can define several styles for different sections of the
document.

The example presented in figure 23.9 is a fairly simple one. It does not extensively modify
the NORMAL template. It represents an invoice form that a small business might use to
invoice one of its regular clients. This document template modifies NORMAL only by
adding a date field, boilerplate text, and a table for entering descriptions of services and
amounts. While not overly complex, it saves several keystrokes each time the client must
be invoiced, as well as the time necessary to locate the information that the template
stores ready for use. You can create one template for each regular client, or you could
use the same template form and add a glossary in which to store each of the addresses. If you use a glossary, it would be attached to the template, enabling you to
choose the client information each time you created a new document using the
template.

To save a document template, use the Save **A**s option from Word's **F**ile menu. Enter
the name for the template in the text box in the Save As dialog box, and make sure
that Save File as **T**ype is set to Document Template. Finally, click on OK to save the
template. To use your new template to create a document, select the **F**ile, **N**ew menu
option, click on the **D**ocument option button in the New dialog box, select your new
template in the appropriate tab, and click on OK. Word will create the new document
on the model defined by your template.

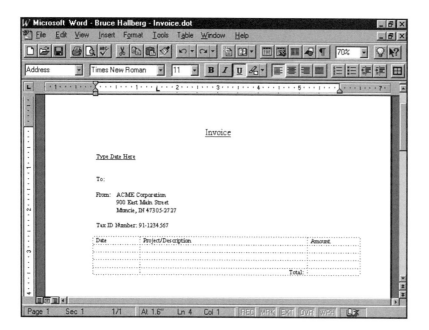

Figure 23.9

Adding boilerplate text to an invoice template.

Tip Save your template to the directory in which you've installed Office, in its Templates subdirectory. You can create a new subdirectory under Templates that causes the File New dialog box to display a corresponding tab from which you can choose whatever templates you've stored in that directory.

Stop When you save your new template, be careful not to overwrite Word's NORMAL template. NORMAL is the template in which Word stores default options and global macros. If you change NORMAL by overwriting it, you could lose your default settings and global macros.

Document templates can have a special relationship with macros. As noted in the section on macros, macros can be stored in a particular document template so that they will be available only in documents created using that template. In addition, document templates can make use of the following special macros:

◆ **AutoNew.** Runs when you create a new document.

◆ **AutoOpen.** Runs when you open an existing document.

◆ **AutoClose.** Runs when you close a document.

By writing macros with these names and assigning them a template context, you can automate the actions taken when creating a document, opening a document, and closing a document. If there are repeated sets of keystrokes or menu actions that must take place at any of these events, creating these macros will automate them for you for any document based on your template.

Tip   Many of the templates included with Word for Windows make use of Wizards to collect common information from the user and insert it into the document. The Letter Wizard template, for instance, is a Wizard that collects the information for the inside address and greeting using dialog boxes.

What Document Templates Can Do for You

Document templates can automate the look and feel of the documents you create using your software. In the Word for Windows example, the document templates manage the visual placement of information on the page, which extensions of Word's capabilities are available as macros to each document, and automatic actions taken at document creation, document opening, and document closing.

You might have imagined a day when, as you create an invoice, your computer offers you a client list from which to select address information, a list of spreadsheets from which to collect the amounts, and a list of services from which to choose. Your computer then inserts the address, collects the amount from the spreadsheet and inserts it into the invoice, and enters the service for which you are invoicing automatically. You can do that today with a document template.

Learning to Think about Compound Documents

In previous chapters, you learned that *compound document* is the name applied to a document that contains information created by several different application programs. The application that creates the document maintains links to the other applications, enabling these applications to update their information when necessary. As you think about integration and automation using compound documents, think in terms of assembling parts. What data is necessary to build the document? Which

applications create and manage different data elements? Which application creates the finished document? Are there any processing steps that must take place along the pathways created by the links? These are the issues that compound documents can assist with in integration and automation.

How to Create Compound Documents

As noted in earlier chapters, you create compound documents (documents made up of components from more than one application) using the Edit menu's Paste **S**pecial option in the application in which you are assembling the document. In the application from which you wish to link data, you select the data and place it on the Clipboard using the standard Cut or Copy commands, as shown in figure 23.10, which uses Excel as the example source application.

Figure 23.10

Copying data to the clipboard to create a compound document.

When the data to be linked is on the Clipboard, use the Paste **S**pecial option from the **E**dit menu to insert the information at the insertion point and create the link. In the Paste Special dialog box, click on the Paste **L**ink option button and then click on OK to create the link, as shown in figure 23.11, which uses Word as the example destination, or receiving, application.

After the link has been created, the information will be updated in the receiving document whenever it is changed in the originating document. As a result, you can build compound documents that assemble data from a variety of resource applications and stay continuously updated. You do not have to manually move data from one application's files to another's—the applications can now handle that for you.

Figure 23.11

*Creating the link
in the Paste
Special dialog
box.*

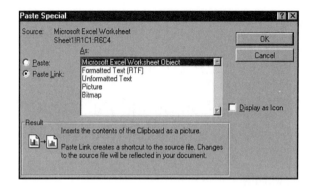

What Compound Documents Can Do for You

Understanding what compound documents can do for you requires you to think in terms of document layers. The lowest layer is the *data origination layer,* at which applications acquire data either through hand data entry or through some form of automated data acquisition. The next layer is the *data manipulation layer,* in which data is transferred from the origination layer applications into a set of documents that manipulate the data by performing calculations or other transformations. The final layer is the *data presentation layer,* the set of documents that you use to communicate with others about the data.

The hierarchy just described is not rigid. Data origination and presentation all might occur within a set of documents managed by one application using Windows' multiple document interface schema. One Word document might be embedded in another, for instance. In addition, the data manipulation layer might merge with the data presentation layer so much that you cannot distinguish between the two of them.

However, the value of this hierarchy is that it aids your thinking as you plan ways to solve problems by integrating applications and automating tasks. If you split your view into these three layers, you are likely to see how you can link data among applications to accomplish very complex tasks automatically. The example of building a letterhead, which begins in the following section, provides a simple demonstration of these concepts. The purpose of the scenarios in the next section of the book is to help you to see ways of using compound documents to solve larger, more complex problems.

Building a Simple Compound Document: A Letterhead

A letterhead need not be a compound document. You can simply build a document template that contains all the requisite items and use that template for all your correspondence. You might, however, want to update parts of a letterhead on occasion. Maintaining those parts as a single file that is linked to all the document templates where the information needs to appear makes the maintenance task easier. You update a single file, and each of the document templates to which the file is linked is automatically updated, including all current correspondence on your hard disk.

Typical items that you would want to be able to update in this way are address and telephone information. All employees could maintain their own letterhead templates on their own machines and customize the address file to suit their needs. On the other hand, if the company were not large, you might want to be able to add an 800 telephone number or a fax number as the company added these services. Linking these items into the document template using DDE makes carrying out such changes as easy as editing a file or two.

Another item that might change occasionally is the company logo. As a result, it would be useful to include the graphics file in the document template. You can do so using either OLE or DDE, but each has a disadvantage to consider. If you use DDE, you will not be able to resize the object, except by resizing it in the application that drew it. (If you use DDE, of course, the advantage is that updating the graphics file automatically updates the image in the document template file.) If you use OLE, you will be able to resize the image at will, but you will have to manually update the image from its source file in each document in which the image is used.

In the example presented here, OLE is the better choice, because the image was originally drawn as an icon for an application. It is a bit map 64 pixels × 64 pixels in size in the original drawing program, and cannot be resized by the original drawing application. Using Paintbrush, which is an OLE client application, you can import the image and resize it. In order to avoid the disadvantage of using OLE, however, the graphics image is embedded into a file that is then linked to the letterhead template. As a result, updating still can be handled from a single file. In planning linkings and embeddings, therefore, it is important to keep in mind that objects can be embedded in files that are then linked.

Creating the Template

The first step in creating the letterhead compound document is creating the document template that you will use to construct letterhead documents. For all practical purposes, this template will serve as the presentation layer. Construct this template as you did earlier in this chapter, using NORMAL as the template. Access the File, New command, select the NORMAL template, select the Template option button, and then click on OK. Figure 23.12 demonstrates this process.

Figure 23.12

Creating the letterhead document template.

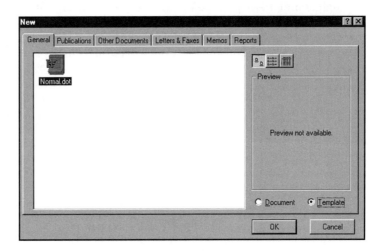

Next, give the new template the name NEWWELET.DOT by saving it using the Save As option on Word's File menu. Type **Write Environment Letterhead.DOT** in the text box and click on OK (see fig. 23.13).

Figure 23.13

Naming the letterhead document template.

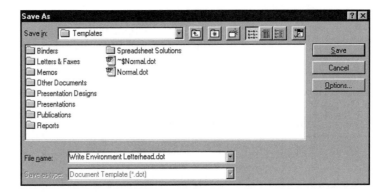

Tip   Saving your documents before creating DDE links among them is a good habit to get into. If you save first, you cannot accidentally break a link by forgetting to save a file when you exit an application. This habit is especially important when you are creating links among several applications and choose to exit Windows from a crowded desktop. As the save queries appear from various applications, you could make a costly mistake.

Linking the Name and Address

The first step in linking the address for the letterhead is to create a new file to hold the address information. This file and others like it serve as the data acquisition layer for the template. Click on the New File button on the toolbar to open a new file. (The New File button is the first one on the left end of the toolbar.) Next, create a 1×2 table on the first line of the address file. Use the table button on the toolbar to insert the table (see fig. 23.14).

Figure 23.14

Inserting a table in the address file.

Click on the right cell of the table to place the insertion point there. Enter the following address information, right-justified, for the company Write Environment. Use a larger font for the company name. Save the address information using the Save **A**s option on the **F**ile menu, giving the file the name WE Address.DOC. Use the Select **A**ll option on the **E**dit menu to select the table and characters you have entered, and select **C**opy to copy them to the Clipboard.

> Write Environment
> 900 East Jefferson
> Muncie, IN 47305-2727
> 317-555-1212

Use Word's **W**indow menu to switch to the document window that contains Write Environment Letterhead.DOT. Use the **E**dit menu's Paste **S**pecial option to paste the address information into the cell. When the Paste Special dialog box appears (see fig. 23.15), select Formatted Text in the list box, then select the Paste **L**ink option button before clicking on OK. The address information appears right-justified in the right cell of the table, and it is linked with DDE to the file WE Address.DOC.

Figure 23.15

Linking the address file.

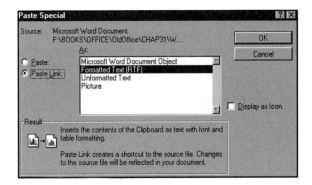

Linking the Footer Information

You might want to display additional information in the footer that appears on the first page of any correspondence. This information also is a good candidate for DDE linking because it might change from time to time. The company Write Environment displays its e-mail addresses in this area. You can link them in following steps very like those used to link in the address information.

First, open the footer for the first page of the document created using the template. Make sure you are in the document window that contains Write Environment Letterhead.DOT, and use the **H**eader/Footer option on the **V**iew menu to make the header and footer visible. Select the Switch Between Header and Footer button on the Header and Footer toolbar to jump from the header to the footer. Then, click on the Page Setup button on the Header and Footer toolbar to display the Page Setup dialog box. In the **L**ayout tab of the Page Setup dialog box (see fig. 23.16), select the check box labeled Different **F**irst Page and click on OK.

Figure 23.16

Opening the first footer.

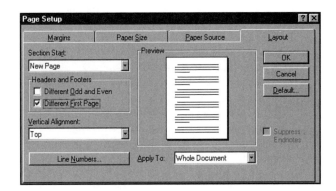

Next, create a new file by clicking on the New File button on the toolbar. (This is another file in the data acquisition layer.) Type the information shown in figure 23.17. Save this file using the Save **A**s option on the **F**ile menu, giving it the name WEFOOT.DOC. Use the Select **A**ll option on the **E**dit menu to select the characters you have entered, and copy them to the Clipboard.

Write Environment E-mail: postmaster@write.com

Figure 23.17

Entering the information for the footer.

Use Word's **W**indow menu to switch to the document window that contains Write Environment Letterhead.DOT. Make sure the insertion point is located in the First Page Footer window. Use the **E**dit menu's Paste **S**pecial option to paste the address information into the First Page Footer window. When the Paste Special dialog box appears, select Formatted Text in the list box and select the Paste **L**ink option button before clicking on OK. The address information appears in the First Page Footer window, and it is linked with DDE to the file WEFOOT.DOC (see fig. 23.18).

Figure 23.18

The linked information in the First Page Footer window.

Embedding the Logo

To embed the logo, use the **W**indow menu to switch to the document window that contains WE Address.DOC. Place the insertion point in the left cell of the table you created, and click select **O**bject from the **I**nsert menu. When the Object dialog box appears, select Paintbrush Picture in the list box and then click on OK to open Paintbrush. Next, choose Paste **F**rom on the **E**dit menu. When the Paste From dialog box appears, select the file WE.BMP and click on OK. Next select the **U**pdate option on the **F**ile menu. The graphic will be embedded in the table.

Note   Adding the logo with Paintbrush adds a new layer to the set of documents that make up the letterhead compound document. The graphics file is in the data acquisition layer, and Paintbrush is an application that is in the data manipulation layer. Paintbrush takes the graphic in its native format and prepares it (by changing its format) to be embedded in the WE Address.DOC document. As you plan integration and automation with compound documents, you often will use an application like Paintbrush to take in data in one format from one application and prepare it to be used in another format by another linked application.

After you have embedded the graphic, click on the **U**pdate option in the **F**ile menu, and then click on E**x**it. Then, in Word, click on the logo once to select it. Size it by dragging the boxes on its frame so that it looks appropriate opposite the address text, as in figure 23.19. Save the file using the **S**ave option on the **F**ile menu.

Figure 23.19

The embedded logo graphic.

Now use the **W**indow menu to change to the document window that contains Write Environment Letterhead.DOT. Notice that it should already have updated the graphic from the source file, WE Address.DOC. If the graphic has not been updated, then you will need to do it manually.

Click on the **E**dit menu and choose the **L**inks option to display the Links dialog box (see fig. 23.20). In the Links dialog box, click on the link for WE Address.DOC in the list box and then click on the **U**pdate Now button. The table, complete with the embedded graphic, now appears in your letterhead template.

Figure 23.20

Using the Links dialog box to manually update the link to Write Environment Letterhead.DOT.

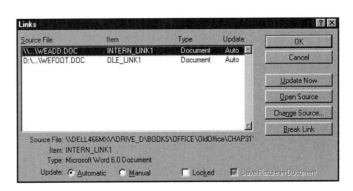

Automating Document Tasks with Macros

The basic look and feel of the letterhead for Write Environment is complete. You might, however, want to add to it using macros so that additional tasks of writing a letter can be automated.

A common task in writing a letter is adding the date and inside address, a task macros can automate considerably. To add the date to a letter automatically, all you need to do is add a date field to the letterhead template. On creation of a letterhead document, Word inserts the current date automatically.

To add the date, first position the insertion point at the location you want the date to appear in the Write Environment Letterhead.DOT file. Next, select the Field option from the Insert menu. When the Field dialog box appears, select the Date and Time category in the Categories list box and then CreateDate in the Field Names list box, as shown in figure 23.21. Click on OK, and Word inserts a macro that automatically displays the current date. (You can see this macro if you select the Field Codes option on the View page of the Tools Options menu.)

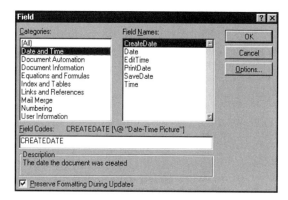

Figure 23.21

Inserting a date field.

C H A P T E R

24

Workgroup Computing with Office

Many people use Microsoft Office at work and, consequently, interact with others in the company that also use Office. Wouldn't it be nice if Office helped those people work more collaboratively within their company? What if it let you manage shared files more effectively, for example? Fortunately, it does all this and more, and this chapter covers all these topics.

In this chapter you learn about the following:

- ◆ Sharing Office files on a network

- ◆ Tracking control information for shared files

- ◆ Preserving the security of your files

- ◆ Using Shared Lists in Excel

- ◆ Creating customized templates for your workgroup

One of the biggest benefits that networks bring companies is the capability to rapidly share and process information within workgroups. Most tightly knit groups within a company that use a network set up and use shared areas on the common fileserver in which everyone in the workgroup can access and save files. This sort of structure greatly expands the ability of the workers in the department to get their jobs done, particularly in organizations that ask every worker to get more done with less. Taking advantage of the power of your network to enable your peers to work more smoothly together can pay large, if subtle, dividends.

The Office suite of applications supports this model of information sharing. Individual applications let you take advantage of features that make working together easier and more manageable.

Sharing Files on a Network

If you often work on files that are stored in areas to which many others have access, you will often try to open a file that someone else is already working on, or they will try to open a file that you are using and changing. Dealing with this simple and common occurrence is important in making sure that confusion doesn't ensue.

All of the Office applications warn you when you try to open a file that someone else is already using. When someone first opens a file for editing, that file is locked on the fileserver, such that another user cannot modify it while it's locked. Office helps you to deal with this gracefully by warning you with the dialog box shown in figure 24.1.

Figure 24.1

When you try to open a file that someone else is using, you see this dialog box.

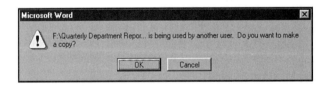

Note The figures in this section use Microsoft Word for their examples. All the Office applications, however, behave the same way in how they deal with already-opened files.

You have three ways of dealing with the dialog box shown in figure 24.1. You can select Cancel and try again later, hoping that the file is free then; you can call the other person on the phone (if you know who it is) and ask them to close the document so you can use it; or you can click on the OK button and make a copy of the document.

Making a copy of the document means that whatever is saved to the disk at that moment will be loaded into your computer, with the indicator (**Copy**) appearing after the file name in the title bar of the application. You can then freely edit the file.

When you go to save the file, two possible things will happen:

◆ If the file is still open by another user, you'll see the dialog box shown in figure 24.2. This dialog box means that, to save the file, you'll have to save it using a different file name or save it to a different directory than the original. Selecting OK brings up the Save As dialog box automatically so you can choose a new file name or location.

◆ If the other person editing the file has finished their work and closed it, you'll see the dialog box shown in figure 24.3. This dialog box tells you that someone else has edited the file, and that it probably contains changes that are not reflected in your copy of the file. If you proceed with saving your copy of the file using the **Y**es button, your changes will overwrite their changes, and their changes will be lost.

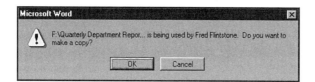

Figure 24.2

Office applications prevent you from overwriting another user's work in progress.

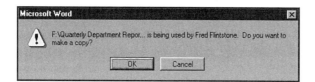

Figure 24.3

If the other user has finished with their changes, you have to decide whether your changes should overwrite theirs or not.

Note   The person's name that appears in the dialog box shown in figure 24.2 is generated by the name stored in the **O**ptions dialog box of the user's Office application. For this reason, you should not use a generic name there, such as your company name.

Using Word's Workgroup Features

Word specifically contains two features that make collaborating on word processing documents easier: annotations and revisions.

Annotations are notes attached to specific parts of a document's text. These notes are identified by the writer's initials. To insert an annotation, access the **I**nsert menu and choose **A**nnotations. Type your comment in the window provided, then click the **C**lose button to save your annotation note.

To view existing annotations (they do not normally appear), pull down the **V**iew menu and choose **A**nnotations. You'll see the window shown in figure 24.4, which is the same window as you use to insert new annotations. Each annotation is indicated with the writer's initials and a sequence number.

Figure 24.4

The Annotations window lets you see and add new annotations to a Word file.

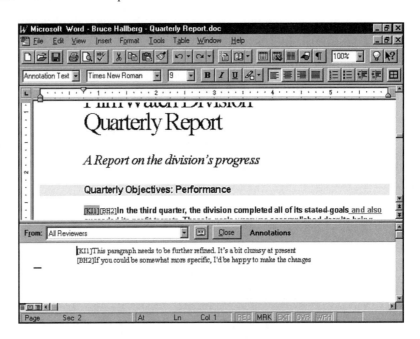

Note The initials used for the annotations are controlled in the **O**ptions dialog box on the User Info page of the dialog box.

Word also contains a feature that keeps track of revisions to a document automatically. You enable this feature by selecting the Re**v**isions command in the **T**ools menu. Check the **M**ark revisions box to cause any changes you make to the document to be tracked. These revisions appear as shown in figure 24.5. New text is shown with an underline, and deleted text appears with strikethrough. Also, each author's changes are marked in a different color.

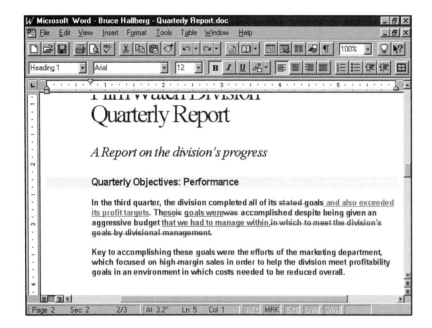

Figure 24.5

Text additions are underlined and deletions are in strikeout when using revision marks.

You can easily review each revision by author. To do this, reaccess the Re**v**isions command in the **T**ools menu. Click on the **R**eview button. This brings up the Review Revisions dialog box shown in figure 24.6. In this dialog box, you successively click on the **F**ind button to move to each revision. For each revision found, it is highlighted on the screen, and the dialog box shows you who made the change and when they made it.

Figure 24.6

Use the Review Revisions dialog box to see who has made what changes, and when they made them.

Using Excel's Shared Lists

New to Excel 95 is the ability for more than one person to edit a single file at the same time, much like a multiuser database program. To do this productively, however, you need to understand how the feature works.

Shared lists only let you add, change, or delete data. You cannot make formatting changes to the shared list file, or add or change formulas. This is why these workbooks are called *shared* lists: they are primarily used for list management duties within Excel. Following are two good examples of where you want to use this feature:

◆ A workgroup may keep a schedule of their shared "to-do" items in Excel (a finance department's period closing schedule would be a good example). Shared lists let all the members maintain the list simultaneously, adding and deleting items as needed.

◆ You might have some kind of departmental database that you keep in Excel workbooks. Perhaps it is a list of people who request information from different people within the department. Each person can add the relevant data simultaneously. The person who is responsible for sending the information out can also access the file to see what they have to do.

Anytime you maintain lists of data in Excel where you want more than one person to access and maintain the data simultaneously is potentially a candidate for the shared list feature.

The first person who opens a workbook has the responsibilty for turning on the Shared Lists feature so that others can have concurrent access to the file. You do this through the File menu's Shared Lists command. Selecting this for the first time brings up the dialog box shown in figure 24.7.

Figure 24.7

Before using a Shared List workbook, you must enable multi-user editing with the check box shown in the Shared Lists dialog box.

Note   Once you designate a workbook as a Shared List, the setting persists until you turn off the feature.

After turning on the multi-user check box, Excel immediately does a Save As of the file so that the file on the shared network drive is immediately saved with the Shared List setting enabled. This first save after enabling multiuser access is required in order for others to access the file in a multiuser fashion.

New Riders Publishing
INSIDE
SERIES

Note   You can change the formatting and formulas in a shared list workbook, but only after turning off the shared lists feature. When you finish your formula or formatting changes, you can re-enable Shared Lists so that others can access the revised file.

The key to understanding shared list workbooks is knowing how conflicts within a file are sorted out. Some are sorted out automatically. Others require intervention when you save the file. Both cases are examined here.

First, say that two people are working on a single workbook. One person inserts a row of data and saves their copy of the file. The other person has not inserted that new row. What happens when the second person goes to save their version of the file? The answer is that the new row added by the first person is automatically inserted into the second person's workbook during the save. Inserting a row would not generally cause a conflict with any other work the second person did, so it's updated automatically. Excel does tell you when it does this, however, with the message box shown in figure 24.8.

Figure 24.8

Changes that do not present an inherent conflict are updated automatically by Excel at the time of saving the file.

More tricky is the case where a change that the first user makes conflicts with something the second user has done within the file. For example, the first person changes the text in a cell in one way, while the second person makes a different change to the same cell. How does Excel handle that?

When the second person goes to save their copy of the workbook and there is a conflict, they see the Conflict Resolution dialog box shown in figure 24.9.

This dialog box is relatively self-explanatory. You can choose to do one of the following:

◆ Make your change succeed, in which the first person's change is overwritten.

◆ Use the other person's change, in which your change is overwritten.

◆ Save the file with your changes with a new file name that doesn't conflict with the main file. This is a good strategy when you're not sure which change should prevail or when you simply want to save your changes for reference, but want to accept the other person's changes for the time being.

Figure 24.9

Trying to save information that conflicts with what another user has done raises this dialog box.

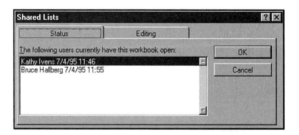

You can also click on the two bottom buttons in the dialog box in which you elect to resolve all conflicts with the other person's changes or with your own changes.

There are two tools that Excel offers you that let you more easily manage Shared Lists: the ability to view who is using the file at any given time, and the Conflict History sheet.

At any time that you're working on a shared list workbook, you can see who else is working on it by accessing the S**h**ared Lists command in the **F**ile menu. The Status tab (see fig. 24.10) shows you who has the file open for editing, and when they opened it.

Figure 24.10

The Shared Lists dialog box shows you who else is using the file.

Excel also lets you keep track of any conflicts in the file, as a sort of audit trail that can help you sort out problems. To see this, make sure the Show **C**onflict History check box (on the Editing tab of the Shared Lists dialog box) is selected. When you do this, your workbook will have a Conflict History sheet, like the one shown in figure 24.11.

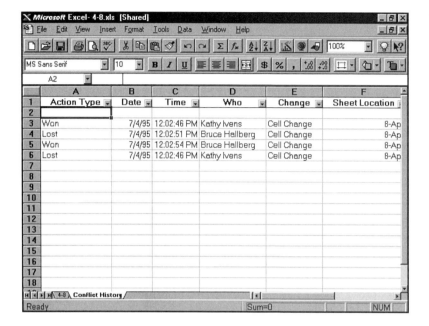

Setting Document Properties

One of the tricks to making effective use of Office applications in a shared environment involves using the file properties to track information about a particular file. With these properties, you can track items such as the following:

◆ Author

◆ Subject

◆ Keywords

◆ Comments

◆ Custom properties, such as editor, client name, and a host of other choices

To access the file's properties, pull down the **F**ile menu and choose Proper**t**ies. The Summary tab contains the main tracking information, shown in figure 24.12.

Figure 24.12

*You can save
summary
information
about the files
you work on in
the Summary tab.*

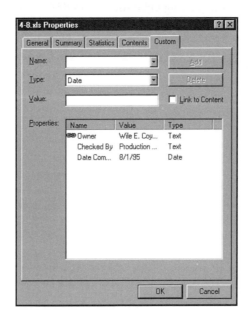

Office applications also include a host of custom file properties that you can make
good use of. These are found in the Custom tab of the Properties dialog box and are
shown in figure 24.13.

Figure 24.13

*Use custom
properties to track
more detailed
information
about your files.*

Access the custom properties using the **N**ame drop-down list. There are over 25 different properties available to you. After choosing a custom property, choose its data type in the **T**ype drop-down list (choose from Text, Number, Date, or Yes/No). Then, type the information into the **V**alue field. Finally, click on the **A**dd button to store the property. Existing properties show in the **P**roperties window.

You can develop some more complicated mechanisms using the **L**ink to Content check box. When selected, you can link a property to data contained in the file itself. For instance, you can reference named cells in Excel or bookmarks in Word. You must have defined the named cells or bookmarks first, however.

Routing Files

If you use Microsoft Exchange, or a similar compatible e-mail system, you can route your Office files to others in the company. You access this feature by choosing Add **R**outing Slip in the **F**ile menu. You see the Routing Slip dialog box shown in figure 24.14.

Figure 24.14

Use Routing Slips to easily distribute Office information to others in the company.

Add recipients using the **A**ddress button. Type a subject and message text so that the recipients will know why they are getting the file. Then, choose your routing method. You can choose to send the file to A**ll** at once or **O**ne after another. Selecting the Trac**k** Status check box causes an e-mail message to be automatically sent to you each time a recipient forwards the file onto the next person. You also can choose to have the file automatically sent back to you once the last person is finished with it.

After filling in the Routing Slip, choose the **A**dd Slip button to store the routing slip, or the **S**end button to put the file into your e-mail outbox.

Maintaining Security

When working in a shared environment, protecting the security of your documents can be important. You can do this with your Office files with file-specific passwords.

Word and Excel let you use passwords to control access to your files. Schedule+ has much more complicated security that is covered separately in the section on that

Figure 24.15

Use the Save Options dialog box to add password protection to your files.

Save Options

☐ Always Create **B**ackup

File Sharing
Protection Password: [XXXXXX]
Write Reservation Password: [XXXXXXXX]
☑ **R**ead-Only Recommended

OK
Cancel

program. PowerPoint does not use password protection.

To add a password to a Word or Excel file, simply choose the Save **A**s command in the **F**ile menu. Then, click on the **O**ptions button to reveal the dialog box shown in figure 24.15.

There are two different passwords you can set: **P**rotection Password and **W**rite Reservation Password. The protection password denies access to the file entirely unless the individual knows the password. The write reservation password lets anyone open the file in read-only mode, but they can only make changes to the file if they know the write reservation password.

You also can specify that a file be **R**ead-Only Recommended. If this check box is selected, Excel warns the person opening the file that they should open it in read-only mode. Although they have the choice of going ahead and opening it with write access, this check box causes Excel to remind them that they should be careful in doing so.

Setting Up Workgroup Templates

In any of the Office applications, when you go to create a new file using the **N**ew command in the **F**ile menu, you see a tabbed dialog box that lists possible files and templates on which you can base your new file. Office creates the standard tabs and files when you first install it.

A workgroup may have many additional files that they specifically use within the group. You can create special Workgroup Templates that contain these group-specific files. When you do this, they appear in the New File dialog box as if they are part of Office.

To set this up, first create a folder on a shared disk that will contain your template folders. In that main folder, create a subfolder for each tab you want to appear in the New File dialog box. In this example, a Workgroup Templates folder was created in the root directory, and in that a My Workgroup folder was created. Whatever name you assign to the subfolders will be used as the names for the tabs in the New File dialog. In each subfolder, place all of the template files that your group uses.

After this is done, each user in the group sets up their system so that it automatically uses that shared location for group-specific templates. They do this by following these steps:

1. Start the Office Toolbar if it's not already started.

2. Click in the control menu of the Office Toolbar (the very upper left corner) and access the **C**ustomize command shown in figure 24.16.

Figure 24.16

Use the Customize command to set the location for Workgroup Templates.

Figure 24.17

Select the top-level folder in which you've placed the actual template folders that you want to appear.

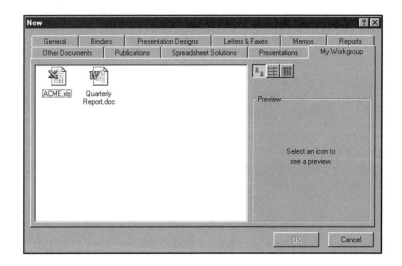

3. Move to the Setting tab.

4. Select the Item Workgroup Templates Location, then click on the **M**odify button to set it. You will see a modified File Open dialog box in which you can locate the folder that contains the templates. In this example, you choose the folder directly off the root directory called Workgroup Templates. See figure 24.17 for an example. Click on the **A**dd button when done.

5. Close the Customize dialog box.

After setting this property, any time you use the **F**ile, **N**ew command in any Office application, or from the Office Toolbar, you will automatically see tabs that contain your workgroup templates.

Index

Symbols

A

Graph **785**

N

PLUG YOURSELF INTO...

The Macmillan USA Information SuperLibrary (tm)

See the new SuperLibrary Newsletter

THE MACMILLAN
INFORMATION SUPERLIBRARY™

**Free information and vast computer resources from
the world's leading computer book publisher—online!**

FIND THE BOOKS THAT ARE RIGHT FOR YOU!
A complete online catalog, plus sample chapters and tables of contents!

- STAY INFORMED with the latest computer industry news through our online newsletter, press releases, and customized Information SuperLibrary Reports.

- GET FAST ANSWERS to your questions about Macmillan Computer Publishing books.

- VISIT our online bookstore for the latest information and editions!

- COMMUNICATE with our expert authors through e-mail and conferences.

- DOWNLOAD SOFTWARE from the immense Macmillan Computer Publishing library:
    - Source code, shareware, freeware, and demos

- DISCOVER HOT SPOTS on other parts of the Internet.

- WIN BOOKS in ongoing contests and giveaways!

TO PLUG INTO MCP:

WORLD WIDE WEB: **http://www.mcp.com**

FTP: ftp.mcp.com

WANT MORE INFORMATION?

CHECK OUT THESE RELATED TOPICS OR SEE YOUR LOCAL BOOKSTORE

CAD and 3D Studio

As the number one CAD publisher in the world, and as a Registered Publisher of Autodesk, New Riders Publishing provides unequaled content on this complex topic. Industry-leading products include AutoCAD and 3D Studio.

Networking

As the leading Novell NetWare publisher, New Riders Publishing delivers cutting-edge products for network professionals. We publish books for all levels of users, from those wanting to gain NetWare Certification, to those administering or installing a network. Leading books in this category include *Inside NetWare 3.12*, *CNE Training Guide: Managing NetWare Systems*, *Inside TCP/IP*, and *NetWare: The Professional Reference*.

Graphics

New Riders provides readers with the most comprehensive product tutorials and references available for the graphics market. Best-sellers include *Inside CorelDRAW! 5*, *Inside Photoshop 3*, and *Adobe Photoshop NOW!*

Internet and Communications

As one of the fastest growing publishers in the communications market, New Riders provides unparalleled information and detail on this ever-changing topic area. We publish international best-sellers such as *New Riders' Official Internet Yellow Pages, 2nd Edition*, a directory of over 10,000 listings of Internet sites and resources from around the world, and *Riding the Internet Highway, Deluxe Edition*.

Operating Systems

Expanding off our expertise in technical markets, and driven by the needs of the computing and business professional, New Riders offers comprehensive references for experienced and advanced users of today's most popular operating systems, including *Understanding Windows 95*, *Inside Unix*, *Inside Windows 3.11 Platinum Edition*, *Inside OS/2 Warp Version 3*, and *Inside MS-DOS 6.22*.

Other Markets

Professionals looking to increase productivity and maximize the potential of their software and hardware should spend time discovering our line of products for Word, Excel, and Lotus 1-2-3. These titles include *Inside Word 6 for Windows*, *Inside Excel 5 for Windows*, *Inside 1-2-3 Release 5*, and *Inside WordPerfect for Windows*.

Orders/Customer Service **1-800-653-6156**   Source Code **NRP95**

New Riders Publishing   201 West 103rd Street ◆ Indianapolis, Indiana 46290 USA

REGISTRATION CARD

Inside Microsoft Office for Windows 95

Name _____ Title _____

Company _____ Type of business _____

Address _____

City/State/ZIP _____

Have you used these types of books before? ☐ yes ☐ no

If yes, which ones? _____
_____

How many computer books do you purchase each year? ☐ 1–5 ☐ 6 or more

How did you learn about this book? _____

Where did you purchase this book? _____

Which applications do you currently use? _____
_____

Which computer magazines do you subscribe to? _____
_____

What trade shows do you attend? _____
_____

Comments: _____
_____
_____

Would you like to be placed on our preferred mailing list? ☐ yes ☐ no

☐ **I would like to see my name in print!** You may use my name and quote me in future New Riders products and promotions. My daytime phone number is: _____

New Riders Publishing   201 West 103rd Street ◆ Indianapolis, Indiana 46290 USA

Fax to **317-581-4670**   Orders/Customer Service **1-800-653-6156**   Source Code **NRP95**

Fold Here

- -

BUSINESS REPLY MAIL

FIRST-CLASS MAIL PERMIT NO. 9918 INDIANAPOLIS IN

POSTAGE WILL BE PAID BY THE ADDRESSEE

**NEW RIDERS PUBLISHING
201 W 103RD ST
INDIANAPOLIS IN 46290-9058**